Lecture Notes in Artificial Intelligence 4065

Edited by J. G. Carbonell and J. Siekmann

Subseries of Lecture Notes in Computer Science

T0134662

Petra Perner (Ed.)

Advances
in Data Mining

Applications in Medicine, Web Mining, Marketing, Image and Signal Mining

6th Industrial Conference on Data Mining, ICDM 2006
Leipzig, Germany, July 14-15, 2006
Proceedings

 Springer

Series Editors

Jaime G. Carbonell, Carnegie Mellon University, Pittsburgh, PA, USA
Jörg Siekmann, University of Saarland, Saarbrücken, Germany

Volume Editor

Petra Perner
Institute of Computer Vision and Applied Computer Sciences, IBaI
Körnerstr. 10, 04107 Leipzig, Germany
E-mail: pperner@ibai-institut.de

Library of Congress Control Number: 2006928502

CR Subject Classification (1998): I.2.6, I.2, H.2.8, K.4.4, J.3, I.4, J.6, J.1

LNCS Sublibrary: SL 7 – Artificial Intelligence

ISSN   0302-9743
ISBN-10   3-540-36036-0 Springer Berlin Heidelberg New York
ISBN-13   978-3-540-36036-0 Springer Berlin Heidelberg New York

Springer is a part of Springer Science+Business Media

springer.com

© Springer-Verlag Berlin Heidelberg 2006
Printed in Germany

Typesetting: Camera-ready by author, data conversion by Scientific Publishing Services, Chennai, India
Printed on acid-free paper   SPIN: 11790853   06/3142   5 4 3 2 1 0

Preface

The Industrial Conference on Data Mining ICDM-Leipzig was the sixth event in a series of annual events which started in 2000. We are pleased to note that the topic data mining with special emphasis on real-world applications has been adopted by so many researchers all over the world into their research work. We received 156 papers from 19 different countries.

The main topics are data mining in medicine and marketing, web mining, mining of images and signals, theoretical aspects of data mining, and aspects of data mining that bundle a series of different data mining applications such as intrusion detection, knowledge management, manufacturing process control, time-series mining and criminal investigations.

The Program Committee worked hard in order to select the best papers. The acceptance rate was 30%. All these selected papers are published in this proceedings volume as long papers up to 15 pages. Moreover we installed a forum where work in progress was presented. These papers are collected in a special poster proceedings volume and show once more the potentials and interesting developments of data mining for different applications.

Three new workshops have been established in connection with ICDM: (1) Mass Data Analysis on Images and Signals, MDA 2006; (2) Data Mining for Life Sciences, DMLS 2006; and (3) Data Mining in Marketing, DMM 2006. These workshops are developing new topics for data mining under the aspect of the special application. We are pleased to see how many interesting developments are going on in these fields.

We would like to express our appreciation to the reviewers for their precise and highly professional work. We appreciate the help and understanding of the editorial staff at Springer and in particular Alfred Hofmann, who supported the publication of these proceedings in the LNAI series.

We wish to thank all speakers, participants, and industrial exhibitors who contributed to the success of the conference.

We are looking forward to welcoming you to ICDM 2007 (www.data-mining-forum.de) and to the new work presented there.

July 2006   Petra Perner

Table of Contents

Theoretical Aspects of Data Mining

Data Mining in Marketing

Mining Signals and Images

Aspects of Data Mining

Using Prototypes and Adaptation Rules for Diagnosis of Dysmorphic Syndromes

Rainer Schmidt and Tina Waligora

Institute for Medical Informatics and Biometry, University of Rostock, Germany
rainer.schmidt@medizin.uni-rostock.de

Abstract. Since diagnosis of dysmorphic syndromes is a domain with incomplete knowledge and where even experts have seen only few syndromes themselves during their lifetime, documentation of cases and the use of case-oriented techniques are popular. In dysmorphic systems, diagnosis usually is performed as a classification task, where a prototypicality measure is applied to determine the most probable syndrome. These measures differ from the usual Case-Based Reasoning similarity measures, because here cases and syndromes are not represented as attribute value pairs but as long lists of symptoms, and because query cases are not compared with cases but with prototypes. In contrast to these dysmorphic systems our approach additionally applies adaptation rules. These rules do not only consider single symptoms but combinations of them, which indicate high or low probabilities of specific syndromes.

1 Introduction

When a child is born with dysmorphic features or with multiple congenital malformations or if mental retardation is observed at a later stage, finding the correct diagnosis is extremely important. Knowledge of the nature and the etiology of the disease enables the pediatrician to predict the patient's future course. So, an initial goal for medical specialists is to diagnose a patient to a recognised syndrome. Genetic counselling and a course of treatments may then be established.

A dysmorphic syndrome describes a morphological disorder and it is characterised by a combination of various symptoms, which form a pattern of morphologic defects. An example is Down Syndrome which can be described in terms of characteristic clinical and radiographic manifestations such as mental retardation, sloping forehead, a flat nose, short broad hands and generally dwarfed physique [1].

The main problems of diagnosing dysmorphic syndromes are as follows [2]:

- more than 200 syndromes are known,
- many cases remain undiagnosed with respect to known syndromes,
- usually many symptoms are used to describe a case (between 40 and 130),
- every dysmorphic syndrome is characterised by nearly as many symptoms.

Furthermore, knowledge about dysmorphic disorders is continuously modified, new cases are observed that cannot be diagnosed (it exists even a journal that only publishes reports of observed interesting cases [3]), and sometimes even new

P. Perner (Ed.): ICDM 2006, LNAI 4065, pp. 1–9, 2006.

syndromes are discovered. Usually, even experts of paediatric genetics only see a small count of dysmorphic syndromes during their lifetime.

So, we have developed a diagnostic system that uses a large case base. Starting point to build the case base was a large case collection of the paediatric genetics of the University of Munich, which consists of nearly 2000 cases and 229 prototypes. A prototype (prototypical case) represents a dysmorphic syndrome by its typical symptoms. Most of the dysmorphic syndromes are already known and have been defined in the literature. And nearly one third of our entire case base has been determined by semiautomatic knowledge acquisition, where an expert selected cases that should belong to same syndrome and subsequently a prototype, characterised by the most frequent symptoms of his cases, was generated. To this database we have added cases from "clinical dysmorphology" [3] and syndromes from the London dysmorphic database [4], which contains only rare dysmorphic syndromes.

1.1 Diagnostic Systems for Dysmorphic Syndromes

Systems to support diagnosis of dysmorphic syndromes have already been developed in the early 80's. The simple ones perform just information retrieval for rare syndromes, namely the London dysmorphic database [3], where syndromes are described by symptoms, and the Australian POSSUM, where syndromes are visualised [5]. Diagnosis by classification is done in a system developed by Wiener and Anneren [6]. They use more than 200 syndromes as database and apply Bayesian probability to determine the most probable syndromes. Another diagnostic system, which uses data from the London dysmorphic database was developed by Evans [7]. Though he claims to apply Case-Based Reasoning, in fact it is again just a classification, this time performed by Tversky's measure of dissimilarity [8]. The most interesting aspect of his approach is the use of weights for the symptoms. That means the symptoms are categorised in three groups – independently from the specific syndromes, instead only according to their intensity of expressing retardation or malformation. However, Evans admits that even features, that are usually unimportant or occur in very many syndromes sometimes play a vital role for discrimination between specific syndromes.

In our system the user can chose between two measures of dissimilarity between concepts, namely of Tversky [8] and the other one of Rosch and Mervis [9]. However, the novelty of our approach is that we do not only perform classification but subsequently apply adaptation rules. These rules do not only consider single symptoms but specific combinations of them, which indicate high or low probabilities of specific syndromes.

1.2 Case-Based Reasoning and Prototypicality Measures

Since the idea of Case-Based Reasoning (CBR) is to use former, already solved solutions (represented in form of cases) for current problems [10], CBR seems to be appropriate for diagnosis of dysmorphic syndromes. CBR consists of two main tasks [11], namely retrieval, which means searching for similar cases, and adaptation, which means adapting solutions of similar cases to the query case. For retrieval usually explicit similarity measure or, especially for large case bases, faster retrieval algorithms like Nearest Neighbour Matching [12] are applied. For adaptation only few general techniques exist [13], usually domain specific adaptation rules have to be acquired.

In CBR usually cases are represented as attribute-value pairs. In medicine, especially in diagnostic applications, this is not always the case, instead often a list of symptoms describes a patient's disease. Sometimes these lists can be very long, and often their lengths are not fixed but vary with the patient. For dysmorphic syndromes usually between 40 and 130 symptoms are used to characterise a patient.

Furthermore, for dysmorphic syndromes it is unreasonable to search for single similar patients (and of course none of the systems mentioned above does so) but for more general prototypes that contain the typical features of a syndrome. Prototypes are a generalisation from single cases. They fill the knowledge gap between the specificity of single cases and abstract knowledge in the form of cases. Though the use of prototypes had been early introduced in the CBR community [14, 15], their use is still rather seldom. However, since doctors reason with typical cases anyway, in medical CBR systems prototypes are a rather common knowledge form (e.g. for antibiotics therapy advice in ICONS [16], for diabetes [17], and for eating disorders [18]).

So, to determine the most similar prototype for a given query patient instead of a similarity measure a prototypicality measure is required. One speciality is that for prototypes the list of symptoms is usually much shorter than for single cases.

The result should not be just the one and only most similar prototype, but a list of them – sorted according to their similarity. So, the usual CBR methods like indexing or nearest neighbour search are inappropriate. Instead, rather old measures for dissimilarities between concepts [8, 9] are applied and explained in the next section.

2   Diagnosis of Dysmorphic Syndromes

Our system consists of four steps (fig.1). At first the user has to select the symptoms that characterise a new patient. This selection is a long and very time consuming process, because we consider more than 800 symptoms. However, diagnosis of dysmorphic syndromes is not a task where the result is very urgent, but it usually requires thorough reasoning and afterwards a long-term therapy has to be started. Since our system is still in the evaluation phase, secondly the user can select a prototypicality measure. In routine use, this step shall be dropped and instead the measure with best evaluation results shall be used automatically. At present there are three choices. As humans look upon cases as more typical for a query case as more features they have in common [9], distances between prototypes and cases usually mainly consider the shared features.

The first, rather simple measure (1) just counts the number of matching symptoms of the query patient (X) and a prototype (Y) and normalises the result by dividing it by the number of symptoms characterising the syndrome.

This normalisation is done, because the lengths of the lists of symptoms of the various prototypes vary very much. It is performed by the two other measures too.

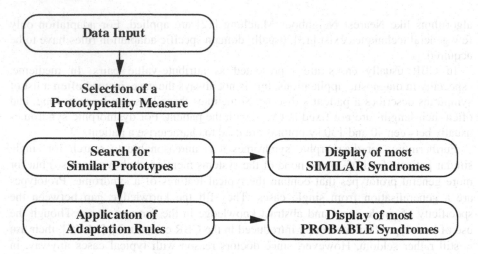

Fig. 1. Steps to diagnose dysmorphic syndromes

The following equations are general (as they were originally proposed) at the point that a general function "f" is used, which usually means a sum that can be weighted. In general these functions "f" can be weighted differently. However, since we do not use any weights at all, in our application "f" means simply a sum.

$$D(X,Y) = \frac{f(X+Y)}{f(Y)} \tag{1}$$

The second measure (2) was developed by Tversky [8]. It is a measure of dissimilarity for concepts. In contrast to the first measure, additionally two numbers are subtracted from the number of matching symptoms. Firstly, the number of symptoms that are observed for the patient but are not used to characterise the prototype (X-Y), and secondly the number of symptoms used for the prototype but are not observed for the patient (Y-X) is subtracted.

$$D(X,Y) = \frac{f(X+Y) - f(X-Y) - f(Y-X)}{f(Y)} \tag{2}$$

The third prototypicality measure (3) was proposed by Rosch and Mervis [9]. It differs from Tversky's measure only in one point: the factor X-Y is not considered:

$$D(X,Y) = \frac{f(X+Y) - f(Y-X)}{f(Y)} \tag{3}$$

In the third step to diagnose dysmorphoic syndromes, the chosen measure is sequentially applied on all prototypes (syndromes). Since the syndrome with maximal

Table 1. Most similar prototypes after applying a prototypicality measure

Most Similar Syndromes	Similarity
Shprintzen-Syndrome	0.49
Lenz-Syndrome	0.36
Boerjeson-Forssman-Lehman-Syndrome	0.34
Stuerge-Weber-Syndrome	0.32

similarity is not always the right diagnosis, the 20 syndromes with best similarities are listed in a menu (table 1).

2.1 Application of Adaptation Rules

In the fourth and final step, the user can optionally choose to apply adaptation rules on the syndromes. These rules state that specific combinations of symptoms favour or disfavour specific dysmorphic syndromes. Unfortunately, the acquisition of these adaptation rules is very difficult, because they cannot be found in textbooks but have to be defined by experts of paediatric genetics. So far, we have got only 10 of them and so far, it is not possible that a syndrome can be favoured by one adaptation rule and disfavoured by another one at the same time. When we, hopefully, acquire more rules, such a situation should in principle be possible but would indicate some sort of inconsistency of the rule set.

How shall the adaptation rules alter the results? Our first idea was that the adaptation rules should increase or decrease the similarity scores for favoured and disfavoured syndromes. But the question is how. Of course no medical expert can determine values to manipulate the similarities by adaptation rules and any general value for favoured or disfavoured syndromes would be arbitrary.

So, instead the result after applying adaptation rules is a menu that contains up to three lists (table 2).

On top the favoured syndromes are depicted, then those neither favoured nor disfavoured, and at the bottom the disfavoured ones. Additionally, the user can get information about the specific rules that have been applied on a particular syndrome (e.g. fig. 2).

Table 2. Most similar prototypes after additionally applying adaptation rules

Probable prototypes after application of adaptation rules	Similarity	Applied Rules
Lenz-Syndrome	0.36	Rule-No.6
Dubowitz-Syndrom	0.24	Rule-No.9
Prototypes, no adaptation rules could be applied		
Shprintzen-Syndrome	0.49	
Boerjeson-Forssman-Lehman-Syndrome	0.34	
Stuerge-Weber-Syndrome	0.32	
Leopard-Syndrome	0.31	

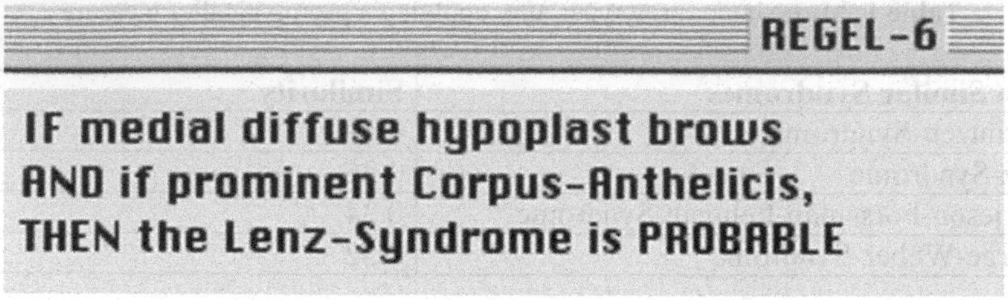

REGEL-6

**IF medial diffuse hypoplast brows
AND if prominent Corpus-Anthelicis,
THEN the Lenz-Syndrome is PROBABLE**

Fig. 2. Presented information about the applied adaptation rule

In the example presented by tables 1 and 2, and figure 2 the correct diagnosis is Lenz-syndrome. The computation of the prototypicality measure of Rosch and Mervis determines Lenz-syndrome as the most similar but one syndrome (here Tversky's measure provides a similar result, only the differences between the similarities are smaller). After application of adaptation rules, the ranking is not obvious. Two syndromes have been favoured, the more similar one is the right one. However, Dubowitz-syndrome is favoured too (by a completely different rule), because a specific combination of symptoms makes it probable, while other observed symptoms indicate a rather low similarity.

3   Results

Cases are difficult to diagnose when patients suffer from a very rare dysmorphic syndrome for which neither detailed information can be found in literature nor many cases are stored in our case base. This makes evaluation difficult. If test cases are randomly chosen, frequently observed cases resp. syndromes are frequently selected and the results will probably be fine, because these syndromes are well-known. However, the main idea of the system is to support diagnosis of rare syndromes. So, we have chosen our test cases randomly but under the condition that every syndrome can be chosen only once.

For 100 cases we have compared the results obtained by both prototypicality measures (table 3).

Table 3. Comparison of prototypicality measures

Right Syndrome	Rosch and Mervis	Tversky
on Top	29	40
among top 3	57	57
among top 10	76	69

The results may seem to be rather poor. However, diagnosis of dysmorphic syndromes is very difficult and usually needs further investigation, because often a couple of syndromes are very similar. The first step is to provide the doctor with information about probable syndromes, so that he gets an idea about which further investigations are appropriate. That means, the right diagnose among the three most probable syndromes is already a good result.

Obviously, the measure of Tversky provides better results, especially when the right syndrome should be on top of the list of probable syndromes. When it should be only among the first three of this list, both measures provide equal results.

Adaptation rules. Since the acquisition of adaptation rules is a very difficult and time consuming process, the number of acquired rules is rather limited, namely at first just 10 rules. Furthermore, again holds: the better a syndrome is known, the easier adaptation rules can be generated. So, the improvement mainly depends on the question how many syndromes involved by adaptation rules are among the test set. In our experiment this was the case only for 5 syndromes. Since some had been already diagnosed correctly without adaptation, there was just a small improvement (table 4).

Table 4. Results after applying adaptation rules

Right Syndrome	Rosch and Mervis	Tversky
on Top	32	42
among top 3	59	59
among top 10	77	71

Some more adaptation rules. Later on we acquired eight further adaptation rules and repeated the tests with the same test cases. The new adaptation rules again improved the results (table 5).

Table 5. Results after applying some more adaptation rules

Right Syndrome	Rosch and Mervis	Tversky
on Top	36	44
among top 3	65	64
among top 10	77	73

It is obvious that with the number of acquired adaptation rules the quality of the program increases too. Unfortunately, the acquisition of these rules is very difficult and especially for very rare syndromes probably nearly impossible.

4   Conclusion

Diagnosis of dysmorphic syndromes is a very difficult task, because many syndromes exist, the syndromes can be described by various symptoms, many rare syndromes are still not well investigated, and from time to time new syndromes are discovered.

We have compared two prototypicality measures, where the one by Tversky provides slightly better results. Since the results were rather pure, we additionally have applied adaptation rules (as we have done before, namely for the prognosis of influenza [19]). We have shown that these rules can improve the results. Unfortunately, the acquisition of them is very difficult and time consuming. Furthermore, the main problem is to diagnose rare and not well investigated syndromes and for such syndromes it is nearly impossible to acquire adaptation rules.

However, since adaptation rules do not only favour specific syndromes but can be used to disfavour specific syndromes, the chance to diagnose even rare syndromes also increases by the count of disfavouring rules for well-known syndromes. So, the best way to improve the results seems to be to acquire more adaptation rules, however difficult this task may be.

References

1. Taybi, H., Lachman, R.S.: Radiology of Syndromes, Metabolic Disorders, and Skeletal Dysplasia. Year Book Medical Publishers, Chicago (1990)
2. Gierl, L., Stengel-Rutkowski, S.: Integrating Consultation and Semi-automatic Knowledge Acquisition in a Prototype-based Architecture: Experiences with Dysmorphic Syndromes. Artificial Intelligence in Medicine 6 (1994) 29-49
3. Clinical Dysmorphology. htp://www.clyndysmorphol.com (last accessed: April 2006)
4. Winter R.M., Baraitser M., Douglas J.M.: A computerised data base for the diagnosis of rare dysmorphic syndromes. Journal of medical genetics 21 (2) (1984) 121-123
5. Stromme P.: The diagnosis of syndromes by use of a dysmorphology database. Acta Paeditr Scand 80 (1) (1991) 106-109
6. Weiner F., Anneren G.: PC-based system for classifying dysmorphic syndromes in children. Computer Methods and Programs in Biomedicine 28 (1989) 111-117
7. Evans C.D.: A case-based assistant for diagnosis and analysis of dysmorphic syndromes. International Journal of Medical Informatics 20 (1995) 121-131
8. Tversky, A.: Features of Similarity. Psychological Review 84 (4) (1977) 327-352
9. Rosch E., Mervis C.B.: Family Resemblance: Studies in the Internal Structures of Categories. Cognitive Psychology 7 (1975) 573-605
10. Kolodner, J.: Case-Based Reasoning. Morgan Kaufmann Publishers, San Mateo (1993)
11. Aamodt, A., Plaza, E.: Case-Based Reasoning: Foundation issues, methodological variation, and system approaches. AICOM 7 (1994) 39-59
12. Broder, A.: Strategies for efficient incremental nearest neighbor search. Pattern Recognition 23 (1990) 171-178
13. Wilke, W., Smyth, B., Cunningham, P.: Using configuration techniques for adaptation. In: Lenz, M. et al. (eds.): Case-Based Reasoning technology, from foundations to applications. Lecture Notes in Artificial Intelligence, Vol. 1400, Springer-Verlag, Berlin Heidelberg New York (1998) 139-168
14. Schank, R.C.: Dynamic Memory: a theory of learning in computer and people. Cambridge University Press, New York (1982)
15. Bareiss, R.: Exemplar-based knowledge acquisition. Academic Press, San Diego (1989)
16. Schmidt, R., Gierl, L.: Case-based Reasoning for antibiotics therapy advice: an investigation of retrieval algorithms and prototypes. Artificial Intelligence in Medicine 23 (2001) 171-186

17. Bellazzi, R., Montani, S., Portinale, L.: Retrieval in a prototype-based case library: a case study in diabetes therapy revision. In: Smyth, B., Cunningham, P. (eds.): Proc European Workshop on Case-Based Reasoning. Lecture Notes in Artificial Intelligence, Vol. 1488, Springer-Verlag, Berlin Heidelberg New York (1998) 64-75
18. Bichindaritz, I.: From cases to classes: focusing on abstraction in case-based reasoning. In: Burkhard, H.-D., Lenz, M.: (eds.): Proc German Workshop on Case-Based Reasoning, University Press, Berlin (1996) 62-69
19. Schmidt, R., Gierl, L.: Temporal Abstractions and Case-based Reasoning for Medical Course Data: Two Prognostic Applications. In: Perner P (eds.): Machine Learning and Data Mining in Pattern Recognition, MLDM 2001. Lecture Notes in Computer Science, Vol. 2123, Springer-Verlag, Berlin Heidelberg New York (2001) 23-34

OVA Scheme vs. Single Machine Approach in Feature Selection for Microarray Datasets

Chia Huey Ooi, Madhu Chetty, and Shyh Wei Teng

Gippsland School of Information Technology
Monash University, Churchill, VIC 3842, Australia
{chia.huey.ooi, madhu.chetty,
shyh.wei.teng}@infotech.monash.edu.au

Abstract. The large number of genes in microarray data makes feature selection techniques more crucial than ever. From rank-based filter techniques to classifier-based wrapper techniques, many studies have devised their own feature selection techniques for microarray datasets. By combining the OVA (one-vs.-all) approach and differential prioritization in our feature selection technique, we ensure that class-specific relevant features are selected while guarding against redundancy in predictor set at the same time. In this paper we present the OVA version of our differential prioritization-based feature selection technique and demonstrate how it works better than the original SMA (single machine approach) version.

Keywords: molecular classification, microarray data analysis, feature selection.

1 Feature Selection in Tumor Classification

Classification of tumor samples from patients is vital for diagnosis and effective treatment of cancer. Traditionally, such classification relies on observations regarding the location [1] and microscopic appearance of the cancerous cells [2]. These methods have proven to be slow and ineffective; there is no way of predicting with reliable accuracy the progress of the disease, since tumors of similar appearance have been known to take different paths in the course of time. Some tumors may grow aggressively after the point of the abovementioned observations, and hence require equally aggressive treatment regimes; other tumors may stay inactive and thus require no treatment at all [1]. With the advent of the microarray technology, data regarding the gene expression levels in each tumor samples now may prove a useful tool in aiding tumor classification. This is because the microarray technology has made it possible to simultaneously measure the expression levels for thousands or tens of thousands of genes in a single experiment [3, 4].

However, the microarray technology is a two-edged sword. Although with it we stand to gain more information regarding the gene expression states in tumors, the amount of information might simply be too much to be of use. The large number of features (genes) in a typical gene expression dataset (1000 to 10000) intensifies the need for feature selection techniques prior to tumor classification. From various filter-based procedures [5] to classifier-based wrapper techniques [6] to filter-wrapper

P. Perner (Ed.): ICDM 2006, LNAI 4065, pp. 10–23, 2006.

hybrid techniques [7], many studies have devised their own flavor of feature selection techniques for gene expression data. However, in the context of highly multiclass microarray data, only a handful of them have delved into the effect of redundancy in the predictor set on classification accuracy.

Moreover, the element of the balance between relative weights given to relevance vs. redundancy also assumes an equal, if not greater importance in feature selection. This element has not been given the attention it deserves in the field of feature selection, especially in the case of applications to gene expression data with its large number of features, continuous values, and multiclass nature. Therefore, to solve this problem, we introduced the element of the DDP (degree of differential prioritization) as a third criterion to be used in feature selection along with the two existing criteria of relevance and redundancy [8].

2 Classifier Aggregation for Tumor Classification

In the field of classification and machine learning, multiclass problems are often decomposed into multiple two-class sub-problems, resulting in classifier aggregation. The rationale behind this is that two-class problems are easier to solve than multiclass problems. However, classifier aggregation may increase the order of complexity by up to a factor of B, B being the number of the decomposed two-class sub-problems. This argument for the single machine approach (SMA) is often countered by the theoretical foundation and empirical strengths of the classifier aggregation approach. The term single machine refers to the fact that a predictor set is used to train only one classifier. Here, we differentiate between internal and external classifier aggregation.

Internal classifier aggregation transpires when feature selection is conducted once based on the original multiclass target class concept. The single predictor set obtained is then fed as input into a single multiclassifier. The single multiclassifier trains its component binary classifiers accordingly, but using the same predictor set for all component binary classifiers. *External classifier aggregation* occurs when feature selection is conducted separately for each two-class sub-problem resulting from the decomposition of the original multiclass problem. The predictor set obtained for each two-class sub-problem is different from the predictor sets obtained for the other two-class sub-problems. Then, in each two-class sub-problem, the aforementioned predictor set is used to train a binary classifier.

Our study is geared towards comparing external classifier aggregation in the form of the one-vs.-all (OVA) scheme against the SMA. From this point onwards, the term *classifier aggregation* will refer to external classifier aggregation. Methods in which feature selection is conducted based on the multiclass target class concept are defined as SMA methods, regardless of whether a multiclassifier with internal classifier aggregation or a direct multiclassifier (which employs no aggregation) is used. Examples of multiclassifier with internal classifier aggregation are multiclass SVMs based on binary SVMs such as DAGSVM [9], "one-vs.-all" and "one-vs.-one" SVMs. Direct multiclassifiers include nearest neighbors, Naïve Bayes [10], other maximum likelihood discriminants and true multiclass SVMs such as BSVM [11].

Various classification and feature selection studies have been conducted for multiclass microarray datasets. Most involved SMA with either one of or both direct and internally aggregated classifiers [8, 12, 13, 14, 15]. Two studies [16, 17] did implement external classifier aggregation in the form of the OVA scheme, but only on a single split of a single dataset, the GCM dataset. Although in [17], various multiclass decomposition techniques were compared to each other and the direct multiclassifier, classifier methods, and not feature selection techniques, were the main theme of that study.

This brief survey of existent studies indicates that both the SMA and OVA scheme are employed in feature selection for multiclass microarray datasets. However, none of these studies have conducted a detailed analysis which applies the two paradigms in parallel on the same set of feature selection techniques, with the aim of judging the effectiveness of the SMA against the OVA scheme (or vice versa) on feature selection techniques for multiclass microarray datasets. To address this deficiency, we devise the OVA version of the DDP-based feature selection technique introduced earlier [8].

The main contribution of this paper is to study the effectiveness of the OVA scheme against the SMA, particularly for the DDP-based feature selection technique. A secondary contribution is an insightful finding on the role played by aggregation schemes such as the OVA in influencing the optimal value of the DDP.

We begin with a brief description of the SMA version of the DDP-based feature selection technique, followed by the OVA scheme for the same feature selection technique. Then, after comparing the results from both SMA and OVA versions of the DDP-based feature selection technique, we discuss the advantages of the OVA scheme over the SMA, and present our conclusions.

3   SMA Version of the DDP-Based Feature Selection Technique

For microarray datasets, the term *gene* and *feature* may be used interchangeably. The training set upon which feature selection is to be implemented, T, consists of N genes and M_t training samples. Sample j is represented by a vector, $\mathbf{x}_j$, containing the expression of the N genes $[x_{1,j}, ..., x_{N,j}]^T$ and a scalar, y_j, representing the class the sample belongs to. The SMA multiclass target class concept $\mathbf{y}$ is defined as $[y_1, ..., y_{Mt}]$, $y_j \in [1, K]$ in a K-class dataset. From the total of N genes, the objective is to form the subset of genes, called the predictor set S, which would give the optimal classification accuracy. For the purpose of defining the DDP-based predictor set score, we define the following parameters.

- V_S is the measure of relevance for the candidate predictor set S. It is taken as the average of the score of relevance, $F(i)$ of all members of the predictor set [14]:

$$V_S = \frac{1}{|S|} \sum_{i \in S} F(i) \tag{1}$$

$F(i)$ indicates the correlation of gene i to the SMA target class concept $\mathbf{y}$, i.e., ability of gene i to distinguish among samples from K different classes at once. A popular parameter for computing $F(i)$ is the BSS/WSS ratios (the F-test statistics) used in [14, 15].

- U_S is the measure of antiredundancy for the candidate predictor set S. U_S quantifies the *lack of redundancy* in S.

$$U_S = \frac{1}{|S|^2} \sum_{i, j \in S} 1 - |R(i, j)| \qquad (2)$$

$|R(i,j)|$ measures the similarity between genes i and j. $R(i,j)$ is the Pearson product moment correlation coefficient between genes i and j. Larger U_S indicates lower average pairwise similarity in S, and hence, smaller amount of redundancy in S.

The measure of goodness for predictor set S, $W_{A,S}$, incorporates both V_S and U_S.

$$W_{A,S} = (V_S)^\alpha \cdot (U_S)^{1-\alpha} \qquad (3)$$

where the power factor $\alpha \in (0, 1]$ denotes the degree of differential prioritization between maximizing relevance and maximizing antiredundancy.

Decreasing the value of α forces the search method to put more priority on maximizing antiredundancy at the cost of maximizing relevance. Raising the value of α increases the emphasis on maximizing relevance (at the same time decreases the emphasis on maximizing antiredundancy) during the search for the optimal predictor set. A predictor set found using larger value of α has more features with strong relevance to the target class concept, but also more redundancy among these features. Conversely, a predictor set obtained using smaller value of α contains less redundancy among its member features, but at the same time also has fewer features with strong relevance to the target class concept.

The SMA version of the DDP-based feature selection technique has been shown to be capable of selecting the optimal predictor set for various multiclass microarray datasets by virtue of the variable differential prioritization factor [8]. Results from the application of this feature selection technique on multiple datasets [8] indicate two important correlations to the number of classes, K, of the dataset: As K increases,

1. the estimate of accuracy deteriorates, especially for K greater than 6; and
2. placing more emphasis on maximizing antiredundancy (using smaller α) produces <u>better</u> accuracy than placing more emphasis on relevance (using larger α).

From these observations, we conclude that as K increases, for majority of the classes, features highly relevant with regard to a specific class are more likely to be 'missed' by a multiclass score of relevance (i.e., given a low multiclass relevance score) than by a class-specific score of relevance. In other words, the measure of relevance computed based on the SMA multiclass target class concept is not efficient enough to capture the relevance of a feature when K is larger than 6.

Moreover, there is an imbalance among the classes in the following aspect: For class k ($k = 1, 2, ..., K$), let h_k be the number of features which have high class-specific (class k vs. all other classes) relevance and are also deemed highly relevant by the SMA multiclass relevance score. For all benchmark datasets, h_k varies greatly from class to class. Hence, we need a classifier aggregation scheme which uses class-specific target class concept catering to a particular class in each sub-problem and is thus better able to capture features with high correlation to a specific class. This is where the proposed OVA scheme is expected to play its role.

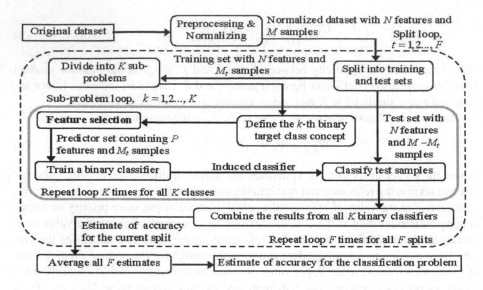

Fig. 1. Feature selection using the OVA scheme

4　OVA Scheme for the DDP-Based Feature Selection Technique

In the OVA scheme, a K-class feature selection problem is divided into K separate 2-class feature selection sub-problems (Figure 1). Each of the K sub-problems has a target class concept different from the target class concept of the other sub-problems and that of the SMA. Without loss of generality, in the k-th sub-problem ($k = 1, 2, ..., K$), we define class 1 as encompassing all samples belonging to class k, and class 2 as comprising of all samples *not* belonging to class k. In the k-th sub-problem, the target class concept, $\mathbf{y_k}$, is a 2-class target class concept.

$$\mathbf{y_k} = \begin{bmatrix} y_{k,1} & y_{k,2} & \cdots & y_{k,M_t} \end{bmatrix} \tag{4}$$

where

$$y_{k,j} = \begin{cases} 1 & \text{if} \quad y_j = k \\ 2 & \text{if} \quad y_j \neq k \end{cases} \tag{5}$$

In solving the k-th sub-problem, feature selection finds the predictor set S_k, the size of which, P, is generally much smaller than N. Therefore, for each tested value of $P = 2, 3, ..., P_{max}$, K predictor sets are obtained from all K sub-problems. For each value of P, the k-th predictor set is used to train a component binary classifier which then attempts to predict whether a sample belongs or does *not* belong to class k. The predictions from K component binary classifiers are combined to produce the overall prediction. In cases where more than one of the K component binary classifiers proclaims a sample as belonging to their respective classes, the sample is assigned to the class corresponding to the component binary classifier with the largest decision value.

Equal predictor set size is used for all K sub-problems, i.e., the value of P is the same for all of the K predictor sets.

In the k-th sub-problem, the predictor set score for S_k, W_{A,S_k}, is given as follows.

$$W_{A,S_k} = \left(V_{S_k}\right)^\alpha \cdot \left(U_{S_k}\right)^{1-\alpha} \tag{6}$$

The significance of α in the OVA scheme remains unchanged in the general meaning of the SMA context. However, it must be noted that the power factor $\alpha \in (0, 1]$ now represents the degree of differential prioritization between maximizing relevance *based on the 2-class target class concept*, y_k, (instead of relevance based on the K-class target class concept y of the SMA) and maximizing antiredundancy.

Aside from these differences, the role of α is the same in the OVA scheme as in the SMA. For instance, at $\alpha = 0.5$, we still get an equal-priorities scoring method, and at $\alpha = 1$, the feature selection technique becomes rank-based.

The measure of relevance for S_k, V_{S_k}, is computed by averaging the score of relevance, $F(i,k)$ of all members of the predictor set.

$$V_{S_k} = \frac{1}{|S_k|} \sum_{i \in S_k} F(i,k) \tag{7}$$

The score of relevance of gene i in the k-th sub-problem, $F(i,k)$, is given as follows.

$$F(i,k) = \frac{\sum_{j=1}^{M_t} \sum_{q=1}^{2} I\left(y_{k,j} = q\right)\left(\bar{x}_{iq} - \bar{x}_{i\bullet}\right)^2}{\sum_{j=1}^{M_t} \sum_{q=1}^{2} I\left(y_{k,j} = q\right)\left(x_{ij} - \bar{x}_{iq}\right)^2} \tag{8}$$

$I(.)$ is an indicator function returning 1 if the condition inside the parentheses is true, otherwise it returns 0. $\bar{x}_{i\bullet}$ is the average of the expression of gene i across all training samples. $\bar{x}_{iq}$ is the average of the expression of gene i across training samples belonging to class k when q is 1. When q is 2, $\bar{x}_{iq}$ is the average of the expression of gene i across training samples *not* belonging to class k.

The measure of antiredundancy for S_k, U_{S_k}, is computed the same way as in the SMA.

$$U_{S_k} = \frac{1}{|S_k|^2} \sum_{i,j \in S_k} 1 - |R(i,j)| \tag{9}$$

For search method, in the k-th sub-problem, we use the linear incremental search [14] given below. The order of computation is $O(NKP_{max})$.

1. For $k = 1, 2, ..., K$, do
    1.1. Choose the gene with the largest $F(i,k)$ as the first member of S_k.

1.2. For $P = 2, 3, \ldots, P_{\max}$

    1.2.1. Screen the remaining $(N - P + 1)$ genes one by one to find the gene that would enable S_k to achieve the maximum W_{A,S_k} for the size P.

    1.2.2. Insert such gene as found in 1.2.1 into S_k.

5 Results

Feature selection experiments were conducted on seven benchmark datasets using both the SMA and the OVA scheme. In both approaches, different values of α from 0.1 to 1 were tested with equal intervals of 0.1. The characteristics of microarray datasets used as benchmark datasets: the GCM [16], NCI60 [18], lung [19], MLL [20], AML/ALL [21], PDL [22] and SRBC [23] datasets, are listed in Table 1. For NCI60, only 8 tumor classes are analyzed; the 2 samples of the prostate class are excluded due to the small class size. Datasets are preprocessed and normalized based on the recommended procedures in [15] for Affymetrix and cDNA microarray data.

Table 1. Descriptions of benchmark datasets. N is the number of features after preprocessing.

Dataset	Type	N	K	Training:Test set size
GCM	Affymetrix	10820	14	144:54
NCI60	cDNA	7386	8	40:20
PDL	Affymetrix	12011	6	166:82
Lung	Affymetrix	1741	5	135:68
SRBC	cDNA	2308	4	55:28
MLL	Affymetrix	8681	3	48:24
AML/ALL	Affymetrix	3571	3	48:24

With the exception of the GCM dataset, where the original ratio of training to test set size used in [16] is maintained to enable comparison with previous studies, for all other datasets we employ the standard 2:1 split ratio. The DAGSVM classifier is used throughout the performance evaluation. The DAGSVM is an all-pairs SVM-based multiclassifier which uses less training time compared to either the standard algorithm or Max Wins while producing accuracy comparable to both [9].

5.1 Evaluation Techniques

For the OVA scheme, the exact evaluation procedure for a predictor set of size P found using a certain value of the DDP, α, is shown in Figure 1. In case of the SMA, the sub-problem loop in Figure 1 is conducted only once, and that single sub-problem represents the (overall) K-class problem. Three measures are used to evaluate the overall classification performance of our feature selection techniques. The first is the *best averaged accuracy*. This is simply taken as the largest among the accuracy obtained from Figure 1 for all values of P and α. The number of splits, F, is set to 10.

The second measure is obtained by averaging the estimates of accuracy from different sizes of predictor sets ($P = 2, 3, ..., P_{max}$) obtained using a certain value of α to get the *size-averaged accuracy* for that value of α. This parameter is useful in predicting the value of α likely to produce the optimal estimate of accuracy since our feature selection technique does not explicitly predict the best P from the tested range of $[2, P_{max}]$. The size-averaged accuracy is computed as follows. First, for all predictor sets found using a particular value of α, we plot the estimate of accuracy obtained from the procedure outlined in Figure 1 against the value of P of the corresponding predictor set (Figure 2). The size-averaged accuracy for that value of α is the area under the curve in Figure 2 divided by the number of predictor sets, ($P_{max}-1$).

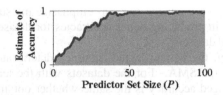

Fig. 2. Area under the accuracy-predictor set size curve

The value of α associated with the highest size-averaged accuracy is deemed the empirical optimal value of the DDP or the empirical estimate of α^*. Where there is a tie in terms of the highest size-averaged accuracy between different values of α, the empirical estimate of α^* is taken as the average of those values of α.

The third measure is *class accuracy*. This is computed in the same way as the size-averaged accuracy, the only difference being that instead of overall accuracy, we compute the class-specific accuracy for each class of the dataset. Therefore there are a total of K class accuracies for a K-class dataset.

In this study, P_{max} is deliberately set to 100 for the SMA and 30 for the OVA scheme. The rationale for this difference is that more features will be needed to differentiate among K classes at once in the SMA, whereas in the OVA scheme, each predictor set from the k-th sub-problem is used to differentiate between only two classes, hence the smaller upper limit to the number of features in the predictor set.

5.2 Best Averaged Accuracy

Based on the best averaged accuracy, the most remarkable improvement brought by the OVA scheme over the SMA is seen in the dataset with the largest number of classes ($K = 14$), GCM (Table 2). The accuracy of 80.6% obtained from the SMA is increased by nearly 2% to 82.4% using the OVA scheme. For the NCI60, lung and SRBC datasets there is a slight improvement of 1% at most in the best averaged accuracy when the OVA scheme is compared to the SMA. The performance of the SMA version of the DDP-based feature selection technique for the two most challenging benchmark datasets (GCM and NCI60) has been compared favorably to results from previous studies in [8]. Therefore it follows that the accuracies from the OVA scheme compare even more favorably to accuracies obtained in previous studies on these datasets [12, 14, 15, 16, 17].

Naturally, the combined predictor set size obtained from the OVA scheme is greater than that obtained from the SMA. However, we must note that the predictor set size *per component binary classifier* (i.e., the number of genes per component binary classifier) associated with the best averaged accuracy is smaller in case of the OVA scheme than the SMA (Table 2). Furthermore, we consider two facts: 1) There are K component binary classifiers involved in the OVA scheme where the component DAGSVM reverts to a plain binary SVM in each of the K sub-problems. 2) On the other hand, there are $^KC_2$ component binary classifiers involved in the multiclassifier used in the SMA, the all-pairs DAGSVM. Therefore, 1) the smaller number of component binary classifiers and 2) the smaller number of genes used per component binary classifier in the OVA scheme serve to emphasize the superiority of the OVA scheme over the SMA in producing better accuracies for datasets with larger K such as the GCM and NCI60 datasets.

For the PDL dataset, the best averaged accuracy deteriorates by 2.8% when the OVA scheme replaces the SMA. For the datasets with the least number of classes ($K = 3$), the best averaged accuracy is the same whether obtained from predictor set produced from feature selection using the SMA or the OVA scheme.

Table 2. Best averaged accuracy ($\pm$ standard deviation across F splits) estimated from feature selection using the SMA and OVA scheme, followed by the corresponding differential prioritization factor and predictor set size ('gpc' stands for 'genes per component binary classifier')

Dataset	SMA	OVA
GCM	$80.6 \pm 4.3\%$, α=0.2, 85 gpc	$82.4 \pm 3.3\%$, α=0.3, 24 gpc
NCI60	$74.0 \pm 3.9\%$, α=0.3, 61 gpc	$75.0 \pm 6.2\%$, α=0.3, 19 gpc
PDL	$99.0 \pm 1.0\%$, α=0.5, 60 gpc	$96.2 \pm 1.1\%$, α=0.6, 16 gpc
Lung	$95.6 \pm 1.6\%$, α=0.5, 31 gpc	$96.0 \pm 1.7\%$, α=0.5, 14 gpc
SRBC	$99.6 \pm 1.1\%$, α=0.7, 13 gpc	$100 \pm 0\%$, α=0.8, 2 gpc
MLL	$99.2 \pm 1.8\%$, α=0.6, 12 gpc	$99.2 \pm 1.8\%$, α=0.7, 4 gpc
AML/ALL	$97.9 \pm 2.2\%$, α=0.8, 11 gpc	$97.9 \pm 2.2\%$, α=0.6, 6 gpc

5.3 Size-Averaged Accuracy

The best size-averaged accuracy for the OVA scheme is better for all benchmark datasets except the PDL and AML/ALL datasets (Table 3). The peak of the size-averaged accuracy plot against α for the OVA scheme appears to the right of the peak of the SMA plot for all datasets except the PDL and lung datasets, where they stay the same for both approaches (Figure 3). This means that the value of the optimal DDP (α^*) when the OVA scheme is used in feature selection is greater than the optimal DDP (α^*) obtained from feature selection using the SMA, except for the PDL and lung datasets. In Section 6, we will look into the reasons for the difference in the empirical estimates of α^* between the two approaches of the SMA and the OVA scheme.

Table 3. Best size-averaged accuracy estimated from feature selection using the SMA and OVA scheme, followed by the corresponding DDP, α^*. A is the number of times OVA outperforms SMA, and B is the number of times SMA outperforms OVA, out of the total of tested values of $P = 2, 3, \ldots, 30$.

Dataset	SMA	B	OVA	A
GCM	68.2%, α^*=0.2	0	76.0%, α^*=0.5	29
NCI60	60.1%, α^*=0.3	0	64.4%, α^*=0.6	29
PDL	94.0%, α^*=0.5	0	92.3%, α^*=0.5	19
Lung	91.8%, α^*=0.6	1	92.3%, α^*=0.6	12
SRBC	97.3%, α^*=0.6	0	99.9%, α^*=0.9	26
MLL	96.8%, α^*=0.7	0	97.4%, α^*=0.8	12
AML/ALL	95.9%, α^*=0.8	0	95.6%, α^*=0.9	9

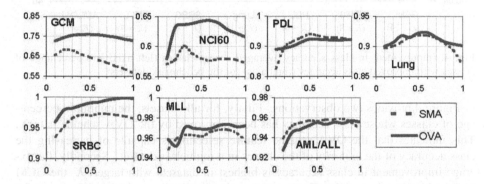

Fig. 3. Size-averaged accuracy plotted against α

We have also conducted statistical tests on the significance of the performance of each of the approaches (SMA or OVA) over the other for each value of P (number of genes per component binary classifier) from $P = 2$ up to $P = 30$. Using Cochran's Q statistic, the number of times the OVA approach outperforms the SMA, A, and the number of times the SMA outperforms the OVA approach, B, at 5% significance level, are shown in Table 3. It is observed that $A > B$ for all seven datasets, and that A is especially large (in fact, maximum) for the two datasets with largest number of classes, the GCM and NCI60 datasets. Moreover, A tends to increase as K increases, showing that the OVA approach increasingly outperforms the SMA (at 5% significance level) as the number of classes in the dataset increases.

5.4   Class Accuracy

To explain the improvement of the OVA scheme over the SMA, we look towards the components that contribute to the overall estimate of accuracy: the estimates of the class accuracy. Does the improvement in size-averaged accuracy in the OVA scheme translate to similar increase in the class accuracy of each of the classes in the dataset?

To answer the question, for each class in a dataset, we compute the difference between class accuracy obtained from the OVA scheme and that from the SMA using corresponding values of α^* from Table 3. Then, we obtain the average of this difference from all classes in the same dataset. **Positive** difference indicates **improvement** brought by the OVA scheme against the SMA. For each dataset, we also count the number of classes whose class accuracy is better under the OVA scheme than in the SMA and divide this number by K to obtain a percentage. These two parameters are then plotted for all datasets (Figure 4).

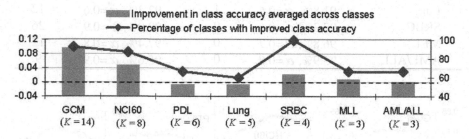

Fig. 4. Improvement in class accuracy averaged across classes (left axis) and percentage of classes with improved class accuracy (right axis) for the benchmark datasets

Figure 4 provides two observations. Firstly, for **all** datasets, the minimum percentage of classes whose class accuracy has been improved by the OVA scheme is 60%. This indicates that the OVA scheme feature selection is capable of increasing the class accuracy of the *majority* of the classes in a multiclass dataset. Secondly, the average improvement in class accuracy is highest in datasets with largest K, the GCM and the NCI60 (above 4%). Furthermore, only one class out of 14 and 8 classes for the GCM and NCI60 datasets respectively does not show improved class accuracy under the OVA scheme (compared to the SMA). Therefore, the OVA scheme brings the largest amount of improvement over the SMA for datasets with large K.

In several cases, improvement in class accuracy occurs only for classes with small class sizes, which is not sufficient to compensate for the deterioration in class accuracy for classes with larger class sizes. Therefore, even if majority of the classes show improved class accuracy under the OVA scheme, this does not get translated into improved overall accuracy (PDL and AML/ALL datasets) or improved averaged class accuracy (PDL and lung datasets) when a few of the larger classes have worse class accuracy.

6 Discussion

For both approaches, maximizing antiredundancy is less important for datasets with smaller K (less than 6) – therefore supporting the assertion in [24] that redundancy does not hinder the performance of the predictor set when K is 2. In the SMA feature selection, the value of α^* is more strongly influenced by K compared to the case in the OVA scheme feature selection. The correlation between α^* and K in the SMA is found to be −0.93, whereas in the OVA scheme the correlation is −0.72. In both cases, the general picture is that of α^* decreasing as K increases.

However, on a closer examination, there is a marked difference in the way α^* changes with regard to K between the SMA and the OVA versions of the DDP-based feature selection technique (Figure 5). In the SMA, α^* decreases in accordance with every step of increase in K. In the OVA scheme, α^* stays near the range of equal-priorities predictor set scoring method (0.5 and 0.6) for the four datasets with larger K (the GCM, NCI60, PDL and lung datasets). Then, in the region of datasets with smaller K, α^* in the OVA scheme increases so that it is nearer the range of rank-based feature selection technique (0.8 and 0.9 for the SRBC, MLL and AML/ALL datasets).

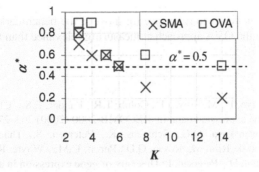

Fig. 5. Optimal value of DDP, α^*, plotted against K for all benchmark datasets

The steeper decrease of α^* as K increases in the SMA implies that the measure of relevance used in the SMA fails to capture the relevance of a feature when K is large. In the OVA scheme, the decrease of α^* as K increases is more gradual, implying better effectiveness than the SMA in capturing relevance for datasets with larger K.

Furthermore, for **all** datasets, the value of α^* in the OVA scheme is greater than or equal to the value of α^* in the SMA. Unlike in the SMA, the values of α^* in the OVA scheme never fall below 0.5 for all benchmark datasets (Figure 5). This means that the measure of relevance implemented in the OVA scheme is more effective at identifying relevant features, regardless of the value of K. In other words, K different groups of features, each considered highly relevant based on a different binary target class concept, $\mathbf{y_k}$ ($k = 1,2,...,K$), are more capable of distinguishing among samples of K different classes than a single group of features deemed highly relevant based on the K-class target class concept, $\mathbf{y}$.

Since in none of the datasets has α^* reached exactly 1, antiredundancy is still a factor that should be considered in the predictor set scoring method. This is true for both the OVA scheme and the SMA. Redundancy leads to unnecessary increase in classifier complexity and noise. However, for a given dataset, when the optimal DDP leans closer towards maximizing relevance in one case (Case 1) than in another case (Case 2), it is usually an indication that the approach used in measuring relevance in Case 1 is *more effective* than the approach used in Case 2 at identifying truly relevant features. In this particular study, Case 1 represents the OVA version of the DDP-based feature selection technique, and Case 2, the SMA version.

7 Conclusions

Based on one or more of the following criteria: class accuracy, best averaged accuracy and size-averaged accuracy, the OVA version of the DDP-based feature selection technique outperforms the SMA version. Despite the increase in computational cost and predictor set size by a factor of K, the improvement brought by the OVA scheme in terms of overall accuracy and class accuracy is especially significant for the datasets with the largest number of classes and highest level of complexity and difficulty, such as the GCM and NCI60 datasets. Furthermore, the OVA scheme brings the degree of differential prioritization closer to relevance for most of the benchmark datasets, implying better efficiency in the OVA approach at measuring relevance than the SMA.

References

1. Slonim, D.K., Tamayo, P., Mesirov, J.P., Golub, T.R., Lander, E.S.: Class prediction and discovery using gene expression data. In: RECOMB 2000 (2000) 263–272
2. Garber, M.E., Troyanskaya, O.G., Schluens, K., Petersen, S., Thaesler, Z., Pacyna-Gengelbach, M., van de Rijn, M., Rosen, G.D., Perou, C.M. , Whyte, R.I., Altman, R.B., Brown, P.O., Botstein, D., Petersen, I.: Diversity of gene expression in adenocarcinoma of the lung. Proc. Natl. Acad. Sci. 98(24) (2001) 13784–13789
3. Schena, M., Shalon, D., Davis, R.W., Brown, P.O.: Quantitative monitoring of gene expression patterns with a complementary DNA microarray. Science 270 (1995) 467–470
4. Shalon, D., Smith, S.J., Brown, P.O.: A DNA microarray system for analyzing complex DNA samples using two-color fluorescent probe hybridization. Genome Research 6(7) (1996) 639–645
5. Yu, L., Liu, H.: Redundancy Based Feature Selection for Microarray Data. In: Proc. 2004 ACM SIGKDD International Conference on Knowledge Discovery and Data Mining (2004) 737–742
6. Li, L., Weinberg, C.R., Darden, T.A., Pedersen, L.G.: Gene selection for sample classification based on gene expression data: study of sensitivity to choice of parameters of the GA/KNN method. Bioinformatics 17 (2001) 1131–1142
7. Xing, E., Jordan, M., Karp, R.: Feature selection for high-dimensional genomic microarray data. In: Proc. 18th International Conference on Machine Learning (2001) 601–608
8. Ooi, C.H., Chetty, M., Teng, S.W.: Relevance, redundancy and differential prioritization in feature selection for multiclass gene expression data. In: Oliveira, J.L., Maojo, V., Martín-Sánchez, F., and Pereira, A.S. (Eds.): Proc. 6th International Symposium on Biological and Medical Data Analysis (ISBMDA-05) (2005) 367–378
9. Platt, J.C., Cristianini, N., Shawe-Taylor, J.: Large margin DAGs for multiclass classification. Advances in Neural Information Processing Systems 12 (2000) 547–553
10. Mitchell, T.: Machine Learning, McGraw-Hill, 1997
11. Hsu, C.W., Lin, C.J.: A comparison of methods for multiclass support vector machines. IEEE Transactions on Neural Networks 13(2) (2002) 415–425

12. Li, T., Zhang, C., Ogihara, M.: A comparative study of feature selection and multiclass classification methods for tissue classification based on gene expression. Bioinformatics 20 (2004) 2429–2437
13. Chai, H., Domeniconi, C.: An evaluation of gene selection methods for multi-class microarray data classification. In: Proc. 2nd European Workshop on Data Mining and Text Mining in Bioinformatics (2004) 3–10
14. Ding, C., Peng, H.: Minimum redundancy feature selection from microarray gene expression data. In: Proc. 2nd IEEE Computational Systems Bioinformatics Conference. IEEE Computer Society (2003) 523–529
15. Dudoit, S., Fridlyand, J., Speed, T.: Comparison of discrimination methods for the classification of tumors using gene expression data. JASA 97 (2002) 77–87
16. Ramaswamy, S., Tamayo, P., Rifkin, R., Mukherjee, S., Yeang, C.H., Angelo, M., Ladd, C., Reich, M., Latulippe, E., Mesirov, J.P., Poggio, T., Gerald, W., Loda, M., Lander, E.S., Golub, T.R.: Multi-class cancer diagnosis using tumor gene expression signatures. Proc. Natl. Acad. Sci. 98 (2001) 15149–15154
17. Linder, R., Dew, D., Sudhoff, H., Theegarten D., Remberger, K., Poppl, S.J., Wagner, M.: The 'subsequent artificial neural network' (SANN) approach might bring more classificatory power to ANN-based DNA microarray analyses. Bioinformatics 20 (2004) 3544–3552
18. Ross, D.T., Scherf, U., Eisen, M.B., Perou, C.M., Spellman, P., Iyer, V., Jeffrey, S.S., Van de Rijn, M., Waltham, M., Pergamenschikov, A., Lee, J.C.F., Lashkari, D., Shalon, D., Myers, T.G., Weinstein, J.N., Botstein, D., Brown, P.O.: Systematic variation in gene expression patterns in human cancer cell lines, Nature Genetics 24(3) (2000) 227–234
19. Bhattacharjee, A., Richards, W.G., Staunton, J., Li, C., Monti, S., Vasa, P., Ladd, C., Beheshti, J., Bueno, R., Gillette, M., Loda, M., Weber, G., Mark, E.J., Lander, E.S., Wong, W., Johnson, B.E., Golub, T.R., Sugarbaker, D.J., Meyerson, M.: Classification of human lung carcinomas by mRNA expression profiling reveals distinct adenocarcinoma subclasses. Proc. Natl. Acad. Sci. 98 (2001) 13790–13795
20. Armstrong, S.A., Staunton, J.E., Silverman, L.B., Pieters, R., den Boer, M.L., Minden, M.D., Sallan, S.E., Lander, E.S., Golub, T.R., Korsmeyer, S.J.: MLL translocations specify a distinct gene expression profile that distinguishes a unique leukemia. Nature Genetics 30 (2002) 41–47
21. Golub, T.R., Slonim, D.K., Tamayo, P., Huard, C., Gaasenbeek, M., Mesirov, J.P., Coller, H., Loh, M.L., Downing, J.R., Caligiuri, M.A., Bloomfield, C.D., Lander, E.S.: Molecular classification of cancer: Class discovery and class prediction by gene expression monitoring. Science 286 (1999) 531–537
22. Yeoh, E.-J., Ross, M.E., Shurtleff, S.A., Williams, W.K., Patel, D., Mahfouz, R., Behm, F.G., Raimondi, S.C., Relling, M.V., Patel, A., Cheng, C., Campana, D., Wilkins, D., Zhou, X., Li, J., Liu, H., Pui, C.-H., Evans, W.E., Naeve, C., Wong, L., Downing, J. R.: Classification, subtype discovery, and prediction of outcome in pediatric lymphoblastic leukemia by gene expression profiling. Cancer Cell 1 (2002) 133–143
23. Khan, J., Wei, J.S., Ringner, M., Saal, L.H., Ladanyi, M., Westermann, F., Berthold, F., Schwab, M., Antonescu, C.R., Peterson, C., Meltzer, P.S.: Classification and diagnostic prediction of cancers using expression profiling and artificial neural networks. Nature Medicine 7 (2001) 673–679
24. Guyon, I., Elisseeff, A.: An introduction to variable and feature selection. Journal of Machine Learning Research 3 (2003) 1157–1182

Similarity Searching in DNA Sequences by Spectral Distortion Measures

Tuan D. Pham[1,2]

[1] Bioinformatics Applications Research Centre
[2] School of Information Technology
James Cook University
Townsville, QLD 4811, Australia
tuan.pham@jcu.edu.au

Abstract. Searching for similarity among biological sequences is an important research area of bioinformatics because it can provide insight into the evolutionary and genetic relationships between species that open doors to new scientific discoveries such as drug design and treament. In this paper, we introduce a novel measure of similarity between two biological sequences without the need of alignment. The method is based on the concept of spectral distortion measures developed for signal processing. The proposed method was tested using a set of six DNA sequences taken from *Escherichia coli* K-12 and *Shigella flexneri*, and one random sequence. It was further tested with a complex dataset of 40 DNA sequences taken from the GenBank sequence database. The results obtained from the proposed method are found superior to some existing methods for similarity measure of DNA sequences.

1 Introduction

Given the importance of research into methodologies for computing similarity among biological sequences, there have been a number of computational and statistical methods for the comparison of biological sequences developed over the past decade. However, it still remains a challenging problem for the research community of computational biology [1,2]. Two distinct bioinformatic methodologies for studying the similarity/dissimilarity of sequences are known as alignment-based and alignment-free methods. The search for optimal solutions using sequence alignment-based methods is encountered with difficulty in computational aspect with regard to large biological databases. Therefore, the emergence of research into alignment-free sequence analysis is apparent and necessary to overcome critical limitations of sequence analysis by alignment.

Methods for alignment-free sequence comparison of biological sequences utilize several concepts of distance measures [3], such as the Euclidean distance [4], Euclidean and Mahalanobis distances [5], Markov chain models and Kullback-Leibler discrepancy (KLD) [6], cosine distance [7], Kolmogorov complexity [8], and chaos theory [9]. Our previous work [10] on sequence comparison has some strong similarity to the work by Wu et al. [6], in which statistical measures

P. Perner (Ed.): ICDM 2006, LNAI 4065, pp. 24–37, 2006.

of DNA sequence dissimilarity are performed using the Mahalanobis distance and the standardized Euclidean distance under Markov chain model of base composition, as well as the extended KLD. The KLD extended by Wu et al. [6] was computed in terms of two vectors of relative frequencies of n-words over a sliding window from two given DNA sequences. Whereas, our previous work derives a probabilistic distance between two sequences using a symmetrized version of the KLD, which directly compares two Markov models built for the two corresponding biological sequences.

Among alignment-free methods for computing distances between biological sequences, there seems rarely any work that directly computes distances between biological sequences using the concept of a distortion measure (error matching). If a distortion model can be constructed for two biological sequences, we can readily measure the similarity between these two sequences. In addition, based on the principles that spectral distortion measures are derived [11], their use is robust for handling signals subjected to noise and having significantly different lengths; and for extracting good features in order to enable the task of a pattern classifier much more effective.

In this paper we are interested in the novel application of some spectral distortion measures to obtain solutions to difficult problems in computational biology: i) studying the relationships between different DNA sequences for biologcal inference, and ii) searching for similar library sequences stored in a database to a given query sequence. These tasks are designed to be carried out in such a way that the computation is efficient and does not depend on sequence alignment.

In the following sections we will firstly discuss how a DNA sequence can be represented as a sequence of corresponding numerical values; secondly we will then address how we can extract the spectral feature of DNA sequences using the method of linear predictive coding; thirdly we will present the concept of distortion measures of any pair of DNA sequences, which serve as the basis for the computation of sequence similarity. We have tested our method with six DNA sequences taken from *Escherichia coli* K-12 and *Shigella flexneri*, and one simulated sequence to discover their relations; and a complex set of 40 DNA sequences to search for most similar sequences to a particular query sequence. We have found that the results obtained from our proposed method are better than those obtained from other distance measures [6,10].

2   Numerical Representation of Biological Sequences

One of the problems that hinder the application of signal processing to biological sequence analysis is that either DNA or protein sequences are represented by characters and thus do not make themselves ready for numerical signal-processing based methods [16,17]. One available and mathematically sound model for converting a character-based biological sequence into a numeral-based biological one is the resonant recognition model (RRM) [12,13]. We therefore adopted the RRM to implement the novel application of the linear predictive coding and its cepstral distortion measures for DNA sequence analysis.

The resonant recognition model (RRM) is a physical and mathematical model which can extract protein or DNA sequences using signal analysis methods. This approach can be divided into two parts. The first part involves the transformation of a biological sequence into a numerical sequence – each amino acid or nucleotide can be represented by the value of the electron-ion interaction potential (EIIP) [14] which describes the average energy states of all valence electrons in a particular amino acid or nucleotide. The EIIP values for each nucleotide or amino acid were calculated using the following general model pseudopotential [12,14,15]:

$$< k + q[w]k >= \frac{0.25 Z \sin(\pi \times 1.04 Z)}{2\pi} \tag{1}$$

Where q is a change of momentum of the delocalised electron in the intreaction with potential w, and

$$Z = \frac{(\sigma Z_i)}{N} \tag{2}$$

where Z_i is the number of valence electrons of the ith component, N is the total number of atoms in the amino acid or nucleotide. Each amino acid or nucleotide can be converted as a unique number, regardless of its position in a sequence (see Table 1).

Numerical series obtained this way are then analyzed by digital signal analysis methods in order to extract information adequate to the biological function. Discrete Fourier transform (DFT) is applied to convert the numerical sequence t o the frequency domain sequence. After that, for the purpose of extracting mutual spectral characteristics of sequences, having the same or similar biological function, cross-spectral function is used:

$$S_n = X_n Y_n^* \qquad n = 1, 2, \ldots, \frac{N}{2} \tag{3}$$

where X_n is the DFT coefficients of the x_m, Y_n^* is the complex conjugate DFT coefficients of the $y(m)$. Based on the above cross-spectral function, we can obtain a spectrum. In the spectrum, peak frequencies, which are assumed that mutual spectral frequency of two analyzed sequences, can be observed [13].

Additionally, when we want to examine the mutual frequency components for a group of protein sequences, we usually need to calculate the absolute values of multiple cross-spectral function coefficients M:

$$|M_n| = |X1_n| \cdot |X1_n| \ldots |XM_n| \qquad n = 1, 2, \ldots, \frac{N}{2} \tag{4}$$

Furthermore, a signal-to-noise ratio (SNR) of the consensus spectrum (the multiple cross-spectral function for a large group of sequences with the same biological function, which has been named *consensus spectrum* [13]), is found as a magnitude of the largest frequency component relative to the mean value of the spectrum. The peak frequency component in the consensus spectrum is considered to be significant if the value of the SNR is at least 20 [13]. Significant frequency component is the characteristic RRM frequency for the entire group of biological sequences, having the same biological function, since it is the strongest frequency component common to all of the biological sequences from that particular functional group.

Table 1. Electron-Ion Interaction Potential (EIIP) values for nucleotides and amino acids [13,15]

Nucleotide	EIIP
A	0.1260
G	0.0806
T	0.1335
C	0.1340

Amino acid	EIIP
Leu	0.0000
Ile	0.0000
Asn	0.0036
Gly	0.0050
Val	0.0057
Glu	0.0058
Pro	0.0198
His	0.0242
Lys	0.0371
Ala	0.0373
Tyr	0.0516
Trp	0.0548
Gln	0.0761
Met	0.0823
Ser	0.0829
Cys	0.0829
Thr	0.0941
Phe	0.0946
Arg	0.0959
Asp	0.1263

Apart from this approach to the analysis of biological sequences, the RRM also offers some physical explanation of the selective interactions between biological macromolecules, based on their structure. The RRM considers that these selective interactions (that is the recognition of a target molecule by another molecule, for example, recognition of a promoter by RNA polymerase) are caused by resonant electromagnetic energy exchange, hence the name *resonant recognition model*. According to the RRM, the charge that is being transferred along the backbone of a macromolecule travels through the changing electric field described by a sequence of EIIPs, causing the radiation of some small amount of electromagnetic energy at particular frequencies that can be recognized by other molecules. So far, the RRM has had some success in terms of designing a new spectral analysis of biological sequences (DNA/protein sequences) [13].

3   Spectral Features of DNA Sequences

Having pointed out that the difficulty for the application of signal processing to the analysis of biological data is that it deals with numerical sequences rather than character strings. If a character string can be converted into a numerical sequence, then digital signal processing can provide a set of novel and useful tools for solving highly relevant problems. By making use of the EIIP values for DNA sequences, we will apply the principle of linear predictive coding (LPC) to extract the spectral feature of a DNA sequence known as the LPC cepstral coefficients, which have been successfully used for speech recognition.

We are motivated to explore the use of the LPC model because, in general, time-series signals analyzed by the LPC have several advantanges as follows. First, the LPC is an analytically tractable model which is mathematically precise and simple for computer implementation. Second, the LPC model and its LPC-based distortion measures have been proved to give excellent solutions to many problems concerining with pattern recognition [19].

3.1   Linear Prediction Coefficients

The estimated value of a particular nucleotide s_m at position or time n, denoted as $\hat{s}(n)$, can be calculated as a linear combination of the past p samples. This linear prediction can be expressed as [18,19]

$$\hat{s}(n) = \sum_{k=1}^{p} a_k \, s(n-k) \tag{5}$$

where the terms $\{a_k\}$ are called the linear prediction coefficients (LPC).

The prediction error $e(n)$ between the observed sample $s(n)$ and the predicted value $\hat{s}(n)$ can be defined as

$$e(n) = s(n) - \hat{s}(n) = s(n) - \sum_{k=1}^{p} a_k \, s(n-k) \tag{6}$$

The prediction coefficients $\{a_k\}$ can be optimally determined by minimizing the sum of squared errors

$$E = \sum_{n=1}^{N} e^2(n) = \sum_{n=1}^{N} \left[s(n) - \sum_{k=1}^{p} a_k \, s(n-k) \right]^2 \tag{7}$$

To solve (7) for the prediction coefficients, we differentiate E with respect to eack a_k and equate the result to zero:

$$\frac{\partial E}{\partial a_k} = 0, \; k = 1, \ldots, p \tag{8}$$

The result is a set of p linear equations

$$\sum_{k=1}^{p} a_k \, r(|m-k|) = r(m), \; m = 1, \ldots, p \tag{9}$$

where $r(m - k)$ is the autocorrelation function of $s(n)$, that is symmetric, i.e. $r(-k) = r(k)$, and expressed as

$$r(m) = \sum_{n=1}^{N-m} s(n)\, s(n + m), \quad m = 0, \ldots, p \tag{10}$$

Equation (9) can be expressed in matrix form as

$$\mathbf{R}\,\mathbf{a} = \mathbf{r} \tag{11}$$

where $\mathbf{R}$ is a $p \times p$ autocorrelation matrix, $\mathbf{r}$ is a $p \times 1$ autocorrelation vector, and $\mathbf{a}$ is a $p \times 1$ vector of prediction coefficients:

$$\mathbf{R} = \begin{bmatrix} r(0) & r(1) & r(2) & \cdots & r(p-1) \\ r(1) & r(0) & r(1) & \cdots & r(p-2) \\ r(2) & r(1) & r(0) & \cdots & r(p-3) \\ \cdot & \cdot & \cdot & \cdots & \cdot \\ r(p-1) & r(p-2) & r(p-3) & \cdots & r(0) \end{bmatrix}$$

$$\mathbf{a}^T = \begin{bmatrix} a_1 & a_2 & a_3 & \cdots & a_p \end{bmatrix}$$

where $\mathbf{a}^T$ is the tranpose of $\mathbf{a}$, and

$$\mathbf{r}^T = \begin{bmatrix} r(1) & r(2) & r(3) & \cdots & r(p) \end{bmatrix}$$

where $\mathbf{r}^T$ is the tranpose of $\mathbf{r}$.

Thus, the LPC coefficients can be obtained by solving

$$\mathbf{a} = \mathbf{R}^{-1}\,\mathbf{r} \tag{12}$$

where $\mathbf{R}^{-1}$ is the inverse of $\mathbf{R}$.

3.2 LPC Cepstral Coefficients

If we can determine the linear prediction coefficients for a biological sequence s_l, then we can also extract another feature as the cepstral coefficients, c_m, which are directly derived from the LPC coefficients. The LPC cepstral coefficients can be determined by the following recursion [19].

$$c_0 = \ln(G^2) \tag{13}$$

$$c_m = a_m + \sum_{k=1}^{m-1} \left(\frac{k}{m}\right) c_k a_{m-k}, \quad 1 \leq m \leq p \tag{14}$$

$$c_m = \sum_{k=1}^{m-1} \left(\frac{k}{m}\right) c_k a_{m-k}, \quad m > p \tag{15}$$

where G is the LPC gain, whose squared term is given as [20]

$$G^2 = r(0) - \sum_{k=1}^{p} a_k r(k) \tag{16}$$

4 Spectral Distortion Measures

Methods for measuring similarity or dissimilarity between two vectors or sequences is one of the most important algorithms in the field of pattern comparison and recognition. The calculation of vector similarity is based on various developments of distance and distortion measures. Before proceeding to the mathematical description of a distortion measure, we wish to point out the difference between distance and distortion functions [19], where the latter is more restricted in a mathematical sense.

Let $\mathbf{x}$, $\mathbf{y}$, and $\mathbf{z}$ be the vectors defined on a vector space V. A metric or distance d on V is defined as a real-valued function on the Cartesian product $V \times V$ if it has the following properties:

1. Positive definiteness: $0 \leq d(\mathbf{x}, \mathbf{y}) < \infty$, $\mathbf{x}, \mathbf{y} \in V$ and $d(\mathbf{x}, \mathbf{y}) = 0$ iff $\mathbf{x} = \mathbf{y}$;
2. Symmetry: $d(\mathbf{x}, \mathbf{y}) = d(\mathbf{y}, \mathbf{x})$ for $\mathbf{x}, \mathbf{y} \in V$;
3. Triangle inequality: $d(\mathbf{x}, \mathbf{z}) \leq d(\mathbf{x}, \mathbf{y}) + d(\mathbf{y}, \mathbf{z})$ for $\mathbf{x}, \mathbf{y}, \mathbf{z} \in V$.

If a measure of dissimilarity satisfies only the property of positive definiteness, it is referred to as a distortion measure which is considered very common for the vectorized representations of signal spectra [19] In this sense, what we will describe next is the mathematical measure of distortion which relaxes the properties of symmetry and triangle inequality. We therefore will use the term D to denote a distortion measure. In general, to calculate a distortion measure between two vectors $\mathbf{x}$ and $\mathbf{y}$, $D(\mathbf{x}, \mathbf{y})$, is to calculate a cost of reproducing any input vector $\mathbf{x}$ as a reproduction of vector $\mathbf{y}$. Given such a distortion measure, the mismatch between two signals can be quantified by an average distortion between the input and the final reproduction. Intuitively, a match of the two patterns is good if the average distortion is small. The long-termed sample average can be expressed as [21]

$$\lim_{n \to \infty} \frac{1}{n} \sum_{i=1}^{n} D(\mathbf{x}_i, \mathbf{y}_i) \tag{17}$$

If the vector process is stationary and ergodic, then the limit exists and equals to the expectation of $D(\mathbf{x}_i, \mathbf{y}_i)$. Being analogous to the issue of selecting a particular distance measure for a particular problem, there is no fixed rule for selecting a distortion measure for quantifying the performance of a particular system. In general, an ideal distortion measure should be [21]:

1. Tractable to allow analysis,
2. Computationally efficient to allow real-time evaluation, and
3. Meaningful to allow correlation with good and poor subjective quality.

To introduce the basic concept of the spectral distortion measures, we will discuss the formulation of a ratio of the prediction errors whose value can be used to expressed the magnitude of the difference between two feature vectors.

Consider passing a sequence $s(n)$ through the inverse LPC system with its LPC coefficient vector $\mathbf{a}$. This will yield the prediction error, $e(n)$, which can be alternatively defined by

$$e(n) = -\sum_{i=0}^{p} a_i s(n-i) \tag{18}$$

where $a_0 = -1$.

The sum of squared errors can be now expressed as

$$E = \sum_{n=0}^{N-1+p} e^2(n) + \sum_{n=0}^{N-1+p} \left[-\sum_{i=0}^{p} a_i s(n-i) \right] \left[-\sum_{j=0}^{p} a_j s(n-j) \right]$$

$$= \sum_{i=0}^{p} a_i \sum_{j=0}^{p} a_j \sum_{n=0}^{N-1+p} s(n-i) s(n-j) \tag{19}$$

We also have

$$\sum_{n=0}^{N-1+p} s(n-i) s(n-j) = \sum_{n=0}^{N-1+p} s(n) s(n-j+i) = r(|i-j|) \tag{20}$$

Therefore,

$$E = \sum_{i=0}^{p} a_i \sum_{j=0}^{p} a_j r(|i-j|) = \mathbf{a}^T \mathbf{R}_s \mathbf{a} \tag{21}$$

Similarly, consider passing another sequence $s'(n)$ through the inverse LPC system with the same LPC coefficients $\mathbf{a}$. The prediction error, $e'(n)$, is expressed as

$$e'(n) = -\sum_{i=0}^{p} a_i s'(n-i) \tag{22}$$

where $a_0 = -1$.

Using the same derivation for $s(n)$, the sum of squared errors for $s'(n)$ is

$$E' = \sum_{i=0}^{p} a_i \sum_{j=0}^{p} a_j r'(|i-j|) = \mathbf{a}^T \mathbf{R}_{s'} \mathbf{a} \tag{23}$$

where

$$\mathbf{R}_{s'} = \begin{bmatrix} r'(0) & r'(1) & r'(2) & \cdots & r'(p-1) \\ r'(1) & r'(0) & r'(1) & \cdots & r'(p-2) \\ r'(2) & r'(1) & r'(0) & \cdots & r'(p-3) \\ \cdot & \cdot & \cdot & \cdots & \cdot \\ r'(p-1) & r'(p-2) & r'(p-3) & \cdots & r'(0) \end{bmatrix}$$

It can be seen that E' must be greater than or equal to E because E is the minimum prediction error for the LPC system with the LPC coefficients $\mathbf{a}$. Thus, the ratio of the two prediction errors, denoted as D, can be now defined by

$$D = \frac{E'}{E} = \frac{\mathbf{a}^T \mathbf{R}_{s'} \mathbf{a}}{\mathbf{a}^T \mathbf{R}_s \mathbf{a}} \geq 1 \tag{24}$$

By now it can be seen that the derivation of the above distortion is based on the concept of the *error matching measure*.

4.1   LPC Likelihood Distortion

Consider the two spectra, magnitude-squared Fourier transforms, $S(\omega)$ and $S'(\omega)$ of the two signals s and s', where ω is the normalized frequency ranging from $-\pi$ to π. The log spectral difference between the two spectra is defined by [19]

$$V(\omega) = \log S(\omega) - \log S'(\omega) \tag{25}$$

which is the basis for the distortion measure proposed by Itakura and Saito in their formulation of linear prediction as an approximate maximum likelihood estimation.

The Itakura-Saito distortion measure, D_{IS}, is defined as [22]

$$D_{IS} = \int_{-\pi}^{\pi} [e^{V(\omega)} - V(\omega) - 1] \frac{d\omega}{2\pi} = \int_{-\pi}^{\pi} \frac{S(\omega)}{S'(\omega)} \frac{d\omega}{2\pi} - \log \frac{\sigma_\infty^2}{\sigma_\infty'^2} - 1 \tag{26}$$

where σ_∞^2 and $\sigma_\infty'^2$ are the one-step prediction errors of $S(\omega)$ and $S'(\omega)$, respectively, and defined as

$$\sigma_\infty^2 \approx \exp \left\{ \int_{-\pi}^{\pi} \log S(\omega) \frac{d\omega}{2\pi} \right\}. \tag{27}$$

It was pointed out that the Itakura-Saito distortion measure is connected with many statistical and information theories [19] including the likelihood ratio test, discrimination information, and Kullback-Leibler divergence. Based on the notion of the Itakura-Saito distortion measure, the LPC likelihood ratio distortion between two signals s and s' is derived and expressed as [19]

$$D_{LR} = \frac{\mathbf{a}'^T \mathbf{R}_s \mathbf{a}'}{\mathbf{a}^T \mathbf{R}_s \mathbf{a}} - 1 \tag{28}$$

where $\mathbf{R}_s$ is the autocorrelation matrix of sequence s associated with its LPC coefficient vector $\mathbf{a}$, and $\mathbf{a}'$ is the LPC coefficient vector of signal s'.

4.2   LPC Cepstral Distortion

Let $S(\omega)$ be the power spectrum of a signal. The complex cepstrum of the signal is defined as the Fourier transform of the log of the signal spectrum:

$$\log S(\omega) = \sum_{n=-\infty}^{\infty} c_n e^{-jn\omega} \tag{29}$$

where $c_n = -c_n$ are real and referred to as the cepstral coefficients.

Consider $S(\omega)$ and $S'(\omega)$ to be the power spectra of the two signals and apply the Parseval's theorem [23], the L_2-norm cepstral distance between $S(\omega)$ and $S'(\omega)$ can be related to the root-mean-square log spectral distance as [19]

$$D_c^2 = \int_{-\pi}^{\pi} |\log S(\omega) - \log S'(\omega)|^2 \frac{d\omega}{2\pi}$$

$$= \sum_{n=-\infty}^{\infty} (c_n - c_n')^2 \tag{30}$$

where c_n and c_n' are the cepstral coefficients of $S(\omega)$ and $S'(\omega)$ respectively.

Since the cepstrum is a decaying sequence, the infinite number of terms in (30) can be truncated to some finite number $L \geq p$, that is

$$D_c^2(L) = \sum_{m=1}^{L} (c_m - c_m') \tag{31}$$

5   Experiments

We have carried two experiments to test and compare the proposed method with other existing approaches. The first test was carried out to find out the phylogenetics between the thrA, thrB and thrC genes of the threonine operons from Escherichia coli K-12 and from Shigella flexneri; and one random sequence. The second test involves a complex set of 40 DNA sequences, which was used for searching similar sequences to a query sequence.

5.1   Phylogenetic Study of DNA Sequences

The algorithm was tested with 6 DNA sequences, taken from the threonine operons of Escherichia coli K-12 (gi:1786181) and Shigella flexneri (gi:30039813). The three sequences taken from each threonine operon are thrA (aspartokinase I-homoserine dehydrogenase I), thrB (homoserine kinase) and thrC (threonine synthase), using the open reading frames (ORFs) 3372799 (ec-thrA), 28013733 (ec-thrB) and 37345020 (ec-thrC) in the case of E.coli K-12, and 3362798 (sf-thrA), 28003732 (sf-thrB) and 37335019 (sf-thrC) in the case of S.flexneri. All the sequences were obtained from GenBank (www.ncbi.nlm.nih.gov/Entrez). In addition, we compared all six sequences with a randomly generated sequence (rand-thrA), using the same length and base composition as ec-thrA.

To compare our proposed technique with other methods, we calculated the sequence similarity or sequence distance using alignment-based methods. All seven sequences have been aligned using CLUSTALW [24]. The multiple sequence alignment has then been used to calculate an identity matrix and the distance matrix using DNADist from the PHYLIP package [25] and the modification of the Kimura distance model [26]. The DNADist program uses nucleotide sequences to compute a distance matrix, under the modified Kimura model of nucleotide substitution. Being similiar to the Jukes and Cantor model [27], which constructs the transition probability matrix based on the assumption that a base change is independent of its identity, the Kimura 2-paramter model allows for a difference between transition and transversion rates in the construction of the DNA distance matrix.

The results obtained using all the presented spectral distortion measures agree with the SimMM [10] and the chaos game representation [9] even though we used seven sequences as test sets; where ec-thrA is closer to ec-thrC than to ec-thrB, and ec-thrB is closer to ec-thrA than to ec-thrC. This relationship was found within both species, E.coli K-12 and S.flexneri. We need to point out that this agreement between these models does not confirm any hypothesis about the relationships of these threonine operons since we have found no current phylogenetic study of these threonine operons in the literature. The alignment-based methods, on the other hand, show a slightly different relationship between the three different sequences. The calculations from both the identity and distance matrices place the thrA sequences closer to thrB than to thrC, and thrB closer to thrC than to thrA. However, the identity-matrix based model places rand-thrA closer to the two thrA sequences, whose relationship is not supposed to be so.

5.2   Database Searching of Similar Sequences

The proposed spectral distortion measures were further tested to search for DNA sequences being similar to a query sequence from a database of 39 library sequences, of which 20 sequences are known to be similar in biological function to the query sequence, and the remaining 19 sequences are known as being not similar in biological function to the query sequence. These 39 sequences were selected from mammals, viruses, plants, etc., of which lengths vary between 322 and 14 121 bases. All of these sequences can be obtained from the GenBank sequence database (http://www.ncbi.nlm.nih.gov/Entrez/). The query sequence is HSLIPAS (Human mRNA for lipoprotein lipase), which has 1612 bases.

The 20 sequences, which are known as being similar in biological function to HSLIPAS are as follows: OOLPLIP (Oestrus ovis mRNA for lipoprotein lipase, 1656 bp), SSLPLRNA (pig back fat Sus scrofa cDNAsimilar to S.scrofa LPL mRNA for lipoprotein lipase, 2963 bp), RATLLIPA (Rattus norvegicus lipoprotein lipase mRNA, complete cds, 3617 bp), MUSLIPLIP (Mus musculus lipoprotein lipase gene, partial cds, 3806 bp), GPILPPL (guinea pig lipoprotein lipase mRNA, complete cds, 1744 bp), GGLPL (chicken mRNA for adipose lipoprotein lipase, 2328 bp), HSHTGL (human mRNA for hepatic triglyceride lipase, 1603 bp), HUMLIPH (human hepatic lipase mRNA, complete cds, 1550 bp), HUMLIPH06 (human hepatic lipase gene, exon 6, 322 bp), RATHLP (rat hepatic lipase mRNA, 1639 bp), RABTRIL [Oryctolagus cuniculus (clone TGL-5K) triglyceride lipase mRNA, complete cds, 1444 bp], ECPL (Equus caballus mRNA for pancreatic lipase, 1443 bp), DOGPLIP (canine lipase mRNA, complete cds, 1493 bp), DMYOLK [Drosophila gene for yolk protein I (vitellogenin), 1723 bp], BOVLDLR [bovine low-density lipoprotein (LDL) receptor mRNA, 879 bp], HSBMHSP (Homo sapiens mRNA for basement membrane heparan sulfate proteoglycan, 13 790 bp), HUMAPOAICI (human apolipoprotein A-I and C-III genes, complete cds, 8966 bp), RABVLDLR (O.cuniculus mRNA for very LDL receptor, complete cds, 3209 bp), HSLDL100 (human mRNA for apolipoprotein B-100, 14 121 bp) and HUMAPOBF (human apolipoprotein B-100 mRNA, complete cds, 10 089 bp).

The other 19 sequences known as being not similar in biological function to HSLIPAS are as follows: A1MVRNA2 [alfalfa mosaic virus (A1M4) RNA 2, 2593 bp], AAHAV33A [Acanthocheilonema viteae pepsin-inhibitorlike- protein (Av33) mRNA sequence, 1048 bp], AA2CG (adeno-associated virus 2, complete genome, 4675 bp), ACVPBD64 (artificial cloning vector plasmid BD64, 4780 bp), AL3HP (bacteriophage alpha-3 H protein gene, complete cds, 1786 bp), AAABDA[Aedes aegypti abd-A gene for abdominal-A protein homolog (partial), 1759 bp], BACBDGALA [Bacillus circulans beta-d-galactosidase (bgaA) gene, complete cds, 2555 bp], BBCA (Bos taurus mRNA for cyclin A, 1512 bp), BCP1 (bacteriophage Chp1 genome DNA, complete sequence, 4877 bp) and CHIBATPB (sweet potato chloroplast F1-ATPase beta and epsilon-subunit genes, 2007 bp), A7NIFH (Anabaena 7120 nifH gene, complete CDS, 1271 bp), AA16S (Amycolatopsis azurea 16S rRNA, 1300 bp), ABGACT2 (Absidia glauca actin mRNA, complete cds, 1309 bp), ACTIBETLC (Actinomadura R39 DNA for beta-lactamase gene, 1902 bp), AMTUGSNRNA (Ambystoma mexicanum AmU1 snRNA gene, complete sequence, 1027 bp), ARAST18B (cloning vector pAST 18b for Caenorhabditis elegans, 3052 bp), GCALIP2 (Geotrichum candidum mRNA for lipase II precursor, partial cds, 1767 bp), AGGGLINE (Ateles geoffroyi gamma-globin gene and L1 LINE element, 7360 bp) and HUMCAN (H.sapiens CaN19 mRNA sequence, 427 bp).

Sensitivity and selectivity were computed to evaluate and compare the performance of the proposed models with other distance measures [6]. Sensitivity is expressed by the number of HSLIPAS related sequences found among the first closest 20 library sequences; whereas selectivity is expressed in terms of the number of HSLIPAS-related sequences of which distances are closer to HSLIPAS than others and are not truncated by the first HSLIPAS-unrelated sequence. Among several distance measures introduced by Wu et al. [6], they concluded that the standardized Euclidean distance under the Markov chain models of base composition was generally recommended, of which sensitivity and selectivity are 18 and 17 sequences respectively, of order one for base composition, and 18 and 16 sequences, respectively, of order two for base composition; when all the distances of nine different word sizes were combined. Both sensitivity and selectivity obtained from SimMM are 18 sequences. The sensitivity and selectivity obtained from the LPC likelihood distortion are 19 and 18 sequences respectively; whereas the LPC cepstral distortion achieved 20 sequences for both sensitivity and selectivity. The results obtained from the distortion measures show their superiority over the other methods for database searching of similar DNA sequences.

6   Conclusions

Comparison between sequences is a key step in bioinformatics when analyzing similarities of functions and properties of different sequences. Similarly, evolutionary homology is analyzed by comparing DNA and protein sequences. So far, most such analyses are conducted by aligning first the sequences and then comparing at each position the variation or similarity of the sequences. Multiple sequence alignments of several hundred sequences is thereby always a bottleneck, first due to long computational time, and second due to possible bias of multiple sequence alignments for multiple occurrences of highly similar sequences. An alignment-free comparison method is therefore of great value as it reduces the technical constraints as only pairwise comparisons are necessary, and is free of bias. Non-alignment methods are designed to compare each pair unrelated to other pairwise comparisons, and the distortion measures can compute pair-wise sequence similarity in such fashion. Given an appropriate numerical representation of DNA sequences, the performance of the new approach for DNA sequence comparison has been found to be better than that of other existing non-alignment methods. Spectral distortion measures are computationally efficient, mathematically tractable, and physically meaningful.

Some issues for future investigations will include further exploration of models for numeral representation of biological sequences – the current experimental results analyzed by the LPC-based distortion measures are affected by the RRM which is not a unique way for expressing character-based biological sequence in terms of numerical values. The application of vector quantization (VQ) [21] of LPC coefficients, where the distance measure is the distance between two LPC vectors, can be a potential approach for improving the calculation of similarity. This can also be readily extended to the use of VQ-based hidden Markov models [19] for similarity searching.

References

1. Ewens, W.J. and Grant,G.R.: Statistical Methods in Bioinformatics. Springer, NY, 2001.
2. Miller,W.: Comparison of genomic DNA sequences: solved and unsolved problems. Bioinformatics **17** (2001) 391397.
3. Vinga,S. and Almeida,J.: Alignment-free sequence comparisona review. Bioinformatics **19** (2003) 513523.
4. Blaisdell, B.E.: Ameasure of the similarity of sets of sequences not requiring sequence alignment. Proc. Natl Acad. Sci. USA **83** (1986) 51555159.
5. Wu,T.J., Burke,J.P. and Davison,D.B.: A measure of DNA sequence dissimilarity based on Mahalanobis distance between frequencies of words. Biometrics **53** (1997) 14311439.
6. Wu,T.J., Hsieh,Y.C. and Li,L.A.: Statistical measures of DNA dissimilarity under Markov chain models of base composition. Biometrics **57** (2001) 441448.
7. Stuart,G.W., Moffett,K. and Baker,S.: Integrated gene and species phylogenies from unaligned whole genome protein sequences. Bioinformatics **18** (2002) 100108.
8. Li,M., Badger,J.H., Chen,X., Kwong,S., Kearney,P. and Zhang,H.: An information-based sequence distance and its application to whole mitochondrial genome phylogeny. Bioinformatics **17** (2001) 149154.
9. Almeida,J.S., Carrico,J.A., Maretzek,A., Noble,P.A. and Fletcher,M.: Analysis of genomic sequences by chaos game representation. Bioinformatics **17** (2001) 429437.
10. Pham, T.D., and Zuegg, J.: A probabilistic measure for alignment-free sequence comparison. Bioinformatics **20** (2004) 34553461.

11. Nocerino, N., Soong, F.K., Rabiner, L.R. and D.H. Klatt, D.H.: Comparative study of several distortion measures for speech recognition, *IEEE Proc. Int. Conf. Acoustics, Speech, and Signal Processing* **11.4.1** (1985) 387-390.

12. Veljkovic, V. and Slavic, I: General model of pseudopotentials, *Physical Review Lett.* **29** (1972) pp. 105-108.

13. Cosic, I.: Macromolecular bioactivity: Is it resonant interaction between macromolecules? – theory and applications, *IEEE trans. Biomedical Engineering* **41** (1994) 1101-1114.

14. Veljkovic, V., Cosic, I., Dimitrijevic, B. and Lalovic, D.: Is it possible to analyze DNA and protein sequences by the methods of digital signal processing? *IEEE Trans. Biomed. Eng.* **32** (1985) 337-341.

15. C.H. de Trad, Q. Fang, and I. Cosic, Protein sequence comparison based on the wavelet transform approach, *Protein Engineering* **15** (2002) 193-203.

16. Anatassiou, D.: Frequency-domain analysis of biomolecular sequences, *Bioinformatics* **16** (2000) 1073-1082.

17. Anatassiou, D.: Genomic signal processing, *IEEE Signal Processing Magazine* **18** (2001) 8-20.

18. Makhoul, J.: Linear prediction: a tutorial review, *Proc. IEEE* **63** (1975) 561-580.

19. Rabiner, L. and Juang, B.H.: *Fundamentals of Speech Recognition.* New Jersey, Prentice Hall, 1993.

20. Ingle, V.K. and Proakis, J.G.: *Digital Signal Processing Using Matlab V.4.* Boston, PWS Publishing, 1997.

21. Gray, R.M.: Vector quantization, *IEEE ASSP Mag.* **1** (1984) 4-29.

22. Itakura, F. and S. Saito, S.: A statistical method for estimation of speech spectral density and formant frequencies, *Electronics and Communications in Japan* **53A** (1970) 36-43.

23. O'Shaughnessy, D.: *Speech Communication – Human and Machine.* Reading, Massachusetts, Addison-Wesley, 1987.

24. Thompson, J.D., Higgins, D.G. and Gibson, T.J.: CLUSTALW: improving the sensitivity of progressive multiple sequence alignment through sequence weighting, position-specific gap penalties and weight matrix choice. Nucleic Acids Res. **22** (1994) 4673-4680.

25. Felsenstein, J.: PHYLIP (Phylogeny Inference Package), version 3.5c. Distributed by the Author, Department of Genetics, University of Washington, Seattle, WA, 1993.

26. Kimura, M.: A simple method for estimating evolutionary rate of base substitutions through comparative studies of nucleotide sequences. J. Mol. Evol. **16** (1980) 111-120.

27. Jukes, T.H. and Cantor, C.R.: Evolution of protein molecules. In Munro,H.N. (ed.), Mammalian Protein Metabolism. Academic Press, NY, pp. 21-132, 1969.

Multispecies Gene Entropy Estimation, a Data Mining Approach

Xiaoxu Han

Department of Mathematics and Bioinformatics Program
Eastern Michigan University, Ypsilanti, MI 48197
xiaoxu.han@emich.edu

Abstract. This paper presents a data mining approach to estimate multispecies gene entropy by using a self-organizing map (SOM) to mine a homologous gene set. The gene distribution function for each gene in the feature space is approximated by its probability distribution in the feature space. The phylogenetic applications of the multispecies gene entropy are investigated in an example of inferring the species phylogeny of eight yeast species. It is found that genes with the nearest K-L distances to the minimum entropy gene are more likely to be phylogenetically informative. The K-L distances of genes are strongly correlated with the spectral radiuses of their identity percentage matrices. The images of identity percentage matrices of the genes with small K-L distances to the minimum entropy gene are more similar to the image of the minimum entropy gene in their frequency domains after fast Fourier transforms (FFT) than the images of those genes with large K-L distances to the minimum entropy gene. Finally, a K-L distance based gene concatenation approach under gene clustering is proposed to infer species phylogenies robustly and systematically.

1 Introduction

Entropy is a measure of the average amount of unpredictability conveyed by an information source. For a sequence of symbols $x = x_1 x_2 ... x_m, x_i \in \Gamma$, where Γ is an alphabet and $|\Gamma|$ is the size of the alphabet, the Shannon entropy can be defined as

$$H(x) = -\sum_{i=1}^{|\Gamma|} p_i \log p_i \tag{1}$$

The p_i is the probability of the occurrence of the ith symbol in the alphabet. If the alphabet is defined as a set of nucleotides : $\Gamma = \{A, T, C, G\}$, then $H(x)$ describes the information of randomness or state of order conveyed by a DNA sequence. Because the single character based Shannon entropy analysis is far from sufficiency to explore the information conveyed by a DNA sequence [1,2], it is often generalized to a block entropy to investigate more structural information embedded in a DNA sequence; that is,

$$H_n(x) = -\sum_{i=1}^{|\Sigma|} p_i^{(n)} \log p_i^{(n)} \tag{2}$$

P. Perner (Ed.): ICDM 2006, LNAI 4065, pp. 38–52, 2006.

Where $p_i^{(n)}$ is the probability of occurrence of the ith symbol block with n nucleotides in the symbol space Σ. The symbol space Σ with size 4^n, is a set of all possible combinations of n nucleotides and also called a sequence space. It is easy to prove that the block entropy is a non-decreasing function of block length n : $H_n(x) \le H_{n+1}(x)$. In the actual entropy calculation, the n-block probability $p_i^{(n)}$ is generally approximated by its corresponding relative frequency: $p_i^{(n)} \approx f_i^{(n)} = \frac{k_i}{L}$, where k_i is the number of occurrence of ith symbol block and L is the sequence length. Such an approach will systematically underestimate the block entropies and suffers from slow convergence [3,4,5]. Despite the finite sample effect problem in the block entropy estimation, the block entropy and its variants are widely applied in gene prediction, intron / exon comparison, codon usage bias measuring, sequence motif modeling and protein structure prediction [5,6,7].

1.1 Multispecies Gene Entropy

Although there are a lot of methods proposed and applications developed related to DNA entropy, there is little work on the gene entropy especially multispecies gene entropy in bioinformatics research. Genes are essential components and genetic information "carriers" of DNA sequences and play important roles in the protein synthesis and cell functionality regulation. A multispecies gene refers a set of genes from different species. The mostly important multispecies genes are homologous genes, the genes sharing a same ancestor in the evolution. In this paper, we refer a multispecies gene as a set of aligned homologous genes for the convenience of discussion. For a multispecies gene x with n aligned nucleotides of m species ($m \ge 2$), it is a $m \times n$ dimension character matrix where each row is a gene sequence of a species and each column is called a site or character. Aligned homologous genes are employed to infer the species phylogenies of a set of organisms in phylogenetics. It is interesting to investigate phylogenetically informative genes in the species phylogeny reconstruction from the point view of the gene entropy. The gene entropy of a single-species gene is same as the definition of the DNA entropy. However, how to define gene entropy for a multispecies gene? We introduce the gene distribution in the sequence space before defining the multispecies gene entropy.

For a multispecies gene $x = x_1 x_2 ... x_n$ with m species and gene length n, where $x_i, i = 1,2...n$ is a column in the character matrix, the gene distribution of the gene x in the sequence space Σ is a collection of probabilities of each m-block in the sequence space; that is, the *gene distribution* of a multispecies gene x is the probability density function $p(x)$ for gene x in the sequence space.

If we treat each site x_i in a multispecies gene x as a block with size m, then a multi-species gene is equivalent to a *special* DNA sequence with length $n \times m$. We define the multi-species gene entropy as

$$H(x) = -\sum_{i=1}^{|\Sigma|} p(x_i) \log p(x_i)$$ (5)

Where $p(x_i), i = 1,2...$ is the gene distribution in the sequence space Σ. Although it seems that the multispecies gene entropy estimation can be conducted by DNA block entropy estimation approaches theoretically from this definition, such estimation may not be a good choice to compute a multispecies genes entropy. In addition to the fact that blocks in a multispecies gene are much more homogeneous than the blocks in a general DNA sequence. The sequence space size for a multispecies gene is generally a huge number and the gene length after alignment is relatively a small number. The finite sample effect problem will be more dangerous under such a situation because the relative frequency based approximation of the probability distribution of all sites in the huge sequence space is no longer reasonable.

We develop a data mining approach to estimate the multispecies gene entropy in this work. The idea is to employ a self-organizing map (SOM) to mine a set of homologous genes to compute their prototypes. The homologous gene set can be viewed as a large sample from the sequence space. The prototypes obtained after SOM mining are the feature data of the original gene set. The feature data share a similar probability density function with that of the original dataset although some data samples in the original dataset drawn with a high probability of occurrence may have better resolution on the SOM plane than those samples drawn with a low probability of occurrence [8,9,10]. The probability density function $p(x)$ of a gene x in the sequence space can be approximated by its corresponding density function $p'(x)$ in the feature space. The gene distribution function $p'(x)$ is computed by tracing the distributions of the prototype of each gene site on the SOM plane. Finally, the entropy for a multispecies gene x can be estimated by the following equation, where k is the number of neurons on the SOM plane,

$$H(x) = -\sum_{i=1}^{k} p'(x_i) \log p'(x_i) \tag{6}$$

We also apply the multispecies gene entropy and relative entropy to find phylogenetically informative genes in in the species phylogeny inference [11,12,13]. Under a same dataset, our relative entropy based gene concatenation approach performs better and more efficient than the original gene concatenation method given by Rokas *et al* [14].

This paper is organized as follows. The basic self-organizing map mining is introduced in the section 2. Section 3 presents the details to estimate the multispecies gene entropy. Section 4 investigates applications of multispecies gene entropy and relative entropy in resolving the incongruence between the gene trees and species trees in phylogenetics.

2 Self-Organizing Map Principles

Self-organizing map (SOM) is a well-known data analysis algorithm for feature selection, data clustering and information visualization. It employs competitive unsupervised learning to partition original data space into a set of corresponding representative prototypes; that is, it maps a dataset X to its prototype or feature data $W : T_{som} : X \rightarrow W$. A self-organizing map (SOM) consists of an input dataset X, a SOM plane P, which is the input and also the output plane, and an unsupervised learning algorithm l.

The input data set X is a $n \times m$ matrix. Each column data in X is called a variable or component and each row data is referred as a sample. In our SOM based gene entropy estimation, the input data matrix X is a set of encoded homologous genes. Each row in X represents a gene sample and four columns represent a species that is due to our encoding scheme. A multispecies gene generally takes from several to many rows. If we view each multispecies gene as a block in the input data matrix X, then input data matrix X consists of many blocks. The SOM plane P is generally a set of neurons (map units) placed on a two dimensional lattice. For each neuron i ($i = 1,2...k$) on the SOM plane, there is a reference vector w_i with same dimensions as each site (gene sample). A reference vector matrix W can be obtained by collecting all reference vectors w_i ($i = 1,2...k$) on the SOM plane. Obviously, the reference matrix W is a $k \times m$ dimensional matrix. After the SOM finishes learning, the reference vector matrix W stores prototypes of the original input data matrix X that is the extracted feature-data of the input dataset. The unsupervised learning algorithm l takes the winner-take-all-rule in the learning. It consists of loops of competition, cooperation and adjusting in addition to the initialization stage at the beginning of the self-organizing learning. The time complexity of each epoch in the SOM learning is $O(nmk)$, where k is the number of neurons on the SOM plane and $n \times m$ is the dimension of the input dataset X.

SOM and its variants are widely applied in gene expression data clustering bioinformatics data visualization, protein structure analysis, time series predictions and commercial database mining [15,16,17,18,19].

3   Gene Entropy Estimation

Our SOM based entropy estimation method is to map a set of homologous genes in the sequence space Σ to its feature data in the feature space Λ. The n-block gene distribution function $p(x_i)$, $i = 1,2..., N$ in the sequence space S is approximated by computing its corresponding gene distribution function $y_j = p(x_i)$, $j = 1,2..., k$ in the feature space Λ. Such a gene entropy estimation approach avoids the finite effect problem in the traditional block entropy estimation by estimating the gene distribution function in the feature space. We have the following steps to estimate gene entropy for a multispecies gene.

1.   Concatenate a set of homologous genes of a group of organisms into a super-gene G.
2.   Encoding the super-gene G into a corresponding digit X to be mined by a self-organizing map.
3.   Conduct the SOM mining for the numeric matrix X.
4.   Computing gene distribution $p'(x)$ on the SOM plane for each gene x by retrieving the frequency of sites in the gene hitting their best match unit (BMU) on the SOM plane.
5.   Estimating the multispecies gene x entropy by Equation 6.

3.1 SOM Mining of a Homologous Gene Set

The first step gene concatenation is to concatenate a set of homologous multispecies genes as a super-gene $G = g_1 g_2 ... g_M$ simply. The super-gene is called a $m \times n$ character matrix for the convenience of discussion. The super-gene works as a large sample from the sequence space. The feature data obtained after SOM mining is a sample in the total feature space of all homologous genes for the group of organisms.

The second step is to mine the super-gene by the self-organizing map (SOM). Before mining the super-gene, we transpose the super-gene G to a $n \times m$ character matrix G^T. The character matrix G^T is transformed into the input dataset X for the SOM mining by encoding four nucleotides by four orthogonal vectors as follows.

$$A = (1,0,0,0)^t, \quad T = (0,1,0,0)^t$$
$$C = (0,0,1,0)^t, \quad G = (0,0,0,1)^t \tag{7}$$

Missing nucleotides and gaps are encoded as a vector with four zeros entries. After encoding, the input dataset X is a $n \times (4m)$ digit matrix where a sample/site is a $4 \times m$ row vector. In the SOM mining, we employ the sequence learning algorithm to avoid potential local minimum trap problem in the batch learning. The reference vectors are initialized by principal component analysis [8,9]. The neighborhood kernel function used is a Gaussian function. After the SOM mining, all features of the super-gene are extracted and stored in the reference matrix W ($k \times (4m)$); that is, the final reference matrix W is the prototype indicating the intrinsic statistic features of the super-gene and the feature data is placed on the SOM plane in a topologically sorting style.

3.2 Gene Entropy Estimation

Our goal is to get the gene distribution function $p'(x)$ for gene x in the feature space to approximate the gene distribution function $p(x)$ in the sequence space. How can we get the gene distribution on the SOM plane? We give the definitions about "hit" and "hit-rate" before we give the formal definition of gene distribution on the SOM plane.

If a neuron j on the SOM plane is acknowledged as the *best match unit* (BMU) of sample/site x_i in the gene x after the SOM mining, we say that the gene sample x_i hits the neuron j. For a neuron j on the SOM plane hit by n_j number of sites in a gene x with l sites after SOM mining, the *hit-rate* for neuron j from the gene x is the fraction between n_j and total site number l, which is just the total hit number of the gene on the SOM plane.

The sites of a gene will hit different neurons according to different nucleotide patterns they contain. The distribution of the neurons hit by sites from a gene on the SOM plane is an approximation of the underlying distribution of the gene in the sequence space. Then the distribution of the neurons hit by a gene on the SOM plane can be represented as the hit-rates of all the map units from the gene. We give definition for a gene distribution on SOM plane as follows.

For a gene $x = x_1 x_2 ... x_l$, its gene distribution $y = y_1 y_2 ... y_k$ on the SOM plane is a vector of hit-rates of neurons hit by the gene, where the number of neurons on the SOM plane is k and y_i is the hit-rate on i^{th} neuron. The gene distribution on the SOM plane for a gene can be computed by tracing the original image of the reference vector associative with each neuron on the SOM plane from the gene. If we reproject reference vector in each map unit to the input data space, we can find a set of samples of the input dataset X. Actually, it is a set of gene samples of the super-gene since X is the encoding of the super-gene. These gene samples may distribute over different genes in the super-gene. If we just trace the original image for the reference vector of each neuron on the SOM plane in a *single* gene x, we can get corresponding number of sites hitting each neuron. Thus, we can compute the corresponding hit-rate for this gene by dividing hitting number in each neuron by the total sites number of the gene.

The gene probability density function $p'(x)$ of gene x on the SOM plane after SOM mining can be represented as $y = y_1 y_2 ... y_k$, where y_i is the hit-rate for the neuron i neuron on the SOM plane. Let h_i be the cardinality of set s_i, a set of samples in the gene x acknowledging the neuron i as their best match unit; that is, a set of sites hitting the neuron i.

$$s_i = \{e \mid \arg \min_{j} \| e - w_j \| = i, j = 1,2...k\} \tag{8}$$

Then, $y_i = h_i / \sum_{i=1}^{k} h_i$, $i = 1,2...k$ and the total number of sites from the gene x is the total hitting number $l = \sum_{i=1}^{k} h_i$. The gene probability is no longer the naïve frequency of sites in the gene but the frequency of the features contained in this gene in the total feature space. The total sampled feature space is the feature data of the super-gene, which is the combination of a set of homologous genes.

After the gene probability density function $p(x)$ in the sequence space Σ is approximated by the gene distribution function $p'(x)$ on the SOM plane with k neurons for each gene, we can estimate entropy for a multispecies gene x as:

$$H(x) = -\sum_{i=1}^{k} p'(x_i) \log p'(x_i) \tag{9}$$

In the actual entropy estimation, we compute gene entropy values by $p'(x)$ from the SOM mining on different sizes of SOM lattices several times. The final entropy value of a gene is the mean of all gene entropy estimations for the gene.

3.3 A Species Phylogeny Inference Problem

Our data is a 106 homologous (orthologous) gene dataset with 127026 bps of seven Saccharomyces species (*S. cerevisiae, S. paradoxus, S. mikatae, S. kudriavavzevii, S. bayanus, S. castellii, S. kluyveri*) and the other species *Candida albicans* from their genome data [14]. The genes are carefully selected widely-distributed orthologous genes in the eight genomes to overcome the incongruence between gene trees and species trees.

Rokas *et al.* pointed out that the phylogenetic analysis (ML, MP) [20] of a gene set with at least twenty (an experimental number) randomly selected genes from this gene set always lead to a species tree with the maximum support on each inferred branch. Their method suffers from the ad-hoc mechanism and is hard to generalize to other dataset because all genes are assumed equally phylogenetically informative in the concatenation and following phylogenetic tree reconstruction. Actually, different genes may have different evolutionary history. To apply the method to other data sets, the experimental number in the method has to be computed by large scale phylogenetic computing. Such a computing will be prohibitive with increase of the taxa number. It is necessary to find phylogenetically informative genes to overcome the ad-hoc mechanism of the method. For the convenience of discussion, we give the definition about congruent genes and tree credibility.

A gene under a phylogenetic reconstruction model R is a congruent gene if its gene tree is congruent with the species tree. Otherwise the gene is called an incongruent gene. There are 45 congruent genes and 61 incongruent genes from Bayesian analysis [21] under GTR+Γ model [13,20]. Such classification result of ours is confirmed by the Shimodaira-Hasegawa test (SH test) [22] under the GTR+Γ model with reestimated log likelihoods (RELL) approximation for 21 tree topologies for each gene (bootstrap replicates: 1000).

A gene is called a phylogenetically informative gene if its corresponding phylogenetic tree is nearest to the species tree in the robustness test (for example, KH, SH test [13,20,22]). Obviously, all congruent genes are phylogenetically informative genes.

For each phylogenetic tree inferred from Bayesian analysis, tree credibility is defined as the product of all posterior probabilities of its inferred branches: $t_p = \prod_{i=1}^{|B_I|} b_p^i$,

where the b_p^i is the posterior probability in the ith inferred branch and B_I is the set of all inferred branches. The tree credibility t_p of the phylogenetic tree of a congruent gene is in the interval $(0,1]$. The tree credibility t_p of the phylogenetic tree of an incongruent gene is zero.

3.3.1 A "worst"Scenario Under the Random Gene Concatenation Case

We give the case of the Bayesian analysis of thirty random concatenation cases of the 61 incongruent genes among the 106 gene dataset used by Rokas et al. [14] under GTR+Γ model. For each random concatenation case, there are 10 random gene sets generated (10 trials). We observed that the tree credibility t_p for each case increases with increasing gene concatenation number. However, there were still generally at least 10% of the gene combination sets whose gene trees are not species tree if the gene combination sets have less than 28 genes (The species tree is showed in Figure 7). This simulation can be seen as the "worst scenario" in the random gene concatenation method (The simulation takes 10 days running under Sun Grid system on a cluster machine with 16 CPUs). Considering the nature of the incongruent genes and the small trial number generated in our experiment, it is possible that such "worst" case will happen often in the random gene concatenation of incongruent genes.

We also did the similar experiments for the congruent genes and random genes. We found it to make each inferred branch reaching its maximum support, there needs at least 4 congruent genes or at least 15 random genes in the combination. However, under the incongruent gene concatenation, it needs at least 28 genes to reach the maximum support for each inferred branch. Considering the congruent genes are phylogenetically informative genes, we can see that gene concatenation method to resolve the incongruence between the species tree and gene trees can be efficient and robust if we can find phylogenetically informative genes among the gene set.

The gene/species trees problem for a group of organisms actually is a black box problem and the worst gene combination case is unavoidable in the ad-hoc gene combination approach because investigators have little knowledge about which genes are more informative in the molecular evolution. On the other hand, each gene in the random gene concatenation method is assumed to have equally positive contribution to the final phylogenetic tree. Under such assumption, it is possible to trap in the case where many genes with noise data are combined but the final tree is a species tree with poor support or even a wrong species tree because of the accumulation of the noise data in the gene concatenation. The ad-hoc mechanism of this method lies that investigators have little knowledge about if a gene is phylogenetically informative or not. In the following sections, we are going to develop an entropy based approach to identify potential informative genes and overcome the ad-hoc mechanism.

3.3.2 Gene Entropy Analysis of the 106 Orthologous Genes

After encoding the character matrix (a super-gene) of the 106 genes into a 127026×32 digit matrix X in the SOM mining, we conduct SOM mining three times on a SOM plane with 15×15, 20×20 and 25×25 neurons respectively. The entropy value of a gene is the mean of three gene entropy values calculated from each SOM mining:

$$H(x) = -\frac{1}{3} \sum_{j=1}^{3} \sum_{i=1}^{|P_j|} p'_j(x_i) \log p'_j(x_i) \tag{10}$$

The probability density functions $p'_j(x), j = 1,2,3$ are the approximations of the gene distribution function in the sequence space on the three SOM planes; $|P_j|, j = 1,2,3$ is the number of neurons on the SOM plane in the training. From the gene entropy plot and their histogram, it is easy to verify that the distribution of the gene entropy of the 106 genes is nearly subject to a normal distribution. However, contrary to our initial expectation, gene entropy seems only dependent on the nucleotide patterns presented or sequence complexity for the multiple aligned genes rather than on the gene length factor. The R square value from the regression between gene entropy and gene length under the 95% confidence interval is only 0.115.

4 Applications of Gene Entropy in the Phylogenetics

Our goal is to employ gene entropy to find the phylogenetically informative genes to resolve incongruence between the gene trees and species trees problem efficiently. What are the potential connections between this measure and the phylogenetic characteristics of a gene? Is it possible to use gene entropy or its variants to identify phylogenetically informative genes such that we can have a systematic resolution to reconstruct the species tree to overcome the incongruence between the gene trees and species trees?

To answer these questions, we first check the basic statistics analysis of the gene entropy. All gene entropy values fall within the interval of the 2 standard deviation of the gene entropy mean: [4.8043-2×0.2459, 4.8043+2×0.2549], except the two genes with the minimum entropy gene: *YMR186W* (entropy value 3.9911) and *YDL126C* (entropy value 4.1345). The phylogenetic trees of these two minimum entropy genes constructed from Bayesian analysis and Maximum Likelihood (bootstrap replicates: 100) are the species tree with maximum support 1.0 on each inferred branch! It is obvious that these two genes are "best" phylogenetically informative genes.

To investigate if minimum entropy genes are phylogenetically informative genes, we sort the gene entropy values in an ascendant order and check the tree credibility t_p of their phylogenetic tree inferred through Bayesian analysis and delta log likelihood value $\Delta \ln L$ (which measures the evolution distance between its gene tree to the species tree (ML tree)) in the SH-test. From the table of the entropy values $H(x)$, tree credibility t_p and $\Delta \ln L$ of the top 10 minimum entropy genes, we can see that 6/10 genes are congruent genes in these genes. We built the same table for the top ten genes with maximum entropy values and found there were 7 incongruent genes among the ten maximum entropy genes. It looks like that the minimum entropy genes are more likely to be phylogenetically informative genes than maximum entropy genes. Although a minimum entropy gene is potential to be a phylogenetically informative gene, it is still far from drawing such a conclusion for us because of lacking robust statistics support (this is partially because our sample size is not big enough). Figure 1 shows that the relationship between the gene entropy $H(x)$ with respect to the $\Delta \ln L$ value in the SH test. We can see the phylogenetically informative genes distributed even more on the relatively high entropy gene zone although most genes in the low entropy zone are phylogenetically informative (their $\Delta \ln L$ value is small) and even the first minimum entropy genes are best phylogenetically informative genes.

Since there is no enough statistical support for our initial guess about phylogenetically informative genes, we do the following query: what are the relationships between the minimum entropy gene, which is one if the best phylogenetically informative genes we already identified in the basic statistical analysis for gee entropy values, with the other genes? However, gene entropy measure itself can not tell us the relationships between these the minimum entropy gene and other genes. To answer this query, we calculate the relative entropy for each gene with respective to the minimum entropy genes. The relative entropy, also called Kullback-Leibler (K-L) distance, measures the similarity between different distributions. It has been used to identify unusual patterns in biological sequence analysis [23]. The relative entropy (K-L distance) between gene distribution $p(x)$ and $q(x)$ is defined as:

$$H(p \parallel q) = -\sum_{i=1} p(x_i) \log \frac{p(x_i)}{q(x_i)} \qquad (11)$$

The $q(x)$ is the gene distribution on the SOM plane of the minimum entropy gene *YMR186W* and the $p(x)$ is the gene distribution of any gene in our gene set on the SOM plane. Figure 2 describes the relationships between the relative gene entropy value for each gene with respect to the minimum entropy gene *YMR186W* and $\Delta \ln L$ value in the SH test. It is interesting to see that $\Delta \ln L$ value decreases statistically with decreasing of the relative entropy; that is, genes more similar to the minimum entropy gene are more likely to be phylogenetic informative: their gene trees are more likely to be a species tree. All the top ten genes with nearest K-L distance with the minimum entropy gene *YMR186W* and 8/10 genes are incongruent genes in the top ten maximum entropy genes.

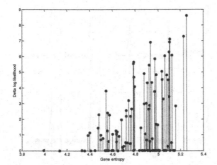

Fig. 1. Gene entropy vs. delta log likelihood in the SH-test

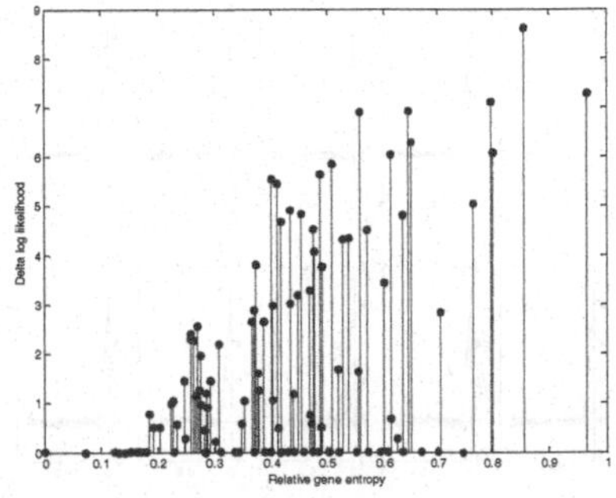

Fig. 2. Gene K-L distance with .respective to the minimum entropy gene vs. delta log likelihood in the SH-test

To explore the characteristics of genes measured by K-L distance to the minimum entropy gene further, we introduce the concept of the identity percentage matrix (IPM) for each multispecies gene. The IPM is a matrix describing the identity percentages between the aligned species sequences of a multi-species gene. Each entry in the IPM is the identity percentages between sequences i, j, where $ham(i, j)$ is the hamming distance between the sequences.

$$IPM(i, j) = \frac{1 - ham(i,j)}{length(i)} \qquad (12)$$

After visualizing IPM for the minimum entropy gene (Figure 3), we can even guess the correct species tree for the eight species from its IPM plot: $(Sklu,(Scas,(Sbay,(Skud,(Smik,(Scer,Spar)))))),Calb)$. We also compute the spectral radius for identity percentage matrix, which is the maximum eigenvalue of the IPM

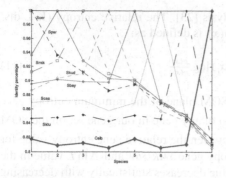

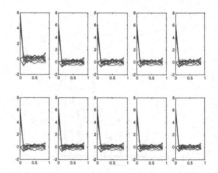

Fig. 3. The minimum entropy gene identity percentage matrix

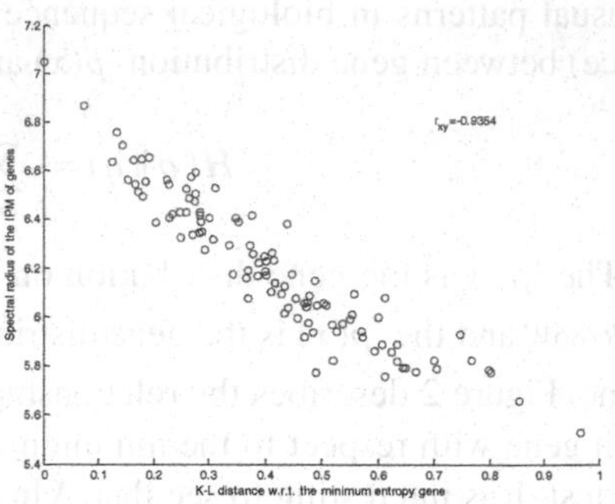

Fig. 4. Scatter plot of the KL-distance of each gene with respective to the minimum entropy gene and the spectral radius of the identity percentage matrix of each gene

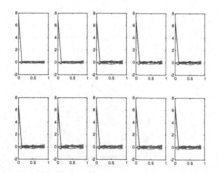

Fig. 5. FFT transforms of the identity percentage matrices of ten genes nearest

Fig. 6. FFT transforms of the identity percentage matrices of ten genes farthest to the minimum entropy genes

and indicates the magnitute in the maximum changeable direction. It is interesting to see that the K-L distance of each gene with respect to the minimum entropy gene is strongly negatively-correlated with the spectral radius of its identity percentage matrix (Figure 4). It implies that a gene with larger K-L distances to the minimum entropy gene will be more potential to change / evolve in a relatively large maganitude than the minimum entropy gene. The gene will have less potential to share a same evolution path with the "best" phylogenetically informative gene. In our context, it means its gene tree will be less likely to have near statistical distance with the species tree.

We also employ the Fast Fourier transform (FFT) [24] to translate the identity percentage matrix to its frequency domain. It is interesting to see that the images of the identity percentage matrices of genes nearest to the minimum entropy gene in K-L distance are more similar to that of the identity percentage matrix of the minimum entropy gene than those genes far from the minimum entropy gene in the frequency domain. Figure 5 and Figure 6 show the FFT transforms of the identity percentage matrices of first 10 genes with nearest K-L distances to the minimum entropy gene and the last 10 genes with farthest maximum K-L distances to the minimum entropy gene. The blue and red colors indicate the real and imaginary part of the FFT transform respectively.

4.3 Reconstructing Species Tree by K-L Distance Based Gene Concatenation Under Gene Clustering

We can construct the species tree of a set of organisms based on entropy estimation since the genes near to the minimum entropy gene in the K-L distance are more likely to be phylogenetic informative. In our method, we selectively concatenate the genes which are more likely to be phylogenetically informative. For the same dataset, we concatenate first 10 genes nearest to the minimum entropy gene (these genes include the minimum gene itself) to be a super-gene and then conduct phylogenetic analysis (Bayesian analysis, ML) for the super-gene, we have an inferred phylogenetic tree, which is the species tree with maximum support in each inferred branch in the Bayesian analysis and ML with bootstrap replicates 100 (Figure 7). We did similar experiments for the first 2 to 9 genes with nearest to the minimum entropy gene and obtained the same results. Compared with the random gene combination approach, our method is systematic and easy to extend to other datasets.

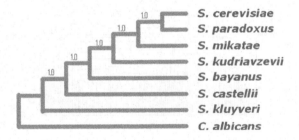

Fig. 7. The species tree constructed by combining 10 genes with minimum K-L distance to the minimum entropy gene

Some investigators may challenge the K-L distance based gene concatenation since the first ten genes with minimum K-L distances all are congruent genes in this dataset. If there were incongruent genes appearing in the gene combination, would the K-L distance based gene concatenation still be effective? To answer this question, we hierarchically cluster the gene set. Since we already have the gene distribution for each gene on the SOM plane in the SOM mining, it is easy for us to cluster the feature data of genes hierarchically. After hierarchically clustering, we pick the gene with minimum K-L distances from each cluster. The selected minimum K-L distance genes are then concatenated to conduct Bayesian analysis. We choose the cutoff as the number of clusters in the hierarchical clustering, which is selected from 2-12 (examples indicated in Figure 8). It is interesting to see the two minimum entropy genes (*YMR186W* and *YDL126C*) are clustered in a cluster, which is indicated in red color, and other 104 genes are clustered in another "*big cluster*" if there are only two clusters. The selected genes with minimum K-L distances are *YMR186W* and *YGR094W*. The gene *YGR094W* is not a congruent gene but it has relatively small statistical distance to the species tree in the SH-test. Under the same computational models, the phylogenetic analysis of the concatenation of the two genes leads to a species tree with maximum support. We keep this procedure until the cutoff value is 12; the phylogenetic tree reconstructed from the super-gene concatenated by genes with minimum K-L distances to the minimum entropy gene is always a species tree with maximum support on each inferred branch! For example, when the cutoff number is 12, the super-gene is the concatenation of genes *YGR094W, YMR186W, YGL225W, YDL215C, YJL085W, YDR484W, YDR531W, YDR361C, YCL054W, YAL053W, YBR070C, YGR005C* and there are six congruent genes among them. The corresponding phylogenetic tree for this super-gene is the species tree with the maximum support. Such results give support to the K-L distance based gene concatenation method to overcome the incongruence between the species tree and gene trees.

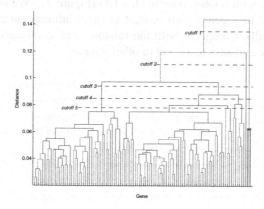

Fig. 8. Hiearchical gene clustering of 106 genes

Here we claim this K-L distance based gene concatenation under gene clustering is easy to extend to other data set and it overcomes the ad-doc problem in the original gene concatenation method. It is reasonable to have the hypothesis that genes in a cluster may share similar phylogenetic characteristics because we found that genes with clusters entropy values were more likely to fall in a same cluster in the hierarchical clustering. Gene clustering can not only organize genes but also can work as a "*pre-screening process*" before any phylogenetic analysis. The K-L distance based gene selection selects the most likely phylogenetically informative gene from each cluster, which conquers the "blindness" in the phylogeny reconstruction. Compared with the original gene concatenation method, there is no experimental number to be computed, which prevents the possible heavy phylogenetic computing and makes the resolution of the gene tree and species tree problem efficiently and systematically.

5 Conclusions

In this study, we give first approach to estimate multispecies gene entropy and explore its applications in the phylogenetics. A K-L distance based gene concatenation under gene clustering approach is proposed to overcome the incongruence between the species tree and gene tree in molecular phylogenetics. Such K-L distance based gene concatenation approach conquers the ad-hoc mechanism in the Rokas *et al* 's approach [14] and avoid possible heavy phylogenetic computing by selecting phylogenetically informative genes from the data set. In our following work, in addition to investigating the entropy values of the corresponding protein genes of the Rokas' dataset [14], we are also working for a new eight species aligned gene set obtained by *S. cerevisiae* microarray data to apply our method. Moreover, we also plan to integrate other knowledge discover mining methods in phylogenetics [25] into our current approach, in addition to applying it to other datasets to investigate the applications of multispecies gene entropy in phylogenetics.

References

1. Schmitt, A. and Herzel, H.: Estimating the Entropy of DNA Sequences. Journal of Theoretical Biology, 188, (1997) 369-377.
2. Lio, P., Politi, A. Buiatti, M. and Ruffo, S.: High Statistics Block Entropy Measures of DNA Sequences, Journal of Theoretical Biology, 180, 151-160. (1996).
3. Lanctot, J., Li, M. and Yang, E.: Estimating DNA sequence entropy, Proceedings of the eleventh annual ACM-SIAM symposium on Discrete algorithms. (2000) 409-418
4. Herzel, H., Ebeling, W., Schmitt, A.O.: Entropies of biosequences: the role of repeats. Phys. Rev. E 50, (1994) 5061–5071
5. Vinga, S. and Almeida, J.: Renyi continuous entropy of DNA sequences, Journal of Theoretical Biology, 231, (2004) 377-388
6. Yeo, G. Burge, C.: Maximum entropy modeling of short Sequence motifs applications to RNA splicing signals, RECOMB'03 Berlin, Germany, (2003) 322-331
7. Weikl, T. and Dill, K.: Folding rates and low-entropy-loss routes of two-state Proteins. J. Mol. Biol. 329, (2003) 585–598
8. Haykin, S.: Neural Networks: A Comprehensive Foundation, 2nd Edition. Prentice-Hall (1999)
9. Kohonen, T.: Self-Organizing Maps, 3rd edition. Berlin: Springer-Verlag. (2001)
10. Ritter, H., Martinetz, T. and Schulten, K.: Neural Computation and Self-Organizing Maps: An introduction, Reading, MA: Addison-Wesley. (1992)
11. Maddison, W.P.: Gene trees in species trees. *Syst. Biol.* 46, (1997) 523-536
12. Page R. and Holmes, E.: Molecular evolution, a phylogenetics approach, Blackwell Science (1998).
13. Nei, M. and Kumar, S.: Molecular Evolution and Phylogenetics 2nd Edition, Oxford University Press. (2000)
14. Rokas A, Williams B, King N, Carroll S.: Genome-scale approaches to resolving incongruence in molecular phylogenies. *Nature.* 425, 798-804. (2003)
15. Tamayo, P., Solni, D., Mesirov, J., Zhu, Q., Kitareewan,K., Dmitrovsky, E., Lander, E. and Golub, T.: "Interpreting Patterns of Gene Expression with Self-Organizing Maps: Methods and Application to Hematopoietic Differentiation," Proc. Nat'l Academy of Sciences of the United States of Am., vol. 96, no. 6, (1999) 2907-2912.

16. Nikkila, J., Toronen,, P., Kaski, S., Venna, J., Castren, E. and Wong, G.: Analysis and visualization of gene expression data using self-organizing maps. Neural Networks, 15, Special issue on New Developments on Self-Organizing Maps, (2002) 9530-966

17. Kohonen, T. and Somervuo, P.: How to make large self-organizing maps for nonvectorial data, Neural Networks 15, (2002) 945-952

18. Yanikoglu, B. and Erman, B.: Minimum Energy Configurations of the 2-Dimensional HP-Model of Proteins by Self-Organizing Networks, Journal of Computational Biology, 9: 4, (2002) 613-620,

19. Dunham, M.: Data mining introductory and advanced topics. Prentice Hall. (2002)

20. Felsentein, J.: Inferring Phylogenies, Sinauer Associates, Inc. (2004)

21. Huelsenbeck, J. and Ronquist, F. MRBAYES: Bayesian inference of phylogenetic trees. Bioinformatics. 17, (2001) 754-755.

22. Shimodaira, H., and Hasegawa, M.: Multiple comparisons of log-likelihoods with applications to phylogenetic inference. Mol Biol. Evol. 16, 1114-1116. (1999).

23. Durbin, R., Eddy, S., Krogh, A. and Mitchison, G.: Probabilistic models of proteins and nucleic acids. Cambridge University Press. (1998)

24. Walker, J.: Fast Fourier Transforms, CRC Press. (1996)

25. Bichindaritz, I. and Potter, S: Knowledge Based Phylogenetic Classification Mining. In: P. Perner,.Advances in Data Mining, Applications in Image Mining, Medicine and Biotechnology, Management and Environmental Control, and Telecommunications, Lecture Notes in Computer Science, 3275, Springer Verlag, (2004) 163-172

A Unified Approach for Discovery of Interesting Association Rules in Medical Databases

Harleen Kaur[1], Siri Krishan Wasan[1], Ahmed Sultan Al-Hegami[2], and Vasudha Bhatnagar[3]

[1] Department of Mathematics, Jamia Millia Islamia, New Delhi-110 025, India
harleen_k1@rediffmail.com, skwasan@yahoo.com
[2] Department of Computer Science, Sana'a University, Sana'a, Yemen
ahmed_s_gamil@yahoo.com
[3] Department of Computer Science, University of Delhi, New Delhi-110 007, India
vbhatnagar@cs.du.ac.in

Abstract. Association rule discovery is an important technique for mining knowledge from large databases. Data mining researchers have studied subjective measures of interestingness to reduce the volume of discovered rules and to improve the overall efficiency of the knowledge discovery in databases process (KDD). The objective of this paper is to provide a framework that uses subjective measures of interestingness to discover interesting patterns from association rules algorithms. The framework works in an environment where the medical databases are evolving with time. In this paper we consider a unified approach to quantify interestingness of association rules. We believe that the expert mining can provide a basis for determining user threshold which will ultimately help us in finding interesting rules. The framework is tested on public datasets in medical domain and results are promising.

Keywords: Knowledge discovery in databases (KDD), data mining, association rule, domain knowledge, interestingness, medical databases.

1 Introduction

The vast search space of hidden patterns in the massive databases is a challenge for the KDD community [19]. However, a vast majority of these patterns are pruned by the objective measures such as score functions engaged in the mining algorithm. To avoid computing the score function for the entire search space, optimization strategies are used. For example, in association rule mining, confidence is the commonly used score function and the anti monotonic property of frequent itemsets is the optimization strategy [3].

Despite massive reduction of search space by employing suitable score functions and optimization strategies, all of the discovered patterns are not useful for the users. Consequently, researchers have been strongly motivated to further restrict the search space, by putting constraints [1,2,4,5,6,7] and providing good measures of interestingness [8-18].

Commonly used techniques to discover interesting patterns in most KDD endeavors are partially effective unless combined with subjective measures of interestingness

P. Perner (Ed.): ICDM 2006, LNAI 4065, pp. 53–63, 2006.

[22,24,25,26]. Subjective measures quantify interestingness based on the user under-standability of the domain. Capturing the user subjectivity in dynamic environment requires a great deal of knowledge about databases, the application domain and the user's interests at a particular time [21,22,23]. Therefore, it is difficult for the user to analyze the discovered patterns and to identify those patterns that are interesting from his/her point of view.

In this paper we introduce a unified approach to quantify interestingness of asso-ciation rules. The user domain knowledge is provided in terms of expert mining rules. Such expert rules are needed in order to capture the subjectivity of medical experts. The paper introduces a technique that efficiently mines the expert knowl-edge to form a constraint to the proposed approach. We believe expert mining can provide a basis for determining user threshold which will ultimately help as in find-ing interesting rules.

2 Related Works

Most existing approaches of finding subjectively interesting association rules ask the user to explicitly specify what types of rules are interesting and uninteresting. In tem-plate-based approach, the user specifies interesting and uninteresting association rules using templates [14,15,16]. A template describes a set of rules in terms of items oc-curring in the conditional and the consequent parts. The system then retrieves the matching rules from the set of discovered rules.

There are various techniques for analyzing the subjective interestingness of classi-fication rules [10,11,13,14]. However, those techniques cannot work for analyzing association rules. Association rules require a different specification language and different ways of analyzing and ranking the rules. Padmanabhan and Tuzhilin have proposed a method of discovering unexpected patterns that considers a set of expecta-tions or beliefs about the problem domain [14,15,16]. The method discovers unex-pected patterns using these expectations to seed the search for patterns in data that contradict the beliefs. However, this method is generally not as efficient and flexible as our post-analysis method unless the user can specify his or her beliefs or expecta-tions about the domain completely beforehand, which is very difficult, if not impossi-ble [9]. Typically, the user must interact with the system to provide a more complete set of expectations and find more interesting rules. The proposed post-anlaysis method facilitates user interaction because of its efficiency. Padmanabhan and Tuz-hilin's approach also does not handle user's rough or vague feelings, but only precise knowledge. User's vague feelings are important for identifying interesting rules be-cause such forms of knowledge are almost as important as precise knowledge.

However, all works stated in the literature are generally not flexible to handle the evolving nature of data as the post-analysis method, unless the user can freely specify his or her beliefs or his/her background knowledge about the domain, which is very difficult. Liu et al. [9,10,11] proposed a post analysis method that considers vague feelings for identifying interesting rules. However, the work does not consider the degree of interestingness and the fact that the user background knowledge changes with the time.

3 The Unified Approach to Quantify Interestingness of Association Rules

An association rule is of the form: Å → C where Å denotes an antecedent and C denotes a consequent. Both Å and C are considered as a set of conjuncts of the form $c_1, c_2, ..., c_k$. The conjunct c_j is of the form $< A = I>$, where A is an item name (attribute), Dom (A) is the domain of A, and I (value) ∈ Dom (A).

Given a dataset D collected over the time $[t_0, t_1, t_2, ... t_n]$. At each time instance t_j, an incremental dataset D_j , j ∈ {j,...,n}, is collected and stored in D. The incremental D_i is subjected to the mining algorithm resulting in the discovery of set of rules (model) {R_i}. The proposed framework process interesting rules from the discovered rules.

Data-mining research has shown that we can measure a rule's interestingness using both objective and subjective measures [7-18]. To the end user, rules are interesting if:

(i) The rules contradict the user's existing knowledge or expectations (Unexpected).

(ii) Users can do something with them and benefit (Actionable).

(iii) They add knowledge to the user prior knowledge (Novel).

Although novelty, actionability and unexpectedness of the discovered knowledge are the basis of the subjective measures, their theoretical treatment still remains a challenging task [13,20,25]. Actionability is the key concept in most applications. Actionable rules let users do their jobs better by taking some specific actions in response to the discovered knowledge. Actionability, however, is an elusive concept because it is not feasible to know the space of all rules and the actions to be attached to them. Actionability is therefore is implicitly captured by novelty and unexpectedness [25].

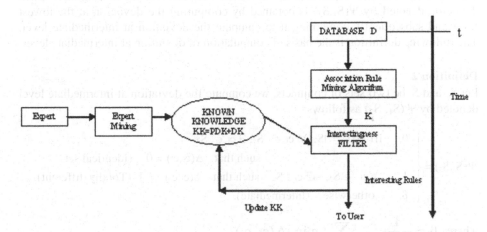

Fig. 1. Interestingness as post analysis filter for KDD process

In this work we introduce a comprehensive interestingness measure that quantifies the unexpectedness and novelty by involving the user background knowledge and the previously discovered knowledge. The framework computes the deviation of discovered rules with respect to the domain knowledge and previously discovered rules. Subsequently the user determines a certain threshold value to report interesting rules. The general architecture of the proposed framework is shown in Fig. 1.

At time t_i, database D_i is subjected to the association rule mining algorithm, resulting into discovery of knowledge K_i. The proposed interestingness filter processes K_i, in the light of knowledge extracted from expert and the previously discovered knowledge *(known knowledge)* to deliver rules that are of real interest to the user.

3.1 Deviation at Lowest Level

Degree of deviation at the lowest level represents the deviation between conjuncts. The deviation between a conjunct c_i and conjuncts c_j is computed on the basis of the result of comparison between the items of the two conjuncts.

Definition 1
Let c_1 and c_2 be two conjuncts ($A_1 = I_1$) and ($A_2 = I_2$) respectively. The deviation of c_1 with respect to c_2 is defined as a Boolean function as follows:

$$\Delta(c_1,c_2) = \begin{cases} 0, & \text{if } A_1 = A_2, \text{ and } I_1 = I_2 \quad \text{(Identical items).} \\ 1, & \text{if } A_1 = A_2, \text{ and } I_1 \neq I_2 \quad \text{(Different items).} \end{cases}$$

The possibilities of deviation at the lowest level as defined in Definition 1 has deviation degree 0 which indicates no deviation exists between the two conjuncts and deviation degree 1 which indicates different conjuncts.

3.2 Deviation at Intermediate Level

This type of deviation represents the deviation between the set of conjuncts. Such deviation denoted by $\Psi(S_1, S_2)$ is obtained by computing the deviation at the lowest level and subsequently combining it to compute the deviation at intermediate level. The following definition is the basis of computation of deviation at intermediate level.

Definition 2
Let S_1 and S_2 be two sets of conjuncts, we compute the deviation at intermediate level denoted by $\Psi(S_1, S_2)$ as follows:

$$\Psi(S_1,S_2) = \begin{cases} 0, & \text{iff } |S_1| = |S_2|, \forall\, c_i \in S_1, \exists\, c_j \in S_2 \\ & \quad \text{such that } \Delta(c_i,c_j) = 0 \quad \text{(Identical sets).} \\ 1, & \forall c_i \in S_1, \neg\exists\, c_j \in S_2 \text{ such that } \Delta(c_i,c_j) = 1 \quad \text{(Totally different).} \\ \beta, & \text{otherwise (Intermediate).} \end{cases}$$

where $\quad \beta = \dfrac{1}{|S_1|} \sum_{c_i \in S_1,\, c_j \in S_2} \min \Delta(c_i, c_j)$

As per Definition 2, $\Psi(S_1, S_2) = 0$ indicates that S_1 and S_2 are identical, $\Psi(S_1,S_2) = 1$ indicates the extreme deviation and the computed value of β, quantifies an intermediate degree of deviation. The value of β is computed as a linear combination of the minimum deviation at the lowest level that represents each conjunct of the S_1 with respect to S_2 divided by the number of conjuncts of S_1.

4 Interestingness of Discovered Knowledge

Having obtained the deviation at lowest and the intermediate level, the deviation at rule level (high level) is to be evaluated as both antecedents and consequents of rules are considered to be sets of conjuncts. The computation of deviation at high level is performed against the rules extracted from experts as well as the rules discovered earlier. The interestingness of a rule is therefore, obtained by comparing the deviation at the highest level (rule level) with respect the user given threshold value. A rule is considered to be interesting if its deviation at the high level exceeds a user threshold value.

Interestingness of a rule R_1 with respect to another rule R_2 is calculated as follows:

Definition 3
Let r: $Å_r \rightarrow C_r$ be a rule whose interestingness is to be computed with respect to the rule set R. Then

$$
I_r^R = \begin{cases}
0 & \text{if } \Psi(A_r, A_s) = 0 \,\&\, \Psi(C_r, C_s) = 0 \\
(\min_{S \in R} \Psi(A_r, A_s) + \Psi(C_r, C_s))/2 & \text{if } \Psi(A_r, A_s)) \geq \Psi(C_r, C_s) \\
(\Psi(A_r, A_s) + \min_{S \in R}(\Psi(C_r, C_s))/2 & \text{if } \Psi(A_r, A_s)) < \Psi(C_r, C_s) \\
1 & \text{if } \Psi(A_r, A_s) = 1 \,\&\, \Psi(C_r, C_s) = 1
\end{cases}
$$

As per Definition 3, $I_r^R = 0$ indicates that R_1 and R_2 are identical, $I_r^R = 1$ indicates the extreme deviation between R_1 and R_2. ($\min_{s \in R} \Psi(A_r,A_s) + \Psi(C_r,C_s))/2$ and ($\Psi(A_r,A_s) + \min_{s \in R} \Psi(C_r,C_s))/2$ indicates the intermediate degree of deviation of R_1 with respect to R_2. The user specifies the threshold to select interesting rules based on the computation of I_r^R.

After rule interestingness is computed, we have to decide either the rule is interesting or simply a deviation of an existing rule. Whether a rule is interesting or not depends on the user feeling about the domain, which is determined by a certain threshold value. The following definition is the basis of determining interesting rules.

Definition 4
Let R_1: $Å_1 \rightarrow C_1$ and R_2: $Å_2 \rightarrow C_2$ be two association rules. R_1 is considered interesting with respect to R_2, if $I_{R_1}^{R_2} > \Phi$, where Φ is a user threshold value, otherwise it is considered conforming rule.

As per Definition 4, the computed value $I_{R_1}^{R_2}$ which indicates the interestingness of R_1 with respect to R_2 is compared against the user threshold value Φ to determine either R_1 is interesting with respect to R_2 or otherwise. The R_1 is interesting if its deviation with respect to R_2 exceeds Φ.

5 Expert Mining Using Mathematical Techniques

Most Association rule algorithms employ support-confidence threshold to exclude uninteresting rules but in medical data mining, many rules satisfying minimum confidence and minimum support may not be interesting in view of expert's experience of critical cases. It is only the user (medical expert) who can judge if the rule is interesting or not. The judgment being subjective, will vary from expert to expert.

Traditionally, medical expert system extract knowledge using IF-THEN diagnostic rules, where as data mining algorithms use large databases to discover a set of rules. Machine learning techniques too rely on available databases. In case of medical databases, it is possible that there are many missing or incomplete records. On the other hand a medical expert because of his limited experience may arrive at incorrect rule. Therefore, it is desirable to compare rules generated by data mining algorithms with rules generated by experts. Subsequently, contradictions can be identified and eliminated to discover interesting rules.

We may extract rules from medical experts using mathematical techniques. Kovalerschuk et al. have applied monotonicity of Boolean functions in the breast cancer problem by evaluating calcifications in a mammogram [27]. Suppose we identify n attributes say $x_1, x_2, x_3 \ldots x_n$ to diagnose a particular disease D. Without loss of generality, we assume these attributes take binary values yes or no i.e. 1 or 0 then there are 2^n combinations of these attributes. We can extract rules by interviewing medical experts on these 2^n combinations of the values of the attributes. By using monotonicity in some form on these 2^n vectors, we may minimize the number of questions. One simple way of defining monotonicity is as follows:

$$(x_1, x_2, x_3 \ldots x_n) \leq (y_1, y_2, y_3 \ldots y_n)$$
$$\text{iff } x_i \leq y_i$$

Now questions to expert will depend on answer to the previous question. Chain of monotonic values of $(x_1, x_2, x_3 \ldots x_n)$ represents a case using Hansel chain [28].

6 Implementation and Experimentation

The proposed approach is implemented and tested on several public medical datasets available at http://kdd.ics.uci.edu using C programming language. The datasets are partitioned into three groups representing instances arrived at time T_1, T_2 and T_3 respectively. The rules are generated using WEKA-associate [29] for each partition of the datasets, with 0.1% and 1% to indicate minimum confidence and minimum support respectively. Subsequently, their interestingness is quantified using the proposed framework. Based on the specified threshold the rules are categorized either as interesting or conforming (Definition 4).

6.1 Experiment I

The objective of the first experiment is to show the effectiveness of the approach in reducing the number of discovered rules. It is expected that the number of discovered rules that are interesting keeps on decreasing over the time. We work with five datasets and assume that the interestingness threshold value (Φ) = 0.6. The values in the third column of Table 1 represent the number of rules discovered, using WEKA, at a given partition and the values in the fourth column represent the interesting rules discovered by our approach. It is observed that the number of interesting rules decreases in contrast to the number of conforming rules which increases as expected. Intuitively, the

Table 1. The discovered medical rules at time T_1, T_2, and T_3

Dataset	Time	Discovered AR's	Interesting rules	Conforming rules
Lymph	T_1	32000	18230	13770
	T_2	28562	12003	16559
	T_3	26781	2010	24771
Breast	T_1	802	320	482
	T_2	725	180	545
	T_3	540	73	467
Hepatitis	T_1	1207	800	407
	T_2	980	430	550
	T_3	626	228	398
Heart	T_1	987	564	423
	T_2	566	320	246
	T_3	207	118	89
Sick	T_1	4502	2876	1635
	T_2	2709	1078	1631
	T_3	986	401	585

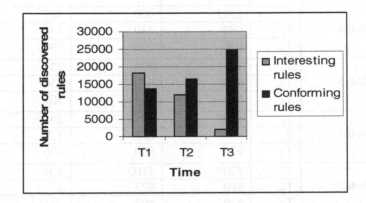

Fig. 2. Graphical representation of discovered rules of Lymph dataset

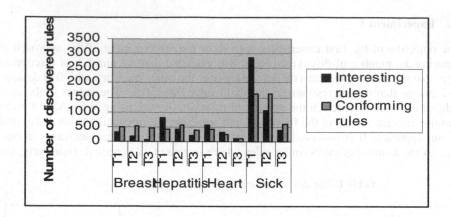

Fig. 3. Graphical representation of discovered rules of different datasets

Table 2. Discovered rules at time T_1, T_2 and T_3 for different (Φ)

Interesting Degree (Φ)	Time	Discovered Rules	Interesting	Conforming
Φ=0.9	T_1	1207	291	913
	T_2	980	160	820
	T_3	626	119	507
Φ=0.8	T_1	1207	311	896
	T_2	980	259	721
	T_3	626	156	470
Φ=0.7	T_1	1207	417	790
	T_2	980	388	592
	T_3	626	214	412
Φ=0.6	T_1	1207	800	407
	T_2	980	430	550
	T_3	626	228	398
Φ=0.5	T_1	1207	976	231
	T_2	980	530	450
	T_3	626	324	302
Φ=0.4	T_1	1207	1016	191
	T_2	980	860	120
	T_3	626	520	106
Φ=0.3	T_1	1207	1103	104
	T_2	980	923	57
	T_3	626	602	24

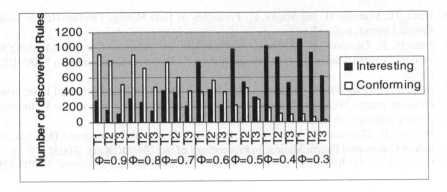

Fig. 4. Graphical representation of discovered rules

interesting rules discovered at time T_1 become known knowledge at time T_2 and hence no more interesting. The conforming rules are shown in the rightmost column of Table 1. Figures 2 and 3 shows the graphical representation of Table 1.

6.2 Experiment II

The second experiment was performed using 'Hepatitis' dataset to study the effectiveness of interestingness threshold (Φ) on the number of discovered rules. It is expected that as the interestingness threshold value (Φ) decreases, the number of rules increases. Intuitively, a higher value of Φ indicates that the user background knowledge about the domain is high and therefore number of interesting rules is reduced. In contrast, a lower value of Φ indicates that the user background knowledge about the domain is low and therefore number of interesting rules is increased. Table 2 shows the result of this experiment. Fig. 4 shows the graphical representation of the results.

7 Conclusions

In this paper, we proposed framework to quantify the interestingness of association rules in evolving medical databases. The approach is post-analysis filter that is used in analysis stage of KDD process. It is based on computation of the deviation of the currently discovered association rules with respect to expert rules and previously discovered knowledge. The user subjectivity is captured the by constructing the expert rules. The framework is implemented and evaluated using five medical datasets and has shown encouraging results.

Currently we are trying to integrate the framework into the Apriori algorithm (mining algorithm), thus using it in the mining stage of the KDD process.

References

1. Han, J. and Kamber, M.: Data Mining: Concepts and Techniques. San Francisco, Morgan Kauffmann Publishers, (2001)
2. Dunham M. H.: Data Mining: Introductory and Advanced Topics. 1st Edition Pearson ygEducation (Singapore) Pte. Ltd. (2003)

3. Hand, D., Mannila, H. and Smyth, P.: Principles of Data Mining, Prentice-Hall of India Private Limited, India, (2001)
4. Bronchi, F., Giannotti, F., Mazzanti, A., Pedreschi, D.: Adaptive Constraint Pushing in Frequent Pattern Mining. In Proceedings of the 17th European Conference on PAKDD03 (2003)
5. Bronchi, F., Giannotti, F., Mazzanti, A., Pedreschi, D.: ExAMiner: Optimized Level-wise Frequent pattern Mining with Monotone Constraints. In Proceedings of the 3rd International Conference on Data Mining (ICDM03) (2003)
6. Bronchi, F., Giannotti, F., Mazzanti, A., Pedreschi, D.: Exante: Anticipated Data Reduction in Constrained Pattern Mining. In Proceedings of the 7th PAKDD03 (2003)
7. Freitas, A. A.: On Rule Interestingness Measures. Knowledge-Based Systems. 12:309-315 (1999)
8. Klemetinen, M., Mannila, H., Ronkainen, P., Toivonen, H., Verkamo, A. I.: Finding Interesting Rules from Large Sets of Discovered Association Rules. In Proceedings of the 3rd International Conference on Information and Knowledge Management. Gaithersburg, Maryland (1994)
9. Liu, B., Hsu, W., Chen, S., Ma, Y.: Analyzing the Subjective Interestingness of Association Rules. IEEE Intelligent Systems (2000)
10. Liu, B., Hsu, W.: Post Analysis of Learned Rules. In Proceedings of the 13th National Conference on AI (AAAI'96) (1996)
11. Liu, B., Hsu, W., Lee, H-Y., Mum, L-F.: Tuple-Level Analysis for Identification of Interesting Rules. In Technical Report TRA5/95, SoC. National University of Singapore, Singapore (1996)
12. Liu, B., Hsu, W.: Finding Interesting Patterns Using User Expectations. DISCS Technical Report (1995)
13. Liu, B., Hsu, W., Chen, S.: Using General Impressions to Analyze Discovered Classification Rules. In Proceedings of the 3rd International Conference on Knowledge Discovery and Data mining (KDD 97) (1997)
14. Padmanabhan, B., Tuzhilin, A.: Unexpectedness as a Measure of Interestingness in Knowledge Discovery. Working paper # IS-97-. Dept. of Information Systems, Stern School of Business, NYU (1997)
15. Padmanabhan, B., Tuzhilin, A.: A Belief-Driven Method for Discovering Unexpected Patterns. KDD-98 (1998)
16. Padmanabhan, B., Tuzhilin, A.: Small is Beautiful: Discovering the Minimal Set of Unexpected Patterns. KDD-2000 (2000)
17. Piatetsky-Shapiro, G., Matheus, C. J.: The Interestingness of Deviations. In Proceedings of AAAI Workshop on Knowledge Discovery in Databases (1994)
18. Piatetsky-Shapiro, G.: Discovery, Analysis, and Presentation of Strong Rules. In Knowledge Discovery in Databases. The AAAI Press (1991)
19. Psaila, G.: Discovery of Association Rules Meta-Patterns. In Proceedings of 2nd International Conference on Data Warehousing and Knowledge Discovery (DAWAK99) (1999)
20. Agrawal, R., Imielinski, T. and Swami, A.: Mining Association Rules between Sets of Items in Large Databases, In ACM SIGMOD Conference of Management of Data. Washington D.C., (1993)
21. Silberschatz, A., Tuzhilin, A.: On Subjective Measures of Interestingness in Knowledge Discovery. In Proceedings of the 1st International Conference on Knowledge Discovery and Data Mining (1995)
22. Silberschatz, A., Tuzhilin, A.: What Makes Patterns Interesting in Knowledge Discovery Systems. IEEE Trans. and Data Engineering. V.5, no.6 (1996)

23. Suzuki, E., Kodratoff, Y.: Discovery of Surprising Exception Rules Based on Intensity of Implication. In Proceedings of the 2nd European Symposium, PKDD98, Lecture Notes in Artificial Intelligence (1998)
24. Liu, B., Hsu, W., Chen, S., and Ma Y.: Analyzing the Subjective Interestingness of Association Rules. IEEE Intelligent Systems (2000)
25. Al-Hegami, A. S., Bhatnagar, V. and Kumar, N.: Novelty Framework for Knowledge Discovery in Databases. In Proceedings of the 6th International Conference on Data warehousing and Knowledge Discovery (DaWak 2004). Zaragoza, Spain, pp 48-55 (2004)
26. Bhatnagar, V., Al-Hegami, A. S. and Kumar, N.: Novelty as a Measure of Interestingness in Knowledge Discovery. In International Journal of Information Technology, Volume 2, Number 1 (2005)
27. Kovalerchuk, B., Triantaphyllou, E., Despande, A. and Vtyaev, E.: Interactive Learning of Monotone Boolean Function. Information Sciences, 94 (1-4):87-118 (1996)
28. Hansel, G.: Sur le nombre des functions Boolenes Monotones den variables. C.R. Acad. Sci. Paris, 262(20):1088-1090 (in French) (1966)
29. Witten, I.H. and Frank, E.: Data Mining: Practical machine learning tools and techniques with Java implementations. Morgan Kaufmann, San Francisco (2000)

Named Relationship Mining from Medical Literature

Isabelle Bichindaritz

University of Washington, Institute of Technology, 1900 Commerce Street,
Box 358426, Tacoma, WA 98402, USA
ibichind@u.washington.edu

Abstract. This article addresses the task of mining named relationships between concepts from biomedical literature for indexing purposes or for scientific discovery from medical literature. This research builds on previous work on concept mining from medical literature for indexing purposes and proposes to learn semantic relationships names between concepts learnt. Previous ConceptMiner system did learn pairs of concepts, expressing a relationship between two concepts, but did not learn relationships semantic names. Building on ConceptMiner, RelationshipMiner is interested in learning as well the relationships with their name identified from the Unified Medical Language System (UMLS) knowledge-base as a basis for creating higher-level knowledge structures, such as rules, cases, and models, in future work. Current system is focused on learning semantically typed relationships as predefined in the UMLS, for which a dictionary of synonyms and variations has been created. An evaluation is presented showing that actually this relationship mining task improves the concept mining task results by enabling a better screening of the relationships between concepts for relevant ones.

Keywords: Medical Informatics, Text Mining, Semantic Web, Knowledge Discovery, Information Retrieval.

1 Introduction

The idea of mining concepts and relationships from medical literature comes from Swanson [13, 14], who ignited the interest of researchers who followed in his trace [15]. Since then, text mining research from biomedical literature has developed as a promising new area to make sense of the exponentially increasing amount of information made available in particular through biomedical literature [3]. Given the vast amount of information in an area, researchers are more and more constrained to specialize, thus abstracting themselves from other domains. Therefore text mining systems are needed to enable researchers to rapidly apprehend the knowledge in a domain, and to discover relationships between concepts from different domains. It is very likely that the research of different research groups could be of interest to one another, nevertheless they may never become aware of one another without the assistance of computer supported knowledge discovery systems [8]. The goal of text mining from literature databases is to discover novel and interesting knowledge in the form of concepts, patterns, and relations [6, 7, 9]. Swanson [13, 14] for example de-

P. Perner (Ed.): ICDM 2006, LNAI 4065, pp. 64–75, 2006.
© Springer-Verlag Berlin Heidelberg 2006

scribes a data mining system that brought forth seven medical discoveries later published in relevant medical journals. Nevertheless, previous systems focus mainly on learning links between concepts, and not the relationships names themselves [13, 14, 15], for example by specializing in a type of relationship such as a causal relationship [13, 14].

The RelationshipMiner system presented here proposes to automate the process of mining for named semantic relationships between concepts from biomedical literature. It builds on a concept miner system mining for unnamed relationships between concepts, such as the relationship between caloric restriction and aging, in order to learn concept pairs, and not isolated concepts. This approach significantly reduced the number of concepts found in documents. The system also restricted its concept learning process by focusing on the figure and table legends in the documents. The next section presents the ConceptMiner system at the basis of this work. The third section introduces the Unified Medical Language System (UMLS) as the ontology guiding the discovery process. The fourth section sets forth the RelationshipMiner system architecture and different components. The fifth section presents an evaluation of the system. It is followed by a discussion and a conclusion.

2 ConceptMiner System

The ConceptMiner system [2] presented serves as the basis for RelationshipMiner, while expanding it to incorporate semantic naming of relationships. While ConceptMiner could process only figure and table legends, RelationshipMiner can be run to specifically process figure and table legends, document parts, or full documents.

ConceptMiner was initially developed for the Telemakus system [5], which consists of a set of domain documents (original focus was the biology of aging), a conceptual schema to represent the main components of each document, and a set of tools to query, visualize, maintain, and map the set of documents through their concepts and research findings [5]. For that purpose, this system mines and maps research findings from research literature. At present, knowledge extraction resorts to systems with both manual and automated components. A key area of current work is to move towards automating the research concept identification process, through data mining [5]. This is exactly why ConceptMiner was developed.

Concept mining involves processing articles already stored in a domain-specific database (DSDB). These articles actually do not comprise the full text of the original articles, only the tables and figures descriptions, referred to as *legends*, which are considered the most probable placeholders for research findings. It has been established by Telemakus project team that the most interesting information about research literature is usually found in legends [5].

ConcepMiner process flow is illustrated in Fig.1. The system processes through several steps, the main ones being syntactic analysis, semantic analysis, and concept mapping and association.

Given an article or a set of articles, the system starts by extracting all legends already stored in the database, processes each legend by identifying interesting relationships, filters relationships,   ranks those relationships based on a number of

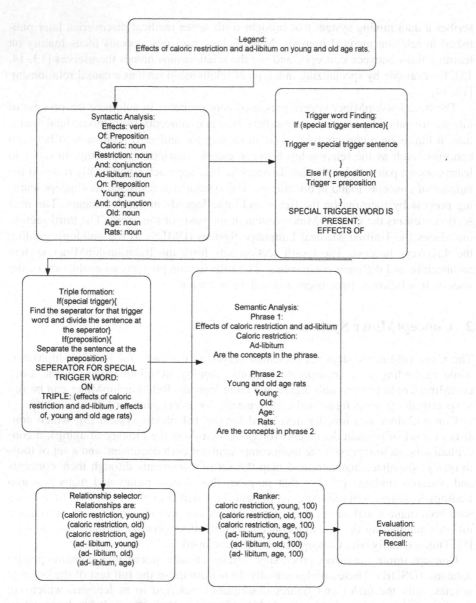

Fig. 1. ConceptMiner system process flow

parameters, and finally writes the resulting relationships to an XML file for later use. For comparison purposes, precision and recall are also computed by the system on a per-article basis.

2.1 Syntactic Analysis

The process of concept extraction and association is applied at the sentence level. Each sentence is parsed and grammatical structures are extracted. From the concept association perspective, each sentence is made up of a connector phrase, called a *trigger phrase*, and the two phrases connected by that trigger phrase. An example of trigger phrase shown on Fig. 1 is "effects of". These trigger phrases are usually prepositions, but human experts have also provided special phrases that act as triggers, such as "effect of". A trigger phrase may contain a connector phrase that separates the remaining part of the sentence into two phrases. After a trigger is found in a sentence, the remaining sentence is split into two phrases optionally connected by a connector phrase. This phase of the system is called *syntactic analysis* in a broad sense. The connector word and two phrases together are called a *triple*.

This project makes use of a *bottom-up analyzer* API available from the National Library of Medicine called *Specialist Text Tools* API [10]. This parser is a minimal commitment barrier category parser. Using the *Specialist lexicon*, the part of speech and other syntactic information are analyzed. This analysis is specific to biomedical field. The results of this phase are a set of *triples* (see Fig. 1 for an example) such as the triple *<effects of, caloric restriction and ad-libitum, young and old age rats>*.

2.2 Semantic Analysis

After triples are built, each triple is further analyzed by *semantic analysis*. This involves looking for concepts in each phrase, and is accomplished by applying a domain specific natural language processing tool. From each phrase, a candidate list of concept phrases from the UMLS is extracted. The semantic analysis is made possible by the National Library of Medicine (NLM)'s UMLS project [12]. UMLS ultimate goal is to facilitate the development of computer systems that behave as if they "understand" the meaning of the language of biomedicine and health.

Although the *Specialist Text Tools* also resort to UMLS, it is a foremost knowledge source for semantic analysis. The words or phrases are considered as concepts in the medical domain if said words or phrases can be found in the metathesaurus of the UMLS. The metathesaurus is one of the three UMLS knowledge sources, and is the central vocabulary component of the UMLS [12].

Semantic analysis is performed on the results of syntactic analysis of the legends to determine the meaning of the words in the sentence. In this step, the semantics of each word or phrase is evaluated. This project uses *MMTx* tool [11] as it is specifically developed for the biomedical field. The main purpose of *MMTx* semantic analysis is to find out the phrases and their variants and then match these to the phrases or words in the UMLS knowledge-base. The words or phrases successfully mapped to the UMLS database can be considered as concepts in the biomedical or health field. The concept mapping process produces a list of concepts for each phrase (see Fig. 1 for an example). For example, the phrase *"caloric restriction and ad-libitum"* is mapped into the list *"caloric restriction"* and *"ad-libitum"*.

2.3 Concept Mapping and Association

The list of candidate concepts is refined in multiple steps, including removing duplicates or substrings, substituting expressions by their preferred form in the domain (for example, "free access to food" is replaced with "ad libitum"), and generating a list of relationships by recombining the concepts in triples.

The list of candidate relationships is further condensed by regrouping expressions, for example resulting into *<caloric restriction, young age rats>*, *< caloric restriction, old age rats>*, *<ad-libitum, young age rats>*, and *< ad-libitum, old age rats>*.

At the article level, all unique relationships from constituent sentences are aggregated. This list is again refined to remove partial matches. The resulting list of relationships is ranked based on the importance of concepts, in particular based on the presence of the concepts in the domain-specific database.

3 UMLS Project

The "Unified Medical Language System" (UMLS) from the National Library of Medicine (NLM) [12], a specialized ontology in biomedicine, provides standardized concepts for the creation of a controlled domain vocabulary. The UMLS provides a very powerful resource for rapidly creating a robust scientific thesaurus in support of precision searching. Further, the semantic type descriptors for each concept and semantic network (see Fig. 2) may offer some interesting opportunities for intelligent searching and mapping of concepts representing research findings, and their relationships.

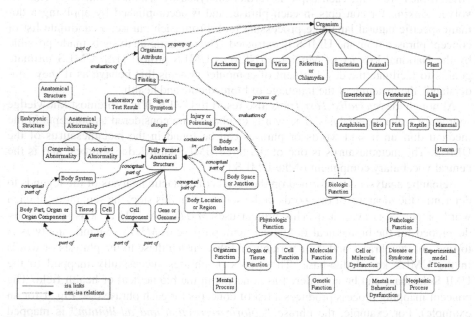

Fig. 2. Extract from the UMLS semantic network showing main concepts and semantic relationships between them (from NLM's UMLS project [12])

Syntactic and semantic analysis tools for automated Natural Language Processing (NLP) are also provided by the National Library of Medicine's UMLS project [10, 11]. UMLS ultimate goal is to facilitate the development of computer systems that behave as if they "understand" the meaning of the language of biomedicine and health.

By navigating the semantic network provided, it is possible to know which concepts extracted by the NLM tools from biomedical documents correspond to diseases, which correspond to findings, which correspond to medications, and so forth. It is also possible to know which relationships connect different concepts. There are a total of 135 semantic types. Figure 3 displays a partial list of the 54 relationships from the UMLS semantic network, and figure 4 how relationships can be refined through specialization/generalization links in the semantic network. Additionally, it is possible to extend the semantic network, both concepts and relationships, for instance for our purpose with a semantic network of planning actions that can be connected by a 'treat' relationship with other concepts.

4 RelationshipMiner system

RelationshipMiner system improves ConceptMiner by keeping the names of the relationships mined, and not only the concepts. For instance, the list of candidate relationships provided in the previous example results in <*effects of, caloric restriction,*

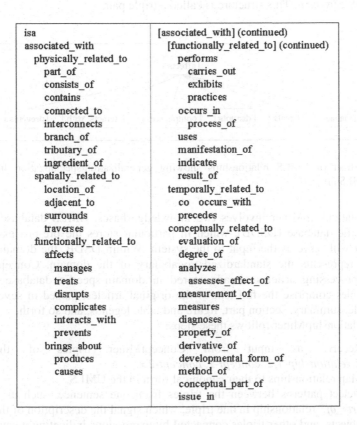

isa	[associated_with] (continued)
associated_with	[functionally_related_to] (continued)
physically_related_to	performs
part_of	carries_out
consists_of	exhibits
contains	practices
connected_to	occurs_in
interconnects	process_of
branch_of	uses
tributary_of	manifestation_of
ingredient_of	indicates
spatially_related_to	result_of
location_of	temporally_related_to
adjacent_to	co occurs_with
surrounds	precedes
traverses	conceptually_related_to
functionally_related_to	evaluation_of
affects	degree_of
manages	analyzes
treats	assesses_effect_of
disrupts	measurement_of
complicates	measures
interacts_with	diagnoses
prevents	property_of
brings_about	derivative_of
produces	developmental_form_of
causes	method_of
	conceptual_part_of
	issue_in

Fig. 3. Extract of UMLS relationships (from NLM's UMLS project [12])

young age rats>, <effects of, caloric restriction, old age rats>, <effects of, ad-libitum, young age rats> , and *<effects of, ad-libitum, old age rats>*, by keeping the "effects of" relationship name.

RelationshipMiner resorts to the UMLS also for this task of mining for relationship names. First, the project team has created a list of potential trigger words for relationships. This list is long, and comprises of course the relationship names from the UMLS (see Fig. 3), but many others as well, such as synonyms, and variations. *MMTx* semantic analyzer [12], augmented by a domain dependent thesaurus including additional relationships, maps all these relationship names into their preferred form in the UMLS, called a canonical form. Canonical forms are the 54 relationship types in the UMLS semantic network.

More generally, RelationshipMiner mines for triples < *relationship-1,2, concept-1, concept-2>* from a document. It also attaches a condition to a triple when it finds it to represent the information that IF a condition occurs, THEN an action or test is undertaken. This can be represented as < *relationship-1,2, concept-1, concept-2>* IF < *relationship-3,4, concept-3, concept-4>*. An example can be < *startTreatment, Patient, PrednisoneAndCyclosporineTherapy>* IF *<property_of, ImmunosuppressantAgentNOS, absent >*. This structure is called a triple pair.

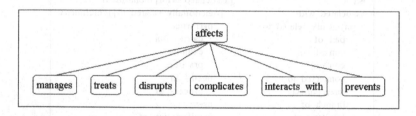

Fig. 4. Extract of UMLS relationships showing generalization/specialization links (from NLM's UMLS project)

The RelationshipMiner involves two knowledge bases, UMLS database, and domain specific database (DSDB), which in particular stores the pre-processed documents that will serve as the input to the system. Within DSDB, the domain specific thesaurus represents the standardized vocabulary of the domain. Concept mining involves processing articles already stored in domain-specific database (DSDB). These articles comprise the full text of the original articles, parsed in several parts, such as title, summary, section part, figure and table legends, and so forth.

The RelationshipMiner follows these steps:

1. Receive as input from ConceptMiner triples of the form < *relationship-1,2, concept-1, concept-2>*.
2. Map relationships to their canonical form in the UMLS.
3. Detect patterns between the triples from one sentence, such as a *"property_of"* relationship in one triple, which signal the description of the state of objects, and other triples connected by expressions indicating a causal or sequential interaction, such as *"if… then … else …"* , or their variants.

4. Group corresponding triples into pairs of triples, in the form of
   < relationship-1,2, concept-1, concept-2> IF < relationship-3,4, concept-3, concept-4>,
   such as
   < startTreatment, Patient, PrednisoneAndCyclosporineTherapy>
   IF <property_of, ImmunosuppressantAgent-NOS, absent >.
5. Produce as output triples organized in a semantic network through their association with other triples in pairs of triples.

Linking the relationships produces a semantic network representing the knowledge conveyed by a document, which can serve information retrieval purposes. The evaluation of this system in the next section focuses on evaluating the indexing capability of this approach.

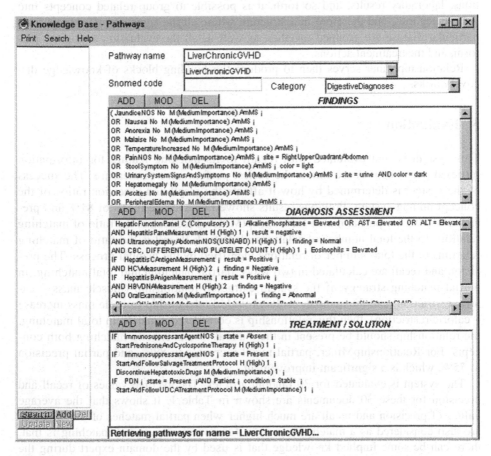

Fig. 5. Example of a prototypical case as it can be mined based on RelationshipMiner learnt relationships

Rule mining is another example of knowledge mined from the article, since the pair of triples above can be represented in the form of a rule:

IF < relationship-3,4, concept-3, concept-4> THEN < relationship-1,2, concept-1, concept-2>,
   such as the example
   IF <property_of, ImmunosuppressantAgentNOS, absent > THEN < startTreatment, Patient, PrednisoneAndCyclosporineTherapy>.

For other types of tasks such as knowledge discovery, it is interesting to merge the networks obtained from separate documents to build a semantic network representing a domain.

Yet other applications of the relationships mined for are to build higher levels of structures, such as prototypical cases (see fig. 5) and cases for instance. Combined with the information in the UMLS about diagnoses, signs and symptoms, medications, laboratory results, and so forth, it is possible to group related concepts into these categories, and therefore in a structure where all the signs and symptoms for a particular disease are grouped together, as well as all the evaluation actions to perform, and the treatment actions.

RelationshipMiner serves then to produce the building blocks of knowledge discovery tasks.

5   Evaluation

This system is first evaluated with regard to its indexing feature for information retrieval purposes because this is the easiest performance to measure. The success of the system is determined by how it affects the recall and precision ratios of the concept mining system. Previous results showed an average recall of 81% and precision of 50% for partial match for ConceptMiner. Precision is the ratio of matching relations to the total number of relations identified. Recall is the ratio of matching relations to the total number of relations identified by the manual process. The precision and recall are calculated in two ways: partial matching and total matching. In partial matching strategy, if the system extracted relationship (muscle mass – caloric restriction) and the manual results provided relationship (muscle mass increase – caloric restriction), then this relationship is considered a match. In total matching, the relationship should be present in the manual results exactly matching both concepts. For RelationshipMiner, partial recall increases to 82%, and partial precision to 75%, which is a significant improvement.

The system is evaluated for 30 random articles. The average values of recall and precision for these 30 documents are shown in Table 1. It shows that the average values of precision and recall are much higher when partial matches of the concepts are also considered as a match. The reason for considering partial matching is that, there can be some implied knowledge that is used by the domain expert during the manual process, but that kind of knowledge is either not available to this system or hard to automate.

Table 1. Precision and recall ratios

Number of Documents	Total Recall	Total Precision	Partial Recall	Partial Precision
ConceptMiner	53%	35%	81%	50%
RelationshipMiner	63%	51%	82%	75%

The interpretation of why the precision in particular is significantly increased is that the system is able to better determine which pairs of concepts correspond to research findings, versus to background knowledge or other information. Human indexers were specifically trained at retaining from the documents their research findings, as the most interesting information for researchers to get from the articles. This was a notable limitation of ConceptMiner to not be able to discriminate enough between research findings and other types of information from the research articles, and one of the motivation to add the semantic relationships types dimension to the text mining process. One of the main issues to solve in data mining is to be able to discriminate among the knowledge learnt which is important and novel. In a system such as the concept miner, many more pairs of concepts are generated by the automatic process than by the human experts. Therefore, a ranking system permits, with different criteria such as repetition and location in the document among others, to rank the pairs of concepts as being more or less important. The improvement to this ranking is in RelationshipMiner that the type of relationship is an essential criteria for assessing the importance of a relationship learnt.

Research findings have been identified here as their relationship types being within the groupings of *"functionally_related_to"*, *"temporally_related_to"*, and some of the *"conceptually_related_to"* (see figure 3). Exclusion of semantic types such as *"physically_related_to"* and *"spatially_related_to"* has proved to be a major advance in this system. Further tests are under way to refine more which relationship types are the most pertinent to keep. This analysis is not straight forward since the human indexers did not record the semantic types of the relationships, but only that there was a relationship between for example "caloric restriction" and "aging", without further precision. Therefore it is by testing the level of recall and precision when adding or removing certain types of relationships that it is possible to learn which ones should be kept in priority.

Although the results of 82% in recall and 75% in precision are not perfect, in terms of information retrieval they are quite acceptable – 60% precision is a minimum success threshold. Moreover, the system proposes a new functionality in terms of learning named relationships, which is a difficult task that few systems have been tackling.

6 Conclusion

RelationshipMiner system presented here is a knowledge discovery system from biomedical literature that learns from a document the main relationships between pairs of concepts in this document and the names or semantic types of these relationships.

Mining for typed or named relationships from biomedical literature is made possible by the availability of an ontology of the medical domain (the UMLS [12]). Researchers have stressed the importance of semantic information processing in many medical informatics tasks [1]. Future directions for this research are very promising. The capability of the system to connect concepts within relationships, and to organize these relationships into more complex structures such as the pairs of triples presented here, can be generalized to build higher level structures such as molecular pathways [4], prototypical cases, and cases [16]. In addition to information retrieval pertinence, this knowledge discovery process will permit to better synthesize the knowledge gained from one domain, to transmit this knowledge in electronic form to knowledge-based systems and experience-based systems, thus spreading their development and dissemination, and to build creative analogies between different domains.

References

1. Bichindaritz, I.: Mémoire: Case-based Reasoning Meets the Semantic Web in Biology and Medicine. In: Funk, P., Gonzàlez Calero, P.A. (eds.): Proceedings of ECCBR 2004. Lecture Notes in Artificial Intelligence, Vol. 3155. Springer-Verlag, Berlin, Heidelberg, New York (2004) 47-61
2. Bichindaritz I., Akineni S.: Case Mining from Biomedical Literature. In: Perner, P., Imiya, A.(eds.): Proceedings of MLDM 05. Lecture Notes in Artificial Intelligence, Vol. 3587. Springer-Verlag, Berlin, Heidelberg, New York (2005) 682-691
3. Dorre, J., Gerstl, P., Seiffert, R.: Text mining: finding nuggets in mountains of textual data. In: Chaudhuri, S., Madigan, D., and Fayyad, U. (eds.): Proceedings of the fifth ACM SIGKDD International Conference on Knowledge Discovery and Data Mining. ACM press, New York (1999) 398-401
4. Friedman, C., Kra, P., Yu, H., Krauthammer, M., Rzhetsky, A.: GENIES: a natural-language processing system for the extraction of molecular pathways from journal articles. Bioinformatics 17, Suppl 1 (2001) S74-S82
5. Fuller, S., Revere, D., Bugni, P., Martin, G.M.: A knowledgebase system to enhance scientific discovery: Telemakus. Biomed Digit Libr. Sep 21;1(1):2 (2004)
6. Han, J., Kamber, M.: Data mining concepts and techniques, first edition. Morgan Kaufmann, San Mateo, CA (2000)
7. Hearst, M.A.: Untangling Text Data Mining. In: Dale, R., Church, K. (eds.): Proceedings of the 37th Annual Meeting of the Association for Computational Linguistics. Association for Computational Linguistics, Morristown, NJ (1999) 3-10
8. Hristovski, D., Peterlin, B., Mitchell, J.A., Humphrey, S.M.: Using literature-based discovery to identify disease candidate genes. International Journal of Medical Informatics, 74 (2-4) (2005) 28-98
9. Nasukawa T., Nagano, T.: Text Analysis and Knowledge Mining System. Knowledge management Special Issue. IBM systems journal Vol. 40 (2001) 967-984
10. National Library of Medicine: The Specialist NLP Tools. http://specialist.nlm.nih.gov [Last access: 2005-04-01] (2004)
11. National Library of Medicine: MetaMap Transfer (MMTx), http://mmtx.nlm.nih.gov [Last access: 2005-04-01] (2005)
12. National Library of Medicine: The Unified Medical Language System. http://umls.nlm.nih.gov [Last access: 2005-04-01] (2005)

13. Swanson, D.R.: Information discovery from complementary literatures: Categorizing viruses as potential weapons. Journal of the American Society for Information Science Vol. 52(10) (2001) 797-812
14. Swanson, D.R., Smalheiser, N.R.: An interactive system for finding complementary literatures: a stimulus to scientific discovery. Artificial Intelligence Vol.9 (1997), 183-203
15. Weeber, M., Vos, R., De Jong-van Den Berg, L.T., Aronson, A.R., Molena, G.: Generating hypotheses by discovering implicit associations in the literature: a case report of a search for new potential therapeutic uses for thalidomide. J Am Med Inform Assoc, May-Jun, 10(3), (2003) 252-259
16. Yang, Q., Hong, C.: Case Mining from Large Databases. In: Ashley, K., Bridge, D.G. (eds.): Proceedings of ICCBR 03. Lecture Notes in Artificial Intelligence, Vol. 2689. Springer-Verlag, Berlin, Heidelberg, New York, (2003) 691-702

Experimental Study of Evolutionary Based Method of Rule Extraction from Neural Networks in Medical Data

Urszula Markowska-Kaczmar and Rafal Matkowski

Wroclaw University of Technology
Medical University of Wroclaw Poland
urszula.markowska-kaczmar@pwr.wroc.pl

Abstract. In the paper the method of rule extraction from neural networks based on evolutionary approach, called GEX, is presented. Its details are described but the main stress is focussed on the experimental studies, the aim of which was to examine its usefulness in knowledge discovery and rule extraction for classification task of medical data. The tests were made using the well-known benchmark data sets from UCI, as well as two other data sets collected by Lower Silesian Oncology Center.

1 Introduction

Neural networks (NN) are widely used in many real problems. They have become so popular because of their ability to learn from data instead to perform strictly the algorithm, which is sometimes difficult to define or to implement. During processing new data they can generalize knowledge they achieved in training procedure. Their ability to remove noise from data is well known, as well.

But there is a big disadvantage of neural networks (NN), which arrest the development of applications based on neural networks in many domains. It is the lack of ability to explain in what way they solve the problem. The medicine is an example of such a domain where the explanation of the final decision is very important in a computer supporting system based on neural network. The rise of the user trust is the main reason of development of the methods of knowledge extraction from neural networks. A brief survey of existing methods, their advantages and drawbacks are presented in the next section

The main part of the paper presents the method of rule extraction called GEX. The main emphasis is focused on the experimental study performed with the application of the method. They have two reasons. The first one was to test its skill to describe the performance of neural network solving the medical classification problem. The tests were made on the benchmark data sets from UCI and the results are compared to other methods.

GEX is developed in this way that by the setting its parameters it is possible to influence on the coverage of examples by a given rule. Rules that cover less examples but more than the value indicated by the user can contain new knowledge. An evaluation of the ability of GEX in this area was the second reason of

P. Perner (Ed.): ICDM 2006, LNAI 4065, pp. 76–90, 2006.

the experimental study. The evaluation of novelty needs the help of an expert so these tests were made on the data collected by Lower Silesian Oncology Center and in cooperation with its expert.

The paper is organized as follows. At the beginning the problem of rule extraction from neural network is presented. It creates the background for the description of GEX, which is presented in the next section. Then the experimental study is shown. Its first part is dedicated to the experiments testing the power of GEX in searching rules describing classification task made by a neural network. The second one investigates its ability in knowledge discovery.

2   The Problem of the Rule Extraction from Neural Networks

The typical feedforward neural network is presented in Fig. 1. Neurons in this network create layers. One neuron calculates the total activation (*net*) as the sum of the weighted signals that reach it and transforms it by the activation function f, which is usually nonlinear. In each layer information is processed in parallel, so it is difficult to describe in which way the network produces the final response. Knowledge about the problem which is solved by a neural network lies in its architecture, and the parameters: weights assigned to the connections, activation functions, biases and in the set of training patterns. That is why all these elements are considered in the rule extraction methods.

The taxonomy distinguishes two main approaches. The global methods treat a neural network as a black box and in the searching rules they use the patterns processed by the network. We can mention here: KT [1], NeuroRule [2], Partial and Full-Re [3] or for regression problem - [4].

The second group describes the activity of each neuron in the form of a rule and by aggregation of these rules the set of rules specifying the performance of the trained neural network is obtained. Between these methods we can cite methods from: [5], [3], [6]. From this short survey one can notice that many methods of rule extraction exist. They differ from each other on the achieved

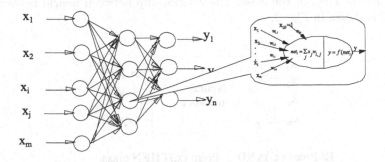

Fig. 1. The scheme of a feedforward neural network with detailed operations of one neuron

results. Some of them are dedicated to the special type of the neural network, some need a retraining of the neural network during the rule extraction or a special rule of the neural network training or they are dedicated to the special type of neural network attributes, so the need to design the method that are free from the above mentioned disadvantage still exists.

Andrews [7] has formulated the following criteria that allow to evaluate acquired set of rules.

- *fidelity* – expresses the way, in which the set of rules mimics the neural network performance;
- *accuracy*– describes the quality of new patterns classification;
- *consistency* – it exists when during different rule extraction session the produced sets of rules give the same classification;
- *comprehensibility* – is expressed in terms of the number of rules and the number of premises in the rules.

In real applications the weight of each criterion can be different. Citing after [6] suitable algorithm of the rule extraction should posses the following features: it should be independent of the architecture of neural network, it should not require its retraining and it should characterise by high accuracy and fidelity.

In the paper the problem of knowledge extraction from a neural network is formulated as follows. The trained neural network that solves classification task and the set of training patterns are given. The designed method should find a set of prepositional rules, that describes the performance of this neural network satisfying the criteria given by Andrews. Other representation of the neural network description are also used, for example decision trees [8], but because of the comprehensibility we focus on the prepositional rules that take the following form:

$$IF\ premise_1\ AND\ premise_2...premise_n\ THEN\ class_v, \qquad (1)$$

the i–th premise corresponds to the i–th neural network input. The premise specifies a condition put on the values of the input attribute of neural network to satisfy the rule. After THEN stands a conclusion, which is unambiguously defined by the label of the class. The relationship between neural network and the rule is shown in Fig. 2.

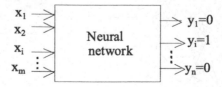

IF Prem (x_1)**AND** ... Prem (x_j)**THEN** class$_i$

Fig. 2. The relationship between the rule and the neural network

In the classification problem the output of neural network is locally encoded. It means that to designate i-th class only i-th output is equal to 1, the remaining outputs are equal to 0.

Taking into account the number of the neural network inputs and the type of attributes that can be not only binary but nominal or real one, searching for some limitations in premises of the rules can be seen as the NP - hard problem. That is why evolutionary approach can be useful in this case. The idea is not new [9]. Unfortunately, the level of complexity of this problem prevents the application of a simple genetic algorithm, so existing methods applying a genetic algorithm differ in the way of coding and obtaining the final set of rules [10], [11], [12].

3   The Basic Concepts of GEX

In GEX the formation of species by simultaneously evolving subpopulations is introduced (Fig. 3). The individuals in subpopulation can evolve independently or optionally migration of individuals is possible. Each species contains individuals corresponding to one class, which is recognized by the NN. One individual in a subpopulation encodes one rule. The form of the rule is described by (1). The premise in a rule expresses a condition, which has to be satisfied by the value of the corresponding input of the neural network in order to classify the pattern to the class indicated by the conclusion of the rule. The form of the premise is depending on the type of attribute, which is included in the pattern. In practice the i-th pattern is identified by the vector x_i (2):

$$\mathbf{x}_i = [x_{i,1}, x_{i,2}, ..., x_{i,n}], \tag{2}$$

where $x_{i,j}$ is the value of the attribute (feature) X_j. Each pattern is the element of Cartesian product:

$$d(X_1) \times d(X_2) \times ... \times d(X_n) \tag{3}$$

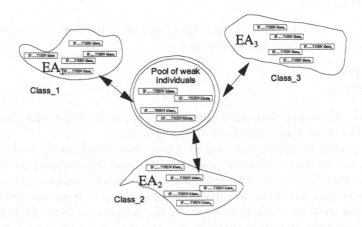

Fig. 3. The idea of GEX method

and $d(X_j)$ is the domain of the feature X_j.
In GEX we concern the following types of attributes:

- *real* $X_j \in V_r \Rightarrow X_j \in \Re$.
  Between them two types are distinguished:
  - *continuous* - V_c: their domain is defined by a range of real numbers:
    $X_j \in V_c \Leftrightarrow d(X_j) = (x_{jmin}; x_{jmax}) \in \Re$.
  - *discrete* V_d: the domain creates a countable set W_d of values w_i and the order relation is defined on this set
    $X_j \in V_d \Leftrightarrow d(X_j) = \{w_i \in \Re, i = 1, ...k, k \in \aleph\}$.
- *nominative* V_w: the domain is created by a set of discrete unordered values
  $X_j \in V_w \Leftrightarrow d(X_j) = \{w_1, w_2, ...w_w\}$, where w_i is a symbolic value.
- *binary* V_b: the domain is composed of only two values *True* and *False*
  $X_j \in V_b \Leftrightarrow d(X_j) = \{True, False\}$.

A condition in the premise differs depending on the type of the attribute. For a real type of the attribute (discrete and continuous) the following premises are covered:

- $\Rightarrow x_i < value_1$,
- $\Rightarrow x_i < value_2$,
- $\Rightarrow x_i > value_1$,
- $\Rightarrow x_i > value_2$,
- $\Rightarrow value_1 < x_i \bigwedge x_i < value_2$,
- $\Rightarrow x_i < value_1 \bigvee value_2 < x_i$.

For a discrete attribute, instead of $(<, >)$ inequalities $(\leq, \geq)$ are used.
For enumerative attributes – only two operators of relation are used $\{=, \neq\}$, so the premise has one of the following form:

- $x_i = value_i$,
- $x_i \neq value_i$.

For boolean attributes there is only one operator of relation $=$. It means that the premise can take the following form:

- $x_i = True$,
- $x_i = False$.

All rules in one subpopulation have identical conclusion. The evolutionary algorithm (EA) is performed in a classical way (Fig. 4).

First, the initial population is created. Then, the individuals are evaluated and the best rules are the candidates to send to the final set of rules that describes the performance of the neural network. They become a members of this set when they are more general than the rules existing in this set. It means that the less general rules are removed from it. Next, by the selection of individuals from the current population and after applying genetic operations (crossover, mutation and optionally migration) the offspring population is created.

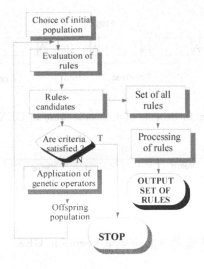

Fig. 4. The schema of evolutionary algorithm in GEX

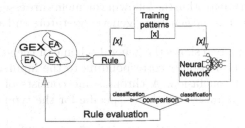

Fig. 5. The rule evaluation in GEX

It can be noticed that the only difference between classical performance of evolutionary algorithm and the proposed one lies in the evaluation of individuals, which requires the existence of decision system based on the rule processing. In each generation (after decoding) rules are evaluated by the comparison of the neural network answer and classification of patterns made upon the rules (Fig. 5). To realize it a decision system consisting in searching the rule that covers the given pattern is implemented. Classification made by the neural network serves as an oracle for the evaluated rules. The comparison of the results of classification is the basis for the evaluation of each rule, which is expressed by the value of a fitness function. Evolutionary algorithm performing in the presented way will look for the best rules that cover as many patterns as possible. In this case the risk exists that some patterns never would be covered by any rule. To solve this problem in GEX the niche mechanism is implemented. The final set of rules is created on the basis of the best rules found by evolutionary algorithm but also some heuristics are developed in order to optimize it.

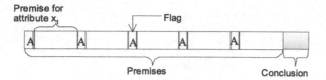

Fig. 6. Scheme of a chromosome in GEX

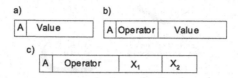

Fig. 7. The designed genes in GEX

3.1   Evolutionary Algorithm

To apply evolutionary algorithm the following elements are essential to design: representation of solution in the genotype, genetic operators and a fitness function.

The Genotype. Figure 6 shows the general scheme of the genotype in GEX. It is composed of the chromosomes corresponding to the inputs of neural network and a single gene of conclusion. A chromosome consists of gene being a flag and genes encoding premises, which are specific for the type of attribute of the premise it refers to.

The existence of flag assures that the rules have a different length, because the premise is included in the body of the rule if the flag is set to 1, only. In order to reflect the condition in the premise the chromosome is designed dependently on the type of attribute (Fig.7). For the real type of attribute the chromosome consists of the code of relation operator and two values determining the limits of range (Fig.7c). For the nominal attribute there is a code of operator and value (Fig.7b). Figure 7a represents a chromosome for the binary attribute. Besides the gene of flag, it consists of one gene referring to the value of attribute.

Selection and Genetic Operators. The initial population is created randomly with the number of individuals equal to *StartSize*. The basic operators used in GEX are a crossover and a mutation. They are applied after a selection of individuals that creates a pool of parents for the offspring population. In the selection a roulette wheel is used. The individuals that are not chosen to become parents are moved to the pool of weak individuals (Fig. 3). In each generation the size of a population is decreased by 1. When the population size reaches the value defined by the parameter *MinSize* migration operator becomes active. It consists in taking individuals from the pool of weak individuals (Fig. 3) to increase the size of the population to *Nsize*. In case the migration is inactive a kind of macromutation is used.

Although in the application of GEX we can choose between one point, two points and uniform crossover in the presented experiments the two-points crossover was used. It relies on the choice of a couple of the parent genotypes with the probability p_{c-w}, then two points are chosen in random and information is exchanged. These points can only lie between chromosomes. It is not allowed to cut the individuals between genes in the middle of the chromosome.

The mutation is specifically design for each type of a gene and is strongly dependent on the type of the chromosome (premise) it refers to. It changes information contained in the gene. The following parameters define this operator:

- p_{mu-op} - the probability of mutation of the relation operator or binary value,
- $p_{mu-range}$ - the probability of mutation of the range limits,
  p_{mu-act} - the probability of mutation of value for genes in chromosomes for nominative attributes,
- r_{ch} - the change of the range.

The mutation of the flag A relies in the change of its actual value to the opposite one with probability p_{mu-op}. The mutation of the gene containing $value$ in the chromosome of the binary attribute is realized as the change of the gene $value$ to its opposite value with the probability p_{mu-op} (True to False or False to True). The mutation of the gene $Operator$ independently of the chromosome consists in the change of the operator to other operator defined for this type of premise with the probability p_{mu-op}. The mutation of gene referring to the $value$ in the chromosomes for the nominative attribute is realized as the change of the actual value to the other one specified for this type with the probability p_{mu-act}. The mutation of the gene encoding the limits of a range in chromosomes for the real attributes consists in the change of $value_1$ and $value_2$. It is realized distinctly for continuous and discrete values. For continuous attributes the limits are changed into new values by adding a value from the following range (4).

$$(-(x_{imax} - x_{imin}) \cdot r_{ch}; (x_{imax} - x_{imin}) \cdot r_{ch}), \tag{4}$$

where x_{imax} and x_{imin} are respectively the maximal and minimal values of i-th attribute, r_{ch} is the parameter, which defines how much the limits of range can be changed. For the discrete type the new value is chosen in random from the values defined for this type.

Fitness Function. The assumed fitness function, is defined as the weighted average of the following parameters: accuracy (acc), classCovering ($classCov$), inaccuracy ($inacc$), and comprehensibility ($compr$):

$$Fun = \frac{A * acc + B * inacc + C * classCov + D * compr}{A + B + C + D} \tag{5}$$

Weights (A, B, C, D) are implemented as the parameters of the application. *Accuracy* measures how good the rule mimics knowledge contained in the neural network. It is defined by (6).

$$acc = \frac{correctFires}{totalFiresCount}, \tag{6}$$

where $totalFiresCount$ is the number of patterns covered by the evaluated rule, $correctFires$ is the number of patterns covered by the rule that are classified by the neural network in the same way as specifies the conclusion of evaluated rule. $Inaccuracy$ is a measure of incorrect classification made by the rule. It is expressed by eq. (7).

$$inacc = \frac{missingFires}{totalFiresCount} \tag{7}$$

Parameter $classCovering$ contains information about the part of all patterns from a given class, which are covered by the evaluated rule. It is formally defined by eq. (8);

$$classcov = \frac{correctFires}{classExampelsCount}, \tag{8}$$

where $classExamplesCount$ is a number of patterns from a given class.
The last parameter - $comprehensibility$ is calculated on the basis of eq. (9).

$$compr = \frac{maxConditionCount - ruleLength}{maxConditionCount. - 1}, \tag{9}$$

where $ruleLength$ is the number of premises of the rule, $maxConditionsCount$ is the maximal number of premises in the rule. In other words, it is the number of inputs of the neural network.

3.2   The Set of Rules

During an evolution the set of rules is updated. Some rules are added and some are removed. In each generation individuals with $accuracy$ and $classCovering$ greater than $minAccuracy$ and $minClassCovering$ are the candidates to update the set of rules. The values $minAccuracy$ and $minClassCovering$ are the parameters of the method.

The rules are added to the set of rules when they are more general than the rules actually being in the set of rules. Rule r_1 is more general than rule r_2 when the set of examples covered by r_2 is a subset of the set of examples covered by r_1. In case the rules r_1 and r_2 cover the same examples, the rule that has the bigger fitness value is assumed as more general one. Furthermore, the less general rules are removed. After presentation of all patterns for each rule $usability$ is calculated according to eq.(10).

$$usability = \frac{usabilityCount}{examplesCount} \tag{10}$$

All rules with $usability$ less then $minUsability$, which is a parameter set by the user, are removed from the set of rules. We can say that optimization of the set of rules consists in removing less general and rarely used rules and in the supplying it by more general rules from the current generation.

The following statistics characterize the quality of the set of rules. The value $covering$ defines the percentage of the classified examples from all examples used in the evaluation of the set of rules (eq. 11).

$$covering = \frac{classifiedCount}{examplesCount} \tag{11}$$

Fidelity expressed in (eq.12) describes the percentage of correct (according to the neural network answer) classified examples from all examples classified by the set of rules.

$$fidelity = \frac{correctClassifiedCount}{classifiedCount} \tag{12}$$

Covering and *fidelity* are two measures of quality of the acquired set of rules that say about its accuracy generalization. Additionally, the *performance* (eq.13) is defined, which informs about the percentage of the correct classified examples compared to all examples used in the evaluation process.

$$performance = \frac{correctClassifiedCount}{examplesCount} \tag{13}$$

4   Experimental Studies

The experimental studies have two aims. First, its efficiency in describing classification decision made by the neural network on the medical data was tested. In these experiments we used the data sets collected in UCI repository [13]. The results are compared with other known methods of the rule extraction.

The second series of experiments was made with using the data sets collected by Lower Silesian Oncology Center. The first one contains 527 records of patients with *Primary cancer of the cervix uteri*, the second one contains 101 records describing patients with *Ductal breast cancer* treated in this Oncology Center. They are described in subsection 4.2.

On the basis of the preliminary experiments with GEX we observed that one can influence on the set of acquired rules by:

- the fitness function (the part *comprehensibility* - as shorter the rule is - the more general it is, the shorter set of rules we obtain in the consequence),
- the assumed value of *minaccuracy*, (a value less than 1, allows to acquire rules that cover more patterns but some of them are covered incorrectly),
- the value of *minusability* parameter – its value defines the minimal number of the covered patterns by each rule to become a member of the final set of rules. When it is high we expect to obtain very general rules.

In classification task we are interested in acquiring rules that are very general. It means, they cover many patterns with high accuracy. It is in contrast to knowledge discovery, when we are looking for rules that cover less patterns but the rules point at new knowledge, so novelty is essential in this case. The second goal of our experiments was to test possibility in application of GEX to knowledge discovery. Because the novelty of acquired knowledge has to be evaluated we use the data from Oncology Center and a help of an expert.

Table 1. The result of experiments of GEX with assumed performace=98% using 10 − *cross validation*; NG - number of generations, NR - number of rules for files from UCI repository with different types of attributes

file	NR	NG	covering	fidelity
Breast Cancer	18,6± 2,04	61,8± 29,9	0,975±0,022	0,982±0,018
WDBC	27,52± 4,19	1789,8± 191,4	0,486±0,125	0,968±0,031
Pima	28.36± 3.04	1477± 332.4	0,81 ±0,099	0,975±0,022
Liver	31,92± 4,01	1870,9± 121,5	0,173±0,102	0,674±0,291
Dermatology	20,24± 2,76	949,3± 452,3	0,829± 0,067	0,981±0,022
Heart	28.36± 3.04	1477± 332.4	0,921±0,048	0,836±0,089
Hypothyroid	21.96± 20.67	316.0± 518.9	0.960±0.048	0.996±0.004

Table 2. The comparison of GEX and *NeuroRule* on the *Breast cancer* data set

NeuroRule	GEX			
	Minusab=1		Minusab=10	
Accuracy	Accuracy	number of rules	Accuracy	number of rules
98,10	98,71± 0,0057	10.30± 2,31	97,5± 0,072	4,2± 0,63

4.1   The Ability of GEX to Describe Classification Made by the Neural Network

In the first experiment we applied GEX for the well known medical data from UCI [13] such as: *Breast Cancer, Wisconsin Breast Cancer, Liver, Hypothyroid, Heart, Dermatology*. The parameters of the method were as follows: p_{mu-op}=0.2, $p_{mu-range}$=0.2, p_{mu-act}=0.2, r_{ch}=0.1, niching=on, migration=on, weights in the fitness function: A=2, B=2, C=-2, D=1, p_{c-w}=0,5, $Nsize = startsize$=40, $minsize = 30$ individuals, $minaccuraccy$=1 and $minusability$=1.

In the experiments the evolution was stopped when the set of acquired rules has reached the performance 98% or when during 250 generations there was no progress in the evolution. 10 *fold cross validation* was applied to evaluate the final set of rules. The results are shown in Table 1. For each file the first column in this table describes the number of the acquired rules (NR) in the final set of rules, the second one is the number of generations (NG) needed to reach this performance. The third and fourth columns refer to covering and fidelity, respectively. One can notice that independently of the type of attributes, that are contained in the experimental data GEX was able to extract rules. Let us emphasize, the aim of this experiment was not to search for the set with the minimal number of rules.

In order to compare the result of GEX to other methods, the experiments were repeated trying to keep the same conditions. Table 2 presents the comparison to the result of *NeuroRule* described in [2]. The *Breast Cancer* data set was split into two equal parts - the training and the testing sets. The quality of the set of rules was measured by its accuracy. Table 2 shows two results of GEX obtained with different parameters settings. With *MinUsabilty*=10 the average

Table 3. The comparison of GEX and *FullRe* on the *Breast cancer* data set

FullRe		GEX	
fidelity		fidelity	
training set	testing set	training set	testing set
96,77	95,61	98,36± 0,99	95,60± 0,87

number of acquired rules was equal to 4.2 and the accuracy was slightly smaller than for *Minusability*=1. Comparing both results to *NeuroRule* one can say that accuracy is comparable. The number of rules for *NeuroRule* was equal to 5 but this method assumes the default rule, which is used in case when none of the extracted rules could be fired.

The comparison with the results of FullRe [3] made on the *Breast cancer* data set is showed in Table 3. The data set is split fifty-fifty in the training and the testing set. The results for GEX are the average from 50 runs after 2000 generations. They were obtained with the parameters described above. The only difference was the value of weight D=10. The FullRe method, like NeuroRule, extracts rules using a default class rule. Taking into account the quality of acquired rules expressed by performance we can say that the results are comparable, but GEX deliver the description for each class.

4.2   The Ability of GEX to Acquire New Knowledge

The experiments described in this section were made on the basis of two data files from Lower Silesian Oncology Center. The first one comes from 5-year observation of 527 patients with primary cancer of the Cervix uteri treated in 1996, 1997 and 1998. The clinical and pathological data available on these patients include: the date of birth and the patients age, FIGO stage of the disease (according to FIGO Staging, 1994), tumor size, histological type of the tumor, the degree of differentiation of the tumor, interval between diagnosis and first treatment (both dates), the type of a surgical treatment, the type of a performed radiotherapy,the duration of radiotherapy, the assessment of the response to a treatment, the date of the end of hospitalization, the last known vital status or the date of death, the relapse-free survival, the overall survival.

The second data set contains 5-year observation of 101 patients with *Primary ductal breast cancer* (stage II) treated in 1993 and 1994. ER and nm23 expression was analyzed by immunohistochemical procedures. The other clinical and pathological data available on these patients included: Bloom and Richardson's grade, the tumor size, the status of axillary lymph nodes, the relapse-free survival, the overall survival, the body mass index, the hormonal status and several other data from anamnesis and family history.

The role of the specified parameters for both distinguished cases (classification and knowledge discovery) was examined on the basis of data with *Primary cancer of the cervix uteri*. In both data sets two classes were distinguished: the first one refers to the patients who after 5 years starting from the treatment were

Table 4. The result of experiments for different values of parameters

Parameters	Experiment1	Experiment2	Experiment3	Experiment4
D	20	10	8	6
Minaccuracy	0.8	1.0	0.95	0.95
Minusability	20	10	10	1
Number of rules	3	10	10	47
Total covering[%]	96	75	87	96.5
number of patterns in class$_1$				
correct covered	154	123	139	164
incorrect covered	36	0	17	11
uncovered	6	73	40	40
number of patterns in class$_2$				
correct covered	286	254	277	294
incorrect covered	22	0	3	11
uncovered	13	67	41	16

alive (for *Cervix uteri* data set 321 patterns), and the second class containing the patients who died ahead 5 years (for *Cervix uteri* data set 196). Table 4 presents the example of the results for different values of parameters. We can observe that the less is the value of *minusability*, the more rules arrives in the final set of rules. This phenomena is also connected with the weight D in the fitness function and *minaccuracy* (47 rules for *minusabilty*=1 and D=6 *minaccuracy*=0,95 but only 3 rules for *minusabilty*=20 and D=20, *minaccuracy*=0,8). The shorter is the rule, the more general it is, in consequence the less number of rules is needed to cover the patterns.

This statement gives the start point to the next step of experiment, where we tried to evaluate the extracted rules in the sense of knowledge they bring for the end user. To realize it we collected rules extracted in the experiment1 and experiment4 from the table 4 and gave to the expert for evaluation. In the same way we have extracted rules for the second data - *Ductal breast cancer*, as well.

For experiment1 the example of the rule for *Cervix uteri* data set is shown bellow:

IF (*DegreeOfDifferentiation* >= 1, 00 *and* *DegreeOfDifferentiation* <= 3, 00) **AND** *histotype* <> 1 **AND** (*TimeDiagnosis−Treatment* >= 50, 28 *and* *TimeDiagnosis − Treatment* <= 586, 28) **AND** *SurgicalCode* = 3 **AND** (*ResponseToTreatment* >= 1, 00 *and* *ResponseToTreatment* <= 2, 00) **THEN** 1

The comment of the expert was as follows: this rule describes in the accurate way the factors of a good prognosis for a patient: the low illness advance, the radical surgical treatment and the effective radiotherapy gives a good chance to survive.

For all rules obtained in the experiment1 the comments of the expert was similar to the one above. It means that rules describe dependence between class and attributes in the way that is confirmed by the experience of the physician. It is very important aspect of GEX application because it can increase the trust of the user to the system. From the other hand, these rules are not revealing. They contain general knowledge only.

To discover new knowledge the parameters of GEX described for experiment4 demonstrates their superiority. For example for the *Primary ductal breast cancer* data set the following rule was found:

IF$(age >= 20, 00$ *and age* $<= 50, 96)$ **AND** $(ER >= 3, 00$ *and ER* $<= 11, 00)$ **AND** $(sizeoftumor >= 0, 00$ *and sizeoftumor* $<= 3, 00)$ **AND** $(birthrate$ $>= 1, 00$ *and birthrate* $<= 2, 00)$ **AND** $(numberoftreatments >= 0, 00$ *and numberoftreatments* $<= 5, 00)$ **AND** $(timeoftreatments >= 237, 58$ *and timeoftreatments* $<= 3400, 00)$ **THEN** 0

The rule was commented by the expert as follows: It is surprising. I would rather think, that the prognosis would be high because ER is positive. Since it refers to the relatively large number of patients it should be widely examined.

The experimental study confirms that by appropriate setting parameters of GEX method we can extract rules for the classification task made by the neural network but also GEX can be seen as a tool for knowledge discovery. For the first case of application of GEX we can suggest that the value of *minusability* and weight D should be high. In this case we obtain rules which are as general as possible, but it is rather difficult to expect they deliver nontrivial dependencies. For the less value of parameter D in the fitness function the rules with more number of premises arrive. This fact combined with the low value of *minusability* explains the high number of rules for the experiment4. We can filter rules from the acquired set rules that have sufficient support to give physicians.

5 Conclusion

The experiments have shown that by affecting on the parameters of the proposed method that control the number of examples covered by the rules GEX can be the useful tool to deliver rules describing classification task made by the neural network and also to discover dependence hidden in data processed by the neural network. In the paper GEX is compared to other methods. Its results are similar or even better comparing to other methods, but it has not default rule, giving in the consequence the description of classification for each class. In comparison to other rule extraction methods the novelty of GEX lies in the design of genotype that enables to process various types of attribute and heuristics that optimize the final set of rules.

Although the tests examining the consistency of GEX remain for the future, on the basis of the experiments that has been doing so far we can conclude that independence of the type of attributes, ability to control the number of the patterns covered by the rules in the final set of rules (that enables to use GEX in rule extraction for classification made by a neural network as well as for knowledge discovery), independence of the neural network architecture and nonexistence of default rule make GEX very attractive alternative to other rule extraction methods.

References

1. Fu, L.M.: Rule generation from neural network. IEEE. Transactions on Systems, Man and Cybernetics **vol. 24** (1994) 1114–1124
2. Lu, H., Setiono, R., Liu, H.: Neurorule: a connectionist approach to datamining. In: Proc. 21 st Conference on very Large Databases, Zurich. (1995)
3. Taha, I., Ghosh, J.: Symbolic interpretation of artificial neural networks. Technical report, The Computer and Vision Research Center, University of Texas, Austin (1996)
4. Setiono, R., Thong, J.: An approach to generate rules from neural networks for regression problems. European Journal of Operational Research **155** (2004) 239–250
5. Palade, V., Neagu, D.C., Patton, R.J.: Interpretation of trained neural networks by rule extraction. Fuzzy Days 2001, LNC 2206 (2001) 152–161 Springer-Verlag Berlin Heilderberg 2001.
6. Thrun, S.B.: Extracting rules from artificial neural networks with distributed representation, advances. Neural Information Processing Systems **vol. 7** (1995)
7. Andrews, R., Diederich, J., Tickle, A.: A survey and critique of techniques for extracting rules from trained neural networks. Knowledge-Based Systems **8** (1995) 373–389
8. Craven, M., Shavlik, J.: Extracting tree-structured representations of trained networks. Advances Information Processes Systems **Vol. 8** (1996.) MIT Press, Cambridge, MA.
9. Vinterbo, S. Ohno-Machado, L.: A genetic algorithm approach to multi-disorder diagnosis. Artificial Intelligence in Medicine **18** (2000) 117–132
10. Francisci, D., Brisson, L., Collard, M.: A scalar evolutionary approach to rule extraction. Technical report, ISRN I3S/RR-200312-FR (2003)
11. Fidelis, M., Lopes, H.S., Freitas, A.: Discovering comprehensible classification rules with genetic algorithm. In: Proc. Congress on Evolutionary Computation (CEC-2000). (2001) 805–810
12. Arbatli, D.A., Akin, L.H.: Rule extraction from trained neural network using genetic algorithm. Nonlinear Analysis, Theory Methods and Application **30** (1997) 1639–1648
13. Murphy, P.M., Aha, D.W.: UCI repository of machine learning databases. PhD thesis, Department of Information and Computer Science, University of California, Irvine, CA (1998)

HTTPHunting: An IBR Approach to Filtering Dangerous HTTP Traffic

F. Fdez-Riverola[1], L. Borrajo[1], R. Laza[1], F.J. Rodríguez[1], and D. Martínez[2]

[1] Dept. Informática, University of Vigo, Escuela Superior de Ingeniería Informática,
Edificio Politécnico, Campus Universitario As Lagoas s/n, 32004, Ourense, Spain
{riverola, lborrajo, rlaza, franjrm}@uvigo.es
[2] Supercomputing Center of Galicia,
Avenida de Vigo, s/n Campus Sur, 15705, Santiago de Compostela, A Coruña, Spain
macada@sing.ei.uvigo.es

Abstract. Recently, there has been significant interest in applying artificial intelligence techniques to intrusion detection problem. To find the solution to the difficulties in acquiring and representing existing knowledge in almost systems, we proposed a novel instance-based intrusion detection system called HTTPHunting. It will provide a framework to intrusion detection problem, incorporating several artificial intelligence techniques that help to overcome some of those limitations. HTTPHunting is able to classify in real time, traffic data arriving at the network interface of the host that is protecting, detecting anomalous traffic patterns. From our initial experiments, we can conclude that there are important key benefits of such an approach to network traffic-filtering domain.

1 Introduction and Motivation

Everyday there are attacks to computer systems taking place with more frequency. It is due, mainly, to the huge increase experienced by communication nets. The effects that produce these attacks are often unpredictable and can include several aspects as confidentiality, integrity, readiness or control of the computer system. Several methods and techniques have been used to carry out these attacks being characterized by a constant and quick evolution. In this context, a key element to minimize attack effects entails detecting them immediately. With this purpose, a great amount of artificial intelligence (AI) models and filtering applications has been built in the area of Intrusion Detection Systems (IDS).

An intrusion can be defined as an unauthorized access or usage of the resources belonging to a computer system [1]. Therefore, an intrusion detection system can be viewed as a security network tool. Such systems have to monitorize, analyze and process each event in every one of the computers owned by an organization in order to find and detect new intrusion attempts. Traditionally, two main approaches have been adopted to tackle the problem of intrusion detection taking into account how the collected data from the supervised system are analysed: (*i*) *misuse* detection system and (*ii*) *anomaly* detection system.

P. Perner (Ed.): ICDM 2006, LNAI 4065, pp. 91–105, 2006.

A misuse detection system, also known as a signature-based intrusion detection system, identifies intrusions by watching for patterns of traffic or application data presumed to be malicious. This kind of systems is presumed to be able to detect only previously *known* attacks. However, depending on their rule set, signature-based IDSs can sometimes detect new attacks that share characteristics with old ones. The IDS analyses the information it gathers and compares it to large databases of attack signatures. Essentially, the IDS looks for a specific attack that has already been documented. Like a virus detection system, misuse detection software is only as good as the database of attack signatures that it uses to compare traffic packets.

On the other hand, anomaly-based intrusion detection systems recognize intrusions by identifying content that is presumed to be different from *normal* activity on the network. In anomaly detection, the system administrator defines the baseline, or normal state of the network's traffic load, breakdown, protocol and typical packet size. The anomaly detector monitors network segments to compare their state to the normal baseline looking for anomalies.

Regardless of the method used for detecting attacks, an IDS can be classified as either host-based (HIDS, *Host Intrusion Detection System*) or network-based (NIDS, *Network Intrusion Detection System*) depending on its source of input data. This feature imposes a division in current systems between those that use the events taking place within a given host (i.e., executed programs, user activity, etc.), and those that make use of network traffic as the main source of data. Snort [2], Bro [3] and Netstat [4] are well-known examples of network-based IDSs.

Another possible classification is based on the IDS in front of a possible attack: (*i*) *passive* IDSs detect a possible violation of the security, register the information and generate an alert while (*ii*) *reactive* IDSs are designed to respond before an illegal activity, for example, throwing out the user of the system or by means of the reprogramming of the firewalls to prevent the traffic from a hostile source.

Nowadays, one of the more active investigation lines in the IDS system context is the definition of hybrid systems able to endow IDS with intelligence and adaptability. The purpose is to obtain systems capable of adapting themselves to the quick dynamics that governs the evolution of the attack techniques. Current IDS base their operation on a static outline that transforms them into very inefficient systems when an attacker codes input data. The databases of the IDS suffer the same inconveniences that antivirus databases: if the database is outdated, it is very probable that a system being attacked will not be detected. Additionally, the time among the discovery of a new attack, the publication of the data patterns and their inclusion in the IDS is quite long, keeping in mind that the time between the publication of the attack and the undue use on the part of a possible attacker is very short.

In this context, this paper reviews the problems that current IDSs present and proposes a novel approach to filtering network communications. The proposed system is able to evaluate the traffic of HTTP streams arriving to a server and to detect the possible attacks automatically. The rest of the paper is organized as follows: Section 2 describes current techniques applied in intrusion detection; Section 3 explains the phases needed to obtain the available data and the stream preprocessing carried out; In Section 4 the proposed instance-based model is explained in detail, while in Section 5 the results coming from the experiments are presented and discussed. Finally, Section 6 summarizes the conclusions and details future work.

2 Current Techniques in Intrusion Detection

During last years, several AI techniques have been applied to intrusion detection problem: rule-based systems, artificial neuronal networks and case-based reasoning approaches constitute some examples of the great amount of previously developed systems.

In recent times, rule-based and model-based expert systems have been proven useful for intrusion detection [5, 6]. Expert system applications also provide a way of attaching meaning to the alarms raised and they allow the generation of appropriate responses to the perceived security threats in a dynamic way. An intrusion detection expert system may recognize single events that represent significant danger to the system, or recognize sequences of events that stand for an entire penetration scenario. Examples of intrusion detection expert systems include IDES (*Intrusion Detection Expert System*) [7], NADIR [8], W&S (*Wisdom and Sense*) [9], MIDAS (*Multics Intrusion Detection and Alerting System*) [10], USTAT [11] and AID (*Adaptive Intrusion Detection System*) [12].

Rule-based expert systems (RBES) represent the knowledge, acquired from experts in the field, as a set of rules. One important aspect of a RBES is that it can use rules containing uncertain or ambiguous terms and make conclusions with a certain degree of uncertainty. However, a major disadvantage of rule-based expert systems is that the existing knowledge needs to be reduced into a set of rules. This is considered a major bottleneck in their implementation.

On the other hand, model-based expert systems attempt to model intrusions by representing their characteristic behaviour at a high level of abstraction. In this approach, intrusion scenarios are modelled abstractly and network attacks are identified through the process of model-based reasoning [13]. Building and using reasonably complete domain models can be extremely difficult due to inexpressive representation languages.

Other approaches are centred in applying artificial neuronal networks (ANN) for the detection of intruders. In the work of Torres [14], the use of an Elman ANN is proposed. The architecture of this network allows considering its use for a variety of problems where the processing of inputs, which are presented in sequence, is carried out. A typical example of this network is the analysis of calls to the operating system kernel to determine behaviour patterns and to detect attacks in progress [15].

The learning process in ANNs can be reached by training the network with the ultimate available information. However, most of the neuronal networks only learn in the training phase. Once this stage finishes, the weights are fixed and learning does not take place during the phase of network operation [16]. In this case, it would be necessary to allow continuous training of the network architecture and this operation cannot be leaved in inexperienced hands. In addition, it is impossible to effectively train a neuronal network if one does not have data reflecting a structure.

Another successful example of AI techniques applied to the IDS problem is the distributed IDS based on multiple independent autonomous agents presented by Spafford and Zamboni [17]. A more recent approach to the development of operative systems applied to IDS is the utilisation of case-based reasoning (CBR) systems [18], which has been proven effective in many experimental and applied IDS systems [1, 19, 20, 21]. The CBR attempts to solve a problem by matching the current situation with previous known cases stored in the knowledge base of the system. Case-based reasoning is most suitable when it is difficult or impossible to break down the knowledge into a set of rules and only records of prior cases exist.

In this paper, an Instance-Based Reasoning (IBR) system is proposed to solve the intrusion detection problem. Instance-based reasoning is a specialization of case-based reasoning. This type of CBR system focuses on problems in which there are a large number of instances which are needed to represent the whole range of the domain and where there is a lack of general background knowledge. The case (instance) representation can be made with plain feature vectors and the whole CBR life cycle is normally automated as much as possible, eliminating human intervention.

3   Problem Description and Data Gathering

Network data mining attempts to extract implicit, previously unknown, and potentially useful information from data. Web servers are surely the richest and the most common source of data. They can collect large amounts of information in their web activity log files and in the log of the databases they use. These logs usually contain basic information (i.e., name and IP of the remote host, date and time of the request, the request line exactly as it came from the client, etc.) and it is usually stored in a standard format. As stated by Facca and Lanzi [22], the preprocessing of web logs is usually complex and time demanding. It comprises four different tasks: (*i*) data cleaning, (*ii*) identification and reconstruction of user sessions, (*iii*) information retrieval regarding page content and structure and (*iv*) data formatting.

Apart from web logs, users behaviour can also be tracked down on the server side by means of TCP/IP packet sniffers. In fact, these applications provide the possibility of (*i*) collecting data in real time and (*ii*) easily merging it into unique log information coming from different web servers.

In these sense, the following subsection explains in detail the steps carried out in order to build a representative instance-base of network knowledge. This collection of vulnerable and safety network streams will constitute the base of the test bed experimentation carried out within our HTTPHunting network filtering system.

3.1   Available Data and Stream Preprocessing

The data used to construct the model was obtained from an experimental real network during the following phases:

 i. Vulnerable HTTP requests were obtained using Nikto (see Figure 1). Nikto is an open source web server scanner, which performs comprehensive tests against web servers for multiple items, including over 3200 potentially dangerous files/CGIs, versions on over 625 servers and version specific problems on over 230 servers. Scan items and plug-ins are frequently updated. Figure 2 shows part of the Nikto file containing attacks rules. Figure 3 shows Nikto HTTP attacks that are based on these rules.

Fig. 1. Scheme of the attack generated by Nikto

```
"generic","/databases/","200","GET","Databases? Really??"
"generic","/databse.sql","200","GET","Database SQL?"
"generic","/db.sql","200","GET","Database SQL?"
"iis","/_vti_bin/admin.pl","200","GET","Default FrontPage CGI found."
"iis","/_vti_bin/cfgwiz.exe","200","GET","Default FrontPage CGI found."
"iis","/_vti_bin/CGImail.exe","200","GET","Default FrontPage CGI found."
"iis","/_vti_bin/contents.htm","200","GET","Default FrontPage CGI found."
"iis","/_vti_bin/_vti_cnf/","200","GET","FrontPage directory found."
"iis","/_vti_cnf/_vti_cnf/","200","GET","FrontPage directory found."
"iis","/_vti_inf.html","200","GET","FrontPage may be installed."
"iis","/_vti_log/_vti_cnf/","200","GET","FrontPage directory found."
"lotus","/vpuserinfo.nsf","200","GET","This database can be read without
authentication."
"lotus","/web.nsf","200","GET","This    database    can    be    read    without
authentication."
"lotus","/webadmin.nsf","200","GET","The server admin database can be accessed
remotely."
"novell","/perl/files.pl","200","GET","This might be interesting..."
"novell","/perl5/files.pl","200","GET","This might be interesting..."
"novell","/scripts/convert.bas","200","GET","This might be interesting..."
"oracle","/owa_util%2esignature","200","GET","unknown--may be interesting"
"website","/cgi-dos/args.bat","200","GET","This might be interesting..."
"website","/sam","200","GET","This might be interesting..."
"website","/sam.bin","200","GET","This might be interesting..."
```

Fig. 2. Snapshot of Nikto rules

```
GET /intranet/sam._?server=<script>alert('Vulnerable')</script>
GET /hidden/ion-p.exe?page=c:\winnt\repair\sam
..........
..........
GET /hidden/foxweb.exe?page=../../../../../../../../../../boot.ini
GET    /databases/wwwadmin.pl?sid=\"><Img    Src=javascript:alert('Vulnerable')><Img
Src=\"
GET /hidden/showcode.asp?|-|0|404_Object_Not_Found
GET /cgi-bin/dcshop/auth_data/cgimail.exe?Template=c:\boot.ini
............
............
GET /porn/seite=;cat%20eshop.pl|?|=../../../../../../../../../etc/passwd
GET /dcshop/auth_data/databse.sql?../../../../../../../etc/passwd
GET /cgi/cfdocs/expeval/oracle?about
```

Fig. 3. Summary of Nikto HTTP attacks

ii.   The previous requests flow from Nikto (HTTP client) to a HTTP server
       through the network. The final goal is to cause a strong damage in real
       servers. Between Nikto and the HTTP server, a firewall has been installed
       with Snort-Mysql detecting these attacks (see Figure 4). Snort-Mysql is
       an open source network intrusion prevention and detection system
       utilizing a rule-driven language, which combines the benefits of

signature, protocol and anomaly based inspection methods. With millions of downloads to date, Snort is the most widely deployed intrusion detection and prevention technology worldwide and has become the facto standard for the industry.

To detect attacks, Snort-Mysql is based on rules (see Figure 5) and it stores these detections in Mysql tables with some relevant information related to attacks and keywords of IDS.

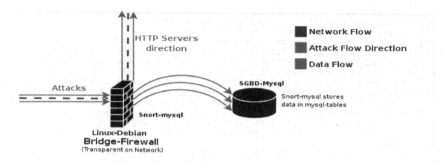

Fig. 4. Snort detection scheme

```
alert tcp $EXTERNAL_NET $HTTP_PORTS -> $HOME_NET any (msg:"WEB-CLIENT JPEG
  parser heap overflow attempt"; flow:from_server,established; content:"image/";
  nocase;          pcre:"/^Content-Type\s*\x3a\s*image\x2fp?jpe?g.*\xFF\xD8.{2}
  .*\xFF[\xE1\xE2\xED\xFE]\x00[\x00\x01]/smi";          reference:bugtraq,11173;
  reference:cve,2004-0200;
  reference:url,www.microsoft.com/security/bulletins/200409_jpeg.mspx;
  classtype:attempted-admin; sid:2705; rev:4;)
alert tcp $EXTERNAL_NET $HTTP_PORTS -> $HOME_NET any (msg:"WEB-CLIENT JPEG
  transfer";      flow:from_server,established;      content:"image/";      nocase;
  pcre:"/^Content-Type\s*\x3a\s*image\x2fp?jpe?g/smi";    flowbits:set,http.jpeg;
  flowbits:noalert; classtype:protocol-command-decode; sid:2706; rev:2;)
alert tcp $EXTERNAL_NET $HTTP_PORTS -> $HOME_NET any (msg:"WEB-CLIENT JPEG
  parser    multipacket    heap    overflow";    flow:from_server,established;
  flowbits:isset,http.jpeg;                                    content:"|FF|";
  pcre:"/\xFF[\xE1\xE2\xED\xFE]\x00[\x00\x01]/";          reference:bugtraq,11173;
  reference:cve,2004-0200;
  reference:url,www.microsoft.com/security/bulletins/200409_jpeg.mspx;
  classtype:attempted-admin; sid:2707; rev:2;)
alert tcp $EXTERNAL_NET any -> $HTTP_SERVERS $HTTP_PORTS (msg:"WEB-CGI swc
  access";      flow:to_server,established;      uricontent:"/swc";      nocase;
  reference:nessus,10493; classtype:attempted-recon; sid:1478; rev:5;)
```

Fig. 5. Snort-Mysql detection rules

iii.   All these detections are extracted from Mysql using AcidBase interface. BASE stands for *Basic Analysis and Security Engine*. It is based on the code from the ACID (*Analysis Console for Intrusion Databases*) project. This application provides a web front-end to query and analyze the alerts coming from a SNORT IDS system.

Several components for AcidBase have been developed to create .CSV files (see Figure 6) containing the instances of vulnerabilities (*vulnerable* instance-base) which will take part on the HTTPHunting system.

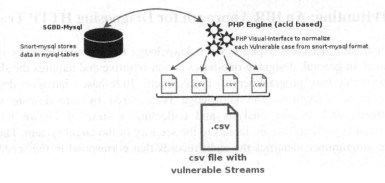

Fig. 6. CSV file with vulnerable streams

In order to obtain safety instances, several log files from different public and private HTTP servers were processed, creating .CSV files which contain those safety instances found (*safety* instance-base) (see Figure 7).

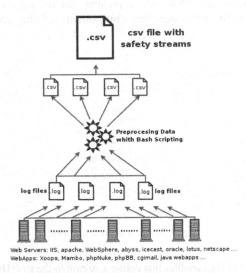

Fig. 7. CSV file with safety streams

Finally, .CSV files, Safety and Vulnerable streams were mixed and the main instance-base repository was created (see Figure 8).

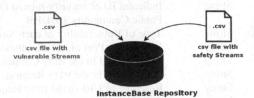

Fig. 8. Building our final instance-base network repository

4   HTTPHunting: An IBR Approach for Diagnosing HTTP Traffic

Current intrusion detection expert systems knowledge base is neither easily created nor updated. In general, designing rule-bases is non-intuitive and requires the skills of experienced rule-base programmers to update them. Rule-based intrusion detection systems are no exception. The knowledge is acquired by interviewing system administrators and security analysts and collecting a suite of known intrusion scenarios and key events that are threats to the security of the target system. Then, the rule-base programmer identifies the audit records that correspond to the scenario or key event, and constructs rules to represent the intrusions based on the expected audit records [1].

This section introduces an approach to intrusion detection that improves some of the weaknesses found in current IDSs. The aim is to design and develop a prototype for an intrusion detection system that uses inexact and IBR techniques to incorporate learning capability and achieve high reliability in intrusion detection. An IBR system is presented as a filtering solution for detecting attacks to a server via HTTP protocol. Next subsections illustrate how we represent each stream and the existing relationships between the processes and components of the proposed hybrid IBR system.

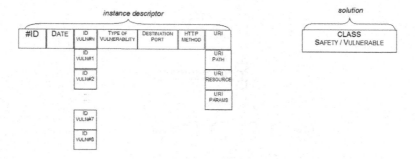

Fig. 9. Instance representation

Table 1. Description of the variables that define a stream in the HTTPHunting IDS system

Variable	Type	Description
#ID	Integer	Unique descriptor of the stream
Date	Date	Date in which the Stream was detected
ID Vuln#1..8	String	Indicates ID of security-related facts of different Public Community's DDBB
Type of Vulnerability	String	Type of Vulnerability of each Stream
Destination Port	Integer	Destination Port of HTTP Connexion
HTTP Method	String	HTTP Method in the HTTP Connexion
URI Path	String	Path of URI in the HTTP Request
URI Resource	String	Resource of URI in the HTTP Request
URI Params	Integer	Parameters of URI in the HTTP Request
Class	Boolean	Stream classification: 0 for Safety, 1 for Vulnerable

4.1 Instance Representation

The structure of each stream represented as an instance in our HTTPHunting system is shown in Figure 9. On the other hand, Table 1 indicates the description of each parameter from every instance belonging to the memory of the system.

4.2 Model Overview

This section describes our IBR system in detail. The life cycle of the system begins every time that a new HTTP stream arrives to the server in which HTTPHunting is running. The reasoning process of the model follows the classic life cycle of a CBR/IBR system, as it is shown in Figure 10. In the following, each one of the steps is analyzed in detail:

i.   *Retrieval phase:* when a new HTTP stream arrives to the server, the system should recover from the knowledge base the most similar instances corresponding to the new petition. HTTPHunting encodes a group of 'experts' (which use different metrics) to carry out the retrieval stage. The metrics that have been used are the following:
  • **URIMatch:** retrieves those streams that exactly match the input stream.
  • **URILong:** retrieves those streams that match the URI length.
  • **PathMatch:** retrieves those streams matching the path.
  • **PathLong:** retrieves those streams that match the path length.
  • **ResourceMatch:** retrieves those streams matching the resource name.
  • **ResourceLong:** retrieves those streams that match the resource name length.
  • **ParamsMatch:** retrieves those streams that present the same parameters.
  The instances retrieved by each expert will correspond to a percentage of safety streams and the rest to vulnerabilities. Each expert should analyze the instances that have retrieved. If the percentage of vulnerable streams is higher than 50%, the expert will determine that the new input stream will be a vulnerability stream, and otherwise, the expert will decide that it is a safety stream.

ii. *Reuse phase:* once each 'expert' has made a decision, each one expresses his vote. The peculiarity of this voting is that not all the votes have the same importance. The decision of each 'expert' is pondered in function of the trust deposited in this expert. This trust (or weight) was determined in a heuristic way. In this sense, considering the votes of all the experts and their corresponding weight, the final decision is obtained. This decision represents the solution proposed by the system to the present HTTP stream.

iii. *Revision phase:* the input stream is presented to the server and it is proven whether the stream is vulnerable or not. The obtained real result is compared with the result proposed by the system. When the system detects that its accuracy in predicting the vulnerability of the streams decrease under 95%, the weights assigned to the 'experts' are readjusted.

iv.   *Retention phase:* the new stream is stored with its real solution (safety or vulnerable classification) in the instance base, increasing the knowledge of the HTTPHunting system.

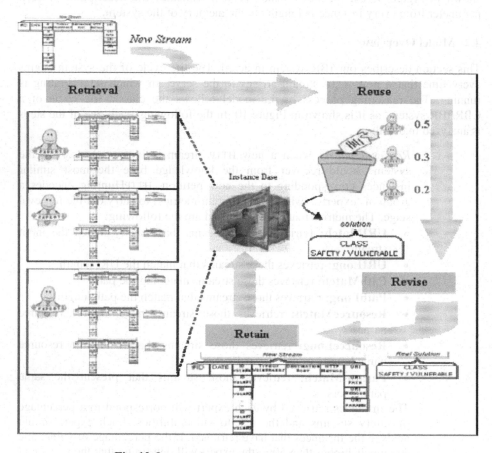

Fig. 10. Instance-base reasoning process and life cycle

5   System Evaluation

The final objective of our experiments is to measure the accuracy of the HTTPHunting system when it is applied to a real-data environment. Therefore, we use our experimental instance-base stream data generated as explained in Section 3. For this purpose, we have designed two different scenarios: (*i*) taking into account the weight assigned to each 'expert' (in the reuse phase) and (*ii*) without applying any relevance value to our metrics.

Five well-known metrics have been used in order to evaluate the performance (efficacy) of the analysed model: absolute error (ABS), percentage of correct classifications (%OK), percentage of False Positives (%FP) and percentage of False Negatives (%FN).

The existing data that constitutes our instance-base (256000 streams) was partitioned into a training (75% of instances) and a test (25% of instances) set taking into account the initial data distribution: 79% of vulnerable streams and 21% of safety streams. All the experiments carried out were executed in a Pentium IV 3.0 GHz processor with HT (Hyper-Threading) technology running with Windows 2003. Our HTTPHunting system was programmed in Java using JDK 1.4.2.

5.1 Experiments and Results

Once the HTTPHunting system is executed and appropriate data is entered, it shows the results that were used to obtain the data presented in Table 2 (see Figure 11).

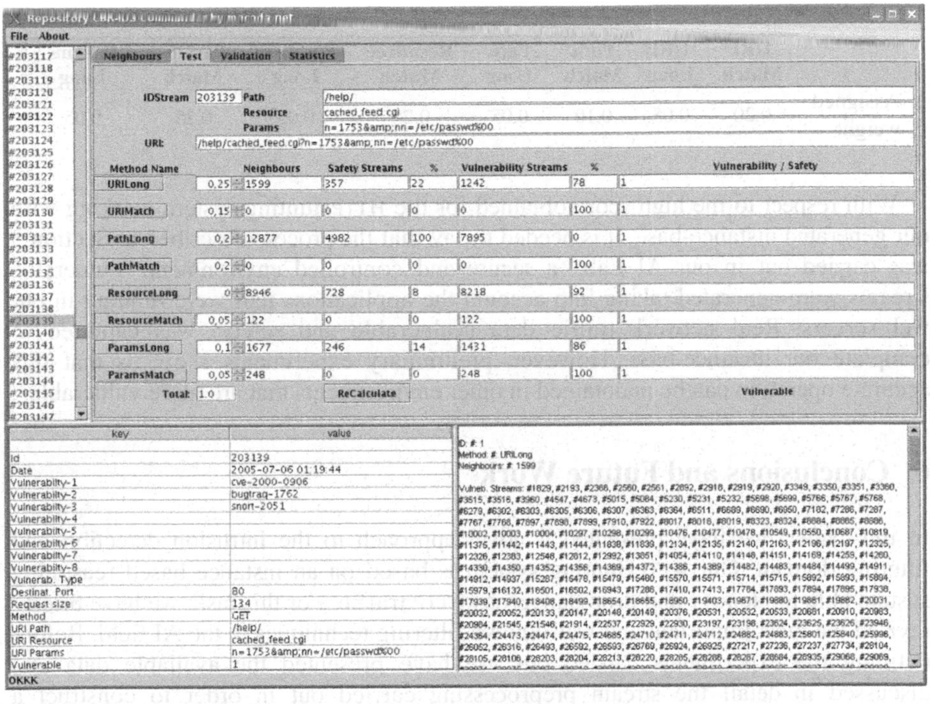

Fig. 11. HTTPHunting system snapshot showing execution results

Table 2 summarizes the percentage of correct stream classifications (%OK), percentage of error (%ERR), false positive rate (%FP), false negative rate (%FN) and absolute stream misclassifications belonging to the analysed model over the defined scenarios.

From Table 2, one can realise that HTTPHunting system is surprisingly accurate. The proposed system is able to correctly classify up to the 99% of the incoming streams and successfully discriminates vulnerable from safety streams. The best results of the system are achieved when weights are applied to the outcome generated by each 'expert'. In these sense, Table 3 show the assigned 'expert' scores for the first scenario.

Table 2. Performance evaluation of the HTTPHunting system

Scenario	[%OK]	[%ERR]	[%FP]	[%FN]	[ABS]
(i) With weighting	99.9658%	0.0342%	0.0054%	0.1429%	2188/64055
(ii) Without weighting	99.9595%	0.0405%	0.0050%	0.0355%	2597/64055

An important characteristic of the proposed HTTPHunting system is the possibility of establishing different values for the experts in the reuse stage. Those values can be modified as part of the retain (learning) stage of the whole system, adapting the internal-state of the model to the actual-state of the network in a continuous way.

Table 3. Weights assigned to the experts in the reuse stage of the HTTPHunting system

	URI Match	URI Long	Path Match	Path Long	Resource Match	Resource Long	Params Match	Params Long
Assigned weight	0.20	0.05	0.10	0.05	0.25	0.05	0.25	0.05

With respect to the high score obtained for the HTTPHunting system working with our generated instance-base, it is needed to say that the process described in Section 3 was carried out in our AI Lab., a secure and controlled environment. Vulnerable streams were generated taking into account the applications that were running in our web-servers. Real network traffic data (vulnerable and safety) was captured to complete our instance-base. However, preliminary experiments show us that this accurate operation can be maintained in other environments that are more vulnerable.

6   Conclusions and Future Work

In this paper, we have presented a novel approach to the intrusion detection and filtering domain. Our HTTPHunting system is based on an instance based reasoning system able to identify and drop dangerous HTTP traffic. For this task, we have briefly revised the most important and well-known filtering techniques in the AI field. Before defining the experiments carried out, we have presented the available data and discussed in detail the stream preprocessing carried out in order to construct a representative instance-base.

In order to define the experiments, we have considered two different scenarios and five standard scores to measure performance among the test bed. The same data distribution was maintained in order to increase the confidence level of the results obtained. From the analysis of these results, we can infer valuable information about the adaptation of our retrieval metrics to the problem domain, needed in order to accurately weighting the proposed reuse model.

There are important key benefits of such an approach to network traffic filtering. Firstly, we have shown that the use of lazy learner algorithms (like HTTPHunting) can handle the inherent variability in stream data, allowing for easy updating as new types of vulnerabilities arrive. Secondly, the instance-based approach to network filtering allows for the sharing of instances and thus a sharing of the effort of discovering new undocumented attacks. Thirdly, an IBR approach facilitates the incorporation of new techniques when they are available without any complex model rebuild (like the implementation of the revise stage of our HTTPHunting system). The main conclusion of this work is that IBR systems are able to adequately tackle the problem of network filtering due to its capacity of on-line learning and their suitability to manage great amounts of data with flexible data structures.

In order to increase HTTPHunting system performance over recent datasets, we are working in new improvements for the retrieval phase of our system. This current research includes the definition of new retrieval mechanisms based on clustering techniques [23-26]. The resultant algorithm will retrieve the most similar cluster of streams (instances with the highest similarity value).

The main objective will be to identify clusters formed with similar streams. The instances will be classified in two mutually exclusive groups: safety or vulnerable. To improve the retrieval phase it is necessary both (*i*) a good clustering technique and (*ii*) that these clusters have to be classified with real domain information or knowledge.

As it has been exposed in Section 2, the main disadvantage of rule-based expert systems is that the knowledge about the problem domain needs to be reduced into a set of rules. This can be avoided with the identification and utilisation of ontologies [27], another introduced line of future work.

In the literature we can found the proposal of several attack taxonomies using some descriptive language and classification schemes [28, 29]. An ontology, unlike taxonomies, provides powerful constructs that include machine interpretable definitions of concepts in a domain within the relations between them.

Our future work will define an ontology that embodies several *concepts* about HTTP attacks. These concepts were established by a human study of the 9999999 vulnerabilities cases in the system. The purpose of this ontology would be to create domain related clusters of vulnerabilities instances able to (*i*) increase system knowledge about individuals and (*ii*) provide software systems with the ability to share a common understanding of the information at issue.

The ontology will be implemented using Protégé (a knowledge-base editing environment developed at Stanford University) and it will be described in OWL (*Ontology Web Language*).

Acknowledgments

This work has been supported by the Spanish Council for Science and Technology (MEC) in projects TIC2003-07369-C02-02.

References

1. Esmaili, M., Balachandran, B., Safavi-Naini, R., Pieprzyk, J.: Case-Based Reasoning for Intrusion Detection. 1063-9527/96 IEEE (1996).
2. Roesch, M.: Snort—lightweight intrusion detection for networks. Proceedings of USENIX LISA 99, USENIX Association, Berkeley, (1999), 229–238. Also available online at <http://www.snort.org>.
3. Paxson, V.: Bro: a system for detecting network intruders in real-time. Proceedings of the 7th USENIX Security Symposium, San Antonio, TX, USENIX Association, Berkeley, (1998) 31–51.

4. Vigna, G., Kemmerer, R.A.: NetSTAT: a network-based intrusion detection system. Journal of Computer Security 7 (1) (1999) 37–71.
5. Denning, D. E., Neumann, P. C.: Requirements and models for IDES - A real-time intrusion detection system. Tech. Rep., CSL, SRI International, (1985).
6. Teng, H. S.: An expert system approach to security inspection of a VAXNMS system in a network environment. Proceedings of the 10th National Computer Security Conference, (Baltimore) (1987).
7. Lunt, T. E: IDES: An intelligent system for detecting intruders. Proceedings of the Symposium: Computer Security, Threat and Countermeasures, (Rome, Italy), (1990).
8. Hubbards, B., Haley, T., McAuliffe, N., Schaefer, L., Kelem, N., Walcott, D. , Feiertag, R. Schaefer, M.: Computer system intrusion detection. Tech. Rep. RADC-TR-90-4 13, Final Technical Report, Trusted Information Systems, Inc.,(1990).
9. Vaccaro, H. S., Liepins, G. E.: Detection of anomalous computer session activity. Proceedings of 1989 IEEE Computer Society Symposium on Security and Privacy, (Oakland, California), pp. 280-289, 1-3 (1989).
10. Sebring, M. M., Shellhouse, E., Hanna, M. E., Whitehurst, R. A..: Expert systems in intrusion detection: A case study. Proceedings of the 11th National Computer Security Conference, pp. 74-8 1, (1988).
11. Ilgun, K.: USTAT: A Real-time Intrusion Detection System for UNIX.. Proceedings of the 1993 Computer Society Symposium on Research in Security and Privacy. Oakland, California, (1993) 16-28. Los Alamitos, CA: IEEE Computer Society Press, 1993.
12. Sobirey, M., Fischer-Hübner, S., Rannenberg, K.: Pseudonymous Audit for Privacy Enhanced Intrusion Detection. In: Yngström, L. (Hrsg.) ; Carlsen, J. (Hrsg.): Information Security in Research and Business, Proceedings of the IFIP TC11 13th International Information Security Conference (SEC'97): 14-16 May 1997, Copenhagen, Denmark. London, Chapman & Hall, (1997), ISBN 0-412-8178-02, 151-163.
13. Garvey, T.D., Lunt, T.F.: Model_based intrusion detection. Proceedings of the 14th National Computer Security Conference, (1991) 372-385.
14. Torres, E.: Sistema inmunológico para la detección de intrusos a nivel de protocolo HTTP. Proyecto de grado. Pntificia Universidad Javeriana (Colombia) (2003).
15. Elman, J.: Finding Structure in Time. Cognitive Science, Vol. 14. (1990) 179-211.
16. Zahedi, F.: Intelligent Systems for Business: Expert Systems with Neural Networks. Wadsworth, Belmont, CA. (1993).
17. Spafford, E. H., Zamboni, D.: Intrusion detection using autonomous agents. Computer Networks, 34(4) (2000) 547-570
18. Kolodner J.: Case-Based Reasoning. San Mateo. CA, Morgan Kaufmann. (1993).
19. Esmaili, M., Safavi-Naini, R., Balachandran, B. M.: Autoguard: A continuous case-based intrusion detection system. Twentieth Australasian Computer Science Conference (1997).
20. Schwartz, D.G., Stoecklin, S., Yilmaz, E.: A Case-Based Approach to Network Intrusion Detection. Fifth International Conference on Information Fusion, IF'02, Annapolis, MD, July 7-11, (2002) 1084—1089.
21. Guha, R., Kachirski, O., Schwartz, D.G., Stoecklin, S., Yilmaz, E.: Case-based agents for packet-level intrusion detection in ad hoc networks. ISCIS XVII Seventeenth International Symposium on Computer and Information Sciences October 28-30, Orlando, Florida (2002).
22. Facca, F.M., Lanzi, P.M.: Mining interesting knowledge from weblogs: a survey, Data & Knowledge Engineering Vol. 53 (3) (2005) 225–241.
23. Witten, I., Frank, E.: Data Mining: Practical Machine Learning Tools and Techniques with Java Implementations. Edt. Morgan Kaufmann. (1999). ISBN 1-55860-552-5

24. Jain, A.K., Murty, M.N., Flynn, P.J.: Data clustering: a review. ACM Computing Surveys 31, 3 (1999).264-323

25. Graepel, T.: Statistical physics of clustering algortihms. Technical Report 171822, FB Physik, Institut fur Theoretische Physic, (1998).

26. Jain, A.K., Dubes, R.C.: Algorithms for clustering data. Prentice-Hall advanced reference series. Prentice-Hall, Inc., NJ. (1988).

27. Gruber, T.: Towards Principles for the Design of Ontologies Used for Knowledge Sharing. International Journal of Human and Computer Studies 43 (5/6) (1994).

28. Undercoffer, J., Joshi, A., Finin, T., Pinkston, J.: A Target-Centric Ontology for Intrusion Detection. 18th International Joint Conference on Artificial Intelligence, Acapulco, Mexico. (2004).

29. Mirkovic, J., Reiher, P.: A Taxonomy of DDoS Attacks and DDoS Defense Mechanisms. ACM SIGGCOM Computer Comunications Reviews. Volume 34, Number 2 (2004)

A Comparative Performance Study of Feature Selection Methods for the Anti-spam Filtering Domain

J.R. Méndez[1], F. Fdez-Riverola[1], F. Díaz[2], E.L. Iglesias[1], and J.M. Corchado[3]

[1] Dept. Informática, University of Vigo, Escuela Superior de Ingeniería Informática,
Edificio Politécnico, Campus Universitario As Lagoas s/n, 32004, Ourense, Spain
{moncho.mendez, riverola, eva}@uvigo.es
[2] Dept. Informática, University of Valladolid, Escuela Universitaria de Informática,
Plaza Santa Eulalia, 9-11, 40005, Segovia, Spain
fdiaz@infor.uva.es
[3] Dept. Informática y Automática, University of Salamanca,
Plaza de la Merced s/n, 37008, Salamanca, Spain
corchado@usal.es

Abstract. In this paper we analyse the strengths and weaknesses of the mainly used feature selection methods in text categorization when they are applied to the spam problem domain. Several experiments with different feature selection methods and content-based filtering techniques are carried out and discussed. Information Gain, χ^2-text, Mutual Information and Document Frequency feature selection methods have been analysed in conjunction with Naïve Bayes, boosting trees, Support Vector Machines and ECUE models in different scenarios. From the experiments carried out the underlying ideas behind feature selection methods are identified and applied for improving the feature selection process of SpamHunting, a novel anti-spam filtering software able to accurate classify suspicious e-mails.

1 Introduction and Motivation

Nowadays Internet mail service (e-mail) has become essential in the enterprise and personal productivity. The amount of messages flowing throw the e-mail servers has been increasing during last years. Everyday, Internet mail is used to send a great amount of documents with a wide variety of data and information. However, some of the contents sent across Internet using e-mail servers are useless and unwanted. Frequently they are advertising and/or fraudulent messages known as spam e-mails.

As the amount of spam messages is constantly increasing, a considerable money loss has been caused [1]. Recently, several legal and technical actions have been applied in order to combat spam e-mails. The former ones are based on adjusting the international laws including sanctions for spammers (senders of e-mail messages) whereas the use of anti-spam filtering software are the basis of the later ones. However, the effectiveness of both methods has been very limited.

At the moment anti-spam filtering software seems to be the most viable solution to spam problem. Spam filtering methods are often classified as *collaborative* or *content-based* [2]. The collaborative filtering entails the collecting of some identifying information about spam messages such as the subject, the sender or the result of com-

P. Perner (Ed.): ICDM 2006, LNAI 4065, pp. 106 – 120, 2006.
© Springer-Verlag Berlin Heidelberg 2006

puting a hash function over the body of the message [3]. The collected data is shared with the community in the form of a digital fingerprint of each spam message. The community users can obtain the existing spam message fingerprints and use them for identifying spam e-mails which had been previously received and categorized by other users.

Despite there is no doubt that collaborative techniques help to spam filtering, they are very simplistic and unable to generalize over knowledge. Due to this fact, content-based approaches had become very popular during last years. Content-based techniques are based on analysing intrinsic properties extracted from the messages (e.g. message subject, body contents, structure, etc.) [4]. This kind of approaches is more effective than previous one because new spam messages can be correctly classified by using generalization methods over the extracted features from examined e-mails.

In the framework of content-based techniques, traditionally two main approaches have been adopted to the problem of spam filtering according to how the classification is generated by the system: *eager* vs. *lazy* learning models. The main types of content-based techniques are machine learning (ML) algorithms and case/instance-based (memory-based) reasoning approaches. ML approaches use an algorithm to 'learn' the classification from a set of training messages. On the other hand, memory-based and case-based reasoning techniques store all training instances in a memory structure and try to classify new messages finding similar e-mails on it. Hence, the decision of how to classify an incoming message is deferred until the last moment.

Regardless of the selected learning strategy, in order to train and test content-based filters it is necessary to build a large corpus with spam and legitimate e-mails or use a publicly available corpus. Anyway, e-mails have to be preprocessed to extract their words (*features*) belonging to the message subject, the body and/or the attachments. Also, since the number of features in a corpus can end up being very high, it is common to choose those features that better represent each message before carrying out the filter training to prevent the classifiers from over-fitting [5]. The effectiveness of content-based anti-spam filters relies on the appropriate choice of the features. If the features are chosen so that they may exist both in a spam and legitimate messages then, no matter how good learning algorithm is, it will make mistakes. Therefore, the preprocessing steps of e-mail features extraction and the later selection of the most representative are crucial for the performance of the filter.

For several years we have been working in the identification of techniques to completely automate the reasoning cycle of case based reasoning (CBR) systems [6, 7] and lately we have been applying all this knowledge in the development of an anti-spam filtering software called SpamHunting [8]. Our model implements an instance-based anti-spam system which successfully combine a dynamical *k-nn* strategy to retrieve the most similar messages and an innovative feature selection method based on identifying the most relevant features of each e-mail. As classical feature selection methods are not straightforwardly applicable within our model (due to its underground ideas), we are trying to reach the best conclusions behind them applied on the anti-spam filtering domain in order to improve our newly feature selection method.

In this paper, we analyse what are the strengths and the weaknesses of different feature selection methods employed in text categorization when they are applied to the spam problem domain. Therefore, we will show the results obtained by different well-known content-based techniques when the preprocessing of the training corpus changes. The selected models for the evaluation were Naïve Bayes [9], boosting trees [10], Support Vector Machines [11] and a case-based system for spam filtering named ECUE [12]. The feature selection methods we take into account were *Document Frequency* [13], *Information Gain* [14], *Mutual Information* [15, 16] and a χ^2-*test* [13].

Another relevant issue tackled in this paper is analysing how feature selection methods can be affected by noise data. Several significant terms such as 'viagra' or 'mortgage' are often obfuscated in spam messages ('v1agra', 'm0rtgage') in order to difficult class identification. Spammers are constantly innovating in word hiding tricks in order to decrease the anti-spam filtering software effectiveness. Finally, several attachments of e-mail messages can contain interesting features helpful for classifying it. We are interested in knowing if the results get better when attachments are processed. In this way, experiments have been carried out when incorporating features extracted from the attachments belonging to the messages and without it.

The rest of the paper is structured as follows: Section 2 summarizes previous work on machine learning techniques and case-based systems successfully applied to the anti-spam filtering domain. In Section 3, we describe the selected corpus for empirical model evaluation and discuss several issues related with message representation and feature selection. Then, Section 4 presents the experiments carried out and the results obtained discussing the major findings. Finally, Section 5 outlines the conclusions obtained from experimentation and presents further work.

2 Content-Based Techniques for Spam Filtering

This section introduces a brief description of the most referenced content-based techniques used in the anti-spam filtering domain. Subsection 2.1 presents a short description of classical machine learning models while Subsection 2.2 summarizes a small review of case-based and memory-based methods. Finally, Subsection 2.3 contains a detailed introduction to our Spam-Hunting model for spam labelling and filtering.

2.1 Machine Learning Approaches

Several machine learning algorithms used in text categorization [17] have also been applied to spam filtering due to the fact that classifying spam e-mails based on the textual content of the messages can be seen as a special case of categorization, with the categories being 'spam' and 'legitimate'. Regarding this subject, the most accurate techniques we should mention are Naïve Bayes, Support Vector Machines and Boosting methods because they have lead to successful research activities in the spam filtering domain.

The first research studies primarily focused on the problem of filtering spam were those of Sahami *et al.* [9] and Drucker *et al.* [18]. In [9], the authors trained a Naïve Bayesian (NB) classifier on manually categorized legitimate and spam messages, reporting impressive precision and recall on unseen e-mails. On the other hand, Drucker *et al.* verified the validity of SVMs' effectiveness in spam detection in [18].

SVMs are based on the *Structural Risk Minimization* principle [11] from computational learning theory. The idea behind structural risk minimization is to find a hypothesis for which one can guarantee the lowest true error. The true error is the probability that the hypothesis will make an error on an unseen and randomly selected test example (new e-mail message). The training of a SVM is usually slow but an optimized algorithm called *Sequential Minimal Optimization* (SMO) has demonstrated a good trade-off between accuracy and speed (see [19] for details).

Besides NB and SVM models, boosting methods are also well-known ML techniques used in this field. The purpose of boosting is to find a highly accurate classification rule by combining many *weak learners* (or weak hypotheses), each of which may be only moderately accurate [10]. The main idea of boosting is to combine the hypotheses to one final hypothesis, in order to achieve higher accuracy than the weak learner's hypothesis would have. From the several boosting algorithms that have been applied for classification tasks, we could highlight Adaboost [20].

An important aspect to take into account is that representative features on spam and legitimate messages can change with the course of time. So for example, the presence of the term 'rolex' has been indicative of legitimate e-mails several years ago but nowadays the existence of this feature is a clue for detecting spam e-mails. This kind of changes in the context of spam domain is the cause of the concept drift problem [21]. Recent work in ML techniques applied to spam detection is taking into account this situation in two different ways: (*i*) improving the performance over current ML models [22, 23, 24] and (*ii*) handling the concept drift problem [25, 26, 27].

2.2 Case-Based and Memory-Based Reasoning Approaches

Because of the changing nature of spam, a anti-spam filtering software using some machine learning approach will need to be dynamic. Several researches have suggested that a memory-based approach may work well [12]. Instance-based (or memory-based) methods are characterized by using a memory structure where each training instance is stored. The utilization of a memory structure should make the retrieval of similar instances easier and faster. In the operation mode, e-mails retrieved are used directly for classification purposes. The main advantages derived from the use of instance-based models are its capacity to continuous updating, manage disjoint concepts and handle concept drift.

In [28] a preliminary evaluation of using memory-based models in spam filtering domain is shown. In this work, TiMBL software [29] (which implements several memory-based learning techniques) is used for identifying the set of training instances in the *k* closest distances from the target problem. The solution is computed taking into account the retrieved instances by a voting strategy which gives priority to legitimate e-mails by a weighting process.

Later on, some CBR systems have been successfully adapted in this domain combining ideas from memory-based models and lazy learning. Case-based reasoning (CBR) is a *lazy* approach to machine learning where induction is delayed until run time. In [12] a case-based system for anti-spam filtering called ECUE (*E-mail Classification Using Examples*) is presented. ECUE can learn dynamically and each e-mail is a case represented as a vector of binary features. If the feature exists in the e-mail then the case assigns to the feature a value of *true*, otherwise the value of the feature is set to *false*.

The ECUE system uses a *k-nn* classifier to retrieve the *k* most similar cases to a target case. The similarity retrieval algorithm is based on Case Retrieval Nets (CRN)

[30], which is a memory structure that allows efficient and flexible retrieval of cases. ECUE classifier uses unanimous voting to determine whether a new e-mail is spam or not. In order to classify a new message as spam, all the returned neighbours need to be classified as spam e-mails.

Recently we have developed a novel instance-based anti-spam filtering system called SpamHunting [8]. Next subsection contains a summarized description of the model operation.

2.3 SpamHunting IBR System

Our SpamHunting system is a lazy learning hybrid model based on an Instance Based Reasoning approach able to solve the problem of spam labeling and filtering [8]. This system uses an Enhanced Instance Retrieval Network (EIRN) model that effectively indexes all e-mails in the instance base.

At the preprocessing stage, text is extracted from the body of each message. PDF, images and HTML documents attached to the e-mail are also processed and converted to text. Then, text is tokenized by using space, carriage return and tabulator chars as token separators. Finally, a stopword removal process is performed over identified tokens by using the stopword list given in [31].

The feature selection process is carried out in an independent way for each training and testing e-mail. Therefore, each message has its own relevant features. The main idea behind feature selection in SpamHunting is finding the best fitting features for each e-mail. Currently, the feature selection process is done by computing the set of the most frequent terms which frequency amount is over a given threshold. We had empirically found that best results can be reached by using a threshold of approximately 30% of the frequency amount.

The relevant terms selected from e-mails are represented in the EIRN network as nodes while the messages are interpreted as a collection of weighted associations with term-nodes. The instance retrieval is carried out by projecting the terms selected from the target problem over the network nodes [8]. The set of messages sharing the maximum number of features with the actual target e-mail are selected as the closest e-mails. Finally, these messages are sorted keeping in mind the frequencies of each shared term between the retrieved e-mails and the target message.

As we can see from Figure 1, when a new e-mail arrives, the EIRN network can quickly retrieve the most similar messages stored in the instance base. Then, in the reuse stage, a preliminary solution is generated by using a unanimous voting strategy with all the retrieved e-mails in the previous stage. Finally, meta-rules extracted from e-mail headers are used in order to complete the revise stage.

Our EIRN model can effectively tackle with concept drift problem by using a term confidence metric associated with each node (represented as a color between red and green in Figure 1).

We are currently working on improving the feature selection method used by our SpamHunting system in two ways: (*i*) taking into account the background ideas from the current feature selection methods which has been successfully used for the spam labeling and filtering domain and (*ii*) handling concept drift problem. In this work, we analyze how can the feature selection method of SpamHunting system be improved in order to achieve better results.

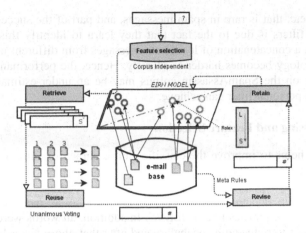

Fig. 1. SpamHunting model architecture

3 Preprocessing of Available Data and Message Representation

In this section we present several evaluation decisions related with feature selection, message representation and ready for use corpus. The following subsections are structured as follows: Subsection 3.1 contains relevant aspects relative to the corpus publicly available, Subsection 3.2 describes the main feature selection methods available in the context of spam filtering. Finally, Subsection 3.3 presents some message representation issues.

3.1 Benchmark Corpus

It is essential to provide content-based filters with an appropriate corpus of e-mails for training and testing purposes. The corpus should contain both spam and legitimate messages. Research on text categorization has been benefited significantly from the existence of publicly available, manually categorized document collections like the Reuters corpora [32], which has been used as standard benchmark. Producing similar corpora for anti-spam filtering is more complicated because of privacy issues. Publicizing spam messages does not pose a problem, since spam messages are distributed blindly to very large numbers of recipients and, hence, they are effectively already publicly available. Legitimate messages, however, in general cannot be released without violating the privacy of their recipients and senders. One way to bypass privacy problems is to experiment with legitimate messages collected from freely accessible news-groups, or mailing lists with public archives.

There are several publicly available corpora of e-mails just as LingSpam, JunkE-mail or PU. In our work, we use the SpamAssassin corpus that contains 2381 spam and 6951 legitimate messages. Legitimate e-mails have been collected from public fore or donated by users with the understanding that they may be made public. SpamAssassin has the disadvantage that its legitimate messages are not indicative of the legitimate messages that would arrive at the mailbox of a single user. Many of the legitimate messages that a user receives contain terminology reflecting his/her profession, interests, etc. that is rare in spam messages, and part of the success of personal learning-based filters is due to the fact that they learn to identify this user-specific terminology. In a concatenation of legitimate messages from different users this user-specific terminology becomes harder to identify. Hence, the performance of a learning-based filter on the SpamAssassin corpus may be an under-estimate of the performance that a personal filter can achieve.

3.2 Preprocessing and Feature Selection

An aspect that helps to improve the classification accuracy of filtering software are the preprocessing steps applied to the training and test corpus. Specially, a relevant issue in natural language processing problems is the tokenizing scheme. In our case, we consider certain punctuations like exclamation points as part of a term since spammers tend to use phrases like '*FREE!!!*'. In addition, all words were converted to lowercase in order to reduce the vocabulary and after that, those terms having smaller semantic contribution are eliminated by using the stopword list given by [21].

Typically, terms are strings of characters where stemming could be applied. Stemming lowers the size of the feature vector but it may be the case that certain forms of a word (such as the active tense) may be important in classification, so we do not stem words here. If the message representation scheme includes all the identified features in the training corpus, then very high-dimensional feature spaces would be generated. Several authors have noted the need for feature selection in order to make possible the use of conventional ML techniques to improve generalization accuracy and to avoid over-fitting the models [13].

The most widely used filter consists on calculating the *Information Gain* (IG) [14] of each term t. IG measures the number of bits of information obtained for category prediction (legitimate and spam) by knowing the presence or absence of a feature in a message. Subsequently, those terms whose value of IG overcomes a certain threshold are selected. Another mechanisms that allow approximating the ideal number of terms can be employed. It is the case of the *Document Frequency* (DF) [13], *Mutual Information* (MI) [15, 16] or the $\chi2$-*test* (CHI2) [13].

DF stands for the number of e-mails in which a feature occurs. We can compute the DF for each unique term in the training corpus and remove from the feature space those terms whose DF is less than some predetermined threshold. The basic assumption is that rare terms are either non-informative for category prediction, or not influential in global performance. Although DF is the simplest technique for vocabulary reduction, it is usually considered an *ad hoc* approach to improve efficiency, not a principled criterion for selecting predictive features [13].

CHI2 measures the lack of independence between a term t and a category c. Just like MI, we can compute for each category the χ^2 *statistic* using a two-way contingency table. IG, CHI2 and DF metrics are the most effective aggressive feature removal methods in the context of text categorization while MI has lower performance due to a bias favouring rare terms and a strong sensitivity to probability estimation errors [13]. Therefore, DF could be used to replace IG and CHI2 when the computation (quadratic) of these measures is too expensive.

3.3 Message Representation

Another relevant issue is the internal structure of the messages used by the different models during training and classification stages. In learning algorithms, training messages are usually represented as a vector of weighted terms like the vector space model in information retrieval [33].

Once carried out the feature extraction process over the whole corpus, the weight of terms in each message need to be calculated. The measure of the weight can be (*i*) binary (1 if the term occurs in the message, 0 otherwise), (*ii*) the *term frequency* (TF) representing the number of times the term occurs in the message, or (*iii*) TF.IDF where IDF means *Inverse Document Frequency* denoting those terms that are common across the messages of the training collection [33]. It is more normal in text classification for lexical features to carry frequency information, but previous evaluations showed that a binary representation works better in this domain [9, 18, 33, 34].

Term frequency is used in order to carry out our experiments with all models except ECUE because, as its author defines it, this model represents each message in a memory structure, which is only able to apply a binary scheme.

4 Experimental Results

The first goal of our experiments is a comparative study of the above feature selection methods (IG, DF, MI and CHI2) when they are applied to the anti-spam filtering domain. Moreover, experimental results will also be useful to improve the feature selection method of our SpamHunting IBR model and they will allow us to know the behaviour of the system in presence of noise data. Finally, these experiments will be useful for giving us an advice about the convenience of parsing e-mail attachments. The experiments have been carried out using implementations of Naïve Bayes, Adaboost, SVM and the ECUE CBR system.

The tests have been carried out for two different scenarios. In the first one, we only consider the features extracted from the subject and the body of the e-mails. Later, we append the features from the attachments. In order to handle the diverse formats of the attached files, we use different techniques for each case, taking into account the 'content-type' header information. So, HTML code was translated into text/plain using HTMLParser tool, images were processed using the Asprise OCR software and the text inside pdf documents was extracted using the PDFBox package.

Six well-known metrics proposed by Androutsopoulos *et al.* [4] have been used in order to evaluate the performance of all the analyzed models: percentage of correct classifications (%OK), percentage of False Positives (%FP), percentage of False Negatives (%FN), spam *recall*, spam *precision* and Total Cost Ratio (TCR). All the experiments have been carried out using a 10-fold stratified cross-validation [35] in order to increase the confidence level of the results obtained.

4.1 Benchmark of the Different Configurations

In this subsection, results from evaluation of the different scenarios using %OK, %FP, %FN, recall and precision metrics are showed and discussed. In this sense, Tables 1 and 2 summarize the results obtained for the evaluated models with and without attachments (w-Att and w/o-Att respectively). In square brackets it is indicated the number of selected features for each tested technique. For this experiment we have selected the best performance model of each approach varying between 100 and 2000 representing features.

Table 1. Mean value of correct classifications, FPs and FNs with 10 fold-cross validation

		NB [1000]		AB [700]		SVM [2000]		ECUE [700]	
		w/o-Att.	w-Att.	w/o-Att.	w-Att.	w/o-Att.	w-Att.	w/o-Att.	w-Att.
%OK									
	IG	849,6	842,8	885,1	885,3	919,1	921,2	893,0	897,4
	DF	849,0	842,7	882,9	878,3	920,7	921,0	863,6	873,9
	MI	694,6	695,2	695,1	695,1	--	--	696,6	696,0
	CHI2	846,8	839,3	887,8	884,5	918,9	919,9	888,7	894,4
%FP									
	IG	48,6	60,9	13,4	12,3	8,7	5,7	6,1	7,9
	DF	48,8	57,9	13,0	12,3	7,0	6,9	5,6	7
	MI	1,8	2,1	0,0	0,0	--	--	46,9	40,3
	CHI2	52,2	64,3	11,8	12,4	8,5	5,8	10,9	12,2
%FN									
	IG	35,0	29,5	34,7	35,6	5,4	6,3	34,1	27,9
	DF	35,4	32,6	37,3	42,6	5,5	5,3	64,0	52,3
	MI	236,8	235,9	238,1	238,1	--	--	189,7	196,9
	CHI2	34,2	29,6	33,6	36,3	5,8	7,5	33,6	26,6

Results in Tables 1 and 2 show that, despite IG has the smallest fail amount, IG, DF and CHI2 have similar effects on the performance of the evaluated classifiers. So, the mean value of correct classifications, FPs (legitimate messages classified as spam) and FNs (spam messages classified as legitimate) are practically the same with any above selection feature measures. These results support previous studies carried out with another classification models when they are applied in text categorization [13].

On the other hand, although MI method achieve the smallest amount of FPs, its fail amount is about 7 times greater than other methods. Therefore, MI method is clearly the worst feature selection method because it is very noise sensitive. If MI method is excluded, then DF achieves the smallest number of FPs.

As it can be seen from Table 1 and 2, SVM model was unable to transform the input space into a new and linearly separable one when using MI method (marked as '--'). Therefore, using MI for spam filtering and labelling is generally a bad idea.

Table 2. Averaged recall and precision scores over 10 fold-cross validation

		NB [1000]		AB [700]		SVM [2000]		ECUE [700]	
		w/o-Att.	w-Att.	w/o-Att.	w-Att.	w/o-Att.	w-Att.	w/o-Att.	w-Att.
Recall									
	IG	0,8530	0,8761	0,8543	0,8505	0,9773	0,9735	0,8568	0,8828
	DF	0,8513	0,8631	0,8433	0,8211	0,9769	0,9777	0,7312	0,7803
	MI	0,0055	0,0092	0,0000	0,0000	--	--	0,2033	0,1730
	CHI2	0,8564	0,8757	0,8589	0,8475	0,9756	0,9685	0,8589	0,8883
Precision									
	IG	0,8071	0,7745	0,9385	0,9431	0,9643	0,9762	0,9711	0,9639
	DF	0,8063	0,7807	0,9394	0,9412	0,9710	0,9713	0,9689	0,9640
	MI	0,0000	0,0000	0,0000	0,0000	--	--	0,5085	0,5059
	CHI2	0,7965	0,7648	0,9457	0,9423	0,9650	0,9756	0,9495	0,9456

4.2 Statistical Analysis of Benchmarking Results

After showing empirical results and several preliminary comments about them, we are going to analyse the generated outcome from a statistical point of view in order to check for the importance of the findings. In this sense, for each analysed algorithm the Cochran Q test shows differences between the proportions of failure or correct decision for all the variants, that is to say, depending on the criterion for selecting relevant terms (CHI2, IG, MI and DF) and the decision of taking or not into account e-mails attachments (w-Att and w/o-Att, respectively).

Table 3. Kappa coefficients of agreement beetween different configurations of the selected methods

	TC	w/o-Att			w-Att		
		AB-χ^2	AB-IG	AB-DF	AB-χ^2	AB-IG	AB-DF
TC	1	0,87	0,86	0,85	0,86	0,86	0,84
w/o-Att AB-χ^2		1	0,98	0,97	0,91	0,91	0,89
AB-IG			1	0,97	0,90	0,90	0,89
AB-DF				1	0,89	0,90	0,89
w-Att AB-χ^2					1	0,98	0,95
AB-IG						1	0,95
AB-DF							1

	TC	w/o-Att			w-Att		
		SVM-χ^2	SVM-IG	SVM-DF	SVM-χ^2	SVM-IG	SVM-DF
TC	1	0,96	0,96	0,96	0,96	0,97	0,97
w/o-Att SVM-χ^2		1	0,99	0,97	0,97	0,97	0,96
SVM-IG			1	0,97	0,97	0,97	0,97
SVM-DF				1	0,97	0,97	0,98
w-Att SVM-χ^2					1	0,98	0,97
SVM-IG						1	0,97
SVM-DF							1

	TC	w/o-Att			w-Att		
		NB-χ^2	NB-IG	NB-DF	NB-χ^2	NB-IG	NB-DF
TC	1	0,76	0,77	0,77	0,75	0,76	0,75
w/o-Att NB-χ^2		1	0,98	0,97	0,89	0,89	0,89
NB-IG			1	0,97	0,87	0,88	0,87
NB-DF				1	0,88	0,88	0,88
w-Att NB-χ^2					1	0,99	0,97
NB-IG						1	0,97
NB-DF							1

	TC	w/o-Att			w-Att		
		ECUE-χ^2	ECUE-IG	ECUE-DF	ECUE-χ^2	ECUE-IG	ECUE-DF
TC	1	0,88	0,87	0,78	0,88	0,89	0,81
w/o-Att ECUE-χ^2		1	0,94	0,80	0,88	0,87	0,81
ECUE-IG			1	0,83	0,89	0,90	0,84
ECUE-DF				1	0,79	0,79	0,86
w-Att ECUE-χ^2					1	0,97	0,84
ECUE-IG						1	0,86
ECUE-DF							1

Given that the MI criterion gives the worst results for all the algorithms, we are interested in the analysis of the rest of factors. We consider each variant as a method, which gives us its opinion about the classification of a message. Now we are interested in knowing the degree of agreement between these methods. In order to do this, we use the Kappa test. Formally, the Kappa test compares the outcome between two methods when the observations are measured on a categorical scale. Both methods must rate the same cases using the same categorical scale to be considered as equivalent. Table 3 shows the Kappa coefficient of agreement between all the possibilities ({CHI2, IG and DF}×{w/o-Att, w-Att}) and the *true class* method (which always gives the true class of the e-mail). The comparison of the Kappa coefficient agreement of each variant with the true class algorithm gives us an idea of the accuracy of each method (bold values in Table 3). The statistical analysis of these values ranks the SVM as the best algorithm, positioning the AB and ECUE methods in second place without significant differences and the NB algorithm in last position.

In order to analyse the impact of each factor for several configurations of the algorithms, the Kappa coefficients of agreement has been statistically analysed by means of a comparison of these indexes by each one of the considered factors. The non-normality of data determines the use of a Kruskal-Wallis test in order to test the null hypothesis (no difference in the Kappa coefficients depending of each factor).

4.3   Analysis of the TCR Scores

In this subsection, TCR scores are calculated and discussed in order to confirm findings reflected in previous subsections. TCR provides a measurement of the spam filter effectiveness keeping in mind the fact that FP errors are more serious that FN. The λ parameter indicates how is the cost of an FP error in relation to an FN.

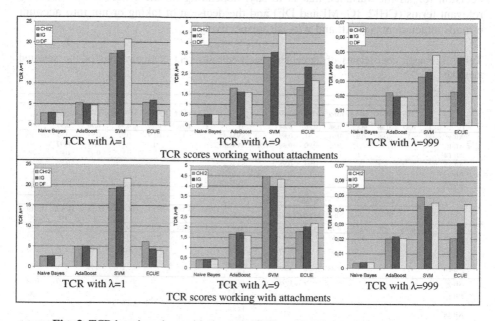

Fig. 2. TCR benchmark considering MI, CHI2 and DF feature selection methods

Figure 2 shows a benchmark of the feature selection methods within different scenarios and models using the TCR score. From results, we can realize that models handling a better capacity of discarding irrelevant features (SVM and AB to a lesser extent) get the best score when attachments are used. Other models, such as NB and AB are not able to avoid or weight down irrelevant terms. Therefore, the SVM input space conversion really complements the use of any feature selection method.

Results from Figure 2 confirm the fact that the processing of the attachment can add irrelevant or confused features to the model input space, making the learning process more difficult. However, if the selected model performs a deeper feature analysis, it can obtain better results by taking advantage of this fact.

4.4   Improving SpamHunting Feature Selection Model

Keeping in mind the background ideas from previous experiments and the existing SpamHunting feature selection model, we had concluded that a feature weight reflecting the classifying capability of a term could be used to improve global performance in the model. Expression (1) defines our proposed measure of a term t for labelling an e-mail e, where $P(t \mid e)$ represents the frequency of the term t in the message e, $P(t \mid s, \mathbf{K})$

and $P(t \mid l, K)$ stand for the document frequency of t in spam and legitimate messages respectively, $P(s \mid K)$ and $P(l, K)$ are the frequency of the spam and legitimate categories and $P(t \mid K)$ represents the document frequency of a term t. In Expression (1), the relevance of a term t within a document e (measured as $P(t \mid e)$) is weighted by a factor that quantifies the classifying capability of the term t computed by the expression inside square brackets. The proposed classifying capability metric will be near to 1 for the most representative terms of each class.

$$TC(t,e) = P(t \mid e) \cdot \left[\frac{\left| P(s,K) \cdot P(t \mid s,K) - P(l,K) \cdot P(t \mid l,K) \right|}{P(t \mid K)} \right] \tag{1}$$

Despite this metric seems to be very noise sensitive, the feature selection over each document prevents the selection of noise terms in all messages belonging the training corpus. The feature selection for each message e is computed by selecting the smallest set of terms from e having the largest TC.

Table 4 shows a comparative performance study of the SpamHunting model when applying both the original feature selection method and the improved one. Results are obtained with and without processing attachments. From Table 4 we can realize that it is possible to obtain better results by applying a feature weighting or finding a feature selection method more accurate than the one currently used in our SpamHunting system. Moreover, we can deduce that our model is able to handle noise data and that it is possible to improve results by processing e-mail attachments. In fact, a similar behaviour with the SVM model is observed when the scenario is changed.

Table 4. Averaged recall and precision scores over 10 fold-cross validation

metric	Original feature selection		Improved feature selection		Metric	Original feature selection		Improved feature selection	
	w/o-Att.	w-Att.	w/o-Att.	w-Att.		w/o-Att.	w-Att.	w/o-Att.	w-Att.
%OK	96,53%	96,30%	96,67%	96,67%	Precision	0,99	0,99	0,99	0,99
%FP	0,19%	0,17%	0,04%	0,19%	TCR λ=1	7,50	7,15	7,79	7,93
%FN	3,28%	3,52%	3,29%	3,14%	TCR λ=9	5,33	5,52	7,19	5,46
Recall	0,87	0,86	0,87	0,88	TCR λ=999	0,87	1,62	5,49	2,12

5 Conclusions and Further Work

In this article, we perform a deeper analysis of feature selection methods in the context of spam filtering using different models and preprocessing scenarios. Finally, findings are used to improve the feature selection method of our SpamHunting filtering software.

The reasons for good or bad accuracy of the evaluated feature selection methods are originated by the criteria they use to choose terms. Those methods with a good performance share the same bias. Therefore, IG, DF and CHI2 score in favour of common terms over rare terms while MI prioritises low frequency terms. As demonstrated in [13], results indicate that common terms are indeed informative for text categorization tasks. Moreover, the result obtained by DF evidences that the use of category information for feature selection does not seem to be crucial for improving accuracy.

MI method is clearly disadvantaged when it is applied to spam filtering. This is motivated because spammers obfuscate terms introducing noise into messages. They spread to include in their messages multiple sequences of special characters and to change characters inside the words for punctuation symbols to make more difficult the detention of their e-mail. This noise can be seen in the quantity of rare features (with very low frequency) included in spam e-mails. Therefore, a way of improving the results obtained by this method is to eliminate those characteristics whose appearance frequency is very low before carrying out the feature selection, just as in [4, 9, 34]. The use of MI with the SVM model is not advisable because the model will probably not be able to complete the training process.

With respect to DF, it is the simplest feature selection method, however, experimental results have shown its good performance when it is applied in spam filtering. Results achieve the smallest amount of false positives probably because a previous stopword removal has been carried out. Without this preprocessing step, the feature selection made will probably contain a lot of semantically empty words.

Talking about IG and CHI2 feature selection methods, results show that generally IG achieves a little bit better precision (security) while CHI2 is slightly superior in recall measure (effectiveness). The experiments carried out have probed that there is no significant differences between this methods regardless of the selected model.

The use of message attachments is useful when it is combined with models, which are able to discard irrelevant or confused features by performing a deeper analysis of the input space in order to detect and remove fake features. Strict methods that use all features from input space achieve poor results because several detected features in the attachment processing are confused or irrelevant. In this sense, SpamHunting feature selection method should be constructed by combining term frequency with a metric able to measure the classification capability of each term. Talking about noise data, as SpamHunting retrieval model is able to distinguish noise data and skip it, this problem can be avoided in our system. The classification capability of each term should be dynamically calculated by using all messages stored in the instance base.

Finally, in order to handle the concept drift problem, a relevant issue is how to give priority to recent e-mails detecting the change of the words representing legitimate and spam classes. Building models and techniques with the capacity of tackling with this problem is the most recent trend in spam research. In this way, several authors have explained the main ideas behind the models, which are able to manage this characteristic of spam filtering problem [21].

Talking about the future work, a new research line in spam filtering has been opened since SpamHunting model introduced the feature selection over each message (and not over the whole training corpus). This way of representing the messages is more effective than others because each document has its own relevant features, allowing continuous updating of the model knowledge and being more suitable for working with disjoint concepts (such as spam). In a first stage we will try to apply the ideas exposed in this paper to improve the feature selection method and later, we will work over the SpamHunting model in order to achieve better results.

References

1. Spam statistics. http://www.theregister.co.uk/security/spam/
2. Oard, D.W.: The state of the art in text filtering. User Modeling and User-Adapted Interaction, Vol.7, (1997) 141–178
3. Wittel, G.L., Wu, S.F.: On Attacking Statistical Spam Filters. Proc. of the First Conference on E-mail and Anti-Spam CEAS, (2004)
4. Androutsopoulos, I., Paliouras, G., Michelakis, E.: Learning to Filter Unsolicited Commercial E-Mail. Technical Report 2004/2, NCSR "Demokritos", (2004)
5. Méndez J.R., Iglesias E.L., Fdez-Riverola, F., Díaz F., Corchado, J.M.: Analyzing the Impact of Corpus Preprocessing on Anti-Spam Filtering Software. Research on Computing Science, To appear. (2005)
6. Corchado, J.M., Corchado, E.S., Aiken, J., Fyfe, C., Fdez-Riverola, F., Glez-Bedia, M.: Maximum Likelihood Hebbian Learning Based Retrieval Method for CBR Systems. Proc. of the 5th International Conference on Case-Based Reasoning, (2003) 107–121
7. Corchado, J.M., Aiken, J., Corchado, E., Lefevre, N., Smyth, T.: Quantifying the Ocean's CO2 Budget with a CoHeL-IBR System. Proc. of the 7th European Conference on Case-based Reasoning, (2004) 533–546
8. Fdez-Riverola, F., Lorenzo, E.L., Díaz, F., Méndez, J. R., Corchado, J.M.: SpamHunting: An Instance-Based Reasoning System for Spam Labelling and Filtering. Decision Support Systems, To Appear (2006)
9. Sahami, M., Dumais, S., Heckerman, D., Horvitz, E.: A Bayesian approach to filtering junk e-mail. In Learning for Text Categorization – Papers from the AAAI Workshop, Technical Report WS-98-05, (1998) 55–62
10. Carreras, X., Màrquez, L.: Boosting trees for anti-spam e-mail filtering. Proc. of the 4th International Conference on Recent Advances in Natural Language Processing, (2001) 58–64
11. Vapnik, V.: The Nature of Statistical Learning Theory. 2nd Ed. Statistics for Engineering and Information Science, (1999)
12. Delany, S.J., Cunningham P., Coyle L.: An Assessment of Case-base Reasoning for Spam Filtering. Proc. of Fifteenth Irish Conference on Artificial Intelligence and Cognitive Science: AICS-04, (2004) 9–18
13. Yang, Y., Pedersen, J.O.: A comparative study on feature selection in text categorization. Proc. of the Fourteenth International Conference on Machine Learning: ICML-97, (1997) 412–420
14. Mitchell, T.: Machine Learning. Mc Graw Hill, (1996)
15. Dumais, S., Platt, J., Heckerman, D., Sahami, M.: Inductive learning algorithms and representations for text categorization. Proc. of the 7th International Conference on Information and Knowledge Management, (1998) 229–237
16. Church, K.W., Hanks, P.: Word association norms, mutual information and lexicography. Proc. of the ACL, Vol.27, (1989) 76–83
17. Sebastiani, F.: Machine Learning in Automated Text Categorization. ACM Computing Surveys, Vol. 34 (1). (2002) 1–47
18. Drucker, H.D., Wu, D., Vapnik, V.: Support Vector Machines for spam categorization. IEEE Transactions on Neural Networks, Vol. 10 (5). (1999) 1048–1054
19. Platt, J.: Fast training of Support Vector Machines using Sequential Minimal Optimization. In Sholkopf, B., Burges, C., Smola, A. (eds.). Advances in Kernel Methods – Support Vector Learning, (1999) 185–208

20. Schapire, R.E., Singer, Y.: BoosTexter: a boosting-based system for text categorization. Machine Learning, Vol. 39 (2/3), (2000) 135–168
21. Tsymbal, A.: The problem of concept drift: definitions and related work, Available at http://www.cs.tcd.ie
22. Graham, P.: Better Bayesian filtering. Proc. of the MIT Spam Conference, 2003
23. Kolcz A., Alspector, J.: SVM-based filtering of e-mail spam with content specific misclassification costs. Proc. of the ICDM Workshop on Text Mining, (2001)
24. Hovold, J.: Naïve Bayes Spam Filtering Using Word-Position-Based Attributes. Proc. of the Second Conference on Email and Anti-Spam CEAS-2005. http://www.ceas.cc/papers-2005/144.pdf
25. Gama, J., Castillo, G.: Adaptive Bayes. Proc. of the 8th Ibero-American Conference on AI: IBERAMIA-02, (2002) 765–774
26. Scholz, M., Klinkenberg, R.: An Ensemble Classifier for Drifting Concepts. Proc. of the Second International Workshop on Knowledge Discovery from Data Streams, (2005) 53–64
27. Syed, N. A., Liu H., Sung. K.K.: Handling Concept Drifts in Incremental Learning with Support Vector Machines. Proc. of the fifth ACM SIGKDD international conference on Knowledge discovery and data mining, (1999) 317–321
28. Androutsopoulos, I., Paliouras, G., Karkaletsis, V., Sakkis, G., Spyropoulos, C.D., Stamatopoulos, P.: Learning to Filter Spam E-Mail: A Comparison of a Naïve Bayesian and a Memory-Based Approach. In Workshop on Machine Learning and Textual Information Access, 4th European Conference on Principles and Practice of Knowledge Discovery in Databases (PKDD) (2000) 1–13
29. Daelemans, W., Jakub, Z., Sloot, K., Bosh, A.: TiMBL. Tilburg Memory Based Learning, version 5.1, Reference Guide. ILK, Computational Linguistics, Tilburg University. http://ilk.uvt.nl/software.html#timbl
30. Lenz, M., Auriol, E., Manago, M.: Diagnosis and Decision Support. Case-Based Reasoning Technology. Lecture Notes in Artificial Intelligence, Vol. 1400, (1998) 51–90
31. Frakes, B., Baeza-Yates, R.: Information Retrieval: Data Structures & Algorithms. Prentice-Hall, (2000)
32. NIST: National Institute of Science and Technology. Reuters corpora. (2004), http://trec.nist.gov/data/reuters/reuters.html
33. Salton, G., McGill, M.: Introduction to modern information retrieval, McGraw-Hill, (1983)
34. Sakkis, G., Androutsopoulos, I., Paliouras, G., Karkaletsis, V., Spyropoulos, C., Stamatopoulos, P. A Memory-Based Approach to Anti-Spam Filtering for Mailing Lists. Information Retrieval, Vol. 6 (1). (2003) 49–73
35. Kohavi, R.: A study of cross-validation and bootstrap for accuracy estimation and model selection. Proc. of the 14th International Joint Conference on Artificial Intelligence: IJCAI-95, (1995) 1137–1143

Evaluation of Web Robot Discovery Techniques: A Benchmarking Study

Nick Geens, Johan Huysmans, and Jan Vanthienen

Department of Decision Sciences and Information Management,
Katholieke Universiteit Leuven, Naamsestraat 69,B-3000 Leuven, Belgium

Abstract. This paper describes part of a web usage mining study executed on log files obtained from a Belgian e-commerce company. From these log files, it can be observed that numerous web robots are active on the site. Most of these robots show a crawling behavior that is radically different from the browsing behavior of human visitors. Because the owners of the e-shop desire information about the paths that human visitors follow through the site, it is of crucial importance to remove these robotic visits from the log files.

Several existing methods for web robot discovery are evaluated and compared, none of them leading to satisfying results. Therefore, a new technique is developed that results in a successful and reliable identification of web robots.

1 Introduction

Web Usage Mining is defined as *the application of data mining techniques to discover usage patterns from web data* [1]. Usually, the web data that is being analyzed consists of log files that store information about the requests made to a particular web server over a certain time interval. In this paper, we discuss the analysis of the log files of a Belgian online shop. During this process the server logs were subjected to the subsequent steps of the typical web usage mining process [2,3,4,5,6]. This process consists of three parts: pre-processing of the data, pattern discovery and pattern analysis. In this paper, we will only describe a certain aspect of pre-processing, more specifically robot discovery. Robot discovery (also called robot identification or detection) is the search for robot sessions in a log file in order to exclude them from the analysis. A formal definition of web robots can be given as follows: *"Web robots are software programs or agents that traverse the hyperlink structure of the World Wide Web by retrieving a document and recursively retrieving all documents that are referenced"* [7]. By doing this, they are capable of automatically locating and retrieving information on the internet.

In the literature, several synonyms can be found for web robots, such as spiders, crawlers or web wanderers. The need for web robots was created by the soaring abundance of information on the internet. Nowadays, it has become an impossible challenge to find the required information on the web without the aid of a search engine. However, only few people realize that search engines succeed

P. Perner (Ed.): ICDM 2006, LNAI 4065, pp. 121–130, 2006.

in structuring this vast amount of information with the aid of web robots. Their crawling operations enable the search engines to store the visited web pages in indices. Besides these indexing robots, there are however plenty of other types of robots with less honorable intentions.

In this paper, we take a closer look at the different types of robots operating on the web and give an overview of several reasons why robot detection is worth the effort. Afterwards, we discuss some robot characteristics and currently applied methods to detect robot sessions. The remaining part of this paper will cover our practical research concerning the evaluation of the different robot detection methods and the development of a new method enabling a more reliable classification of robot sessions.

2   Motivations for Robot Discovery

There are many situations in which it is essential to separate robot sessions from visits of human users. First of all, when performing web usage mining on log files, it is indispensable to remove the robot sessions. The main purpose of this type of analysis is to extract useful information about the behavior of the human visitors of the site. Knowing that robots tend to have totally different browsing patterns compared to those of human visitors, the results of the analysis will be strongly biased because of robot presence.

Secondly, some e-commerce websites may contain information of high strategic value. Web robots can easily collect and aggregate this data, leading to precious business intelligence being exposed. To deal with this problem, preventive solutions will have to be developed in order to deny these robots access to the website.

Thirdly, a multitude of robots are employed by senders of spam to collect all email addresses that appear on web pages. Recognition of these malicious robots, can reduce the amount of spam received. Another possible approach followed by several sites is to show pages with non-existent email addresses when receiving a visit from these robots in order to pollute the databases of the spammers.

Another reason for robot detection is the excessive amount of bandwidth and server resources used by some robots. A great deal of web robots do not make use of these network resources in a responsible way, which can cause serious delays for other users.

Finally, some robots may be employed to perform fraudulent or illegal actions. When an advertising website is paid in relation to the amount of clicks it gets on the banners shown on the website, a robot can be designed to automatically click these advertisements in order to artificially inflate the number of banner clicks.

3   Different Types of Web Robots

As mentioned above, the most important task of robots is retrieving web pages for adding them to search engine indices. These **indexing robots** will be fed with a certain page (the 'seed') as a starting point. Due to the high level of connectivity between websites the robot will be able to take off on its journey through the internet.

Other robots are used to execute **link checking**. Since the internet is a rapidly changing and uncontrolled environment, web pages will be created, moved and deleted at all times. Nothing is more annoying for the visitors of a website to be confronted with links which lead them to the well known 404-page. In order to detect these broken links, robots can automatically check all the hyperlinks on a website and report dead links to the webmaster.

Thirdly, robots can be used to realise **offline browsing**. Users who want to be able to visit a web page at times when they are not online, can create an offline version of this website on their hard disks. All common browsers contain this kind of robot (e.g. MSIECrawler in Internet Explorer) which will download every page, image and other related file of a website. In some cases it might be interesting to duplicate websites or transfer them to another location. These mirrors will be created for websites with a large number of daily visitors in order to spread traffic over more web servers. For the sake of a faster response time, mirrors will sometimes be placed on different continents, enabling interaction with a web server residing nearby the client. Off course the consistency between different mirrors of one website must be guaranteed at all times: this task is perfectly executable by robots.

Another purpose for robots can be found in comparing prices of a given product on several e-commerce websites. The use of these so-called **shopbots** is a great asset for online customers, but will off course push the higher priced products out of the market. Therefore **pricebots** have been created for online merchants. These robots will dynamically adapt the prices of the offered products in function of the observed prices on other websites [8].

Finally, we may not ignore that robots might as well be employed in abusive practices. **Email harvesters** for example, travel through websites to collect email addresses which will be used for marketing and spam purposes.

4   Common Detection Methods Based on Log File Characteristics

We will now take a look at the typical characteristics of robot sessions in a log file. Some current methods for robot discovery based upon these characteristics will be discussed as well as the inherent flaws of these techniques. Related research on this topic was conducted in [9] and [10].

We start with the most frequently used method, which rests on the Robot Exclusion Standard of Koster [11]. This protocol proposes the use of a file named 'robots.txt' to indicate which parts of a website are restricted for robot visits. According to this standard, robots should always consult this file before indexing a website. Since human visitors will, during normal use, never end up at this file, a robots.txt request in the log file is strong evidence for the presence of a robot session. If all robots obeyed the Robot Exclusion Standard, this method would yield a perfect detection and there would be no need for robot discovery research. However, since these rules can not officially be imposed, there is no guarantee that all robots employ this standard.

Another typical robot feature can be found in the user agent field of the log file. Normally, information about the browser type used by the visitor can be found in this field. In the case of robots however, Eichmann [12] has postulated in his Directives for ethical web agents that they should make use of this field to declare their identity. When going through a log file, one will in fact notice that the user agent field in some sessions contains a robot name followed by some additional information. For instance, when Google has indexed a website, the log file will show the visit of their bot as follows: "Googlebot/2.1 (+http://www.googlebot.com/bot.html)". As a consequence, checking these user agent fields for names which are related to robots (e.g. all names containing 'bot', 'spider', 'crawler' etc.) has become a widely applied method for robot discovery. Eichmann's principles however are predestined to the same fate as the Robot Exclusion Standard, because these suggestions are also not enforceable to robot designers. Some robots go even further and try to conceal their identity by mentioning user agent information belonging to regular browsers.

Because the robots.txt request and user agent information are features which can be determined by robot designers themselves, there is clearly a need for methods relying on objective robot identification. From this point of view, the approach has been suggested to create a list containing IP addresses of all known robots and comparing these addresses to the ones in the log file. The soaring amount of robots operating on the web however, makes the maintenance of such a list a virtually impossible task. Moreover, the presence of proxy servers and providers with IP address pools has made it impossible to determine exactly which users belong to which IP addresses.

As stated above, robots will often attempt to remain undetected. This is why some existing methods try to discover robots based on their typical crawling behavior rather than using features referring to their identity. Detecting this robot behavior can first of all be achieved by considering the method (e.g. GET, POST, HEAD etc.) used to perform the HTTP requests. Browsers of human users will always request web pages with the GET method in order to receive the complete HTML page from the server. The task of some robots (e.g. link checking) on the other hand, can in several cases be executed by applying the HEAD method, causing only the header of the HTTP message to be transferred across the network. Another approach takes the referrer field of the logfile into account. This referrer field shows the web page that contains the link followed by the client in order to reach the requested page. In some specific situations however, this referrer field will not be registered, which is denoted by a hyphen. These unassigned referrers will occur when a visitor has manually typed the URL of a page in his browser or when he has reached a given page through his bookmarks. Robots in particular do often not assign a value to the referrer field, leading to all requests of their session having an unassigned referrer.

Three other methods based on the browsing behavior of web robots are related to the time pattern of subsequent requests. First of all, the ethical robot directives state that bandwidth should not be overconsumed at the expense of human users. Therefore, robots would have to operate as much as possible during the night. Secondly, from the same point of view, robots should insert a waiting period between subsequent requests instead of firing requests at the server every other second. If robots employ such a fixed request delay, this will result in a zero standard deviation in the times between subsequent requests. On the other hand, some robots are not considerate of human users and overload a server with requests in a short period of time. That is why a very low average time between subsequent requests is also a strong indication for robot sessions. As we will discover in our practical research however, none of these time-related techniques succeeds in efficiently distinguishing robots from human visitors.

Finally, we mention a last characterizing aspect of robot sessions which has not yet been included in standard robot discovery techniques. Remember that using the HEAD method was justified since for some robot purposes it appeared to be unnecessary to request complete web pages. Furthermore, most robots are also not interested in the images embedded in web pages as they are unable to extract useful information from these images. As a consequence, we can distinguish these robots from human visitors, whose browser will automatically depict all images belonging to a requested web page. The absence of image requests however, is not a guarantee that we are dealing with a web robot, since some visitors may have adjusted their browser settings in such a way that images are not shown.

5   Practical Evaluation of Currently Applied Methods

In order to assess the described methods, we have performed a practical study on the log files of a Belgian e-commerce website. Before discussing the results, we introduce two criteria on which this evaluation will be based. We define recall and precision as follows:

$$\text{Recall} = \frac{\text{number of correctly identified robot sessions}}{\text{total number of actual robot sessions}} \tag{1}$$

$$\text{Precision} = \frac{\text{number of correctly identified robot sessions}}{\text{total number of predicted robot sessions}} \tag{2}$$

In other words, recall yields the percentage of robot sessions that were discovered using a particular method, whereas precision describes the accurateness in terms of the proportion of correct predictions. It is clear that any method, in order to be useful, has to obtain a sufficient score on both metrics. There is no advantage in being able to detect all robot sessions if at the same time half of the predictions is incorrect.

Of course, there is one condition linked to these criteria: we must know exactly which sessions in the log file were created by robots. Therefore, we have manually

Table 1. Evaluation of commonly applied methods

	Correct	Wrong	Recall(%)	Precision
Manual Research	241	0	100	100
Robots.txt	41	0	17.01	100
IP address list	167	0	69.29	99.4
Robotic User Agent	64	0	26.56	100
HEAD method	78	0	32.37	100
Unassigned Referrer(1-100)	232	212	96.27	52.25
No Image Requests	237	77	98.34	75.48
Night	59	58	24.48	50.43
Standard Deviation (3s)	6	0	2.49	100
Average Time (1s)	6	2	2.49	75

checked a period of 5 days, resulting in 241 robot sessions out of a total 8001 registered sessions. In order to be sure about the origin of the visitors, we checked each session on the simultaneous presence of several robot characteristics and made use of DNS reverse look-up when this examination could not give a decisive answer.

Table 1 summarizes the outcome of each of the 9 considered methods. Before evaluating these methods, we quickly go through some implementation details. The list of known robots was based upon the overview available on www.robotstxt.org [13], while the third method scanned the user agents for the following words: bot, crawl, search, seek, archive, scan, link and spider. According to the HEAD method-technique, sessions are considered to be robotic as soon as they contain one occurrence of the HEAD method. Unassigned referrers (1-100) means that we detect sessions satisfying two conditions: the minimum number of requests in the session is 1 and all of the requests (100%) must contain an unassigned referrer. The night feature selects all sessions falling between 00.00 am and 07.00 am. Furthermore, we will consider all sessions as robotic if the period of time between subsequent requests has a standard deviation of less then 3 seconds or an average of less than 1 second. All of these parameter values were deduced from a separately conducted experiment which we will not treat in-depth here.

Considering the results for recall and precision, we can distinguish three groups of methods.

- The first group of 4 methods (robots.txt, IP address list, robotic user agents and HEAD method) are those with a perfect precision, but a rather low recall. A precision of 100% means that during the examined period, these 4 characteristics could only be found in robot sessions, making them very reliable techniques to discover robots. However, regarding the poor recall values, this reliability is not worth a great deal since these methods only detect about 20 to 30% of the robot sessions. Only by using the IP address list a considerably higher recall of 70% could be obtained, but this result must be nuanced knowing that the log files we examined were dated from

3 years before the applied IP address list. This way, all robots operating at the time of the log files, have probably been discovered and registered on the list by now.

- A second coherent group are the methods based on unassigned referrers and the absence of image requests. These techniques manage to discover almost all robot sessions, but also lead to a great amount of false positives.
- Thirdly, we notice that the techniques based on time-related features do not score well at all. A lot of robots seem to operate during the daytime and human visitors tend to execute nocturnal sessions as well. This is not surprising taking the high level of international web traffic into account. The methods 'standard deviation' and 'average time' are also incapable of detecting a sufficient percentage of robot sessions. The main reason for this failure can be found in the presence of the large amount of robot sessions existing out of only one request. Of course this type of sessions can not be detected by methods needing at least two requests to calculate standard deviation and average values. More robots could be discovered by applying higher maximum values for the parameters, but we found that this results in a plummeting reliability, making these methods completely useless.

It is obvious that applying any of the considered methods will result in a large part of the robot sessions remaining undetected or in misclassifying a substantial amount of human users as robots. Notice that the proposed Robot Exclusion Standard results in a very poor detection of only 17% of the robot sessions. The ethical guidelines on the other hand, are also ignored by most of the robots, regarding the low recall values for techniques based on requests during night time and on user agent information. All together, we can conclude that the currently existing techniques are inadequate to execute robot discovery in an accurate fashion.

6 Proposal for a New Robot Discovery Technique

If we want to develop a new method for robot detection, it is essential that it yields a high level of recall and precision at the same time. Thus, our goal is to create one single technique combining the positive effects of both method groups but also excluding their deficiencies.

First of all, the 4 features resulting in a perfect precision will definitely have to be part of the composed method, since they do not damage the final solution in terms of reliability. We combine them into one new technique, which we will be referring to as the 'high precision' method further on. The characteristics are logically combined in such a way that as soon as a session complies with one of the conditions, the session will be labelled as robotic. We know in advance that this technique will yield a 100% precision and the recall value will be at least 69.29% (this is the highest recall of the 4 selected features). When calculating the results, we notice that this method detects 73% of the robots sessions, an increase of only 4% compared to the IP address list method.

Table 2. Evaluation of combined robot discovery methods

	Correct	Wrong	Recall(%)	Precision(%)
Manual Research	241	0	100	100
High Precision (H.P.)	176	0	73.03	100
H.P. or No images	240	77	99.59	75.51
H.P. or Unass. Referrer	236	212	97.93	52.68
H.P. or Unass. Referrer or No Images	241	260	100	48.10
H.P. or (Unass. Referrer and No Images)	235	28	97.51	89.35

In order to achieve a better recognition of robot sessions, we will be obligated to select one of the methods with higher recall values. By adding these less reliable characteristics to our composed technique, we expect our global solution to be penalized in terms of precision. Indeed, the high precision method in combination with the image absence feature delivers an almost perfect detection of 99%, but the precision tumbles to 75%. The same effect can be observed when we apply high precision together with the unassigned referrers characteristic. Recall is improved to almost 98%, while precision drops to 52%, which is even lower than in the previous case. It is remarkable in those two results that precision falls back to a level which more or less corresponds to the individual precision of the added methods. The performance of a combined method seems to be completely determined by the strength of its weakest link. For completeness reasons, we also mention the results of combining all methods in one composed technique, however these results are -as logically expected- even worse than the ones above. If a session is classified as a robot session when it complies with one of the 6 robot features, a recall of 100% and a precision of 48% is obtained.

To upgrade our composed method we will have to look for ways to strengthen the weakest link. Therefore we examine the types of false positives occurring in the individual implementations of the two unreliable methods. On one hand, it can be noticed that 'No images' misjudges sessions of human clients with particular browser settings causing embedded images not to be requested. Incorrect evaluations of 'Unassigned referrer' on the other hand, appear to be short sessions of visitors entering the site by manually typing the site's URL and immediately leaving afterwards. These two types of misclassifications are not correlated, so we may assume that a given session will only coincidentally be misclassified by both methods at the same time. In other words, the cross-section of these two false positives sets will be more or less empty. Considering this observations, it makes perfect sense that by combining methods in the way we did above, the global result of one technique was determined by the weakest link. Remember that the composed methods were based on a logical OR operator: as soon as one of the robot conditions was fulfilled, the session was deemed to be robotic.

In order to exclude all false positives situated outside this cross-section, we now combine the two unreliable methods by means of a logical AND operator before adding them to the High precision technique. The full definition of this technique then becomes:

"Robots.txt OR IP address list OR Robotic user agent OR HEAD method OR (Unassigned referrer AND No images)"

This composed technique should offer the recall power of the methods 'Unassigned referrers' and 'No images' in combination with an acceptable precision. In fact, the practical results showed us a recall value of 97.51% while still guaranteeing a reliability of 89.35%. In comparison to the other composed techniques, this is a stunning improvement, as can be seen in the overview given in Table 2.

7   Conclusion

In this paper, robot discovery as a part of web usage mining was treated and the currently applied techniques for robot detection were discussed. The main part of this paper dealt with the practical evaluation of these methods, which learned us that none of them managed to accurately classify robot sessions. Consequently, we discussed some possible composed techniques in order to obtain better results and proposed the use of a method which succeeds to detect almost every robot session with a reliability reaching up to 90%.

References

1. Srivastava, J., Cooley, R., Deshpande, M., Tan, P.N.: Web usage mining: Discovery and applications of usage patterns from web data. SIGKDD Explorations **1**(2) (2000) 12–23
2. Cooley, R.: Web Usage Mining: Discovery and Application of Interesting Patterns from Web Data. PhD thesis, University of Minnesota (2000)
3. Huysmans, J., Baesens, B., Vanthienen, J.: Web usage mining: a practical study. In: Twelfth Conference on Knowledge Acquisition and Management (KAM 2004). (2004)
4. Perner, P., Fiss, G.: Intelligent e-marketing with web mining, personalization, and user-adapted interfaces. In: Industrial Conference on Data Mining (ICDM02), London, UK, Springer-Verlag (2002) 37–52
5. Blanc, E., Giudici, P.: Sequence rules for web clickstream analysis. In: Industrial Conference on Data Mining (ICDM02), London, UK, Springer-Verlag (2002) 1–14
6. Huysmans, J., Baesens, B., Mues, C., Vanthienen, J.: Web usage mining with time constrained association rules. In: Proceedings of the Sixth International Conference on Enterprise Information Systems (ICEIS 2004), Porto, Portugal (2004) 343–348
7. Heinonen, O., Hatonen, K., Klemettinen, K.: WWW robots and search engines (1996) Seminar on Mobile Code, Report TKO-C79, Helsinki University of Technology, Department of Computer Science.
8. Greenwald, A.R., Kephart, J.O.: Shopbots and pricebots. In: Agent Mediated Electronic Commerce (IJCAI Workshop). (1999) 1–23
9. Almeida, V., Menasce, D.A., Riedi, R.H., Peligrinelli, F., Fonseca, R.C., Jr., W.M.: Analyzing web robots and their impact on caching. In: 6th Web Caching and Content Delivery Workshop. (2001) 299–310

10. Tan, P., Kumar, V.: Discovery of web robot sessions based on their navigational patterns. Data Mining and Knowledge Discovery **6** (2002) 9–35
11. Koster, M.:   The robot exclusion standard (http://www.robotstxt.org/wc/norobots.html) (1994)
12. Eichmann, D.: Ethical Web agents. Computer Networks and ISDN Systems **28**(1–2) (1995) 127–136
13. Koster, M.: The web robots database (http://www.robotstxt.org/wc/active.html) (2004)

Data Preparation of Web Log Files for Marketing Aspects Analyses

Meike Reichle[1], Petra Perner[1], and Klaus-Dieter Althoff[2]

[1] Institute of Computer Vision and Applied Computer Sciences, IBaI, Leipzig
www.ibai-institut.de
[2] University of Hildesheim
www.uni-hildesheim.de

Abstract. This article deals with several aspects of a marketing-oriented analysis of web log files. It discusses their preprocessing and possible ways to enrich the raw data that can be gained from a web log file in order to facilitate a later use in different analyses. Further, we look at the question which requirements a good web log analysis software needs to meet and offer an overview over current and future analysis practices including their advantages and disadvantages.

1 Introduction

Maintaining an online presence offers numerous advantages to an organization or company. The internet offers a relatively cheap and simple way to reach a high number of people, independent of their location or other circumstances, and present them with information, a company's range of products and maybe even the opportunity to buy them online. Such a web presence is advantageous in many aspects: Information needs to be published only once, it is always and easily available; changes are easy to make and come into effect immediately.

There is however more to an online presence than it seems at first glance: a website does not only offer information to the visitor, it also conveys information about the visitors – and thus the company's potential customers – to the company! It should not be forgotten, that the people visiting a company's web pages are the company's clients and clientele and thus any information about them is valuable.

The log files produced by a web server are a useful source of information for this. However, already with middle-rate traffic the log files of a website grow to a size that can no longer be evaluated manually in an acceptable amount of time. Thus a program is needed that can fulfill several tasks in supporting a company's webmaster or marketing personnel with this [1].

In this paper we are focusing on log file data preparation for later analysis. We describe the issues that need to be addressed when preparing a log file in such a way that it can be semantically understood by humans. As a basis for our study we first briefly describe the common log file format in Section 2. Afterwards we review existing freely or commercially available log file analysis tools in Section 3. In conclusion of that we focus on local analysis tools that allow a user to study their logs onsite. The software requirements for these kind of tools are described in Section 4.

P. Perner (Ed.): ICDM 2006, LNAI 4065, pp. 131–145, 2006.

Based on that we develop in Section 5 a system architecture and describe the single components of this architecture exemplarily on samples. Finally, we give an outlook on the analysis of the prepared log file in Section 6. Conclusions about our work are given in Section 7.

2 The Log File

An average web server log consists of one line per executed web server command and is set in the *"(Extended) Combined Log Format"* [2]. It usually looks similar to the example presented in Figure 1.

More data can be included easily, however most ISPs keep more or less to this standard. Additional information could e. g. be the accessed domain or the indication of a proxy.

The single entries are separated by spaces. Multi-word expressions are enclosed in quotes, parentheses or square brackets, other delimiters may occur but are uncommon. An empty entry is usually indicated by a single hyphen.

```
123.45.67.89 - JohnDoe [15/Jan/2005:18:53:37 +0200] "GET /index.html
HTTP/1.1" 200 639 "http://www.google.com/search?q=mydomain+myname"
"Mozilla/5.0 (X11; U; Linux i686; en-US; rv:1.7.12) Gecko/20050919
Firefox/1.0.7"
```

Fig. 1. A log line in Combined Log Format

It includes:

- The **REMOTE HOST'S INTERNET PROTOCOL (IP) ADDRESS:** Each machine connected to the Internet has such an address. It takes the form of four numbers between 0 and 255 separated by dots and identifies each sender or receiver of packets sent across the Internet. In this case the log gives the IP address of the sender, i. e. the address that requested a certain file.

- The **REMOTE LOGIN NAME OF THE USER.** (Usually empty)
- The **AUTH LOGIN.** Set if the page or a file on it is password protected
- The exact **DATE** in a unified format (a.k.a. timestamp). This format can be freely set in the web server's configuration, but most webmasters adhere to the standard presented in the example.
- The **REQUEST.** The exact command that was passed to the web server, stating which file to get and what method to use.
- The **WEB SERVER'S RETURN CODE.** This code indicates whether the request could be carried out successfully. The most common return codes are 200 (OK), 403 (Forbidden) and 404 (Not found).
- The **SIZE OF THE RETURNED FILE** in Bytes
- The **REFERRER** that indicates the website the user came from when requesting this file (not always detectable)
- The **USER AGENT,** usually the browser program or if the visitor it not human a designation of the respective robot or crawler.

Although this standard looks well organized it must be understood, that a web log is a pretty unstructured source of information. The format presented above is merely a recommendation and any webmaster is free to change it according to his or her needs. The given values, their order and formatting can be changed freely and there are only few common standards such as the space as first separator or a hyphen as general place holder for missing values.

Web design and web technologies are ever-changing and these changes will be directly reflected in the web server's log. It is thus important to keep the structure of the program as flexible as possible. The log file has to be considered as a very dynamic source of information in respect to the structure of the data and the content and this has to be taken into account when developing a flexible log file preparation tool and not a special purpose data preparation tool.

3 Related Work

When looking at the current range of web log analysis tools, their supply can be broken down into three different groups: Free web statistics by ISPs, remote analysis services and local software.

When evaluating them we need to consider the difference between a sales oriented website and a site that merely offers information. For a web shop, success can simply be measured in sales. A site that "only" offers information has more complex requirements: A successful page visit does not necessarily end in a purchase or anything else that can be directly measured using the web server logs. For such sites the quality criteria are more fuzzy: How many people visit the site? What do they look at? Where is it linked or referenced? How often are the owners approached on contents within the page and by whom? How quickly do changes or new information get noticed? Also, the line between use and misuse is thin, an informational site wants to be referenced, it does not want its content to be copied or even hot-linked. Thus a thorough analysis of referrers, in this case especially when considering image files or text documents is needed. A simple per page analysis would leave such things unnoticed.

The first group that we looked at, are free web statistics offered by most ISPs for their website hosting customers. These are the most basic analyses. They give a rough overview over the number of requests and some statistics, but lack usability and flexibility. Analyses are presented as-is and the user has no control over what is analyzed and how. Such an analysis can give a quick overview over a page's traffic, it is of no use though for a more thorough analysis or an application in CRM (customer relationship management).

The second group are host based services. These services don't analyze the log files produced by the respective web server. Instead they use a different approach where the webmaster adds to each page that shall be analyzed a remotely hosted element (usually a picture or a java script call). Thus every time the page is requested, the element is requested as well and a log entry is added to the remote service's log. This offers a lot of advantages to the service provider: There is no need to deal with changing log formats, since they only have to parse their own log files, the parsing can be done locally, in real time and on a server rather than a personal computer.

There is but one problem: The company exposes exact and detailed information about it's web presence usage – and thus customers – to another party. Moreover, all analyses can be accessed over the web (usually via a simple username/password authentication) and are thus in the potential danger of being hacked. Many companies may not be willing to take that risk.

This leads us to the third group: Local log file analysis tools. A broad range of analyses is offered by NetLog, made by IBaI Solutions [3]. The program offers access to a whole number of analyses and views accompanied by the according charts. Another possibility is an integrated solution based on the products by Microsoft[4]. They offer a statistical analysis that is based on OLAP and analysis components in their SQL and Commerce Server Products. However, the exemplary statistical analyses we could see showed that they do not process the log file in such a way that more intelligent analyses are possible besides the statistical ones. Other professional solutions are offered by ClickTracks [5], WebTrends [6] and LiveSTATS by DeepMetrix [7]. These programs also incorporate page content modeling (defining the "role" of a site) and customer relationship management (CRM) elements. Their program design mostly aims specifically at web shops and is capable of e. g. recognizing an addition to the shopping basket or a successful purchase. With this information they can distinguish successful from unsuccessful visitor sessions or recognize buying patterns, which, e. g. connected with the entry referrer, allows conclusions as to the effectiveness of a certain ad, or of being referenced on a certain website or portal. Provided with the costs of different ads they can even calculate their ROI (return on investment) based on the actual purchases that resulted from them. An additional feature that can be found in all of them are tied-in CRM tools that can e. g. associate email addresses with visitors using tagged referrers within email campaigns.

These programs offer not only lots of additional eye candy, but also more sophisticated filtering and a large number of criteria that visitors and sessions can be sorted by. As to the actual analysis, all of these programs have a two-fold approach: They offer their analyses either as a client based piece of software, or as a hosted service (as described above). Also, although they do offer the import of raw log files, all of these programs prefer the afore mentioned approach of including a tracking script in each website, that is then either remotely or locally evaluated. This offers numerous advantages, as it again spares having to deal with changing log file formats, funny values, filtering of frames and other nuisances traditional log file analysis brings with it (see further sections). Also, sometimes there is no other choice than to use a remote element for web analyses. For example when a reverse proxy is used that accepts all outside requests and hands them to the respective services. This is a common practice among larger sites in order to deal with load balancing, on-site firewalls and other security measures. In these cases however, the requesting IP is always the IP of the reverse proxy. Here a remote element is one way to get to the actual requesting IP. However, there's also disadvantages to this approach: Firstly it means a lot of initial extra work for the webmaster: The tracking script call has to be inserted into every single page of the web presence. Depending on the number and structure of pages, this can be a wearisome task. In addition an analysis based solely on tracking scripts will only work from the day the scripts were inserted. Months or even years worth of collected logs would remain unused, a considerable waste of information resources. Also, though evaluating the information gathered by a tracking script is much more comfortable, web server logs are still the most detailed source of information available. Their seeming disadvantage is also their biggest advantage: They list everything! This produces a considerable overhead, but also offers the possibility to retrieve information from old logs that maybe didn't seem interesting (and thus wasn't included in the tracking scripts) then, but is in a later point in time. Also the presented professional programs are mostly tailored for web shops and can only partially fulfill the described needs of information-centered web sites, as mentioned in the beginning of this section.

Finally there is one thing, that none of the presented programs offers: All of them can only group sessions by either pre- or user-defined criteria or patterns. A valuable additional source of information would be to see what new correlations or groups can be found. This needs more intelligent analysis methods such as clustering for discovery of groups of users [8] [9], structural analysis for common path recognition or for finding sequence rules in web log files [10].

4 Software Requirements

Web logs offer a great wealth of information, they are however poorly structured. Thus, software that aims to allow it's user to work in a reasonable way with the information they include needs to fulfill certain requirements:

- It needs to be able to handle the dynamic nature of the structure and of the content (semantic) of the data without doing any programming changes.
- It needs to present the information included in the log file in a clear and concise manner, excluding unnecessary information, presenting the remaining data in a clearly semantically understandable way.
- It also needs to offer several different views on the data, depending on what the interest of the user is. Be it the source of a page's visits, which pages attract most attention or how well the pages are covered by search engines and listing services.
- The software needs to support a quick overview just as well as an in-depth investigation. Therefore, the analysis should work on a single or several data base fields as well as on single or consecutive data base entries.
- Since we are dealing with a temporal medium comprised of web server requests in temporal sequence we also have to determine a user session from our raw data. This session represents one single, continuous visit of a person (or robot).
- It needs to extract all additional information that can be gained from the log data and allow their free combination.
- It should allow detecting and filtering out pre-defined patterns in the log file data such as robot accesses to the website.

Generally speaking, it needs to assist the user in drawing conclusions from the data, either by doing that itself or by providing according hints.

5 System Overview

To fulfill the software requirements described in Section 4 a series of steps needs to be carried out in order to get from the original log file to a usable database [11] (see Fig. 2). These steps are (1) Data Preparation, (2) Data Extension, (3) Data Conversion & Extension (4) Data Parsing, and (5) Session Recognition.

The software should be as flexible as possible. Therefore the structure of our tool is similar to a knowledge-based system comprised of an inference engine and a knowledge base [12]. Everything that is flexible or can change over time is represented by facts in the knowledge base. This knowledge base can be edited by a human or can be obtained by extracting facts from the log file and importing them as a text file into the knowledge base. Another feature of the software is an automated look-up of the DNS information from the DNS server to ensure the identification of the visitor by his hostname or DNS entry. In order to work on the log data with reasonable performance the existing text file is first converted into a local database file. A log file is more or less a raw data file where every single line of text represents a future data set and every separated value goes into another column. Once the initial database is filled, further data processing is performed in order to bring the data in a convenient format.

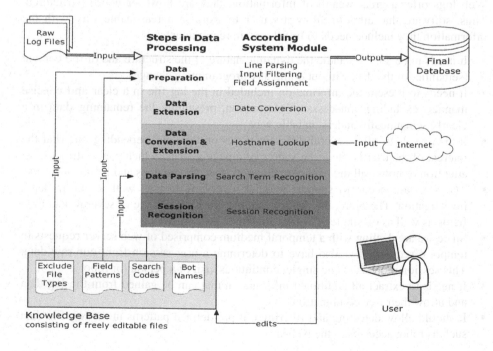

Fig. 2. An Overview over the individual Steps in Data Processing

One of these steps is data parsing where semantically irrelevant data are removed from the data strings in order to get human readable information out of encoded strings, such as the referrer. Date strings are converted to timestamp data types, numeric values (such as IP addresses) are supplemented with symbolic information (in this case the according hostname). This step is referred to as data conversion. Other DNS information leads to data extension since they bring out more information about a visitor such as the company name or the country name. In a last step the data sets are split up into sessions and each session is assigned a unique session ID. After this last step, we have generated a final database that contains all explicit and implicit information that can be gained from the log file. Over this data base we can perform our data analysis.

We would like to point out here that the performance of the software is an important issue that already needs to be considered during the software design phase, otherwise the data preparation step takes too much computation time. Reading values from the database and parsing them or performing a database lookup does not take too much time. However, writing them back takes time. Every new value can only be inserted in the fitting places so with every insertion goes a full database search. Therefore, multithreading techniques should be used and the data base design should be made accordingly. However, since parts of these results depend on each other (e. g. session IDs can only be assigned once the dates have been parsed) this can only be used in some aspects. Thus other sophisticated procedures need to be included. Looking up each individual hostname can cause some delay, especially when an IP cannot be resolved by the "whois" command and it times out. This problem can at least partially be solved by implementing a caching function.

5.1 Creation of the Initial Database

5.1.1 The Database

For reasons of simplicity and portability we are using an embedded database management system, rather than a client server based approach. However, since all database communication is done using simple SQL, interaction with any other database management system is possible too, provided the according driver is included in the program. Storing the data in a SQL database also allows the capable user to not only use the predefined queries in the program, but also freely query the database him-/herself to get whatever information is desired. Doing a direct SQL query, the search can e. g. be reduced to a specific time segment, or limited to datasets matching a certain criterion (e. g. all visitors from a particular country, all accesses of a particular page, or all users who visited more than 5 different pages.). There is literally no limitation to what you can do with the database using SQL. Also data mining methods can work on SQL [13] [14].

5.1.2 Line Parsing and Database Insertion

The creation of the database itself is done by simply parsing line by line of the log file and writing each value into the database. Likewise in any data mining problem we also have to face the problem of missing or unknown data values while parsing the data.

Missing data are data that are not in the log file such as the language of the user agent that is not always indicated.

We consider the unknown data problem as the problem where we cannot parse the data since the parsers has no parsing rules for it. It is clear that this system state cannot remain as it is during the lifetime of system. Therefore our system has the possibility to detect this novel situation and go into a knowledge engineering phase by allowing the user to manually insert the missing parsing rules into the knowledge base.

Thus, the first task that needs to be undertaken is to break each line into its respective elements. The number of these elements is the same in every line, since missing values are replaced by a place holder (usually a hyphen).

In order to distinguish the individual elements during the parsing, we first need to identify the different separators: The default separator is a single space, if an element contains spaces itself, it needs to be enclosed by an additional type of delimiter (see Fig. 3), this can be squared brackets, single or double quotes. Simple parentheses or curly braces are less common but should be considered as well. When doing this, a common mistake is to fall for delimiters within elements, such as within the last element in Fig 3. An element always ends with the delimiter it started with – plus a space.

```
foo bar "a multi word item" baz [there are many different delimiters]
'and yet another item, with "funny" 'stuff'
```

Fig. 3. Different Delimiters

It should also be considered that delimiters that do not break parsing can still cause trouble when feeding the respective string into the database. Especially mixtures or repetitions of quotes and double quotes within a string can interfere with the insertion of that string into the database. Most programming languages offer a quoted string function that can take care of some of these problems. They cannot take care of them all though, and also log data should not be altered too easily since e. g. a referrer url can get useless when exchanging special characters. In these cases a careful choice has to be made between program stability and data integrity.

In order to maintain a database that completely reflects the log file we would now have to stop reading the data, output some kind of error message as to why that log file could not be read and stop the program. However, for the sake of user friendliness and considering that the degree of "data corruption" will most likely remain well below the usually acceptable 5% error rate we simply insert a dummy value for missing values. This ensures that neither session nor path recognition gets broken.

An additional option might be to include some unique key into the replacement string and write both, the key plus the original line into an external file, allowing the user to still look up the full log entry if he/she wishes.

5.1.3 Input Filtering

Already when we are reading in the original log file a first filtering function must be applied in order to reduce the amount of redundant data within the database. For set-up of such a filter we first have to understand the conceptual model of the web site and the user needs for the analysis. It is a difference whether images are pure decorational elements or the main information like in an on-line image gallery.

Log files can easily have tens of thousands of lines and not every line has the desired informational value. Generally speaking, a line is appended to the web server log for every single command the web server carries out whether it sends an html file, images or a css file, containing styling information.

Not all of these actions are of interest to us though. What we most likely want to see is the user's navigation over the different pages. Styling or decorative elements are – under the aspect of a marketing oriented analysis – of only limited informational value. If a visitor accesses a page that has a background image and buttons underlayed with two different bitmaps, this will result in four lines in the log file: one for the actual html file, one for the background image, one for each bitmap, since these are of course also files that have to be retrieved by the web server. These four log entries will however always appear together, since the images will (in most cases) only be requested when a visitor accesses the html page that references them. The three image requests thus add no informational value and need not be included in the database.

Due to this a first input filter can be applied here that controls, which log lines do get included in the database and which are left out all together. This can for example be done by providing a configuration file that lists file extensions that shall be excluded from the database. Typically this file would include image file extensions such as jpg, gif or png, or files that are concerned with scripts or formatting, such as java script or css. In order to adhere to the afore mentioned flexibility it is important to not hard-code these into the actual source code but export them to a freely editable configuration file. Providing this, new additions can be made anytime (e. g. when a site is switched to css) or entries can be taken out.

5.1.4 Field Name Assignment

Once all desired log entries have been inserted into the database, one last problem remains to be solved: As mentioned above there is a common standard for log file formatting, however, no ISP has to stick to it and it is easy to change the log format within a web server application. Thus we can make no assumptions as to which database column represents which value. There are two approaches to dealing with this problem: One would be to adjust the program to the log file format, either by another configuration file or by presenting the user with one or a collection of sample lines, asking him/her to give each entry the according designation. This approach however depends on the quality of the sample line(s) and the user's knowledge on the matter. A second possibility would be an automated approach: Here the program's settings are not changed, instead it tries to guess the according fields itself e. g. using textual pattern recognition. This would be no problem with entries like the IP or the web server command. The recognition however becomes less trivial when it comes to distinguishing e. g. return code from byte size or classifying entries that are arbitrary, like a user's login. Also such a mechanism would have to be provided with all possible fields plus a description of their pattern and could thus not adapt to new database fields. Thus, we would suggest a user-based approach.

5.1.5 Data Extension and Conversion

Once initial data preparation is finished and an initial database has been created, the database is worked over several times in order to include additional information that can be gained from the log file information itself. Firstly the dates that are available only as simple strings (see Figure 4) are converted from a string into a date data type (e. g. DateTime or Timestamp) in order to facilitate working with them in the following process.

```
[15/Sep/2005:08:35:37 +0200]
```

Fig. 4. A typical Time String

Once the database has proper date types, queries like "before", "after" or "between" can easily be carried out on these fields without any need for tedious string parsing.

Additionally every IP is looked up using functions provided by the respective programming language. Often the hostname already tells us what institution or company the visitor came from. If the information is insufficient or a hostname is unavailable a full DSN query can be done. An IP's DNS record can provide much useful information on the owner of an IP, such as the country, a contact address and a description of the institution.

This works of course only if the visitor or his/her company or organization have an IP address of their own. Otherwise the DNS record will show the data of the visitor's internet service provider. This can still be helpful though, since it may be assumed that most people have an ISP within their own country.

5.2 Data Parsing

Another source of information are search machine referrers, since they indicate the search terms with which the webpage was found and sometimes also the position in the search machine's page ranking. It may also be of interest which search machine is most frequently used or what internet portal is most popular with the company's clientele. However, the referrer that includes this information will be rather cryptic. Figure 5 shows three different search engine referrers searching for the same key words from the same browser and the same machine, though they vary considerably since every search engine has it's own way of encoding search queries.

```
http://www.google.com/search?q=ibai+institut&sourceid=mozilla-
search&start=0&start=0&ie=utf-8&oe=utf-8&client=firefox-
a&rls=org.mozilla:de-DE:official

http://suche.web.de/search/web/?mc=hp%40suche.suche%40home&su=ibai+in
stitut&webRb=de

http://search.lycos.com/default.asp?loc=searchbox&tab=web&query=ibai+
institut&submit.x=0&submit.y=0&submit=image
```

Fig. 5. Different Search Engine Referrers

The program now needs to be able to e. g. extract the search terms from every of these referrers, and again, there is no guarantee that a search engine will not change it's encoding or a new one will come up. This problem is solved by again outsourcing the descriptors that indicate the actual search terms (in this case "q=", "su=" and "query=") into an external file, so that new descriptors can be included and existing ones changed. To further illustrate this, we will demonstrate the exact parsing process in detail with the first referrer.

The full version is:

```
http://www.google.com/search?q=ibai+institut&sourceid=mozilla-
search&start=0&start=0&ie=utf-8&oe=utf-8&client=firefox-
a&rls=org.mozilla:de-DE:official
```

We perform a search over it with the search word descriptors we know and cut it from there, which leaves us with:

```
q=ibai+institut&sourceid=mozilla-search&start=0&start=0&ie=utf-
8&oe=utf-8&client=firefox-a&rls=org.mozilla:de-DE:official
```

We also know that the ampersand ("&") is in pretty much every encoding used to append the different elements of a query. Thus we also make a cut before the first ampersand:

```
q=ibai+institute
```

With this cut-out we have almost reached our target. Now all we have to do is to remove the search word descriptor and use a url decoding function on the remaining text. Url decoding [15] is used to encode special characters within urls. (Unfortunately not every site uses them as they should, otherwise a lot of the above mentioned parsing problems wouldn't exist. However we may assume that at least all reasonable search machines use url encoding for their search expressions.) A few examples for url encoding can be seen in Figure 6.

Search term encoded	Search term decoded
ibai+institute	ibai institut
%22ibai+institut%22	"ibai institut"
ibai%2Binstitut	ibai+institut
%27ibai+institut%27	'ibai institut'

Fig. 6. A few Examples on URL Encoding

Once the url decoding is successfully finished, the original search terms are extracted from the search machine's referrer and can be presented to the user, statistically analyzed etc.

Of course extracting the search terms isn't the only information that can be gained from a search engine's referrer. Providing some more previous knowledge on the structure of a certain search machine's queries we can also extract additional information such as the browser language or a page's position within the search engine's page ranking system. This information shows another possibility of data extension but is however not provided by every search machine and should hence not be generally expected.

5.3 Session Recognition

Once all above mentioned steps are carried out, every data set is assigned a session ID (SID). A session is understood as a single visitor's contiguous path over the different pages. Thus we define a session as a set of log entries where every entry has the same origin IP address, and the time interval between two consecutive entries is never above twenty minutes.

6 Views and Analyses

Up until now we have realized two different kind of web log data analyses: statistical analyses and views.

The statistical analyses don't present the log data themselves but meta information about them, such as the number of entries, the number of pages, the number of unique or recurring visitors, average length of stay or the amount of generated traffic. Another common task are rankings: The most popular referrer, hostname, search terms or, in a multi domain log, the most popular domain. Any database field can be ranked like this, though it of course doesn't make sense for all of them. This data representation is most suited to give a quick overview on the general numbers and popularity of a specific website or an entire web presence.

Views present the actual log content but in a more tailored fashion. This can mean rearranging individual columns, filtering or grouping the data. An example for filtering would be excluding automated page hits from entities like crawlers, bots or other information harvesting scripts. The more up-to-date a search engine wants to be, the more crawlers it needs to send out. This can cause a considerable impact on your website's log. You also might want to exclude your own page accesses. Many companies maintain the practice to set their own site as every web browser's starting page. That is okay as long as it points to a local copy or the intranet. Setting it to the company's internet address tends to tamper website statistics, hit counters and other statistical analyses. An example for grouping data would be a session view. Here, instead or presenting every single dataset, the log entries are combined to sessions, which can then again be compared, evaluated or sorted by all desired criteria.

7 Analysis Obstacles

A data analysis like the one presented in this paper offers high informational value to the owner of a web presence. It is not trouble-free though. During the first testing phase we noticed several factors that can tamper or complicate a proper site analysis.

A first obstacle is the use of frames. This means that a site does not consist of only one html document, as it usually is, but it consist of several frames, that each contains an html document. Typically there may be one frame containing the menu, another one for the title or footer and a third one that holds the actual content. Thus, when entering a site the server has to send three html documents for the user to see a (seemingly) single page.

Frames should generally no longer be employed for a number of reasons: First of all they tend to cause confusion to the user himself because they appear as one single site, though they are not. This can cause problems with a number of things like printing (many browsers put one frame per page.), bookmarking (the bookmarked page will be a different one depending where the focus is at the time of the bookmark's creation) or interaction with other software like screen readers or hardware like a Braille terminal. Also navigation can be made difficult because the functioning of the "forward" and "back" buttons is affected by frames as well. Badly implemented "nesting" frames can even render a page completely useless. These navigation problems also affect crawlers that try to index the site for a search machine. Also, there are also still browsers around, that don't support frames. All this has led to a dislike of frames among the wider internet "population". They are today regarded bad style and "old hat".

Additionally to all this they also complicate a proper path analysis since there is no way to tell whether a given frame offers content, navigational elements or pure decoration, say, a fancy title. So instead of a clear path like this:

```
index -> products -> product1 -> contact -> email_form
```

you might end up with a path like this one:

```
menu -> top -> index -> menu -> top -> products -> product_footer ->
menu -> top -> product1 -> product_footer -> menu -> top -> contact -
> menu -> top -> email_form
```

Thus, used on a page structure that employs frames the software would have to be adapted individually to each frame that is used and does not contain path-relevant content.

Another problem, not for the path analysis but for it's use by a human, are content management systems (CMS) and their automatically generated page names, that leave you with a path like

```
1/1 -> 16/7 -> 16/12 -> 8/1 -> 2/4
```

Here the generated path is valid but does not allow any conclusion as to the site's actual content. There are several ways for solving this, such as configuring the content management system to use descriptive page names or mapping the individual page names to a more meaningful "translation" within the program.

A last factor that should be considered are people who deliberately hide their identity when online, be it for privacy reasons or on a certain purpose. Measures like e. g. using an anonymizing HTTP proxy or forging a browser's user-agent signature can effectively hide a user's identity from web server logs. Other measures like setting cookies or using java scripts to track a visitor can also be evaded easily. It should also be kept in mind, that tracking techniques, when used too aggressively, can also have a deterring effect since nobody likes to by "spied" upon. It needs to be decided individually which tracking techniques are adequate and what conclusions can be drawn from the number of visitors evading them.

8 Conclusion and Outlook

Our objective is, to find a way to present the vast but incomprehensible data that are provided by a web server's log file in a clear and concise way, but without reducing it's informational value or making any kind of data inaccessible. In order to achieve this, the interface was designed to be simple and flexible because a one-size-fits-all approach is not feasible in this application. There can be only little prediction as to a user's intention. He or she might just want to get a quick overview or – in the opposite – trace a specific user's behavior, thus a good log analysis software needs to meet all these requirements.

We have described our work on web server log data preparation. Our intension was to develop a flexible software tool that meets the requirements posed by the dynamic nature in structure and content of a web log file. Therefore we developed an architecture for the system that is similar to a knowledge-based system comprised of a inference engine and a knowledge base. The knowledge base contains information about the parsing criteria and the set up of the filters. These information can be easily changed or up-dated by hand or semi-automatically. We have also point out the special software development requirements to ensure acceptable run-time performance. The missing and unknown data problem was described and method to handle that for log file data. Finally, we presented our first analysis methods. Further work will be done to develop more intelligent analysis methods such as user profiling, path analysis and association mining.

References

1. P. Perner and G. Fiss, Intelligent E-marketing with Web Mining, Personalization, and User-Adpated Interfaces, In: P. Perner (Ed.) Advances in Data Mining, Applications in E-Commerce, Medicine, and Knowledge Management, lnai 2394, Springer Verlag 2003, p. 37 – 52.
2. Apache HTTP Server Documentation Project: Combined Log Format. http://httpd. apache.org/docs/1.3/logs.html#combined (accessed Jan 23rd 2006)
3. P. Perner, Einrichtung zur automatischen Ermittlung der Nutzung von Web-Präsentationen und/oder On-line Verkaufsmodellen, Patent D 198 01 400.7-08
4. Microsoft SQL Server Analysis Services http://www.microsoft.com/sql/technologies/ analysis/default.mspx
5. Clicktracks Software http://www.clicktracks.com/
6. Webtrends Software http://www.webtrends.com
7. Deepmetrix Software http://www.deepmetrix.com
8. Scherbina and S. Kuznetsov, Clustering of Web Session Using Levenshtein Metric, In: P. Perner (Ed.), Advance in Data Mining, Applications in Image Minnig, Medicine and Biotechnology, Management, Environmental Control, and Telecommunications, lnai 3275, Springer Verlag 2004, p. 127-133.
9. M. Halvey, M.T. Keane, and B. Smyth, Birds of a Feather Surf Together: Using Clustering Methods to Improve Navigation Prediction from Internet Log Files, In: P. Perner and A. Imiya (Eds.) Machine Learning and Data Mining in Pattern Recognition, lnai 3587, Springer Verlag 2005, p. 174-183

10. E. Blanc and P. Giudici, Sequence Rules for Web Clickstream Analysis, In: P. Perner (Ed.) Advances in Data Mining, Applications in E-Commerce, Medicine, and Knowledge Management, Springer Verlag, lnai 2394 , 2002 p. 1-14
11. Ahlemeyer-Stubbe, Analyseorientierte Informationssysteme = Data Warehouse, In: P. Perner (Ed.) Data Mining, Data Warehouse, and Knowledge Management, Proc. Industrial Conference on Data Mining ICDM, IBaI-Report 2001, ISSN 1431–2360, p. 30-39
12. J. Rech and K.-D. Althoff, Artificial Intelligence and Software Engineering - Status and Future Trends, Special Issue on Artificial Intelligence and Software Engineering, Zeitschrift Künstliche Intelligenz (3)2004, p. 5-11
13. R. Meo, P. Luca Lanzi, M. Klemettinen (Eds.), Database Support for Data Mining Applications: Discovering Knowledge with Inductive Queries, Springer Verlag 2004, lnai 2682
14. R. Meersman, K. Aberer, Th. Dillon (Eds.), Semantic Issues in e-Commerce Systems, Vol. 111, 2003
15. W3 Schools: HTML URL-encoding Reference. http://www.w3schools.com/tags/ref_urlencode.asp (accessed Jan 23rd 2006)

UP-DRES
User Profiling for a Dynamic REcommendation System

Enza Messina[1], Daniele Toscani[1,2], and Francesco Archetti[1,2]

[1] DISCO, Università degli Studi di Milano Bicocca,
Via Bicocca degli Arcimboldi, 8
20126 Milano, Italy
messina@disco.unimib.it
[2] Consorzio Milano Ricerche, Via Cicognara 7,
20129 Milano, Italy
{archetti, toscani}@milanoricerche.it

Abstract. The WWW is actually the most dynamic and attractive information exchange place. Finding useful information is hard due to huge data amount, varied topics and unstructured contents. In this paper we present a web browsing support system that proposes personalized contents. It is integrated in the content management system and it runs on the server hosting the site. It processes periodically site contents, extracting vectors of the most significant words. A topology tree is defined applying hierarchical clustering. During online browsing, viewed contents are processed and mapped in the vector space previously defined. The centroid of these vectors is compared with the topology tree nodes' centroids to find the most similar; its contents are presented to the user as link suggestions or dynamically created pages. Personal profile is saved after every session and included in the analysis during same user's subsequent visits, avoiding the cold start problem.

1 Introduction

Today's world is sometimes called "the information society", to point out the growing importance that information is assuming. It is easy for everyone to consult knowledge sources and to publish them. Automatic systems help in this process, but they also generate a huge amount of monitoring and derived data. The practical effect is that, at a certain stage, people will be confronted with more information than they can effectively process: this situation is known as information overload [4] [17]. This means that part of that information will be ignored, forgotten, distorted or otherwise lost. The web is the most evolving media and reflects these trends: finding information on it is becoming more and more difficult and time consuming.

Users want to find "useful" and "interesting" contents during the navigation; on the other hand, portal administrators of e-commerce and services sites want to attract visitors. Every person perceives the definition of "useful" and "interesting" in a different way: this is the reason why systems that provide personalized suggestions based on user preferences, a.k.a. recommendation systems, are required. In [37] we find the description of an architecture to improve e-commerce web sites functionalities, allowing platform adaptation to user's needs. Data about user's behaviour can be

P. Perner (Ed.): ICDM 2006, LNAI 4065, pp. 146–160, 2006.
© Springer-Verlag Berlin Heidelberg 2006

collected automatically but are needed web profiling techniques that will use these data to infer customer's characteristics.

In order to derive models for representing web users and identifying their interests three different approaches may be found in the literature: collaborative filtering, content-based analysis, browsing behaviour modelling; this classification depends on the basis of the data source used.

People interacting with collaborative filtering based systems have to actively express an interest, rating the contents they are viewing. This allows the system to give "friendly suggestions" (filter) based on the opinions of others users of the same service (from this the term "collaborative"). In [12], for example, the authors proposed an email filter which asks a small group of users to formulate queries in a special language, in order to determine the email usefulness.

Other collaborative filtering systems have been proposed in [18] and [25]. Even in these cases, an active and explicit participation from the user community is required: each user has to rate the content of Usenet news articles. A form of automation is introduced here by applying a k-nearest neighbour algorithm to find groups with similar interests.

In [24] rating weights are defined to be proportional to the time spent viewing a page. In [31] the Usenet news posting are used to rate the liking of web sites, creating a list of the top endorsed sites.

In a recent work of Sugiyama [30] user's profiles are derived from the choices made after a query submission to a search engine and from the contents of the pages selected from the query results. A modified collaborative filtering is then applied to a user-term matrix (instead of user-item matrix in classic collaborative filtering). Users' term vectors are then clusterized to find homogeneous communities.

Content based recommendation systems build a model of the web pages contents and compare them with the contents which are of interest for the user. Collaborative filtering is here implicit, in the sense that user's choices are helpful to state the relevance of similar items. The main techniques applied in this field can be grouped in clustering [3] [6], bayesian networks [6] and rule-based systems [27].

A content based approach to learn human interests automatically through a divisive hierarchical clustering algorithm has been proposed in [16]. Each page can be assigned to one or more nodes in the hierarchy, which is used for learning and predicting interests: the root is the user's general long-term interest and leaves represent short-term specific domains.

In [28] information coming from multiple information resources is aggregated in order to create a recommendation list as reply to queries in which different query elements can be assigned by the user.

An interesting application can be found in [13] where a system which presents links of interest in a box integrated into the Internet Explorer browser is presented. Here an ontology is built by clustering vectors of words extracted from web pages. In [23] the computer science ontology described in [22] is used for bootstrapping the current user's interests, in order to overcome the "cold start" problem arising when the user is unknown to the system. Documents viewed by the user are associated to a topic by using a variant of the nearest neighbour algorithm. Collaborative filtering is then performed on a user-topic matrix.

In another system the content based approach is combined with collaborative filtering [1]. It ranks web pages through a topic filter and this information is reinforced by the user's feedbacks.

Content personalized web pages present different information to different users and diverge from link personalization, which only adapts the link anchor structure and leaves unmodified the substantial information part. Early studies in [5] present the idea of a newspaper that allows for interactive personalization. In My Yahoo! [21] user's preferences are collected from explicit indication or semi-automated inference from navigation activity, asking the user to choose from general areas to more specific topics.

The browsing behaviour modelling approach analyzes the interactions between the user and the web. In [36] are presented some methodologies for the click stream analysis based on association rules and expert systems. Here the data mining conclusions drawn on the basis of the association rules, which are local models, are compared with the global probabilistic expert system model to find which better represents frequent navigation patterns. Like in [35] web-server logs are used as data source to track user's browsing pattern into web sites. These logs, that are collected automatically from web server applications, provide information about activities performed by a user from the moment he/she enters a web site to the moment he/she leaves it [8], including time spent viewing a page, and allow us to separate browsing sessions.

Sessions' clustering is useful to discover both groups of users, exhibiting similar browsing patterns, and groups of pages, with related contents (pages are clusterized on the basis of how often they appear together across navigation patterns). Algorithms for sessions clustering can be classified into two approaches: similarity-based and model-based (or probabilistic) [7].

Compared to similarity-based methods, which assign user to a cluster only on the basis of a given session similarity measure, model-based methods offer better interpretability: each model directly characterizes the corresponding cluster. Model-based clustering techniques have been widely used and have shown promising results in many applications involving web data [2] [33]. More specifically, in the model based approach the users' sessions clusters are generated as follows:

1. A user arrives at the web site in a particular time and is assigned to a cluster with some probability. The number of clusters is determined by using several probabilistic methods, such as BIC (Bayesian Information Criterion), bayesian approximations, or bootstrap methods [11].
2. The behaviour of each cluster is governed by a statistical model and the user's behaviour is generated from this model.

Each cluster has a data-generating model with different components. Clusters are defined by learning the parameters of one or more (in the case of a mixture) probability distribution function, used to assign people to the various clusters, and the number of components. The number of components of the model can be determined by model selection techniques and parameters can be estimated using maximum likelihood algorithms, e.g. the EM (Expectation-Maximization) [9].

Other approaches that don't need user's active participation to the model creation are WebWatcher [14] and Letizia [19] [20], which extract information on users from their browsing behaviour. Some critics can be moved to the fact that they propose a persistent model and don't care about user's interest changes. For a complete review of the system based on implicit user participation see [15].

In this paper we propose a web profiling system particularly suitable for improving the services offered by dynamic web sites, whose contents are composed from a repository of documents related to different arguments. It combines the content based analysis with browsing behaviour modelling, in the sense that we follow the users during their visits and, on the basis of the contents that they are viewing, we identify their behaviour and consequently their interests.

Sometimes people have to answer many questions about preferences or demographic data when they register to a web site. Profiles created in this way are generally static and have to be kept updated under the responsibility of the user. However, only few of them are willing to spend time doing seemingly useless operations, also if this will ensure a better personalization. The results are incomplete, unreliable profiles.

The proposed approach does not require human interaction, because it extracts information about user preferences from the contents of the visited web pages. Another advantage of our system is that, being integrated in the content management application, it operates online, collecting the requests made by user without the need of web server logs data. In fact, log files ideally represent a good source of data to infer the browsing behaviour but practically, as stated in [2][33], they have to be cleaned and processed to reconstruct the users' navigation sessions; this process can be very hard and sometimes impossible, due to technical reasons concerned mainly with privacy and security procedures that hide personal data. In addition, today the world wide web is migrating towards a dynamic structure, in which pages are not published in simple HTML format, but contains executable code and dynamic access to resources, and logs are losing the traditional function of "lists of requested web pages", to become "records of content management applications status", from which it is difficult to obtain useful information.

The rest of the paper is organized as follows: the general architecture of the system is described in Section 2, where we introduce all of its modules: Content Extractor, responsible to manage documents and convert them in a machine-tractable form, Taxonomy Builder, that creates a document hierarchy based on topics, Recommendation Manager, which creates Short and Long Term Profiles of users, on the basis of contents that they view. In sections 3 to 5 are given detailed descriptions of each of these modules. Finally, in Section 6 we present our conclusions and future work directions.

2 The Proposed System

In this section we present a synthesis of the architecture of the system that allows us to profile web users dynamically, in order to help them during the navigation process. In Fig. 1 we show the system's main modules: Content Extractor, Taxonomy Builder and Recommendation Manager. The activation of these modules and the data exchanges between them are governed by the super-module UP-DRES, which acts as a supervisor.

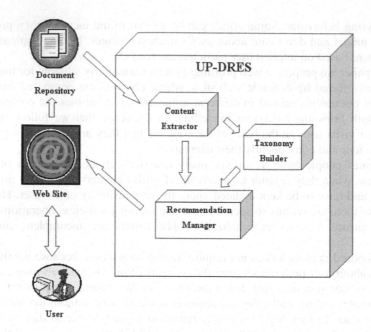

Fig. 1. Overview of the system

Some external elements take part in UP-DRES functioning. The Document Repository contains all the textual elements that can be used to compose the Web Site pages. The application that manages the Web Site is able to intercept the User's request and send them to the Document Repository, in order to select the documents to introduce to the UP-DRES system for the classification process.

The system, through the Recommendation Manager module, combines the user's Short Term Profile (STP), obtained by analysing the user behaviour during the current session, with a Long Term Profile (LTP) built as a weighted sum of the previously constructed user's STPs.

Typical web pages are composed of text, images, multimedia contents and applications stored in a file system area called Document Repository.

Profiles are obtained by considering the contents of the pages visited by the user. They are used by the Recommendation Manager Module to decide, through a maximization matching procedure, which information to present next on the web site by choosing it from the currently available Document Repository.

Contents shown on the web page should therefore automatically capture the visitor's preferences by using as indicator of interest the choices made by the user by clicking on a given page and the time spent visiting such page.

The system runs on the server side, as a process integrated in the content management system which manages the web pages publication.

In order to maximize the matching between the user's preferences expressed during the navigation pattern and the information currently available in the Document Repository, the Content Extractor browses periodically (off-line) the Document Repository to take "snapshots" of the web site contents and it builds a matrix, which is its vector space representation, as described in Section 3. This matrix is then used as input by the Taxonomy Builder module to generate the Web Site Taxonomy, as explained in Section 4.

As a visiting session starts, the sequence of pages viewed by the user are processed by the Content Extractor and a STP is dynamically updated at each click. The Recommendation Manager combines opportunely the STP with the Long Term Profile, as described in section 5.

This profile combination produces as output a vector of terms which is classified according to the Web Site Taxonomy in order to find the taxonomy node whose contents best matches the user's browsing behaviour and his/her general interests. Recommendation is therefore made generating a self-adapting, personalized web site: contents of the matching class are presented to the user as link suggestion or composed dynamically in a web page.

At the end of each session, the STP is integrated in the LTP, which synthesizes the user's browsing history which will be used in the next sessions to refine the recommendation process.

3 Content Extractor

The Content Extractor module takes as input web documents from the Document Repository and processes them. During the off-line phase it analyzes all the documents in the Repository and it processes the new ones, while during the online phase it parses only pages visited by the user. Documents are then represented in the Vector Space Model [26] following the approach proposed in [38].

Each document d^j, $1 \leq j \leq D$. of n^j words (terms) is represented as a vector of $|w|$ components defined as:

$$d^j_i = TF(w_i, d^j) \cdot IDF(w_i) , \quad 1 \leq i \leq |w| \tag{1}$$

Where:

- w_i is the ith word of the vector space
- $TF(w_i, d^j)$ is the Term Frequency, i.e. the number of times the word w_i occurs in document d^j
- $DF(w_i)$ is the Document Frequency, i.e. the number of documents in which word w_i occurs at least once
- $$IDF(w_i) = \log \frac{D}{DF(w_i)}$$

Smaller vectors ensure less noise, lower computational times and a more reliable clusterization. For these reasons it is necessary to select only the most significant words of the document set. Before the vector representation, raw text is processed to remove stop words and a stemming procedure is applied.

After this, the total number of words is reduced substantially; however, the word vectors may still be too large. For this reason we apply a feature selection technique known with the name of Term Variance Quality Selection [10] [38]. Given the Term Frequency TF (w_i, d^j) and the Document Frequency DF(w_i), we calculate a Quality Measure q_w for each term w_i with the formula:

$$q_{w_i} = \sum_{k=1}^{DF(w_i)} TF(w_i, d^k)^2 - \frac{1}{DF(w_i)}\left[\sum_{k=1}^{DF(w_i)} TF(w_i, d^k)\right] \tag{2}$$

The assumption is that words with higher quality value q_w have a higher discriminatory power. It is then possible to choose a threshold in order to discard terms with low quality value or fix the maximum number of accepted terms ordered by decreasing quality measure.

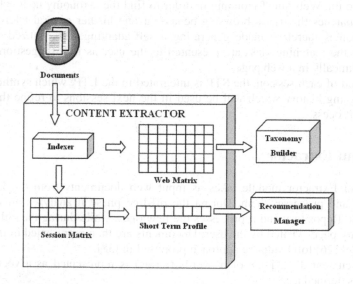

Fig. 2. Schema of Content Extractor module functionalities

In Fig. 2 we show the main functions of the Content Extractor and its relations with other modules. The vectorial representation of documents gives the input to build some of the data structures needed for the following processing phases. In particular, the TFIDF Web Matrix is constructed off-line, taking as input all the documents in the Document Repository; it contains all the TFIDF word vectors, extracted from documents. The STP is obtained as the centroid of each person's TFIDF Session Matrix, which is composed taking as input only the documents visited by the user during the current navigation session.

4 Taxonomy Builder

The sequence of steps described before leads to a vector space representation of the web site, which is apt to be processed by a clustering algorithm. The Taxonomy Builder module is the software component that helps to organize the unstructured elements of the web site in a hierarchical taxonomy tree.

If viewed as a "black box", the Taxonomy Builder receives as input the matrix of vectors representing indexed documents and it gives as output a data structure named

Web Site Taxonomy. This hierarchical structure has the form of a tree; its nodes are groups (clusters) of vectors representing documents.

The root node will contain all the documents in the collection (belonging to the Document Repository) while leaves will contain documents having a common subject.

Each node may have two or more children nodes: elements contained in the parent node are assigned to different children depending on their topics. Each node is characterized by a centroid vector that synthesizes the documents belonging to it.

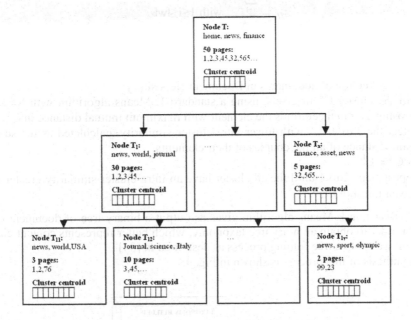

Fig. 3. Data Structure of the *Web Site Taxonomy*

Fig. 3 presents graphically an example of a taxonomy structure, with the root T. The root has *a* children nodes, $T_1, T_2, .., T_a$; each of them has a different number of second-level children (e.g. node T_1 has *b* child nodes). The figure shows that every node contains its name, the number of elements (each of them is addressed by the corresponding index assigned by the Content Extractor) and it is labelled with the L most characterizing words of its centroid.

In order to obtain this Taxonomy, we clusterize the indexed documents through a modified version of the well known Bisecting K-means that has been inspired by the *Induced Bisecting K-Means* [38]. This algorithm, proposed by Archetti et al., has shown good performances in classification accuracy and computational time. It is stable w.r.t. noisy data and is particularly suitable for web applications, where heterogeneous text have to be manipulated and compared.

A cluster C is a set of words vectors of the form:

$$C=(d^1, d^2, ... d^N) \qquad (3)$$

And each document vector has the form:

$$d^j=(d^j_1,d^j_2,..,d^j_{|w|}) \text{ with } 1{\leq}j{\leq}N \qquad (4)$$

We define $centr^C$ as the centroid of C defined as:

$$centr^C=(\mu_1, \mu_2,..,\mu_{|w|}) \qquad (5)$$

Where each μ_i is given by:

$$\mu_i = \frac{\sum_{j=1}^{N} d_i^{\,j}}{N} \text{ with } 1{\leq}i{\leq}|w| \qquad (6)$$

In our implementation the steps of the process are:

1. The initial cluster C* contains all the rows of the Web Matrix, representing the whole collection of documents in Document Repository;
2. Split the cluster C* in 2 sets, using a standard K-Means algorithm with K=2 and choosing as initial centroids the element with maximum mutual distance in C*.
3. Select the cluster C^L with lower intra-cluster similarity, calculated as the sum of cosine distance of all the couples of their elements.
4. Set $C* = C^L$
5. Repeat steps 2 to 4 until the all cluster have an intra-cluster similarity greater than a given threshold τ.

The Bisecting k-Means algorithm gives as output a binary tree of document clusters. In order to obtain an n-ary tree taxonomy, which better represents content classification, we apply a tree folding process as described in [34].

A synthesis of this process is shown in Fig. 4.

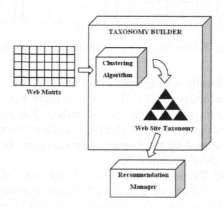

Fig. 4. *Taxonomy Builder* Functionalities

5   Recommendation Manager

The Recommendation Manager is the module that presents to the user the result of recommendation process. It takes in input the STPs from the Content Extractor Module; its functions are to update the LTPs, taking into account the Profile History, and to combine Short and LTPs in order to obtain a dynamic Profile which will be used to give recommendations, as depicted in Fig. 5.

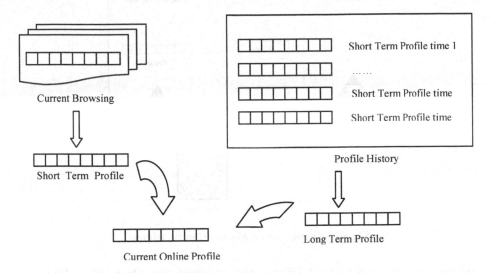

Fig. 5. Combination of *STP* with *LTP* to create the *Online Profile*

This allows us to solve the problem arising when a user has just started to navigate the web site. In this case the information acquired is not enough to properly understand the visitor's hidden characteristics and it is hard to give a good recommendation. This is known as the cold-start problem [23] and has a negative effect on user's trust of the recommendation system: wrong recommendation can confuse the visitor, annoy him or give him a false impression of the site.

For this reason we proposed to enhance the system complexity, introducing the concept of STP and LTP. The STP is a synthetic representation of current user interests expressed implicitly during navigation by clicks on web pages. If the site provides a personal identification access system it is possible to recognize users during different visits and to create for each of them a LTP: a vector whose values are the average values of each coordinate of the STPs. In this way we build user profiles that consider the browsing history. The basic assumption is that, although each browsing session can be generated by different needs and governed by the short term behaviour, we can take a general view about user persistent preferences that are common to all or most of the sessions. These general interests can be captured only analyzing different sessions and trying to discover common patterns and recurrent elements, represented here by words that occur very frequently and emerge as the most meaningful elements of the Long Term Profile (Fig. 6).

The Recommendation Manager is a daemon process that runs on the server hosting the web site. When a new navigation session starts, the Recommendation Manager receives the STP from the Content Extractor module and, if the user is known, it

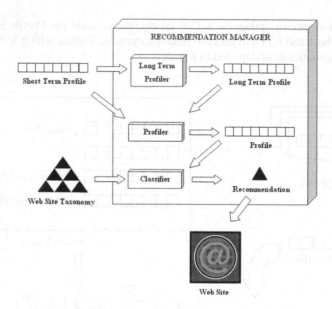

Fig. 6. *Recommendation Manager* functionalities

combines this one with his/her LTP, through a weighted sum. The resulting Profile is represented by a vector that is classified comparing it with the centroids of the Web Site Taxonomy nodes. Once identified the cluster most similar to the current profile, the system chooses from its elements those that have a distance from the Profile vector below a given threshold and recommend them to the user.

The STP is fed by the Content Extractor module at fixed intervals. We define the Profiling Window size (PF) as the number of "clicks" that rules the frequency of the recommendation. A new STP is calculated every PF requests of the navigation session. Typically $3 \leq PF \leq 8$. Every time a STP arrives, a new Online Profile P is built through a weighted average between STP and LTP, as described in Fig. 6.

We define Tset as the set of taxonomy nodes, Tset= $\{T, T_1, T_2, .., T_a, T_{11}, T_{12}..T_{1b}, T_{21}...\}$, and CentrSet as the set of centroids that characterize each element of Tset; CentrSet=$\{Centr^T, Centr^T_1, Centr^T_2,..., Centr^T_a, Centr^T_{11}, Centr^T_{12}.. Centr^T_{1b}, Centr^T_{21}...\}$.

The Recommendation System operates with the following steps:

1. Calculate the cosine distance from P and each element of CentrSet.
2. Find the element $Centr^T_{min}$ in CentrSet that has minimum distance from P
3. Select the taxonomy node T_{min} that corresponds to $Centr^T_{min}$
4. Label user profile with the label words associated with T_{min}
5. The H elements of T_{min} closest to P are recommended to the user.

The system presents the recommended contents in a frame of the web page, as a "Suggested Links" box. The recommended documents are ordered by decreasing distance from the STP P; each link is labelled with the L words that have the highest TFIDF value in the corresponding vector. Another way to present the profiling results is through dynamic creation of web pages. Pages elements and frames are filled composing the contents that are closest to the user's inferred interests. Like a custom made newspaper built of clipped out articles, web pages become different for each user. The first representation mode is less invasive and lets the user free to choose whether to continue the browsing in the current page or to follow the link suggestions. In the second mode, however, a real personalization of the web is achieved, generating views that fit each user's needs.

We keep track of a fixed number M of STPs for each user, generating a time-window history of word vectors P_m, $1 \leq m \leq M$. Changes on the M value influences the sensibility with respect to the user actions: a small window assigns greater importance to the last expressed preferences, allowing rapid adaptation to behaviour changes. Nevertheless, a longer history ensures a higher robustness to temporary facts and a stronger personal characterization. When a person ends his M+1th visit, his last STP P_{M+1} is inserted into the STPs queue and the oldest P_1 is discarded. After every navigation session, we update the LTP. This history is useful in situation where it is necessary to change the time interval included in the LTP calculation. E.g. further to user's behaviour permanent changes, the calculated LTP can be very different from LTPs; in this situation the presence of a profile history allows to reduce the number of profiled used to calculate the LTP and adapt it more quickly to new browsing patterns.

The LTP plays an important role in the personalization process. At the beginning of the navigation session the STP weight is much less than the LTP weight for determining the Profile P; the cold start problem is solved and the user receives suggestions that are close to his/her general interests. While the session becomes longer, the weight of the STP increases and the weight of the LTP decreases: this means that the user behaviour during the current session drives the recommendation process.

6 Conclusions and Future Work

In this paper we described a web user profiling system, integrated in the content management application of a web server, called UP-DRES. UP-DRES operates in two phases: the first step is the analysis of the web site documents, to group them in clusters on the basis of their contents and to produce a hierarchical taxonomy tree. The second phase is activated during each visitor's navigation session: the system is able to recognize his/her interests on the basis of the viewed contents. Similarities between the browsed documents and the web site taxonomy are found and the contents that best fit the user's preferences are presented to him/her.

This approach is novel in the sense that it combines a static taxonomization of the published information with the dynamical analysis of the browsed web pages. STPs creation allows us to model human interests in a synthetically and powerful way. LTPs history and their global treatment allows to obtain a profiling system that resists to local behaviour changes and is reliable also in the presence of scarce browsing data.

Many other web recommendation systems, like those based on the collaborative filtering, rely on explicit human supervision of the contents. UP-DRES, instead, works in a totally unsupervised way, inferring implicit user's interests through his behaviour, analyzing and grouping documents only on the basis of their contents. UP-

DRES can be integrated in every web site, because its functioning doesn't require domain-dependent configuration, and it is particularly suitable in highly dynamical web sites, in which collaborative suggestions are ineffective due to their slow responses to the frequent content changes.

Many issues are still open. As a first question, during the text extraction phase we apply standard techniques to reduce the number of words, like stop words eliminations and stemming. An interesting opportunity is given by ontology dictionaries either generic or domain specific. Through domain specific ontologies and public services (e.g. WordNet [32]) it is possible to incorporate concept definition and synonym identification in the selection process; different terms that identify the same concept are grouped together, in order to drastically reduce their number without loosing information.

The clustering algorithm could also be improved. In this paper we presented a modified version of the well known bisecting K-means algorithm as divisive partitioning engine. However other clustering techniques, either divisive or agglomerative, should be considered to investigate the effects on the recommendation performance, as explained in [29].

References

1. M. Balabanovic and Y. Shoham, Fab: Content-Based, Collaborative Recommendation, Communications of the ACM, 40(3) pp. 66–72, 1997.
2. P. Baldi, P. Frasconi, and P. Smyth. Modeling the Internet and the Web, Wiley, 2003.
3. C. Basu, H. Hirsh and W. Cohen, Recommendation as Classification: Using Social and Content-Based Information in Recommendation, In Proc. of the 15th National Conference on Artificial Intelligence (AAAI '98), pp. 714–720, 1998.
4. H. Berghel, Cyberspace 2000: dealing with information overload, Communications of the ACM 40 (2), pp. 19-24. 1997
5. K. Bharat, T. Kamba and M. Albers, Personalized Interactive News on the Web, Multimedia Systems, 6(5) pp. 349–358, 1998.
6. J. S. Breese, D. Heckerman, and C. Kadie, Empirical Analysis of Predictive Algorithms for Collaborative Filtering, In Proc. of the 14th Conference on Uncertainty in Artificial Intelligence (UAI '98), pp. 43–52, 1998.
7. S. Chakrabarti, Mining the web. Discovering knowledge from hypertext data. Morgan Kaufmann, 2003
8. Z. Chen, A. Wai-Chee Fu and F. Chi-Hung Tong, Optimal algorithms for finding user access sessions from very large Web logs, World Wide Web: Internet and Information Systems 6, pp. 259-279, 2003.
9. A. P. Dempster, N. M. Laird and D. B. Rubin, Maximum likelihood from incomplete data via the EM algorithm, Journal of the Royal Statistical Society B 39, pp. 1-38, 1997.
10. I. Dhillon, J. Kogan, C. Nicholas, Feature Selection and Docuement Clustering, in Survey of Text Minng, Springer-Verlag, New York, Chapter 4, pp. 73-100, 2004
11. C. Fraley and A. Raftery, How many clusters? Which clustering method? Answers via model based cluster analysis, Computer Journal, 41(8) pp. 578-588, 1998.
12. D. Goldberg, D. Nichols, B. M. Oki and D. B. Terry, Using Collaborative Filtering to Weave an Information Tapestry, Communications of the ACM, 35(12) pp. 61–70, 1992.

13. M. Grcar, D. Mladenic, M. Grobelnik, User profiling for interest-focused browsing history, in Proc. 2nd Annual ESWC (European Semantic Web Conference) June 2005
14. T. Joachims, D. Freitag and T. M. Mitchell, WebWatcher: A Tour Guide for the World Wide Web, In Proc. of the 15th International Joint Conference on Artificial Intelligence (IJCAI'97), pp. 770–777, 1997.
15. D. Kelly and J. Teevan, Implicit Feedback for Inferring User Preference: A Bibliography, SIGIR Forum, 37(2) pp. 18–28, 2003.
16. H.R. Kim and P. K. Chan, Learning Implicit User Interest Hierarchy for Context in Personalization. Proc. of the 8th international conference on Intelligent user interfaces Miami, Florida, USA, pp. 101-108, 2003
17. D. Kirsh, A few thoughts on cognitive overload, Intellectica, pp. 19-51, 2000
18. J. A. Konstan, B. N. Miller, D. Maltz, J. L. Herlocker, L. R. Gordon, and J. Riedl, GroupLens: Applying Collaborative Filtering to Usenet News, Communications of the ACM, 40(3) pp. 77–87, 1997.
19. H. Lieberman, Letizia: An Agent That Assists Web Browsing, In Proc. of the 14th International Joint Conference on Artificial Intelligence (IJCAI '95), pp. 924–929, 1995.
20. H. Lieberman, Autonomous Interface Agents, In Proc. of the Conference on Human Factors in Computing Systems (CHI '97), pp. 67–74, 1997.
21. U. Manber, A. Patel and J. Robison, Experience with Personalization on Yahoo! Communications of the ACM, 43(8) pp. 35–39, 2000.
22. McCallum, A. K. Nigam, K. Rennie, J. Seymore, K. Automating the Construction of Internet Portals with Machine Learning, Information Retrieval 3(2), pp. 127-163, 2000
23. S. E. Middleton, N. R. Shadbolt, D. C. De Roure, Capturing Interest through Inference and Visualization: Ontological User Profiling in Recommender Systems. In Proc. 2nd Conference on Knowledge Capture, pp. 62-69, 2003
24. M. Morita and Y. Shinoda, Information Filtering Based on User Behavior Analysis and Best Match Text Retrieval, In Proc. of the 17th Annual International ACM SIGIR Conference on Research and Development in Information Retrieval (SIGIR '94), pp. 272–281, 1994.
25. P. Resnick, N. Iacovou, M. Suchak, and J. R. P. Bergstorm. GroupLens: An Open Architecture for Collaborative Filtering of Netnews. In Proc. of the ACM 1994 Conference on Computer Supported Cooperative Work (CSCW '94), pp. 175–186, 1994.
26. G. Salton and C. Buckley, Term Weighting Approaches in Automatic Text Retrieval, Technical Report, COR-87-881, Department of Computer Science, Cornell University. 1987
27. B. M. Sarwar, G. Karypis, and J. A. Konstan, Analysis of Recommendation Algorithms for E-commerce, In Proc. of the 2nd ACM Conference on Electronic Commerce (EC '00), pp. 158–167, 2000.
28. J. B. Schafer, J. A. Konstan, and J. Riedl, Meta-recommendation Systems: User-controlled Integration of Diverse Recommendations, In Proc. of the 11th International Conference on Information and Knowledge Management (CIKM '02), pp. 43–51, 2002.
29. M. Steinbach, G. Karypis and V. Kumar, A comparison of Document Clustering Techniques, in Proc. of KDD-2000 Workshop on Text Mining, pp. 109–110. 2000
30. K. Sugiyama, K. Hatano, M. Yoshikawa, Adaptive Web Search Based on User Profile Construction without Any Effort from Users, in Proc. of 13th International World Wide Web Conference, pp. 675-684, 2004
31. L. Terveen, W. Hill, B. Amento, D. McDonald and J. Creter, PHOAKS: A System for Sharing Recommendations, Communications of the ACM, 40(3) pp. 59–62, 1997.
32. WordNet: An Electronic Lexical Database, ed. C. Fellbaum, MIT Press, 1998

33. I. V. Cadez, D. Heckerman, C. Meek, P. Smyth, and S. White, Model-based clustering and visualization of navigation patterns on a Web site, Data Mining and Knowledge Discovery, 7(4) pp. 399-424 2003.
34. V. Kashyap, C. Ramakrishnan, C. Thomas, D. Bassu, T.C. Rindflesch, A. Sheth, TaxaMiner: An Experimentation Framework for Automated Taxonomy Bootstrapping, International Journal of Web and Grid Services, Special Issue on Semantic Web and Mining Reasoning, September 2005 (to appear)
35. I. V. Cadez, D. Heckerman, C. Meek, P. Smyth, and S. White, Model-based clustering and visualization of navigation patterns on a Web site, Data Mining and Knowledge Discovery, 7(4) pp. 399-424 2003.
36. E. Blanc and P. Giudici, Sequence Rules for Web Clickstream Analysis, Advances in Data Mining 2002, LNAI 2394, pp. 1-14, 2002.
37. P. Perner and G. Fiss, Intelligent E-Marketing with Web Mining, Personalization and User-adpated Interfaces, Data Mining in E-Commerce, Medicine, and Knowledge Management, LNAI 2394, 2002
38. F. Archetti, P. Campanelli, E. Fersini, E. Messina, A Hierarchical Document Clustering Environment based on the Induced Bisecting k-Means, to appear in Lecture Notes in AI, In Proc. of 7th International Conference on Flexible Query Answering Systems, Università degli studi di Milano-Bicocca, 7-10 June 2006

Improving Effectiveness on Clickstream Data Mining

Cristina Wanzeller[1] and Orlando Belo[2]

[1] Departamento de Informática, Instituto Superior Politécnico de Viseu,
Escola Superior de Tecnologia de Viseu, Campus Politécnico de Repeses,
3505-510 Viseu, Portugal
cwanzeller@di.estv.ipv.pt
[2] Departamento de Informática, Escola de Engenharia,
Universidade do Minho, Campus de Gualtar,
4710-057 Braga, Portugal
obelo@di.uminho.pt

Abstract. Developing and applying data mining processes are often very complex tasks to users without deep knowledge in this domain, particularly when such tasks involve *clickstream* data processing. One important and known challenge arises in the selection of mining methods to apply on a specific data analysis problem, trying to get better and useful results for a particular goal. Our approach to address this challenge relies on the reuse of the acquired experience from similar problems, which had provided successful mining processes in the past. In order to accomplish such goal, we implemented a prototype mining plans selection system, based on the Case-Based Reasoning paradigm. In this paper we explain how this paradigm and the implemented system may be explored to assist decisions on the data mining or Web usage mining specific scope. Additionally, we also identify the underlying issues and the approaches that were followed.

1 Introduction

Web Usage Mining (WUM) concerns to the application of mining methods to data related to the interaction processes between visitors and Web sites. This data, as we know, is usually called as *clickstream* or usage data. The WUM aim is to discover relevant usage patterns, to understand and satisfy what a site visitor wants, as an insight to improve site user friendliness and effectiveness levels. This knowledge is quite useful to support decisions on several application areas, such as Web personalization, business intelligence, site restructuring and content alteration and system performance improvement [20]. The basic intention behind all of this consists of catching and keeping attention from visitors to the promoted contents, in order to reach the goals established for the web sites by their managers and administrators.

Data Mining (DM) and WUM tools are becoming increasingly important to a variety of users with different levels of knowledge in the area. Indeed, any user inside the organization can be, in general terms, an informal analyst. Nevertheless, such tools are usually too complex to be used without the aid of a specialist in the area. A common known challenge is related with the selection of suitable methods to apply on a specific data analysis problem, in order to improve the quality of results for a particu-

P. Perner (Ed.): ICDM 2006, LNAI 4065, pp. 161–175, 2006.
© Springer-Verlag Berlin Heidelberg 2006

lar goal defined for a specific site. This challenge is the main motivation of our work, which aims at promoting a more effective, productive and simplified exploration of such data analysis potentialities. The way defended to achieve this goal consists in assisting the development and the application of DM processes, using the experience acquired in the past when we solved similar problems applying successful mining processes. This is a typical strategy based on the principles that we recognize that *Case Based Reasoning* (CBR) presents to us [1,11,19]. Based on such principles, we designed and implemented a prototype recommendation system, which is able to propose the most suited mining plans to a specific *clickstream* data analysis problem, given a high level description of the problem. The case based representation models can also act as exploration and sharing bases over knowledge repositories, promoting sustained learning and best practices adoption involving usage data exploitation.

Assisting decisions within DM applications and knowledge discovery processes is not a new initiative. There are some that explore also the CBR paradigm to undertake related purposes. The Mining Mart project [16], for instance, represents several efforts devoted to the reuse of successful data pre-processing processes, appealing to a case based metadata repository. However, this system does not explore the meta-model potentialities neither the typical CBR methods to help users on establishing the mapping between the problem that we have and the stored ones. Moreover, this project is centred in pre-processing activities, not in DM processes. Another example is the METAL project [14], which involved multiple research and development initiatives, some of them based on the CBR paradigm (e.g. [6,13]). Generally, the main aim of these initiatives was to assist users in model selection – one of the steps of a conventional knowledge discovery process –, and they focused mainly on the algorithms selection issue, within regression and classification problems. Conversely, our work has a different perspective and scope. The system implemented previews assistance on DM models selection, comprising diverse DM functions, and covers support to processes involving transformation operations and multiple stages, according to real-life applications requirements. Besides, the intended DM task specification reaches a greater level of abstraction. This paper explains our view of the mining methods selection challenge, discussing how it may be handled exploring the CBR paradigm and the implemented system. We also describe the system developed, identifying the main issues faced to fulfil the establish requirements and the approaches followed to accomplish this task.

2 The Challenge

Selecting the most suitable methods to apply on a specific data analysis problem is an important and known challenge of DM and WUM processes development. *Clickstream* data is a very rich and valuable source of information. It captures every trace of the interaction process, allowing revealing the behaviour of Web users, besides the traditional elements of the performed transactions. Potentially, this data can provide enormous discoveries, and the insights can easily be turned into actions [3]. Though, usage data brings up new issues. A huge amount of labour-intensive pre-processing is required to prepare it for mining. Even so, extracting meaning from this data is very difficult, due to their subtle nature, intrinsic complexity and large volume and number of variables. Koutri et al [12] provide a survey very useful to explain the faced challenge. They discuss the major WUM techniques that can be applied for building adaptive hypermedia systems, identifying:

- the most prominent DM functions (clustering, association rule and sequential pattern mining);
- three specific aspects of adaptation, as the result of Web usage patterns application [15] (personal recommendation, dynamic adjustment and static page/site adjustment);
- some important types of usage patterns revealed from WUM (clusters of Web documents references, clusters of user visits, associations among Web documents and sequences of frequently accessed documents).

The above pattern types were also correlated with the identified adaptation aspects, describing the interpretation of each pattern type and the kind of decision support provided, in order to point out the most appropriate context(s) of each pattern use. In addition, the usage pattern types were compared based on the involved requirements and precision levels. For instance, the sequential patterns were considered the most accurate, since they are more informative, but they require richer datasets to capture the diversity of the behaviour of Web users and being the most difficult to obtain.

We described a few issues involved on one type of WUM application (or three more specific types of adaptation applications). The challenge increases by other kinds of issues faced in real-life scenarios. Among them are the requirements of identifying precisely the business problem, transforming some data to answer the problem and the technical understanding of the mining methods. Usually, DM and WUM tools provide a reduced and abstracted offer, as a set of available DM models. Yet, each model's characteristics constraint its applicability and impose distinct configurations. Furthermore, individual models of the same functions are, usually, more suited for distinct purposes. For example, within classification function, decision trees are descriptive models, being more appropriated for interpreting purposes than neural network models. So, if it is more important to understand the influent factors, than to develop an accurate predictive model, the analyst would prefer the former model.

Our real challenge is to find out some ways to empower analysts, in the sense they are able to serve themselves [3]. The followed approach consists in providing a system with the ability to assist them in two different ways:

1. organizing and storing on a shared repository the examples of successful WUM processes;
2. proposing the mining plans most suited to one *clickstream* data analysis problem, given a high level description of the problem.

Examples of past successful solved problems might be the most helpful and convincing form of aid in this scope. They may: (i) simplify the underlying complexity, providing at the same time the details of a tested and solved situation; (ii) yield context information, making possible to report the solutions along with the respective justifications and obtained discoveries; (iii) promote the mapping of the current problem, against the existent ones, when a more direct form of reuse is not possible. In fact, a straight reuse of one solution is quite possible, since recurrent problems are common on this domain. In addiction, the system can be incrementally improved by adding new experiences. This particularity is of great importance, as new solving approaches, DM models, application areas, and WUM problems, are always coming up, being hereby automatically integrated.

To better show our point of view, we consider a typical and simple WUM example problem. This problem is centred on obtaining feedback about how visitants are using a Web site, to improve navigation convenience. Namely, the intended action is to add relevant links between some Web pages which are visited together. The analyst wants to find out which Web pages are the best ones to include as links and within which pages, tacking into account pages' importance from the visitants' point of view. In the following sections this example will be further developed, in terms of its treatment exploring the implemented system.

We previewed two exploitation scenarios for our system: the exploratory and the problem solving ones. The former involves the use of the system to gain insights about features of interest, typically through an incomplete description of the problem. For instance, the analyst might wish to know what kind of goals and intents or other categorizations have been used to describe related experiences, with the purpose to learn how to better specify the current problem. The analyst might also wish to find out which data elements or sources were used on similar problems, to decide whether usage data is enough (and on what granularity) or other related data must be integrated. Conversely, the problem solving scenario supposes the knowing of the current problem and its submission to the system using a more focused description, in order to obtain more selective solutions.

3 The Mining Plans Selection System

A CBR application can be described by a cycle comprising four processes, usually assigned by the four R's [1]: (i) retrieve cases similar to the current problem; (ii) reuse the information and knowledge of the retrieved case(s) to solve the problem at hand; (iii) revise or adapt the proposed solution to better fit the current problem, if necessary; (iv) retain the confirmed experience parts that might be useful in future problems solution. A case is usually viewed as a problem specification and a described solution of this problem. In the current scope, a case represents and describes one knowledge discovery process, in terms of two factor sets having higher influence in this scope: (i) analysis requirements and characteristics of the target dataset; (ii) experience about the application of DM functions and models and other operations. The items belonging to the first factor set define the CBR problem description, being useful descriptors to retrieve similar cases. The remaining factors belong to the data analysis problem solution, being retained and used to produce a solution description.

Fig. 1 shows the main functional components of the system and their interconnections, inputs and outputs. The CBR engine is the system's core component and the one that performs the inference processes. Currently, this component implements the retrieve and the retain processes and uses a Database Management System (DBMS) to manage the acquired knowledge - other CBR processes will be considered in future work.

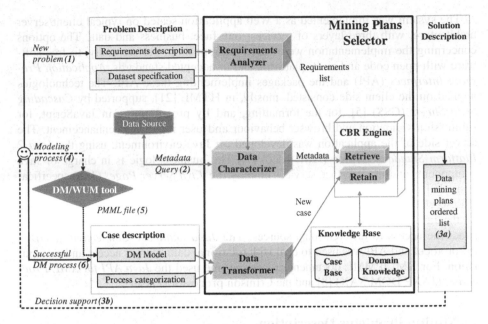

Fig. 1. The system's components

The most typical use of the system can be described by the following steps:

1. the analyst enters a new data analysis problem (1) through the dataset specification and the analysis requirements description;
2. the **data characterizer** component analyses the dataset and extracts the
   most relevant metadata (2), to the purpose of WUM processes selection;
3. the **requirements analyzer** component handles the analysis requisites description, to get and systemize the embedded constraints;
4. the **retrieve module** matches the incoming descriptions of the new problem
   against the (potential useful) existent cases, to find out the most similar
   cases;
5. the most similar cases are organized and then presented to the analyst, providing a suggested solution description, which comprises an ordered list of
   the most suited DM plans (3a);
6. the DM plans are reused to assist the analyst (3b), which develops and sub-
   mits the DM process (4), appealing to a DM or WUM tool;
7. if the DM tool supports the Predictive Model Markup Language (PMML)
   standard [17], it can provide a DM model description through a file in the
   PMML format (5);
8. a successfully DM process (6) may become a new case to retain;
9. the **data transformer** component analyses and assembles the data of the
   new case specification, including the DM model description (e.g. PMML
   files) and the process categorization (complementary descriptions);
10. the **retain module** is then evoked to structure and store the new case, finish-
   ing the cycle.

The system was implemented as a Web application seated on typical client/server architecture, with three layers of services: interface, business and data. The options concerning the implementation were based on appealing, preferentially, to free software with open code and multi-platform, and to accepted standards, *Application Program Interfaces* (API) and the packages implementing these API. The technologies applied on the client side consisted, mostly, in HTML [21], supported by *Cascading Style Sheets* (CSS) [5], for the formatting, and by programming in JavaScript, for submission validation and browser behaviour and user interaction enhancement. The server side of the application was developed on Java environment, using the *Java 2 Platform Standard Edition* (J2SE 1.5.0) [7]. The business logic is in charge of Java components and the interface services employ the *Java Server Pages* (JSP) specification [10]. The publication and deployment of these services is assured by the JSP/Servlets container Apache Tomcat (version 5.5) [4]. The data services, developed on the Java platform, were implemented exploring different API, to support and abstract the access to different data sources. The *Java Database Connectivity* (JDBC) [9] protocol and API was used to deal with relational data sources access and manipulation. For XML/PMML document processing one used the *Java API for XML Processing* (JAXP DOM/SAX) [8] and the Crimson processor (Parser).

4 Mining Problems Description

Problem description involves the specification of the current problem's characteristics and a set of constraints, based on the analysis nature and on the analyst's preferences. The main elements of a WUM problem description are shown on Fig. 2 (in bold), along with the specification of some values of the example problem (referred before). The target dataset consists in *clickstream* data (a server log file), describing information (8 variables) at page view/access level (granularity). One important issue is to capture the relevant dataset properties to the particular purpose of DM methods selection. A common data characterization approach builds upon general measures, statistical (numerical attributes) and theoretical information (symbolic attributes) [13]. This approach has been frequently and successfully used in Meta-Learning, to select adequate learning algorithms. Though, those measures are numerous, complex and diverse and the proposals about their content have been used for a subgroup of DM functions. To accomplish datasets characterization we identified a simple set of descriptors, involving metadata automatically extracted by the system and properties values indicated by the analyst. These descriptors are of two main types: (i) DM generic characteristics, collected at dataset level and at individual variables level; (ii) WUM specific characteristics, obtained almost all at dataset level, except the variables' semantic category. The system also provides means to indicate the relevant items or the desirable proprieties, in terms of the dataset variables.

The major requirement regarding the WUM task is to support high level descriptions, through abstractions related to the real problems to solve. A description based on DM functions (or models) cannot abstract the complexity and might exclude processes involving other alternative functions (or models). So, this specification relies on the data analysis goals, which have two distinct perspectives in real-life applications: the business and the WUM ones. The business point of view is meant as the analysis intention or possible uses of the discoveries, being assigned by application area. The WUM perspective stands for the mining result type to get and the sort of analysis approach to explore, in order to satisfy business goals. This point of view is called goal, since it reflects a kind of WUM problem, and implies that each new case to retain must be related to a specific goal and to one or more application areas. To allow several levels of subdivision in more specific sub-areas, and its definition according to organization needs, the application areas are organized in a dynamic hierarchy. Thus, the DM task specification becomes the selection of the most relevant goal(s) and application area(s), in levels of detail closer to the problem to solve.

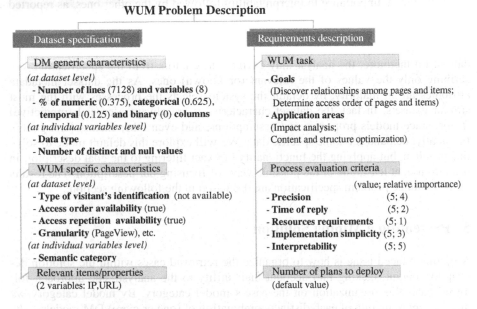

Fig. 2. Main elements of a WUM problem description

At the moment, our case base contains a small number of cases. This fact and the (current) intentional generality restrict the diversity of goals and application areas. Namely, the existent hierarchy of application areas comprises only two levels with three top areas (including few sub-areas): (i) adaptability (e.g. dynamic adjustment and personalization); (ii) business intelligence (e.g. profiling & targeting and initiatives evaluation & planning); (iii) quality of service (e.g. impact analysis and content & structure optimization). For instance, the quality of service area focuses actions of systems and Web site improvement, involving basic expectations and affecting all the visitants. Therefore, we selected the two exemplified sub-areas of the quality of service area to define the example problem, since they are both relevant and the closest ones to the intended actions. In terms of goals we used all the ones that might provide information about relationships among pages. Other existent goals include Distinguish visits based on target events and Identify & characterize different types of visits and visitants.

Concerning the evaluation criteria of DM processes, we adopted the usual performance indicators. As the most promising, the ones shown on Fig. 2 had been chosen. To simplify the specification of the intended evaluation criteria and to deal with its subjectivity, we establish an ordinal and limited scale for all indicators ([1-5]), where greater (>) always means better. Moreover, the values specified by the analyst are meant as lower bounds. In other words, what matters is a value being lower (worst) than the searched one. So, the analyst might describe what he considers acceptable, defining the lower bounds of the relevant indicators and imposing priorities among them through relative importance. Within the specification of the example problem we assigned the value 5 (maximum) to all the evaluation criteria and the greatest relative importance to interpretability followed by the other ones, as reported in the figure.

Finally, the problem description supports the specification of exact filtering criteria and descriptors importance levels, to enable the improvement of the problem specification. Furthermore, the analyst may exclude descriptors from the specification, describing only the values of the relevant (or known) ones. As the dataset metadata attributes are in majority, by default the system selects the processes with the most similar datasets. In fact, the dataset characteristics are always a crucial (predictive) factor, since models properties and assumptions, and even other factors (e.g. goals), frequently, demand for some specific data. We will explore this default mode to solve this problem, but applying the functionality of exact filtering to the goal descriptor, in order to use, at least, one of the possible ways of focusing our description. The results of the example problem specification are discussed in the following section.

5   Presenting a Mining Solution

A pertinent faced issue is how to organize the retrieved cases within the solution description output, tacking into account their utility to the analyst. The approach followed basis this organization on the case's model category. By model category we mean a representation of each distinct combination of (one or more) DM models – the most important applied methods – occurring among the stored cases.

Fig. 3 illustrates a (small) possible solution description for the example problem. The figure presents the mining plans of three model categories (column D), instantiated with the most similar case of the category (column A). The column (B) shows the similitude between the target and each instantiated case. The hyperlinks of the cases (A) provide direct access to the respective detailed information. The combo boxes (A) show the similarity with the remaining retrieved cases of the model category (expanded on E). These combo boxes allow to access further information about such cases, through the selection among the available options. The column C depicts the average values of each evaluation criteria, respecting to all the retrieved cases of the model category. The interpretability criterion is the first one, because previously, we gave it the greatest relative importance. Using the described organization, the analyst can see several alternative solutions of the same problem, as well several instances of one solution of particular interest. Hereby, we maximize the solutions utility simultaneously for two distinct purposes: diversity of alternative solutions and variety of instances of a solution of particular interest.

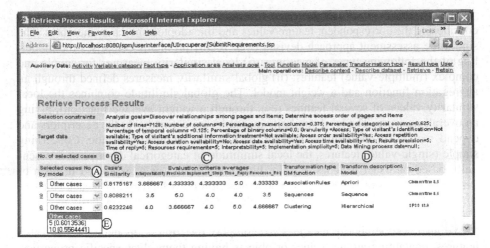

Fig. 3. Example of a description for a solution

All the suggested models are suited to the problem at hand. The association rules option is a good compromise between precision and coverage: it is more informative and precise (e.g. provides rules and the respective support and confidence) than the hierarchical clustering; generally, it provides better overall coverage than the sequence model, although being less informative than such model, which yields more fine-grained information (e.g. ordering among accessed pages). As expected, the system (on the default mode) gives emphasis to the similarity between datasets. The similitude of the cases from the hierarchical clustering is substantially inferior, since this model was applied to datasets with very different properties (e.g. binary matrix of pages × sessions). Conversely, the analyses from cases 8 and 9 were performed using datasets similar to the target one. However, the inclusion of the hierarchical clustering model within the solution is useful, since it is possible to transform the target dataset into the format commonly used to explore this model.

The strategy to undertake the retrieve process comprises the following major steps:

1. cases pre-selection, given the exact filtering criteria;
2. similarity estimation between the cases pre-selected and the target;
3. cases grouping by model category and determination of the evaluation criteria averages;
4. deployment of the firsts K groups, ordered (on first place) by the greatest similarity within the group and (on second place) by the evaluation criteria averages of the group.

Step 1 selects the WUM processes applicable on the current problem. Step 2 evaluates the proximity level of each retrieved case in relation to the target, pointing out the processes potentially more effective. Step 3 provides a global evaluation perspective of each model category, and, finally, step 4 allows the presentation of the K most promise mining plans, according to the similarity level and the model category evaluation criteria, which is most relevant to the analyst.

The similitude of each pre-selected case's problem to the target one is computed considering the correspondent feature values and the adopted similarity measures. The similitude assessment approach devised over WUM problems comprises the modelling of the following types of measures: (i) local similarity measures for simple and complex (multiple-value) features; (ii) global similarity measures defined through an aggregation function and a weight model. The global similitude combines the local similarity values of several features (e.g. through a weight average function), giving an overall measure. The local similarity measures are defined over the descriptors and depend mainly on the features domain, besides the intended semantic. Concerning simple (single-value) features, the local similitude of categorical descriptors is essentially based on exact matches (e.g. for binary attributes) or is expressed in form of similarity matrices (e.g. for some symbolic descriptors), which establish each pairwise similitude level. To compare numeric simple features, we adopted similarity measures mainly based on the normalized *Manhattan* distance.

We also need similarity measures for complex descriptors, modelled as set–value features, containing atomic values or objects having themselves specific properties. Indeed, this need was the main issue faced under the similarity assessment. For instance, it appears when matching the variables from the target and each case. We have to compare two sets of variables, with inconstant and possibly distinct cardinality, where each variable has its own features. There are multiple proposals in the literature to deal with related issues. Even so, we explored a number of them and the comparative tests performed lead us into tailored (extended) measures, better fitting our purposes.

6 Describing a Mining Experience

As shown in Fig. 4, case description comprises the DM model and the process categorization. This subdivision is justified by the intent to support the data model submission using files in PMML format. PMML [17] is a XML-based standard which provides a way to define statistical and DM model and to share them among PMML compliant applications. This standard is supported by a high and raising number of DM tools, even if with some limitations (e.g. versions supported). So, it represents an opportunity to automate some data gathering processes. Yet, it is necessary to obtain other data elements, about items unavailable in PMML files (e.g. configuration parameters and transformation operations), being required to provide a complementary form of data submission. Furthermore, the PMML file may not be available.

Despite we only show the most important elements, one concern was to capture a wide characterization of each WUM process, since it is essential to store the specific context required to find, interpret and evaluate the solutions. The DM model represents the modelling stages of the processes, where each instance comprises the major elements of the modelling description, extracted from PMML files or obtained directly from the analyst. A modelling stage involves the application of a DM model, belonging to a DM function, appealing to a DM tool, as well the configuration of a particular set of parameters and the use of a set of variables performing different roles. Categorization represents complementary information about the WUM processes, specifically, the data elements which can not be extracted from PMML files.

The dataset item includes the elements previously discussed, collected during the problem description specification. The transformation operations item respects to data preparation stages, described mainly in terms of the used tool, type of operation (e.g. derive new variable) and the set and roles of the involved variables (e.g. input and output variables). The discoveries item concerns to results provided by the process. Finally, the process classification regards to its categorization in terms of features such as evaluation criteria, application areas and analysis goals.

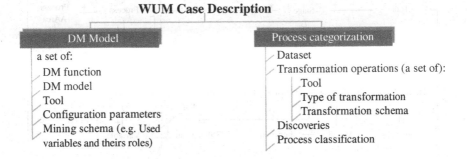

Fig. 4. Main elements of a WUM case description

7 Knowledge Representation

In CBR systems the primary kind of knowledge is contained on the specific cases, stored and organized in a case base. While traditionally viewed as data or information, rather than knowledge, concrete descriptions of past problem solving episodes became knowledge for CBR methods, since these methods are able to use cases for reasoning [2]. Besides case's specific knowledge, other and more general types of knowledge may be integrated within the CBR process, with varying levels of richness, degree of explicit representation and role [1]. Richter [18] introduced a model that identifies four knowledge containers in CBR systems: 1) vocabulary; 2) similarity measures; 3) solution transformations; and 4) case base. The first three containers represent compiled (more stable) knowledge, while the cases contain interpreted (dynamic) knowledge. This knowledge container view received wide acceptance, becoming the natural approach for knowledge representation structuring in CBR systems.

Our system's knowledge base integrates two components: the case base and the domain knowledge. The case base consists in a metadata repository, supported by a relational DBMS (involving about forty tables), where each case represents a successful DM process description. The domain knowledge concerns to knowledge about this particular scope of application, covering items as the specification of concepts and attributes (namely of problem description), mostly in terms of properties required to interpret, compare and retrieve the cases. This component provides knowledge items belonging to the vocabulary and similarity measures containers, since our system does not transforms solutions. The former container includes, for instance, items which define descriptor types and domains and establish the mappings between the relational schema and the case descriptors. The knowledge involved in the retrieval and comparison approaches (e.g. weights and similarity functions) is held by the second type of container. Fig. 5 shows an excerpt of the cases representation conceptual metadata model, using a class diagram in *Unified Modeling Language* (UML) simplified notation.

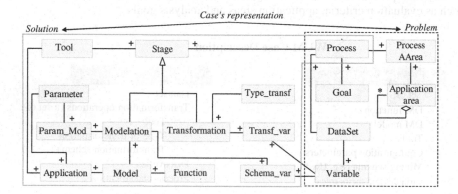

Fig. 5. Excerpt of the cases representation conceptual metadata model

The main components of a case's description are the following ones:

- *Process* - central class that represents an individual DM process and establishes the connection between classes concerning the problem and solution description. This class includes attributes that describe and characterize each process (e.g. evaluation criteria).
- *DataSet and Variable* – classes that embody the dataset and the variables characteristics.
- *Stage, Transformation* and *Modelation* - classes regarding to a DM process development phase; the superclasse Stage represents the shared parts or properties of each phase, while the Transformation and Modeling subclasses concern to the specific ones.
- *Model and Function* - classes that establish categorizations of the DM models and functions provided by tools.
- *Goal, Application_Area and Process_AArea* - classes covering, respectively, the analyses goals, the hierarchy of application areas and the association between processes and Application_Area.

The conceptual model presented provides the support to attend the established requisites, although being in continuous refinement. One of the refinements accomplished was the inclusion of the context of the datasets and the facts related to them and to the DM processes. This refinement intends to improve the cases description and to minimize the data redundancy. Other extensions consists on the inclusion of classes about sources (e.g. dataset and PMML files and database tables used), DM processes authors, DM processes discoveries and theirs relationships with existent facts.

8   Conclusions and Future Work

The WUM exploration is one important instrument to organizations involved in Web sites optimization and truly concerned on achieving their goals. Web site design, administration and improvement are complex tasks, which demand deep decision support, reaching an increasing ample and diversified population of users. However, DM and WUM tools and their concepts and techniques are too complex to be effectively explored without the aid of specialists on the area. The developed work aims at contributing to a more simplified, productive and effective exploration of WUM potentialities. As referred before, the main idea is to assist analysts through examples of solved similar analysis problems, promoting the reapplication of its best practices in the current situation. This approach seems to be the most opportune, according to accepted facts related to these processes nature. In DM and WUM domains, recurrent problems and methods repetitive use are quite common. Additionally, the experience and acquired know-how have a prominent value. Besides, examples of successfully solved problems are the most useful and convincing form of aid. To achieve this aim, we implemented a prototype system, which should suggest the mining plans more adjusted to one *clickstream* data analysis problem, given the respective description. This system is also based on abstractions related to the real problems to solve, meaning that it could serve the particular needs of less knowledge analysts, who wish to learn how to handle a concrete problem, being also useful to specialists interested in reminding and reusing successful solutions, instead of solving the problems from scratch.

The decision support involving discovering processes is an important working area, being, thus, the focus of multiple research projects. The CBR paradigm exploration is used too in efforts devoted to analogous purposes. Though, the work developed can be distinguished from the main related work on several features, namely, the support of multiple stage processes, the extended aid involving different DM functions selection, the integration of transformation operations (even if simplified) and, primary, the attempt to reach high abstraction levels in the intended DM task specification. Additionally, the system proposed is particularly devoted to the specific WUM domain and previews support over realistic exploration scenarios.

In this paper we described the system that we implemented to fulfil requirements and goals that we presented before, giving emphasis to their main characteristics and to the vision of its practical use to assist some steps within a WUM process development. A key factor to the system efficacy is a coherent and well structured definition of the analysis goals and application areas descriptors. The approach provided to support theirs definition and use is simple, flexible and effective. One drawback to point out is the treatment of the analysis goal descriptors, which is only suited to a moderate number of items. Even so, the potential of the approach has not been explored. Greater level of abstraction might be achieved developing further these descriptors and, thus, a better support is a possible future direction of work. This may be realised through some form of goals grouping, namely, an overlapping one. Additionally, the system has been tested using a small sample of simple WUM processes. In fact, the most exhaustive tests performed concern to the comparison between datasets and they point to the efficacy of the system. As previously mentioned we conducted a comparative study over several similarity measures and already integrated the obtained results within our system. Nonetheless, the activities concerning the preparation of more cases, comprising WUM process with higher complexity are still occurring. Afterwards, a more systematic evaluation of the system becomes possible and necessary. Furthermore, other planed and related activity is to explore additional data mining algorithms, specifically, approaches able of better fitting the properties of Web usage data, preferentially appealing to free software.

Acknowledgments. The work of Cristina Wanzeller was supported by a grant from PRODEP (Acção 5.3, concurso nº02 /2003).

References

1. Aamodt, A. and Plaza, E.: Case-Based Reasoning: Foundational Issues, Methodological Variations and Systems Approaches. In Artificial Intelligence Communications (AICom), IOS Press, Vol. 7, No 1 (1994) 39-59.
2. Aamodt, A.: Knowledge Acquisition and Learning by Experience - The Role of Case Specific Knowledge. In Machine Learning and Knowledge Acquisition, Academic Press, Integrated Approaches (1995) 197-245.
3. Ansari, S., Kohavi, R., Mason, L. and Zheng, Z.: Integrating E-Commerce and Data Mining: Architecture and Challenges. In Proc. 2001 IEEE International Conf. on Data Mining, IEEE Comput. Soc. (2001) 27–34.
4. Apache Jakarta Tomcat. http://tomcat.apache.org/. Access April 2006.
5. Bos, B.: W3C. Web Style Sheets – Home Page. http://www.w3.org/Style/. Access April 2006.
6. Hilario, M. and Kalousis, A.: Fusion of Meta-Knowledge and Meta-Data for Case-Based Model Selection. In Proc. of the 5th European Conference on Principles and Practice of Knowledge Discovery in Databases (PKDD '2001), Springer (2001) 180-191.
7. Java 2 Platform, Standard Edition (J2SE). Sun Microsystems. http://java.sun.com/javase/index.jsp. Access April 2006.
8. Java API for XML Processing (JAXP). Sun Microsystems http://java.sun.com/webservices/jaxp/. Access April 2006.
9. Java Database Connectivity, JDBC Data Access API. Sun Microsystems. http://www.javasoft.com/products/jdbc/index.html. Access April 2006.
10. Java Server Pages. Sun Microsystems. http://java.sun.com/products/jsp/. Access April 2006.
11. Kolodner, J.: Case-Based Reasoning, Morgan Kaufman, San Francisco, CA (1993).
12. Koutri, M., Avouris, N. and Daskalaki, S.: A Survey on Web Usage Mining Techniques for Web-Based Adaptive Hypermedia Systems. In S. Y. Chen and G. D. Magoulas (eds.), Adaptable and Adaptive Hypermedia Systems, Idea Publishing Inc., Hershey (2005).
13. Lindner, C. and Studer, R.: AST: Support for algorithm selection with a CBR approach. In Proc. of the 3rd European Conf. on Principles of Data Mining and Knowledge Discovery (PKDD'1999), Springer (1999) 418-423.
14. MetaL project http://www.metal-kdd.org/ Access April 2006.
15. Mobasher, B., Berendt, B. and Spiliopoulou, M.: KDD for Personalization. In PKDD 2001 Tutorial (2001).
16. Morik, K. And Scholz, M.: The MiningMart Approach to Knowledge Discovery in Databases. In N. Zhong and J. Liu (eds.), Intelligent Technologies for Information Analysis, Springer (2004).

17. Predictive Model Markup Language. Data Mining Group. http://www.dmg.org/index.html. Access April 2006.
18. Richter, M.: The Knowledge Contained in Similarity Measures. (Invited Talk) at the First International Conference on Case-Based Reasoning, ICCBR'95, Lecture Notes in Artificial Intelligence 1010, Springer Verlag (1995).
19. Riesbeck, C.K. and Schank, R.C.: Inside Case-Based Reasoning. Lawrence Erlbaum Associates, Hillsdale, NJ, US (1989).
20. Srivastava, J., Cooley, R., Deshpande, M. and Tan P.-N.: Web Usage Mining: Discovery and Applications of Usage Patterns from Web Data. In SIGKDD Explorations, Vol. 1, No 2 (2000) 1–12.
21. W3C HTML Working Group. HyperText Markup Language (HTML) – Home Page. http://www.w3.org/MarkUp/. Access April 2006.

Conceptual Knowledge Retrieval with FooCA: Improving Web Search Engine Results with Contexts and Concept Hierarchies

Bjoern Koester

Webstrategy GmbH, Darmstadt, Germany
bjoern.koester@webstrategy.de
http://www.webstrategy.de

Abstract. This paper presents a new approach to accessing information on the Web. FooCA, an application in the field of Conceptual Knowledge Processing, is introduced to support a holistic representation of today's standard sequential Web search engine retrieval results. FooCA uses the itemset consisting of the title, a short description, and the URL to build a context and the appropriate concept hierarchy. In order to generate a nicely arranged concept hierarchy using line diagrams to retrieve and analyze the data, the prior context can be iteratively explored and enhanced. The combination of Web Mining techniques and Formal Concept Analysis (FCA) with contextual attribute elicitation gives the user more insight and more options than a traditional search engine interface. Besides serving as a tool for holistic data exploration, FooCA also enables the regular user to learn step by step how to run new, optimized search queries for his personal information need on the Web.

1 Introduction

Access to information through Web data plays an important role today [13]. While facing a rapidly growing flood of information on the World Wide Web, we see an increasing need for advanced tools that guide us to the kind of information we are looking for. Retrieval results of major search engines are growing every day. Especially searches for general terms usually end up with over one million results.

Judging over a larger, sequential list of results is almost impossible with the current user interfaces provided by major Web search engines today. Inspired by a discussion with Prof. Rudolf Wille who criticized the way society has been 'googlelized' by limiting searches to the first few pages retrieved via a regular Web search, this work aims at introducing an alternative way of retrieving Web search results.

The challenge for this explorative work was to see whether Google's three-row result itemset consisting of the title, a short description (a so-called snippet), and the URL could be used to build a meaningful context and an appropriate concept hierarchy.

P. Perner (Ed.): ICDM 2006, LNAI 4065, pp. 176–190, 2006.

In earlier stages of the project ([17], [18]), it had turned out that the presentation of the retrieved search engine results within a context already gives a valuable and holistic overview of information units and their relations. Now, the additional perspective of the corresponding concept hierarchy further improved and elaborated this effort.

This paper presents a new approach to accessing information on the Web. Conceptual Knowledge Processing is derived from a pragmatic understanding of knowledge according to which human knowledge is acquired and supported in a process of human thinking, reasoning, and communicating [23]. Methods and tools supporting conscious reflection, judgment and action are proposed that facilitate such a form of information gathering. This understanding of knowledge processing serves as the background of FooCA.

FooCA stands for a word combination of FCA and Google, the described FCA mechanisms having first been applied to a standard Google search. Since all major search engines do not differ significantly in the way they present their search results, FooCA aims at supporting a general approach for search engines.

The first part of FooCA uses a regular Web search engine for the retrieval of potential Web objects[1]. Giving autonomy and thus the decision-making ability back to the user, the second part is an interactive interface that allows the searcher to participate in selecting, filtering and choosing the best methods for customizing the results according to his information need. The user can choose among multiple search strategies and select those preferences best suited for his search interest. Depending on the strategies he has chosen, the search can range between being more accurate but slower, and less accurate but faster. After sending his search request the system assists the user in further refining his search query.

Search engine retrievals will be visualized first in a context to assist in further refining the search and reducing the complexity. Later, when the context has been successfully refined, the data can be visualized by a line diagram to establish a concept hierarchy.

Many expressions used in this paper are based on the terminology of Conceptual Knowledge Processing introduced in [24]. In general, when speaking about a *concept lattice*, we will refer to it by using the more general term *concept hierarchy*.

2   Formal Concept Analysis (FCA)

Formal Concept Analysis aims at gaining concepts and hierarchical implications out of data [14]. FCA studies how objects can be hierarchically grouped together according to their common attributes. We give a brief introduction.

---

[1] The term 'Web objects' is used throughout this paper to address various types of media that can be accessed via a URL (Unified Resource Locator). These are mainly Web pages, PDF documents or images.

Formal Context. A formal context $\mathbb{K} := (G, M, I)$ is composed of a set of objects G, a set of attributes M, and a binary relation $I \subseteq G \times M$. We call I the 'incidence relation' and read $(g, m) \in I$ as 'object g has the attribute m'.

A context $\mathbb{K}$ can be visualized by a two dimensional table, a cross table, containing crosses which indicate the incidence relation.

Derivation Operators. For a subset $A \subseteq G$ of the objects we define the set of attributes common to the objects in A as

$$A' := \{m \in M \mid gIm \ for \ all \ g \in A\} \tag{1}$$

respectively, for a subset $B \subseteq M$ of the attributes we define a set of objects which have all attributes in B as

$$B' := \{g \in G \mid gIm \ for \ all \ m \in B\} \tag{2}$$

From a Galois Connection to a Formal Concept. The pair of the derivation operators form a *Galois connection*. Thus the following statements are true for a given context (G, M, I), its subsets $A, A_1, A_2 \subseteq G$ of objects as well as its subsets $B, B_1, B_2 \subseteq M$ of attributes:

$$A_1 \subseteq A_2 \Rightarrow A_2' \subseteq A_1' \ and \ B_1 \subseteq B_2 \Rightarrow B_2' \subseteq B_1' \tag{3}$$

$$A \subseteq A'' \ and \ B \subseteq B'' \tag{4}$$

$$A' = A''' \ and \ B' = B''' \tag{5}$$

$$A \subseteq B' \Leftrightarrow B \subseteq A' \Leftrightarrow A \times B \subseteq I \tag{6}$$

Both, the derivation operators and the formed Galois connection now allow us to define a formal concept as follows.

Formal Concept. In a philosophical sense a concept consists of two parts: the extension and the intension. The extension covers all objects belonging to this concept and the intension comprises all attributes valid for all those objects.

A formal concept of the corresponding context $\mathbb{K} := (G, M, I)$ is composed of a pair (A, B) consisting of an extension $A \subseteq G$ and an intension $B \subseteq M$, to which the following apply:

$$A' = B \ and \ B' = A \tag{7}$$

We denote by $\mathfrak{B}(G, M, I)$ the set of all concepts of the context (G, M, I) and write $\mathfrak{B}(\mathbb{K})$ for short.

Concept Hierarchy. An important structure can be obtained by defining a subconcept-superconcept relation building a formal order relation on $\mathfrak{B}(G, M, I)$ which then enables us to form a mathematical lattice denoted by $\underline{\mathfrak{B}}(G, M, I)$. Such a lattice structure[2] can be visualized by line diagrams, as shown in Figure 2. A further mathematical introduction into these structures would lead far beyond the scope of this paper. Readers interested in a deeper insight into FCA are referred to [14].

3 Retrieval Via a Standard Web Search Engine

Our approach[3] is to launch a search request using the official programming interfaces provided by the search engines. The returned set of ranked items is then analyzed by means of Web Mining and FCA.

We first obtain ranked items that match the criteria of the internal and unrevealed ranking algorithms of the search engine. Since the search engine market has become competitive, the exact algorithms used for the ranking of Web results are classified.

3.1 Query Evaluation

For our frequent use of the term 'query' and its fundamental operations in the context of FooCA, we would like to propose a short introduction first.

Query. A query Q_i is a list of terms forming a request for information from a database. In almost all Web search engines, the entered query is parsed and segmented into terms. Adding additional terms to the query means that each term should appear in a document. We would like to simplify our understanding of a query as a list of terms with two operations only, the concatenation and explicit exclusion of terms:

Implicit AND Operator. The query 'data mining' results in a search for pages containing the words 'data' and 'mining'. Since there is no 'and' operator between the terms, this notation is called implicit AND. The focus of an AND query is to add more terms to establish a 'list of terms' that specializes or characterizes the search concept.

---

[2] We prefer using the more general term *concept hierarchy* instead, as this paper would like to address and inspire a broader group of people outside of abstract algebra as well.

[3] One other way of retrieving Web objects is to implement just another Web crawling agent that spiders and indexes all Web pages it can possibly find. But this approach would involve not only considerable cost through having to run the hardware and storage systems but also intensified internet traffic. In addition, it would take some time to make a crawler robust enough and the indexing fast enough. And then, we would lose a lot of time implementing a general retrieval task as it has already been done by so many institutions and companies worldwide.

Query Term Negation. Instead of adding terms to a query, it sometimes seems necessary to avoid the appearance of specific terms. As an example, a query for the term 'data mining' will return a lot of Web objects about data and mining in general (also mineral mining). Assuming that we are primarily interested in data mining, we could use the negation operator to exclude a term from the search by simply adding '-minerals' to our search query resulting in the following query that better suits our information need: 'data mining -minerals'. All pages returned contain 'data' and 'mining' and no instance of the term 'minerals'.

3.2   From Ranked Lists to Conceptual Structures

Considering the fact that we obtain a ranked set of documents which ran through a completely automated machinery, how would the automated system know exactly what the user really wants? A user might search for a term and get back more than one million documents matching his query. Now he has the option of clicking sequentially through all the results lists, checking each item and hopefully finding the relevant pages he was looking for. An alternative would be to further specify the query to limit results. This, however, requires a degree of familiarity with techniques for narrowing down a search query.

Hence, new ways of controlling and obtaining an overview of information need to be established to guide and assist the user instead of ignoring human skills, such as the intuitive understanding of a concept.

This paper proposes a vision as well as a working prototype that shows how traditional, sequential lists can indeed be replaced by conceptual structures.

4   Conceptual Knowledge Retrieval with FooCA

As introduced above, FooCA uses the search facilities provided by a standard Web search engine and enriches them by assisting the user and enabling him to control the search in more advanced ways.

4.1   Architecture

FooCA runs on a standard Linux system and is written in Perl. It communicates with the search engines using their official APIs.[4]

In a query result, we are interested in the general items returned by the Web search engine to a normal user: the title of the Web document, its URL, and the snippet that represents the semantic context in which the search query (or parts of it) occurred.

As shown in Figure 1, FooCA enables the user to interact with the search engine. The user has a specific but informal concept in mind that he wants to

---

[4] More information on the API for Google can be obtained at http://www.google.com/apis/reference.html, the API for Yahoo can be downloaded at http://developer.yahoo.net.

Fig. 1. FooCA interacts between the user and the search engine. Queries are passed to the search engine along with additional options. The results are then post-processed for visualization to the user.

search for. He then enters an approximate query that represents his concept, along with chosen options for later FooCA processing. FooCA then receives that information, evaluates the personal options for that user and re-submits his query to the search engine which interprets the query as if it were a normal search and processes it, returning the results in a ranked order to FooCA. Using the personal options and the search results retrieved, FooCA now generates its internal representation of the context and presents it to the user in a visualized form. From this point on, the user can refine his search with the FooCA interface.

4.2   Basic Feature Extraction Operations

In order to process attributes within FooCA, we need to identify word tokens. Therefore, some basic feature extraction operations are applied to the standard Web search engine retrieval results: Identification of tokens divided by space or punctuation, stripping of all HTML format tags, transforming all characters from upper- to lower-case and finally removing all special characters except for '-'. Using these basic operations,[5] a list of useful word tokens originating from the snippet can easily be generated.

4.3   From a Web Search Engine Retrieval to a Context

FooCA lets the user enter a query Q_i which is directly passed on to the Web search engine without modification. Web search engines usually offer the user a short excerpt of words before and after the occurrence of a term that appears in the query. This short excerpt is called a 'snippet'. The idea is to use that snippet as a starting point since it provides us with a short, non-formal context in which the search query (or parts of it) are embedded. In cases where no snippet is retrieved, the page title is used instead. After extracting feature terms from the retrieved snippets, we gain a context $\mathbb{K}$ considering the URLs as objects G and the extracted feature terms as attributes M as follows: $\mathbb{K}(Q_i) := (G, M, I)$.

---

[5] When using FooCA in German, an additional processing step to rewrite the German umlauts such as 'ö' or 'ä' to 'oe' and 'ae' is provided to map different writings of the same tokens onto one single attribute.

4.4 Representing the Context in a Cross Table

Once the user has enabled or disabled specific search strategies and entered the search query, FooCA presents the retrieved results in an interactive two-dimensional cross table. The row headers are object names, which are clickable numbers in our case, representing the ranked Web object search results. Columns are headed by attributes which are the extracted feature terms of the snippets. The incidence relation I of the context $\mathbb{K}$ between the Web objects G and its attributes M is marked by a cross '$\times$' in the table. The ith Web object possesses the jth attribute indicated by a cross in the (i, j) position.

The cross table can be navigated using the mouse. As the mouse cursor moves along the table, the underlying row is highlighted indicating the Web object. The user can click anywhere inside the table and is promptly directed to the related Web object.

Apart from navigating inside the table by way of the incidence relation of the context, another navigation method using query refinement is offered. The user can click on any listed attribute name in order to either search for that name directly, launching a new query with that attribute only, or he can include or exclude an attribute by further qualifying the previous query.

4.5 Search Preferences and Strategies

To cope with the rising flood of information in almost every field, the user has surrendered a part of his own authority of judgment to an automated evaluation process that makes decisions and acts based on certain rules.

FooCA gives the searcher the possibility to gain more control over the decision-making process by using methods and operations that are usually processed automatically in general search engines without human intervention. Those methods and operations provided by the FooCA application are described in the following subsections:

Choice of Search Engine. The user has the choice between a set of pre-integrated Web search engines. In fact, any search engine providing a sequential listing of search retrievals and a snippet can be integrated into FooCA by building a specific interface. As for the moment, interfaces for the two most popular search engines, Google and Yahoo, have been deployed successfully and tested thoroughly. More interfaces will be provided in the short term.

By using different search engines as the input source of the FooCA system, various different contexts can be generated and explored.

Language Restriction. Both, Google and Yahoo offer the possibility to restrict the search to a predefined subset of its Web object index. FooCA supports the search in English and German. However, depending on the facilities of the underlying search engine, other languages could easily be integrated as well.

Removal of Stop Words. Common words in a language that occur frequently but are insignificant for searching purposes can simply be removed. English stop words are, for instance, 'I', 'you', 'are', 'it', 'the', 'and', 'on' and 'of'. FooCA provides a list of general stop words for English and German.

Stemming. Stemming means reducing words to their respective grammatical root. This is accomplished either by using a rule-based stemming algorithm (such as the Porter stemmer [20]) or a knowledge base consisting of words and their related root forms. FooCA uses Porter stemming.

Clarification of the Context. The context $\mathbb{K} := (G, M, I)$ can be attribute-clarified to a context $(G, M/\sim, \tilde{I})$, where $\sim$ is the equivalance relation with $m \sim n :\Longleftrightarrow m' \sim n'$. A corresponding clarification of objects cannot be implemented due to the line-based navigation within the cross table which associates each line with a distinct Web object.

User-Based Query Refinement. In FooCA, we understand a query Q_i to be a set of attributes of our attribute set M, $Q_i \subseteq M$. Although this is a very simplified view on queries – we are not considering any advanced operations here – we gain a lot of power by simply adding and removing attributes from an attribute set.

By letting the user decide about the importance or unimportance of the attributes presented, the system enables him to refine the search space accordingly and trigger a new information retrieval process. Just as in the process of adding new query terms into the Web search engine form, the user can simply click an attribute representing a query term and decide to either include or exclude that term in a new search process. The main difference between the FooCA-based refinement process for a query and the manual refinement using the original Web search interfaces consists in the set of given attributes. Typically, the user is not entirely clear from the beginning which term(s) are needed to narrow a specific search. With FooCA presenting the attributes in an attribute-object relation, the user is able to inspect the context and make his decision based on that specific contextual knowledge. Furthermore, new relationships or erroneous relationships become apparent in a holistic way.

In our approach, removed attributes are not actually removed from the retrieved document collection; instead a new query is defined explicitly excluding that removed attribute. A new context for the new, refined query is then generated and displayed.

For easy navigation and intuitive handling of the refinement process when the query refinement option is enabled, each attribute column is headed by a big green checkmark followed by a red cross. When the user wants to refine his search by accepting the whole concept formed by the attribute set contained in a column, he can simply click on the green checkmark. The next iteration of the search is then refined including all search attributes shown underneath the previously clicked checkmark. Correspondingly, clicking on the big red cross, the search is refined by excluding all listed attributes within that column. For a more subtle refinement, a smaller green plus and a red minus symbol are placed behind each attribute to initiate a single-attribute refinement.

Limiting by an Object Count for Attributes. A reduction of the corresponding context seems appropriate. The user can limit his view of the context by increasing the object count for attributes. The default value for the object count corresponds to the full context. Increasing the object count decreases the number of attributes shown in the context and hence makes visualization easier when concentrating on the more prominent attributes only.

Minimum Attribute Length. In most cases it seems necessary to filter out tokens that are small in size, especially words with less than three characters. However, in some search scenarios even small words are relevant. The user decides whether he wants to use this option to remove all words with less than n characters.

Attribute Ranking. FooCA retrieves Web object references in a pre-ranked order based on the search engine's own ranking criteria. A hybrid approach for ranking seems to be a pragmatic solution, since we can maintain the ranking for the objects and combine them with a new ranking of the related attributes. This approach seems natural as we read from top left to bottom right. The goal is to achieve a diagonal area of crosses in the cross table starting from the upper left to the lower right. To that end, attributes are ranked first by the number of objects they are related to and second by the sum of the ranking positions of the related objects. The latter corresponds to, and respects, the prior ranking of the search engine.

Exporting the Context. In addition to FooCA, the corresponding lattice visualization of a context, the explored formal context can easily be exported into your favorite visualization program for further operations. FooCA offers an export interface using the Burmeister Format (CXT). We have tested importing contexts generated by FooCA in ToscanaJ/Siena[6] [2].

4.6   Visualization of the Concept Hierarchy Using FlashLattice

Finally, after successfully refining the context $\mathbb{K}$, its concept hierarchy $\mathfrak{B}(\mathbb{K})$ can be visualized by a line diagram using FlashLattice as used in SurfMachine[10] and D-SIFT[11], which has been contributed as a plugin for FooCA by Jon Ducrou from the University of Wollongong, Australia. FlashLattice provides the ability to visualize the prior refined context in a corresponding concept hierarchy, where each circle represents a concept, and lines between the concepts represent their subconcept-superconcept relation as shown in [8]. When clicking a concept button, the URLs attached to it will be opened in separate browser windows.

5   Example of a FooCA Web Search Analysis

5.1   Stepwise Context Size Reduction Via a Cross Table

Figure 2 shows the results for the query 'ICDM 2006' in FooCA. The context has already been refined by allowing only a minimum of four objects per attribute

---

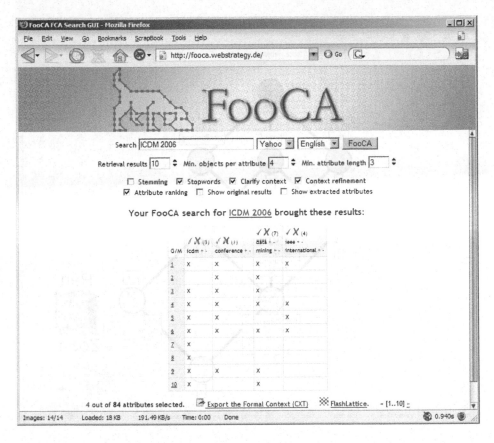

Fig. 2. FooCA result for the query 'ICDM 2006' on ten Yahoo results after a human-oriented context refinement process

and at least three characters of size for the attributes. Further optional preferences such as enabling stopword filtering, clarification of the context, query refinement and attribute ranking have been enabled in this example.

5.2 Visualization of the Concept Hierarchy Using a Line Diagram

In order to support data analysis, and hence, enable judgment over Web search engine data retrieval, data is presented to the user in the expanded form of a 'landscape structure'. Fortunately, FCA provides us with methods to support such a structured visualization. Every (finite) context can be represented by a concept hierarchy which is best visualized by a line diagram. A concept hierarchy represents the subconcept-superconcept relation. Concepts are represented by circles, whereas the relationships between concepts are symbolized by lines. Object labels are attached below the circles, whereas attribute labels are attached above attributes. These labels allow the diagram to be read and interpreted in two ways. As stated earlier in the FCA introductory section, the

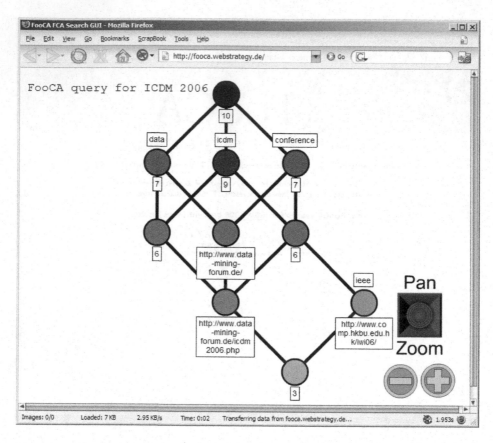

Fig. 3. FooCA showing the concept hierarchy for the query 'ICDM 2006' of ten Yahoo results. All Web objects can be opened by clicking on a concept. New or previously unknown relationships within the data set such as that there are two conferences on different continents called 'ICDM 2006' have been made visible.

extension covers all objects belonging to a concept and the intension comprises all attributes valid for all those objects. The extension of a distinct concept can then be read in a line diagram by starting at the very concept, following the objects downward along the path. An equivalent procedure can be done on the intension of a certain concept by following the attributes upward along the path.

The line diagram in Figure 3 can be read as follows: attributes, which are labeled above the circles, are 'data', 'icdm', 'conference' and 'ieee'. Labeled below the circles are the objects. At first, the objects are hidden behind a white label only indicating the count of objects that are clustered within or below the concept. By clicking at the label, the label window opens showing all objects associated with that specific object. In this example two object labels have been opened to reveal different semantics for the search query 'ICDM 2006': Considering the attributes 'data' and 'conference', the top concept for the object URL http://www.data-mining-forum.de is visualized right in the center of the hierarchy. The web page behind that URL is the host of the ICDM 2006 conference in Leipzig, Germany. Right below this concept, the official ICDM 2006 homepage can be found. The difference between them is the attribute 'icdm' which does not belong to the host web page, but instead to the official conference web page at http://www.data-mining-forum.de/icdm2006.php. All attributes except for 'ieee' are in its intension. If you look on the right hand side, you will find the two labels 'ieee' and the URL http://www.comp.hkbu.edu.hk/iwi06 attached to a concept which is just another conference called ICDM hosted in China. By clicking on one of the concepts, a new browser window opens directing right to the URLs represented by the related Web objects.

6   Conclusion and Discussion

In this paper, we have presented an approach combining Formal Concept Analysis with Web Mining techniques to build a tool that applies Conceptual Knowledge Processing in information retrieval.

In FooCA as well as in any other information retrieval system, the user enters his own concepts in the form of a query of terms into the system. New with FooCA are the pre- and post-processing steps. A query is submitted along with user-selected options and the results are post-processed in order to obtain conceptual information.

After submitting the query, the user receives feedback in the form of a re-trieval result presented in a context as shown in Figure 1 and represented by a line diagram of the concept hierarchy as shown in Figure 2. By his evaluation of, and judgment on, a larger conceptual presentation of terms and their rela-tions to certain objects, the user learns to refine his query, developing similar or closely related queries and exploring their results interactively to define entirely new queries. By personally influencing the refining process using the interactive cross table, the user therefore not only finds new queries but also develops and adapts new concepts of thinking. The graphical representation of a line diagram uncovers conceptual structures that are closely related to cognitive structures of the human mind [21]. FooCA has indeed shown that it not only allows new con-cepts to be explored by searching for related queries using the query refinement mechanism, but that it also supports a holistic interpretation of, and judgment over, a larger amount of data by visualizing conceptual structures.

Consequently, using FooCA involves a learning process whereby the user un-derstands how to close the systematically-evolving, semantic-pragmatic gap as described by Andelfinger [1].

According to Weber [22], the Kantian capacity to judge [16], whereby symbols involve a double judgment, is extended by a new technological dimension that unfolds in three steps:

> First, the capacity to judge applies a concept of a model to an object of sensible intuition. Then, it applies the mere rule of reflection to a different object of which the first is only a symbol. Finally, it establishes a relationship allowing the model to affect the object.

As a result, FooCA is a highly supportive tool assisting a user in assessing search retrievals. It gives the user more insight and an increased range of active possibilities than he would have with a traditional search engine interface.

Consequently, there is a definite need for establishing the idea of Conceptual Knowledge Processing in a next generation of information retrieval systems, a need for solutions that offer assistance. Further research in this area would appear appropriate.

6.1   Related Work

Approaches to enhancing information retrieval results have been studied for some time. Hearst [15] gives a general overview of user interfaces for information retrieval systems. Marchionini et. al. [19] have reported on ongoing efforts to develop and test generalizable user interfaces that provide interactive overviews for large-scale Web sites and portals.

Carpineto and Romano [6,7] introduced an FCA approach in 2004 with CREDO.[7] However, CREDO presents results in the look of a cluster-based search engine such as Clusty.[8] Although hierarchically focussing on specialized concepts, the user is confronted with a standard sequential list view consisting of title, link and a text snippet.

6.2   Future Work

FooCA has shown a successful way of giving structure to mostly unstructured or poorly structured data. The quality of the concept hierarchy and its corresponding line diagram can of course be heavily increased by obtaining more background knowledge. A possible approach to obtain background knowledge is inherent in the Web itself. Due to its inherent knowledge, a huge variety of freely-available knowledge bases can either be used or newly created by means of (semantic) Web Mining [3]. In Tim Berners-Lee's vision of the Semantic Web [4], all information on the World Wide Web can be connected. As for today, the Semantic Web is still a vision. Furthermore, doubts have arisen regarding the practicability of the Semantic Web approach [9].

Nevertheless, once we have a knowledge base that is suitable for a specific search domain, interfaces can be implemented. Knowledge bases could consist of domain-specific vocabularies or thesauri that limit the attributes in our example to the desired topic or domain, such as the online thesaurus that contains information about synonyms and hypernyms, WordNet.[9]

We hope we have been able to show new ways of combining fast search results, giving the user full control over fundamental searching strategies, and unlocking data through new forms of representation such as contexts and concept hierarchies with FooCA.

In a nutshell, FooCA is an innovative, practical implementation of Conceptual Knowledge Processing.

---

[7] http://credo.fub.it
[8] http://www.clusty.com
[9] http://wordnet.princeton.edu

Acknowledgments

We would like to thank Prof. Rudolf Wille[10] and Joachim Hereth Correia[11] for their support throughout the project. We also thank Jon Ducrou[12] for his contribution of the Web-based Flash application called FlashLattice which has been integrated into FooCA as a plugin.

References

1. Andelfinger, U.: Diskursive Anforderungsanalyse. Ein Beitrag zum Reduktionsproblem bei Systementwicklungen in der Informatik. Peter Lang, Frankfurt 1997 (in German).
2. Becker, P., Hereth Correia, J.: The ToscanaJ Suite for Implementing Conceptual Information Systems. In Ganter, B., Stumme, G. and Wille, R. (Eds.): Formal Concept Analysis, Foundations and Applications. Springer-Verlag, Berlin, 2005.
3. Berendt, B., Hotho, A., Stumme, G.: Towards Semantic Web Mining. In International Semantic Web Conference, ISWC02, Springer-Verlag, Berlin, 2002.
4. Berners-Lee, T.: Weaving the Web: The Past, Present and Future of the World Wide Web by its Inventor. Texere, London, 1999.
5. Brin, S., Page, L.: The anatomy of a large-scale hypertextual Web search engine. In Computer Networks and ISDN Systems, Elsevier, Amsterdam, 1998.
6. Carpineto, C., Romano, G.: Concept Data Analysis: Theory and Applications. John Wiley & Sons, Chichester, 2004.
7. Carpineto, C., Romano, G.: Exploiting the Potential of Concept Lattices for Information Retrieval with CREDO. In Journal of Universal Computer Science, Springer-Verlag, Berlin, 2004.
8. Cole, R., Ducrou, J., and Eklund, P.: Automated Layout of Small Lattices Using Layer Diagrams. In Missaoui, R., Schmid, J. (Eds.): Formal Concept Analysis, 4th International Conference, ICFCA 2006, Dresden, Germany, Proceedings. Springer-Verlag, Berlin, 2006.
9. de Moor, A.: Patterns for the Pragmatic Web. In Dau, F., Mugnier, M., Stumme, G. (Eds.): Conceptual Structures: Common Semantics for Sharing Knowledge, ICCS05, Springer-Verlag, Berlin, 2005.
10. Ducrou, J., Eklund, P.: Combining Spatial and Lattice-based Information Landscapes. In Ganter, B., Godin, R. (Eds.): Proceedings of the 3rd Int. Conference on Formal Concept Analysis, ICFCA 2005, Springer-Verlag, Berlin, 2005.
11. Ducrou, J., Wormuth, B., Eklund, P.: D-SIFT: A Dynamic Simple Intuitive FCA Tool. In Dau, F., Mugnier, M., Stumme, G. (Eds.): Conceptual Structures: Common Semantics for Sharing Knowledge: Proceedings of the 13th International Conference on Conceptual Structures, Springer-Verlag, Berlin 2005.
12. Eklund, P., Ducrou, J., Brawn, P.: Concept Lattices for Information Visualization: Can novices read line diagrams. In Eklund, P. (Ed.): Proceedings of the 2nd International Conference on Formal Concept Analysis, ICFCA 2004, Springer-Verlag, Berlin, 2004.

---

[10] AG Algebra und Logik, Darmstadt University of Technology, Germany
[11] Institut für Algebra, Technische Universität Dresden, Germany
[12] School of Economics and Information Systems, University of Wollongong, Australia

13. Fürnkranz, J.: Web Mining. In Maimon, O. and Rokach, L. (Eds.), Data Mining and Knowledge Discovery Handbook, Springer-Verlag, Berlin, 2005.
14. Ganter, B., Wille, R.: Formal Concept Analysis: Mathematical Foundations. Springer-Verlag, Berlin, 1999.
15. Hearst, M.: User interfaces and visualization. In Modern Information Retrieval, edited by R. Baeza-Yates and B. Ribeiro-Neto. ACM Press, New York, 1999.
16. Kant, I.: Kritik der Urteilskraft. Ed.: Wilhelm Weischedel. Suhrkamp, Frankfurt am Main, 2004 (in German).
17. Koester, B.: Conceptual Knowledge Processing with Google. In Bauer, M., Fürnkranz, J., Kröner, A. et. al. (Eds.): Lernen, Wissensentdeckung und Adaptivität, LWA 2005, GI Workshops, Saarbrücken, October 10th-12th, 2005.
18. Koester, B.: FooCA: Enhancing Google Information Research by Means of Formal Concept Analysis. In Ganter, B., Kwuida, L. (Eds.): Contributions to ICFCA 2006, Verlag Allgemeine Wissenschaft, Mühltal, 2006.
19. Marchionini, G. and Brunk, B.: Towards a General Relation Browser: A GUI for Information Architects. Journal of Digital Information, Volume 4 Issue 1, Texas A&M University Libraries, 2003.
20. Porter, M.F.: An Algorithm for Suffix Stripping. In Readings in information retrieval. Morgan Kaufmann Multimedia Information And Systems Series, San Francisco, 1997.
21. Seiler, Th. B.: Begreifen und Verstehen. Ein Buch über Begriffe und Bedeutungen. Verlag Allgemeine Wissenschaft, Mühltal, 2001 (in German).
22. Weber, D.: Kybernetische Interventionen. Zum Kritischen Verständnis des immanenten Verhältnisses von Multimedia und Pädagogik. Verlag für Sozialwissenschaften, Wiesbaden, 2005 (in German).
23. Wille, R.: Conceptual Knowledge Processing in the Field of Economics. In Ganter, B., Stumme, G., Wille, R.: Formal Concept Analysis. Foundations and Applications. Springer-Verlag, Berlin, 2005.
24. Wille, R.: Methods of Conceptual Knowledge Processing. In In Missaoui, R., Schmid, J. (Eds.): Formal Concept Analysis, 4th International Conference, ICFCA 2006, Dresden, Germany, Proceedings. Springer-Verlag, Berlin, 2006.

A Pruning Based Incremental Construction Algorithm of Concept Lattice*

Zhang Ji-Fu[1,2], Hu Li-Hua[1], and Zhang Su-Lan[1]

[1] School of Computer Science and Technology, Tai-Yuan University of Science and Technology, Tai-Yuan 030024, P.R. China
[2] National Laboratory of Pattern Recognition, Institute of Automation, Chinese Academy of Sciences, Beijing 100080, P.R. China
jifuzh@sina.com

Abstract. The concept lattice has played an important role in knowledge discovery. However due to inevitable occurrence of redundant information in the construction process of concept lattice, the low construction efficiency has been a main concern in the literature. In this work, an improved incremental construction algorithm of concept lattice over the traditional Godin algorithm, called the pruning based incremental algorithm is proposed, which uses a pruning process to detect and eliminate possible redundant information during the construction. Our pruning based construction algorithm is in nature superior to the Godin algorithm. It can achieve the same structure with the Godin algorithm but with less computational complexity. In addition, our pruning based algorithm is also experimentally validated by taking the star spectra from the LAMOST project as the formal context.

Keywords: concept lattice, pruning, redundant information, incremental construction algorithm, star spectra.

1 Introduction

From a philosophical point of view, a concept is a unit of thoughts consisting of two parts, the extension and the intension. Based on the philosophical understanding of concept, the formal concept analysis [1] was introduced by Wille.R in 1982, and later used to detect, sort and display of concepts. Based on the formal concept analysis, the extension covers all objects belonging to this concept and the intension comprises all attributes valid for all those objects, by which the philosophical understanding of concept was realized. By nature, concept lattice describes the relationship between objects and attributes, indicates the relationship of generation and specialization between concepts. Besides, its Hasse diagram is an effective tool of data visualization. Thanks to its straightness, simplicity and completeness of knowledge expressing, the concept lattice has been widely applied in software engineer, knowledge engineer, knowledge discovery and so on [2], [3], [11], etc.

* This paper is supported by the National Natural Science Foundation of P.R.China (60573075).

P. Perner (Ed.): ICDM 2006, LNAI 4065, pp. 191–201, 2006.
© Springer-Verlag Berlin Heidelberg 2006

At present, broadly speaking, there are two kinds of concept lattice construction algorithms: The incremental algorithm [4], [5], [6] and the patch algorithm [8]. The basic idea of the patch algorithm is to generate all concepts at first, then according to the relationship of generation and specialization, to generates edges, then form concept lattice. Such algorithms include Bordat algorithm, OSHAM algorithm, Chein algorithm, Ganter algorithm, Nourine algorithm and so on [8]. The basic idea of the incremental construction algorithm is to initialize a null concept at first, then gradually form concept lattice by adopting different suitable operations based on the intersection difference between the attributes of a newly added object with the intension of the original concept lattice nodes. Such algorithms include Godin, Gapineto and T.B.Ho algorithm [2], [8]. Many researchers have proposed some improvements on the above algorithms, such as the fast incremental algorithm for building concept lattice [9] and so on. Lots of experiments show that the incremental construction algorithm is a promising one, and the Godin algorithm is a typical incremental construction algorithm.

In many cases, concept lattice construction uses mass, high-dimensional data as formal context. For the analysis of mass data, usually too many nodes are generated due to the completeness requirement of concept lattice, which in turn causes large storage and low construction efficiency during the incremental construction process, because the attributes of a newly added object must be compared with the intension of the original concept lattice nodes one by one. As a result, with more added objects, the updating efficiency of concept lattice becomes worse. In reality, in the process of incremental construction, much redundant information is generated, which unnecessarily increases the comparing times of concept lattice intension but has no effect on the resulting structure. Hence how to eliminate or reduce the redundant information in the concept lattice construction process is a key issue to increase its construction efficiency. To this end, we propose a technique, coined as "pruning", to eliminate possible redundant information in this work, and the proposed algorithm is shown to work satisfactorily. In particular, our experiments show that our proposed algorithm (PCL) could improve the construction efficiency by above 15 % than the Godin algorithm, a popular algorithm in the literature.

2 Basic Concept of the General Concept Lattice and Its Incremental Construction

Definition 1. A formal context is defined as a triplet K=(O, D R), where O is a set of objects, D is a set of attributes and R is a binary relation between O and D, which describes the inherent lattice structure and defines the natural groupings and relationships between the objects and their attributes. This structure is known as a concept lattice or Galois lattice L.

Definition 2. Given a concept lattice L constructed from formal context K, each one of its nodes is a couple, denoted as C (A, B), where $A \in P$ (O) is called the extension of concept, $B \in P$ (D) called the intension of concept. P(O) and P(D) are power sets of O and D respectively.

Definition 3. Concept lattice L must be a complete couple with respect to R. that means for each node C (A, B), following two conditions are both satisfied:

(1) $A=B'=\{a\in O|\ \forall b\in B,\ a\ R\ b\}$

(2) $B=A'=\{b\in D|\ \forall a\in A,\ a\ R\ b\}$

Definition 4. In the concept lattice L, if a node Ci (Ai, Bi) satisfies the following condition, it is defined as the supremum of this node, denoted as Sup(Ci). J is the alphabetical order set of concept lattice L.

$$\underset{i\in J}{\vee}(A_i,B_i)=\left(\left(\underset{i\in J}{\cap}B_i\right)',\underset{i\in J}{\cap}B_i\right)$$

Definition 5. If C1=(A1, B1) and C2=(A2, B2) are two different nodes, then $C1<C2 \Leftrightarrow A1\subset A2 \Leftrightarrow B2\subset B1$. If there does not exist other node C3=(A3,B3) in the lattice such that C1<C3<C2, we say C1 is the sub(child) concept of C2 , denoted as C1=child(C2) ; C2 is the super (parent) concept of C1, denoted as C2=father (C1).

In general, the formal context of concept lattice is represented by a table as shown in Table 1, where the rows represent objects, and the column represent attributes. As an example, the corresponding concept lattice of Table 1 is shown in Fig. 1.

Table 1. Formal Context

O D	A	B	C	D	E
1	√	√			
2		√		√	√
3		√	√		
4	√			√	
5			√		

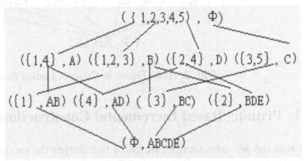

Fig. 1. Hasse Figure of General Concept Lattice

Given a concept lattice L, constructed from the formal context K=(O, D, R), the incremental construction is such a process that while a new object x is added (S is the set of attributes of x), the concept lattice L is modified according to the relationship between the attributes of the object x and the intension of the original concept lattice nodes at the new formal context K'=(O $\cup$ {x}, D, R). In the process of incremental construction, according to the attribute set S of the newly added object and the intension of the original concept lattice nodes, concept lattice nodes can be classified into three cases: old node, modified node and newly added node. Their definitions are:

Definition 6. Let C (A, B) be a node of concept lattice L, if the intersection between B and S is NULL, denoted as B∩S=Φ, then C is called an old node.

Definition 7. Let C (A, B) be a node of concept lattice L, if B is a subset of S, i.e., B⊆S, then C is called a modified node.

Definition 8. Let C (A, B) be a node of concept lattice L, if the intersection between B and S, H=B∩S, is not NULL, denoted as H≠Φ, and then C is called a generated node. Additionally if the following two conditions are both satisfied:

    (1)   H is not equal to the intension of any nodes of concept lattice L.
    (2)   The intersection of S with any super node C_1 of C is not equal to H, i.e., $B_1 \cap S \neq H$,

Then $C_1=(A \cup \{x\}, H)$ is called a newly added node of concept lattice L.

Fig2 shows the old nodes, modified nodes, and newly added nodes by the incremental construction algorithm. Fig. 2. is generated from Fig .1. by adding a new object x (6, {A, E}). The node ({2,6}, E) is a new node; all the other nodes are old ones.

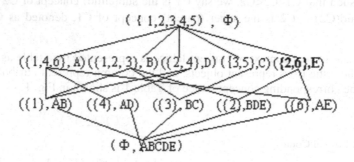

Fig. 2. Hasse Figure of Concept Lattice from a New Object

3 Pruning Based Incremental Construction of Concept Lattice

From the previous section, we know that during the incremental construction, the nodes and edges corresponding to modified nodes or newly added nodes should be modified. As a result, it is possible that unnecessary comparisons between S and B occur. Hence by eliminating or avoiding such unnecessary comparisons, the construction efficiency could be improved.

Definition 9. Let C (A, B) be a node of concept lattice L, C1 (A1, B1) and C2 (A2, B2) are two sub (child) nodes of C, C1=child(C), C2=child(C), C1 and C2 are called the sibling nodes. The sub (child) nodes C1 or C2, denoted as offs(C), offs(C) are called the offspring nodes of C.

Definition 10. Let C (A, B) be a node of concept lattice L, the number of the objects contained in A is called the support of extension of concept C, denoted as |A|. The number of the attributes contained in B is called the support of intension of concept C, denoted as |B|.

Definition 11. Let C (A, B) be a node of concept lattice L and C be a modified node with respect to a newly added object x during the incremental construction process, if C is modified as C_1 (A_1, B_1), where $A \subset A_1$ and $B_1=B$, then C_1 (A_1, B_1) is called the redundant information.

Theorem 1. Let C=(A, B) be a node of concept lattice L, x is a newly added object (its attributes set is S), if C is modified to C_1 (A_1, B_1), and B is not equal to Sup (S), then C_1 (A_1, B_1) must be redundant information.

Proof. Since B is not equal to Sup (S), there must exist a node C_2 (A_2, B_2) such that $B_2 \subset B$ and $A \subset A_2$ in the concept lattice L. Since C is a modified node, we have $B \subseteq S$, then $B_2 \subseteq S$. Node C_1 (A $\cup$ {x}, S) could be generated from the newly added object x and C, and node C_3 ($A_2 \cup$ {x}, S) could be generated from x and C_2. By definition 11, C_1 is redundant information.

Definition 12. In the incremental construction process of concept lattice, the operations of eliminating redundant information is called pruning.

Theorem 2. The pruning of concept lattice does not disrupt the completeness of concept lattice.

Proof. Suppose redundant information C_1 (A_1, B_1) is generated during the incremental construction process of concept lattice L, from theorem 1, C_1 (A $\cup$ {x}, S) and C_3 ($A_2 \cup$ {x}, S) are generated also. Hence after the pruning of concept lattice, redundant information is eliminated, and C_3 ($A_2 \cup$ {x}, S) is generated from the newly added object x and C_2. So the pruning of concept lattice does not disrupt the completeness of concept lattice.

From Theorem 2, redundant information only adds comparing times of concept lattice intension; it does not affect the structure of concept lattice.

The comparisons of the attribute set S of the newly added object x with the intension B of a node C (A, B) of concept lattice can be listed as the following 4 cases:

1) B is a subset of S ($B \subset S$)

If $B \subset S$, it indicates that the generated nodes by adding object x are the parent nodes of C. In this case, it is unnecessary to compare with the child or offspring nodes of C;

2) S is the supermum of B

If B=Sup(S), it indicates the generated nodes by adding object x is the child nodes of C. No further operation is needed;

3) B=S

In this case, it suffices to modify node C and the extensions of all the parent nodes of C.

4) $B \cap S \neq \Phi$ and $B \not\subset S$

In this case, a new node should be added, and at the same time, this newly added node should be compared with the existing nodes.

Based on the above analysis, we can see that the process of pruning can reduce the redundant information, decrease the comparing times of concept lattice intension without affecting its structure during the construction of concept lattice. And additionally, its completeness is also preserved. Hence by combining with the Godin algorithm, the basic principle of the pruning based incremental construction of concept lattice can be outlined as:

If the attribute set of a newly added object is a subset of the intension of concept lattice nodes, it will generate redundant information from theorem 1 when compared with the sub concepts of the concept lattice nodes. In order to eliminate such redundant information, we can use the pruning of concept lattice to find the subset of the newly added object such that it does not need to compare with sub nodes and offspring nodes. Similarly if the attribute set of a newly added object is equal to the intension of concept lattice nodes, no comparison with sub nodes and offspring nodes is needed either.

The above process is an improvement of the Godin algorithm. It is capable of eliminating redundant information during the construction process, and consequently enhancing the construction efficiency. In addition, the construction process is a top-down process.

Theorem 3. In the construction process of concept lattice by the pruning based incremental construction algorithm, if no redundant information is generated, the pruning based algorithm is degenerated to the Godin algorithm.

Proof. If no redundant information is generated, it means there is no super-node relationship between the newly added object with the other nodes, i.e., comparisons with the offspring of node C do not occur, hence the construction process by the pruning based algorithm is identical to that by the Godin algorithm, and the two algorithms also possess the same time complexity.

Theorem 4. The construction efficiency of the pruning based algorithm is better than that of the Godin algorithm.

Proof. If redundant information is generated in the incremental construction process, according to theorem 1 and theorem 2, the pruning process reduces the number of the comparisons between the intensions, hence its computational efficiency is better than that of the Godin algorithm. On the other hand, if no redundant information is generated in the incremental construction process, according to theorem 3, the two construction algorithms have the same computational complexity. Combining these two cases, we can see that the construction efficiency of the pruning based algorithm is no worse than that of the Godin algorithm in all possible cases.

4   Pruning Based Incremental Construction Algorithm of Concept Lattice Entries

A pseudo-code of our pruning based incremental construction algorithm of concept lattice (PCL in short) could be described as follow:

```
PCL (The pruning based concept lattice) algorithm:
Input:The original concept lattice and a new added object,
the nodes of the original concept lattice are sorted in the
deceasing order of their support of intensions.
output : A new concept lattice
/* inte: the intension of a concept lattice node; exte: the
extension of a concept lattice node; father: the super node
of a concept lattice node; child : the sub node of concept
lattice node; now:is the current label number of the concept
lattice node */
```

```
(1)  Input a new object
(2)  Search the concept lattice nodes from top to down, and
       compare the attribute set of the new object with the
       intension of the current concept lattice.
(3)  Set the new object to a new node new c, its intension
       is new, its extension is code, its super node is
       newfather, its sub node is newchild
(4)  for I=now to 1
(5)    determine the relationship between new and inte
(6)        call procedure "judge" (new,inte) ;
(7)  next I
(8)  end PCL;
     judge(new,inte)
(1)   if  new⊆inte then
(2)          fetch newfahter
(3)        if I∉newfather then
(4)            add a new edge I->new
(5)            code=exte∪code
(6)            father=father∪code
(7)          newchild=newchild∪code
(8)          end if
(9)          exit for
(10)   elseif inte⊆new then
(11)          fetch newchild
(12)        if I∉newchild then
(13)            add a new edge new->I
(14)            newfather=I∪newfather
(15)            exte=exte∪code
(16)            child=child∪code
(17)          end if
(18)   elseif inte=new then
(19)        fetch I and the extension exte of all its
       supernodes
(20)          exte=exte∪code
(21)          delete node new
(22)          exit for
(23)   elseif  inte∩new≠Φ then
(24)        add a new concept lattice node newjoin, the
       intersection intension is join
(25)          for j=1 to now
(26)            if  j≠now then
(27)                if  join=inte  then
(28)                    update j
(29)                    delete node newjoin
```

```
(30)                    end if
(31)                  end if
(32)            next for
(33)      if not exist equal then
(34)              njexte=code∪exte
(35)              njinte=join
(36)              njchild=code∪I
(37)              determine   the   superconcept   relationship
          between newjoin and other concept lattice nodes
(38)            if ∃newjoin's  super node,  then
(39)                repeat the above modifying operations of the
          super node
(40)              end if
(41)            end if
(42)          end if;
(43)   end judge;
```

In the process of the traditional incremental construction, when a new object is added to the formal context, it must be compared with all the nodes of the original concept lattice. As a result, the algorithm computational complexity increases exponentially at the worst case. More specifically, time complexity of the general concept lattice is O ($2^K|U|$).

For our PCL, when a newly added object is compared with the current concept lattice nodes, if it exists the relationship of the super nodes as before, it becomes unnecessary to continue the comparison process. As a result, it can reduce the comparisons, and the time complexity of our PCL algorithm PCL is no larger than O ($2^K|U|$).

5   Experiment Analysis

Now a large telescope called LAMOST (Large Sky Area Multi-Object Fiber Spectroscopic Telescope) is under construction in the National Observatory in Beijing, China. After its scheduled completion in 2006, it is expected to collect more than 40,000 spectrums in a single observation night Such voluminous data demand automatic spectrum processing and data mining [12]. In this section, we will give some results of our experiments on the concept lattice construction from the observed celestial spectrums.

The experiment setup is: PentiumIII-1.0G CPU, 256M memory, Windows 2000 operating system and ORACLE 9i DBMS. Both the PCL algorithm and the Godin algorithm are coded in Visual Basic 6.0. The star spectra are treated by the following steps, then used as the formal context:

1)   For each star spectrum, choose 200 wave-length from 3510 A to 8330 A at a step of 20 A as its attributes set.

2)   At the above each chosen wave length, the corresponding flux, peak width and shape information of the spectrum are quantified respectively into one of the 13 different intervals in total.

Table2 are the results of the concept lattice construction, where 150 wave-lengths are used as the attribute set, 500, 1000, 1500, 2000, 2404 B-type star spectra are used as the data objects. Table 3 are the construction results of concept lattice, where the size of the attributes set is 100, 125, 150, 175, 200, and 1500 B-type star spectra are used as the objects.

Table 2. Experimental Comparison of Various Object SetsBetween the Godin and PCL Algorithms

The number of objects	Godin algorithm (seconds)	PCL algorithm (seconds)	The number of nodes
500	108	75	1035
1000	409	348	1462
1500	830	724	1652
2000	1511	1368	2051
2404	2639	2452	2997

Table 3. Experimental Comparison of Various Attribute Sets Between the Godin and PCL Algorithms

The number of attributes	Godin algorithm (seconds)	PCL algorithm (seconds)	The number of nodes
100	123	96	227
125	195	147	373
150	830	724	1652
175	1577	1450	2393
200	2533	2278	3259

From Table2 and Table3, it can be concluded that:

(1) The Godin algorithm and the PCL algorithm can construct the same concept lattice. In other words, the number of the constructed nodes, the corresponding intension, extension, and father-son relationships are the same for both the two algorithms. This verifies the theoretical correctness of the PCL algorithm;

(2) The PCL algorithm is more efficient than the Godin algorithm. This indicates that in the incremental construction process, redundant information is indeed generated for newly added objects, and by pruning, such redundant information is indeed removed.

(3) Dependent on formal context, the efficiency improvement of the PCL algorithm over the Godin algorithm varies. But on average, a 15% improvement is obtained. In addition, since redundant information could occur only for modified nodes, the improvement of the PCL algorithm is only related to the modified nodes, not the total nodes. For example, in Table2, when the number of objects is 2404, the efficiency improvement is not as significant as the other cases. In Table3, the improvement for the case of 175 attributes is not as significant as that for the case of

125 attributes. Their underlying main reason is that although the newly added nodes are large in these cases, the modified nodes are relatively small, as a result, the chance of generating redundant information is relatively small, hence small improvements of their computational efficiency.

6 Conclusions

An improved algorithm to the Godin algorithm, a benchmark of the incremental construction of concept lattice in the literature, is proposed in this work. The key novelty of our proposed algorithm is that during the construction process of concept lattice, a pruning process is activated to detect and eliminate possible generated redundant information, by which the number of the comparisons of concept lattice intensions is largely reduced when a new node is added, and the construction efficiency is consequently increased. In addition, our pruning based incremental construction algorithm is tested using the star spectra from the LAMOST project as the formal context. The preliminary experimental results show that our pruning based algorithm could have a 15% improvement on average on the construction efficiency over the Godin Algorithm. Finally, as the performance of our pruning based algorithm depends crucially on the formal context, and our currently used attributes of spectra are rather simple, our future work will focus on how to select more appropriate attributes to further boost the construction efficiency in the star spectra mining for the LAMOST project.

References

1. Wille R, Restructuring Lattice Theory: An Approach Based on Hierarchies of Concepts. In: Rival I ed. Ordered sets, M. Dordrecht:Reidel, (1982) 415–470
2. Wille R, Knowledge Acquisition by Methods of Formal Concept Analysis. In: Diday E ed. Data Analysis, Learning Symbolic and Numeric Knowledge, C. New York: Nova science publisher, (1989) 365–380
3. Belen Diaz-Agudo, Pddro A. Gonzalez-Calero. Formal Concept Analysis As a Support Technique for CBR, In: Knowledge-based systems, Vol 14. (2001) 163–171
4. Godin R, Missaoue R. An Incremental Concept Formation Approach for Learning From Database. Theoretical Computer Science, Vol. 133. (1994) 387–419
5. Godin R, Missaoue R, Alaui H. Incremental Concept Formation Algorithms Based on Galois (Concept) lattice. Computational Intelligence, Vol 1(2). (1995) 246-267
6. Nourine L. Raynaud O. A Fast Algorithm for Building Lattices. In: Workshop on Computational Graph Theory and Combinatories, C. Victoria, Canada, May(1999)1-12
7. J. Han, M. Kambr. Data Mining Concepts and Techniques. In: Morgan Kaufmann Publishers, M. (2000)
8. Hu Ke -Yun, Lu Yu-Chang, Shi Chun-Yi. Advances in Concept Lattice and Its Application. Tsinghua Univ (Sci & Tech), Vol 40(9). (2000) 77-81
9. Xie Zhi-Peng, Liu Zong-Tian. A Fast Incremental Algorithm for Building Concept Lattice. Chinese Journal of Computers, Vol 25(5). (2002) 490-496

10. Wang Zhi-Hai, Hu Ke-Yun, Hu Xue-Gang et al. General And Incremental Algorithms of Rule Extraction Based On Concept Lattice. Chinese Journal of Computers, Vol 22(1). (1999) 66-70

11. Hu Ke-Yun, Lu Yu-Chang, Shi Chun-Yi. An Integrated Mining Approach for Classification and Association Rule Based on Concept Lattice. Chinese Journal of Software, Vol 11(11). (2000)1478-1484

12. QIN Dong-Mei. Studies on Automated Spectral Recognition of Celestial Objects. Ph.D.Thesis. Institute of Automation, Chinese Academy of Sciences,(2003)

Association Rule Mining with Chi-Squared Test Using Alternate Genetic Network Programming

Kaoru Shimada, Kotaro Hirasawa, and Jinglu Hu

Graduate School of Information, Production and Systems, Waseda University
2-7 Hibikino, Wakamatsu-ku, Kitakyushu-shi, Fukuoka, 808-0135, Japan

Abstract. A method of association rule mining using Alternate Genetic Network Programming (aGNP) is proposed. GNP is one of the evolutionary optimization techniques, which uses directed graph structures as genes. aGNP is an extended GNP in terms of including two kinds of sets of node functions. The proposed system can extract important association rules whose antecedent and consequent are composed of the attributes of each family defined by users. The method measures the significance of association via chi-squared test using GNP's features. Rule extraction is done without identifying frequent itemsets used in Apriori-like methods. Therefore, the method can be applied to rule extraction from dense database, and can extract dependent pairs of the sets of attributes in the database. Extracted rules are stored in a pool all together through generations and reflected in genetic operators as acquired information. In this paper, we describe the algorithm capable of finding the important association rules and present some experimental results.

1 Introduction

Association rule mining is the discovery of association relationships or correlations among a set of attributes (items) in a database [1]. Association rule in the form of 'If X then Y $(X \Rightarrow Y)$' is interpreted as "database tuples satisfying that X are likely to satisfy Y". The most popular model for mining association rules from databases is Apriori algorithm [2]. This model measures the uncertainty of an association rule with two factors: support and confidence. Association rules are widely used in marketing, decision making and business management.

A method of association rule mining using Genetic Network Programming (GNP) [3,4] has already been proposed [5,6,7]. GNP is one of the evolutionary optimization techniques, which uses the directed graph structures as genes. GNP is composed of two kinds of nodes: judgement node and processing node. Attributes in a database correspond to judgement nodes in GNP. Association rules are represented by the connections of nodes. The method calculates support and confidence of association rules directly using GNP. Candidates of important rules are obtained by genetic operations. The algorithm extracts the important association rules in the case of both free consequent and fixed consequent. The features of the method are as follows:

- Rule extraction is done without identifying frequent itemsets used in Apriori-like methods. The method can be applied to rule extraction from dense databases, where many frequently occurring items are found in each tuple.

P. Perner (Ed.): ICDM 2006, LNAI 4065, pp. 202–216, 2006.

- Conditions of important association rules are defined flexibly. The definition can include the minimum threshold chi-squared value. Chi-squared value of each rule is measured by the feature of GNP's structure.
- Extracted rules are stored in a pool through generations. GNP evolves in order to store new interesting rules in the pool, not to obtain the individual with high fitness value. The method cannot extract all the rules meeting given the definitions of importance, but extracts important rules sufficiently enough for user's purpose.
- Extracted important association rules in a pool are reflected in genetic operators as acquired information. Mutation changes the contents of the nodes using the knowledge of interesting rules acquired in the pool.
- The proposed method can easily extract positive and negative association rules just by defining the judgement nodes including negative attributes.

Conventional association rule mining techniques have not considered the properties of each attribute. Attributes in the database in rule extraction is dealt with uniformly except association rules for classification. Users cannot define explicitly which set of attributes composes antecedent or consequent. For example, some medical databases include items of environments, items of medical histories and genotypes. Therefore, if we can extract interesting rules from such databases considering the properties of each item, then we can discover the following association relationships or correlations in life science entities effectively.

(an itemset of genotype) $\Rightarrow$ (an itemset of environments or medical histories),
(an itemset of environments or medical histories) $\Rightarrow$ (an itemset of genotype)

In this paper, we propose an algorithm capable of extracting important association rules whose antecedent and consequent are composed of the attributes of each family defined by users. The new algorithm uses Alternate GNP (aGNP). aGNP is an extended GNP in terms of including two kinds of sets of node functions. The method measures the significance of association via chi-squared test. Therefore, dependent pairs of the sets of attributes between attribute families in dense database can be extracted.

This paper is organized as follows: In the next section, some related concepts and definitions on association rules are presented. The outline of Genetic Network Programming (GNP) is reviewed briefly and Alternate GNP (aGNP) is proposed in Section 3. The conventional algorithm on association rule mining using GNP is described in Section 4. In section 5, a new algorithm capable of finding the important association rules between attribute families using aGNP is described. Performance results are presented in Section 6, and conclusions are given in Section 7.

2   Association Rules

The following is a formal statement of the problem of mining association rules. Let $I = \{i_1, i_2, \ldots, i_l\}$ be a set of literals, called items or attributes. Let G be a set of transactions, where each transaction T is a set of items such that $T \subseteq I$. Associated with each transaction is a unique identifier whose set is called TID. We say that a transaction T contains X, a set of some items in I, if $X \subseteq T$. An association rule is an implication of the form $X \Rightarrow Y$, where $X \subset I$, $Y \subset I$, and

$X \cap Y = \emptyset$. X is called antecedent and Y is called consequent of the rule. In general, a set of items is called an itemset. Each itemset has an associated measure of statistical significance called support. If the fraction of transactions containing X in G equals t, then we say that $support(X) = t$. The rule $X \Rightarrow Y$ has a measure of its strength called confidence defined as the ratio of $support(X \cup Y)/support(X)$. An example is shown below using Table 1. Let item universe be $I = \{A, B, C, D\}$ and transaction universe be $TID = \{1, 2, 3, 4\}$. In order to extend our research to dense databases, we indicate the items of the transaction by 1 or 0 as shown in Table 1. In Table 1, itemset $\{A, C\}$ occurs in two transactions of 1 and 3 in TID. So, its frequency is 2, therefore, its support, that is, $support((A = 1) \wedge (C = 1))$ becomes 0.5. Itemset $\{A, C, D\}$ occurs in the transaction of 3 in TID. Its frequency is 1, so its support, i.e., $support((A = 1) \wedge (C = 1) \wedge (D = 1))$ becomes 0.25. Therefore, $support((A = 1) \wedge (C = 1) \Rightarrow (D = 1)) = 0.25$, and $confidence((A = 1) \wedge (C = 1) \Rightarrow (D = 1)) = 0.5$.

The most popular model for mining association rules from databases is Apriori algorithm, the support-confidence framework proposed by Agrawal et $al.$ [2]. The Apriori algorithm searches large (frequent) itemsets in databases and finds all the rules meeting user-specified constraints such as minimum support or minimum confidence. However, this algorithm may suffer from large computational overheads when the number of frequent itemsets is very large. There have been published numerous papers showing improvements on mining itemsets of interest [8,9,10]. There has been a recent trend in applying the rule mining to dense databases [11], such as census data analysis [12], where any or all of the following properties are found: many frequently occurring items; strong correlations between several items; many items in each tuple.

Brin et $al.$ made the suggestion to measure the significance of association via the chi-squared test for correlation used in classical statistics [12]. Calculation of χ^2 value of the rule $X \Rightarrow Y$ is described as follows. Let $support(X) = x$, $support(Y) = y$, $support(X \cup Y) = z$ and the number of database tuples equals N. If events X and Y are independent then $support(X \cup Y) = xy$. Table 2 is the contingency of X and Y: the upper parts are the expectation values under the assumption of their independence, and the lower parts are observational. Now, let E denote the value of the expectation under the assumption of independence and O the value of the observation. Then the chi-squared statistic is defined as follows:

$$\chi^2 = \sum_{AllCells} \frac{(O - E)^2}{E}. \tag{1}$$

We can calculate χ^2 using x, y, z and N of Table 2 as follows:

$$\chi^2 = \frac{N(z - xy)^2}{xy(1 - x)(1 - y)}. \tag{2}$$

This has 1 degree of freedom. If it is higher than a cutoff value (3.84 at the 95% significance level, or 6.63 at the 99% significance level), we should reject the independence assumption.

Table 1. An example of database

TID	A	B	C	D
1	1	0	1	0
2	0	1	1	1
3	1	1	1	1
4	0	1	0	1

Table 2. The contingency of X and Y

	Y	$\neg Y$	$\sum_{row}$
X	Nxy Nz	$N(x - xy)$ $N(x - z)$	Nx
$\neg X$	$N(y - xy)$ $N(y - z)$	$N(1 - x - y + xy)$ $N(1 - x - y + z)$	$N(1 - x)$
$\sum_{col}$	Ny	$N(1 - y)$	N

(N: the number of tuples ($= |TID|$))

3 Alternate Genetic Network Programming (aGNP)

In this section, the outline of conventional Genetic Network Programming (GNP) [3,4] is reviewed briefly and Alternate GNP (aGNP) is proposed.

3.1 Conventional GNP

GNP is one of the evolutionary optimization techniques, which uses the directed graph structures as solutions. The basic structure of GNP is shown in Fig.1. GNP is composed of two kinds of nodes: judgement node and processing node. Judgement nodes correspond nearly to elementary functions of Genetic Programming (GP). Judgement nodes are the set of $J_1, J_2, \ldots, J_p$, which work as *if-then* type decision making functions. On the other hand, processing nodes are the set of $P_1, P_2, \ldots, P_q$, which work as some kind of action/processing functions. The practical roles of these nodes are predefined and stored in the library by supervisors. Once GNP is booted up, firstly the execution starts from the start node, secondly the next node to be executed is determined according to the connection from the current activated node. GNP is useful because it can not only form the optimal structure effectively, but it can also avoid the premature convergence.

The genotype expression of GNP node is shown in Fig.2. This describes the gene of node i, then the set of these genes represents the genotype of GNP individuals. NT_i describes the node type, $NT_i = 0$ when node i is start node, $NT_i = 1$ when node i is judgement node and $NT_i = 2$ when node i is processing node. ID_i is an identification number, for example, $NT_i = 1$ and $ID_i = 1$ mean node i is J_1. $C_{i1}, C_{i2}, \ldots$, denote the nodes which are connected from node i firstly, secondly, $\ldots$, and so on depending on the number of the arguments of node i. All programs in a population have the same number of nodes. The following genetic operators are used in GNP. Crossover operator affects two parent individuals. All the connections or contents of the uniformly selected

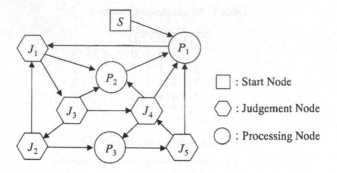

Fig. 1. Basic structure of GNP individual

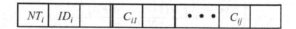

Fig. 2. Gene structure of GNP (node i)

corresponding nodes in two parents are swapped each other by crossover rate P_c. Mutation operator affects one individual. All the connections of each node are changed randomly by mutation rate of P_m.

3.2   Alternate GNP (aGNP)

aGNP is an extended GNP in terms of including two kinds of sets of node functions. aGNP is divided into two sections: GNPsA and GNPsB. GNPsA is composed of judgement nodes and processing nodes using one set of node functions. GNPsB is composed using the other set of node functions. Each node in aGNP belongs to one of the two sets of node functions, while in conventional GNP, a node belongs to a total set of node functions.

A transition in one section is just a fragment of a function, however a transition through two sections makes a function. aGNP is different from GNP with functional localization (GNP with FL) [13], because GNP with FL is composed of plural GNPs and each GNP has its own distinct task.

Judgement node has plural connections to the next node and processing node has a singular connection to the next node also in aGNP. The connections of nodes are not restricted to the nodes in their section. The genotype expression of aGNP node is the same as shown in Fig.2. NT_i describes the node type, for example, $NT_i = 1$ when node i is judgement node in GNPsA. ID_i is an identification number and describes the node function. Genetic operators of aGNP are the same as conventional GNP.

4   Association Rule Mining Using GNP

In this section, a conventional method of association rule mining using GNP [7] is explained. Let A_i be an attribute (item) in a database and its value be 1 or 0. The method extracts the following association rules with chi-squared test:

$(A_j = 1) \wedge \cdots \wedge (A_k = 1) \Rightarrow (A_m = 1) \wedge \cdots \wedge (A_n = 1)$
(briefly, $A_j \wedge \cdots \wedge A_k \Rightarrow A_m \wedge \cdots \wedge A_n$).

4.1 GNP for Association Rule Mining

Attributes and their values correspond to the functions of judgement nodes in GNP. The connections of nodes are represented as association rules. Fig.3 shows a basic structure of GNP for association rule mining. P_1 is a processing node and is a starting point of association rules. "$A = 1$", "$B = 1$", "$C = 1$" and "$D = 1$" in Fig.3 denote the functions of judgement nodes. The connections of these nodes represent association rules, for example, $A \wedge B \wedge C \Rightarrow D$, $A \wedge B \Rightarrow C \wedge D$ and $A \Rightarrow B \wedge C \wedge D$. The details of it are described in the next subsection.

GNP examines the attribute values of database tuples using judgement nodes and calculates the measurements of association rules using processing nodes. Judgement node determines the next node by a judgement result of Yes or No, and has Yes-side and No-side. Yes-side of the judgement node is connected to another judgement node. Judgement nodes can be reused and shared with some other association rules because of GNP's feature. As a result, candidates of rules are obtained effectively.

Each processing node has an inherent numeric order (P_1, P_2, ..., P_s) and is connected to a judgement node. Start node connects to P_1. Examinations of attribute values start at each processing node. No-side of the judgement node is connected to the next numbered processing node. For example, in Table 1, the tuple $1 \in TID$ satisfies $A = 1$ and $B \neq 1$, therefore, the node transition from P_1 to P_2 occurs in Fig.3 in this case. If the examination of attribute values from the starting point P_s ends, then GNP examines the tuple $2 \in TID$ from P_1 likewise. Thus, all tuples in the database will be examined. If transition using Yes-side connection of judgement nodes continues and the number of the judgement nodes from the processing node becomes a cutoff value (maximum number of attributes in extracted association rules given by users), then Yes-side connection is transferred to the next processing node obligatorily.

4.2 Extraction of Association Rules

The total number of tuples moving to Yes-side at each judgement node is calculated for every processing node, which is a starting point for calculating association rules. In Fig.3, N is the number of total tuples, and a, b, c and d are the numbers of tuples moving to Yes-side at each Judgement node, respectively. The measurements are calculated by these numbers. Table 3 shows the measurements of the support and confidence of association rules.

The method measures the significance of associations via the chi-squared test for correlation. For example, if we change the connection of P_1 node from '$A = 1$' node to '$B = 1$' node in Fig.3, we are able to calculate the support of B, $B \wedge C$ and $B \wedge C \wedge D$ in the next examination. As a result we will obtain χ^2 value of $A \Rightarrow B \wedge C \wedge D$ and so on. In addition, we can examine new rules such as $B \Rightarrow C$, $B \wedge C \Rightarrow D$. If we change the connection of P_1 node from '$B = 1$' node to '$D = 1$' node, then χ^2 value of rules such as $B \wedge C \Rightarrow D$ are obtained. The method repeats this like a chain operation at each generation. The change of the connection of processing nodes at each generation is one of the feature of the proposed method.

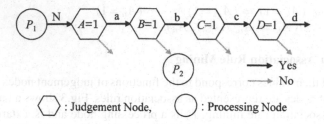

⬡ : Judgement Node,   ◯ : Processing Node

Fig. 3. GNP for association rule mining

Now, we define important association rules as the ones which satisfy the following:

$$\chi^2 > \chi^2_{min},\tag{3}$$

$$support \geq sup_{min},\tag{4}$$

χ^2_{min} and sup_{min} are the minimum threshold chi-squared and support value given by supervisors. If required, we can also add the condition of confidence to the definition of important association rules. The extracted important association rules are stored in a pool all together through generations and reflected in genetic operators as acquired information. When an important rule is extracted by GNP, the overlap of the attributes is checked and it is also checked whether the important rule is new or not, i.e., whether it is in the pool or not.

4.3 Genetic Operators

The connections of the nodes and the functions of the judgement nodes at an initial generation are determined randomly for each of the GNP individual. GNP needs not include all functions of judgement node at an initial generation and the number of each function is not fixed.

Fitness of GNP is defined as

$$F = \sum_{i \in I}\{\chi^2(i) + 10(n_{ante}(i) - 1) + 10(n_{con}(i) - 1) + \alpha_{new}(i)\}\tag{5}$$

The symbols in (5) are as follows:

I : set of suffixes of important association rules which satisfy (3) and (4) in a GNP (individual)
$\chi^2(i)$: chi-squared value of rule i.
$n_{ante}(i)$: number of attributes in the antecedent of rule i.
$n_{con}(i)$: number of attributes in the consequent of rule i.
$\alpha_{new}(i)$: additional constant defined as

$$\alpha_{new}(i) = \begin{cases} \alpha_{new} & \text{(rule } i \text{ is new)} \\ 0 & \text{(rule } i \text{ has been already extracted)} \end{cases}\tag{6}$$

$\chi^2(i)$, $n_{ante}(i)$, $n_{con}(i)$ and $\alpha_{new}(i)$ are concerned with the importance, complexity and novelty of rule i, respectively.

Table 3. Measurements of association rules

association rules	support	confidence
$A \Rightarrow B$	b/N	b/a
$A \Rightarrow B \wedge C$	c/N	c/a
$A \Rightarrow B \wedge C \wedge D$	d/N	d/a
$A \wedge B \Rightarrow C$	c/N	c/b
$A \wedge B \Rightarrow C \wedge D$	d/N	d/b
$A \wedge B \wedge C \Rightarrow D$	d/N	d/c

At each generation, individuals are replaced with new ones by the selection rule and genetic operations. GNP individuals evolve in order to store new interesting rules in the pool, not to obtain the individuals with high fitness value. Therefore, the method is fundamentally different from other evolutionary algorithms in its evolutionary way. When an important association rule is extracted, the rule changing an attribute to another one or the rule adding some attributes can be candidates of important rules. We can obtain these rules effectively by genetic operations of GNP, because mutation and crossover change connections or contents of the nodes. We use three kinds of genetic operators;

- Crossover: Crossover we used is the uniform crossover. Judgement nodes are selected as crossover nodes with the probability of P_c. Two parents exchange the gene of the corresponding crossover nodes.
- Mutation-1: Mutation-1 operator affects one individual. The connection of the judgement nodes is changed randomly by mutation rate of P_{m1}.
- Mutation-2: Mutation-2 operator affects one individual. This operator changes the function of the judgement nodes by a given mutation rate P_{m2}. All programs in a population have the same number of nodes, but the node with the same node number needs not have the same function due to mutation-2.

The individuals are ranked by their fitnesses and upper 1/3 individuals are selected. After that, they are reproduced three times, then the above three kinds of genetic operators are executed to them. These operators are executed for the gene of judgement nodes of GNP. All the connections of the processing nodes are changed randomly in order to extract rules efficiently.

4.4 Use of Acquired Information

As one of the features of our method, we can select the functions by the mutated judgement nodes using the frequency of attributes of the extracted rules in the pool. We define the probability of selecting the attribute A_j for judgement nodes by the following P_j^g, when mutation-2 is carried out:

$$P_j^g = \frac{n_g(A_j) + c}{\sum_{k \in K} (n_g(A_k) + c)}, \tag{7}$$

where P_j^g is the probability of selecting A_j using the acquired information on the association rules extracted in the latest g generations. $n_g(A_j)$ is the frequency of the attribute A_j in the rules extracted in the latest g generations. K is the set of suffixes of attributes. c is a constant given by users. If no rules are extracted in the recent g generations, then P_j^g is equal to the inverse of the number of attributes. We can use all the extracted rules in the pool, however, it has been found that using extracted rules in some of the latest generations is better than using all the rules [7].

5   Association Rule Mining Between Attribute Families Using aGNP

In this section, a method of association rule mining using Alternate GNP (aGNP) is proposed. The proposed system can extract important association rules whose antecedent and consequent are composed of the attributes of each different family defined by users.

5.1   aGNP for Association Rule Mining

Let A_i or B_i be an attribute (item) in a database and its value be 1 or 0. The database includes attributes family A $(A_1, A_2, \ldots, A_M)$ and attributes family B $(B_1, B_2, \ldots, B_N)$. The new method extracts the following association rules with chi-squared test using aGNP:
$$(A_j = 1) \wedge \cdots \wedge (A_k = 1) \Rightarrow (B_m = 1) \wedge \cdots \wedge (B_n = 1),$$
$$(B_m = 1) \wedge \cdots \wedge (B_n = 1) \Rightarrow (A_j = 1) \wedge \cdots \wedge (A_k = 1)$$
(briefly, $A_j \wedge \cdots \wedge A_k \Rightarrow B_m \wedge \cdots \wedge B_n$, $B_m \wedge \cdots \wedge B_n \Rightarrow A_j \wedge \cdots \wedge A_k$)
As a result, dependent pairs of the sets of attributes in database are obtained.

The proposed method is an extended one described in the preceding section. The features of the proposed method using aGNP are as follows:

- The connection of judgement nodes in a section represents antecedent of association rules and goes into another section. The connections of judgement nodes in both sections represent antecedent and consequent of a rule, respectively.
- A processing node in a section cooperates with the corresponding processing node in another section for rule extraction like chain operations. The changes of the connection of these processing nodes are linked each other.

An aGNP includes two sections: GNPsA and GNPsB. GNPsA is composed of processing nodes $P_1, P_2, \ldots, P_s$ and judgement nodes related to attribute family A. GNPsB is also composed of processing nodes $Q_1, Q_2, \ldots, Q_s$ and judgement nodes related to attribute family B. Each processing node has an inherent numeric order. The number of processing nodes in GNPsA equals the one in GNPsB. aGNP examines the attribute values of database tuples using judgement nodes. A judgement node in GNPsA examines an attribute value in family A, and a judgement node in GNPsB examines an attribute value in family B. Judgement node determines the next node by a judgement result of Yes or No. Each judgement node has two Yes-sides: the connection to a judgement node in its own section and one to another section. No-side of the judgement node is connected to the next numbered processing node in its own section. The processing node is connected to a judgement node in its own section.

P_k in GNPsA cooperates with Q_k in GNPsB for rule extraction like chain operations. The changes of the connection of these processing nodes are linked each other.

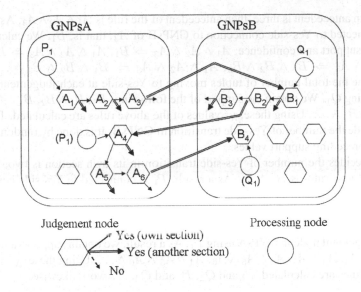

Fig. 4. Alternate GNP for association rule mining between attribute families

Each processing node is not only a starting point of association rules, but also decides the number of Yes-side transition in its own section, that is, the number of attributes in antecedent. For instance, if P_1 decides that the number of Yes-side transition in GNPsA is three, then the third Yes-side judgement node from P_1 in GNPsA connects to a judgement node in GNPsB, to which Q_1 also connects. Equally, if Q_1 decides that the number of Yes-side transition in GNPsB is two, then the second Yes-side judgement node from Q_1 in GNPsB connects to a judgement node in GNPsA, to which P_1 also connects.

5.2   Extraction of Association Rules

Using the above node connections, aGNP examines a number of tuples moving to Yes-side at each judgement node. Node transition is done actually as follows. No-side of the judgement node is connected to the next numbered processing node in its own section, that is, if P_k (Q_k) is a starting point, then it connects to P_{k+1} (Q_{k+1}). If transition using Yes-side connection of judgement nodes continues and the number of the judgement nodes becomes a cutoff value, then Yes-side connection is transferred to the next processing node obligatorily.

The examination of attribute values in a tuple is done using all the processing nodes in a section. Start node is connected to P_1 in GNPsA. If the examination of attribute values from the starting point P_s ends, then return to P_1 and aGNP examines the next tuple. Thus, all tuples in the database will be examined.

Fig.4 shows a basic structure of aGNP for association rule mining between attribute families. We demonstrate the above more concretely using Fig.4. For instance A_1, B_1 denote the function of judgement nodes $A_1 = 1$ and $B_1 = 1$, respectively. If P_1 decides the number of Yes-side transition in its own section is three, that is, the number of attributes in antecedent is three, then antecedent of the rule is $A_1 \wedge A_2 \wedge A_3$. As a result, Q_1 is connected to Yes-side connection to GNPsB of A_3, that is, B_1. We calculate the following support and confidence: $A_1 \wedge A_2 \wedge A_3 \Rightarrow B_1$, $A_1 \wedge A_2 \wedge A_3 \Rightarrow B_1 \wedge B_2$, $A_1 \wedge A_2 \wedge A_3 \Rightarrow B_1 \wedge B_2 \wedge B_3$, $A_1 \wedge A_2 \wedge A_3 \Rightarrow B_1 \wedge B_2 \wedge B_3 \wedge \dots$. Now, we examine the total number of tuples moving to Yes-side at each judgement node in GNPsB using Q_1. We obtain the support of the following: B_1, $B_1 \wedge B_2$, $B_1 \wedge B_2 \wedge B_3$, $B_1 \wedge B_2 \wedge B_3 \wedge \dots$. Using these, χ^2 values of the above rules are calculated. Then, Q_1 has to decide the number of Yes-side transition in GNPsB. It is done by randomly or by using the preceding support values.

If Q_1 decides the number of Yes-side transition in its own section is two, then antecedent of new rules is $B_1 \wedge B_2$. As a result, P_1 is connected to Yes-side connection to GNPsA of B_2, that is, A_4. Then, we obtain the following support and confidence: $B_1 \wedge B_2 \Rightarrow A_4$, $B_1 \wedge B_2 \Rightarrow A_4 \wedge A_5$, $B_1 \wedge B_2 \Rightarrow A_4 \wedge A_5 \wedge A_6$, $B_1 \wedge B_2 \Rightarrow A_4 \wedge A_5 \wedge A_6 \wedge \dots$. We can also examine the total number of tuples moving to Yes-side at each judgement node in GNPsA using P_1. As a result, we obtain support values of the following: A_4, $A_4 \wedge A_5$, $A_4 \wedge A_5 \wedge A_6$, $A_4 \wedge A_5 \wedge A_6 \wedge \dots$. Using these, χ^2 values of the above rules are calculated. P_2 and Q_2, P_3 and Q_3, $\dots$ work likewise.

5.3 Evolution of aGNP

The connections of the nodes and the functions of the judgement nodes at an initial generation are determined randomly for each of aGNP individual.

We define important association rules using (3) and (4). The selection and the genetic operation are done in the same way described in subsection **4.3**. The fitness value of aGNP individual is calculated by (5). If acquired information are reflected in mutation-2, we use the probability $P^g_{A_i}$ or $P^g_{B_j}$ for selecting the attribute A_i or B_j as follows:

$$P^g_{A_i} = \frac{n_g(A_i) + c}{\sum_{k \in K}(n_g(A_k) + c)}, \tag{8}$$

$$P^g_{B_j} = \frac{n_g(B_j) + c}{\sum_{h \in H}(n_g(B_h) + c)}, \tag{9}$$

where, $n_g(A_i)$ and $n_g(B_j)$ are the frequency of the attribute A_i and B_j in the rules extracted in the latest g generations, respectively. K and H are the set of suffixes of attributes in family A and family B, respectively. c is a constant given by users.

6   Simulations

We have performed experiments and estimated the performance of our algorithm. All the experiments were run on synthetic data.

6.1   Conditions

Synthetic database we used is the following joins of DB1 and DB2. Each attribute value in the database is 1 or 0. This is considered as a dense database.

DB1 includes 20 attributes (C_j, $j = 1, 2, \ldots, 20$) and 683 tuples. DB1 is a transformed dataset using the dataset named *breast-w* from UCI ML Repository [14]. Discretization of continuous attributes is done using the Entropy Method. DB1 includes strong correlations between several attributes.

DB2 includes 32 attributes (R_j, $j = 1, 2, \ldots, 32$) and 683 tuples. DB2 was compounded by random numbers ($support(R_j = 1) = 0.33$, $j = 1, 2, \ldots, 32$).

We have performed three cases, DB-20.6/0.26, DB-10.16/10.16 and DB-18.8/2.24.

- DB-20.6/0.26
  Family A includes C_j ($j = 1, 2, \ldots, 20$), R_j ($j = 1, 2, \ldots, 6$),
  Family B includes R_j ($j = 7, 8, \ldots, 32$)
- DB-10.16/10.16
  Family A includes C_j ($j = 1, 2, \ldots, 10$), R_j ($j = 1, 2, \ldots, 16$),
  Family B includes C_j ($j = 11, 12, \ldots, 20$), R_j ($j = 17, 18, \ldots, 32$)
- DB-18.8/2.24
  Family A includes C_j ($j = 1, 2, \ldots, 18$), R_j ($j = 1, 2, \ldots, 8$),
  Family B includes C_j ($j = 19, 20$), R_j ($j = 9, 10, \ldots, 32$)

In simulations, the following rules are extracted:

$$(A_j = 1) \wedge \cdots \wedge (A_k = 1) \Rightarrow (B_m = 1) \wedge \cdots \wedge (B_n = 1),$$
$$(B_m = 1) \wedge \cdots \wedge (B_n = 1) \Rightarrow (A_j = 1) \wedge \cdots \wedge (A_k = 1)$$

We use (3) ($\chi^2_{min} = 6.63$), (4) ($sup_{min} = 0.2$), (5) and (6) ($\alpha_{new} = 150$). In addition, the added conditions of extracting association rules in the simulations are as follows: $n_{ante}(i) + n_{con}(i) \geq 6$, $n_{ante}(i) \leq 5$, $n_{con}(i) \leq 5$

The set of rules satisfy these conditions is denoted by I in (5).

The population size is 120. The number of processing nodes in section A, section B, the number of judgement nodes in section A and section B are 10, 10, 40 and 40, respectively. The number of changing the connections of the processing nodes at each generation described in subsection **5.2** is 5. The new connection of the processing node is selected randomly among five judgement nodes connected from the processing node. The conditions of crossover and mutation are $P_c = 1/5$, $P_{m1} = 1/3$ and $P_{m2} = 1/5$. We used two set of probabilities of P^0 ($P^0_{A_i}$, $P^0_{B_j}$) and P^5 ($P^5_{A_i}$, $P^5_{B_j}$, $c = 1$) for selecting the attributes of judgement nodes in mutation-2. $P^0_{A_i}$ and $P^0_{B_j}$ mean the probability of selecting each attribute is identical. All algorithms were coded in C. Experiments were done on a 1.50GHz Pentium M with 504MB RAM.

6.2 Simulation Results

First of all, we did the important rule extraction using DB-20.6/0.26. Attribute values of family B in this dataset are compounded by random numbers. No important rules were extracted in the pool at 1000th generation in ten simulations.

In next experiment, the proposed method is applied to the DB-10.16/10.16. Fig.5 and Fig.6 show the number of important association rules obtained in the pool in ten simulations under P^0 and P^5, respectively. The results show that proposed method can extract important association rules whose antecedent and consequent are composed of

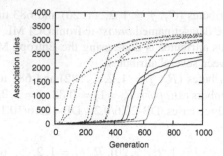

Fig. 5. Number of association rules in the pool in ten simulations (DB-10.16/10.16, P^0)

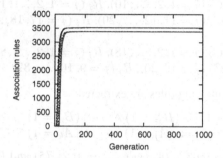

Fig. 6. Number of association rules in the pool in ten simulations (DB-10.16/10.16, P^5)

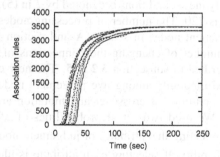

Fig. 7. Number of association rules in the pool versus run-time in ten simulations (DB-10.16/10.16, P^5)

the attributes of each family. Especially the mechanism with P^5 is useful for acquiring many important rules, because the variance of the obtained data on the number of rules is smaller and is able to obtain many rules than with P^0. When using P^0, the break-through generation when rule extraction starts effectively varies trial by trial. However, the proposed method extracts rules at a stretch in the case of P^5. Fig.7 shows the number of association rules versus run-time in the same experiment as Fig.6. Although the increase of the number of the rules in the pool requires much run-time, Fig.6 and Fig.7 show the proposed method is efficient.

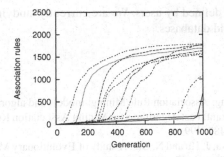

Fig. 8. Number of association rules in the pool in ten simulations (DB-18.8/2.24, P^0)

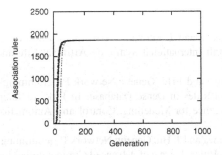

Fig. 9. Number of association rules in the pool in ten simulations (DB-18.8/2.24, P^5)

We have estimated the performance of the rule extraction using DB-18.8/2.24. Fig.8 and Fig.9 show the number of important association rules obtained in the pool in ten simulations under P^0 and P^5, respectively. This database includes only a few attributes composing important rules in family B. Therefore, the rule extraction is imagined to be more difficult than using DB-10.16/10.16. It is clear from Fig.8 and Fig.9 that, if we do not use the acquired information, then it is not easy to extract the rules from DB-18.8/2.24. Using acquired information, the proposed evolutionary method becomes useful for rule extraction from the database including only a few strong correlated attributes in an attribute family.

7 Conclusions

In this paper, we describe the algorithm capable of finding the important association rules between attribute families using Alternate Genetic Network Programming (aGNP). The method measures the significance of association via chi-squared test using aGNP's features. The proposed system evolves itself by an evolutionary method. Extracted association rules are stored in a pool all together through generations and reflected in genetic operators as acquired information. We have performed experiments and estimated the performance of our algorithm. The results showed that proposed method can extract important association rules whose antecedent and consequent are composed of the attributes of each family defined by users. We are currently studying the applications of our method to real world databases.

References

1. C. Zhang and S. Zhang: Association Rule Mining: models and algorithms, Springer (2002)
2. R.Agrawal and R.Srikant: Fast Algorithms for Mining Association Rules, In Proc. of the 20th VLDB Conf. (1994) 487–499
3. T. Eguchi, K. Hirasawa, J. Hu and N. Ota: A study of Evolutionary Multiagent Models Based on Symbiosis, IEEE Trans. on System, Man and Cybernetics, -PART B-, Vol.35, No.1 (2006) 179–193
4. K. Hirasawa, M. Okubo, H. Katagiri, J. Hu and J. Murata: Comparison between Genetic Network Programming (GNP) and Genetic Programming (GP), In Proc. of Congress of Evolutionary Computation (2001) 1276–1282
5. K. Shimada, K. Hirasawa and T. Furuzuki: Association rule mining using genetic network programming, The 10th International Symp. on Artificial Life and Robotics 2005 (2005) 240–245
6. K.Shimada, K.Hirasawa and J.Hu: Genetic Network Programming with Acquisition Mechanisms of Association Rules in Dense Database, In Proc. of International Conference on Computational Intelligence for Modelling, Control and Automation - CIMCA'2005, Vol.2 (2005) 47–54
7. K. Shimada, K. Hirasawa and J. Hu: Genetic Network Programming with Acquisition Mechanisms of Association Rules, Journal of Advanced Computational Intelligence and Intelligent Informatics, Vol.10, No.1 (2006) 102–111
8. J. S. Park, M. S. Chen and P. S. Yu: An Effective Hash-Based Algorithm for Mining Association Rules, In Proc. of the 1995 ACM SIGMOD Conf. (1995) 175–186
9. A. K. H. Tung, H. Lu, J. Han and L. Feng: Efficient Mining of Intertransaction Association Rules, IEEE Transactions on Knowledge and Data Engineering, Vol. 15, No. 1 (2003) 43–56
10. X. Wu, C. Zhang and S. Zhang: Efficient Mining of Both Positive and Negative Association Rules, ACM Transactions on Information Systems, Vol.22, No.3 (2004) 381–405
11. R. J. Bayardo Jr., R. Agrawal and D. Gunopulos: Constraint-Based Rule Mining in Large, Dense Databases, In Proc. of the 15th International Conf. on Data Engineering (1999) 188–197
12. S. Brin, R. Motwani and C. Silverstein: Beyond market baskets: generalizing association rules to correlations, In Proc. of ACM SIGMOD (1997) 265–276
13. S. Eto, H. Hatakeyama, S. Mabu, K. Hirasawa and J. Hu: Realizing Functional Localization Using Genetic Network Programming with Importance Index, Journal of Advanced Computational Intelligence and Intelligent Informatics, Vol. 10 (2006) (to appear)
14. C.Blake and C. Merz. UCI repository of machine learning databases. http://www.ics.uci.edu/ mlearn/MLRepository.html.

Ordinal Classification with Monotonicity Constraints

Tomáš Horváth[1] and Peter Vojtáš[2]

[1] Institute of Computer Science,
Faculty of Science,
Pavol Jozef Šafárik University,
Košice, Slovakia
horvath@ics.upjs.sk
[2] Institute of Computer Science,
Czech Academy of Sciences,
Prague, Czeh Republic
Peter.Vojtas@mff.cuni.cz

Abstract. Classification methods commonly assume unordered class values. In many practical applications – for example grading – there is a natural ordering between class values. Furthermore, some attribute values of classified objects can be ordered, too. The standard approach in this case is to convert the ordered values into a numeric quantity and apply a regression learner to the transformed data. This approach can be used just in case of linear ordering. The proposed method for such a classification lies on the boundary between ordinal classification trees, classification trees with monotonicity constraints and multi-relational classification trees. The advantage of the proposed method is that it is able to handle non-linear ordering on the class and attribute values. For the better understanding, we use a toy example from the semantic web environment - prediction of rules for the user's evaluation of hotels.

Keywords: Monotone, monotonicity constraints, classification, ordinal data.

1 Introduction

Classification algorithms map attribute values to a categorical target value, represented by a class attribute. Sometimes the class attribute is called dependent or head attribute. The other attributes are called independent or body attributes. The values of the class attribute are often called classes. In many real-word situations the dependent attribute have ordered values (ordinal classes) and some of the independent attributes can be ordered, too.

We introduce an illustrative example of 10 hotels (table 1, figure 1). The independent attributes of an hotel is its name, distance from the city center in meters and the price of accommodation in US dollars. The dependent attribute is the user's evaluation of appropriateness of the hotel. The user classifies every hotel into one of the three classes (categories): poor, good and excellent. Note that this evaluation is subjective and depends on the preferences of an given user but it is not important in our case.

P. Perner (Ed.): ICDM 2006, LNAI 4065, pp. 217–225, 2006.

Our aim is to find prediction rules for user's classification of hotels into the mentioned classes based on the attributes of hotels.

Table 1. Illustrative example of hotels with attributes name, distance, price and users evaluation

hotel name	distance (m)	price ($)	user's evaluation
danube	1300	120	good
iris	1100	35	excellent
linden	1200	60	excellent
oak	500	149	good
poplar	100	99	good
rose	500	99	excellent
spruce	300	40	good
themse	100	149	poor
tulip	800	45	excellent
grape	900	130	excellent

The specific property of the classification of hotels from our example is the natural order among the different classes – an excellent hotel fulfills requirements for good and poor classes of hotels and the good hotel fulfills requirements for a poor one. The converse does not hold. So, we can say in brief, that an excellent hotel is "at least" good and the good hotel is "at least" poor. Moreover there is a monotonicity (or ordering) in attributes, too: the distance 900 m is "at least" as far as 800 m, 500 m, and so on. Similarly, the price 99 $ is "at least" as cheap as 120 $, 130 $, etc. In other words, if 500 m (120 $) is far (cheap) so it will 800 m (99 $), etc.

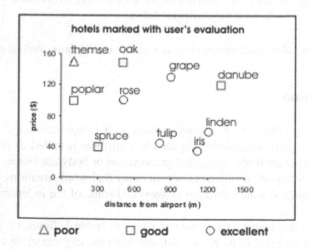

Fig. 1. The graphical representation of the illustrative example from Table 1

The natural meaning of this ordering is that we determine the relations "better" or "worst" between two values of an given attribute.

Such an ordinal classification is quite common, e.g. we classify students in school by grades, hotels by *, **, ***, investment safety of countries ranging from AAA to FFF, or a granulation of user's preferences of price of a product... in all this cases a higher classification inherits all properties of a lower classification.

The paper is structured as follows. In section 2 we describe several approaches to solve this classification problem, namely induction of decision trees, ordinal classification, monotone classification. In section 3 we propose our method of ordinal classification with monotonicity constraints. Section 4 summarizes the contributions made in this paper.

2 Ordinal Classification Approaches

The following approaches we present are based on classification and regression trees. Just the prediction rules for the "at least" excellent and "at least" good classes are presented, since every hotel belongs to the "at least" poor class.

2.1 Classification and Regression Trees

The method of induction of decision trees [8] is designed to solve a standard classification task. However, the application to ordinal classification problems without any modification is not suitable. In this case the classes are nominal (poor, good, excellent), not incorporating any ordering. On the figure 2 the computed prediction rules from applying classification tree induction method are presented:

```
evaluation=excellent IF distance>650;

evaluation=good IF distance>200 AND distance<650;
```

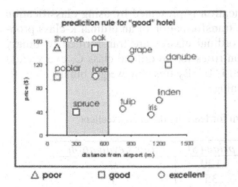 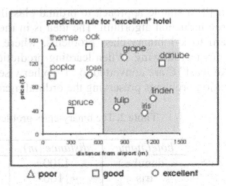

Fig. 2. Results of applying classification tree induction method with nominal class values

If we perceive these rules in an ordinal meaning, we see the following. The prediction rule for good hotel is right in an ordinal meaning, since it covers "at least" good hotels. Its gap is that it covers just a few hotels (2 good and 1 excellent hotel from 9 "at least" good hotels). On the other side the prediction rule for excellent hotel covers 4 from 5 "at least" excellent ones, but it covers one good hotel. This fact breaks the ordinal meaning, since not every covered hotels are "at least" excellent.

We can transform the nominal classes to numbers (1 = poor, 2 = good, 3 = excellent). The prediction rules computed by a regression tree induction method are illustrated on figure 3. The rules are the following (after transforming back numerical classes to nominal ones):

```
evaluation=excellent IF distance> 400 AND price< 109.5;

evaluation=good IF distance> 400 AND price> 109.5;
```

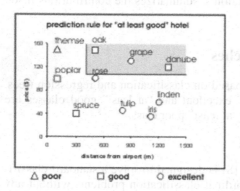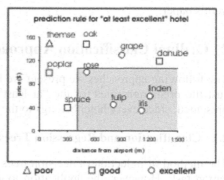

Fig. 3. Results of applying regression tree induction method with numerical class values

In this case the prediction rules are right and the ordinal meaning is preserved. The only lack is the low coverage of prediction rule for "at least good" hotel.

2.2 Ordinal Classification

In [2] a simple approach to ordinal classification is presented by using classification tree induction algorithm. The idea is in the transformation of an ordinal k-class problem to k-1 binary-class problems, where ordinal classes are transformed to binary ones in following. When learning prediction rules for an ordinal class C, every class "at least" C are converted to "1", otherwise to "0". By this way we get binary classification problems preserving the ordinal meaning.

Table 2. The binary-class problem for learning the class excellent

hotel name	distance (m)	price ($)	user's evaluation
danube	1300	120	0
iris	1100	35	1
linden	1200	60	1
oak	500	149	0
poplar	100	99	0
rose	500	99	1
spruce	300	40	0
themse	100	149	0
tulip	800	45	1
grape	900	130	1

Table 3. The binary-class problem for learning the class good

hotel name	distance (m)	price ($)	user's evaluation
danube	1300	120	1
iris	1100	35	1
linden	1200	60	1
oak	500	149	1
poplar	100	99	1
rose	500	99	1
spruce	300	40	1
themse	100	149	0
tulip	800	45	1
grape	900	130	1

In case of our example we transform the ordinal 3-class problem to two binary-class problems. In table 2 the binary-class problem for learning the class excellent is presented.

The rule for the binary-class problem from the table 2 is the following (presented in the right part of the figure 4):

```
evaluation=excellent IF distance>400 AND price<109.5;
```

In table 3 the binary-class problem for learning the class good is presented. There are no rules for this binary-class problem (presented in the left part of the figure 4).

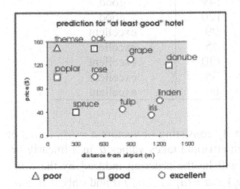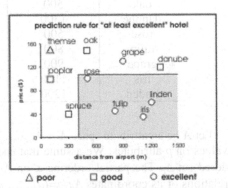

Fig. 4. Results of applying ordinal classification

If we use regression in place of classification to binary-class problems from table 2 and 3 the results are a little bit different from previous ones (illustrated on figure 5):

```
evaluation=excellent IF distance>400 AND price < 109.5;

evaluation=good IF distance>200;
```

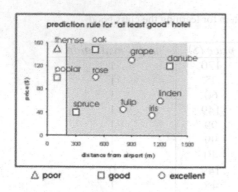 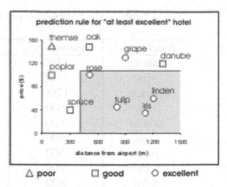

Fig. 5. Results of applying ordinal regression

2.3 Monotone Classification Trees

In [7] the methods for solving classification problems with monotonicity constraints are presented.

Table 4. Hotels from the illustrative example, ordered by the class attribute

hotel name	distance (m)	price ($)	user's evaluation
themse	100	149	poor
poplar	100	99	good
spruce	300	40	good
oak	500	149	good
danube	1300	120	good
rose	500	99	excellent
tulip	800	45	excellent
grape	900	130	excellent
iris	1100	35	excellent
linden	1200	60	excellent

Let A be an attribute space $A = A_1 \times \ldots \times A_p$ consisting of vectors $a = (a_1, \ldots, a_p)$ of values on p attributes. We assume that each attribute takes values a_i in a linearly ordered set A_i. The partial ordering $\leq$ on A will be the ordering induced by the order relations of its coordinates A_i: $a=(a_1, \ldots, a_p) \leq a'=(a_1', \ldots, a_p')$ if and only if $a_i \leq a_i'$ for all i. Furthermore, let C be a finite linearly ordered set of classes.

A monotone classification rule is a function $f: A \rightarrow C$, for which

$$a \leq a' \Rightarrow f(a) \leq f(a')$$

where a, a' $\in$ A. It is easy to see that a classification rule on attribute space is monotone if and only if it is non-decreasing in each of its attributes, when the remaining attributes are held fixed.

This problem setting is not appropriate for our example, since our attribute space is not monotone, i.e. not non-decreasing in each of its attributes (see the table 4).

3 Ordinal Classification with Monotonicity Constraints

Our approach, presented in this section lies on the boundary between the described methods in section 2. It combines their advantages.

Furthermore, it is able to induce first-order rules, since it is based on Inductive Logic Programming ILP framework [1], containing the advantage of multi-relational decision tree learning [6], involving complex, relational data structures.

Inductive logic programming (ILP) is concerned with finding a hypothesis H (a definite clause program) from a set of true and false examples T and F (logical facts) under the presence of the background knowledge B (a definite clause program) that is provided to the ILP system and fixed during the learning process. It is required that the hypothesis H together with the background knowledge B *cover* all true examples in T and none of the false examples in F.

The main idea of our approach is similar to ordinal classification. We transform the k-class learning problem to several binary-class learning problems like described in section 2. The difference is in data preparation, during which there are two important steps.

The first one is the discretization of the continuous attribute domains. It is very important because of ILP but furthermore, by correct discretization we can eliminate some little deviations in monotonicity of the attribute space, mentioned in section 2.3. For illustration, see the figure 6, where the attribute space is not non-decreasing in attribute. By discretizing the values of attribute into classes $1 = <1;2)$ and $2 = <2;3)$ the attribute space become non-decreasing in attribute.

attribute	class		attribute	class
1.4	1		1	1
1.3	2	$\Rightarrow$	1	2
2.6	3		2	3
2.5	4		2	4

Fig. 6. The illustration of discretization of attributes and its impact to monotonicity

The second important step in data preparation is the determination of order relations of an attribute space, for every attribute a_i. In this case we determine an ordering of discretized attribute values. Notice, that there can be nominal attributes except the ordinal ones what need no discretization - in that case the order relation for this attribute is empty. We notate the order relation for an attribute i as $_i\leq^*$. Differently from the order relation mentioned in section 2.3 we don't require just the ordering $\leq$ on the attribute space. For illustration, consider that we have discretized the attribute values to three classes { near, middle, far }. The different orderings of this classes are:

near $\leq^*$ middle $\leq^*$ far (non-decreasing)

near $\leq^*$ far $\leq^*$ middle

far $\leq^*$ middle $\leq^*$ near (non-increasing)

far $\leq^*$ near $\leq^*$ middle

middle $\leq^*$ near $\leq^*$ far (the middle values are "better" than near or far)

middle $\leq^*$ far $\leq^*$ near

These orderings can be clearly represented by definite clause programs, so the use of ILP is advantageous. On the other side the computation in ILP takes much time and are more complex than the decision tree algorithms.

The prediction rules for our illustration example are illustrated on figure 7:

evaluation=excellent IF distance>=500 AND price<=99;

evaluation=good IF disance>=500;

evaluation=good IF price<=99;

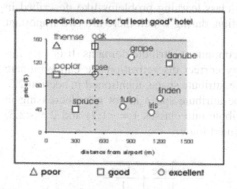
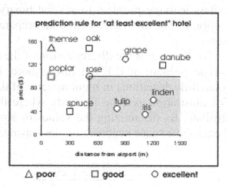

Fig. 7. Results of applying ordinal classification with monotonicity constraints

The ordinal meaning in results from figure 7 are preserved and the coverage is better than in the case of other approaches. These types of rules preserve the monotonicity (both in the directions down and up depending on the directions of the monotonicity of attributes).

4 Conclusions

We describe several approaches to learn ordinal classification rules. These are based on decision tree learning algorithm. These approaches have several lack. The approach of classical decision tree is not convenient for this task. With the use of regression tree learner we can achieve better results, but it can only be applied in conjunction with a regression scheme. The ordinal classification approach is better, but it don't consider ordering of attribute space. The monotone classification approach deal with an order relation, but it must be non-decreasing in all attributes, what is not the common case. Finally, our approach improve and combine the mentioned methods. Furthermore, it is able to learn multi-relational rules, what makes this method more flexible than the other methods [3,4,5]. We tried our and the ordinal classification approaches on the well-known IRIS database (we omit the data description) from UCI machine learning repository. The result of our approach were similar to ordinal classification approach.

Acknowledgement. Partially supported by Czech project 1ET 100300517 and Slovak project VEGA 1/3129/06.

References

1. Džeroski S., Lavrač N.: An introduction to inductive logic programming. Relational data mining, S. Džeroski, N. Lavrač eds., Springer 2001, 48-73.
2. Frank E., Hall E.: A Simple Approach to Ordinal Classificaiton. In Proceedings of the 12th European Conference on Machine Learning, 2001, ISBN 3-540-42536-5,p:145-156.
3. Horváth T., Vojtáš P.: Fuzzy induction via generalized annotated programs. In: 8th International Conference on Computational Intelligence (Fuzzy Days, Dortmund '04), Dortmund, Germany, 2004: Springer, 2005, ISBN 3-540-22807-1, p:419-433.
4. Horváth T., Sudzina F., Vojtáš P.: Mining rules from monotone classification measuring impact of information systems on business competitiveness. In: 6th International Conference on Information Technology for Balanced Automation Systems (BASYS '04), Wien, Austria, 2004: Springer, 2004, ISBN 0-387-22828-4, p:451-458.
5. Horváth T., Krajči S., Lencses R., Vojtáš P.: An ILP model for a graded classification problem. J. KYBERNETIKA 40 (2004), No. 3, AV ČR, Czech Republic, 2004, ISSN 0023-5954, p:317–332.
6. Leiva H. A.: MRDTL: A multi-relational decision tree learning algorithm. MSc Thesis, Iowa State Univerity, Ames, Iowa, 2002.
7. Potharst R., Feelders A. J.: Classification Trees for Problems with Monotonicity Constraints. SIGKDD Explorations, Volume 4, Issue 1, 2002, p: 1-10.
8. Quinlan J. R.: Induction of decision trees. Machine Learning, 1, 1986, ISSN 0885-6125, p:81-106.

Local Modelling in Classification on Different Feature Subspaces

Gero Szepannek and Claus Weihs

Department of Statistics
University of Dortmund 44227 Dortmund
szepannek@statistik.uni-dortmund.de

Abstract. Sometimes one may be confronted with classification problems where classes are constituted of several subclasses that possess different distributions and therefore destroy accurate models of the entire classes as one similar group. An issue is modelling via local models of several subclasses.

In this paper, a method is presented of how to handle such classification problems where the subclasses are furthermore characterized by different subsets of the variables. Situations are outlined and tested where such local models in different variable subspaces dramatically improve the classification error.

1 Introduction

In order to minimize the misclassification error in a $C-$class classification problem one aims at searching for a classification rule

$$\hat{c} = \arg \max_{c=1,\ldots,C} P(c|x) \tag{1}$$

that maximizes the conditional posterior probability given the observation x. It may be the case that a class c is composed of several "subclasses" with different distributions. For an accurate estimation of $P(c|x)$ these subclasses have to be modelled separately by *local models*. During this paper, we assume all the subclass-memberships in the training data to be known, whereas these memberships in the test data - of course - are not known (else the class of the observation would also be given!). If the subclasses are not known in advance clustering methods can be used to investigate if the data of some class are composed from several subgroups of data.

We call $k \in \{1,\ldots,K\}$ the index of all subclasses. There is existing a (surjective) relationship $f : \{1,\ldots,K\} \rightarrow \{1,\ldots,C\}$. Given the posterior probabilities of the membership of any of the subclasses $P(k|x)$, the classification rule for any class c is given by

$$\hat{c} = \arg \max_{c=1,\ldots,C} \sum_k I_{\{c\}}(f(k)) * P(k|x) \ . \tag{2}$$

Moreover, the subclasses may be characterized by different variables in the data. If size of training set is not very large, a variable selection may particularly be useful to model only such variables that are relevant to the classification problem.

P. Perner (Ed.): ICDM 2006, LNAI 4065, pp. 226–238, 2006.

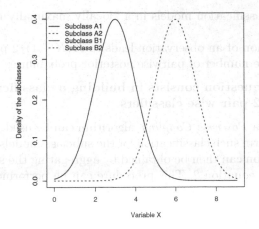

Fig. 1. Example of a '2 classes with 2 subclasses each' problem as introduced in example 1. Only half of the subclasses can be separated by differing distributions in this variable.

Table 1. $+/-$ indicates whether variable X in example 1 serves for discrimination of two subclasses or not. Parentheses indicate the same class ($c = A \, or \, B$). Only half of the subclass-pairs can be discriminated in this variable.

Subclass	A_2	B_1	B_2
A_1	(+)	-	+
A_2		+	-
B_1			(+)

Example 1. Imagine the case of two classes A and B each consisting of two subclasses A_i and B_i, $i = 1, 2$. Let now the distribution of the subclasses in variable X $f(X|A_i) = f(X|B_i)$, $i = 1, 2$. Figure 1 shows this example for subclasses being normally distributed with unit variance but differing means μ_i. In such case subclasses A_1 and B_2 can be discriminated, as can be subclasses A_2 and B_1. For discrimination of the subclasses A_1 and B_1 as well as A_2 and B_2 this variable contributes no information and should therefore preferably be omitted. This reflection is summarized in the matrix of Tab. 1.

If any preceeding variable selection in local modelling is desired, this usually has to be performed globally, since comparing local models in different variable subsets is a difficult task. This problem is outlined in Szepannek et al. (7).

Szepannek and Weihs (8) proposed a method of pairwise variable selection (PVS). By this method, the simulated misclassification test-error in the well-known *Waveform* data set (see Breiman et al., 3) for Linear Discriminant Analysis (which works quite well on this task) has been reduced from 20.02% to 16.96% (being bounded by 14.9% Bayes error from below). A K-class problem is splitted into $K(K-1)/2$ two-class-problems. For any of these class pairs a classification rule is built after some variable selection procedure. The result consists of $K(K-1)/2$ classification models in a "locally maximally reduced" variable space.

Such classification of an observation leads to $K(K-1)/2$ pairwise decisions, returning the same number of pairwise posterior probabilities.

The remaining question consists in building a classification rule from these $K(K-1)/2$ pair wise classifiers.

To solve this task a *Pairwise Coupling* algorithm can be used. It is described in Sect. 2. If we perform such classification for the subclass-models $k = 1, \ldots, K$ the desired classification can then be obtained by aggregating the subclass-posterior probabilities as in equation 2. This procedure can be performed principally for any classification method returning posterior probabilities in combination with any meaningful method of variable selection.

The following pseudo-code summarizes the steps of the suggested proceeding:

Build.classification.model *(data [containing the subclass.labels], f, classification.method, variable.selection.method)*

f is the function labelling the subclasses to the classes.

1. For each pair of two subclasses do
2. (a) Remove temporarily all observations that do not belong to one of both subclasses from *data*: return *newdata*.
   (b) Perform *variable.selection.method* on *newdata*:
   return *subspace.of.subclass-pair*.
   (c) Perform *classification.method* on *newdata* only considering *subspace.of.subclass-pair*: return *model.of.subclass-pair*.
   (d) Return *subspace.of.subclass-pair* and *model.of.subclass-pair* for this pair of two subclasses.
3. Return the whole model consisting of: f and for all pairs of subclasses the *subspace.of.subclass-pair* and *model.of.subclass-pair*.

Predict.class *(new.object, subspaces.of.subclass-pairs, models.of.subclass-pairs,f)*

1. For each pair of subclasses do
2. (a) Calculate the class pairwise posterior probabilities for *new object* assuming the object being of in one of the actually considered two subclasses according to *model.of.subclass-pair* on *subspace.of.subclass-pair*.
   (b) Return the *subclass.pair.posterior.probabilities*.
3. Use the Pairwise Coupling algorithm to calculate the posterior probabilities for all K subclasses from the set of all estimated pairs of conditional *subclass.pair.posterior.probabilities*, return: *subclass.posterior.probabilities*.
4. Calculate the *class.posterior.probabilities* using the class-labelling function f according to equation 2.
5. Return the predicted class c with maximal *class.posterior.probability*.

The following section describes a solution to the question of gaining the vector of subclass-posterior probabilities form the pairwise classifications built on the different selected variable subsets. Section 3 briefly describes some variable selection methods that are used in the studies in this paper. In Sect. 4, a simulation study is performed that shows possible benefit of such local variable reduction. In Sect. 5, the method is applied to some real world data.

2 Pairwise Coupling

2.1 Definitions

We now tackle the problem of finding posterior probabilities of a K-(sub)class classification problem given the posterior probabilities for all $K(K-1)/2$ pairwise comparisons. Let us start with some definitions.

Let $p(x) = p = (p_1, \ldots, p_K)$ be the vector of (unknown) posterior probabilities. p depends on the specific realization x. For simplicity in notation we will omit x. Assume the "true" conditional probabilities of a pairwise classification problem to be given by

$$\mu_{ij} = Pr(i|i \cup j) = \frac{p_i}{p_i + p_j} \ . \tag{3}$$

Let r_{ij} denote the estimated posterior probabilities of the two-class problems. The aim is now to find the vector of probabilities p_i for a given set of values r_{ij}.

Example 2. Given $p = (0.7, 0.2, 0.1)$. The μ_{ij} can be calculated according to equation 3 and can be presented in a matrix:

$$\{\mu_{ij}\} = \begin{pmatrix} . & 7/9 & 7/8 \\ 2/9 & . & 2/3 \\ 1/8 & 1/3 & . \end{pmatrix} \tag{4}$$

Example 3. The inverse problem does not necessarily have a proper solution, since there are only $K-1$ free parameters but $K(K-1)/2$ constraints. Consider

$$\{r_{ij}\} = \begin{pmatrix} . & 0.9 & 0.4 \\ 0.1 & . & 0.7 \\ 0.6 & 0.3 & . \end{pmatrix} \tag{5}$$

where the row i contains the estimated conditional pairwise posterior probabilities r_{ij} for class i. From Machine Learning, majority voting ("Which class wins most comparisons ?") is a well known approach to solve such problems. But here, it will not lead to a result since any class wins exactly one comparison. Intuitively, class 1 may be preferable since it dominates the comparisons the most clearly.

2.2 Algorithm

In this section we present the Pairwise Coupling algorithm of Hastie and Tibshirani (6) to find p for a given set of r_{ij}. They transform the problem into an iterative optimization problem by introducing a criterion to measure the fit between the observed r_{ij} and the $\hat{\mu}_{ij}$, calculated from a possible solution $\hat{p}$. To measure the fit they define the weighted Kullback-Leibler distance:

$$l(\hat{p}) = \sum_{i<j} n_{ij} \left(r_{ij} * log \left(\frac{r_{ij}}{\hat{\mu}_{ij}} \right) + (1 - r_{ij}) * log \left(\frac{1 - r_{ij}}{1 - \hat{\mu}_{ij}} \right) \right) . \tag{6}$$

n_{ij} is the number of objects that fall into one of the classes i or j.

The best solution $\hat{p}$ of posterior probabilities is found as in Iterative Proportional Scaling (IPS) (for details on the IPS-method see e.g. Bishop, Fienberg and Holland, 1975). The algorithm consists of the following three steps:

1. Start with any $\hat{p}$ and calculate all $\hat{\mu}_{ij}$.
2. Repeat until convergence $i = (1, 2, \ldots, K, 1, \ldots)$:

$$\hat{p}_i \leftarrow \hat{p}_i * \frac{\sum_{j \neq i} n_{ij} r_{ij}}{\sum_{j \neq i} n_{ij} \hat{\mu}_{ij}} , \tag{7}$$

    renormalize $\hat{p}$ and calculate the new $\hat{\mu}_{ij}$.
3. Finally scale the solution to $\hat{p} \leftarrow \frac{\hat{p}}{\sum_i \hat{p}_i}$.

Motivation of the algorithm: Hastie and Tibshirani (6) show that $l(p)$ increases at each step. For this reason, since it is bounded above by 0, if there exists a proper solution $\hat{p}$ providing $\hat{\mu}_{ij} = r_{ij} \, \forall i \neq j$, it will be found.

Even if the choice of $l(p)$ as optimization criterion is rather heuristic, it can be motivated in the following way: consider a random variable $n_{ij} r_{ij}$, being the number of observations of class i among the n_{ij} observations of class i and j. This random variable can be considered to be binomially distributed $n_{ij} r_{ij} \sim B(n_{ij}, \mu_{ij})$ with "true" (unknown) parameter μ_{ij}. Since the same (training) data is used for all pairwise estimates r_{ij}, the r_{ij} are not independent, but if they were, $l(p)$ of equation 6 would be equivalent to the log-likelihood of this model (see Bradley and Terry, 2). Then, maximizing $l(p)$ would correspond to maximum-likelihood estimation for μ_{ij}.

Going back to example 3, we obtain $\hat{p} = (0.47, 0.25, 0.28)$, a result being consistent with the intuition that class 1 may be slightly preferable.

In Wu et al. (11) several methods for multi-class probability by Pairwise Coupling algorithms are presented and compared. In the simulations of this paper, the method of Hastie and Tibshirani (6) is used.

3   Validation of the Principle

In this section, the suggested procedure of a subclass pairwise variable selection combined with Pairwise Coupling [PVS] is compared to classification using linear and quadratic Discriminant Analysis [LDA, QDA] with global variable subset selection.

Variable selection: The method of variable selection in our implementation is a quite simple one. We used subclass pairwise Kolmogorov-Smirnov tests (see Hajek, 5, pp.62–69) to check whether the distributions of two subclasses differ in a variable or not. For every subclass pair and every variable, the statistic

$$D = \max_{x} |F_{n_{k_1}}(x) - F_{n_{k_2}}(x)| \tag{8}$$

is calculated, where the $F_{n_{k_i}}(x)$ are the empirical distributions of subclass k_i, $i = 1, 2$. A variable is taken into a pairwise model if its p value strongly indicates differing densities. Of course, any other variable selection could be used instead.

Especially one could refer here to the *stepclass* method (see Weihs et al., 10) which is a prediction orientated method of variable selection. Variables are included in the model if they improve some predefined measure like e.g. the misclassification rate on the cross-validated data set. This method possesses the advantage that it is adaptive to the specifics of any classification method.

3.1 A First Example

Our first example is chosen according to the introducing example 1 in Sect. 1 to again illustrate the problem. Data are simulated in 3 classes (à 3 subclasses each) and 8 variables. Subclass k is distributed according to $X \sim N(2 * 1.64 * e_k, I)$ if $k < 9$ and $X \sim N(0, I)$, if $k = 9$. Here e_k represents the standard basis vector, 0 is the 0 vector and I is the identity matrix.

This means, two subclasses $k \neq l$, $k, l < 9$ differ in their distributions in only 2 variables (k and l). Subclass 9 can be discriminated from any other class k only in variable k. Subclasses $k = 1$ to 3 are subclasses of class $c = 1$. Subclasses $k = 4, 5$ and 6 belong to class $c = 2$, so do subclasses $k = 7, 8$ and 9 to class $c = 3$.

By construction, no variable can be omitted. For that reason, "global" variable selection will not remove any of the variables, using Linear Discriminant Analysis.

Variable selection is especially useful if there are few training examples in the data for estimating the structure of the classes. If classes consist of several subclasses, the amount of available data is further reduced since there are more

Table 2. Averaged error rates of LDA, QDA and PVS at varying subclass sizes

size	LDA	QDA	PVS (with LDA)
4	0.186	-	0.154
6	0.140	-	0.110
8	0.123	-	0.096
10	0.112	0.416	0.096
15	0.098	0.240	0.087
20	0.095	0.185	0.086
50	0.084	0.105	0.079

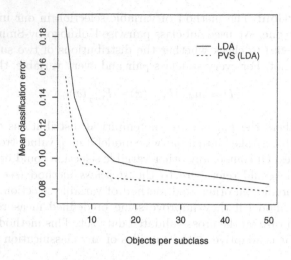

Fig. 2. Averaged error rates on test data in simulation 3.1

populations to be fitted with the same amount of data. We therefore computed simulations with varying (equal) (sub)class sizes in the training data to investigate the effect of sparse data. In the test data each subclass contains 50 objects. Error rates are averaged over 50 repetitive simulations of the data set. The results are given in Tab. 2. The QDA classification rules can only be built having enough data. Even at larger class sizes QDA error rates are still very high. The PVS approach shows systematically lower error rates on the test data than LDA with "global" variable selection, especially if there are only few observations in the training data. For larger class sizes the differences of both methods in the error rates are still present but seem to vanish.

3.2   Differing Variances

We now extend the situation of the first example. In real life it may be possible that one is confronted with data where one of the (sub)classes is strongly concentrated in a specific variable. Of course, this class can be more easily identified by its realizations in this variable. Using LDA will fail to detect this property by pooling all classes' covariances.

We modelled this situation with data consisting of 3 classes each consisting of 3 subclasses (as in the previous example) in 9 variables. Subclass k is distributed following $X \sim N(2e_k, \Sigma)$ with Σ being the identity except from $(\sigma)_{kk} := 0.1$.

An illustration of the phenomenon is given in Fig. 3 where the vertical line in the left plot indicates the wrong 'optimal decision' if wrongly assuming equal covariances as in the right plot. Intuitively, QDA seems to be more appropriate in this situation. The results for varying training data sizes are shown in Fig. 4.

Astonishingly, here LDA still shows smaller error rates than QDA. For QDA, there does not seem to be enough data. Both methods can be largely improved by a class pairwise variable selection using QDA. But note that such variable selec-

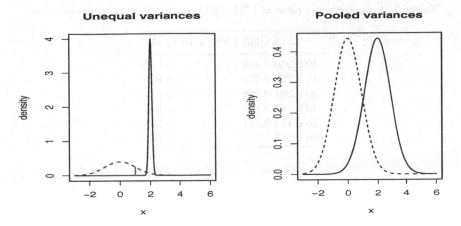

Fig. 3. Example of unequal variances and their pooled estimators (by LDA)

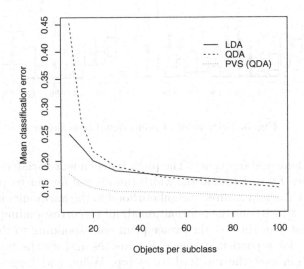

Fig. 4. Averaged error rates on test data in example 3.2

tion simply using the KS-test statistic will fail to detect situations of correlation between variables.

3.3 Real World Data

The method is now applied to some real world data. The task is register classification (i.e. correct labelling into high and low pitch) of singers and instruments by pitch-independent features. As predictor variables characteristics of the fundamental and the first 12 harmonics are used. The fundamental $[F0]$ of a sound is exactly its pitch frequency, where the harmonics $[F1, F2, \ldots]$ are all integer multi-

Table 3. Averaged error rates of LDA, QDA and PVS at varying class sizes

	LDA	QDA	PVS (with QDA)
10	0.250	0.453	0.177
15	0.226	0.273	0.161
20	0.201	0.218	0.151
30	0.182	0.190	0.145
50	0.174	0.171	0.143
100	0.157	0.151	0.133

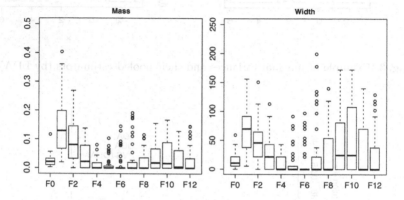

Fig. 5. Voice print of professional bass singer

ples of the fundamental frequency. The pitch-independent variables are the mass of the harmonics $F0$ to $F12$ and the width (number of fourier frequencies above some specified threshold in direct neighbourhood to the harmonics in the normalized periodogram) without the information about its corresponding frequency.

Figure 5 illustrates the so-called voice print corresponding to the whole song "Tochter Zion" for a particular singer. For masses and widths boxplots are indicating variation over the involved tones (cp. Weihs and Ligges, 9). For the analyses of this paper we use these characteristics of the voice print for individual tones per harmonic and singer or instrument.

This classification problem may be an example for local modelling as it is described in the previous sections, since apart from the classes (namely: *high* and *low* register) and the 26 variables also the subclass, i.e. the instrument-type, may influence the distribution of the data. For this reason, local modelling has already been shown here to improve the results.

The data set consists of 432 observations. The subclasses $k := (i, c)$, $i \in \{all\ instruments\}$, $c \in \{low, high\}$ are all combinations of instrument i AND register c and contain between 9 and 90 observations. A detailed description of the classification problem as well as a description of the data set and the results of global and local modelling are described in Szepannek et al. (7). In that paper Linear Discriminant Analysis and Decision Trees are used to build both local and global classification rules. It turned out that the best results are obtained using local LDA-classifiers. Several methods are derived to build classification rules from the local LDA-models for each instrument. The error rates (estimated by leave one out cross validation) have been improved up to 26.9%.

Two of the winner-classification rules are briefly described here:

The first one is referred to as *average density rule*. The estimated multivariate normal densities of the local instrument-subclasses as they are returned by LDA are summed up for the classes, leading to the classification rule:

$$\hat{c} = \arg\max_c \sum_k p(x|k) I_{\{c\}}(f(k)) \tag{9}$$

where $f(k) = f(i,c) = c$ is the function that labels the subclasses $k = (i,c)$ to the corresponding classes c as it is introduced in Sect. 1 and $p(x|k)$ is the estimated density of the observation given the subclass $k = (i,c)$. Since comparing densities on different variable subsets is questionable the local models here have to be built on a globally chosen variable subspace.

The second method will be called *global weighting of local posteriors*. It makes use of the fact, that each of the instruments (i.e. the subclasses) appears in combination with all registers in an attribute-like manner and therefore an additional "global" classification into the correct (unknown) instrument-subclass can be performed. Local LDA classification rules are built for every instrument separately. The obtained local posterior probabilities for the register of a new object are then weighted by some *global weights* that are gained by the posterior probabilities of the "global" classification into the instrument-subclass. The classification rule can be described by

$$\hat{c} = \arg\max_c \sum_i P(c|i,x) * P(i|x) \tag{10}$$

which is an applicaton of Bayes' theorem. i here denotes the index of the subclass-attribute (instrument). This method turned out to render the smallest obtained error rate. The different local models (given the instrument-subclass) can be built on different variable subsets. But for calculation of the global classification posterior probabilities into the right instrument-subclass of course for all instruments the same variables have to be taken into account.

For comparison, an analysis has been performed using external knowledge about the instrument for the prediction (i.e. an object is classified with respect to the correct local model). Using this extra information the error rates can be improved up to 15% which can be considered as a "lower bound" for the error rates.

While the *average density rule* does not allow modelling on different variable subsets, the method of *global weighting of local posteriors* does allow models on different feature subsets for different instruments but for the global instrument-classification for all instruments the variables must be the same. For application of this method, it is necessary that the subclasses possess an attribute-like

Table 4. Leave one out cross validated error rates for the different methods

method	l1o error rate
global LDA	0.345
average density rule	0.301
global weighting of local posteriors	0.269
PVS (with LDA)	0.243
"lower bound"	0.150

structure. Implementing the PVS method leads to pairwise comparisons of any combinations (i, c) of instrument and register on possibly differing variables.

Using now the *PVS* approach (with LDA) one observes a further slight improvement of the error rate up to 24.3%. A summary of the different modelling results is given in Tab. 4.

Remark: Relationship between the PVS-method and the 'winner model'. By definition the conditional probability of register, given instrument (and observation x) is given by

$$P(c|i, x) = \frac{P(i, c|x)}{P(i|x)} \ . \tag{11}$$

This changes the classification rule of the "winner model" of *global weighting of local posteriors* in equation 10 into

$$\hat{c} = \arg\max_c \sum_i P(c, i|x) \ . \tag{12}$$

Using the function $f(k) = f(i, c) = c$ as it is defined above, then our classification rule becomes

$$\hat{c} = \arg\max_c \sum_{(i, c^*)} I_{\{c\}}(f(i, c^*))P(c^*, i|x) \ . \tag{13}$$

This classification rule is of the same form as it is introduced in equation 2 in Sect. 1 for local modelling by the PVS approach. It can be seen, that in both methods modelling is essentially done in the same way. The difference is in estimating the local membership probabilities. The PVS method here only uses those variables that are important for decision between two subclasses. This explains why the result of the winner rule is even slightly improved by using the proposed method.

Additionally, the proposed PVS method is more flexible since it can also be applied to subclasses that do not possess an attribute-like character as the subclasses in the example do.

4   Summary

The problem is tackled to perform local modelling for classification where the variable subspaces of the different local models can differ. An approach of pairwise variable selection [PVS] is suggested to perform the maximal possible variable selection by splitting a K-subclass classification problem into $K(K-1)/2$

subclass pairwise classification problems. An algorithm is presented to build a classification rule from the results using this method. This principle can be applied to any classification method returning class-membership posterior probabilities in combination with any (meaningful) variable selection procedure.

Situations are outlined where such proceeding is strongly beneficial. The method is investigated on different simulated and real world data sets using (linear and quadratic) Discriminant Analysis and the results are compared to their original results using global variable selection. Gain in classification error rate can be noticed, especially if the number of observations is not very large.

Additionally, the pairwise variable subset selection can give interpretational insight into which features characterize the differences between two (sub)classes.

On the other hand, the computation time grows since there have to be built $K(K-1)/2$ classification models. Furthermore, the classification rule of each object has to be iteratively evaluated by the Pairwise Coupling algorithm.

Finally, it should be referred to another approach to solving multiclass-classification problems by transforming them into several binary classification problems using the method of *Error-Correcting Output Codes* (Dietterich and Bakiri, 4). There basically, in every binary classification problem the K classes are grouped into two sets of classes which are classified. The result is a sequence of classifiers into the different groups of classes. Each of the classes is then represented by a codebook of its (binary) group-labels. Prediction of an object is done by assigning it to the class with the most similar codebook vector. The binary classifiers may also be performed on different feature subspaces. This may be topic of further investigation.

Acknowledgment. This work has been supported by the Collaborative Research Center 'Reduction of Complexity in Multivariate Data Structures' (SFB 475) of the German Research Foundation (DFG).

References

Bishop, Y., Fienberg, S. and Holland, P.: Discrete multivariate analysis. MIT Press, Cambridge 1975.

Bradley, R. and Terry, M.: The rank analysis of incomplete block designs, i. the method of paired comparisons. Biometrics (1952) 324–345.

Breiman, L., Friedman, J., Olshen, R. and Stone, C.: Classification and regression trees. Wadsworth Publishing Co Inc. 1984.

Dietterich, T. and Bakiri, G.: Solving Multiclass Learning Problems via Error-Correcting Output Codes. Journal of Artificial Intelligence Research 2 (1995) 263–286.

Hajek, J.: A course in nonparametric statistics. Holden Day, San Francisco 1969.

Hastie, T. and Tibshirani, R.: Classification by Pairwise Coupling. Annals of Statistics **26(1)** (1998) 451–471.

Szepannek, G., Ligges, U., Luebke, K., Raabe, N. and Weihs, C.: Local Models in Register Classification by Timbre. Technical Report 47/2005, SFB 475, Fachbereich Statistik, Universität Dortmund.

Szepannek, G. and Weihs, C.: Variable Selection for Discrimination of more than two Classes where Data are Sparse. In: Spiliopoulou, M., Kruse, R., Nürnberger, A., Borgelt, C. and Gaul, W. (Eds.): From Data and Information Analysis to Knowledge Engineering. Springer-Verlag, Heidelberg (2006) 700–707.

Weihs, C. and Ligges, U.: Voice Prints as a Tool for Automatic Classification of Vocal Performance. In: Kopiez, R., Lehmann, A., Wolther, I. and Wolf, C. (Eds.): Proceedings of the 5th Triennial ESCOM Conference. Hannover University of Music and Drama, Germany, 8-13 September 2003, 332–335.

Weihs, C., Ligges, U., Luebke, K. and Raabe, N.: klaR Analyzing German Business Cycles. In: Baier, D., Becker, R. and Schmidt-Thieme, L. (Eds.): Data Analysis and Decision Support, Springer, Berlin (2005) 335–343.

Wu, T.-F., Lin, C.-J. and Weng, R.: Probability Estimates for Multi-class Classification by Pairwise Coupling. Journal of Machine Learning Research **5** (2004) 975–1005.

Supervised Selection of Dynamic Features, with an Application to Telecommunication Data Preparation

Sylvain Ferrandiz[1,2] and Marc Boullé[1]

[1] France Télécom R&D
2, avenue Pierre Marzin,
22307 LANNION Cedex, France
[2] Université de Caen, GREYC,
Campus Côte de Nacre,
boulevard du Maréchal Juin BP 5186
14032 Caen Cedex, France
sylvain.ferrandiz@francetelecom.com
marc.boulle@francetelecom.com

Abstract. In the field of data mining, data preparation has more and more in common with a bottleneck. Indeed, collecting and storing data becomes cheaper while modelling costs remain unchanged. As a result, feature selection is now usually performed. In the data preparation step, selection often relies on feature ranking. In the supervised classification context, ranking is based on the information that the explanatory feature brings on the target categorical attribute.

With the increasing presence in the database of feature measured over time, *i.e.* dynamic features, new supervised ranking methods have to be designed. In this paper, we propose a new method to evaluate dynamic features, which is derived from a probabilistic criterion. The criterion is non-parametric and handles automatically the problem of overfitting the data. The resulting evaluation produces reliable results. Furthermore, the design of the criterion relies on an understandable and simple approach. This allows to provide meaningful visualization of the evaluation, in addition to the computed score. The advantages of the new method are illustrated on a telecommunication dataset.

1 Data Preparation and Feature Ranking

In a data mining project, the data preparation step is a cornerstone. It aims at providing a dataset for the modelling step, that is a row/column table, from primary collected data [3]. Typically, topics like instance representation, instance selection and/or aggregation, missing values handling, feature selection, are to be dealt with. We focus in this paper on feature selection, in the context of supervised classification.

In [7], a check list of the different problems to tackle when performing feature selection is provided. According to this list, we consider in the present paper that :

P. Perner (Ed.): ICDM 2006, LNAI 4065, pp. 239–249, 2006.
© Springer-Verlag Berlin Heidelberg 2006

- we have domain knowledge : the whole search space may be of very large size and domain knowledge limits the evaluation to meaningful features,
- features are commensurate : no normalization has to be carried out preliminarily,
- we are to select subsets of the input variables : the context is that of large databases,
- we assess features individually : for the sake of simplicity and scalability,
- we do not focus on the prediction performance : the context is that of data preparation,
- we cannot make hypotheses on the interdependence or the "noisiness" of the features : this must be detected not hypothesized,
- we want a stable solution : extracted information must be general, not valid on the data at hand only.

Assessing the features individually, more than being simple and scalable, is well-suited to the data preparation step. Indeed, following the classification of [9], this is a filter method, being independent of the choice of a predictor. We can think of the problem as a variable ranking problem. We assume that a high score describes a valuable variable and that variables are sorted decreasingly. As an application, nested subsets progressively incorporating more and more variables of decreasing relevance can be defined in order to build predictors. Classical scoring paradigms are described in the section 2.

With the increasing collecting and storing capacity of many computerized systems, data-miners have to deal with more and more heterogeneous data and face new challenges. As an example, while features used to be static, they are becoming more and more dynamic, being measured over time. To each instance can be associated static continuous values (like the age of the patient), static categorical values (like the hospital in which the patient is being treated), and dynamic features (like an ECG, an EEG). We discuss the problematic of supervised selection of dynamic features in the section 3.

In the static case, the approach adopted in [2] for discretization of a continuous feature and in [1] for grouping the values of a categorical feature provides the user with an evaluation of the amount of information the feature contains relating to the target attribute. As dynamic features are innerly multivariate, any extended version of these static methods to the multivariate case allows to evaluate dynamic features. In [5], the approach is adapted to the case of multivariate features. It relies on partitioning the set of instances and designing a criterion for the evaluation of different partitions. We derive from it a method to evaluate dynamic features in the section 4. For the convenience of the reader, the technicalities around the criterion are postponed to the section 5.

In the section 6, we illustrate the advantages of the new criterion for supervised selection of dynamic features on a telecommunication dataset. As this dataset contains continuous data only, we restrict ourselves to this kind of data in the following. But, as it will become clearer, the proposed indicator can deal with any kind of data.

2   Classical Evaluation Paradigms

Let us consider a continuous explanatory random variable X and a target attribute Y. We describe in this section the classical approaches for designing a measure of interest of X relating to Y.

In a two-class classification problem, the values of Y can be mapped to the values ± 1. Then, the squared correlation coefficient between X and Y can be used to score the variable X. It can be shown that this correlation coefficient is closely related to the ratio of the between-class variance to the within-class variance, that is to Fisher's criterion, and to the Student's T-test. Variable ranking can thus be turned into classical statistical testing. This approach is limited to two-class problems, is parametric (in the algorithmic and statistical sense) and relies on an asymptotic approximation.

In the considered supervised context, many scores are based on the individual predictive performance of X. Once X is turned into a classifier, the error rate evaluated on a separated validation sample measures such a performance. For example, in a two-class problem, a classifier is obtained by setting a threshold on the values of X. Varying the threshold allows to perform a ROC analysis, measuring the performance of X with the area under the ROC curve [4]. Cutting a continuous attribute into more than two intervals is a discretization problem. By considering more complex cuttings, one has to prevent from overfitting the data [10]. In case of large number of variables, ranking criteria based on predictive performance cannot separate the top ranking variables.

The maximum margin principle can be applied as well. The margin of an instance is the absolute difference between its distance to the nearest example of the same class and its distance to the nearest example of another class. Considering the sum of the margins on X provides an evaluation of X. This evaluation extends straightforwardly to the multivariate case. The resulting feature subset selection problem is tackled in [6]. The use of margins comes with distribution-free generalization bound. These bounds can be very loose in practice.

Another well-known approach is the information theoretic one. It relies on the maximization of the mutual information, which measures how far the joint distribution of X and Y is from independency. The main difficulty is to empirically estimate the mutual information, as it considers the joint distribution and the marginal distributions simultaneously. Some might say that the problem is easier in the categorical case, as the integral becomes a sum. Discretization is then applied, with an information preserving goal, this time. Once again, one has to prevent from overfitting the data [10].

3   When Features Are Dynamic

In the classical case, a feature is static : the marital status, the gender, the salary, etc. As collecting and storing data becomes cheaper, it is more and more usual to monitor features over time. While gender cannot fluctuate over time, the salary and marital status do. The salary curve then has to be considered as a fully qualified feature. This is what we will refer to as a dynamic feature.

Thus, beside static features, the data-miner now encounters dynamic features. While the overall problematic of the data mining tasks remains unchanged (building a classifier, in the supervised classification context, for example), the introduction of such features raises new questions that require a particular treatment. Especially, the question of the representation is strengthened.

While the representation problem for continuous static features is usually turned into a discretization problem, and is quite less considered for categorical static features, the range of possibility is dramatically enlarged for dynamic features :

– the time scale is fixed according to technical constraints and can be unrelevant for the data-mining task,
– data can be noisy,
– relevant information can be hidden,
– ...

Segmentation, denoising, Fourier's transform and many other algorithms are applied to the primary data and produce different representations. It means that, when ranking features, different representations of the same dynamic feature have to be evaluated too. Indeed, for a particular supervised study, the Haar's transform might be better than the Fourier's one. In the supervised context, such transformations are applied according to the domain knowledge, disregarding the target attribute.

As an example, let us consider head related transfer functions (HRTFs), which describe the acoustic filtering properties of a listener's external auditory periphery and are used in 3-D audio systems. An HRTF results from the application of the Fourier's transform to a particular head-related impulse response. The domain knowledge leads to work with the log of the Fourier's coefficient (as our auditive scale is closer to a logarithmic scale than a linear one), and to adopt a threshold (which corresponds to a threshold of hearing). The distance between HRTFs is usually measured by the euclidean distance. Studies show that weighting schemes produce similarity measure closer to the properties of our auditive system.

A dynamic feature is represented by a new set of explanatory attributes : the Fourier's coefficients, the segment means, etc. Then, a similarity measure between instances is usually defined. This measure itself is part of the representation. Supervised ranking of dynamic features amounts to the evaluation of a set of attributes equipped with a similarity measure.

4   Evaluation of Dynamic Features

Let us consider that a representation of a dynamic feature is given by a set of descriptive attributes and a similarity measure. In the static case, it is proposed in [2] to consider the problem of the discretization of a continuous attribute as a modelling problem. A model is a partition of the attribute into a set of intervals. The most probable given the data is selected. The originality of the method relies

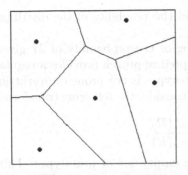

Fig. 1. Examples of synthetic and real Voronoi partitions for the euclidean metric

on the definition of the probability of a model given the data, compromising between the complexity of the model (*i.e.* the number of intervals) and goodness of fit to the data (*i.e.* the purity of the target attribute in each interval). In [5], the approach is extended in order to deal with the multivariate case, provided that a similarity measure is defined.

While intervals are considered in the static case, partitions are made up with Voronoi cells in the multivariate case. Given a set P of instances, the *Voronoi cell* induced by $p \in P$ contains the points x whose p is the most similar element in P, with respect to a fixed dissimilarity measure. The element p is called the *representative* or the *prototype* of its cell. Examples of Voronoi partitions are given in the Figure 1. The problem of selecting the most probable partition given the data is then turned into an instance selection problem.

In order to perform instance selection, a representation must be fixed, that is a set of attributes and a similarity measure. In this context, a model is no other than a set of prototypes, *i.e.* a subset of the set of instances. For a given representation R and any set of prototypes M, let us evaluate the quality of M with the supervised criterion $c(R, M)$, the definition of which is postponed to the next section. Instance selection is performed by minimizing this criterion and we denote $c^*(R)$ the minimum value of $c(R, M)$:

$$c^*(R) = min_M c(R, M).$$

The resulting evaluation function c^* can be used and helpful for ranking representations : for a given representation, apply a combinatorial optimization algorithm for instance selection and evaluate the representation according to the minimum encountered criterion value. The technicalities of the criterion and the optimization algorithm are discussed in the next section.

The proposed primary criterion $c(M, R)$ sets a compromise between the size of M and the discrimination of the target attributes. Every instance in the database has a nearest prototype, according to the representation R. Each prototype thus supports the distribution of the labels of the instances lying in its Voronoi cell. Increasing the size of M produces distributions that are purer and purer but supported by less and less instances. The criterion $c(M, R)$ quantifies the compromise between the size of M and the reliability of the distributions, in a principled manner.

The criterion $c(M, R)$ is the negative log of the probability of M given the representation R and the data. As the adopted approach provides a regularized criterion, the search for the best set of prototypes is not prone to overfitting. In order to provide a normalized indicator, we consider the following transformation of c^* :

$$g^*(R) = 1 - \frac{c^*(R)}{c_0(R)},$$

where $c_0(R)$ is the criterion value for the empty set of prototypes. This can be interpreted as a compression gain, as negative log of probabilities are no other than coding lengths [11]. The compression gain $g^*(R)$ is greater than 0 (as soon as the empty set is evaluated during the optimization) and less than 1. If $g^*(R) = 0$, the representation R brings no information on the target attribute. The nearer $g^*(R)$ is from 1, the more separable the labels are.

The use of a validation set is very constraining. It limits the size of the training set and introduces useless variance in the result. Cross-validation is often used in order to reduce the variance effects, but is time consuming. Unlike performance based criteria, the compression gain is validation free.

The use of margins is validated by the fact that they provide distribution-free bounds on the generalization performance. In practice, these bounds are often very loose and margins are not innerly meaningful. The compression gain makes sense by quantifying a simple compromise between complexity of the hypotheses and discrimination of the target attribute.

Informational criteria and statistical tests often rely on statistical parametric assumptions (the probability laws are supposed to have a predetermined parametric shape) and possess an asymptotic validity. For a particular finite dataset, the quality of the estimations is not guaranteed or can be very loose as well. Unlike informational criteria or statistical tests, the compression gain is a finite-data criterion.

5   Instance Selection: Criterion and Algorithm

In this section, we describe the criterion and the algorithm from which is derived the new method to evaluate dynamic features.

5.1   Evaluation of Sets of Prototypes

We first set the notations. We have a finite sample $D = \{X_n, Y_n\}$ of N labelled instances. We denote $D^{(x)} = \{X_n\}$ the set of instances and $D^{(y)} = \{Y_n\}$ the set of labels. The labels lie in an alphabet of size J and the instances in a space $\mathbb{X}$. A dissimilarity measure $\delta : \mathbb{X} \times \mathbb{X} \to \mathbb{R}_+$ is given.

For a set of prototypes $M = \{p_1, \ldots, p_K\} \subset \mathbb{X}$, K is the size of M, N_k ($1 \leq k \leq K$) is the number of instances whose nearest prototype is p_k and N_{kj} denotes the number of such instances in the jth class. Thus, $N = N_1 + \cdots + N_K$ and $N_k = N_{k1} + \cdots + N_{kJ}$.

The approach adopted in [5] leads to the following supervised evaluation of M :

$$c(M) = \log N + \log \binom{N + K - 1}{K} + \sum_{k=1}^{K} \log \binom{N_k + J - 1}{J - 1} + \log \frac{N_k!}{N_{k1}! \ldots N_{kJ}!}.$$

This value can be interpreted as the negative log of $p(D^{(y)}, M/D^{(x)})$. The first term of the criterion stands for the choice of the number K of prototypes, the second term for the choice of the K prototypes and the third term for the choice of the output label distributions in each cell. The last sum over the cells, according to the Stirling's approximation $\log x! \approx x \log x - x + O(\log x)$, behaves asymptotically as N times the conditional entropy of the distribution of the Y_n's given the clusters assignment function :

$$\frac{1}{N} \sum_{k=1}^{K} \log \frac{N_k!}{N_{k1}! \ldots N_{kJ}!} \approx - \sum_{k=1}^{K} \sum_{j=1}^{J} \frac{N_{kj}}{N} \log \frac{N_{kj}}{N_k}.$$

The criterion thus evaluates the discrimination of the distributions with a finite-data entropy-related term balanced with a structural weight, which quantifies the complexity of the partitioning. This prevents from overfitting the data.

5.2   The Optimization Heuristic

In this section, an optimization algorithm is described. It consists in a greedy optimization of a set of prototypes, the complexity of which can be reduced by exploiting the properties of the descriptive criterion. This greedy search is embedded into a meta-heuristic in order to further optimize the criterion.

The greedy heuristic Greedy(M) applies to every set M of p prototypes. Every subset resulting from the removal of an element in M is evaluated. Among those subsets, the winner is the one minimizing the criterion. This process is iterated and applied to every successive winners, until a singleton has been evaluated. The best encountered subset is returned. This method considers $O(p^2)$ subsets and each evaluation requires a search of the nearest prototype for each instance. A straightforward implantation of Greedy(M) has a complexity down to $O(Np^3)$. The properties of the models and the criterion allows to reduce this complexity to $O(Np \log p)$.

The greedy heuristic thus performs many evaluations quickly, as long as the number p of prototypes is not too large. It is then natural to think about applying this algorithm repeatedly. This is done according to the Variable Neighborhood Search (VNS) meta-heuristic [8], which consists in applying the primary heuristic (i.e. the greedy one) to a neighbor of the solution. If the new solution is not better, a bigger neighborhood is considered. Otherwise, the algorithm restarts with the new best solution and a minimal size neighborhood. The process is controlled by specifying the maximum length of the series of growing neighborhoods to explore.

6   Application

We illustrate the advantages of the new evaluation method for dynamic features on a real dataset. The problem is that of dynamic feature selection for data preparation, in the context of supervised classification. The target attribute is a four-class attribute and the distribution of the labels is uniform : 25% of the instances are in class A, 25% in class B, 25% in class C and 25% in class D. We aim at scoring 24 dynamic features. The 24 features are themselves well-ordered and indexed from 1 to 24. Each feature is represented by 7 continuous attributes. Experiments are carried out with the L_1 and L_2 metrics alternatively.

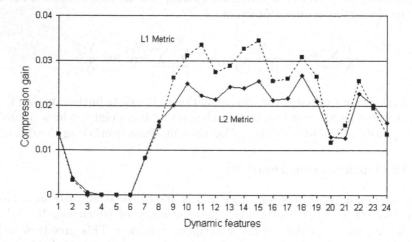

Fig. 2. Evaluation of the 24 dynamic features

The scoring curve of the dynamic features is plotted in the figure 2. In the case of the L_1 metric, the compression gain of the features from 3 to 6 is null. This means that these dynamic features are uncorrelated with the target attribute. Automatically and with few risks of taking a wrong decision, the data-miner can eliminate those features.

Considering the L_1 and the L_2 metric alternatively, compression gain is higher when using the first one. Under such a hypothesis, the data-miner can perform metric selection according to the compression gain. Here, the L_1 metric should be prefered.

The partition comes with a set of prototypes. The predictive accuracy of the nearest neighbor rule on this set of prototypes is reported on the figure 3 for every dynamic feature. The accuracy is measured by the prediction rate estimated on a separate test set. As can be noticed, the prediction accuracy and the compression gain exhibit the same global behavior.

Furthermore, the number of final prototypes is very low. This allows to provide the user with a visualization of the discrimination. The relating distribution of

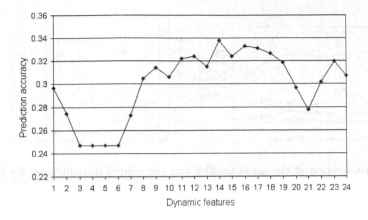

Fig. 3. Prediction accuracy of the 24 dynamic features

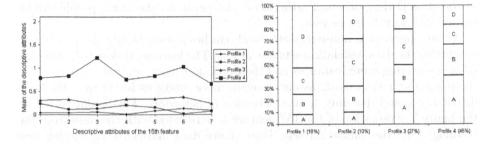

Fig. 4. Visualization of the mean profiles and the related distributions, for the 15th feature. The method select four prototypes. To each prototype p is associated a mean profile : the average of the instances the nearest prototype of which is p. The four extracted profiles are plotted on the left. The labels of the instances can be collected and attributed to the nearest prototype and the four resulting frequential distributions are plotted on the right. The support of each prototype is reported too (Profile 1 (18%) means that the first prototype is the nearest prototype of 18% of the instances).

the target attribute can be plotted. Working with continuous attributes, for a prototype p, the instances whose nearest prototype is p can be averaged. The resulting mean profile assigned to each prototype can be plotted as well. This is done for the 15th feature, which is the most relevant one, in the figure 4. The four classes are very mixed, and none of them clearly dominate the others. This is often the case in practice. In such situations, notions like prediction accuracy and margins are likely to be less meaningful.

Owing to the provided visualization, the approach adopted in this paper allows to make more than dynamic feature ranking. Useful and reliable general knowledge can be extracted. While the B class is not discriminated (for every prototypes, the proportion of instances labelled B is about 25%), the proportion

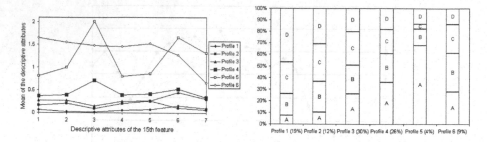

Fig. 5. Visualization of the mean profiles and the related distributions, for the 15th feature, with more data

of the D class ranges from 52% to 16%. Coupling this information on the distributions with the mean profiles allows the data-miner to draw the conclusion that instances with profile 4 on the 15th dynamic feature are more likely to be in the class D than others. Furthermore, the peaks on the mean profile can be turned into knowledge as well.

As the approach is non-parametric and handles automatically the problem of overfitting the data, validation sets are useless. The learning task usually benefits from considering more instances and then produces more accurate classifiers. In the present situation, more instances means more robust estimations of the label distributions and, possibly, a finer detection of behaviors. This is illustrated on the figure 5. Evaluation of the 15th feature is performed with the data from the training AND the validation sets. Using more data allows to distinguish new profiles (6 instead of 4) and the data-miner is able to extract more knowledge, which is still reliable.

7   Conclusion and Further Work

In this paper, we have discussed the ranking paradigm for feature selection and the particular problem raised by the presence of dynamic features in the database, especially in the context of data preparation. We proposed a new scoring method for such features, based on a criterion applying to instance selection for the nearest neighbor rule. The advantages of the new method fonction are illustrated on a real telecommunication dataset.

Being non-parametric, the method does not require a validation set. The method is able to take advantage of the presence of more instances. As the criterion handles automatically the problem of overfitting the data, the results are reliable. Furthermore, the underlying instance selection, which is performed when evaluating a feature, allows to produce a visualization in addition to the computed score. Finally, although the criterion does not focus on the prediction accuracy, the adopted target discrimination principle exhibits a strong correlation to the accuracy.

References

[1] Boullé, M.: A grouping method for categorical attributes having very large number of values. In: P. Perner and A. Imiya (Eds.), Machine Learning and Data Mining in Pattern Recognition, Springer Verlag, lnai 3587, MLDM 2005, (2005), 228–242

[2] Boullé, M.: A bayesian approach for supervised discretization. Data Mining V, Zanasi and Ebecken and Brebbia, WIT Press (2004) 199–208

[3] Chapman, P., Clinton, J., Kerber, R., Khabaza, T., Reinartz, T., Shearer, C., Wirth, R.: CRISP-DM 1.0 : step-by-step data mining guide. Applied Statistics Algorithms (2000)

[4] Fawcett T.: ROC Graphs : notes and practical considerations for reseachers. Technical report HPL-2003-4 (2003).

[5] Ferrandiz S., Boullé M.: Supervised evaluation of Voronoi partitions. Journal of intelligent data analysis (2006), to be published

[6] Gilad-Bachrach R., Navot A., Tishby N.: Margin based feature selection - theory and algorithms. Proceedings of the 21'st international conference on machine learning (2004)

[7] Guyon I., Elisseeff A.: An introduction to variable and feature selection. Journal of machine learning research 3 (2003) 1157–1182

[8] Hansen P., Mladenovic N.: Variable neighborhood search: principles and applications. European journal of operational research 130 (2001) 449–467

[9] Kohavi R., John G.H.: Wrappers for Feature Subset Selection. Artificial Intelligence 97 (1997) 273–324

[10] Kohavi R., Sahami M.: Error-based and entropy-based Discretization of continuous features. Proceedings of the 2'nd international conference on knowledge discovery and data mining (1996) 114–119

[11] Shannon C.E.: A mathematical theory of communication. Bell systems technical journal 27 (1948) 379–423 and 623–656

Using Multi-SOMs and Multi-Neural-Gas as Neural Classifiers

Nils Goerke and Alexandra Scherbart

Div. of Neural Computation, Dept. of Computer Sciene,
University of Bonn, Bonn, Germany
{goerke, scherbart}@nero.uni-bonn.de
http://www.nero.uni-bonn.de

Abstract. Within this paper we present the extension of two neural network paradigms for clustering tasks. The Self Organizing feature Maps (SOM) are extended to the Multi SOM approach, and the Neural Gas is extended to a Multi Neural Gas. Some common cluster analysis coefficients (Silhouette Coefficient, Gap Statistics, Calinski-Harabasz Coefficient) have been adapted for the new paradigms. Both new neural clustering methods are described and evaluated briefly using exemplary data sets.

1 Classification with Neural Networks

The task of classifying data points, and finding clusters within data sets is an application where neural networks can be successful applied. To complete the task of data clustering the following two subtasks have to be realised:

A) Find a set of classes that represents the given set of data points adequate.
B) Assign a given data point to that class, that is representing this point best.

Neural networks, as learning function approximators have been applied in various ways for the task of classification. Depending on the existence of pre-classified patterns (examples) different types of learning paradigms for the neural networks apply.

Supervised learning is used if already classified data points are available. The neural network is trained to realise a mapping from the data space onto the space of classes, with respect to the given data points, and the given classification for these data points. Typical neural network paradigms applied are: Multi Layer Perceptrons (MLPs), Radial Basis Function Networks (RBF) and Learning Vector Quantisation (LVQ), [12], [5], [8].

The training algorithm is imprinting shape and position of the classes (task A) into the neural network by adapting the internal network parameters (weights). Once the training is complete, the neural network is capable of performing the classification by associating a class to a given data point (task B).

In the case that no classified data points are available, unsupervised or self organising neural paradigms apply. Based only on the given data points, the neural systems can learn to build a classifier, e.g. Adaptive Resonance Theory (ART) and Self Organising Feature Maps (SOMs, Kohonen maps) [12], [5], [8].

P. Perner (Ed.): ICDM 2006, LNAI 4065, pp. 250–263, 2006.

2   Multi-SOMs

Multi SOMs are an extension of the Self Organising (feature) Maps (SOMs) of T. Kohonen [7]. Based on the classical SOM idea, the Multi-SOM approach takes a set of several SOMs, combine them to the Multi-SOM, and train them using a slightly modified SOM learning. Multi-SOMs are specially designed to represent data distributions that are non-contiguous [3].

2.1   Self Organising Feature Maps (SOMs)

A self organising (feature) map (SOM), is a neural network that is capable of adapting part of its structure in accordance to the statistical properties of the data provided. A SOM consists of N neurons that receive an D-dimensional input $\mathbf{P}$. Each neuron n has an D-dimensional center vector $\mathbf{C}_n$ which is compared to the input pattern $\mathbf{P}$ yielding the neural response. The neuron with the largest response within the SOM is called the winner neuron i. In addition, the SOM neurons are connected to each other via a grid structure $\mathcal{G}$, defining a neighborhood between the neurons and a topology in feature space.

During the SOM training, the center vectors $\mathbf{C}_n$ of the N neurons are adapted with respect to the provided training data. Learning means, that the center vector $\mathbf{C}_n$ of each neuron n is pulled toward the input pattern $\mathbf{P}$. The center $\mathbf{C}_i$ of the winner neuron i is adapted the most, the center vectors $\mathbf{C}_n$ of the other neurons n are adapted with respect to the neighborhood function $h(i, n, t)$, which uses the topological distance on the grid $\mathcal{G}$ between the winner i and the neuron n to adapt. The learning rule for a SOM is updating the center $\mathbf{C}_n$ of the neuron n with respect to the input $\mathbf{P}$ and the winner neuron i:

$$\mathbf{C}_n(t+1) \quad = \quad \mathbf{C}_n(t) + \eta(t) \cdot h(t, i, n) \cdot (\mathbf{P} - \mathbf{C}_n(t) \tag{1}$$

Once a SOM is trained, each neuron has to be *labeled*. Labeling a SOM means, that each neuron is assigned to a data set which this neuron is responsible for. Typically, the labels for the neurons are the names or the indexes of classes.

In the recall phase, an input pattern, or input vector $\mathbf{P}$ is applied to the SOM, yielding a winner neuron i. The output of such a SOM is the number of the winning neuron, and thereby the label associated with this very winner neuron, e.g. a class label. Thus, SOMs have the capability to map patterns from the D-dimensional input space to the feature space, (classes).

It has been shown that self organising feature maps have the capability to adapt to the distribution of the training data. For a detailed discussion of the SOM capabilities see the book from T.Kohonen [8].

2.2   Multi SOM Principle

The multi-SOM approach is the extension of the SOM neural network to several SOMs. An M-SOM consists of K individual partner SOMs. Each of these K partner SOMs is a SOM of its own, and treated exactly like a classical SOM: center vectors, response, winner neuron, topological grid structure. Only the learning algorithm has to be adapted slightly in the following way: Adaptation of the centers of the M-SOM neurons is restricted to that neurons, that are in the same partner SOM than the winner i. Only the winning SOM is adapted, using the classical SOM learning; the neurons from all other, non-winning partner-SOMs are kept unchanged.

M-SOM Architecture

A Multi-SOM is consisting of K partner SOMs. Each of these partner SOMs contains an individual number N_k of neurons, It is not necessary that all partner-SOMs within a Multi-SOM are identical, they can be different in topology, size and dimension. For example, a set of 2-dimensional partner-SOMs can be used to represent a data distribution in 2-dimensions (see Fig. 1 and 2) or can be trained to represent a 3-dimensional data set as depicted in Fig. 2.

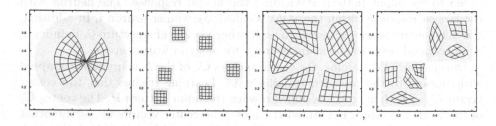

Fig. 1. Diffferent M-SOMs in 2 dimensions depicting different results of M-SOM data representation. From left to right: 1-9x9, 6-5x5, 5-6x6, 7-4x4.

It has been found useful to define all partner SOMs equal in size, dimension and topology. It showed to be easier for a human operator to interpret and judge the solution found by the M-SOM if all partner SOMS are alike in size and topology.

Is is easy to argue, that an M-SOM with an individual topology for each partner SOM can improve the mapping capabilities of the complete M-SOM, if the topology is aligned to the data set. This requires some a-priori knowledge about the underlying data distribution. If this knowledge is not available, it is a good advice to keep all partner SOMs equal.

The number K and the size, dimension, and topology of the partner SOMs are parameters that have to be chosen carefully. In case a Multi-SOM is applied for mapping the D-dimensional input patterns onto a feature space with lower dimension, the dimensionality of the partner SOMs should be chosen as the dimension of the prospective feature space. As a rule of thumb, keep the size of the partner SOMs small, to avoid the effect of getting a twisted SOM (see Fig. 1 left). The two extreme configurations of M-SOM, demonstrate the range of paradigms that can be realised with an M-SOM. With $K = 1$ the complete M-SOM consists of just one single SOM. In this case the M-SOM is identical to a classical SOM. The other extreme situation, with K partner SOMs that have the minimal size of $N_k = 1$, the M-SOM is identical to a K-Means clustering algorithm.

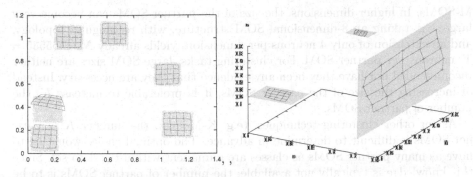

Fig. 2. Left: 6-5x5 M-SOM in 2D during learning, one of the partner SOMs has not yet completely adapted to the data distribution. Right: a 3-5x5 M-SOM representing three 2-dimensional data sets within the 3-dimensional input space.

M-SOM Learning

The learning procedure of an M-SOM is following the learning rule for a classical SOM. The only extension to the classical SOM algorithm is, that only the winner SOM is learning, and only the winner SOM neurons have to be adapted. As for the classical SOMs, it is a good advice to reduce the learning rate $\eta(t)$, and the size of the neighborhood $h(i, n, t)$ with time ([2], [8]). During the learning process, the mean difference between the pattern $\mathbf{P}$ and the winning neuron $\mathbf{C}_i$ is a good measure to monitor, and determine the learning progress. With the learning time, this deviation will decrease, and finally converge (see left part of Fig. 3).

2.3   M-SOMs for Classification

When using the M-SOMs for classification, and unsupervised clustering, the task of the M-SOM is covering both aspects of classification in the following way:

A: Find a set of classes that represents the given set of data points in an adequate way.
    This is performed with the M-SOM by changing the centers of the neurons with respect to the given data points. The connections between the neurons (grid structure $\mathcal{G}$), take care that the topological properties of the input data is well represented by the SOMs.
B: Assign a given data point to that class, that is representing this data point best.
    This is performed by the SOMs, directly by finding the winner neuron i, and thereby by finding the winner SOM that stands for the class determined.

When using the M-SOM for classification tasks, the choice of the dimension for the partner SOMs is not critic. Of course, it is a good advice to use any available a priori knowledge about the data distribution. Partner SOM sizes from one single neuron $N_k = 1$ per partner SOM, to mid-size sizes like $N_k = 49 = 7 \times 7$ in 2 dimensions, or $N_k = 125 = 5 \times 5 \times 5$ in 3 dimensions are usual choices for

M-SOMs. In higher dimensions, the size of the partner SOMs can become very large, e.g. taking an 8-dimensional SOM structure, with rectangular topology, and an extension of only 4 neurons per dimension, yields already $N_k = 65535 = 4^8$ neurons per partner SOM. For clustering tasks, large SOM sizes are neither recommended nor have they been any evidence that they are necessary. Instead of increasing the size of the partner SOMs, it is preferable to increase K, the number of partner SOMs.

As for other clustering techniques, (e.g. K-Means), the number K of partner SOMs is difficult to determine in advance. The optimal choice would be to have as many partner SOMs as classes are immanent within the data set. Since this knowledge is typically not available, the number of partner SOMs is to be determined during the adaptation process.

The case that the number K of partner SOMs is too small, means that there are fewer partner SOMs than clusters within the data distribution. Then, the M-SOM is trying to represent the data as a classical SOM would do. The effect would be, that some of the partner SOMs are representing more than one cluster. Still, the SOM learning procedure is generating a distribution of neurons that is concentrated, and well aligned with the clusters of the data, but an easy, direct alignment between the partner SOMs and the clusters is no longer possible (see Fig. 6.

The case that the number K of partner SOMs is too large, means that there are more partner SOMs than clusters. Then, more than one partner SOM is available to represent a data cluster. This situation does not get a direct mapping from partner SOM to class either, since some classes will be represented by several SOMs. This situation is preferable to having too few partner SOMs, because different clusters yield different winner SOMs, and typically the clusters are still separated (see Fig. 6).

Clustering with the extreme M-SOM configuration, $K = 1$ realises a classical SOM. After all, a classical SOM is not a bad approach to unsupervised clustering. The other extreme configuration with $N_k = 1$ implements a set of N neurons. The centers of these neurons are driven towards the center of gravity of the data distribution, which is exactly what K-Means clustering does. Both extreme M-SOM configurations implement clustering methods that are established, and well respected. A typical M-SOM configuration can do better.

3   Multi-NeuralGas

Following the basic idea of Multi-SOMs [3] to have several disconnected neural networks that are treated individually, the Neural Gas approach [9] has been extended to a Multi-Neural Gas neural network (Multi-NGas, M-NGas).

3.1   Neural Gas

A neural gas is an ensemble of N neurons, that are acting in the D-dimensional input space. Each neuron has a D-dimensional center vector $\mathbf{C}$. An input pattern $\mathbf{P}$ is compared to each of the center vectors $\mathbf{C}_n$. The winner neuron

i is that neuron that has the smallest distance between input pattern $\mathbf{P}$ and center vector $\mathbf{C}_i$. This is the same procedure as for the self organising feature maps (SOMs).

The distance, between the input pattern $\mathbf{P}$ and the center $\mathbf{C}_n$, yields an order among the N neural gas neurons, beginning with the winner i. The winner neuron i has the first position within the sorted list $\mathbf{L}$ of neurons.

Learning the neural gas is performed similar to the learning procedure of a SOM, with the difference, that the neighborhood function $h(t, s)$ is determined with respect to the position s within the sorted list $\mathbf{L}$.

It has been shown in the literature, that the neural gas neurons converge to the data points (patterns), and that the neural gas structure represents the data distribution correctly [9], [2].

3.2   Multi-Neural Gas Principle

The Multi-NGas is an extension of the Neural Gas approach, where several (K) neural gas networks (partner neural gas networks) exist in parallel. Similar to the M-SOM, only the neurons from the winner neural gas are adapted according to the normal rules of neural gas learning. Once again, the K different partner neural gas networks, are used to define the clusters for the classification task. Compared to the M-SOM approach, the M-NGas has no underlying grid structure, which showed to be a disadvantage when applied for mapping data from the input space to a feature space. Used for unsupervised and self organising clustering, the grid structure is not missing, and the M-NGas provides a good approach to clustering data.

M-NGas Architecture. Since the M-NGas has no inner structure to take care for, only the number of neurons (N_k) per partner neural gas, and the number K of partner neural gas networks has to be determined.

As for K-Means clustering and for the M-SOMs, the number K of neural gas networks is the crucial parameter to adjust. Without any prior knowledge, K can only be determined experimentally while during the clustering process.

The M-NGas extreme configuration $N_k = 1$ with just one single neuron per partner gas, yields the K-Means clustering method. The other extreme configuration with $K = 1$, implements a normal neural gas. This configuration is a good choice to represent the data with the neurons, but is not providing enough information to apply for clustering.

M-NGas Learning. Training the M-NGas is performed in the same way as a normal neural gas, with the difference, that only the neurons from the winning gas are trained. Compared to a neural gas with the same number N of neurons than all partner neural gas neurons together N_k, the M-NGas has the advantage that only a fraction of the neurons have to be updated. Since building and sorting the list L has to be only performed for the winning gas, the speed-up by using an M-NGas is respectable.

3.3   M-NGas for Classification

Multi-neural gas networks can be easily applied to clustering and classification. It is obvious, that the center of the neurons are tending towards the patterns provided.

When using the M-NGas both aspects of classification and clustering are covered in analogy to the M-SOM:

A: Find a set of classes that represents the given set of data points in an adequate way.

This is performed with the neural gas by adapting the centers of the neurons with respect to the given data points.

B: Assign a given data point to that class, that is representing this data point best.

This is performed by the neural gas neurons, directly by finding the winner neuron i, and thereby by finding the winner gas.

4   Quality Measures

Unsupervised clustering methods depend only on the input patterns; no class information is provided with the patterns. Therefore, the quality of the data clustering can only be evaluated by statistical properties of the found clustering (cluster analysis [11]). Several indicators and coefficients can be found in the literature for judging the quality of the clustering, dedicated to determine the optimal number K of active clustering centers (e.g. Silhouette-coefficient for K-Means Clustering) [6], [11].

To evaluate the presented methods for unsupervised clustering, M-SOM and M-NGas, the question of how to determine the optimal number K^* for the Multi-SOMs and Multi-NGas networks is still open. The idea is, to make use of the developed cluster analysis methods [11] and expand them to the M-SOM and M-NGas approach. In addition, we have investigated if these coefficients can be used as a quality measure for the clustering process, to monitor the progress of the clusters during the adaptation process.

Mean Deviation, Variance

While training the M-SOM and the M-NGas neurons the distance (deviation, error e) between the pattern $\mathbf{P}$ and the center vector $\mathbf{C}_i$ of the winner neuron i is calculated. The error $e(r)$, averaged over all R available data points $\mathbf{P}_r$ is indicating how good the patterns are represented by the winning neurons. The mean deviation $\bar{E}$ is the average error that is made by taking the center vector $\mathbf{C}_i$ of the respective winning neuron $i = i(r)$, instead of taking the data point $\mathbf{P}$ itself.

The variance is a second indicator to evaluate whether the patterns are correctly represented by the centers of the respective winner neurons. The variance S^2 is the mean of the sum of the squared errors e.

$$\bar{E} = \frac{1}{R} \cdot \sum_{r=1}^{R} \|\mathbf{P}_r - \mathbf{C}_{i(r)}\| \qquad S^2 = \frac{1}{R} \cdot \sum_{r=1}^{R} \|\mathbf{P}_r - \mathbf{C}_{i(r)}\|^2 \qquad (2)$$

Typically the Euclidean distance($\| \ \|_2$) is used to calculate the error $e = \|\mathbf{P}_r - \mathbf{C}_{i(r)}\|$, but other distance measures apply as well. Mean deviation and variance, are good indicators for the advances of the clustering process. During the learning process of the M-SOM and the M-NGas the mean deviation $\bar{E}$, and the variance S^2 are decreasing constantly and converge to minimum values see left diagram of Fig. 3.

Silhouette Coefficient

The Silhouette Statistics $s(r)$ is a widely used coefficient to monitor the performance of the clustering with respect to k [6]. We have adjusted the silhouette statistics for the M-SOM, and M-NGas networks, in such a way, that the distances are not calculated to the centers of the clusters, but to the respective closest neurons. Accordingly the distance to the closest neuron of the own M-SOM, and the distance to the closest neuron of one of the the the other M-SOMs is used. For pattern number r, the error $e(r)$ is the distance between pattern $\mathbf{P}_r$ and the winner neuron i. The secondary cluster distance $g(r)$ is the distance between pattern $\mathbf{P}_r$ and that neuron j that is the closest neuron not belonging to the same partner SOM, or partner gas than the winner i. This yields the extended silhouette statistics $s(r)$, and averaged over all R patterns the silhouette coefficient SK:

$$\text{SK} \ = \ \frac{1}{R}\sum_{r=1}^{R} s(r) \ = \ \frac{1}{R}\sum_{r=1}^{R} \frac{g(r) - e(r)}{\max\{e(r), g(r)\}} \tag{3}$$

A large $s(r)$ indicates that the pattern $\mathbf{P}_r$ is well clustered. A large SK indicates a better clustering for the complete data set. For extreme M-SOM, and M-N-Gas configurations with just one neuron per partner SOM/Gas, the adjusted silhouette coefficient is exactly the classical silhouette coefficient for a K-means clustering solution.

Gap-Statistic

The gap statistics [11] calculates the compactness of the clusters by calculating the Within-Cluster Sum of Squares W_k, and compares it to the expectation $E^*(W_k)$ of the Within-Cluster Sum of Squares for a "cluster free" reference distribution with respect to the number K of clusters. The W_ks are small for data distributions that are very dense, and large if the data points are well distributed. For M-SOMs and M-NGas networks, the Within-Cluster Sum of Squares W_k are determined for different numbers k of partner SOM/gas networks by taking the distance between the patterns and the respective winner neurons instead of taking the center of gravity for the clusters.

$$W_k \ = \ \sum_{m=1}^{k}\sum_{j \epsilon \text{SOM}} \|\mathbf{P}_j - \mathbf{C}_{i(j)}\|^2 \tag{4}$$

$$\text{Gap}_R(k) = E_R^*(\log(W_k)) - log(W_k) \ \approx \ \frac{1}{B}\sum_{b=1}^{B}(\log(W_{kb})) - log(W_k) \tag{5}$$

The smallest k such that $\text{Gap}(k) \geq \text{Gap}(k+1) - s_{k+1}$ is the proposed number of clusters to use; see [11] for details.

Calinski, Harabasz Coefficient

The Calinski, Harabasz Coefficient (CH) is the ratio between the normalised Between-Cluster Sum of Squares B_k and the normalised Within-Cluster Sum of squares W_k. [1] (after [11])

$$CH(k) = \frac{B_k/(k-1)}{W_k/(n-k)} \tag{6}$$

For the M-SOMs the B_k become the Inter-SOM-Distances and the W_k become the Intra-SOM-Distances (and respectively for the M-NGas networks).

5   Results of Experiments

To evaluate the capabilities of our approach we have conducted several series of experiments with different data distributions, applying the two proposed approaches, Multi-SOMs and Multi Neural Gas, and calculated the values for the described quality measures.

Learning

One series of tests was performed with a data distribution in 2 dimensions, with 4 clearly separated clusters; blue shaded areas in Fig. 6 and Fig. 7. The corresponding values of the quality measures are depicted in Fig. 3 during the learning phase. The Mean Deviation $\bar{E}$ shrinks, indicating a shrinking error. The Silhouette Coefficient is increasing, and tending towards a maximal value and thus indicating a better clustering. The Gap statistics is decreasing, and the Calinski-Harabasz Coefficient is increasing, these two coefficients are not very helpful for evaluating the learning process. They show their potential with respect to finding the optimal K^*.

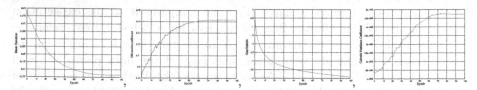

Fig. 3. Development of the quality measures while the M-SOM is learning the 4-cluster test data; from left to right: Mean Deviation, Silhouette Coefficient, Gap value, Calinski-Harabasz Coefficient

Different K

With respect to different numbers K of partner SOMs and partner NGas the quality measures have been evaluated, as proposed for finding the optimal K^* for the clustering see Fig. 4 and Fig. 5. Evaluating the Silhouette Coefficient and the Gap Statistic for the M-SOMs and the M-NGas one can find, that all four curves are indicating the correct cluster number of $K^* = 4$. The Mean Deviation and the Variance decrease with rising K. The curves show a "knee" as soon as

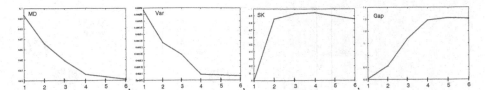

Fig. 4. Quality measures with respect to the number K of partner SOM after clustering the 4-cluster test data; from left to right: Mean Deviation, Variance, Silhouette Coefficient, Gap value

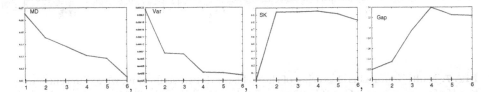

Fig. 5. Quality measures with respect to the number K of partner Neural Gas networks after clustering the 4-cluster test data; from left to right: Mean Deviation, Variance, Silhouette Coefficient, Gap value

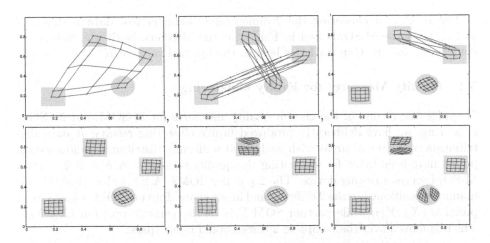

Fig. 6. Multi-SOM clustering of the 4 cluster data distribution, with different number K of partner SOMs of K-5x5 type. For K=1 the 5x5 SOM is divided between the 4 clusters. For K=2, each SOM is responsible for 2 clusters, for K=3 one SOM is spread over 2 clusters, the other 2 SOMs fit well into the data; for K=4 the optimal clustering is reached; for K=5 and K=6 some clusters are represented by more than one partner SOM.

K reaches the optimal value K^*. A closes investigation of this effect will lead to another indicator for the correct cluster number K^*. Further investigations to clarify this are in progress.

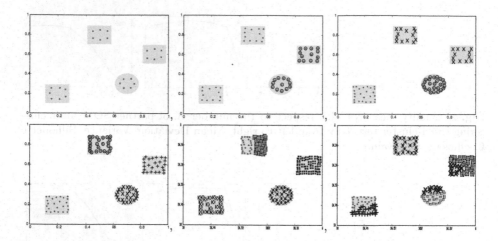

Fig. 7. Multi Neural Gas clustering of the 4 cluster data distribution, with different number K of partner Neural Gas of K-25 type, For K=2 and K=3 the different partner Neural Gas neurons have been marked with different symbols. For K=4 all 4 clusters are covered perfectly by a NGas of their own. For K=5, the upper, middle cluster is represented by 2 NGas, for K=6 the lower left cluster is represented by 2, and one NGas is spread over the two right clusters, cluster boundaries have been marked where necessary.

The results for clustering the 2-dimensional 4-cluster test data is depicted in Fig. 6 for the M-SOMs and in Fig. 7 for the M-NGas. Both, the Silhouette coefficient, and the Gap statistics lead to the optimal value of $K^* = 4$.

5.1   Quality Measures for Faulty Clustering

To judge the results of the chosen quality measures for M-SOM and M-NGas clustering, we have deliberately produced faulty clustering results. A data distribution of 2 circular areas with each 5000 uniformly distributed random data points have been taken for evaluating the quality measures. A $K = 2, 2 - 3 \times 3$ M-SOM serves a testing device. The 2 partner SOMs (A,B) of this M-SOM, are manually positioned in the 2 dimensional input space. Partner SOM A has a fixed position (X_A, Y_A), while partner SOM B is at the variable position (X_B, Y_B), which is moved over the complete 2 dimensional input space.

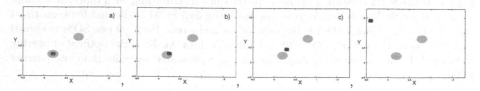

Fig. 8. The two circular data spots, with each 5000 data points, and the 4 positions for the partner SOM A, from left to right: a) optimal, b) slightly deviated, c) wrong, but close d) completly wrong

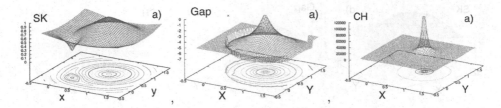

Fig. 9. Situation a): Location $(X - B, Y_B)$ dependent Quality Measures (Silhouette Coefficient SK, Gap Statistics, Calinski-Harabasz Coefficient CH) for optimal placement of (X_A, Y_A). All three coefficients have a maximum at the optimal position, The silhouette coefficient has a clear minimum at the position (X_A, Y_A), indicating a poor clustering.

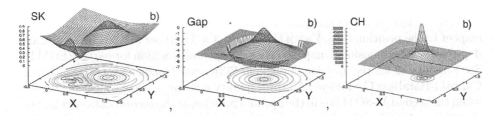

Fig. 10. Situation b): Location $(X - B, Y_B)$ dependent Quality Measures (SK,Gap, CH) for a slightly deviated placement of (X_A, Y_A). All three coefficients gain a maximum at the optimal position. The Silhouette coefficient has a smaller maximum at the center of the data spot A.

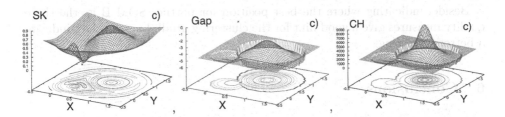

Fig. 11. Situation c): Location $(X - B, Y_B)$ dependent Quality Measures (SK, Gap, CH) for a wrong, but close placement of (X_A, Y_A). The maximum is again found at the optimal position. The silhouette coefficient established a clear second maximum at the position of data spot A. The Gap statistics, and the CH coefficient show a small deviation at data spot A as well.

The location (X_A, Y_A) of partner SOM A can be one of the following four positions; see Fig. 8.

a) optimal positioned in the center of one data spot
b) slightly deviated from the optimal position a), but still in the data spot

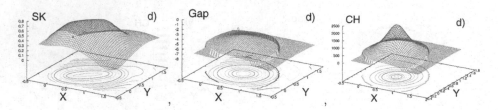

Fig. 12. Situation d): Location $(X - B, Y_B)$ dependent Quality Measures (SK, Gap, CH) for completely wrong placement of (X_A, Y_A). All three coefficients show a maximum value between the two data spots.

c) outside the data spot, but close to it,

d) completely wrong, far away from the optimal position.

With a fixed (X_A, Y_A) the quality measures (SK,Gap,CH) are evaluated with respect to the position (X_B, Y_B) of the second 3×3 partner SOM. The results are depicted in a 2 dimensional map, showing the optimal position for partner SOM B. See Fig. 9 to 12 for the location dependent Silhouette Coefficient, Gap Statistics, Calinski-Harabasz Coefficient. All three quality measures, show a clear maximum when the second M-SOM B is in the optimal position at the second data spot for the situations a,b,and c. The situation d) with a completely wrong positioned M-SOM A, shows a maximum value just in-between the two data spots.

The silhouette coefficient shows a minimum, if the second partner SOM B is positioned in the vicinity of partner SOM A (see Fig. 9, 10, and 11. For the situation d), no minimum is visible, because partner SOM A lies outside the area where partner SOM B is positioned.

Beside, indicating where the best position for partner SOM B is, the three quality measures give a good hint for the clustering at all. Larger values indicate a better clustering.

6   Conclusions

The proposed extensions Multi-SOM to the Self Organising feature Maps, and Multi Neural Gas to the Neural Gas paradigm has been shown to be a valuable neural network tool for unsupervised, and self organising clustering. The common cluster analysis coefficients Mean Deviation, Variation, Silhouette Coefficient, Gap Statistics, Calinski-Harabasz Coefficient, have been adjusted for the proposed paradigms. The experiments with clustering data have demonstrated the capabilities of the two proposed new methods, and have shown that the quality measures are valuable coefficients for judging the quality of the reached clustering, and for determining the optimal number of partner networks K^*.. The systematic evaluation even, of faulty clustering solutions gave further insight into the properties of the methods used, and the chosen quality measures. Applying the M-SOMs and the M-NGas to classification of robot sensor time series is in progress, and one of the topics of our current work.

References

1. Calinski, R.B.; Harabasz, J.: "A Dendrite Method for Cluster Analysis", Communications in statistics, Vol. 3, pp. 1-27, (1974).
2. Fritzke, B.: "Wachsende Zellstrukturen - ein selbstorganisierendes neuronales Netzwerkmodell", PhD Thesis, Erlangen (1992).
3. Goerke, N.; Kintzler, F.; Eckmiller, R.: "Self Organized Partitioning of Chaotic Attractors for Control", In: Proc. of the Int. Conf. on Artificial Neural Networks (ICANN'01), Springer, LNCS 2130, pp. 851-856, (2001).
4. Goerke, N.; Kintzler, F.; Brueggemann, B.: "Multi-SOMs for Classification", In: Proc. of the Int. Workshop on Automatic Learning and Real-Time, ALaRT'05, pp. 99-107, (2005).
5. Haykin, S.: "Neural Networks: A Comprehensive Foundation", Prentice Hall, Erlangen (1999).
6. Kaufman, L.; P.J. Rousseeuw, P.J.: "Finding Groups in Data: An Introduction to Cluster Analysis", Wiloy, New York, (1990).
7. Kohonen, T.: "Self-Organized Formation of Topologically Correct Feature Maps", *Biological Cybernetics*, Vol. 43, pp.59-69, 1982.
8. Kohonen, T.: "Self-Organizing Maps", Springer, Berlin Heidelberg 1995.
9. Martinetz, Th.; Schulten, K.: "Neural-Gas Network Learns Topologies", Artificial Neural Networks, Vol. I, pp. 397-402, (1991).
10. Martinetz, Thomas M.; Berkovich, Stanislav G.; Schulten, Klaus J.: "Neural Gas: Network for Vector Quantization and its Application to Time-Series Prediction", IEEE 1993.
11. Tibshirani, R.; Walther, G.; Hastie, T.: "Estimating the Number of Clusters in a Dataset via the Gap Statistics", Tech. Rep. 208, Dept. of Statistics, Stanford University, (2000).
12. Zell, A.; "Simulation Neuronaler Netze", Oldenbourg Verlag, 2000.

Derivative Free Stochastic Discrete Gradient Method with Adaptive Mutation

Ranadhir Ghosh, Moumita Ghosh, and Adil Bagirov

School of Information Technology and Mathematical Sciences,
University of Ballarat, P.O. Box 663, Ballarat 3353, Australia
{r.ghosh, m.ghosh, a.bagirov}@ballarat.edu.au

Abstract. In data mining we come across many problems such as function optimization problem or parameter estimation problem for classifiers for which a good learning algorithm for searching is very much necessary. In this paper we propose a stochastic based derivative free algorithm for unconstrained optimization problem. Many derivative-based local search methods exist which usually stuck into local solution for non-convex optimization problems. On the other hand global search methods are very time consuming and works for only limited number of variables. In this paper we investigate a derivative free multi search gradient based method which overcomes the problems of local minima and produces global solution in less time. We have tested the proposed method on many benchmark dataset in literature and compared the results with other existing algorithms. The results are very promising.

1 Introduction

Although a wide spectrum of methods exist for unconstrained optimization, they can broadly be categorized in terms of using the derivative information. Gradient-based methods are generally more efficient when the function to be minimized is continuous in its first derivative. Solution methods for non-linear optimization problems can be classified into local and global methods. Local optimization methods such as gradient descent method and Newton's method use local information such as first and second order gradient information to perform descents and converge to a local minimum. Local optimization methods converge to local minima. For some applications, local optima are good enough. Still local optimization methods have got few disadvantages on many applications. The ill conditioned problem is a phenomenon, which badly affects minimization. It occurs when the function being minimized has a wide range of curvatures. That means a small change in decision variables causes large error in the function value that is to be minimized. Due to the complexity of the surface it is sometimes very hard and costly to compute the derivative for that. Especially when the values of the model function are noisy the first or the higher order partial derivatives cannot be calculated accurately. Even when the problem functions are not smooth or even discontinuous, derivative or gradient information generally cannot be used to determine the direction in which the function is increasing (or decreasing). In other words, the situation at one possible solution point gives very little information about where to look for a better solution for its next step. The application of gradient-

P. Perner (Ed.): ICDM 2006, LNAI 4065, pp. 264–278, 2006.
© Springer-Verlag Berlin Heidelberg 2006

based methods to non-smooth problems may lead to a failure in convergence, in optimality conditions, or in gradient approximation.

In the last decade, derivative-free or direct search methods have attracted increasing attention. These methods are especially useful, when Newton-type searches are inapplicable.

Powell [1] has outlined a method for finding minima without calculating derivatives. The method proceeds in stages. Each stage consists of a sequence of $n+1$ one-dimensional searches. The one-dimensional searches are conducted by finding the exact minimizer of a quadratic interpolant computed for each direction. The first n searches are along each of a set of linearly independent directions. The last search is along the direction connecting the point obtained at the end of the first n searches with the starting point of the stage. At the end of the stage, one of the first n search directions is replaced by the last search direction. The process then repeats at the next stage. But Powell's method [1] is quite unreliable and become inefficient when the size of the problem increases.

The discrete gradient [2] is a finite difference estimate to a sub-gradient. Unlike many other finite difference estimates to sub-gradient, the discrete gradient is defined with respect to a given direction, which allows one to get good approximation for the sub-differential. In the algorithm for the calculation of the descent direction of a locally lipschtiz function by using discrete gradients is proposed. This calculates discrete gradients step by step, and after a finite number of iterations either the descent direction is calculated or it is found that the current point is an approximate stationary point. In Discrete gradient method Armijo's algorithm is used for a line search. Hence at a given approximation, the method calculates the descent direction by calculating the discrete gradients step by step, and improving the approximation of the Demyanov-Rubinov quasi-differential. Once the descent direction is calculated, Armijo's algorithm is used for line search. This local minimum is chosen as the next approximation. The discrete gradient method is a derivative free method and it can be applied both to smooth and non-smooth optimization problems.

The main advantage of the Discrete gradient method is that the method approximates the descent direction with respect to the discrete gradient in a particular direction. Hence we do not require the gradient information. So the algorithm is suitable for non-smooth optimization where the derivative does not exists at certain points. The other advantage is that as Discrete gradient method is a local search technique hence it takes much less time compare to other global optimization methods. With a good initial guess the method converges to a near optimal solution with high accuracy.

The main disadvantage is that the algorithm is very much sensible to initial guess. The algorithm finds out the solution across the neighbourhood of the initial point. The initial guess determines whether or not a good or the best solution is found. Thus bad starting point can take a very long time to converge. If the initial guess is very far away form the local minimiser it doesn't give a good solution. The other disadvantage is that as the algorithm has only downhill movement it can easily get trapped into narrow local minima around the initial point. Often after a small number of iteration the method falls into a local minimum and never escape.

Earlier research has shown that hybridization of discrete gradient method with a stochastic global search method improves the quality of the solution. The most popular hybrid method is to combine an Evolutionary algorithm with the discrete gradient method. Though it improves the solution but it takes long time to converge.

One way to solve the problem is to use a method that uses multiple local searches named as multi start local method. We can apply it for the discrete gradient method. In that case the method will start with more than one initial point and we need to apply discrete gradient method for each of these starting point. We call it Multi start Discrete Gradient method.

But in that case the problem of local minima remains as a disadvantage with the method. Even though we repeat the discrete gradient method for several times it is unable to escape from the local solution and can not improve it further. So the multistart discrete gradient method though is better than discrete gradient method is unable to improve the quality of the solution after the first iteration.

So we need a method that can add stochastic quality in the search direction after each iteration of multi start. The hybrid method of discrete gradient and Evolutionary algorithm (EADG) exists in literature. The algorithm is efficient in terms of reaching the global solution. The algorithm uses crossover operator along with the mutation and selection. The crossover evolves new set of points those are far away form the parents depending on the type of crossover operation. Hence eventually it might jumps to a distant point and takes more time to converge. On the other hand if we only apply the mutation without the crossover, the mutation generates the new point in the neighbourhood of the parent. So it helps the method to overcome the local minima. So we need a method which has the discrete gradient search direction as a local search method with a stochastic process that helps the method to come out form the local minima and moves towards the global one.

In this paper we are introducing the Evolutionary Discrete gradient method. It is a multistart method in which after each generation/iteration we apply only mutation and selection genetic operator. Through mutation we introduce slight variation in the solution points so that in the next iteration the discrete gradient method could escape from the local minima and move towards global one. After each generation we calculate the solution value of each set of solution points and take that vale as fitness value of the individual. Then individuals in a solution set are chosen for next generation on the basis of individuals with higher fitness value. We are using roulette wheel selection scheme. Then we are applying mutation with adaptive mutation rate. At the beginning the mutation rate we kept very high. Then gradually as the method progress, it converges towards the solution and the mutation rate decreases gradually to zero. The method is explained in details in the Methodology section. 2. Methodology.

2.1 Discrete Gradient Method

In this section we will give a brief description of the discrete gradient method. The full description of this method can be found in [2]. The discrete gradient method can be considered as a version of the bundle method [3] when sub-gradients are replaced by their approximations - discrete gradients.

Let f be a locally Lipschitz continuous function defined on R^n. A function f is locally Lipschitz continuous on R^n if in any open bounded subset $S \subset R^n$ there exists a constant $L > 0$ such that

$$\frac{f(x) - f(y)}{\|x - y\|} \le L, \quad \forall x, y \in S. \tag{1}$$

The locally Lipschitz function f is differentiable almost everywhere and one can define for it a set of generalized gradients or a Clarke sub-differential [4], by

$$\partial f(x) = co\{v \in R^n : \exists (x^k \in D(f), x^k \to x, k \to \infty) : v = \lim_{k \to +\infty} \nabla f(x^k)\} \tag{2}$$

Here $D(f)$ denotes the set where f is differentiable, co denotes the convex hull of a set and $\nabla f(x)$ stands for a gradient of the function f at a point $x \subset R^n$.

Let

$$S_1 = \{g \in R_n : \|g\| = 1\} \tag{3}$$

$$G = \{e \in R^n : e = (e_1, e_2, ..., e_n), |e_j| = 1, j = 1, ..., n\} \tag{4}$$

$$P = \{z(\lambda) : z(\lambda) \in R^1, \ z(\lambda) > 0, \ \lambda > 0, \ \lambda^{-1} z(\lambda) \to 0, \ \lambda \to 0\} \tag{5}$$

$$I(g, \alpha) = \{i \in \{1, ..., n\} : |g_i| \ge \alpha\} \tag{6}$$

where $\alpha \in \left(0, n^{-\frac{1}{2}}\right)$ is a fixed number. Here S_1 is the unit sphere, G is a set of vertices of the unit cube in R^n and P is a set of univariate positive infinitesimal functions.

We define operators $H_i^j : R^n \to R^n$ for $i = 1, ..., n, j = 0, ..., n$ by the formula

$$H_i^j g = \begin{cases} (g_1, ..., g_j, 0, ..., 0) & \text{if } j < i, \\ (g_1, ..., g_{i-1}, 0, g_{i+1}, ..., g_j, 0, ..., 0) & \text{if } j \ge i \end{cases} \tag{7}$$

We can see that $H_i^0 g = 0 \in R^n$ for all $i = 0, ..., n$. Let $e(\beta) = (\beta e_1, \beta^2 e_2, ... \beta^n e_n), \ \beta \in (0,1]$. For $x \in R^n$ we will consider vectors

$$x_i^j(g) \equiv x_i^j(g, e, z, \lambda, \beta) = x + \lambda g - z(\lambda) H_i^j e(\beta) \tag{8}$$

where

$$g \in S_1, \ e \in G, \ i \in I(g, \alpha), \ z \in P, \ \lambda > 0, \ \beta \in (0,1], \ j = 0, ..., n, \ j \ne i.$$

Definition 1. The discrete gradient of the function f at the point $x \in R^n$ is the vector

$$\Gamma^i(g,e,z,\lambda,\beta) = \left(\Gamma_1^i, \Gamma_2^i, \ldots\ldots, \Gamma_n^i\right) \in \Re^n, \; g \in S_1, \; i \in I(g,\alpha) \tag{9}$$

with the following coordinates:

$$\Gamma_j^i = \left[z(\lambda)e_j(\beta)\right]^{-1}\left[f\left(x_i^{j-1}(g)\right) - f\left(x_i^j(g)\right)\right], \; j = 1,\ldots\ldots, n, \; j \neq i \tag{10}$$

$$\Gamma_i^i = (\lambda g_i)^{-1}\left[f\left(x_i^n(g)\right) - f(x) - \sum_{j=1, j \neq i}^{n} \Gamma_j^i\left(\lambda g_j - z(\lambda)e_j(\beta)\right)\right] \tag{11}$$

From the definition of the discrete gradient we can see that it is defined with respect to a given direction $g \in S_1$ and in order to calculate the discrete gradient we use step $\lambda > 0$ along this direction. The $n-1$ coordinates of the discrete gradient are defined as finite difference estimates to a gradient in some neighbourhood of the point $x + \lambda g$. The ith coordinate of the discrete gradient is defined so that to approximate a sub-gradient of the function f. Thus the discrete gradient contains some information about the behaviour of the function f in some region around the point x.

Now we will consider the following unconstrained minimization problem:

$$\text{minimize} \; f(x) \text{ subject to } x \in \Re^n \tag{12}$$

where the function f is assumed to be locally Lipschitz continuous. We consider the discrete gradient method for solving this problem. An important step in this method is the computation of a descent direction of the objective function f. So first, we describe an algorithm for the computation of the descent direction of the function f.

Let $z \in P, \lambda > 0, \beta \in (0,1]$, the number $c \in (0,1)$ and a small enough number $\delta > 0$ be given.

Algorithm 1. An algorithm for the computation of the descent direction.

Step 1. Choose any $g^1 \in S_1$, $e \in G$, $i \in I(g^1, \alpha)$ and compute a discrete gradient $v^1 = \Gamma^i(x, g^1, e, z, \lambda, \beta)$. Set $\overline{D}_1(x) = \{v^1\}$ and $k = 1$.

Step 2. Calculate the vector $\|w^k\| = \min\{\|w\| : w \in \overline{D}_k(x)\}$. If

$$\|w^k\| \leq \delta \tag{13}$$

then stop. Otherwise go to Step 3.

Step 3. Calculate the search direction by

$$g^{k+1} = -\|w^k\|^{-1} w^k \tag{14}$$

Step 4. If

$$f(x + \lambda g^{k+1}) - f(x) \le -c\lambda \|w^k\| \tag{15}$$

then stop. Otherwise go to Step 5.

Step 5. Calculate a discrete gradient

$$v^{k+1} = \Gamma^i(x, g^{k+1}, e, z, \lambda, \beta), \; i \in I(g^{k+1}, \alpha) \tag{16}$$

and construct the set

$$\overline{D}_{k+1}(x) = co\{\overline{D}_k(x) \cup \{v^{k+1}\}\} \tag{17}$$

Set $k = k + 1$ and go to Step 2.

The algorithm contains steps, which deserve some explanations. In Step 1 we take any direction $g^1 \in S_1$ and calculate the first discrete gradient. In Step 2 we calculate least distance between the convex hull of the discrete gradients and the origin. This problem is reduced to a quadratic programming problem and can be effectively solved by Wolfe's terminating algorithm [5]. If this distance is less than some tolerance $\delta > 0$, the algorithm stops and we can consider this point as an approximated stationary point. Otherwise, in Step 3, a search direction is calculated. If this direction is a descent direction, the algorithm terminates, otherwise, in Step 5, we calculate a new discrete gradient with respect to this direction to improve the approximation of the set of generalized gradients. Since the discrete gradient contains some information about the behaviour of the function f in some regions around the point x this algorithm allows to find descent directions in stationary points which are not local minima (descent directions in such stationary point always exist). This property makes the discrete gradient method attractive for design of hybrid methods in global optimization. It is proved that Algorithm 1 is a terminating.

Now we can describe the discrete gradient method. Let sequences $\delta_k > 0$, $z_k \in P$, $\lambda_k > 0$, $\beta_k \in (0,1]$, $\delta_k \to +0$, $\lambda_k \to +0$, $\beta_k \to +0$, $k \to +\infty$ and the numbers $c_1 \in (0,1)$, $c_2 \in (0, c_1]$ be given.

Algorithm 2. Discrete gradient method

Step 1. Choose any starting $x^0 \in \Re^n$ and set $k = 0$

Step 2. Set $s = 0$ and $x_s^k = x^k$.

Step 3. Apply Algorithm 1 for the calculation of the descent direction at $x = x_s^k$, $\delta = \delta_k$, $z = z_k$, $\lambda = \lambda_k$, $\beta = \beta_k$, $c = c_1$. After termination of this algorithm for some finite $m > 0$ are computed an element

$$\|v_s^k\| = \min\{\|v\| : v \in \overline{D}_m(x_s^k)\} \tag{18}$$

and a search direction

$$g_s^k = -\left\|v_s^k\right\|^{-1} v_s^k \tag{19}$$

such that either

$$f\left(x_s^k + \lambda_k g_s^k\right) - f\left(x_s^k\right) \le -c_1 \lambda_k \left\|v_s^k\right\| \tag{20}$$

Or

$$\left\|v_s^k\right\| \le \delta_k \tag{21}$$

.
Step 4. If

$$\left\|v_s^k\right\| \le \delta_k \tag{22}$$

then set

$$x^{k+1} = x_s^k, \; k = k+1 \tag{23}$$

and go to Step 2. Otherwise go to Step 5.

Step 5. Construct the following iteration

$$x_{s+1}^k = x_s^k + \sigma_s g_s^k, \tag{24}$$

where σ_s is defined as follows

$$\sigma_s = \arg \max\left\{\sigma \ge 0 : f\left(x_s^k + \sigma g_s^k\right) - f\left(x_s^k\right) \le c_2 \sigma \left\|v_s^k\right\|\right\} \tag{25}$$

Step 6. Set $s = s + 1$ and go to Step 3.

The main steps in this algorithm are Steps 3 and 5. In Step 3 we calculate a descent direction using Algorithm 1. The stepsize is calculated in Step 5. For the point $x^0 \in \Re^n$ we consider the set

$$M\left(x^0\right) = \left\{x \in \Re^n : f(x) \le f\left(x^0\right)\right\} \tag{26}$$

Theorem 1. Assume that the set $M\left(x^0\right)$ is bounded for starting points $x^0 \in \Re^n$. Then every accumulation point of $\left\{x^k\right\}$ belongs to the set.

The main advantage of the Discrete gradient method is that the method approximates the descent direction with respect to the discrete gradient in a particular direction. Hence we do not require the gradient information. So the algorithm is suitable for non-smooth optimization where the derivative does not exists at certain points. The other advantage is that as Discrete gradient method is a local search technique hence it takes much less time compare to other global optimization methods. With a good initial guess the method converges to a near optimal solution with high accuracy.

2.2 Multi-start Discrete Gradient Method

We compare our algorithm with multi start discrete gradient method. In multi start discrete gradient method we start with some number of initial points and apply discrete gradient method for all of them. Then we move towards the next iteration and repeat the discrete gradient methods for the new set solution points provided by the discrete gradient method.

2.3 Evolutionary Discrete Gradient Method

The flow chart of the method is shown in Figure 1. The algorithm starts with a set of initial points. Then we apply the discrete gradient method for each of these points. Then we calculate the fitness for each of them. Here the fitness is the objective function value. Then we apply the selection mechanism to select the solution point from the current set.

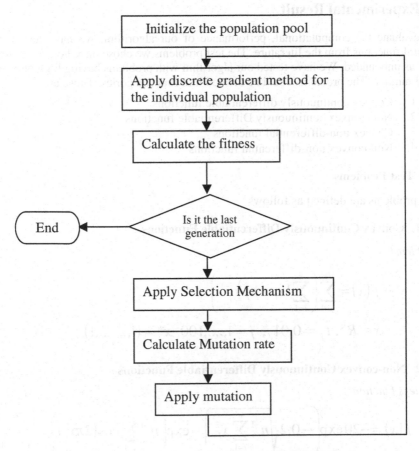

Fig. 1. Flowchart of Stochastic Discrete Gradient Method

We use roulette wheel selection. The method creates a region of a wheel based on the fitness of a population string. All the population strings occupy the space in the wheel based on their rank in fitness. A uniform random number is then generated within a closed interval of [0,1]. The value of the random number is used as a pointer and the particular population string that occupies the number is selected for the offspring generation.

After the selection operator we apply mutation. We change the mutation rate according to the number of generation/iteration. At the first generation we make it 100% mutation and gradually decrease the value as it converges to the solution and at the end the mutation rate becomes zero. According to the mutation rate we apply the mutation on the selected solutions. We select randomly one solution point and modify the value randomly between the upper and lower limit of the variables. After the mutation we again apply the discrete gradient method and check whether it is the last generation or not which is the stopping criterion. If yes we stop there otherwise we keep in repeating the process.

3 Experimental Result

To evaluate the computational; performance of our algorithm, we have tested it on several functions from the literature. The test problems we chose have box constrains as well as unbounded. We have tested our algorithm with problems having high number of local minima. The problems could be divided into four categories. Those are

1. Convex continuously differentiable functions
2. Non-convex continuously Differentiable functions
3. Convex non-differential functions
4. Non-convex non-differential functions

3.1 Test Problems

The problems are defined as follows

3.1.1 Convex Continuously Differentiable Functions
Problem1

$$f(x) = \sum_{j=1}^{100} \left(\sum_{i=1}^{n} (x_i - x_i^*) t_j^{i-1} \right)^2 \tag{27}$$

$$x \in R^n, \ t_j = 0.01j, \ j = 1,....,100, \ x^* = (1,........,1)$$

3.1.2 Non-convex Continuously Differentiable Functions
Ackleys function

$$f(x) = -20\exp\left(-0.2\sqrt{n^{-1}\sum_{i=1}^{n} x_i^2}\right) - \exp\left(n^{-1}\sum_{i=1}^{n}\cos(2\pi x_i)\right) \tag{28}$$

$$x \in R^n, \ t_j = 0.01j, \ j = 1,....,100, \ x^* = (1,........,1)$$

Griewanks function

$$f(x) = \frac{1}{d} \sum_{i=1}^{n} x_i^2 - \prod_{i=1}^{n} \cos\left(\frac{x_i}{\sqrt{i}}\right) + 1$$

$$x \in R^n, \; -500 \le x_i \le 700$$

(29)

Levy Nr 1

$$f(x) = \frac{\pi}{n}\left(10\sin^2(\pi y_1) + \sum_{i=1}^{n-1}(y_i - 1)^2\left(1 + 10\sin^2(\pi y_{i+1})\right) + (y_n - 1)^2\right)$$

(30)

$$y_i = 1 + \frac{x_i - 1}{4}, \; -10 \le x_i \le 10$$

Rastringin

$$f(x) = 10n + \sum_{i=1}^{n}\left(x_i^2 - 10\cos(2\pi x_i)\right),$$

(31)

$$x \in R^2, \; -5.12 \le x_i \le 5.12$$

Levy Nr 2

$$f(x) = \frac{\pi}{n}\left(10\sin^2(\pi y_1) + \sum_{i=1}^{n-1}(y_i - 1)^2\left(1 + 10\sin^2(\pi y_{i+1})\right) + (y_n - 1)^2\right)$$

$$+ \sum_{i=1}^{n} u(x_i, 10, 100, 4)$$

$$y_i = 1 + \frac{x_i - 1}{4}, \; -50 \le x_i \le 50$$

(32)

where

$$u(x_i, a, k, m) = \begin{cases} k(x_i - a)^m, & x_i > a \\ 0, & -a \le x_i \le a, \\ k(-x_i - a)^m, & x_i < -a. \end{cases}$$

3.1.3 Convex Non-differentiable Functions

Problem1

$$f(x) = \max\left\{x_1^2 + x_2^4, (2 - x_1)^2 + (2 - x_2)^2, 2e^{-x_1 + x_2}\right\}, x \in R^2$$

(33)

Problem2

$$f(x) = \max\left\{x_2^2 + x_1^4, (2 - x_1)^2 + (2 - x_2)^2, 2e^{-x_1 + x_2}\right\}, x \in R^2$$

(34)

Problem3

$$f(x) = \max\{5x_1 + x_2, -5x_1 + x_2, x_1^2 + x_2^2 + 4x_2,\}, x \in R^2 \qquad (35)$$

3.1.3 Non-convex Non-differentiable Functions

Problem 1

$$f(x) = |x_1 - 1| + 100|x_2 - |x_1||, x \in R^2 \qquad (36)$$

Problem 2

$$f(x) = |x_1 - 1| + 100|x_2 - |x_1|| + 90|x_4 - |x_3|| + |x_3 - 1|$$
$$+ 10.1(|x_2 - 1| + |x_4 - 1|) + 4.95(|x_2 + x_4 - 2| - |x_2 - x_4|), x \in R^4 \qquad 37)$$

Problem 3

$$f(x) = \sum_{j=1}^{100} \left| \sum_{i=1}^{n} (x_i - x_i^*) t_j^{i-1} \right| - \max\left\{ \left| \sum_{i=1}^{n} (x_i - x_i^*) t_j^{i-1} \right|, j = 1,2,....,100 \right\} \qquad (38)$$

$$x \in R^n, t_j = 0.01j, \; j = 1,....,100, \; x^* = (1,........,1)$$

Dembo3, Dembo 5, Dembo 7
Could be found in [6].

3.2 Results

The results are discussed in the following subsections 2. We have compared the proposed algorithm (SDG) with Multi start Discrete Gradient method (MDG). We have taken 10 identical initial points for both the cases.

3.2.1 Results with Convex Continuously Differentiable Functions

In this section we describe the results obtained for the convex continuously differentiable functions. We are using the function in Equation 27. The minimum value of the function is 0. Table 1 shows the results obtained by the algorithm. The table (Table 1) shows that, all the algorithms have converged to the minimum solution. Hence there is no any difference in terms of the quality of the solution.

Table 1. Results for Convex Continuously differentiable function

Variable	Algorithm	Function Value	Function Value Actual	CPU Time (second)
2	MDG	0	0	10.115
	SDG	0	0	10.64
10	MDG	0	0	12.406
	SDG	0	0	12.52
30	MDG	0	0	15.001
	SDG	0	0	15.27

3.2.2 Results with Non-convex Continuously Differentiable Functions

In this section we describe the results obtained for the non-convex continuously differentiable functions. We have tested on Ackelys, Griewanks, Rastringin, Levy Nr1, Levy Nr2 functions. Table 2 shows the results obtained by the algorithms. The table (Table 2) shows that the Multi start Discrete Gradient algorithm has stuck at a local minimum as the local minima are unevenly distributed for these problems. Hence it is unable to produce the minimum solution for the problem. But when we consider the Stochastic Discrete Gradient algorithm we see that the method easily overcame the local minima and produced better solutions, even the global solution for most of the cases.

Table 2. Results for Non-Convex Continuously differentiable function

Function	Algorithm	Function Value	Function Value Actual	CPU Time (second)
Ackelys(20)	MDG	8.659658	0	10.135
	SDG	4.832105	0	11.844
Griewanks	MDG	50.468437	0	141.75
	SDG	17.236857	0	159.906
Rastringin	MDG	1.991927	0	14.001
	SDG	0	0	14.87
Levy Nr1	MDG	1.929112	0	15.75
	SDG	0	0	15.75
Levy Nr2	MDG	4.898787	0	17.2
	SDG	0	0	11.71

3.2.3 Results with Convex Non-differentiable Functions

In this section we describe the results obtained for the convex non-differentiable functions. We have tested on three convex non-differentiable test functions listed in Equation 33, 34, and 35 respectively. Table 3 shows the results obtained by the algorithms. Table 3 shows that both the have converged to the global minima. As the problems are convex, there exists only one minimum and there is no chance to get stuck.

Table 3. Results for Convex Non-differentiable function

Function	Algorithm	Function Value	Function Value Actual	CPU Time (second)
Problem1	MDG	1.952224	1.952224	5.67
	SDG	1.952224	1.952224	5.859
Problem2	MDG	2	2	4.75
	SDG	2	2	4.86
Problem3	MDG	-3	-3	0.282
	SDG	-3	-3	0.315

3.2.4 Results with Non-convex Non-differentiable Functions

In this section we describe the results obtained for the non-convex non-differentiable functions. We have tested on three non-convex non-differentiable test functions listed in Equation 36, 37, and 38 respectively. Table 2 shows the results obtained by the algorithms. The table (Table 2) shows that the Multi start Discrete Gradient algorithm has stuck at a local minimum as the local minima are unevenly distributed for these problems. Hence it is unable to produce the minimum solution for the problem. But when we consider the Stochastic Discrete Gradient algorithm we see that the method easily overcame the local minima and produced better solutions, even the global solution for most of the cases.

Table 4. Results for Non-Convex Non-differentiable function

Function	Algorithm	Function Value	Function Value Actual	CPU Time (second)
Problem1	MDG	1	0	20.35
	SDG	0	0	23.5
Problem2	MDG	10700.61	0	17.75
	SDG	0	0	22.62
Problem3	MDG	7.165633	0	2945.23
	SDG	0.869910	0	2975.26

4 Analysis and Discussion

In this section we analyze the convergence property of proposed algorithm as well as we have shown the improvement of the solution.

4.1 Convergence

We have compared the solution obtained by both Multi start Discrete Gradient algorithm (MDG) and Stochastic Discrete Gradient algorithm, and plotted in graph.

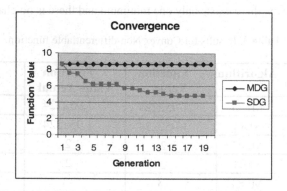

Fig. 2. Convergence of SDG and MDG

Figure 2 shows how the algorithms have improved the quality of the solution in each generation. Figure 2 shows that MDG could not improve the quality of the solution cause it is unable to overcome the local minima. Where as the SDG algorithm as improved the quality gradually and produced the global solution.

4.2 Adaptive Mutation Rate

We have also shown how the adaptive mutation rate affects the quality of the solution and the convergence as well. We have plotted the average solution value in each generation with respect to the mutation rate. We call the SDG with Adaptive mutation rate as SDGA and SDG with fix mutation rate as SDGNA. Figure 3 shows the convergence over the mutation rate in each generation. Figure 3 shows that there was a smooth convergence for average solution value for SDGA, where as with fix mutation rate, the average solution has degraded quite a few times.

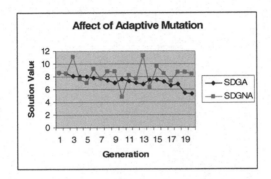

Fig. 3. Affect of Mutation rate on Convergence

5 Conclusion

In this paper we propose a stochastic based derivative free optimization method that is suitable for non-smooth, non-convex optimization. We have used adaptive mutation rate in place of fixed rate and shown that the average quality of the solution has improved significantly. The results are very promising in terms of the solution value. We have compared our results with another existing technique. In terms of the solution value and time complexity our proposed algorithm performs better than the multistart counterpart.

References

1. Fletcher, R.: Practical Methods of Optimization. John Wiley and Sons, se Chichester, second edition (1987).
2. Bagirov, A.M.: Derivative-free methods for unconstrained nonsmooth optimization and its numerical analysis, Investigacao Operacional (1999), 19-75.

278   R. Ghosh, M. Ghosh, and A. Bagirov

3. Hiriart-Urruty, J. B., Lemarechal, C.: Convex Analysis and Minimization Algorithms, Springer-Verlag, Berlin, New York (1993).
4. Clarke, F.: Optimization and Non-smooth Analysis, John Wiley & Sons, New York (1983).
5. Wolfe, P.: Finding the nearest point in a polytope. Mathematical Programming, Vol. 11, No. 2, (1976), 128- 149.
6. Browein J.: A note on the existence of subgradients, Mathematical Programming, Vol. 24, No. 2, (1982), 225-228.

Association Analysis of Customer Services from the Enterprise Customer Management System

Sung-Ju Kim, Dong-Sik Yun, and Byung-Soo Chang

463-1, jeonmin-dong, Yuseong-gu, Daejeon,
KT network technology laboratory, Korea
{Be3sowon, dsyun, bschang}@kt.co.kr

Abstract. The communications market has seen rising competition among businesses. While securing new customers is still important, it is more crucial to maintain and manage existing customers by providing optimized service and efficient marketing strategies for each customer in order to preserve existing customers from business rivals and ultimately maximize corporate sales. This thesis investigates how to obtain useful methodologies for customer management by applying the technological concepts of data-mining and association analysis to KT's secure customer data.

1 Introduction

It has become common sense in the post-2000 business arena that corporations should see everything from the perspective of customers and establish business strategies that take their demands into consideration. This has led to the recognition that the ultimate goal of businesses should be based not on making one-time sales but on establishing a continuous relationship with customers, which provides a strong motivation for the establishment and development of new business strategies. Only through data-mining can managers figure out the interaction between customers and what they will do in the future, as well as related implications and information. [1]

The saying "The only way for a business to survive these days is to know more about customers and execute related plans as early as possible" is ever becoming a reality test for businesses to survive beyond clichés.[2] According to Asron Zornes from the Meta Group, data-mining is the process of discovering knowledge through which potentially executable information is mined from a large amount of database. The Gartner Group's Erick Brethenoux defines it more specifically as the process of discovering useful interrelationships, patterns or trends from large amounts of data through statistical, mathematical and pattern-recognition technologies. [3]

Data-mining employs various models in performing various tasks, among which are the predictive model and the descriptive model. The predictive model is used to predict new data by building a model based on already known results. It includes classification, regression and time series. The descriptive model refers to a model that describes a rule or pattern of data. The discovered patterns or rules are used to support efficient and profitable marketing activities. It includes clustering, association analysis and sequence discovery. [4]

P. Perner (Ed.): ICDM 2006, LNAI 4065, pp. 279–283, 2006.

Association refers to items that happen at the same time in a given event or record. That is, if a certain item A is part of a certain event, item B at the same time with X% in the same event.

Association analysis is also called 'shopping basket analysis'. It should exclude chance occurrences from regular occurrences. When investigating useful elements, Support determines how much transactions include item A and item B, making it possible to see the whole trend of purchasing.

$$S = \Pr(A \cap B) = \frac{Occurrences\ that\ include\ both\ item\ A\ and\ item\ B\ at\ the\ same\ time}{Whole\ occurrences} \qquad (1)$$

Confidence Rate indicates the probability that item B could be included among transactions that include item A, making it possible to understand the level of association.

$$C = \Pr(B/A) = \frac{P(A \cap B)}{P(A)} = \frac{Occurrences\ that\ include\ both\ item\ A\ and\ item\ B\ at\ the\ same\ time}{Occurrences\ that\ include\ item\ A} \qquad (2)$$

Lift Rate indicates the ration in which a certain transaction includes item B when a customer purchases item A, versus the accidental purchase of item B.

$$L = \frac{P(B/A)}{P(B)} = \frac{P(A \cap B)}{P(A)P(B)} \qquad (3)$$

Support and Confidence are stipulated by the law of probability, ranging from 0 to 1. If they are near 1, it means deeper association. If Lift is over 1, it means positive association. If it is less than 1, it means negative association.

This paper aims to investigate the processes of defining problems, preparing related data and deducing final results by tracking down data-mining processes through the Enterprise Customer Management System, which is KT's business support system.

2 Association Analysis and Results

2.1 Enterprise Customer Management System

The Enterprise Customer Management System contains unified information about KT's enterprise customers by linking their communication information to our system, as shown in Figure1. The system is managed by AM/RM and has some 30,000 customers and it provides general information on customers, maintenance, construction and traffic statistics analysis. Figure2 shows the Enterprise Customer Management System through the Web. Marketing activities based on objective data – information about customers' facilities and their dependence on rival communication companies, various emergency situations and follow-up measures, and maintenance and support information – will heighten customer loyalty and help prevent the loss of current customers by enabling the rapid response to their requests and demands.

It will also raise customer satisfaction by improving and suggesting the communication services of KT and its customer companies. It will ultimately help in maintaining customer confidence and securing superior customers, which will in turn increase corporate profitability.

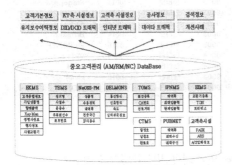

Fig. 1. ECMS Structure

Fig. 2. Facility information related to customers

2.2 Data-Mining Application Analysis

Definition of Purposes

For the successful execution of data-mining, its purposes should be defined first. This paper will determine the associations for the services that enterprise customers are using. KT provides hundreds of services to customers. The complexity and variety of the services make it difficult to comprehend the associations; therefore we classified them into 17 major services such as telephone, Kornet, Megapass, Nespot and VPN.

Data Preparation

This stage requires a lot of time. Sometimes it could be repeatedly performed along with the model construction. In most data-mining projects, this stage is considered very important, requiring 50 to 80 percent of the time and effort. For data collection, data should be collected inside the company first, but sometimes it could also be obtained from the outside. [5]

Here, we took advantage of the customer information and registration product names collected from the EKMSS (Enterprise KT Marketing Support System). We first applied an ID to each customer to make the 'loc-id' column and set up the Primary Key. A code is then applied to each service product, as shown on the mapping table in Figure 2. Group1 is made from the upper classification in areas while Group 2 is made from the lower classification from specific product lines. As extra elements, the usage frequency of the service lines are indicated as the 'line-cnt' column and the specific monthly sales per service is shown in the 'fee-sum' column, all of which are excluded from association analysis. Regarding the quality of data, experience has borne out the truth of the term GIGO (Garbage In, Garbage Out). If the data is not good, its result could not be good either. Therefore, we need to pay special attention to the missing value or the data that does not comply with integrity

Table 1. Customer Use Service Table

LOC_ID	GROUP1	GROUP2	LINE_CNT	FEE_SUM
30035263442	0003	0011	1	31384
30050092286	0001	0008	4	271714
30050092286	0003	0011	1	100750
30034194190	0001	0008	13	549200
30034194190	0003	0011	2	78000
30050375630	0001	0008	12	1148513
30050375630	0003	0011	2	84534
30030696874	0001	0008	9	460500
30030696874	0003	0011	1	33320
30052077077	0001	0008	16	686624
30052077077	0003	0011	1	40630
30034484259	0001	0008	14	162550
30034484259	0003	0011	3	175940

Table 2. Mapping Table for group1, group2

GROUP1	GROUP1_NM	GROUP2	GROUP2_NM
0001	전화	0008	전화
0002	회선설비	0009	국내회선
0003	인터넷	0010	Kornet
0003	인터넷	0011	Megapass
0003	인터넷	0012	Nespot
0003	인터넷	0014	IDC
0003	인터넷	0015	Bizmeka
0003	인터넷	0016	인터넷기타
0004	데이터	0013	VPN
0004	데이터	0017	ATM
0004	데이터	0018	Hinet
0004	데이터	0019	ISDN
0004	데이터	0020	데이터기타

constraints in order to heighten product model quality. After conducting research on loc-id, group1 and group2, which are being used for the purpose of association analysis, we did not find out any non-normal values.

Association Analysis Between Products

We used the tool Enterprise Miner to conduct the association analysis. This tool is used when exploring relations or patterns hidden inside large masses of data and making a model out of it. It can perform large masses of data-modeling in a GUI environment and can have direct access to various DBs (Oracle, Sybase, DB2) and data warehouses for data-extraction and data-mining. Enterprise Miner was developed by SAS. It provides multiple data-mining algorithms including returning analysis, classification and statistical analysis packages. Its major features are its various uses as an analytical tool and the fact that it was made from SAS' long experience in the statistical analysis market. [6]

We selected association analysis in order to figure out the association among the different services adopted by major enterprise customers. We set up each Model Role as the id and target for the columns 'loc-id' and 'group2' and adopted the association for our analysis mode of the environmental variable. We applied 3 percent as the minimum transaction frequency to support the association and 30 as the maximum number of items in an association.

Analysis Result

Table3 shows the results from the analysis of services adopted by KT's major customers while Figure 3 is the graph that shows the results of its association analysis. It shows that some 69.57 percent of customers are using the ISDN and KT local phone service together with Megapass, and its support rate comes to 3.82. And those who use the ISDN and KT phone service indicate a positive rate of 1.37 in the Lift rate. Some 59.88 percent of Nespot customers use the Megapass and KT phone service and shows a positive rate of 1.23 in Lift. When the Relation is 2, some 92.85 percent of Megapass users also use the KT phone service, but its Lift rate only comes to 1.01, implying that Megapass users are not necessarily using the KT phone service.

Through this method, we can identify the associations and interrelationships among the different services for the rest of the results.

Table 3. SAS Association Analysis Result

Relations	Lift	Support(%)	Confidence(%)	Transaction Count	Rule
1	2 1.04	48.66	95.66	5184.0	0011 ==> 0008
2	2 1.04	48.66	52.86	5184.0	0008 ==> 0011
3	2 1.01	7.19	92.85	766.00	0012 ==> 0008
4	2 1.01	7.19	7.81	766.00	0008 ==> 0012
5	2 1.20	4.74	61.21	505.00	0012 ==> 0011
6	2 1.20	4.74	9.32	505.00	0011 ==> 0012
7	2 1.20	3.89	61.24	414.00	0019 ==> 0011
8	2 1.20	3.89	7.64	414.00	0011 ==> 0019
9	3 1.04	4.90	5.32	522.00	0008 ==> 0011 & 0010
10	3 1.04	4.90	95.96	522.00	0011 & 0010 ==> 0008
11	3 1.23	4.64	59.88	494.00	0012 ==> 0011 & 0008
12	3 1.27	4.64	9.12	494.00	0011 ==> 0012 & 0008
13	3 1.06	4.64	5.04	494.00	0008 ==> 0012 & 0011
14	3 1.06	4.64	97.82	494.00	0012 & 0011 ==> 0008
15	3 1.27	4.64	64.49	494.00	0012 & 0008 ==> 0011
16	3 1.23	4.64	0.53	494.00	0011 & 0008 ==> 0012
17	3 1.24	3.82	60.21	407.00	0019 ==> 0011 & 0008
18	3 1.37	3.82	7.61	407.00	0011 ==> 0019 & 0008
19	3 1.07	3.82	4.15	407.00	0008 ==> 0019 & 0011
20	3 1.07	3.82	98.31	407.00	0019 & 0011 ==> 0008
21	3 1.37	3.82	69.57	407.00	0019 & 0008 ==> 0011
22	3 1.24	3.82	7.85	407.00	0011 & 0008 ==> 0019

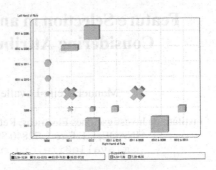

Fig. 3. SAS Association Analysis Graph

2.3 Practical Application

Data-mining for CRM can increase corporate profits through efficient cross-selling by bringing about better understanding through customer classification and product purchase association.

Cross-selling is aimed at leading customers to encourage them to buy additional products. This also induces customers to purchase more profitable products and widen customer transactions by acquiring more loyal customers. Regional Marketers and Network Consultants are taking full advantage of association analysis between the different services in KT's strategic marketing activities.

3 Conclusion

Through the aforementioned process, a few cases of the adoption of the data-mining method in Enterprise Customer Management System for CRM are introduced. Here, we tried to analyze the associations among the different services adopted by major enterprise customers in order to construct various data-mining models based on a data warehouse for enterprise customers in the future. It is expected that this analysis will be used strategically in KT's future marketing activities and contribute a lot in managing enterprise customers and raising corporate profitability.

References

[1] Jun, Heh. Data-mining in Telecommunication Market Telco-CAT (CHURN analysis), pp11
[2] Jun, Heh. Data-mining in Telecommunication Market Telco-CAT (CHURN analysis), pp3
[3] Sung-hyun Kim, Oracle Technical Note Introducing Data-mining, pp.2~3
[4] Margaret H. Dunham, Data mining introductory and advanced topics, pp4~5
[5] Sung-hyun Kim, Oracle Technical Note Introducing Data-mining, pp6
[6] Jiawei Han, Nicheline kamber, Data Mining concepts and techniques, pp461

Feature Selection in an Electric Billing Database Considering Attribute Inter-dependencies

Manuel Mejía-Lavalle[1] and Eduardo F. Morales[2]

[1] Instituto de Investigaciones Eléctricas, Reforma 113, 62490 Cuernavaca, Morelos, México
[2] INAOE, L.E.Erro 1, 72840 StMa. Tonantzintla, Puebla, México
mlavalle@iie.org.mx, emorales@inaoep.mx

Abstract. With the increasing size of databases, feature selection has become a relevant and challenging problem for the area of knowledge discovery in databases. An effective feature selection strategy can significantly reduce the data mining processing time, improve the predicted accuracy, and help to understand the induced models, as they tend to be smaller and make more sense to the user. Many feature selection algorithms assumed that the attributes are independent between each other given the class, which can produce models with redundant attributes and/or exclude sets of attributes that are relevant when considered together. In this paper, an effective best first search algorithm, called buBF, for feature selection is described. buBF uses a novel heuristic function based on *n-way* entropy to capture inter-dependencies among variables. It is shown that buBF produces more accurate models than other state-of-the-art feature selection algorithms when compared on several real and synthetic datasets. Specifically we apply buBF to a Mexican Electric Billing database and obtain satisfactory results.

1 Introduction

Data mining is mainly applied to large amounts of stored data to look for the implicit knowledge hidden within this information. To take advantage of the enormous amount of information currently available in many databases, algorithms and tools specialized in the automatic discovery of hidden knowledge within this information have been developed. This process of non-trivial extraction of relevant information that is implicit in the data is known as Knowledge Discovery in Databases (KDD), in which the data mining phase plays a central role in this process.

It has been noted, however, that when very large databases are going to get mined, the mining algorithms get very slow, requiring too much time to process the information. Another scenario is when acquiring some attributes is expensive. One way to approach this problem is to reduce the amount of data before applying the mining process. In particular, the pre-processing method of feature selection, applied to the data before mining, has been shown to be promising because it can eliminate the irrelevant or redundant attributes that cause the mining tools to become inefficient and ineffective. At the same time, it can preserve-increase the classification quality of the mining algorithm (accuracy) [1].

P. Perner (Ed.): ICDM 2006, LNAI 4065, pp. 284–296, 2006.

Although there are many feature selection algorithms reported in the specialized literature, none of them are perfect: some of them are effective, but very costly in computational time (e.g. wrappers methods), and others are fast, but less effective in the feature selection task (e.g. filter methods).

Specifically, wrapper methods, although effective in eliminating irrelevant and redundant attributes, are very slow because they apply the mining algorithm many times, changing the number of attributes each time of execution as they follow some search and stop criteria [2]. Filter methods are more efficient; they use some form of *correlation* measure between individual attributes and the class [3][4]; however, because they measure the relevance of each isolated attribute, they cannot detect if redundant attributes exist, or if a combination of two (or more) attributes, apparently irrelevant when analyzed independently, are indeed relevant [5].

In this article, we propose a feature selection method that tries to solve these problems in a supervised learning context. Specifically, we use a heuristic search alternative, inspired by the Branch & Bound algorithm, which reduces considerably the search space, thus reducing the processing time. Additionally, we propose a novel evaluation criterion based on an *n-way* entropy measure that, at the same time, selects the relevant attributes and discovers the important inter-dependences among variables of the problem.

To cover these topics, the article is organized as follows: Section 2 surveys related work; Section 3 introduces our feature selection method; Section 4 details the experiments, emphasizing over the Mexican electric billing database; conclusions and future research directions are given in Section 5.

2   Related Work

The emergence of Very Large Databases (VLDB) leads to new challenges that the mining algorithms of the 1990´s are incapable to attack efficiently. According to [6], from the point of view of the mining algorithms, the main lines to deal with VLDB (scaling up algorithms) are: a) to use relational representations instead of a single table; b) to design fast algorithms, optimizing searches, reducing complexity, finding approximate solutions, or using parallelism; and c) to divide the data based on the variables involved or the number of examples. In particular, some of these new approaches in turn give origin to Data Reduction that tries to eliminate variables, attributes or instances that do not contribute information to the KDD process. These methods are generally applied before the actual mining is performed.

In fact, the specialized literature mentions the *curse of dimensionality*, referring to the fact that the processing time of many induction methods grows dramatically (sometimes exponentially) with the number of attributes. Searching for improvements on VLDB processing power (necessary with tens of attributes), two main groups of methods have appeared: wrappers and filters [6]. We focus our research in filter methods because of their relatively low computational cost.

Narendra [7] and others [8], [9], [10] have proposed a filter method for optimal feature selection. In general, they use the Branch & Bound algorithm, starting the search with all the D features and then applying a backward elimination feature strategy, until they obtain d optimal features ($d < D$). Additionally, they use a monotonic subset feature evaluation criterion: e.g., when augmenting (subtracting) one feature to the feature subset, the criterion value function always increases (decreases). The monotonicity property allows us to prune unnecessary sub-trees (e.g. sub-trees that do not improve the solution because they have values less than the bound obtained for another sub-tree). These approaches have demonstrated to be efficient; however, they have several drawbacks, because they need:

- An a priori definition of the number of features d (equal to the maximum tree deep level to consider); this is a problem because, in most cases, the number of relevant attributes is previously unknown,
- To start evaluating all the features (top-down strategy); this strategy represents high computational cost at the beginning of the subset feature search process,
- To use a monotonic subset evaluation criterion: although a monotonic criterion permits safe sub-trees cut offs, it assumes that the features are independent between each other, given the class attribute.

Trying to tackle these problems, in this paper we propose a bottom-up Best First method that is described in the next Section.

3 Bottom-Up Best First

The proposed method has two basic components: a) the evaluation function of each feature subset (in a supervised learning context), and b) the search strategy.

3.1 Evaluation Criterion

With respect to the feature subset evaluation criterion, we proposed a non-monotonic function. This function is calculated in a similar way to the Shannon entropy, only that instead of considering the entropy of one single feature, or attribute, against the class attribute (*2-way* entropy, or traditional entropy), it is calculated considering the entropy of two (or more attributes) against the class (*n-way* entropy). With this approach, we sought to capture the inter-dependences among attributes.

Formally, the traditional entropy H of a variable X after observing values of another variable Y is defined as

$$H(X \mid Y) = -\Sigma_j P(y_j) \; \Sigma_i P(x_i \mid y_j) \; log_2 (P(x_i \mid y_j)), \qquad (1)$$

where $P(x_i \mid y_j)$ is the posterior probabilities of X given the values of Y. We obtain the *n-way* entropy Hn with the same equation but, instead of using the count of only one attribute, we count the number of times that a particular combination of attribute values appears, against the class value, taking into account all the instances of the dataset. In this form, if the *n-way* entropy Hn decreases, using a particular feature subset, means that we have additional information about the class attribute.

For instance, if U and V are different attribute subsets, C is the class attribute, and if $Hn(U|C) > Hn(V|C)$, then we conclude that subset V predicts better than subset U. The idea of calculating in this manner the *n-way* entropy is inspired by the work of

Jakulin and Bratko [11]. Although they calculate this in a more costly way using the concept of Interaction Gain I. For instance, they obtain the 3-way interactions using:

$$I(X; Y; C) = H(X|C) + H(Y|C) - H(X,Y|C) - \{ H(X) + H(Y) - H(X,Y) \}, \quad (2)$$

so, we experiment with the n-way entropy variant Hn because of its simplicity and its relative low computational cost.

Nevertheless, a defect or problem with the n-way entropy Hn is that it decreases quickly when the number of the combined attribute values grows, resulting in a "false" low entropy. In an extreme case, it is possible that we can count as many different combined attribute values as the total number of dataset instances. If we count as many combined attribute values as instances, then the entropy will be zero (perfect). However, this does not necessarily reflect, in an effective way, how that combination of attributes is relevant. The specialized literature has already reported how the entropy tends to prefer those attributes that have many different values, then, an attribute randomly generated could be considered better than another attribute observed from the real system.

Although there are some proposals to mitigate the problem (e.g. gain ratio or symmetrical uncertainty), they usually add an extra computational cost; instead, we directly apply a reward to the n-way entropy considering the number of values that a specific attribute (or attributes) can take. Our proposed evaluation criterion, or metric, is defined as:

$$nwM = \lambda \, (\, Hn\,) + (1 - \lambda)(tot.combined\ attribute\ values\ /\ tot.\ instances) \quad (3)$$

With this metric, a balance between the n-way entropy Hn and the combined attribute values is sought, obtaining a metric, now called nwM, to detect relevant and inter-dependant features. The λ parameter can take values between zero and one and it is defined by the user according to how much weight he desires to give to each term. We empirically test the proposed metric, and obtain very promising results (see Section 4).

3.2 Search Strategy

With respect to the search strategy, we propose to explore a search tree with forward feature selection or bottom-up schema.

The idea consists in using a best first search strategy: always expanding (aggregates a new feature) to the node (attribute subset) whose metric is the best of the brother nodes (node with the smaller nwM) and better than the parent node, stopping the search when none of the expanded nodes is better than the parent node. In this case, following the best first search strategy, the search continues selecting the best non-expanding node, according to the metric, and expanding until none of the children nodes are better than the parent node, and so on.

Thus, the proposed search schema explores the most promising attribute combinations according to the non-monotonic metric, generating several possibly good solutions. At the same time, it carries out sub-tree pruning, when the nwM metric has indicated, heuristically, that continuing to explore some of those sub-trees,

---

Given a dataset with D features and N instances, and $\lambda \in [0,1)$,

1. obtain *nwM* (2-*way* entropy) for each feature in the dataset;
2. while (available memory) or (unexplored nodes) do begin
3.   select for expansion the feature subset F with the best *nwM* and
                                                    better than his parent node;
4.   for $I := 1$ to $(D - \| F \|)$ do begin
5.   obtain *nwM* ($F \cup I \mid I \notin F$);
6.   end;
7. end;
8. show feature subset with the best *nwM*;

Fig. 1. buBF algorithm

maybe will not improve the evaluation criterion. The search process stops due to insufficient memory, or when all the nodes have been expanded. The modified algorithm, called now bottom-up Best First (buBF), is shown in Fig. 1 ($\| . \|$ is the size of a set).

The proposed search seems like a Branch & Bound strategy, in the sense that it prunes sub-trees that maybe will not conduct to better solutions, according to the evaluation criterion. Nevertheless, it is not exactly equal to the feature selection Branch & Bound schema reported in the specialized literature.

The basic differences consist of:

- Instead of removing attributes and evaluating the resulting feature subset (backward elimination), our method adds attributes and evaluates (forward selection). Using forward selection we will be able to process datasets with more features.
- Instead of using a monotonic evaluation criterion, a non-monotonic criterion is employed. Although sub-tree pruning is not safe using a non-monotonic criterion, our heuristic measure captures attributes inter-dependencies.
- Instead of having to define an a priori tree depth, in our case the tree depth search is variable, and depends on the evaluation criterion: this criterion indicates stopping the depth search when none children node is better than the parent node.
- In our case, adding nodes (attributes) is sought to determine not only the relevant attributes, but also their inter-dependences, since other methods reported in the literature assumes attribute independence [9].

4 Experiments

We conducted several experiments with real and synthetic datasets to empirically evaluate if buBF can do better in selecting features than other well-known feature selection algorithms, in terms of learning accuracy and processing time. We choose synthetic datasets in our experiments because the relevant features of these datasets are known beforehand.

4.1 Experimentation Details

The experimentation objective is to observe the buBF behavior related to classification quality and response time.

First, we test our proposed method with a real database with 24 attributes and 35,983 instances; this database contains information of Mexican electric billing costumers, where we expect to obtain patterns of behavior of illicit customers.

Specifically, one of the main Mexican electric utility functions is to distribute to the costumers the electrical energy produced in the different generating plants in Mexico. Related to distribution, this utility faces different problems that prevent it to recover certain amount of "lost income" from the 100% of the total energy for sale.

At present, it loses approximately 21% of the energy for distribution. These losses are mainly due to two kinds of problems: a) technical, and b) administrative. The technical energy losses are usually in the range of 10% and a great investment in new technologies would be needed in the distribution equipment to be able to reduce this percentage.

The other 11% of the losses are due to administrative control problems, and they are classified in three categories of anomalies: a) invoicing errors, b) measurement errors, and c) illicit energy use or fraud. The first two have a minimum percentage impact so the big problem is the illicit use of energy, that is to say, people who steal the energy and therefore they do not pay for it.

The Mexican utility has faced this problem applying different actions (as to increase the frequency of measurement equipment readings of suspect customers, or to install equipment for automatic readings) and has managed to reduce the percentage due to illicit use losses, which represents a recovery of several million dollars.

Since the problem has not been completely solved, it is important to attack it with other technologies and actions, using a knowledge discovery approach based on data mining to obtain patterns of behavior of the illicit customers. This alternative solution does not require a great deal of investment and it has been proven effective in similar cases, like credit card fraud detection.

The subject information to analyze is a sample of a legacy system developed with the COBOL language, it contains around twenty tables with information about contracts, invoicing, and collection from customers across the nation.

This system was not designed with the illicit users discovery in mind; nevertheless, it contains a field called *debit-type* in which a record is made if the debit is due to illicit use of energy. After joining three tables, including the one that has the *debit-type* field, a "mine" was obtained with the following attributes: *Permanent customer registry (RPU), Year, Month, debit-type, Digit, kWh, Energy, Cve-invoicing, Total, Status, Turn, Tariff, Name, Installed-load, Contract-load*, and others. One of the values that the attribute *debit-type* can be assigned is "9", which indicates an illicit use, and it is our class attribute.

To obtain additional evidence, we experiment too using 10 synthetic dataset, each of them with different levels of complexity. To generate the 10 datasets we use the functions described in [12]. Each of the datasets has nine attributes (1.salary, 2.commission, 3.age, 4.elevel, 5.car, 6.zipcode, 7.hvalue, 8.hyears, and 9.loan) plus

---

disposable := (0.67 * (*salary* + *commission*) − 5000 * *elevel* − 0.2 * *loan* − 10000)

IF (disposable > 0) THEN class label := Group "A"
ELSE class label := Group "B"

Fig. 2. A function example

the class attribute (with class label Group "A" or "B"); each dataset has 10,000 instances. The values of the features of each instance were generated randomly according to the distributions described in [12]. For each instance, a class label was determined according to the rules that define the functions. For example, function 9 uses four attributes and classifies an instance following the statement and rule shown in Fig. 2.

Finally, we experiment with the corrAL and corrAL-47 synthetic datasets [13], that has four relevant attributes (A0, A1, B0, B1), plus irrelevant (I) and redundant (R) attributes; the class attribute is defined by the function $Y = (A0 \wedge A1) \vee (B0 \wedge B1)$.

In order to compare the results obtained with buBF, we use Weka's [14] implementation of *ReliefF, OneR* and *ChiSquared* feature selection algorithms. These implementations were run using Weka's default values, except for ReliefF, where we define to 5 the number of neighborhood, for a more efficient response time.

Additionally, we experiment with 7 Elvira's [15] filter-ranking methods: *Mutual Information, Euclidean, Matusita, Kullback-Leibler-1 and 2, Shannon and Bhattacharyya*. To select the best ranking attributes, we use a threshold defined by the largest gap between two consecutive ranked attributes (e.g. a gap greater than the average gap among all the gaps). In the case of buBF, we set λ to 0.85 for all the experiments. All the experiments were executed in a personal computer with a Pentium 4 processor, 1.5 GHz, and 250 Mbytes in RAM. In the following Section, the obtained results are shown.

4.2 Experimental Results

Testing over the electric billing database, we use the selected features for each method as input to the decision tree induction algorithm J4.8 included in the Weka tool (J4.8 is the last version of C4.5, which is one of the best-known induction algorithms used in data mining). We notice that buBF obtains the best accuracy ties with Kullback-Leibler-2, but with less attributes (Table 1). On the other hand, buBF requires more processing time.

We realized an additional experiment with the electric billing database, in order to observe how two approaches that try to mitigate the effect of many attribute values over entropy behave, named *gain ratio* [16] and *symmetrical uncertainty* (SU) [13].

Table 1. J4.8´s accuracies (%) for 10-fold-cross validation using the features selected by each method (electric billing database)

Method	Total features selected	Accuracy (%)	Pre-processing time
buBF	5	97.50	1. 5 mins.
Kullback-Leibler 2	9	97.50	6 secs.
All attributes	24	97.25	0
ChiSquared	20	97.18	9 secs.
OneR	9	95.95	41 secs.
ReliefF	4	93.89	14.3 mins.
Euclidean distance	4	93.89	5 secs.
Shannon entropy	18	93.71	4 secs.
Bhattacharyya	3	90.21	6 secs.
Matusita distance	3	90.21	5 secs.
Kullback-Leibler 1	4	90.10	6 secs.
Mutual Information	4	90.10	4 secs.

Table 2. J4.8´s accuracies (%) for 10-fold-cross validation using the features selected by each method considering adjust for many attribute values (electric billing database)

Method	Total features selected	Accuracy (%)	Pre-processing time
buBF	5	97.50	1. 5 mins.
Gain Ratio *n-way*	1	90.18	1. 8 mins
Gain Ratio *Weka*	1	90.18	1 sec.
SU	3	90.68	1 sec.

We ran two versions of gain ratio: a) *n-way* fashion (we used the same essential buBF program, only changing the evaluation metric), and b) ranking fashion (applying Weka). Results are shown in Table 2.

In this case, *gain ratio n-way* only selects one attribute, because it does a strong penalty when two or more attributes are combined (and consequently, the number of different attribute values increase): this results in a relatively low J4.8 accuracy. Processing time is similar to buBF due to the fact that we used buBF schema but with *gain ratio* instead of *nwM*. Gain Ratio as a filter (Weka) selects the same attribute that *gain ratio n-way,* and it takes only one second. SU metric selects three attributes, resulting in a relatively low J4.8 accuracy.

Table 3. Features selected by different methods (10 synthetic datasets)

Function number	Method											
	Oracle	Mut.Infor	Euclidean	Matusita	Kullback Leibler-1	Kullback Leibler-2	Shannon	Bhattach	ReliefF	OneR	ChiSquar	buBF
1	3	3	3	3	3	9-7-2-8	9-1	3	3	3	3	3
2	1-3	1	2-1	1	1-2	1	9-3-7-1	1	3-1	1	1-2	3-1
3	3-4	4-3	4	4-3	4-3	4-3	3-9-1	4-3	4-3	4-3	4-3	3-4
4	1-3-4	1	2-1	1	1	1	1-9	1	1-4-2	1-2	1-2	4-3-1
5	1-3-9	9-1	9-4	9	9	9-1	1-3	9	9-3-1	9	9	5-2-3-9
6	1-2-3	1-3-2	2	1-3	1-3	1	3	1-3-2	3-1-2	3-1-2	1-3-2	1-2-3
7	1-2-9	9	2-9	9	9-1-2	9	1-9	9-1	9-1-2	9	9-1-2	9-1-2
8	1-2-4	2-1	2-4-1	2-1	2-1-4	2-1	9-3	2-1	1-2-4	-	1-2-4	4-2-1
9	1-2-4-9	9	2-4-9	9-1	9	9	9	9-1	9-1-2	9	9-1-2-4-3	2-1-9
10	1-2-4-7-8-9	4	4	4	4	4	9-1-3	4	8	4	4-8-7-6	6-8-4

Table 4. J4.8´s accuracies (%) using the features selected by each method (10 synthetic datasets)

Function number	Method											
	Oracle	buBF	ReliefF	ChiSquar	Bhattach	Mut.Infor	Kullback Leibler-1	Matusita	OneR	Kullback Leibler-2	Euclidean	Shannon
1	100	100	100	100	100	100	100	100	100	67	100	67
2	100	100	100	73	73	73	73	73	73	73	73	100
3	100	100	100	100	100	100	100	100	100	100	68	59
4	100	100	90	84	84	84	84	84	84	84	84	84
5	100	91	100	74	74	82	74	74	74	82	74	60
6	99	99	99	99	99	99	87	87	99	68	64	69
7	98	98	98	98	94	86	98	86	86	86	88	94
8	100	100	100	100	99	99	100	99	-	99	100	98
9	97	94	94	97	92	85	85	92	85	85	88	85
10	99	99	80	99	97	97	99	97	98	97	97	80
Avg.	99.3	98.1	96.1	92.4	91.2	90.5	89.8	89.2	84.9	84.1	83.6	79.6

Next, to verify if buBF effectively captures attribute inter-dependencies, we experiment with synthetic datasets. The features selected by each method are shown in Table 3, where "Oracle" represents a perfect feature selection method (it selects exactly the same features that each function uses to generate the class label). We can observe that, in some cases, the methods almost select the same features, but there are other functions in which the methods disagree. For function 8, only OneR cannot determine any feature subset, because ranks all attributes equally.

Then, we used the selected features for each method as input to J4.8. We use 10-fold cross validation in order to obtain the average test accuracy for each feature subset (We experiment with other metrics, like Balanced Error Rate, obtaining very similar results). The results are shown in Table 4. The column "Oracle/ All" means accuracy applying the perfect attributes and, in this case, we obtain the same results if we use all the dataset attributes.

To summarize the obtained results in Table 4, we count the times when buBF win, loss or tie versus the other methods. This information is reported in Table 5. In Table 5, we can observe that buBF has a good performance, because there was only loss one time versus ReliefF, and one time versus ChiSquared, but it still maintained good accuracy.

Table 5. buBF accuracy results summary vs. other methods (10 synthetic datasets)

buBF vs.	Method											
	Oracle	OneR	ReliefF	ChiSquar	Bhattach	Mut.Infor	Kullback Leibler-1	Matusita	Shannon	Kullback Leibler-2	Euclidean	Average
Win	0	7	2	3	7	7	5	8	9	9	8	**5.9**
Loss	2	0	1	1	0	0	0	0	0	0	0	**0.4**
Tie	8	3	7	6	3	3	5	2	1	1	2	**3.7**

Table 6. Averaged processing time for each method (10 synthetic datasets)

Exhaustive wrapper	ReliefF	OneR	ChiSquared and Elvira	buBF
1,085,049 secs. (12.5 days)	573 secs. (9.55 mins.)	8 secs.	1 sec.	71 secs. (1.18 mins.)

The processing time is shown in Table 6. Although buBF is computationally more expensive than OneR and ChiSquared, these algorithms cannot detect some attribute inter-dependencies; on the other hand, buBF is faster than ReliefF, but with similar, or better, feature selection performance.

To have a better idea of the buBF performance, we can compare the results presented previously against the results produced by an exhaustive wrapper approach. In this case, we can calculate that, if the average time required to obtain a tree using J4.8 is 1.1 seconds, and if we multiply this by all the possible attribute combinations, then we will obtain that 12.5 days, theoretically, would be required to conclude such a process.

In order to observe how the selected features (Table 3) respond with another classifier, we use these features as input to the Naïve Bayes Classifier (NBC) included in the Weka tool. The results are shown in Table 7. Again, buBF obtains satisfactory accuracy results.

Table 7. NBC's accuracies (%) for 10-fold-cross validation using the features selected by each method (10 synthetic datasets)

Function number	Oracle	buBF	Matusita	Kullback Leibler-1	Bhattach	Mut.Infor	ChiSquar	ReliefF	Euclidean	Kullback Leibler-2	OneR	Shannon
1	89	89	89	89	89	89	89	89	89	67	89	67
2	69	69	69	64	69	69	64	69	64	69	69	68
3	65	65	65	65	65	65	65	65	66	65	65	58
4	76	76	76	76	76	76	70	69	70	76	70	76
5	68	68	68	68	68	68	68	68	68	68	68	60
6	71	71	72	72	71	71	71	71	59	60	71	58
7	89	89	86	89	88	86	89	89	86	86	86	88
8	99	99	98	99	98	98	99	99	99	98	50	98
9	89	88	88	85	88	85	88	88	86	85	85	85
10	98	98	98	98	98	98	97	80	98	98	98	80
Avg.	81.3	81.2	81	81	81	80.5	80	78.7	78.5	77.2	75.1	73.8

Table 8. Features selected by different methods (corrAL and corrAL-47 datasets)

Method	Features selected	
	corrAL	corrAL-47
buBF	B1, B0, A1, A0	A0, A1, B0, B1
ReliefF	R, A0, A1, B0, B1	R,B1$_1$,A0,A0$_0$,B1,B1$_0$,B0,B0$_0$,B0$_2$,A1,A1$_0$
FCBF$_{(log)}$	R, A0	R, A0, A1, B0, B1
FCBF$_{(0)}$	R, A0, A1, B0, B1	R, A0, A1, B0, B1
CFS	A0, A1, B0, B1, R	A0, A1, B0, B1, R
Focus	R	A0, A1, A1$_2$, B0, B1, R
SU	R, A1, A0, B0, B1	A0$_1$, A0, A0$_7$, B01, B0, A1$_1$, A1, R
Gain Ratio (Weka)	R, A1, A0, B0, B1	A0$_1$,A0,A0$_7$,B0,B0$_1$, A1, R, A1$_1$
OneR	R, A1, A0, B0, B1	A0$_1$,A0,A0$_7$,B0$_1$,B0, A1$_1$, A1, R, A0$_5$, B1$_3$
ChiSquared	R, A1, A0, B0, B1	A0$_1$,A0,A0$_7$, B0$_1$,B0, A1$_1$, R, A1, B1$_3$

We tried the Weka´s Logistic Regression classifier (with default parameters), but the predictive accuracy was low (e.g., using Oracle attributes we obtain 77.2% average; with functions 7 to 10 the accuracy was perfect, but with the rest the accuracy was 62.2% average). We tried too with the Weka´s Multilayer Perceptron, but we obtain similar accuracies, with high processing times (e.g., 4.83 minutes to process each function).

Finally, when we test with the corrAL and corrAL-47 datasets [13], our method was the only that can remove the redundant attribute (Table 8); results for FCBF, CFS and Focus methods were taken from [13].

This suggest that our method, although requires more processing time, is a good approach to capture inter-dependencies among attributes. On the other hand, buBF processing time is competitive when we try to use wrapper feature selection methods. We point out that we do not carry out comparisons against Branch & Bound methods because these require a previous definition of the number of attributes to select, which is not necessary with buBF.

5 Conclusions and Future Work

We have presented a new algorithm for feature selection that tries to overcome some drawbacks found in Branch & Bound feature selection algorithms. The proposed method follows a forward attribute selection (instead of backward, like other methods do) finding reductions in processing time, because it is less costly to obtain the evaluation criterion for few attributes than for all the features.

Additionally, we propose a new subset evaluation criterion, that considers a balanced *n-way* entropy with respect to the combined attribute values; this metric is not very expensive and, due to the fact that is non-monotonic, heuristically allows pruning the search tree, with additional processing time savings. Furthermore, the *n-way* entropy considers the inter-dependences among features, obtaining not only isolated relevant features, and doing unnecessary a previously definition of the tree depth.

With the experiments that we performed, we observed that *gain ratio* did not work in a *n-way* schema as expected, because it penalized the evaluation strongly when many attribute-values appears (this happens when we combine two or more attributes); therefore, *gain ratio* as described in [16], is useless in our case.

Discussing about buBF processing times, we point out that buBF is relatively slow, not due to the *nwM* metric, but primarily due to the search strategy that we are currently using (best first) and to the actual implementation (still in a beta stage). We believe that if we use an improved search strategy, we will obtain similar accuracy results but in less time.

From the experimental results, with a real electric billing database and 12 synthetic datasets, the proposed method buBF represents a promising alternative, compared to other methods, because of its acceptable processing time and good performance in the feature selection task.

Some future research issues arise with respect to buBF improvement. For example: experimenting with more real databases; comparing our approach against other similar methods (e.g. Liu´s ABB [17]); using another metric variations to eliminate the data dependent parameter λ (e.g., DKM) and more efficient search methods (e.g., multi-restart hill climbing); characterize the λ parameter according to specific data (e.g., determine the best λ value given the attribute-values quantity for certain dataset); improving the tree pruning strategy and test the method with data sets with more instances and attributes.

Acknowledgements. The authors gratefully acknowledge the support of the Instituto de Investigaciones Eléctricas (Electric Research Institute). We would also like thank our anonymous reviewers.

References

1. Guyon, I., Elisseeff, A., An introduction to variable and feature selection, Journal of machine learning research, 3, 2003, pp. 1157-1182.
2. Kohavi, R., John, G., Wrappers for feature subset selection, Artificial Intelligence Journal, Special issue on relevance, 1997, pp. 273-324.
3. Piramuthu, S., Evaluating feature selection methods for learning in data mining applications, Proc. 31st annual Hawaii Int. conf. on system sciences, 1998, pp. 294-301.
4. Perner, P., Apté, C., Empirical Evaluation of Feature Subset Selection Based on a Real-World Data Set. PKDD 2000, pp. 575-580.
5. Molina, L., Belanche, L., Nebot, A., Feature selection algorithms, a survey and experimental eval, IEEE Int.conf.data mining, Maebashi City Japan, 2002, pp. 306-313.
6. Mitra, S., et.al., Data mining in soft computing framework: a survey, IEEE Trans. on neural networks, vol. 13, no. 1, January, 2002, pp. 3-14.
7. Narendra, P., Fukunaga, K., A branch and bound algorithm feature subset selection, IEEE Trans. computers, vol. 26, no. 9, sept 1977, pp. 917-922.
8. Yu, B., Yuan, B., A more efficient branch and bound algorithm for feature selection, Pattern Recognition, vol. 26, 1993, pp. 883-889.
9. Frank, A., Geiger, D., Yakhini, Z., A distance-B&B feature selection algorithm, Procc. Uncertainty in artificial intelligence, México, august. 2003, pp. 241-248.
10. Somol, P., Pudil, P., Kittler, J., Fast Branch & bound algorithms for optimal feature selection, IEEE Trans. Pattern Analysis and Machine Intelligence, vol. 26, no. 7, july 2004, pp. 900-912.
11. Jakulin, A., Bratko, I., Testing the significance of attribute interactions, Procc. Int. conf. on machine learning, Canada 2004, pp. 409-416.
12. Agrawal, R., Imielinski, T, Swami, A., Database mining: a performance perspective, IEEE Trans. Knowledge data engrg. Vol. 5, no. 6, 1993, pp. 914-925.
13. Yu, L., Liu, H., Efficient feature selection via analysis of relevance and redundancy, Journal of Machine Learning Research 5, 2004, pp. 1205-1224.
14. www. cs.waikato.ac.nz/ml/weka, 2004.
15. www. ia.uned.es/~elvira/ , 2004.
16. Quinlan, J.R., Decision trees and multi-valued attributes. In J.E.Hayes, D.Michie, and J.Richards (eds.), Machine Intelligence 11, Oxford, UK: Oxford University Press, 1988, pp. 305-318.
17. Liu, H. Motoda, and M. Dash. A monotonic measure for optimal feature selection. In Proceedings of European Conference on Machine Learning,, 1998, pp. 101-106.

Learning the Reasons Why Groups of Consumers Prefer Some Food Products

Juan José del Coz[1], Jorge Díez[1], Antonio Bahamonde[1], Carlos Sañudo[2],
Matilde Alfonso[2], Philippe Berge[3], Eric Dransfield[3], Costas Stamataris[4],
Demetrios Zygoyiannis[4], Tyri Valdimarsdottir[5], Edi Piasentier[6], Geoffrey Nute[7],
and Alan Fisher[7]

[1] Artificial Intelligence Center, University of Oviedo at Gijón, 33204 Gijón, Spain
{juanjo, jdiez, antonio}@aic.uniovi.es
[2] Facultad de Veterinaria. University of Zaragoza, Zaragoza (Aragón), Spain
csanudo@unizar.es, matilde_alfonso@ncsu.edu
[3] Unité de Recherches sur la Viande, INRA de Theeix, 63100 St. Genès- Champanelle, France.
Current address: Wageningen UR, 6700 AA wageningen, The Netherlands
{berge, dransf}@clermont.inra.fr
[4] Aristotle University, Department of Animal Health and Husbandry, Thessaloniki, Greece
{stamatar, zygoyan}@vet.auth.gr
[5] Icelandic Fisheries Laboratories, PO Box 1405, 121, Reykjavík, Iceland
maturoglyf@simnet.is
[6] Department de Science della Produzione Animale, University of Udinem, Pagnacco, Italy
edi.piasentier@uniud.it
[7] Department of Food Animal Science, University of Bristol, BS40 5DU, United Kingdom
{geoff.nute, alan.fisher}@bris.ac.uk

Abstract. In this paper we propose a method for learning the reasons why groups of consumers prefer some food products instead of others of the same type. We emphasize the role of groups given that, from a practical point of view, they may represent market segments that demand different products. Our method starts representing in a metric space people preferences; there we are able to define similarity functions that allow a clustering algorithm to discover significant groups of consumers with homogeneous tastes. Finally in each cluster, we learn, with a SVM, a function that explains the tastes of the consumers grouped in the cluster. Additionally, a feature selection process highlights the essential properties of food products that have a major influence on their acceptability. To illustrate our method, a real case of consumers of lamb meat was studied. The panel was formed by 773 people of 216 families from 6 European countries. Different tastes between Northern and Southern families were enhanced.

1 Introduction

Consumer preferences for food products address the strategies of industries and breeders, and should be carefully considered when export and commercial policies are designed. In this paper we present a method to deal with data collected from panels of consumers in order to discover groups with differentiated tastes; these groups may

P. Perner (Ed.): ICDM 2006, LNAI 4065, pp. 297–309, 2006.
© Springer-Verlag Berlin Heidelberg 2006

constitute significant market segments that demand different kinds of food products. Additionally, our approach studies the factors that contribute to the success or failure of food products in each segment.

From a conceptual point of view, the panels are made up of untrained consumers; these are asked to rate their degree of acceptance or satisfaction about the tested products on a scale. The aim is to be able to relate product descriptions (human and mechanical) with consumer preferences. Simple statistical methods can not cope with this task. In fact, this is not a straightforward task; the reason is that when we are aiming to induce a function that maps object descriptions into ratings, we must consider that consumers' ratings are just a way to express their preferences about the products presented in the same testing session. Additionally, it is necessary to realize that numerical ratings do not mean the same for all the people, the scales used may be quite different. Discussions about ratings and preferences can be found in [1], in the context of food preferences in [2, 3, 4].

To illustrate our method, we used a data set that collects the ratings of a panel of lamb meat consumers. Let us recall that the world market for this meat is quite important; in fact, among all meats, lamb meat is the most internationally traded, 15% of total world production is exported.

The panel studied was formed by 216 European families, from 6 countries, that ordered, according to their preferences, 12 kinds of lambs [5, 6]. The purpose of the study was to discover what features of lambs may explain why significant groups of consumers prefer some lamb types. Thus, we start looking for significant *clusters* of families with similar tastes.

The main assumption behind the approach presented in this paper is that we are able to map people's preferences into a metric space in such a way that we can assume some kind of continuity. In the case of lamb meat panel, the mapping can be simply given by a ranking vector of lamb types provided by each consumer or family of consumers.

However, this is not the general case. Thus, we extended the method proposed here to situations where the size of the sample of food prevents panellist from testing all products. We must take into account that usually we can not ask our panellist to spend long periods of time rating the whole set of food samples. Typically, each consumer only participates in one or a small number of testing sessions, usually in the same day. Notice that tasting a large sample of food may result physically impossible, or the number of tests performed would damage the sensory capacity of consumers. In this case we will codify people preferences by the weighting vector of a linear function in a high dimensional space; the space where we represent the descriptions of food products. Thus, the similarity is defined by means of the kernel attached to the representation map. This approach has been successfully applied in [7].

Once we have people's preferences represented in a metric space, and we have defined a similarity function, then we use a clustering algorithm. Although there are other possibilities, we used the nonparametric hierarchical clustering algorithm of Dubnov *et al.* [8] that uses a proximity matrix of pairwise relations that directly captures the intention of the similarity functions. Then in each cluster, we learn a ranking function from the descriptions of each object involved in testing sessions; so we will be able to explain why the group of consumers of the cluster prefers some kind of products instead of others. Moreover, a feature selection algorithm will point out the essential characteristics that make the difference between success and failure in the market segment that clusters represent.

The paper is organized as follows. In the next section we describe how it is possible to measure similarities between preference criteria of two consumers. In the third section we explain the clustering algorithm used. The last section is devoted to report the results achieved in the case of the data from the panel of European lamb meat consumers. We spell out the steps followed by our method in this real world case, and we review the implications both to lamb breeders and to designers of future commercial strategies.

2   Computing Distances Between Preference Criteria

This section is devoted to show how preference criteria of consumers can be mapped into a metric space where it is possible to define a similarity measure. We distinguish two situations. In the first one, each consumer already provides a ranking vector, while we require a kernel based method in the most general case.

2.1   When Everybody Tastes Everything: Using Explicit Rankings

In some cases, we have situations where there are a fixed set of food items that each tester can order in a ranking of preferences. Then, the similarity of tester preferences can be straightforward measured. In this section we analyze one of these cases, the data collected on a large panel of European families testing 12 different types of lambs.

Both lambs and families were selected from 6 different countries: Greece, Italy, and Spain (Southern countries in the European Union), and France, Iceland, and United Kingdom (Northern countries). A total of 36 families in each country rated each lamb sample (a total of 216 families); we considered the average rating of each family as the *unit* expression of their preferences; a total of 773 people were involved in the panel. The decision of averaging the ratings into each family is justified on [5], where it was noticed that there is more agreement in the rates between individuals within a household than between households; that means that there exists an important effect that might be called *family halo* in people's gastronomic preferences.

The panel was asked to rate several aspects of lamb meat on a numerical scale from 0 to 100; however, we are only going to deal with their *overall* judgement. Testing was done over a period between 3 and 6 months depending of the country. Each family received 12 hind leg joints (one from each lamb type), and they were asked to roast the joints using their own cooking criteria. It is important to notice that 108 lambs per type were used, what means 1296 animals, and 2592 hind legs. The sample is a quite wide range of lamb covering different breeds, diets, age at slaughter and weights of carcass; see Table 1 for more details.

Table 1. Description of lamb types in order of increasing carcass weight in Kg. The average age at slaughter is expressed in months.

Country of origin	Breed type	Age at slaughter	Carcass Weight	Main feeding background	Lamb Codes
Spain (ES)	Churra	1.0	5.4	Milk	4
Greece (GR)	Karagouniko	1.7	8.1	Milk	7
Spain (ES)	Rasa Aragonesa	2.8	10.0	Concentrate	3
Italy (IT)	Appenninica	2.4	11.2	Concentrate	12
United Kingdom (GB)	Welsh Mountain	7.4	15.3	Grass	2
France (FR)	Lacaune	3.3	15.3	Concentrate	6
Greece (GR)	Karagouniko	3.5	15.4	Concentrate	8
Iceland (IS)	Icelandic	4.3	15.9	Grass	10
France (FR)	Meat breeds	7.0	16.6	Grass	5
Iceland (IS)	Icelandic	4.3	16.7	Grass	9
United Kingdom (GB)	Suffolk x Mule	4.0	17.8	Grass	1
Italy (IT)	Bergamasca	12.0	30.5	Transhumance	11

The preferences expressed by each family were summarized by the ranking of lamb types ordered according to their rates. Then, the similarity of the preferences of two families was computed as the number of pairs where both rankings coincide in their relative ordering; in this case, an integer from 0 to 66. In symbols, if r_1 and r_2 are two rankings, we define

$$similarity\,(r_1, r_2) = \sum_{t_1, t_2 \in LT, t_1 \neq t_2} 1_{((r_1(t_1) - r_1(t_2))*(r_2(t_1) - r_2(t_2)) \geq 0)} \qquad (1)$$

where LT is the set of lamb types; $1_{(p(x))}$ returns 1 when $p(x)$ is true and 0 otherwise; and $r_i(t_j)$ stands for the ordinal number of lamb type t_j in ranking r_i.

2.2 In a General Case: Using Ranking Functions

In this section we deal with a more general case (see [7]) than that of lambs spelled out in the previous section. Now we assume that the consumers involved in a panel can be divided into sociological categories or *units*, and that each person has rated a limited number of samples in one or a few sessions. Therefore it is not straightforward to compute a ranking of food products for each unit. Instead of that, we are going to induce a function able to captures somehow the criteria used to express unit preferences. Then we will manage to define similarities in the space of those functions.

Although there are other approaches to learn preferences, following [9, 10, 11] we will try to induce a real *preference*, *ranking*, or *utility function* f from the space of object descriptions, say $\mathbf{R}^d$, in such a way that it maximizes the probability of having $f(\mathbf{x}) > f(\mathbf{y})$ whenever $\mathbf{x}$ is preferable to $\mathbf{y}$; we call such pairs, *preference judgments*. This functional approach can start from a set of objects endowed with a (usually ordinal) rating, as in regression; but essentially, we only need a collection of preference judgments.

When we have a set of ratings given by members of a unit u, we most take into account the session where the ratings have been assessed [2, 4]. Thus, for each session we consider the average of all ratings given by members of the unit to each sample presented in the session; then we include in the set of preference judgments PJ_u the pairs $(\mathbf{x}, \mathbf{y})$ whenever the sample represented by $\mathbf{x}$ had higher rating than the sample represented by $\mathbf{y}$. In this way, we can overcome the *batch effect*: a product will obtain a higher/lower rating when it is assessed together with other products that are clearly worse/better. In fact, if we try to deal with sensory data as a regression problem, we will fail [3]; due to the batch effect, the ratings have no numerical meaning: they are only a relative way to express preferences between products of the same session.

In order to induce the ranking function, we can use the approach presented by Herbrich *et al.* in [9]. So, we look for a function F_u: $\mathbf{R^d} \times \mathbf{R^d} \rightarrow \mathbf{R}$ such that

$$\forall \mathbf{x}, \mathbf{y} \in \mathbf{R}^d, \ F_u(\mathbf{x}, \mathbf{y}) > 0 \Leftrightarrow F_u(\mathbf{x}, 0) > F_u(\mathbf{y}, 0) \tag{2}$$

Then, the ranking function f_u: $\mathbf{R^d} \rightarrow \mathbf{R}$ can be defined by $F_u(\mathbf{x}, 0)$ plus any constant.

Given the set of preference judgments PJ_u, we can specify F_u by means of the constraints

$$\forall \ (\mathbf{x}, \mathbf{y}) \in PJ_u, \ F_u(\mathbf{x}, \mathbf{y}) > 0 \text{ and } F_u(\mathbf{y}, \mathbf{x}) < 0 \tag{3}$$

Therefore, PJ_u gives rise to a set of binary classification training set

$$E_u = \{(\mathbf{x}, \mathbf{y}, +1), (\mathbf{y}, \mathbf{x}, -1): (\mathbf{x}, \mathbf{y}) \in PJ_u\} \tag{4}$$

Nevertheless, a separating function for E_u does not necessarily fulfill (2). Thus, we need an additional constraint about the antisymmetrical role that we require for the objects of E_u entries. So, if we represent each object description $\mathbf{x}$ in a higher dimensional feature space by means of $\phi(\mathbf{x})$, then we can represent pairs $(\mathbf{x}, \mathbf{y})$ by $\phi(\mathbf{x}) - \phi(\mathbf{y})$. Hence, a classification SVM can induce the function of the form:

$$F_u(\mathbf{x}, \mathbf{y}) = \sum_{s \in SV_u} \alpha_s z_s \left\langle \phi(\mathbf{x}_s^{(1)}) - \phi(\mathbf{x}_s^{(2)}), \phi(\mathbf{x}) - \phi(\mathbf{y}) \right\rangle \tag{5}$$

where $<\mathbf{x}, \mathbf{y}>$ stands for the inner product of vectors $\mathbf{x}$ and $\mathbf{y}$; SV_u is the set of support vectors, notice that they are formed by two d-dimensional vectors $(\mathbf{x}_s^{(1)}, \mathbf{x}_s^{(2)})$, while the scalars z_s represent the class $+1$ or -1. Trivially, F_u fulfils the condition (2).

Notice that if k is a kernel function defined as the inner product of two objects represented in the feature space, that is, $k(\mathbf{x}, \mathbf{y}) = <\phi(\mathbf{x}), \phi(\mathbf{y})>$, then the kernel function used to induce F_u is

$$K(\mathbf{x}_1, \mathbf{x}_2, \mathbf{x}_3, \mathbf{x}_4) = k(\mathbf{x}_1, \mathbf{x}_3) - k(\mathbf{x}_1, \mathbf{x}_4) - k(\mathbf{x}_2, \mathbf{x}_3) + k(\mathbf{x}_2, \mathbf{x}_4) \tag{6}$$

Usually it is employed a linear or a simple polynomial kernel; that is, $k(\mathbf{x}, \mathbf{y}) = \langle \mathbf{x}, \mathbf{y} \rangle$, or $k(\mathbf{x}, \mathbf{y}) = (\langle \mathbf{x}, \mathbf{y} \rangle + c)^g$, with $c = 1$ and $g = 2$.

Once we have a function F_u for a unit u fulfilling (2), then a utility function f_u is given by

$$f_u(x) = \sum_{s \in SV_u} \alpha_s z_s \left\langle \phi(\mathbf{x}_s^{(1)}) - \phi(\mathbf{x}_s^{(2)}), \phi(\mathbf{x}) \right\rangle = \sum_{s \in SV_u} \alpha_s z_s \left(k(\mathbf{x}_s^{(1)}, \mathbf{x}) - k(\mathbf{x}_s^{(2)}, \mathbf{x}) \right) \tag{7}$$

Therefore, f_u can be represented by the weight vector $\mathbf{w}_u$ in the higher dimensional space of features such that

$$f_u(\mathbf{x}) = <\mathbf{w}_u, \phi(\mathbf{x})>, \tag{8}$$

where

$$\mathbf{w}_u = \sum_{s \in SV_u} \alpha_s z_s \left(\phi(\mathbf{x}_s^{(1)}) - \phi(\mathbf{x}_s^{(2)}) \right) \tag{9}$$

Now we only need to define the distance of unit preferences. Given that preferences are codified by those weighting vectors, we define the similarity of the preferences of units u and u' by the cosine of their weighting vectors. In symbols,

$$similarity(\mathbf{w}_u, \mathbf{w}_{u'}) = \cos(\mathbf{w}_u, \mathbf{w}_{u'}) = \frac{\langle \mathbf{w}_u, \mathbf{w}_{u'} \rangle}{\|\mathbf{w}_u\| * \|\mathbf{w}_{u'}\|} \tag{10}$$

Given that this definition uses scalar products instead of coordinates of weighting vectors, we can easily rewrite (10) in terms of the kernels used in the previous derivations. The essential equality is:

$$
\begin{aligned}
\langle \mathbf{w}_u, \mathbf{w}_{u'} \rangle &= \sum_{s \in SV_u} \sum_{l \in SV_{u'}} \alpha_s \alpha_l z_s z_l \left\langle \phi(\mathbf{x}_s^{(1)}) - \phi(\mathbf{x}_s^{(2)}), \phi(\mathbf{x}_l^{(1)}) - \phi(\mathbf{x}_l^{(2)}) \right\rangle \\
&= \sum_{s \in SV_u} \sum_{l \in SV_{u'}} \alpha_s \alpha_l z_s z_l \mathbf{K}\left(\mathbf{x}_s^{(1)}, \mathbf{x}_s^{(2)}, \mathbf{x}_l^{(1)}, \mathbf{x}_l^{(2)} \right)
\end{aligned}
\tag{11}
$$

3 Generalizing Preferences from Consumers to Groups

Once we have defined a reasonable similarity measure for preference criteria, we proceed to look for clusters of consumers with homogeneous tastes. In principle, we could use any available clustering algorithm. However, we avoided those methods, like k-means, that require frequent recomputations of the centroids of each cluster. The reason is that the updating of (11) would result very uncomfortable. Additionally, we need a mechanism able to estimate a reasonably number of clusters directly from the data, without any explicit manual intervention.

Hence, we applied a nonparametric pairwise algorithm of Dubnov et al. [8], although this is not probably the only possibility. The following paragraphs sketch a description of this algorithm as we used it in the experimental results reported in the last section.

3.1 The Clustering Algorithm

Let $S = (s_{ij})$ be a square matrix where s_{ij} stands for the similarity between data points i and j; in our case, data points are the vectorial representation of the preference criteria of consumer units, and similarities are given by equations (1) or (10). In the following, S will be called the *proximity matrix*.

The matrix S is transformed iteratively, following a two step procedure that makes it to converge to a binary matrix, yielding a bipartition of the data set into two clusters. Then, recursively, the partition mechanism is applied to each of the resulting clusters represented by their corresponding submatrices. To guarantee that only meaningful splits take places, Dubnov *et al.* [8] provide a cross validation method that measures an index that can be read as a significance level; we will only accept splits in which the level is above 95%.

The basic iterative transformation uses the following formulae to go from iteration t to t+1:

$$p_{ij}(t+1) = \frac{s_{ij}(t)}{max\{|s_{ik}(t)| : k\}}$$

$$s_{ij}(t+1) = \frac{1}{2}\sum_k p_{ik}(t+1)\log\frac{p_{ik}(t+1)}{\frac{1}{2}(p_{ik}(t+1)+p_{jk}(t+1))}$$

$$+\frac{1}{2}\sum_k p_{jk}(t+1)\log\frac{p_{jk}(t+1)}{\frac{1}{2}(p_{jk}(t+1)+p_{ik}(t+1))}$$

(12)

The first step gives rise to (p_{ij}) normalizing the columns of the proximity matrix using the L_∞ norm; then the proximities are re-estimated using the Jensen-Shannon divergence. The idea is to formalize that two preference criteria are close (after these two steps) if they were both similar and dissimilar to analogous sets of criteria before the transformation.

This method of clustering preference criteria is quite different from a work presented in [12]. That approach is based on the estimation of learning errors in the data sets of groups; therefore, the method requires a lot of data available, what make difficult its use when we are dealing with sensory data since the amount of data available is usually very scarce. Additionally, that method is a bottom-up clustering algorithm which tends to produce many clusters. In sensorial analysis applications, we don't expect that many market segments exist, so a top-down clustering is more adequate.

3.2 The Preference Function of Groups

Given a set of clusters {Cluster(j): j = 1:n}, we have to explain the reasons that make people of each cluster to have those similar criteria that make them different from people of other clusters. The best way to achieve this is to induce a preference function using product descriptions. The learning algorithm is the SVM explained in section 2.2, but notice that now instead of using the preference judgments PJ_u sets of individual units, we consider for each cluster the union

$$PJ_{cluster(j)} = \bigcup_{u \in cluster(j)} PJ_u$$

(13)

The preference functions (see equation (7)) will be useful for two different things. First, we can compute the average ranking of the cluster, and the estimation of the ranking position of future products given their descriptions. Second, we can determine the influence of each feature that describes food products in the acceptability by consumers of the market segment represented by clusters. Therefore, we will be able to design policies to improve the acceptability by different kinds of consumers.

Feature influence analysis is not a straightforward task and it must be handled with care to obtain useful results. Different approaches must be used depending if we deal with linear or non-linear functions [13, 14, 15, 16]. For the aims of this paper, we use adaptations of these selection algorithms to preference learning [2, 4, 11].

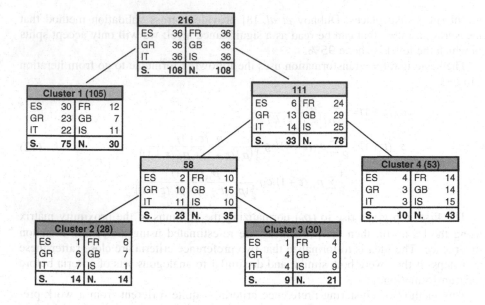

Fig. 1. Trace of the clustering algorithm. In each node we report the total number of families, the number of families of each country, and the sum of families from Southern and Northern European countries.

4 Experimental Results

In this section we report the results obtained with the data base of the European lamb panel. As was described in section 2.1, the distances between the preferences of two families was computed as the number of pairs with a disagreement in their relative order.

The clustering algorithm [8] returns the tree of 4 leaves depicted in Figure 1. All split nodes achieved a high confidence level: 100%, 95% and 97% respectively from top to bottom. Clusters 1 and 4 are the biggest; they sum 105 and 53 families, while the other two clusters represent minority market segments of 28 and 30 families each. The rankings of lamb types that capture the preferences of each cluster are reported at Table 2.

The degree of consensus achieved into the clusters can be estimated by the cross validation error of the classification SVM used to compute the rankings of each cluster when we merged the preference judgments of all families involved. In this case, each lamb type was described by 98 attributes reporting the data included in Table 1, chemical and physical properties of the meat, and a sensory description given by a set of trained experts. The cross validation estimations for these errors are, for cluster 1 to 4, 29.25%, 35.59%, 30.94%, and 36.64%, respectively. It is important to notice here that if, for each pair of lambs, we choose the most frequent relative ordering in each cluster, then the number of disagreements would be, 28.52%, 30.02%, 29.32%, and

32.31%, respectively in the four clusters. Therefore, the estimation of accuracy of the preferences functions induced is quite high.

Additionally, the processes of preference learning provide us the scores reported in Table 2; they are computed as the normalized values (in the range [0, 100]) returned by the corresponding ranking functions f_u (equation 7) of the clusters. These values can be interpreted as the *average* ratings into the clusters, but considering the individual ratings just as preference judgments instead of numeric values.

Table 2. Composition and rankings for each cluster. We report the number of families from South and North European countries. The ranking of lamb types is shown by columns; cells shaded correspond to types with a country of origin in the South of Europe; the score column gives the normalized (between 0 and 100) outputs of the ranking function (learned for the corresponding cluster) in each lamb type.

	Cluster 1		Cluster 2		Cluster 3		Cluster 4	
	# Families	%	# Families	%	# Families	%	# Families	%
South	75	71.4%	14	50%	9	30%	10	18.9%
North	30	28.6%	14	50%	21	70%	43	81.1%
Rank	Lamb type	Score	Lamb type	Score	Lamb type	Score	Lamb type	Score
1	4	100	11	100	11	100	6	100
2	3	84,5	5	62,8	8	72,8	5	89,3
3	12	77,5	1	51,1	2	68,9	8	89,3
4	6	64,9	4	47,1	6	63,6	9	84,7
5	7	62,7	3	46,4	10	58,5	10	70,5
6	8	58,1	2	37,6	3	55,9	1	68,2
7	9	55,4	8	28,7	1	46,8	2	67,8
8	5	51,0	9	18,5	9	46,4	7	59,4
9	1	45,0	6	10,4	5	40,8	12	59,1
10	2	44,6	7	3,5	7	34,5	3	25,8
11	10	44,0	12	1,4	12	30,0	4	23,4
12	11	0	10	0	4	0	11	0

4.1 Implications for Lamb Markets and Breeders

In general, it is well known that meat qualities are mainly the result of a set of complex factors somehow inherent in animal's breed, rearing system, and feeding background. With the panel available, we can try to quantify these biological complexities with the additional difficulty of measuring meat qualities through the sensorial appreciations of people with different geographical extractions.

In this sense, there are several conclusions that can be drawn from Table 2. First, we observe that the lamb type of code 11, the oldest and heaviest (see Table 1), divides the preferences of clusters; so while in clusters 1 and 4 this lamb type is the least appreciated, on the other two clusters, it is the most appreciated lamb type. This is a lamb with a very strong flavor and odor what arouses vivid reactions.

However, the most striking result is that the most representative clusters arrange the majority of families from Southern and Northern European countries respectively. Moreover, lamb types with origin in southern countries are the most appreciated in Southern countries, and the same happens if we refer to Northern countries and lambs.

Most people like best the kind of lambs that they are used to eat at home. In other words, European lamb consumers seem to be very influenced by their culinary and cultural background.

To illustrate this point, we only have to observe the opposite role played by the sequence of lamb types 4, 3, and 12. While they occupy the leading positions in the mainly Southern cluster 1; they are relegated to the bottom of the list in the cluster of the mainly Northern families (clusters 4 and 3). These lamb types are the lightest (if we exclude the type 7) with a milk and concentrate diets.

Another important source of information is the relevancy of the features that take part in the learning process. In this case, the most relevant descriptors of lamb types in each cluster ranking are *phospholipids (php) fraction*, and *neural lipid (nl) fatty acids fraction*. However, from a practical point of view this information is not directly practicable; since it is not obvious at all how we can *improve* the *php* or the *nl* of lambs. Notice that the term 'improve' is a relative expression in this context, since its exact meaning depends on the cluster.

The question is what *visible* lamb features can be identified with people's preferences? Or how can a breeder produce lambs for a given market segment? To answer these questions we have to realize that there are some features like age, weight, and feeding, that are easily modifiable by breeders. Moreover, using only these features and their products, it is possible to explain the rankings of each cluster. Thus, these features are not only visible and modifiable, but they content also enough information so as to approach a guide to breeders and designers of marketing strategies. Table 3 reports the contribution of these features to the ranking of each cluster.

Table 3. Contribution to the preferences in each cluster of the main attributes of lamb types: those where breeders can act over them in order to improve the popularity of their lamb meats

Attribute	Cluster 1		Cluster 2		Cluster 3		Cluster 4	
	Sign	Relevancy	Sign	Relevancy	Sign	Relevancy	Sign	Relevancy
milk	+	4	-	2	-	5	-	1
grass	-	1	+	5	+	3	+	3
concentrate	+	3	-	4	+	2	+	4
age	-	5	+	1	+	4	-	2
weight	-	2	+	3	+	1	+	5

To obtain these data, from the preference judgments expressed by the ranking of each cluster, we built one classification training set. Each lamb type (see Table 1) was described using 5 features: age, weight, and 3 binary features, one to describe if the feeding background was or not milk, another for grass, and a third one for concentrate. Then if t_1 was preferred to t_2, we included $t_1 - t_2$ with class +1, and $t_2 - t_1$ with class −1 in the corresponding training set. Notice that each of these training sets has 132 examples.

According to section 2.2, the coefficients of the hyperplane that separates the positive and negative classes are the weights of the features in the ranking function: a computational model of the preferences of the cluster. In Table 3 we report the signs of these coefficients. Notice that there is not any feature with the same sign in all clusters. On the other hand, we observe that the differences in sign from cluster 1 to the other 3 is the biggest of any single cluster; this would explain, from another point of view, the clustering distribution proposed by the algorithm of Dubnov *et al.* [8]. The split of clusters 2, 3 and 4 can even be conjectured from their sign distributions.

In addition to sign we include in Table 3, the order of relevancy of each of the features. Here we used a procedure based on the Gram-Schmidt orthogonalization, see [16]. The information provided by this ordering allows us to gain insight into the strength of the features of lamb types when they are used to explain the preferences of a cluster.

From cluster 1 and cluster 4, related with South and Northern families respectively, we observe as in the South young animals, with small slaughter weight, reared with milk or concentrate are preferred. Whereas in the North countries, grass or concentrate fed lambs, with high carcass weights, are the most appreciated. These results are related with the culinary habits of the consumers, as was pointed out in [17]; additionally, the results justify the idea that it is necessary to produce lamb meat taking into consideration the destination market.

5 Conclusions

In this paper we propose a method for learning the reasons why groups of consumers prefer some food products instead of others of the same type. To illustrate our method, a real case of consumers of lamb meat was studied and we pointed out some practical conclusions that can allow breeders to design policies to improve the acceptability of lamb meat by different market segments.

The proposed method stresses that it is possible to map with continuity people's preferences into a metric space, where it is possible to compute the similarity between preference criteria. In this context we distinguish two kinds of situations: i) all consumers rate all products, then the similarity is computed as the number of preference judgements pairs where their rankings coincide; and ii) each consumer only rates some products of the sample, then we codify their preferences by linear functions in a high dimensional space and compute the similarity between these ranking functions by means of a kernel based method.

Once we have a reasonable similarity measure for preference criteria, the main goal is to discover different groups of consumers (or market segments) and explain why consumers of each group prefer some kind of products. For this purpose, we use three learning tools: i) to group people with similar preferences, a hierarchical clustering algorithm that directly captures the intention of the similarity functions using a proximity matrix of pairwise relations; ii) a SVM algorithm to learn preferences functions using the descriptions of the products; and iii) a feature selection algorithm to point out the essential characteristics that make the difference between success and failure in the market segment that each cluster represents.

Acknowledgments

The research reported in this paper is supported in part under the grant TIN2005-08288 from the Spanish Ministerio de Educación y Ciencia.

We would like to thank: the authors of Spider [18], a MatLab toolbox that includes kernel based algorithms; and Thorsten Joachims [19] for his SVM^{light}. Those systems were used in the experiments reported in this paper.

References

1. Cohen, W., Shapire, R., Singer, Y.: Learning to order things. Journal of Artificial Intelligence Research, 10 (1999) 243–270.
2. Del Coz, J. J., Bayón, G. F., Díez, J., Luaces, O., Bahamonde, A., Sañudo, C.: Trait selection for assessing beef meat quality using non-linear SVM. Proceedings of the Eighteenth Annual Conference on Neural Information Processing Systems (NIPS 2004). Vancouver, British Columbia, Canada, December (2004) 13–18.
3. Díez, J., Bayón, G. F., Quevedo, J. R., del Coz, J. J., Luaces, O., Alonso, J., Bahamonde, A.: Discovering relevancies in very difficult regression problems: applications to sensory data analysis. Proceedings of the European Conference on Artificial Intelligence (ECAI '04), Valencia, Spain (2004) 993–994.
4. Luaces, O., Bayón, G.F., Quevedo, J.R., Díez, J., del Coz, J.J., Bahamonde, A.: Analyzing sensory data using non-linear preference learning with feature subset selection. Proceedings of the 15th European Conference of Machine Learning (2004) 286–297.
5. Dransfield, E., Martin, J-F., Fisher, A., Nute, G.R., Zygyiannis, D., Stamataris, C., Thorkelsson, G., Valdimarsdottir, T., Piasentier, E., Mills, C., Sañudo, C., Alfonso, M.: Home Placement Testing of Lamb Conducted in Six Countries. Journal of Sensory Studies, 15 (2000) : 421–436.
6. Sañudo, C., Alfonso, M., Sanchez, A., Berge, F., Dransfield, E., Zygoyiannis, D., Stamataris, C., Thorkelsson, G., Valdimarsdottir, T., Piasentier, E., Mills, C., Nute, G., Fisher, A.: Meat texture of lambs from different European production systems. Australian Journal of Agricultural Research, 54 (2003) 551–560.
7. Díez, J., del Coz, J. J., Sañudo, C., Albertí, P., Bahamonde, A.: A Kernel Based Method for Discovering Market Segments in Beef Meat. Proceedings of the 9th European Conference on Principles and Practice of Knowledge Discovery in Databases, (2005) 462–469.
8. Dubnov, S., El-Yaniv, R., Gdalyahu, Y., Schneidman, E., Tishby, N., Yona, G.: A New Nonparametric Pairwise Clustering Algorithm Based on Iterative Estimation of Distance Profiles. Machine Learning, 47 (2002) 35–61.
9. Herbrich, R., Graepel, T., Obermayer, K.: Large margin rank boundaries for ordinal regression. In A. Smola, P. Bartlett, B. Scholkopf, and D. Schuurmans, editors, Advances in Large Margin Classifiers, MIT Press, Cambridge, MA. (2000) 115–132.
10. Joachims, T.: Optimizing search engines using clickthrough data. In: Proceedings of the ACM Conference on Knowledge Discovery and Data Mining (KDD) (2002).
11. Bahamonde, A., Bayón, G. F., Díez, J., Quevedo, J. R., Luaces, O., del Coz, J. J., Alonso, J., Goyache, F.: Feature subset selection for learning preferences: a case study. Proceedings of the 21st International Conference on Machine Learning, ICML (2004) 49–56.
12. Díez, J., del Coz, J.J., Luaces, O., Bahamonde, A.: A clustering algorithm to find groups with homogeneous preferences. In the 26th Annual International ACM Conference on Research and Development in Information Retrieval (SIGIR '03), Workshop on Implicit Measures of User Interests and Preferences, Toronto, Canada, (2003).
13. Guyon, I., Weston, J., Barnhill, S., & Vapnik, V.: Gene selection for cancer classification using support vector machines. Machine Learning, 46 (2002) 389–422.

14. Rakotomamonjy, A.: Variable selection using SVM-based criteria. Journal of Machine Learning Research, 3 (2003) 1357–1370.
15. Degroeve, S., De Baets, B., Van de Peer, Y., Rouzé, P.: Feature subset selection for splice site prediction. Bioinformatics, 18 (2002) 75–83.
16. Stoppiglia, H., Dreyfus, G., Dubois, R., Oussar, Y.: Ranking a Random Feature for Variable and Feature Selection. Journal of Machine Learning Research; 3 (2003) 1399–1414.
17. Sañudo C, Nute GR, Campo MM, María GA, Baker A, Sierra I, Enser M, Wood JD. Assessment of commercial lamb meat quality by British ad Spanish taste panels. Meat Science 48 (1998) 91–100.
18. Weston, J., Elisseeff, A., BakIr, G., Sinz, F.: SPIDER: object-orientated machine learning library. http://www.kyb.tuebingen.mpg.de/bs/people/spider/.
19. Joachims, T.. Making large-Scale SVM Learning Practical. Advances in Kernel Methods - Support Vector Learning, B. Schölkopf and C. Burges and A. Smola (ed.), MIT-Press, (1999).

Exploiting Randomness for Feature Selection in Multinomial Logit: A CRM Cross-Sell Application

Anita Prinzie and Dirk Van den Poel

Department of Marketing, Ghent University, Hoveniersberg 24, 9000 Ghent, Belgium
{Anita.Prinzie, Dirk.VandenPoel}@UGent.be

Abstract. Data mining applications addressing classification problems must master two key tasks: feature selection and model selection. This paper proposes a random feature selection procedure integrated within the multinomial logit (MNL) classifier to perform both tasks simultaneously. We assess the potential of the random feature selection procedure (exploiting randomness) as compared to an expert feature selection method (exploiting domain-knowledge) on a CRM cross-sell application. The results show great promise as the predictive accuracy of the integrated random feature selection in the MNL algorithm is substantially higher than that of the expert feature selection method.

1 Introduction

In data mining classification applications feature and model selection are key tasks [7].

Feature selection pertains to selecting a relevant subset of features from the original feature space. There is a plenitude of reasons for the need of feature selection. Firstly, rapid evolution in computer storage capacity evokes an explosion in available data. However, computer power cannot keep pace with these storage evolutions and with computational requirements of algorithms, thereby implicitly forcing the researcher to reduce the dimensionality of the input space provided to learning algorithms. One such reduction strategy is feature selection. As humans are ineffective in selecting influential features from such huge feature spaces [18], feature selection algorithms are necessary. Secondly, in fields like text mining [17] and genomic analysis [23] the small ratio between the number of available training instances and the number of features necessitates feature selection. Thirdly, in a supervised learning problem mapping the feature space X (M features) into Y (K classes), the attributes providing the algorithm with an optimal description of the classes are a priori unknown. As a result, a number of irrelevant and redundant features are included in the feature space. Unfortunately, many learning algorithms, both in machine learning and statistics, suffer from the curse of dimensionality. Multinomial logit (MNL), a popular method within choice modeling, is no exception to that. In such a case, unnecessary features only increase the learning period as they complicate the learning problem [22]. Furthermore, redundant features introduce multicollinearity, a serious problem for MNL, thereby potentially obstructing the convergence of the learning algorithm. Fourthly, besides the aforementioned reasons, there are also positive

P. Perner (Ed.): ICDM 2006, LNAI 4065, pp. 310–323, 2006.
© Springer-Verlag Berlin Heidelberg 2006

arguments for feature selection. Feature selection speeds up the data mining algorithm, improves mining accuracy [13] and increases comprehensibility [18].

The second task involves the optimization of the classifier with respect to the selected features, i.e. model selection. Both problems, i.e. feature and model selection, should be addressed simultaneously to achieve the best classification results [7].

In this paper, we propose a random feature selection procedure integrated within the MNL classifier to perform both tasks simultaneously. We illustrate this new procedure on a Customer Relationship Management (CRM) cross-sell application (cf. choice modeling). CRM data is characterized by many input variables and consequently, feature selection is a fertile field of research within the CRM domain [7]. Typically, features describing customer behavior are retrieved from a huge transactional database. For instance in choice modeling, a popular application field within the CRM domain, the data mining classification algorithms are employed to predict customer's choices based on a series of explanatory variables. These typically include socio-demographical data and a multitude on purchase-behavior related variables. Random utility (RU) models are well-established methods describing discrete choice behavior. To date, the MNL model is the most popular RU model due to its closed-form choice-probability solution [2]. Moreover, MNL's robustness [1] is greatly appreciated. Unfortunately, MNL suffers from the curse of dimensionality thereby implicitly necessitating feature selection (cf. supra). In glaring contrast to binary logit, to date, software packages mostly lack any feature selection algorithm for MNL. To accommodate this unanswered need for feature selection for MNL, this paper introduces the random feature selection in MNL. Its potential is assessed by com-paring the predictive accuracy of a MNL model with random feature selection (exploiting randomness) to the accuracy of a MNL with expert feature selection (exploiting domain-knowledge).

The remainder of the paper is structured as follows. In the methodology section, we briefly discuss the MNL algorithm. Next, we provide some argumentation for our new random feature selection in MNL and we elucidate the technical properties of the proposed selection procedure. We also elaborate on the MNL with expert feature selection, which serves as benchmark for our new method. In Section 3, we describe the CRM cross-sell application in which we illustrate our new feature selection method. Section 4 discusses the main findings. Finally, the last Section draws conclusions and suggests several avenues for further research.

2 Methodology

2.1 MultiNomial Logit

Within multinomial-discrete choice modeling [5], RU models define a random utility function U_{ik} for each individual i for choice k belonging to choice set D_K with $K > 2$ (cf. multiclass). This random utility is decomposed into a deterministic and stochastic component (1):

$$U_{ik} = \beta' x_{ik} + \varepsilon_{ik} .$$
(1)

where x is a matrix of observed attributes which might be choice (e.g. price of product) or individual specific (e.g. age of customer), β' is a vector of unobserved marginal utilities (parameters) and ε_{ik} is an unobserved random error term (i.e. disturbance term or stochastic component). Different assumptions on the error term of the random utility function U_{ik} give rise to different classes of models. In this paper, we apply the MultiNomial Logit (MNL, independent and i.i.d. disturbances). The probability of choosing an alternative k among K_i choices for individual i can be written as in (2). The classifier predicts the class with the highest posterior probability for individual i.

$$P_i(k) = \frac{\exp(x'_{ik} \beta)}{\sum_{k \in K} \exp(x'_{ik} \beta)}. \tag{2}$$

We will estimate a MNL model incorporating all features. This model might serve as benchmark for the random feature selection in MNL as well as for the MNL with expert feature selection.

2.2 Random Feature Selection in MNL (rfs_MNL)

Feature Selection Algorithm Motivation. Our new random feature selection procedure can be justified based on the unifying platform by Liu and Hu [18]. This platform is a first attempt to create an integrated system automatically recommending the most suitable feature selection algorithm(s) to the user. Starting from this platform, we determined what kind of feature selection algorithm might be appropriate for the application at hand. At the top of the platform, knowledge and data about feature selection are two key factors. The proposed random feature selection method is mainly motivated by the knowledge factor of the platform.

The knowledge factor covers purpose of feature selection, time, expected output type, and m/M ratio, i.e. the ratio between the expected number of selected features m and the total number of features M. The *purpose of feature selection* can be visualization, data understanding, data cleaning, redundancy and/or irrelevancy removal, and performance (e.g. predictive accuracy and comprehensibility) enhancement. In our CRM cross-sell application, the purposes of feature selection are redundancy removal (cf. reducing multicollinearity) and performance enhancement. Given the latter, a wrapper algorithm should be preferred to a filter model as it is better suited to the mining algorithm [16]. In the filter approach, feature selection employs evaluation criteria (e.g. information-gain, distances) independent of the learning algorithm. As such filter approaches disregard the classifier with which the selected features are to be used in the model selection task. Conversely, the wrapper model searches for features better suited to the mining algorithm thereby optimizing the classifiers performance. The *time concern* is whether the feature selection process is time critical or not. In a competitive retail environment like the home-appliances industry (cf. application), time is extremely critical. Therefore, algorithms with sequential search or random search should be selected for fast results [18]. Our new random feature selection method starts with a randomly selected subset and proceeds by generating new subsets in a completely random manner, i.e. random search. This use of randomness helps to escape local optima in the search space and optimality of the selected subset dependent on the resources available. The *output type of feature selection* can be a minimum subset or a ranked list. A minimum subset does not indicate order among the features in the selected subset. In our cross-sell application, we prefer a ranked list to such a minimum subset, as we want to be able to make a cost-benefit analysis (performance/financial cost) of removing features. Finally, the *expected m/M ratio* determines a proper search strategy. In our CRM application, we expect this ratio to be small so a sequential forward search is more appropriate than a sequential backward search. We opt for a random search (cf. supra). To recap, the knowledge factor of the unifying platform advises us to apply a wrapper algorithm (maximization of performance) adopting a sequential or random search method (critical time and small expected m/M ratio) and outputting a ranked list of features. Our random feature selection method in MNL fits in the wrapper approach, adopts a random search method and returns besides a classifier, also a ranked list of features.

Another justification we retrieve from Melgani and Bruzzone [19]. They discuss several strategies to overcome Hughes phenomenon; on increasing the number of features given as input to the classifier over a given threshold (which depends on the number of training instances and the classifier), the classification accuracy decreases. One such strategy is the combination of classifiers. We argue that MNL also suffers from Hughes phenomenon due to its susceptibility to convergence problems because of multicollinearity between the features. Our random feature selection method for MNL combines several MNLs estimated on a random selection of features.

Finally, the random feature selection in MNL does not only exploit randomness by starting from random feature subsets. Traditional feature selection algorithms perform dimensionality reduction no matter the data input. However, feature selection might be enhanced by selecting instances from the data [18]. Therefore, our random feature selection in MNL exploits the potential of random input selection as a second source of randomness (cf. Random Forests [6]). Hence, the random feature selection in MNL performs feature and model selection simultaneously by combining R MNLs estimated on the r-th bootstrap sample including m randomly selected features.

Random Feature Selection in MNL. This paper proposes a random-feature selection wrapper algorithm integrated in MNL performing the feature and model selection tasks simultaneously. The random feature selection in MNL combines R MNLs with m randomly selected features estimated on the r-th bootstrap sample. The combination of MNLs with m randomly selected features addresses the multicollinearity problem. The ensemble of MNLs might contain a collection of highly correlated features, but each MNL is estimated on a selection of features with a total multicollinearity lower than the unknown threshold causing convergence problems for a single MNL, hereby mitigating Hughes phenomenon.

Moreover, this ensemble of MNLs with R * m randomly selected features will output a ranked list of the collection of features used by the ensemble allowing a cost-benefit analysis of inclusion/exclusion of a feature. We use the out-of-bag (oob) data to estimate the feature importances. By presenting each instance i left out of the construction of the r-th multinomial regression to the r-th MNL, we obtain a misclassification rate on oob data. To measure the importance of the v-th unique variable in the ensemble, we randomly permute this variable in the oob data and feed into the corresponding MNL. Subtract the number of votes for the correct class in the variable-v-permuted data from the number of correct votes in the untouched data and average over all R MNLs. This is the raw importance score for variable m from which we infer the standardized importance score z. The wrapper approach of the algorithm boils down to the fact that for each randomly generated subset S_r, the selection algorithm evaluates its goodness by applying the MNL algorithm to the bootstrap data with feature subset S_r and evaluating the predictive accuracy of the r-th MNL. Finally, the random feature selection in MNL classifies instances by delivering their input vector to the R MultiNomial Logits. Let $p_r(x)$ be the class probability distribution predicted by the r-th MNL on example x. The probability distribution vectors returned by the R MNLs are averaged to obtain the class probability distribution of the ensemble of R MNLs (3). This amounts to the adjusted Majority Vote, a refinement of the Majority Vote algorithm suited to learning algorithms producing continuous outcomes. The instance is classified into the class having the highest combined posterior probability.

$$P_{R_{RMNL}} = \frac{1}{R} \sum_{r=1}^{R} p_r(x).$$ (3)

2.3 MNL with Expert Feature Selection

We compare the predictive performance of the random feature selection integrated in MNL (exploiting randomness) with a MNL with feature selection based on human know-how of the CRM domain (exploiting domain-knowledge), i.e. 'MNL with expert feature selection'. Similar to the random feature selection method, we adopt the wrapper approach, selecting features improving the MNL algorithm's performance. The expert feature selection combines sequential search (search per feature block and not over all M) with complete search (within feature blocks). In a first step, the CRM expert relies on his domain-knowledge to extract from the feature space several blocks of features capturing potential influential dimensions of consumer-choice behavior. In a second step, to reduce multicollinearity in the final model, the best set of two features (blocks 1 to 8, cf. infra) or the single best feature (blocks 9 and 10) is selected within each block. In the last step, from the selected features in step 2, the best five features are withdrawn (over blocks 1 to 8). The model selection involves the estimation of the MNL model on the retained features.

2.4 Predictive Model Evaluation: wPCC and AUC

The predictive performance of the random feature selection in MNL and the MNL with expert feature selection is evaluated in terms of wPCC and AUC on a separate test set, i.e. a data set of instances not used for feature and model selection.

In absence of a specific predictive objective, e.g. predict classes k=1 and k=3 well, we evaluate the algorithms in terms of their ability to correctly classify cases in all classes K. Given this objective and the small class imbalance of the dependent (i.e. differences in class prior probabilities biasing predictions towards the dominant class, cf. infra), it is inappropriate [3] to express the classification performance in terms of the average accuracy like the Percentage Correctly Classified (PCC), i.e. the total number of correctly classified relative to the total number of predicted instances [20]. The predictive evaluation of the models should therefore take the distribution of the multinomial dependent variable into consideration [20]. Firstly, we will weigh the class-specific PCCs with regard to the prior class distribution. Each class k ($k \in$ K) of the dependent variable has a strict positive weight w_k (4), with f_k referring to the relative frequency of the class on the dependent variable. The class-specific weights sum to one as in (4). Given the weights, the weighted PCC is (5):

$$w_k = \frac{1-f_k}{\sum\limits_{k=1}^{K} 1-f_k} \qquad \text{s.t.} \quad \sum_{k=1}^{K} w_k = 1 \tag{4}$$

$$wPCC = \frac{\sum\limits_{k=1}^{K} wPCC_k}{K}. \tag{5}$$

with $wPCC_k = w_k * PCC_k$. The weighted PCC favors a model with a smaller PCC but with a greater number of correctly classified on smaller classes, to a model having a higher PCC due to predicting most cases to over represented classes. We penalize models predicting several alternatives (cf. ties on maximum probability) by equally dividing the 100% classified over all alternatives predicted. Our weighted PCC is related to the balanced error rate. Secondly, we benchmark the model's performance to the proportional chance criterion (Cr_{pro}) rather than the maximum chance criterion (Cr_{max}) [20]:

$$Cr_{pro} = \sum_{1}^{K} f_k^2 \tag{6}$$

Besides this wPCC, the predictive performance of both feature selection methods in MNL is assessed by the Area Under the receiver Operating Curve (AUC). The Receiver Operating Characteristics curve plots the hit percentage (events predicted to be events) on the vertical axis versus the percentage false alarms (non-events predicted to be events) on the horizontal axis for all possible cut-off values [11]. The predictive accuracy of a model is expressed by the area under the ROC curve (AUC). The AUC statistic ranges from a lower limit of 0.5 for chance (null model) performance to an upper limit of 1.0 for perfect performance [12]. Although the AUC measure is essentially designed to measure the degree to which a classifier can discriminate between two classes, we apply this binary measure to assess the multiclass classification predictive performance by adopting a one-versus-all (k-versus-K\k) approach and averaging these K AUCs to an overall multiclass AUC. We test the statistical difference between the AUC of the random feature selection in MNL and the AUC of the MNL with expert feature selection by employing the non-parametric test by DeLong et al. [9].

3 A CRM Cross-Sell Application

The methodological framework (random feature selection in MNL and MNL with expert feature selection) is applied to a CRM database of a major home-appliances retailer containing scanner data for over one million customers making purchases from a very broad and deep product assortment ranging from small appliances like food processors to big appliances like dish washers. We analyze these scanner data to amass knowledge on customers' cross-buying patterns in order to support cross-sell actions. Cross-sell strategies aim at the augmentation of the number of products/services customers use from the firm.

The CRM objective is to build the best possible 'Next-Product to Buy' model (NPTB model, [15]) predicting in what product category the customer will acquire his next durable. We partition the home-appliance product space into nine product categories based on four underlying needs: cleaning, communication, cooking and entertainment [4], [14] and [8]. Hence, Y takes discrete values $\{1, 2, ..., 9\}$, K=9 and has following prior distribution: $f_1 = 9.73\%$, $f_2 = 10.45$, $f_3 = 20.49$, $f_4 = 12.64$, $f_5 = 11.70$, $f_6 = 9.74$, $f_7 = 8.67$, $f_8 = 8.13$ and $f_9 = 8.45$. We select customers having at least two previous purchase events and maximum 16 purchase events thereby excluding outliers (median length of 2 + 3 times σ=4.88). Companies are deleted from the analysis. We randomly assigned 37,276 (N_1) customers to the estimation sample and 37,110 (N_2) customers to the test sample. For each of these customers we constructed, based on our CRM domain-knowledge, a number of predictors X about: 1) monetary value, depth and width of purchase behavior - 5 features, 2) number of home-appliances acquired at the retailer – 14 features, 3) socio-demographical information – 5 features, 4) brand loyalty – 21 features, 5) price sensitivity - 25 features, 6) number of home-appliances returned – 3 features, 7) dominant mode of payment – 1 feature, 8) experience of a special life-event – 1 feature, 9) the order of acquisition of durables (ORDER) – 12 features, 10) the time to a first-acquisition or a repeated-acquisition event for a durable (DURATION) – two features. The first eight blocks of features build a general customer profile (NULL). The last two blocks capture sequential patterns (ORDER or DURATION between acquisitions) in customers' purchase behavior. For a more in-depth discussion of these covariates, we refer the interested reader to [21].

4 Results

4.1 MultiNomial Logit (MNL)

We applied the MultiNomial Logit algorithm to our home-appliance scanner data to predict in what category k with K={1, 2, ..., 9} the customer will buy next. In a first step, we estimated a MNL model with all M (89) features. This turned out to be a fruitless attempt, as the model did not converge even after numerous attempts. It confirms our experience that in presence of large feature spaces, MNL forces the researcher to engage in feature selection. Moreover, it stresses the need for a feature selection algorithm for MNL.

4.2 Random Feature Selection in MNL (rfs_MNL)

We illustrate our new random feature selection in MNL on the CRM cross-sell case aiming at building the best possible NPTB model. The random feature selection in MNL combines R MNLs with m randomly selected features estimated on the r-th bootstrap sample. We create R bootstrap samples BS_r by randomly drawing N_1 instances with replacement from the training data. Each r-th MNL model is estimated on the r-th bootstrap sample with m randomly selected features out of the M features in the input space. To classify instances, the R MNLs are combined with an adjusted Majority Voting (MV) combination scheme (cf. supra).

Random Feature Selection in MNL with R=100. Initially, we estimated the predictive accuracy of our new random feature selection in MNL with R=100. We combine 100 MNLs (R=100) estimated on 100 bootstrap samples with m randomly selected features. We take the square root of M; $m=89^{\wedge 1/2}$, as default parameter setting and, subsequently, engage in a grid search with main step size 1/3 of the default setting. This way m spans a range from 3 to 84. Unfortunately, MNL models with more than 48 variables failed to estimate for the same reason (multicollinearity) that we were unable to estimate full MNL model. Table 1, rfs_MNL (R=100) gives an overview of the results. Among the rfs_MNLs with R=100, the highest predictive accuracy is observed for m=48 (wPCCe=21.25, PCCe=26.87, AUCe=0.6491).

Table 1. Predictive performance of random feature selection in MNL on estimation sample

m	rfs_MNL (R=100)			10_rfs_MNL (R=10)		
	wPCCe	PCCe	AUCe	wPCCe	PCCe	AUCe
3	11.53	21.41	0.6163	19.30	23.93	0.6232
6	13.41	22.45	0.6225	18.76	24.42	0.6262
9	15.60	23.62	0.6270	19.69	24.98	0.6315
12	17.52	24.53	0.6300	19.94	25.25	0.6342
15	18.36	24.98	0.6328	20.56	26.33	0.6403
18	18.62	25.15	0.6359	20.42	26.35	0.6419
21	19.33	25.56	0.6390	21.09	26.78	0.6436
24	19.48	25.64	0.6404	21.12	26.77	0.6425
27	19.74	25.90	0.6423	21.14	26.63	0.6435
30	20.17	26.18	0.6443	21.45	27.04	0.6461
33	20.37	26.35	0.6458	21.59	27.13	0.6468
36	20.66	26.54	0.6467	21.55	27.05	0.6469
39	20.73	26.58	0.6472	21.75	27.23	0.6480
42	20.91	26.69	0.6480	21.82	27.31	0.6477
45	21.03	26.73	0.6485	21.87	27.27	0.6478
48	**21.25**	**26.87**	**0.6491**	**22.01**	**27.33**	**0.6489**

Random Feature Selection in MNL combining MNLs with 10% highest wPCC (10_rfs_MNL). Although all 100 MNLs have a performance better than $Cr_{pro}=12.28\%$, combining only very accurate classifiers might improve the performance of the random feature selection in MNL even more [10].

Therefore, in a second step, we combined only the MNL models for a given m with the 10% highest wPCCe, i.e. 10_rfs_MNL. We refrain from evaluating the potential of combining the 10% with highest PCCe or AUCe, as the wPCCe is our main performance criterion. Furthermore, as this paper focuses on illustrating the potential of randomness for Feature Selection in MNL, we refrain from a sensitivity-analysis on the number of classifiers (e.g. 10%) combined. The same range of m values as for random feature selection in MNL with R=100 is considered. Table 1, column 10_rfs_MNL reports the results. Analogous to rfs_MNL with R=100, the highest predictive performance is also attained for m=48 and this performance is, as far as it concerns the wPCCe and the PCCe, slightly higher than the performance of rfs_MNL R=100 (wPCCe +0.76 pctp, PCCe +0.46). Conversely, the AUC statistic is slightly worse (AUCe –0.016 pctp). In sum, combining only a selection of more accurate rfs_MNL models improves upon the performance of a rfs_MNL combining all 100 MNLs. However, how does the predictive accuracy of these rfs_MNL models compare to the accuracy of a MNL model with expert feature selection?

4.3 MNL with Expert Feature Selection (efs_MNL)

As a full MNL model (m=M) failed to estimate, we compare the predictive performance of the random feature selection in MNL with a MNL with Expert Feature Selection (efs_MNL). Firstly, we selected the best features within each of the three different types of covariates aiming to reduce multicollinearity (cf. supra Section 3, A CRM Cross-sell application), i.e. within the NULL, ORDER and DURATION blocks. Within the NULL block, we first selected the best set of two features and subsequently the best set of five features over the retained features, both by applying a complete search method. In the ORDER and DURATION blocks, we select the best feature employing a complete search. Secondly, we compared four NPTB models on their predictive accuracy wPCC, PCC and AUC on the estimation sample: 1) BEST5 model including only 5 selected NULL features, 2) BEST5 + ORDER including only the selected NULL features and selected ORDER feature, 3) BEST5 + DURATION including only the selected NULL features and selected DURATION feature, and 4) BEST5 +ORDER+ DURATION including only the selected NULL features, selected ORDER feature and selected DURATION feature. The BEST5 model with Duration (wPCCe= 19.75%, PCCe=22.00% with $Cr_{pro}=12.28\%$ and AUCe=0.5973) delivered the best possible NPTB model employing the expert feature selection procedure. Notwithstanding this high level of accuracy, its wPCCe, PCCe and AUCe are considerably lower than that of the best random feature selection in MNL; i.e. 10_rfs_MNL: wPCCe –1.5 percentage points (from now on abbreviated to pctp), PCCe –4.87 pctp and AUCe –3.53 ptcp. Moreover, the expert feature selection is very resource consuming (time and computer power) and it cannot guarantee that the optimal subset of features is selected.

These results are promising because on the one hand rfs_MNL accommodate for the feature selection problem of MNL while simultaneously improving the model performance. However, can we replicate these findings when applying the rfs_MNL and efs_MNL algorithms to new unseen data (i.e. test data)?

4.4 Predictive Model Evaluation on Test Data

We assess the robustness of the results on the estimation sample by applying and evaluating the best random feature selection in MNL (m=48, 10_rfs_MNL) and the best MNL with expert feature selection (best5+Duration) on a separate test sample, i.e. a dataset of instances not used for estimation (N_2=37,110). Table 2 and Fig. 1 present the results.

The arrows in Fig. 1 clearly illustrate that the observed higher performance of the best random feature selection in MNL, 10_rfs_MNL (10_rfs in Fig. 1) as compared to that of the best MNL with expert feature selection (efs_MNL in Fig. 1) on the estimation sample is confirmed on the test sample. Table 2 reveals that wPCCt increases by 1.31 pctp, PCCt by 4.57 pctp and AUCt by 3.96. Furthermore, we determine if the AUCs of the MNL with expert feature selection and the best random feature selection in MNL are statistically different. Per product category, we employ the non-parametric test by DeLong et al. [9] to determine whether the areas under the ROC curves (AUCs) within a product category are significantly different. All AUCs on the test set are statistically significant at ε=0.05. Table 3 reports the χ2 statistics.

Table 2. Predictive performance on test data

	wPCCt	PCCt	AUCt
efs_MNL	19.75	21.84	0.5926
10_rfs_MNL	21.06	26.41	0.6322

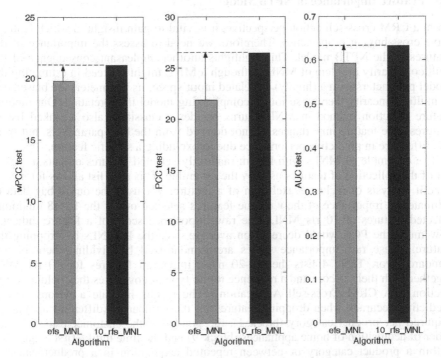

Fig. 1. Test set predictive performance of efs_MNL and 10_rfs_MNL

Table 3. Statistical significance of differences in AUCs on test set

10_rfs_vs_efs	
1	215.15
2	73.01
3	58.84
4	100.01
5	128.63
6	24.12
7	91.90
8	117.49
9	81.45

To recap, on the one hand, the estimation and test results clearly illustrate the potential of random feature selection in MNL to mitigate the curse of dimensionality and the convergence problems due to multicollinearity, both necessitating feature selection. On the other hand, the results indicate that the random feature selection in MNL addresses the feature selection problem while simultaneously improving the performance as compared to the predictive performance of a MNL with expert feature selection.

4.5 Feature Importance in NPTB Model

From a CRM cross-sell action perspective, it is vital to gain insight in which features drive cross-buying propensities. Therefore, we need to assess the importance of the features in the NPTB model. This highlights another unpleasant consequence of the multicollinearity problem of MNL. Although a MNL might succeed in estimating the model parameters with a (highly) correlated input space, its parameters are biased due to multicollinearity thereby seriously complicating model interpretation. Our random feature selection method in MNL returns besides a classifier, also a ranked list of features. The feature importances are not derived from the beta-parameters, but from the difference in predictive performance due to excluding a specific feature.

The ensemble of MNLs with R * m randomly selected features outputs a ranked list of the collection of features used by the ensemble. This rank list allows for a cost-benefit analysis of inclusion/exclusion of a feature. We used the out-of-bag data to estimate the importance of the v unique features selected out of the 10*48 randomly selected features of 10_rfs_MNL. The raw importance score of a feature indicates how much the PCC would decrease on average over the R MNLs by dropping the feature. These raw importance scores are standardized by dividing them by the standard error. Table 4 lists the top-20 most important features for 10_rfs_MNL together with their z-score and a reference to the type of covariates they belong to (cf. Section 3 A CRM Cross-sell Application). The results indicate a serious loss in predictive accuracy when dropping features on the number of (different) appliances acquired per product category (block 1), the gender of the customer (block 3), the order of acquisition of home appliances (block 9) and the time until a first acquisition within a product category or between repeated acquisition in a product category (block 10).

Table 4. Top-20 features for 10_rfs_MNL

Rank	Varname	z	Block	Description
1	productnbr_pc	29.37	1	monetary, depth and width
2	diffproduct_pc	24.91	1	monetary, depth and width
3	gender	19.70	3	socio-demo
4	ORDER Markov 2nd order	16.01	9	order
5	DURATION (surv)	9.48	10	duration
6	ORDER Markov 2nd order	9.21	9	order
7	ORDER dummies	7.69	9	order
8	ORDER Markov for Discrimination	4.86	9	order
9	language	4.84	3	socio-demo
10	nbrdiffbrand	4.74	4	brand loyalty
11	loyal_PANASONIC	4.51	4	brand loyalty
12	ORDER Markov 2nd order	4.44	9	order
13	rnbrreturns	4.41	6	returns
14	nbrabovep90	4.32	5	price sensitivity
15	maxdiffprod	3.96	2	number acquired
16	nbrbelowq1	3.87	5	price sensitivity
17	maxprod	3.74	2	number acquired
18	maxamount	3.38	1	monetary, depth and width
19	DURATION (survdiff)	3.36	10	duration
20	ORDER Markov 2nd order	3.34	9	order

5 Conclusion

Feature selection is a well-studied subject in many fields. Its necessity follows mainly from insufficient computer power and the inclusion of irrelevant and redundant features in the input space due to a priori unknown important features. Within the CRM domain, choice modeling employs data mining algorithms like MNL to predict choice behavior. Anologous to other mining algorithms, MNL suffers from the curse of dimensionality forcing data mining specialists to engage in feature selection. The results strongly support this statement as a full MNL as well as MNLs with more than 48 features failed to estimate. Besides this curse of dimensionality, the sensitivity of the MNL model to dependencies between features (multicollinearity), possibly obstructing model convergence, urges also for feature selection, as removing redundant features reduces multicollinearity. Notwithstanding this overwhelming evidence for the need of feature selection for MNL, to date, in glaring contrast to binary logit, software packages mostly lack any feature selection algorithm for MNL. To accommodate this unanswered need for feature selection for MNL, this paper proposed a random feature selection procedure integrated within the multinomial logit (MNL) classifier. Although the dimensionality limit of MNL could be addressed by choosing a more scalable classifier like SVM or Random Forests, there is a strong call for a scalable version of MNL due to its theoretical foundation explaining choice-behavior from a random-utility perspective [5].

The random feature selection in MNL performs feature and model selection simultaneously by combining R MNLs estimated on the r-th bootstrap sample including m randomly selected features. Our new procedure accommodates for two serious weaknesses of the MNL model: 1) the feature selection attempts to avoid failure of estimation because of the curse of dimensionality, 2) the feature selection in se and the combination of several MNL models estimated on feature subsets tackles the multicollinearity problem. The consequences of multicollinearity are two-fold. On the one hand it might obstruct the estimation of the MNL model. On the other hand, even if the MNL model converges, multicollinearity biases parameter estimates and hence, complicates the interpretation of the model. Our random feature selection method in MNL returns besides a classifier, also a ranked list of features.

The results are very promising. The random feature selection in MNL not only addresses the curse of dimensionality and multicollinearity problems of MNL, but the random search even improves model accuracy. The latter was reflected in the substantially higher predictive performance of the random feature selection in MNL as compared to that of the MNL with expert feature selection. The random search helps to escape local optima in the search space and optimality of the selected subset dependent on the resources available as in the MNL with expert feature selection.

This paper applied random feature selection in MNL. Future work could adopt the random feature selection approach on a multinomial heteroscedastic-extreme-value or probit model. Moreover, the proposed feature selection method might be extended outside the random-utility models to other supervised learning algorithms requiring feature selection. Another interesting direction for further research constitutes a comparison of our random feature selection in MNL with a GA-based feature selection algorithm in MNL. The latters' fitness function would optimize the total predictive accuracy of the MNL ensemble by combining MNL models estimated on feature subsets emerging from applying genetic operators like mutation, cross-over and replication. Finally, future work could explore the potential of random feature selection in MNL by combining MNLs estimated with randomly selected feature subsets of different sizes (m variable within ensemble).

References

1. Agrawal, D., Schorling, C.: Market Share Forecasting: An Empirical Comparison of Artificial Neural Networks and Multinomial Logit Model. Journal of Retailing (1996) 72(4) 383-407
2. Baltas, G., Doyle, P.: Random utility models in marketing: a survey. Journal of Business Research (2001) 51(2) 115-125
3. Barandela, R., Sánchez, J.S., Garcia, V., Rangel, E.: Strategies for learning in class imbalance problems. Pattern Recognition (2003) 36(3) 849-851
4. Barsalou, L.W.: Deriving Categories to Achieve Goals. In: Bower, G.H. (eds.): The Psychology of Learning and Motivation. Academic Press, New York (1991) 1-64
5. Ben-Akiva, M., Lerman, S.R.: Discrete Choice Analysis: Theory and Application to Travel Demand. The MIT Press, Cambridge (1985)
6. Breiman, L.: Random Forests. Machine Learning (2001) 45(1) 5-32

7. Buchtala, O., Klimek, M., Sick, B.: Evolutionary optimization of radial basis function classifiers for data mining classifications. IEEE Transactions on Systems Man and Cybernetics Part B- Cybernetics (2005) 35(5) 928-947
8. Corfman, K.P.: Comparability and Comparison Levels Used in Choices Among Consumer Products. Journal of Marketing Research (1991) 28(3) 368-374
9. DeLong, E.R., DeLong, D.M., Clarke-Pearson, D.L.: Comparing the areas under two or more correlated receiver operating characteristic curves: a nonparametric approach. Biometrics (1988) 44 837-845
10. Dietterich, T.G.: Machine-Learning Research – Four current directions. AI Magazine (1997) 18(4) 97-136
11. Fawcett, T.: ROC Graphs: Notes and Practical Considerations for Researchers. Technical Report HPL-2003-4, HP Laboratories (2003)
12. Green, D., Swets, J.A.: Signal detection theory and psychophysics. John Wiley & Sons, New York (1966)
13. Huang, Y., McCullagh, P., Black, N., Harper, R.: Feature Selection and Classification Model Construction on Type 2 Diabetic Patient's Data. In: Perner, P. (ed.): LNAI, Vol. 3275, Springer-Verlag, Berlin Heidelberg New York (2004) 153)162
14. Johnson, M.D.: Consumer Choice Strategies for Comparing Noncomparable Alternatives. Journal of Consumer Research (1984) 11(3) 741-753
15. Knott, A., Hayes, A., Neslin, S.A.: Next-Product-To-Buy Models for Cross-selling Applications. Journal of Interactive Marketing (2002) 16(3) 59-75
16. Kohavi, R., John, G.H.: Wrappers for Feature Subset Selection. Artificial Intelligence (1997) 97(1-2) 273-324
17. Leopold, E., Kindermann, J.: Text Categorization with Support Vector Machines. How to Represent Texts in Input Space? Machine Learning (2002) 46(1-3) 423-444
18. Liu, H., Yu, L.: Toward Integrating Feature Selection Algorithms for Classification and Clustering. IEEE Transactions on Knowledge and Data Engineering (2005) 17(4) 491-502
19. Melgani, F., Bruzzone, L.: Classification of Hyperspectral Remote Sensing Images with Support Vector Machines. IEEE Transactions on Geoscience and Remote Sensing (2004) 42(8) 1778-1790
20. Morrison, D.G.: On the interpretation of discriminant analysis. Journal of Marketing Research (1969) 6 156-163
21. Prinzie, A., Van den Poel, D.: Incorporating sequential information into traditional classification models by using an element/position-sensitive SAM. Decision Support Systems in press 2006
22. Sindhwani, V., Rakshit, S., Deodhare, D., Erdogmus, D., Principe, J.C., Niyogi, P.: Feature Selection in MLPs and SVMs Based on Maximum Output Information. IEEE Transactions on Neural Networks (2004) 15(4) 937-948
23. Xing, B., Jordan, M., Karp, R.: Feature Selection for High-Dimensional Genomic Microarray Data. Proc. 15th International Conf. Machine Learning (2001) 601-608

Data Mining Analysis on Italian Family Preferences and Expenditures

Paola Annoni, Pier Alda Ferrari, and Silvia Salini

University of Milan, Department of Economics,
Business and Statistics, via Conservatorio 7, 20122 Milano, Italy
{paola.annoni, pieralda.ferrari, silvia.salini}@unimi.it

Abstract. Italian expenditures are a complex system. Every year the Italian National Bureau of Statistics (*ISTAT*) carries out a survey on the expenditure behavior of Italian families. The survey regards household expenditures on durable and daily goods and on various services. Our goal is here twofold: firstly we describe the most important characteristics of family behavior with respect to expenditures on goods and usage of different services; secondly possible relationships among these behaviors are highlighted and explained by social-demographical features of families. Different data mining techniques are jointly used to these aims so as to identify different capabilities of selected methods within these kinds of issues. In order to properly focalize on service usage, further investigation will be needed about the nature of investigated services (private or public) and, most of all, about their supply and effectiveness along the national territory[1].

1 Introduction

The use of new ICT (Information and Communication Technologies) in Public Administration allows government to get large quantity of data. They can be fruitfully used to analyze, asses and improve interventions and services to citizens and companies (i.e. health, school, energy). The process of decision making in the public management should be properly founded on scientific bases, taking into account the multi-dimensionality feature of data.

Data mining techniques in the private sector have been already implemented for business improvement with success. Significant applications are customer relationship management and quality control [5]. For this reason, the need is felt to extend and customize data mining to the public sector too. To this purpose, a review of common data mining techniques and of their evaluation criteria is due. Evidently there are some differences between private and public setting. The most important difference is that public issues have to take into account peculiar variables in the evaluation processes: social utility, risks and benefits for the collectivity are of primary importance in public management. In addition, while the private sector frequently has the use of exhaustive data, such as customer tables, public sector analyses are often based on samples.

---

[1] The project is financially supported by the grant COFIN2004 from *MIUR*, ITALY.

P. Perner (Ed.): ICDM 2006, LNAI 4065, pp. 324–336, 2006.

In spite of the need of decision support in the public sector, for the reasons mentioned above, the measuring process is more complex and still not completely explored. This article is a proposal in this direction. It concentrates on the analysis of Italian families expenditures through a CRISP-DM, i.e. a CRoss Industry Standard Process model for data mining [9]. In Section 2 the definition of the problem is outlined; Section 3 is devoted to data understanding and preparation: Association Rules, factor analysis and k-means cluster are implemented in order to reduce the high dimensionality of data and to go further into data comprehension. In Section 4 peculiar models are detailed, in particular Decision Trees and Canonical Correspondence Analysis, while in Section 5 the evaluation of selected models are described and results are shown and discussed. In the end, section 6 highlights some conclusions and perspectives.

2 Definition of the Problem

Analyses are based on data from the Household Expenditure Survey 2003 by the Italian National Bureau of Statistics (*ISTAT*), which is a yearly survey for the analysis of expenditures of Italian families. The survey regards about 28000 Italian families. The aim is to collect the amount of household expenditure on durable and daily goods and on various services. Particular focus is on social and economical aspects of the household way of life. The survey is repeated each year, thus allowing comparative analyses and data update.

As a first step, the analysis here presented aims to describe the most important characteristics of family behavior with respect to expenditures on goods and usage of services. As a second step, every relationships among these behaviors have to be highlighted and eventually explained by social-demographical characteristic of families.

The final goal is to detect the presence of critical situations and/or social risk factors. Furthermore, regarding to public services it is relevant to identify prospective lacks or deficiencies in order to properly plan public interventions.

3 Data Understanding and Data Preparation

As mentioned above, the data-set is very large: about 28000 records by 400 fields. Each record represents a statistical unit (a family) while each field represents a variable collected for the family. Variables have different measurement scales: categorical, ordinal, numerical and dichotomous. Variables collected regard: social-demographical characteristics of the family (number of components, age, education, etc.); household preferences on durable goods (property of a car, house, computer, etc.); household preferences on services (transport, health, insurances, school, entertainment, culture, etc.); household expenditures on daily goods (foods, drinks, cigarettes, newspapers, etc.). Data are provided on a Ascii format file and data manipulation is needed in order to obtain a *customer table* structure.

Due to the nature of collected variables, the data-set is characterized by prevalence of zeros and of spurious information. As it is always the case in data-mining analyses, data cleaning and filling methods are applied.

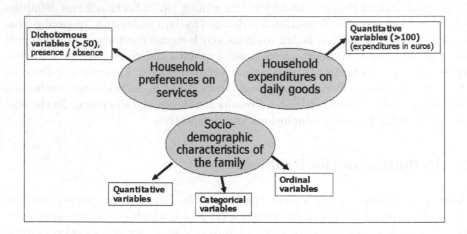

Fig. 1. Data structure: Three sets of variables are defined

Peculiar aspects of the problem suggest us to divide variables into three groups, as sketched in Fig.1: (a) expenditures on daily goods (continuous scale of measurement); (b) preferences on services (dichotomous); (c) social-demographical characteristics of the family (categorical, ordinal, and numeric variables).

This classification is due to various reasons. First of all variables play different roles. Expenditures are response variables which are driven by social-demographical features and, furthermore, they reflect personal choices of the family components. On the contrary, social-demographical variables are explanatory variables and play the role of risk factors. Preferences on services are placed at an intermediate level with respect to the previous variable typologies, because the preference is related on one hand to the effective need of that service (school, mobility, health-care, etc.), which depends on customers, and on the other hand to the service availability, which depends on practical politics.

In addition, statistical issues contribute in discriminating among these different sets of variables. In particular scales of measurement and different variable roles should lead to the proper choice of methods and techniques. Because of both problem complexity and variable typologies, different models have to be alternatively or jointly used. With this regard, data-mining appears particularly suitable.

Once variables have been divided into the sets, as explained above, within each set explorative analyses are applied in order to keep non-redundant data and discard sources of misleading noises. In particular, Association Rules [1] are employed to define different combination of services usage by households (here called 'service profile'), while factor and cluster analysis are used in sequence to identify different combinations of expenditures which characterize families (here called 'expenditure profile'). Service and expenditure profiles actually represent new variables which will be used with social-demographical variables to the final purpose. Methods for setting-up service and expenditure profiles are described in the following.

3.1   Setting-Up of Service Profile of Families: Association Rules

Authors concentrate on the family usage of various type of private or public services. In particular, the focus is on *means of transport, instruction & culture, household & babysitting*. Data are of binary type (family uses or not). Our goal is to find relevant relationships among preferences on different services.

For each different type of service, many variables are available for each family in the sample. For example for the service *means of transport* the following variables are collected: property of a car, a motorcycle, a scooter, a camper or a bicycle, subscription/tickets for buses, trains, airplanes or ferries. In order to identify significant links into multi-ways cross tables, classical approaches involve log-linear models. In this case dimensionality is too high and a classical approach is evidently wasteful, both from the computationally and from the interpretative point of view, hence alternative explorative techniques are needed. Our choice is Association Rules since it is based on the same starting point as log-linear models, i.e. the odds ratio.

Association Rules, usually employed to obtain Market Basket Analyses [9], is here applied taking families as customers and different household preferences on services as products. The algorithm of Association Rules automatically finds associations which can be manually detected using visualization techniques, such as the Web node. An *A-Priori* algorithm is used to extract a set of rules from the data, pulling out those rules with the highest information content. As known, Association Rules are based on statements of the form:

"if antecedent then consequent"

To create an *A-Priori* rules set, one or more Input fields and one or more Output fields are to be defined. Categorical variables can be Input (antecedent), Output (consequent) or Both. *A-Priori* algorithm is particularly suitable in our case because it is fast and it considers various antecedents at a time. The steps here undertaken are as follows: (a) selection of all the variables which indicate household preferences on services, among those indicated above; (b) detection of the most important linkages between antecedents and consequents by symmetric approach, so as not imposing any constraints on the choice of both antecedents and consequents; (c) particular regard to specific groups of preferences by asymmetric approach in order to discard non informative variables. Antecedents/Consequent associations are computed imposing an antecedent support higher than 2% and 10% of minimum rule confidence. A maximum number of five antecedents is imposed. Rules are selected looking at the lift value (lift > 1). Analysis results suggest to recode different types of preferences into two categorical macro-variables *transport* and *instruction&house*. Variable *transport* is defined to have four categories: public, private, both, none, which indicate the preference of the family towards private or public means of transport. Variable *instruction&house* is defined to have the following categories: school, house, both, none, in order to describe the household behavior with respect to expenditures related to instruction, school fees, school-buses, private lessons, etc. and house-care, which include both domestic care and baby-sitting. Unlikely data do not allow to discriminate between public or private school preference.

Family preferences behavior is described by every possible combination of categories of the two new macro-variables. Hence, sixteen family profiles are defined as: PUblic-School, PUblic-House, Private-School, Both-None, etc.

3.2 Setting-Up of Expenditure Profile of Families: Factor and Cluster Analysis

As just mentioned variables which describe family expenses refer to the whole household and not to every single component. In order to identify expenditure profiles, expenses have to be reduced to pro-capite amounts.

If a pro-capite amount of a household is computed by simply dividing the total by the number of components, the implicit assumption is that economies of scale do not exist. That is, each component has equal weight in the computation. However, larger households generally have an actual advantage over smaller households as they can benefit from sharing commodities (such as housing, stoves, furniture, etc.) or from purchasing products in bulk, which is usually cheaper. Hence economies of scale have to enter the analysis. There is no single agreed-upon method to estimate economies of scale in consumption. Equivalence scales are used to enable welfare comparisons across heterogeneous households. Since we are analyzing the Italian scenario we apply the following equivalence scale:

$$X_e = X/(nc)^{0.65} \tag{1}$$

where X is the total expenses of the household and nc is the number of components who belong to the household. The equivalence coefficient 0.65 was specifically estimated for Italian families on the basis of Engel's method [4]. In the following, all expenditures on daily goods are transformed into 'equivalent expenditures' X_e, according to eq.(1) and direct comparisons are allowed.

Factor analysis was applied to 'equivalent expenditures' in order to detect specific combinations of daily consumptions. On the basis of the scree-plot, eight factors are selected. These factors are characterized as follows: 1. primary goods (sugar, bread, oil, milk, etc.); 2. cultural goods (newspapers, books, theater, etc.); 3. domestic goods (soaps, washing powder, toilet paper, etc.); 4. fast food goods (cheese, cold cut, deep-frozen, etc.); 5. vegetables; 6. fresh fruit; 7. luxury goods (champagne, shellfish, caviar, etc.); 8. idle-hours goods (cigarettes, lottery, pubs, etc.). Each family is now described by a particular expenditure profile which is defined by a string of the above factors.

Successively, cluster k-means algorithm is applied to define groups of families homogeneous with respect to expenditure profiles. It emerges that families can

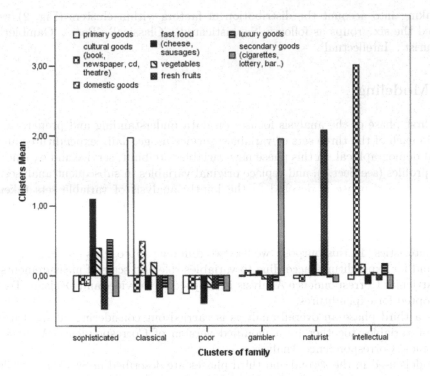

Fig. 2. Means of first eight factors within clusters

Table 1. Frequency distribution of clusters

Cluster	Frequency	Percentage
Sophisticated	4688	16.8
Classical	2442	8.7
Poor	13742	49.1
Gambler	2857	10.2
Naturist	2993	10.7
Intellectual	1259	4.5

be divided into six groups as shown in Table 1. Each group is characterized by a typical expenditure behavior as Fig. 2 makes evident.

How it can be easily seen, all groups, but the third one, show a particular expenditure behavior since one factor is clearly predominant. Specifically the first group represents families whose preference is towards fast food; the second group towards primary goods; the forth towards goods typically consumed during idle-hours. In the fifth group the predominant factor is the fresh fruit factor, while the sixth group is characterized by high values of the cultural factor. The only exception is the third group which is composed by families with low values for every factors.

Taking into account the distribution of factors within clusters (Fig. 2) we named the six groups as follows: 'Sophisticated', 'Classical', 'Poor', 'Gambler', 'Naturist', 'Intellectual'.

4 Modeling

The first phase of the analysis focuses on data understanding and preparation within each of the three sets of variables: service usage, daily expenditures and social-demographical. In this phase new variables are built, service and expenditure profiles (see Sect.3), and replace original variables in subsequent analyses.

The second phase is devoted to the jointly analysis of variable sets taken two at a time: service profiles vs social-demographical characteristic and expenditure profiles vs social-demographical characteristics. The goal is to highlight every possible relationships between services usage or expenditures and family characteristics. To this purpose, we use two different approaches for services usage and for expenditures according to variables role and scale of measurements. In particular Correspondence Analysis is adopted for services and Decision Tree is adopted for expenditures.

As a third phase an overall analysis is carried out considering all the three sets of variables together by a modified version of Correspondence Analysis, Canonical Correspondence Analysis.

Models used in the second and third phases are described in Section 4, while results are pointed out in Section 5.

4.1 Services Usage and Family Characteristics: Correspondence Analysis

Correspondence Analysis [6] is here used in order to highlight relationships between households behavior with respect to services usage and family typologies, so as to identify patterns of service usage and family type. In addition it is our intention to relate those patterns to explanatory variables, which could possibly drive families behavior, as it will be shown in Sect. 4.3.

To this aim a contingency table of service profiles by family typologies is set up. Service profiles are those built in Sect. 3.1, whilst family typologies are from *ISTAT* survey. Families are classified as follows (between brackets names we assigned to *ISTAT* typologies): couple with one child (couple_1); couple with two children (couple_2); couple with three or more children (couple_3); couple without children with reference component of age under 35 (two_35); couple without children with reference component of age between 36 and 65 (two35_64); couple without children with reference component of age over 64 (two_65); single of age under 35 (one_35); single of age between 36 and 65 (one35_64); single of age over 64 (one_65); only one parent (1_parent); other typology (other).

As known Correspondence Analysis (CA) is an ordination technique which could be generally applied to contingency tables. The goal of CA is to reduce dimensionality providing a map, usually in two dimensions, of row and column points where Euclidean distances are proportional to similarities between rows or columns (in term of χ^2 distances). In the case under examination let Y_{mxn} be the service profiles-by-family typologies matrix. Let $M_{mxm} = \text{diag}(y_{k+})$ and $N_{nxn} = \text{diag}(y_{+i})$. Various approaches can be applied to reach CA ordination axes. One of them is called optimal scaling which computes standardized typology scores $\mathbf{x}_{nx1}$ that maximize the dispersion δ of service profile scores $\mathbf{u}_{mx1}$. In matrix notation:

$$\delta = (\mathbf{u}^T \mathbf{M} \mathbf{u})/(\mathbf{x}^T \mathbf{N} \mathbf{x}) \qquad (2)$$

where T stands for transpose and $\mathbf{u} = \mathbf{M}^{-1} \mathbf{Y} \mathbf{x}$. Denominator in eq.2 takes into account the standardization of $\mathbf{x}$, provided $\mathbf{x}$ is centered. Dispersion δ represents the inertia of row scores. The problem of maximizing δ with respect to $\mathbf{x}$ has as a solution the second root λ_2 of the following equation:

$$\mathbf{Y}^T \mathbf{M}^{-1} \mathbf{Y} \mathbf{x} = \lambda \mathbf{N} \mathbf{x} \qquad (3)$$

Hence $\delta = \lambda_2$. The first eigenvector of CA is thus the solution related to the second root of eq.(3), i.e. its first non-trivial solution [6].

4.2   Expenditures and Family Characteristics: Decision Tree

As explained in Sect. 3, expenditures have a response nature (here with notation y_i) and family characteristics are explanatory variables ($\mathbf{x}_i$). The focus is to establish if it is possible to classify households in expenditure profiles by means of social-demographical variables.

Regression approaches, such as logistic regression, linear discriminant analysis play an important role in many data analyses, providing prediction and classification rules, and data analytic tools for understanding the importance of different inputs. Although attractively simple, the traditional parametric linear model often fails in some situation: in real life in general and in social science in particular, effects are often non linear [7]. Non parametric learning methods, for instance neural networks and support vector machine, are flexible and powerful to approximate any type of relationships among any type of variables. The drawback of this approach is the non interpretability of the mapping function that is a sort of black-box.

For our aim the more suitable approach seems to be the Tree-based method. These methods partition the feature space into a set of rectangles, and then fit a simple model in each one. They are conceptually simple yet powerful. The most popular method for tree-based regression and classification is called CART [3]. This algorithm uses binary partitions. A key advantage of the recursive binary tree is its interpretability. If the target is a classification outcome taking values $1, 2, ..., K$, the only changes needed in the tree algorithm pertain to the criteria for splitting nodes and pruning the tree. In a node m, representing a region R_m with N_m observations, the proportion of class k observation in nod m is:

$$\hat{p}_{mk} = \frac{1}{N_m} \sum_{\mathbf{x}_i \in R_m} I(y_i = k) \qquad (4)$$

We classify observations x_i in node m to class $k(m) = \arg\max_k \hat{p}_{mk}$, the majority class in node m. Different measures of node impurity can be used, for example misclassification error, cross-entropy or deviance and Gini index. We choose Gini index because it is more sensitive to changes in node probabilities and for its interesting interpretation. Furthermore, to prevent over-fitting we choose to prune the tree using the standard error criterion.

Furthermore, the tree-based algorithm automatically selects only discriminant variables, due to the iterative procedure and its stopping rules. Discriminant variables are ranked during selection, so as an importance rank is obtained.

4.3   Three-Ways Analysis: Canonical Correspondence Analysis

In order to get a better understanding of patterns of service profiles vs family typologies, some explanatory variables could be integrated into the ordination technique described in Sect.4.1. The goal is to detect patterns of variation in service profiles that are best explained by external variables (covariates) suitable when dealing with response variables that follow an unimodal and symmetric behavior with respect to selected covariates. Two variables are considered here to have an explanatory role: the average age of the reference person in the family, as an indicator of generation behavior and the average equivalent expenditure X_e (eq.(1)), as a rough indicator of richness.

Selected model to embed the two covariates into the bi-dimensional map of service profiles vs family typologies is Canonical Correspondence analysis (see [10] and [11]). The methodology was originally developed to detect relationships between biological species composition and environmental gradients. In this case service profiles play the role of biological species and environmental gradients are defined as 'generation' and richness' indicators.

Canonical Correspondence Analysis (CCA) stems directly from the classical ordination method of Correspondence Analysis, in this sense CCA can be seen as a 'restricted' CA. In fact, CCA selects ordination axes as in CA but imposing that they are a linear combination of covariates. CCA chooses then the best weights for the explanatory variables so as to maximize the dispersion of service profile scores. Being a restricted CA, CCA maximizes eq.(2), provided $\mathbf{x}$ is centered, subject to the constraint $\mathbf{x} = \mathbf{Z}^T \mathbf{c}$, where $\mathbf{Z}_{2xn}$ is the matrix of standardized values of the two covariates and $\mathbf{c}$ is the vector of unknown weights. By inserting $\mathbf{x} = \mathbf{Z}^T \mathbf{c}$ in eq.(2) and maximizing δ with respect to $\mathbf{x}$, it is possible to find the solution of CCA. More precisely, the roots of the following equation:

$$\mathbf{ZY}^T\mathbf{M}^{-1}\mathbf{YZ}^T\mathbf{c} = \lambda\mathbf{ZNZ}^T\mathbf{c} \tag{5}$$

provide the maximization of δ with respect of $\mathbf{x}$, where the maximum δ equals the maximum λ. To each ordination axis corresponds an eigenvalue that represents the amount of inertia explained by the axis, the total inertia being the sum of eigenvalues calculated by the unrestricted procedure, i.e. CA.

5   Evaluation and Results Interpretation

Within each phase, we need to choose among different models. Our choice is based on various criteria. First of all proper statistics criteria (lift, percentage of explained variance, misclassification rate, etc.) are to be taken into account. At the same time, informative criteria (nice interpretability of results) and models compatibility (models can be used in sequence and/or in a jointly way) are adopted. Last but not least, model results should allow direct and effective communication and our choices take into account also this non trivial aspect. For most people, in fact, graphical display are more effective than mathematical formula [8]. Selected models lead to the following results.

5.1   Services Usage and Family Characteristics

Results of Correspondence Analysis are shown in Fig.3, which shows the two-dimensional map of service profile and family typology scores.

In CA computations an asymmetric approach is here chosen, where profiles are at the centroid of family typologies. This is to assign more importance to spatial distribution of service profiles. The cumulative percentage of total inertia explained by the first two CA axes is 96.8% thus indicating a satisfactory representative power of the reduced space.

As it evident from the map in Fig.3, two groups of profiles are evident: the one on the right side of diagram, which represents households with low mobility needs and without school expenditures (family who prefer public means of transport,

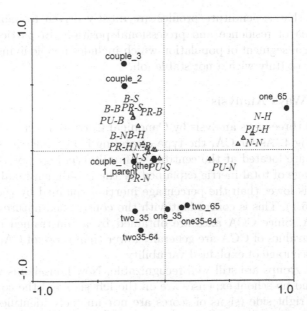

Fig. 3. Two-dimensional diagram of service profiles and family typologies

spend money for domestic cares but not for schools); on the other hand, the group on the left side is composed by families who have high mobility and school needs. Accordingly, the mutual position of service profile and family typology points shows that the right group is composed by older families or families without children, while the left group is evidently mostly composed by couples with children.

5.2 Expenditures and Family Characteristics

The tree expenditures vs social-demographical characteristics has a good classification performance, in fact the percentage of cases predicted in the correct way is 62%. This means that the expenditure choices of the families mainly depend on theirs characteristics. In order to find critical situations in the distribution of Italian families, we look in particular at category *poor*. As shown in Table 1, the total percentage of *poor* is 49.1%. The CART algorithm identifies a leaf, in which the percentage of *poor* is about 68%. The leaf represents almost 9% of overall population and 12.3% within cluster *poor*. The rule that describes this segment is shown in Table 2.

Table 2. Rule for segment 'poor'

Ranking	First	Second	Third
Variables	Family type	Geographical area	Professional position
Category	Single	South and Islands	Precarious workers

It emerges that expenditure profiles are mostly driven by family type, geographical area of residence and professional position. In particular the tree detects a critical segment of population which includes people living alone in the Southern part of Italy with a not stable job.

5.3 Three-Ways Analysis

Results of the three-ways analysis by Canonical Correspondence analysis are illustrated in Fig.4. As for CA, the type of scaling is asymmetric, hence service profile points are located at the centroid of family typology points. The cumulative percentage of total inertia explained by the two-dimensional space is now 70.3%, i.e. it is lower than the percentage inertia explained by the two axes of CA (see Sect.5.1). This is concordant with the constrained nature of CCA with respect to CA. Since CCA axes are obtained by a constrained maximization problem, eigenvalues of CCA are generally lower than those of CA, thus leading to a lower percentage of explained variability.

Two major groups are still well recognizable. Now households with low mobility needs and no school expenses are on the left side and the complementary one is on the right side (signs of scores are not uniquely identified in CA and CCA). It is interesting to note that the two groups are mainly explained by the

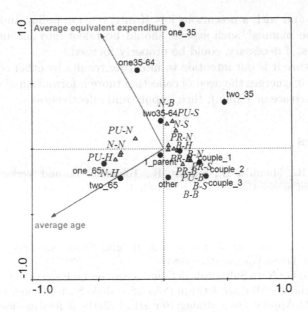

Fig. 4. Two-dimensional diagram of service profiles and family typologies with two covariates

age of the reference component of the family, thus suggesting that the usage of services is mainly driven by the actual household needs of that service and not by economical capabilities. The richness indicator, taken as the average equivalent expenditure, does not seem to influence service profiles pattern. Yet, family typologies could be ordered along the richness axis making evident that young singles have more money to burn than older or numerous families.

6   Conclusion

Italian family expenditure patterns are a complex system. It is important for a Public Administration to know the family behavior and the factors that influence it, in order to plan actions and investments. It is also useful the identification of relevant expenditure patterns and links to family characteristics, also in order to find social and economical critical points. Furthermore it is relevant to know the actual preference for services that could help to avoid situations of social deficiencies.

Univariate and marginal views miss important relations, on the contrary data mining methods aim to discover and highlight relationships and 'hidden evidences'. In this paper a first attempt in this direction is due. The analysis highlights two major aspects: on one hand three-way analysis points out that services usage is mainly driven by the effective household needs and not by its economical capabilities, on the other hand critical situations can be detected within the population which include people living alone in the Southern part of the Country and with a precarious job. If intervention policy and/or prioritization are to be planned, such aspects should be taken into account and further investigations, if necessary, could be properly focused.

In near future it is our intention to integrate results by other sources of data. In particular it emerges the need of collecting more information about the nature of services (private or public), their supply and effectiveness.

References

1. Agrawal, R., Mannila, H., Srikant, R., Toivonen, H. and Verkamo, A. I.: Fast discovery of association rules. Advances in Knowledge Discovery and Data Mining, AAAI/MIT Press, Cambridge, MA (1995)
2. Berry, M.J.A. and Linoff, G.: Data Mining Techniques: for marketing, sales, and customer support. John Wiley and Sons, (1996)
3. Breiman, L., Friedman, J. H., Olshen, R. and Stone, C. J.: Classification and Regression Trees. Wadsworth, (1984)
4. Carbonaro, G.: Nota Sulle Scale di Equivalenza, on La Povertà in Italia, Presidenza del Consiglio dei Ministri, Istituto Poligrafico dello Stato, Rome, (1985)
5. Giudici, P.: Applied Data Mining: Statistical Methods for Business and Industry, John Wiley and Sons, (2003)
6. Greenacre, M. J.: Theory and Applications of Correspondence Analysis. Academic Press, London (1984)
7. Hastie, T., Tibshirani, R., Friedman, J.: The Elements of Statistical Learning: data mining, inference and prediction, Springer-Verlag, New York, (2001)
8. Kenett, R., Thyregod, P.: Aspects of statistical consulting not taught by academia. Neerlandica special issue on Industrial Statistics (2006) (to appear)
9. Perner, P.: Advances in Data Mining. Springer Verlag, Berlin-Heidelberg, (2002)
10. ter Braak, C.J.F.: Canonical community ordination. Part I: Basic theory and linear methods. Ecoscience, $1(2)$ (1994) 127–140
11. ter Braak, C.J.F. and Verdonschot, P.F.M.: Canonical Correspondence Analysis and related multivariate methods in aquatic ecology. Aquatic Sciences, $57/3$ (1995) 255–289

Multiobjective Evolutionary Induction of Subgroup Discovery Fuzzy Rules: A Case Study in Marketing

Francisco Berlanga[1], María José del Jesus[1], Pedro González[1], Francisco Herrera[2], and Mikel Mesonero[3]

[1] Department of Computer Science, University of Jaén, Jaén, Spain
{berlanga, mjjesus, pglez}@ujaen.es
[2] Department of Computer Science and Artificial Intelligence,
University of Granada, Granada, Spain
herrera@decsai.ugr.es
[3] Department of Organization and Marketing,
University of Mondragón, Spain
mmesoner@eteo.mondragon.edu

Abstract. This paper presents a multiobjective genetic algorithm which obtains fuzzy rules for subgroup discovery in disjunctive normal form. This kind of fuzzy rules lets us represent knowledge about patterns of interest in an explanatory and understandable form which can be used by the expert. The evolutionary algorithm follows a multiobjective approach in order to optimize in a suitable way the different quality measures used in this kind of problems. Experimental evaluation of the algorithm, applying it to a market problem studied in the University of Mondragón (Spain), shows the validity of the proposal. The application of the proposal to this problem allows us to obtain novel and valuable knowledge for the experts.

Keywords: Data mining, descriptive induction, multiobjective evolutionary algorithms, genetic fuzzy systems, subgroup discovery.

1 Introduction

Knowledge Discovery in Databases (KDD) is defined as the non trivial process of identifying valid, original, potentially useful patterns which have comprehensible data [1]. Within KDD process the data mining stage is responsible for high level automatic knowledge discovery from information obtained from real data.

A data mining algorithm can discover knowledge using different representation models and techniques from two different perspectives:

- *Predictive induction*, whose objective is the discovery of knowledge for classification or prediction [2].
- *Descriptive induction*, whose fundamental objective is the discovery of interesting knowledge from the data. In this area, attention can be drawn to the discovery of association rules following an unsupervised learning model [3], subgroup discovery [4], [5] and other approaches to non-classificatory induction.

P. Perner (Ed.): ICDM 2006, LNAI 4065, pp. 337–349, 2006.

In subgroup discovery the objective is, given a population of individuals and a specific property of individuals we are interested in, find population subgroups that are statistically "most interesting", e.g., are as large as possible and have the most unusual distributional characteristics with respect to the property of interest.

This paper describes a new proposal for the induction of rules which describe subgroups based upon a multiobjective evolutionary algorithm (MOEA) which combines the approximated reasoning method of the fuzzy systems with the learning capacities of the genetic algorithms (GAs).

The induction of rules describing subgroups can be considered as a multi-objective problem rather than a single objective one, in which the different measures used for evaluating a rule can be thought of as different objectives of the subgroup discovery rule induction algorithm. In this sense, MOEAs are adapted to solve problems in which different objectives must be optimized. In the specialized bibliography can be found several evolutionary proposals for multiobjective optimization [6], [7]. Recently the MOEAs have been used in the extraction of knowledge in data mining [8], [9].

The multiobjective algorithm proposed in this paper defines three objectives. One of them is used as a restriction in the rules in order to obtain a set of rules (the pareto front) with a high degree of coverage, and the other objectives take into account the support and the confidence of the rules. The use of this mentioned objective allows us the extraction of a set of rules with different features and labels for every property of interest.

The paper is arranged in the following way: Section 2 describes some preliminary concepts. The multiobjective evolutionary approach to obtain subgroup discovery descriptive fuzzy rules is explained in Section 3. Finally, Section 4 shows the experimentation carried out and the analysis of results and section 5 outlines the conclusions and further research.

2 Preliminaries

2.1 Subgroup Discovery

Subgroup discovery represents a form of supervised inductive learning in which, given a set of data and having a property of interest to the user (target variable), attempts to locate subgroups which are statistically "most interesting" for the user. In this sense, a subgroup is interesting if it has an unusual statistical distribution respect of the property of interest. The methods for subgroup discovery have the objective of discover interesting properties of subgroups obtaining *simple* rules (i.e. with an understandable structure and with few variables), *highly significant* and *with high support* (i.e. covering many of the instances of the target class).

An induced subgroup description has the form of an implication, $R^i\!: Cond^i \rightarrow Class_j$, where the property of interest for subgroup discovery is the class value $Class_j$ that appears in the rule consequent, and the rule antecedent $Cond^i$ is a conjunction of features (attribute-value pairs) selected from the features describing the training instances.

The concept of subgroup discovery was initially formulated by Klösgen in his rule learning algorithm EXPLORA [4] and by Wrobel in the algorithm MIDOS [5]. In the specialized bibliography, different methods have been developed which obtain descriptions of subgroups represented in different ways and using different quality measures, as SD [10], CN2-SD [11] or APRIORI-SD [12] among others.

One of the most important aspects of any subgroup discovery algorithm is the quality measures to be used, both to select the rules and to evaluate the results of the process. We can distinguish between objective and subjective quality measures. Some of the most used objective quality measures for the descriptive induction process are:

- *Coverage for a rule* [11]: measures the percentage of examples covered on average by one rule R^i of the induced rule set.

$$Cov(R^i) = Cov(Cond^i \rightarrow Class_j) = p(Cond^i) = \frac{n(Cond^i)}{n_s} \qquad (1)$$

where $n(Cond^i)$ is the number of examples which verifies the condition $Cond^i$ described in the antecedent (independently of the class to which belongs), and n_s is the number of examples.

- *Support for a rule*: considers the number of examples satisfying both the antecedent and the consequent parts of the rule. Lavrac et al. compute in [11] the support as:

$$Sup(R^i) = Sup(Cond^i \rightarrow Class_j) = p(Class_j.Cond^i) = \frac{n(Class_j.Cond^i)}{n_s} \qquad (2)$$

where $n(Class_j.Cond^i)$ is the number of examples which satisfy the conditions for the antecedent $(Cond^i)$ and simultaneously belong to the value for the target variable $(Class_j)$ indicated in the consequent part of the rule.

- *Significance for a rule* [4]: indicates how significant is a finding, if measured by the likelihood ratio of a rule.

$$Sig(R^i) = Sig(Cond^i \rightarrow Class_j) = 2 \cdot \sum_{j=1}^{n_c} n(Class_j.Cond^i) \cdot \log \frac{n(Class_j.Cond^i)}{n(Class_j) \cdot p(Cond^i)} \qquad (3)$$

where n_c is the number of values for the target variable and $p(Cond^i)$, computed as $n(Cond^i)/n_s$, is used as a normalized factor.

- *Unusualness for a rule*: is defined as the *weighted relative accuracy* of a rule [13].

$$WRAcc(Cond^i \rightarrow Class_j) = \frac{n(Cond^i)}{n_s} \cdot \left(\frac{n(Class_j.Cond^i)}{n(Cond^i)} - \frac{n(Class_j)}{n_s} \right) \qquad (4)$$

The WRAcc of a rule can be described as the balance between the coverage of the rule $(p(Cond^i))$ and its accuracy gain $(p(Class_j.Cond^i) - p(Class_j))$.

2.2 Disjunctive Normal Form Fuzzy Rules

In the proposal presented in this paper, we use fuzzy rules in disjunctive normal form (DNF fuzzy rules) as description language to specify the subgroups, which permit a disjunction for the values of any variable present in the antecedent part.

We can describe a fuzzy rule R^i as:

$$R^i : Cond^i \rightarrow Class_j$$

where the antecedent describes the subgroup in disjunctive normal form, and the consequent is a value of the target variable.

So, the DNF fuzzy rule can be expressed as:

$$R^i : \text{If } X_1 \text{ is } LL_1^1 \text{ or } LL_1^3 \text{ and } X_7 \text{ is } LL_7^1 \text{ then } Class_j \tag{5}$$

where $LL_{n_v}^{k_{n_v}}$ is the linguistic label number k_{n_v} of the variable n_v.

The fuzzy sets corresponding to the linguistic labels ($LL_v^1 \dots LL_v^{k_v}$) are defined by means of the corresponding membership functions which can be defined by the user or defined by means of a uniform partition if the expert knowledge is not available. In this algorithm, we use uniform partitions with triangular membership functions, as it is shown in Fig. 1 for a variable v with 5 linguistic labels.

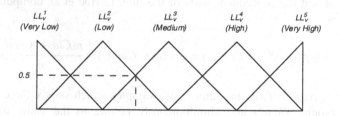

Fig. 1. Example of fuzzy partition for a continuous variable

It must be noted that any subset of the complete set of variables can take part in the rule antecedent, with any combination of linguistic labels related with the operator OR. In this way a subgroup is a compact and interpretable description of patterns of interest in data.

2.3 Multiobjective Genetic Algorithms

GAs are general purpose search algorithms which use principles inspired by natural genetics to evolve solutions to problems [14]. In the area of subgroup discovery any rule induction algorithm must optimize simultaneously several objectives. The more suitable way to approach them is by means of multiobjective optimization algorithms in which we search a set of optimal alternative solutions (rules in our case) in the sense that no other solution within the search space is better than it in all the considered objectives. The expert will use the set of rules obtained to select all or a set of them for the description of the subgroups based on the particular preference information of the problem.

In a formal way, a multiobjective optimization problem can be defined in the following way:

$$\min/\max \vec{y} = f(\vec{x}) = f_1(\vec{x}), f_2(\vec{x}), ..., f_n(\vec{x}))$$ (6)

where $\vec{x} = (x_1, x_2, ...x_m)$ is the decision vector and $\vec{y} = (y_1, y_2, ..., y_n)$ is the objective vector (a tuple with n objectives). The objective of any multiobjective optimization algorithm is to find all the decision vectors for which the corresponding objective vectors can not be improved in a dimension without degrading another, which is denominated optimal Pareto front.

In the last two decades an increasing interest has been developed in the use of GAs for multiobjective optimization. There are multiple proposals of multiobjective GAs [6], [7] as the algorithms MOGA [15], NSGA II [16] or SPEA2 [17] for instance.

The genetic representation of the solutions is the most determining aspect of the characteristics of any GA proposal. In this sense, the proposals in the specialized literature follow different approaches in order to encode rules within a population of individuals. In [18] a detailed description of these approaches is shown. Our proposal follows the *"Chromosome = Rule"* approach, in which each individual codifies a single rule, and a set of rules is codified by a subset of the complete population [19].

3   A Multiobjective Evolutionary Approach to Obtain Descriptive Fuzzy Rules

In this section we describe *MESDIF* (Multiobjective Evolutionary Subgroup DIscovery Fuzzy rules), a multiobjective GA for the extraction of rules which describe subgroups. The proposal extracts rules whose antecedent represents a conjunction of variables and whose consequent is fixed. The objective of this evolutionary process is to extract for each value of the target variable a variable number of different rules expressing information on the examples of the original set. As the objective is to obtain a set of rules which describe subgroups for all the values of the target feature, the algorithm must be carried out so many times as different values has the target feature. This algorithm can generate fuzzy and/or crisp DNF rules, for problems with continuous and/or nominal variables.

The multiobjective GA is based on the SPEA2 approach [17], and so applies the concepts of elitism in the rule selection (using a secondary or elite population) and search of optimal solutions in the Pareto front (the individuals of the population are ordered according to if each individual is or not dominated using the concept of Pareto optimal).

In order to preserve the diversity at a phenotypic level our algorithm uses a niches technique that considers the proximity in values of the objectives and an additional objective based on the novelty to promote rules which give information on examples not described by other rules of the population. Therefore, in a run we obtain a set of rules that provide us knowledge on a property of interest.

Figure 2 shows the scheme of the proposed model.

Step 1. Initialization:
    Generate an initial population P_0 and create an empty
    elite population $P'_0 = \emptyset$. Set t = 0.
Repeat
    Step 2. Fitness assignment: calculate fitness values of
    the individuals in P_t and P'_t.
    Step 3. Environmental selection: copy all non-dominated
    individuals in Pt and P'_t to P'_{t+1}. As the size of P'_{t+1}
    must be exactly the number of individuals to store (N),
    we may have to use a truncation or a filling function.
    Step 4. Mating selection: perform binary tournament
    selection with replacement on P'_{t+1} applying later
    crossover and mutation operators in order to fill the
    mating pool (obtaining P_{t+1}).
    Step 5. Increment generation counter (t = t+1)
While stop condition is not verified.
Step 6. Return the non-dominated individuals in P'_{t+1}.

Fig. 2. Scheme of the proposed algorithm

Once outlined the basis of the model, we will describe in detail some more important topics.

3.1 Chromosome Representation

In a subgroup discovery task, we have a number of descriptive features and a single target feature of interest. As we mentioned previously the multiobjective GA discovers a DNF fuzzy rule whose consequent is prefixed to one of the possible values of the target feature and each candidate solution is coded according to the "*Chromosome = Rule*" approach representing only the antecedent in the chromosome and associating all the individuals of the population with the same value of the target variable.

This representation of the target variable means that the evolutionary multiobjective algorithm must be run many times in order to discover the rules of the different classes, but it assures the knowledge extraction in all the classes.

All the information relating to a rule is contained in a fixed-length chromosome with a binary representation in which, for each feature it is stored a bit for each of the possible values of the feature; in this way, if the corresponding bit contains the value 0 it indicates that the bit is not used in the rule, and if the value is 1 it indicates that the corresponding value is included. If a rule contains all the bits corresponding to a feature with the value 1, this indicates that this feature has no relevance for the information contributed in the rule (all the values or the feature verify the rule condition), and so this feature is ignored. This takes us to a binary representation model with so many genes by variable as possible values exist for the same one. The set of possible values for the categorical features is that indicated by the problem, and for continuous variables is the set of linguistic terms determined heuristically or with expert information.

3.2 Definition of the Objectives of the Algorithm

In the rule induction process we try to get rules with high predictive accuracy, comprehensible and interesting. In our proposal, we have defined three objectives, and the algorithm tries to maximize all the defined objectives.

- *Confidence*. Determines the relative frequency of examples satisfying the complete rule among those satisfying only the antecedent. In this paper we use an adaptation of Quinlan's accuracy expression in order to generate fuzzy classification rules [20]: the sum of the degree of membership of the examples of this class (the examples covered by this rule) to the zone determined by the antecedent, divided the sum of the degree of membership of all the examples that verifies the antecedent part of this rule (irrespective of their class) to the same zone:

$$Conf\ (R^i) = \frac{\sum_{E^S \in E / E^S \in Class_j} APC(E^S, R^i)}{\sum_{E^S \in E} APC(E^S, R^i)} \tag{7}$$

  where *APC* (Antecedent Part Compatibility) is the compatibility degree between an example and the antecedent part of a fuzzy rule, i.e., the degree of membership for the example to the fuzzy subspace delimited by the antecedent part of the rule.

- *Support*. This is the measure of the degree of coverage that the rule offers to examples of that class, calculated as the quotient between the number of examples belonging to the class which are covered by the rule and the total number of examples from the same class:

$$Sup1\ (R^i) = \frac{n(Class_j.Cond^i)}{n(Class_j)} \tag{8}$$

- *Original support*. This objective is a measure of the originality level of the rule compared with the rest of rules. It is computed adding, for each example belonging to the antecedent of the rule, the factor *1/k*, where *k* is the number of rules of the population that describe information on that example. This measure promotes the diversity at the population at a phenotypic level.

The last objective defined, the original support, is a restriction in the rules in order to obtain a set of rules, the pareto front, with a high degree of coverage, and is related with the cooperation between rules; the other objectives take into account the support and the confidence.

3.3 Fitness Assignment

The fitness assignment for the rules extracted is performed in the following way:

- For each individual in the population is computed the value for all the objectives.
- The values reached by each individual in both the population and the elite population are used to compute what individual dominate what other.

- The strength of each individual is computed as the number of individuals that it dominates.
- The raw fitness of each individual is determined as the sum of the strength of its dominators (even in the population as in the elite population).
- The computation of the raw fitness offers a niching mechanism based in the concept of Pareto dominance, but it can fail when much of the individuals are non-dominated. To avoid this, it is included additional information on density to discriminate between individuals with the same values of raw fitness. The density estimation technique used in SPEA2 is an adaptation of the method of the k-th nearest neighbour, where the density in a point is decreasing function of the distance to the k-th nearest point. In this proposal we use the inverse of the distance to the k-th nearest neighbour as density estimation.
- The fitness value of each individual is the sum of its raw fitness value and its density.

3.4 Environmental Selection

This algorithm establishes a fixed length for the elite population, so it is necessary to define a truncation and a fill function. The truncation function allows eliminating the non-dominated solutions of the elite population if it exceeds the defined size. For this purpose it is used a niche schema defined around the density measured by the distance to its k-th nearest neighbour, in which, in an iterative process, in each iteration it is eliminated from the elite population the individual that is nearest of others respect of the values of the objectives. The fill function allows adding dominated individuals from the population and the elite population until the exact size of the set is reached (ordering the individuals according to their fitness values).

3.5 Reproduction Model and Genetic Operators

We use the following reproduction model:

- Join the original population with the elite population obtaining then the non-dominated individuals of the joining of these populations.
- Apply a binary tournament selection on the non-dominated individuals.
- Apply recombination to the resulting population by a two point cross operator and a biased uniform mutation operator in which half the mutations carried out have the effect of eliminating the corresponding variable, in order to increase the generality of the rules.

4 A Case Study in Marketing: Knowledge Discovery in Trade Fairs

In the area of marketing, and specifically in the trade fairs planning, it is important to extract conclusions of the information on previous trade fairs to determine the relationship between the trade fair planning variables and the success of the stand. This problem over the extraction of useful information on trade fairs has been analyzed in the Department of Organization and Marketing of the University of Mondragón, Spain [21].

Businesses consider trade fairs to be an instrument which facilitates the attainment of commercial objectives such as contact with current clients, the securing of new clients, the taking of orders, and the improvement of the company image amongst others [22]. One of the main inconveniences in this type of trade fair is the elevated investment which they imply in terms of both time and money. This investment sometimes coincides with a lack of planning which emphasises the impression that trade fairs are no more than an "expense" which a business must accept for various reasons such as tradition, client demands, and not giving the impression that things are going badly, amongst other factors [23]. Therefore convenient, is the automatic extraction of information about the relevant variables which permit the attainment of unknown data, which partly determines the efficiency of the stands of a trade fair.

A questionnaire was designed to reflect the variables that better allow explaining the trade fair success containing 104 variables (7 of them are continuous and the rest are categorical features, result of an expert discretization). Then, the stand's global efficiency is rated as *high*, *medium* or *low*, in terms of the level of achievement of objectives set for the trade fair. The data contained in this dataset were collected in the Machinery and Tools biennial held in Bilbao in March 2002 and contain information on 228 exhibitors.

For this real problem, the data mining algorithm should extract information of interest about each efficiency group. The rules generated will determine the influence which the different fair planning variables have over the results obtained by the exhibitor, therefore allowing fair planning policies to be improved.

4.1 Results of the Experimentation on the Marketing Dataset

As our proposal is a non-deterministic approach, the experimentation is carried out with 5 runs for each class of the target variable: *low*, *medium* and *high* efficiency. The parameters used in this experimentation are:

- Population size: 100.
- Elite population size: 5.
- Maximum number of evaluations of individual in each GA run: 10000.
- Mutation probability: 0.01.
- Number of linguistic labels for the continuous variables: 3

We have experimentally verified that the approach have a better behaviour using an elite population size of 5 individuals.

Table 1 shows the best results obtained for all the classes of the target variable (*low*, *medium* and *high* efficiency). In this table, it is shown for each rule obtained, the number of variables involved (*# VAR*), the *Support* (*SUP1*) as defined in (8) and used in our proposal, the *Confidence* (*CONF*) of each rule as defined in (7), the *Coverage* (*COV*) as defined in (1), the *Support* (*SUP2*) as defined in (2), the *Significance* (*SIG*) as defined in (3) and the *Unusualness* (*WRACC*) of the rule as computed in (4).

Table 1. Results for *Low*, *Medium* and *High* efficiency

Efficiency	# VAR.	SUP1	CONF	COV	SUP2	SIG	WRACC
Low	8	0.079	0.820	0.026	0.013	5.026	0.007
	4	0.026	1.000	0.004	0.004	3.584	0.001
	5	0.395	0.724	0.127	0.066	25.684	0.042
	6	0.289	0.759	0.088	0.048	19.672	0.031
Medium	6	0.088	0.892	0.658	0.057	6.623	0.008
	1	0.959	0.657	0.947	0.623	0.605	0.004
	2	0.574	0.802	0.469	0.373	12.104	0.065
	2	0.845	0.676	0.811	0.548	3.447	0.017
	4	0.182	0.750	0.158	0.118	2.441	0.011
High	5	0.095	0.595	0.031	0.017	6.565	0.010
	3	0.024	1.000	0.004	0.004	3.383	0.001
	4	0.047	0.722	0.013	0.009	3.812	0.004

It must be noted that high values in support (*SUP1*, expression (8)) means that the rule covers most of the examples of the class, and high values in confidence (*CONF*, expression (7)) means that the rule has few negative examples.

The rules generated have adequate values of confidence (*CONF*, expression (7)) and support (*SUP1*, expression (8)). The algorithm induces set of rules with a high confidence (higher than the minimum confidence value). The rule support, except for some rules, is low. The market problem used in this work is a difficult real problem in which inductive algorithms tend to obtain small disjuncts (specific rules which represent a small number of examples). However, the small disjunct problem is not a determining factor in the induction process for subgroup discovery because partial relations, i.e., subgroups with interesting characteristics, with a significant deviation from the rest of the dataset, are sufficient. The results show that *Low* and *High* efficiency classes are the more interesting for the subgroup discovery task, but also the more difficult.

The knowledge discovered for each one of the target variable values is understandable by the user due to the use of DNF fuzzy rules, and the low number of rules and conditions in the rule antecedents (below 10% of the 104 variables). Moreover, the rules obtained with the *MESDIF* algorithm are very simple.

Tables 2, 3 and 4 show the extracted rules for the three levels of efficiency (*low*, *medium* and *high*).

Marketing experts from Department of Organization and Marketing of the University of Mondragón (Spain) analysed the results obtained and indicated that:

- The exhibitors who obtained worse results were those with a medium or high size of the stand, not using indicator flags in it and with a low or medium valuation of the assembly and disassemble services.
- The companies which obtain medium efficiency are those with none or high satisfaction with the relation maintained with the clients, and medium, high or very high global satisfaction.
- Finally, the exhibitors who obtained better results (high efficiency) are big or huge companies using telemarketing with the quality contacts.

Table 2. Rules for *Low* efficiency

#Rule	Rule
1	IF (Publicity utility = None OR Medium OR High) AND (Number of annual fairs = 2-5 OR 6-10 OR 11-15 OR >15) AND (Use of consultants = NO) AND (Importance improvement image of the company = None OR Low OR Medium) AND (Addressees if only clients = NO) AND (Stand size = Medium OR High) AND (Valuation assembly/disassembly = Low OR Medium) AND (Indicator flags = NO) THEN Efficiency = Low
2	IF (Stand size = Medium OR High) AND (Telemarketing = ALL OR Only quality) AND (Gifts = NO) AND (Indicator flags = NO) THEN Efficiency = Low
3	IF (Use of consultants = NO) AND (Importance improvement image of the company = None OR Low OR Medium) AND (Stand size = Medium OR High) AND (Valuation assembly/disassembly = Low OR Medium) AND (Indicator flags = NO) THEN Efficiency = Low
4	IF (Publicity utility = None OR Low OR High) AND (Importance improvement image of the company = None OR Low OR Medium) AND (Addressees if only clients = NO) AND Stand size = Medium OR High) AND (Valuation assembly/disassembly = Low OR Medium) AND (Indicator flags = NO) THEN Efficiency = Low

Table 3. Rules for *Medium* efficiency

#Rule	Rule
1	IF (Satisfaction relation clients = None OR High) AND (Importance public relations = Very high) AND (Global satisfaction = Medium OR High OR Very high) AND (Quality visitors valuation = Low OR High) AND (Gifts = NO) AND (Inserts = NO) THEN Efficiency = Medium
2	IF (Previous promotion = YES) THEN Efficiency = Medium
3	IF (Satisfaction relation clients = None OR High) AND (Global satisfaction = Medium OR High OR Very high) THEN Efficiency = Medium
4	IF (Global satisfaction = Medium OR High OR Very high) AND (Inserts = NO) THEN Efficiency = Medium
5	IF (Satisfaction relation clients = None OR High) AND (Previous promotion = YES) AND (Company advertising mention = YES) AND (Inserts = NO) THEN Efficiency = Medium

Table 4. Rules for *High* efficiency

#Rule	Rule
1	IF (Importance new contacts = Low OR Medium OR Very High) AND (Visitor information valuation = Medium OR High) AND (Gratefulness letter = All OR Only quality) AND (Telemarketing = None OR Only quality) AND (Little gifts before fair = YES) THEN Efficiency = High
2	IF (Employees = 251-500 OR >500) AND (Follow-up modality = Only quality) AND (Telemarketing = NO OR Only quality) THEN Efficiency = High
3	IF (Employees =251-500 OR >500) AND (Visitor information valuation = Medium OR High) AND (Gratefulness letter = All OR Only quality) AND (Telemarketing = NO OR Only quality) THEN Efficiency = High

5 Conclusions

In this paper we describe an evolutionary multiobjective model for the descriptive induction of fuzzy rules which describe subgroups applied to a real knowledge extraction problem in trade fairs.

The use of a subgroup discovery algorithm for this problem is well suited because in subgroup discovery task the objective is not to generate a set of rules which cover all the dataset examples, but individual rules that, given a property of interest of the data, describe in an interpretable way the more interesting subgroups for the user.

In spite of the characteristics of the problem (elevated number of variables and lost values, low number of examples and few continuous variables) this multiobjective approach to the problem allows to obtain sets of rules, with an appropriate balance between the quality measures specified in the algorithm that are easily interpretable, and with a high level of confidence and support.

DNF fuzzy rules contribute a more flexible structure to the rules, allowing each variable to take more than one value, and facilitating the extraction of more general rules. In this kind of fuzzy rules, fuzzy logic contributes to the interpretability of the extracted rules due to the use of a knowledge representation nearest to the expert, also allowing the use of continuous features without a previous discretization.

As future work, we will study the inclusion in the *MESDIF* algorithm of different quality measures (and combinations of them) as objective functions in order to obtain fuzzy subgroup discovery rules with better properties.

Acknowledgment

This work was supported by the Spanish Ministry of Science and Technology and by the European Fund. FEDER under Projects TIC-2005-08386-C05-01 and TIC-2005-08386-C05-03, and the nets TIN2004-20061-E and TIN2004-21343-E.

References

1. Fayyad, U.M., Piatetsky-Shapiro, G., and Smyth, P., From Data Mining to Knowledge Discovery: An Overview, in Advances in Knowledge Discovery and Data Mining, U. Fayyad, et al., Editors, AAAI Press (1996) 1–30
2. Michie, D., Spiegelhalter, D.J., and Taylor, C.C.: Machine learning, neural and estatistical classification. Ellis Horwood, (1994)
3. Agrawal, R., Mannila, H., Srikant, R., Toivonen, H., and Verkamo, I., Fast Discovery of Association Rules, in Advances in Knowledge Discovery and Data Mining, U. Fayyad, et al., Editors, AAAI Press: Menlo Park, Calif. (1996) 307–328
4. Klösgen, W., Explora: A Multipattern and Multistrategy Discovery Assistant, in Advances in Knowledge Discovery and Data Mining, U. Fayyad, et al., Editors, AAAI Press: Menlo Park, Calif. (1996) 249–271
5. Wrobel, S., An algorithm for multi-relational discovery of subgroups, in Principles Of Data Mining And Knowledge Discovery (1997) 78-87
6. Deb, K.: Multi-Objective Optimization using Evolutionary Algorithms. John Wiley & Sons, (2001)

7. Coello, C.A., Van Veldhuizen, D.A., and Lamont, G.B.: Evolutionary Algorithms for Solving Multi-Objective Problems. Kluwer Academic Publishers, (2002)
8. Ghosh, A. and Nath, B.: Multi-objective rule mining using genetic algorithms. Information Sciences. 163 (2004) 123-133
9. Ishibuchi, H. and Yamamoto, T.: Fuzzy rule selection by multi-objective genetic local search algorithms and rule evaluation measures in data mining. Fuzzy Sets and Systems. 141 (2004) 59-88
10. Gamberger, D. and Lavrac, N.: Expert-guided subgroup discovery: Methodology and application. Journal Of Artificial Intelligence Research. 17 (2002) 1-27
11. Lavrac, N., Kavsec, B., Flach, P., and Todorovski, L.: Subgroup discovery with CN2-SD. Journal of Machine Learning Research. 5 (2004) 153-188
12. Kavsek, B., Lavrac, N., and Jovanoski, V., APRIORI-SD: Adapting association rule learning to subgroup discovery, in Advances In Intelligent Data Analysis V (2003) 230-241
13. Lavrac, N., Flach, P., and Zupan, B., Rule evaluation measures: A unifying view, in Inductive Logic Programming (1999) 174-185
14. Goldberg, D.E.: Genetic algorithms in search, optimization and machine learning. Addison-Wesley, (1989)
15. Fonseca, C.M. and Fleming, P.J. Genetic algorithms for multiobjective optimization: formulation, discussion and generalization. in Fifth International Conference on Genetic Algorithms (ICGA). 1993. San Mateo, CA
16. Deb, K., Pratap, A., Agarwal, A., and Meyarivan, T.: A fast and elitist multiobjective genetic algorithm: NSGA-II. IEEE Transactions on Evolutionary Computation. 6 (2002) 182-197
17. Zitzler, E., Laumanns, M., and Thiele, L., SPEA2: Improving the strength pareto evolutionary algorithm for multiobjective optimisation, in Evolutionary methods for design, optimisation and control, K. Giannakoglou, et al., Editors, CIMNE (2002) 95-100
18. Cordón, O., Herrera, F., Hoffmann, F., and Magdalena, L.: Genetic fuzzy systems: evolutionary tuning and learning of fuzzy knowledge bases. World Scientific, (2001)
19. Wong, M.L. and Leung, K.S.: Data Mining using Grammar Based Genetic Programming and Applications. Kluwer Academics Publishers, (2000)
20. Cordón, O., del Jesus, M.J., and Herrera, F.: Genetic Learning of Fuzzy Rule-based Classification Systems Co-operating with Fuzzy Reasoning Methods. International Journal of Intelligent Systems. 13 (1998) 1025-1053
21. Mesonero, M., Hacia un modelo efectivo de planificación ferial basado en algoritmos genéticos, in Departamento de Organización y Marketing, Universidad de Mondragón: Mondragón (2004)
22. Gopalakrishna, S., Lilien, G.L., Williams, J.D., and Sequeira, I.K.: Do trade shows pay off. Journal of Marketing. 59 (1995) 75-83
23. Millar, S.: How to get the most of the trade shows. NTC Publishing Group, (2003)

A Scatter Search Algorithm for the Automatic Clustering Problem

Rasha S. Abdule-Wahab[1,2], Nicolas Monmarché[2], Mohamed Slimane[2], Moaid A. Fahdil[1], and Hilal H. Saleh[1]

[1] University of Technology, Dept. of Computer Science, Iraq
[2] Université François Rabelais de Tours, Laboratoire d'Informatique, 64 av. Jean Portalis 37200, Tours - France

Abstract. We present a new hybrid algorithm for data clustering. This new proposal uses one of the well known evolutionary algorithms called Scatter Search. Scatter Search operates on a small set of solutions and makes only a limited use of randomization for diversification when searching for globally optimal solutions. The proposed method discovers automatically cluster number and cluster centres without prior knowledge of a possible number of class, and without any initial partition. We have applied this algorithm on standard and real world databases and we have obtained good results compared to the K-means algorithm and an artificial ant based algorithm, the Antclass algorithm.

1 Introduction

Clustering [4] is an important unsupervised classification technique that gathers data into classes (or clusters) such that the data in each cluster shares a high degree of similarity while being very dissimilar to data from other clusters. Formally, clustering can be defined as follows [11]: given a set $\mathcal{X} = \{\mathbf{x}_1, \mathbf{x}_2, .., \mathbf{x}_n\}$ of features vectors, find an integer K ($2 \leq K \leq n$) and the K clusters of $\mathcal{X}$ which exhibit homogeneous subsets.

Multitudes of clustering methods are proposed in the literature [4]. Theses methods can be basically classified into: Partitional, Hierarchical, Density-based and Grid-based clustering. In this paper we are concerned with the former one.

Partitional clustering algorithms obtain a single partition of the data instead of a clustering structure such as the dendrogram produced by a hierarchical technique. Partitional methods show advantages in applications involving large data sets for which the construction of a dendrogram in computationally prohibitive [4]. The best known and commonly used partitioning methods are K-means, H-means and J-means [10]. All these techniques are based on the minimization of the overall sum of the squared errors between each point and the corresponding cluster centres. This can be written as the minimization of the following objective function:

$$E = \sum_{i=1}^{K} \sum_{\mathbf{x}_\ell \in \mathcal{C}_i} ||\mathbf{x}_\ell - \mathbf{g}_i||^2 \tag{1}$$

P. Perner (Ed.): ICDM 2006, LNAI 4065, pp. 350–364, 2006.
© Springer-Verlag Berlin Heidelberg 2006

where $\mathbf{g}_i$ is the centre of the cluster $\mathcal{C}_i$. The methods which minimize this function are not able to predict the correct number of clusters because the evaluation of E requires K to be predefined and fixed. Hence, when K varies, the value of E for a set with optimal number of clusters may not attain the minimum value. For example, if the number of clusters of a set is very close to the number of objects, then the value of E is close to zero. Obviously, this kind of situation may not represent an optimal partition [11]. So, most of the well-known partitional techniques get stuck with problems where the number K is varying. In order to solve this problem and to keep the ability to optimize the number of clusters, different clustering criteria have been defined. In [11], we can find a combination of the Davis-Boulding criteria and E which is used as an objective function to identify the correct number of clusters. Also in [6], are explained a number of related works where the authors have used different criteria functions as objective functions which are based on the intercluster and the intracluster measures.

In this paper we address clustering problem using Scatter Search hybridized with K-means algorithm. The reason for investigating Scatter Search to solve clustering problem is the behavior of this algorithm that has explained its efficiency and ability to yield promising outcomes for solving combination and nonlinear optimization problem [3]. Scatter Search is an evolutionary method that has been successfully applied to hard optimization problems. In contrast with other evolutionary methods like genetic algorithms, Scatter Search is founded on the premise that systematic design and method for creating a new solution afford significant benefits beyond those derived from recourse to randomization. It uses strategies for search diversification that have been proved to be effective in a variety of optimization problems [3]. Thus we should expect some improvement in performance to solve clustering problem from the utilization of this technique. In addition we use a different criteria function which guides the algorithms to choose the correct number of cluster.

The outline of this paper is organized as follows, in section 2 explains the principle of the Scatter Search algorithm. Section 3 develops the algorithm and other new directions. In section 4, results obtained on different kinds of data are presented and finally, section 5 gives the conclusions.

2   Scatter Search Algorithm

Scatter Search was introduced in 1977 by Fred Glover, and derives its foundation from earlier strategies to combine decision rules and constraints. The main goal is to produce better solutions with a procedure that combines original solutions [3]. Basically, Scatter Search algorithm starts with a collection of feasible solutions. At each step, some of the best solutions are extracted from the collection in order to be combined. A trial point is then created by a combination operator and a heuristic operator is applied to the trial point. As a result of the operator, a new feasible solution is obtained which might be included or not (according to some criteria) in the collections. These steps are repeated so that the collection sets created do not change [3].

2.1   Basic Scatter Search Design

The Scatter Search methodology is very flexible, since each of its elements can be implemented in a variety of ways and degrees of sophistication. In the following we explain the template for implementing Scatter Search which consists of five methods [2]:

1. **Diversification Generation Method:** A routine designed to generate a collection of diverse trial solutions.
2. An **Improvement Method:** A routine designed to transform a trial solution into one or more enhanced trial solutions.
3. A **Reference Set Update Method:** A routine designed to maintain and manage a reference set of the best solutions found.
4. A **Subset Generation Method:** A routine designed to produce a subset of the reference set solutions for the purpose of creating combined solutions.
5. A **Solution Combination Method:** A routine designed to transform a given subset of solutions produced into one or more combined solution vectors.

2.2   Diversification Generation Method

The goal of the diversification generator is to produce solutions that differ from each other in significant ways, and that yield productive alternatives in the context of the problem considered. Also, this can be viewed as sampling the solution space in a systematic fashion to identify high quality solutions with controllable degrees of differences. By contrast, the goal of randomization is to produce solutions that may differ from each other in any degree, as long as the differences are entirely unsystematic [2].

2.3   Reference Set Updating Method

The reference set *RefSet* is updated by replacing the reference solutions with the worst objective function value with a new solution that has a better objective function value. Since *RefSet* is always ordered, the best solution can be denoted by x^1 and worst solution by x^b. Then, when a new solution x is generated as a result of the Solutions Combination Method, the objective function value of the new solution is used to determine whether *RefSet* needs to be updated. Various methods for rebuild the reference set can be found in [5], one of them is the same basic principle which will use and explained it in section (3.3).

2.4   Subset Generation Method

This method consists of generating the subsets that will be used for creating new solutions with the Solutions Combinations Method. The Subset Generation Method is typically designed to generate the following types of subsets [5]:

1. Subset Type 1: all 2-element subsets.
2. Subset Type 2: 3-element subsets derived from the 2-element subsets by augmenting each 2-element subset to include the best solution not in this subset.

3. Subset Type 3: 4-element subsets derived from the 3-element subsets by augmenting each 3-element subset to include the best solution not in this subset.
4. Subset Type 4: the subsets consisting of the best 4 elements.

3 Scatter Search Clustering Algorithm (SSC)

In this section we explain the implementation of SSC: our particular implementation uses the five key components of the original Scatter Search algorithm which will presented in the same order as in section 2.1.

3.1 Diversification Generation Method (DGM)

DGM generator is used at the beginning of the search process to generate the Original Set (OS), which is a set of OS_{size} solutions. OS_{size} is typically at least 10 times the size of the Reference Set [7].

This method is based on the same principle which can be found in [5]: a controlled randomization scheme based on a frequency memory is used to generate a set of diverse solutions with different lengths. For M dimensional feature space, each solution is represented as a vector of real values with the length equal to $K' \times M$ where K' is a random value between 2 and a specified positive integer K_{max}. The first M positions represent the M dimensions of the first cluster center; the next M positions represent those of the second cluster center, and so on. A pseudo-code version of the DGM to produce solutions appears in algorithm 1.

DGM is initiated by dividing the data set n (records) into sub-regions, in our approach the number of region is specified to 4. On the other hand the size of each sub-region is approximately equal to n/4. Each solution x is generated with the form: $\{g_1^x, \ldots, g_{K'}^x\}$ with $g_z^x = \{g_1^x, \ldots, g_M^x\}$. Two steps are needed to create g_z^x. First a sub-region j is selected according to the stored value in the frequency memory. The frequency memory avoids the repeated selection that may happen to the same sub-region. The second step randomly generates a value which represents the index of the element (record) that exists in the selected region(see algorithm 1). This value can be determined using the following

$$Index = \left\lfloor \frac{(i+r) \times (n-1)}{4} \right\rfloor \tag{2}$$

where r is uniformly generated in $[0,1]$, n represent the number of element in the datasets. For more explanation, consider the following example: if $K' = 3$ and n=100, the frequency counts are structured in table 1.

To construct the first cluster centers C_1 for a solution x, the number of the sub-region from which the elements (record) will be selected must be specified. Initially if the frequency counts for all sub-regions are equal to zero, then the sub-region number is determined randomly in the range between 1 and 4 and the count of the selected sub-region will be increased. The same process will be

---

Algorithm 1. Diversification Generation Method

1: $K_{index}=\emptyset$ {K_{index} is the set that contains the indexes of selected points}
2: $K'=$ random value between 2 and K_{max}
3: **while** $|\mathcal{K}| < K'$ **do**
4:     Compute the frequency count of $\mathcal{K}^{th}$ which is the sum to the values stored in frequency memory for all regions and is stored in Fc.
5:     **if** frequency count for all region is zero **then**
6:         $i \leftarrow \mathcal{U}(\{1,2,3,4\})$
7:     **else**
8:         $j \leftarrow$ choose a random value between 1 and the frequency count.
9:         $i \leftarrow 1$
10:         **while** $j >$ frequency of region (i) **do**
11:             $j \leftarrow j-($ Fc - the amount of the frequency of region $(i))$
12:             $i \leftarrow i+1$
13:         **end while**
14:     **end if**
15:     $r \leftarrow \mathcal{U}([0;1])${uniform random}
16:     $Index = \left\lfloor \frac{(i+r)\times(n-1)}{4} \right\rfloor$
17:     $K_{index} \leftarrow K_{index} \cup \{Index\}$
18: **end while**

Table 1. Initial frequency count

	C_1	C_2	C_3
Sub_region_1	0	0	0
Sub_region_2	0	0	0
Sub_region_3	0	0	0
Sub_region_4	0	0	0

repeated to the other cluster centers $C_{K'}$ to complete the construction process of the solution x. Table 2 presents the content of the frequency memory after the solution construction process was completed.

According to the values of table 2, solution x is constructed with the form: x = {sub_region$_3(index_{1,...,n/4})$,sub_region$_2(index_{1,...,n/4})$, sub_region$_2(index_{1,...,n/4})$ }. The constructed solution will be considered one of the solutions that contribute to create OS. DGM will continue in constructing other new solutions based on the current contents of frequency memory, which can be done as follows: to construct the first cluster centers C_1, a random value between 1 and F_{C_1} is selected (i.e, $F_{C_K} = \sum_{p=1}^{4}$ (sub_region$_{pK}$)) ,this selected value will guide DGM algorithm to select the appropriate sub_region. This will happen by checking if the selected value is less than the count of sub_region(j) where (j=1,...,4), then select the sub_region(j), else the comparison and decrease in this value will be repeated until the count of reaching sub_region is less than the selected value. The reached sub_region will be taken, then one of the elements within this sub_region will be chosen by specifying its index using Eq(2). Table 3 shows the updated frequency memory where the selected value is equal to 1.

Table 2. Frequency count

	C_1	C_2	C_3
Sub_region_1	0	0	0
Sub_region_2	0	1	1
Sub_region_3	1	0	0
Sub_region_4	0	0	0

Table 3. The updated frequency memory

	C_1	C_2	C_3
Sub_region_1	1	0	0
Sub_region_2	0	1	1
Sub_region_3	1	0	0
Sub_region_4	0	0	0

3.2 Improvement Method

As a meta_heuristic, Scatter Search can house a variety of optimization or heuristic based improvement approaches. This method enhances solutions and converts them into feasible one if it is possible while other components of Scatter Search achieve the global one. Therefore for the sake of space a particular improved method is described that have found to be effective in this technique.

This method improves the generated solutions that are produced by the Diversification Generation Method. These solutions are passed into a local optimizer. The local optimizer that has been chosen is a modified K-means algorithm [12]. The pseudo-code of this algorithm is presented in algorithm 2, which explains the processing that is applied to any solution to be improved.

In this algorithm the value v_{ij} is computed. This value is used as a factor of the movement that may happen between the clusters, for example: let C_ℓ be the cluster to which belongs, then the value of v_{ij} for all other clusters C_j (with $j \neq \ell$) is calculated by using the following formula { This formula is obtained from Späth to simplify the calculation in K-means }[10,12]:

$$v_{ij} = \frac{|C_j| \times ||\mathbf{x}_i - \mathbf{g}_j||^2}{|C_j| + 1} - \frac{|C_\ell| \times ||\mathbf{x}_i - \mathbf{g}_\ell||^2}{|C_\ell| - 1} \tag{3}$$

Then when the negative value of v_{ij} is obtained, the reassignment is done and the cluster centers are updated by using the following formula:

$$\mathbf{g}_\ell = \frac{|C_\ell|\mathbf{g}_\ell - \mathbf{x}_i}{|C_\ell| - 1} \quad and \quad \mathbf{g}_\lambda = \frac{|C_\lambda|\mathbf{g}_\lambda - \mathbf{x}_i}{|C_\lambda| + 1} \tag{4}$$

Locale optimizer stops until reaching a maximum number of iterations. In our approach, a small value is specified as a maximum number of iterations because this method is not responsible for obtaining the global optimality which will be achieved by applying the other components of SSC. After that the competition

Algorithm 2. Solutions improvement

1: **while** a specified iterations limit is not reached **do**
2:    **for** $\ell = 1$ to K' **do**
3:       **for all** $\mathbf{x}_i \in C_\ell$ **do**
4:          **for all** $j = 1$ to K' and $j \neq \ell$ **do**
5:             Calculate v_{ij} (see Eq. 3)
6:          **end for**
7:          Let be $\lambda = \arg\min_{j=1,..,K', j\neq\ell}\{v_{ij}\}$
8:          **if** $v_{i\lambda} < 0$ **then**
9:             Reassign $\mathbf{x}_i$ to C_λ
10:          **end if**
11:       **end for**
12:    **end for**
13:    Compute the fitness of the new created solution
14:    Compare with the original solution, and choose the best one.
15: **end while**

is done between the current solution and the new point that results from passing the current solution to the local optimizer, if the new point is better than the current point, take it and leave the old one, and so on until a specified condition is reached.

The solution obtained by algorithm 2 is checked: empty clusters are removed, this algorithm can sometimes decrease the number of clusters (as K-mean can do).

This method is applied at the beginning through the creation process of initial trial solutions (it is not applied to the solutions created by the solution combination method unlike some version of original Scatter Search). As a general, algorithm 3 presents the pseudo-code used for creating the original set OS.

Algorithm 3. Processing for Creating the Initial Trial Solutions

1: $OS \leftarrow \emptyset$
2: **while** $|OS| < OS_{size}$ **do**
3:    Chose the number of clusters K' randomly between 2 and $K_{\max}$
4:    $X \leftarrow \emptyset$
5:    **for** $k = 1$ to K' **do**
6:       Create (with Diversification Generation method) the k-th cluster centre and add to X
7:    **end for**
8:    Apply algorithm 2 to X to obtain X^*.
9:    **if** $X^* \notin OS$ **then**
10:       $OS \leftarrow OS \cup \{X^*\}$
11:    **end if**
12: **end while**

3.3   Reference Set

Initial Reference Set Building. As explained before, the reference set *RefSet* is a collection of both high quality solutions and diverse solutions that are used to generate new solutions by applying the solutions combination method. In this method, the reference set consists of the union of two subsets $RefSet_1$ and $RefSet_2$ of size b_1 , and b_2 respectively. To create $RefSet_1$, the best b_1 solution is selected from OS. These solutions are added to $RefSet_1$ and deleted them from OS, while $RefSet_2$ initially constructed uses the following steps:

1. Compute the distance d(x,y) between each solution x that exists in OS and each solution y in *RefSet*, where d(x,y) is the Euclidean distance between x and y.
2. Select the solutions that maximize $d(x)$ where $d_{min}(x) = \{d(x, y)\}, y \notin RefSet$

For example, if *RefSet* has the following solution: $RefSet=\{y_1, y_2, y_3\}$ and OS have the following $OS=\{x_1, x_2, \ldots, x_{10}\}$. The first element in $RefSet_2$ is created by calculating the distance between solutions which exist in OS and solutions which exist in the current *RefSet*:

$d_{min}(x_1) = Min\{d(x_1, y_1), d(x_1, y_2), d(x_1, y_3)\}$
$d_{min}(x_2) = Min\{d(x_2, y_1), d(x_2, y_2), d(x_2, y_3)\}$
$\vdots$

after that select the solution that achieves the maximum of $d_{min}(x)$ values, add it to *RefSet* and delete it from OS.

To create other elements in $RefSet_2$, the update process is done on $d_{min}(x)$ values because of the new addition on the current *RefSet*. This process is repeated until b_2 solutions are added to $RefSet_2$. Algorithm 4 presents the necessary steps for generating solutions to $RefSet_2$.

Algorithm 4. Building of $RefSet_2$

1: Start with $RefSet_2 = \emptyset$
2: **while** $|RefSet_2| < b_2$ **do**
3:     $x = \arg\max_{i \in OS}\{\min_{j \in RefSet_1 \cup RefSet_2} d(i, j)\}$
4:     $RefSet_2 \leftarrow RefSet_2 \cup \{x\}$
5: **end while**

Each generated solution is a member in *RefSet* if it is considered to be a new one. Therefore, to verify the new created solutions that does not exist in *RefSet*, a procedure is needed to perform these verifications steps, algorithm 5 explains this procedure.

Reference Set Updating Method. After the initial reference set is constructed, the Solution Combination Method is applied to the subset generated as outlined in the following section. This set is used to update solutions that exists in $RefSet_1$ and $RefSet_2$, so this method is responsible to do that.

Algorithm 5. Verify a new solution Y

Require: M is the number of attributes and $Y = \{\mathbf{g}_1^Y, \ldots, \mathbf{g}_{K'}(Y)^Y\}$ with $\mathbf{g}_i^j = (g_i^j(1), \ldots, g_i^j(M))$

1: new←true
2: **for all** $X \in RefSet_1$ **do**
3:   K_{min}=min($K'(X), K'(Y)$)
4:   **for** $i = 1$ to K_{min} **do**
5:     **for** $j = 1$ to M **do**
6:       **if** $|g_i^X(j) - g_i^Y(j)| \geq$ threshold {the threshold value has been arbitrarily fixed to 1%} **then**
7:         new←true
8:       **else**
9:         new←false, and exit the algorithm
10:      **end if**
11:    **end for**
12: **end for**
13: **end for**

New solution may become a member of $RefSet_1$ if the following condition is satisfied:

new solution x has a better fitness value than x^{b1} (the worst solution of $RefSet_1$) and also is not a member of the current $RefSet_1$.

Or it replace the worst solution in $RefSet_2$ if the following conditions is satisfied.

The new solution x has a better divers value than the worst solution x^{b2} in current $RefSet_2$ and if it is not a member in this set .

In both cases, the new solution replaces the worst and ranking is updated to identify the new worst solution in terms of either quality or diversity.

3.4   Subset Generation Method

This method consists of generating the subset that will be used to create new solutions with the Solution Combination Method. For the purpose of our paper, we limit our scope to type-1 subset consisting of all pair wise combinations of the solutions in $RefSet$.

3.5   Solution Combination Method

This method uses the subset generated with the Subset Generation Method to combine the elements in each subset for creating new trial solutions. In this case we use a linear combination method[5] to generate new trial solutions. Original linear combination process solutions that have fixed length(the same number of clusters), while SSC process solutions which have different number of clusters, therefore some modification is needed to work well with SSC. For the sake of simplicity, the linear combination is referred to ϕ . To perform the combination method between x_1 and x_2 which have lengths equal to l_{x_1} and l_{x_2} respectively (i.e., l_{x_1}, l_{x_2} , represent the number of cluster centers):

$$x_1 = \{\mathbf{g}_1^{x_1}, \mathbf{g}_2^{x_1}, \mathbf{g}_3^{x_1}, \mathbf{g}_4^{x_1}\} \text{ where } K'(x_1) = 4$$
$$x_2 = \{\mathbf{g}_1^{x_2}, \mathbf{g}_2^{x_2}, \mathbf{g}_3^{x_2}\} \text{ where } K'(x_2) = 3$$

the minimum length between l_{x_1} and l_{x_2} will be selected. Based on the selected length, the elements within x_1 and x_2 will be combined which represent the first solution created by this method (let it y_1). The remaining elements within the largest length will be added to y_1, this will be considered the second one (let it y_2).

$$y_1 = \{\phi(\mathbf{g}_1^{x_1}, \mathbf{g}_1^{x_2}), \phi(\mathbf{g}_2^{x_1}, \mathbf{g}_2^{x_2}), \phi(\mathbf{g}_3^{x_1}, \mathbf{g}_3^{x_2})\}$$
$$y_2 = \{\phi(\mathbf{g}_1^{x_1}, \mathbf{g}_1^{x_2}), \phi(\mathbf{g}_2^{x_1}, \mathbf{g}_2^{x_2}), \phi(\mathbf{g}_3^{x_1}, \mathbf{g}_3^{x_2}), \mathbf{g}_4^{x_1}\}$$

Either y_1 or y_2 will be selected, whereas the selection process is done randomly.

3.6   Fitness Function

To quantify the quality of obtained solutions, and in order to create the $RefSet_1$, we have used two criterion which are minimized simultaneously. The first criteria (Eq 5), is used to guide the algorithm to choose the appropriate cluster number from the original set OS. The second criterion concentrates on the competition between solutions that have been added to $RefSet_1$. Therefore to choose the appropriate solutions in $RefSet_1$ we have used the following criterion:

$$D = \sum_{i=1}^{K'} \max_{i \neq j} \left\{ \frac{\Delta(C_i) + \Delta(C_j)}{\delta(C_i, C_j)} \right\} \tag{5}$$

$$\Delta(C) = \frac{2}{|C|} \sum_{\mathbf{x}_\ell \in C} d(\mathbf{x}_\ell, \mathbf{g}) \tag{6}$$

$$\delta(C_i, C_j) = \frac{|C_i|\Delta(C_i) + |C_j|\Delta(C_j)}{2(|C_i| + |C_j|)} \tag{7}$$

This criterion is computed for each element in the original $RefSet$ and are choose b_1 solutions from this set which have the minimum value of D. After creating b_1 solutions to $RefSet_1$, order this set. The ordering process is done by using the following criterion:

$$Fitness = |(D - I) + E| \tag{8}$$

where I is equal to:

$$I = \sum_{i=1}^{K'} \sum_{j=1(j \neq i)}^{K'} \delta(C_i, C_j) \tag{9}$$

and E is aforementioned in Eq 1. In this case the minimum value of $Fitness$ represents the best value in the $RefSet_1$ which represents the first element and the large value of $Fitness$ represent the worst element.

Also, we need to compute the value of fitness (Eq 8) for each solution produced from Solution Combination Method, and which may become members in $RefSet_1$ if the value of the fitness function is smaller than the worst solution in this set and absolutely if theses solution achieved the differential from the solutions that exists in this set.

3.7   Overall Procedure

The proposed procedure is explained in algorithm 6 where: OS_{size} is the size of Original Set, b is the size of the reference set, b_1 is the size of the high-quality subset, b_2 is the size of the diverse subsets and $Iter_{max}$ is maximum number of iteration.

Algorithm 6. The Pseudo-Code of the Overall Procedure

1: Build the Original Set OS
2: Compute the Fitness value for each solution in OS (formula 5)
3: Build $RefSet = RefSet_1 \cup RefSet_2$ from OS. $RefSet_1$ is made of the first b_1 elements of OS which is ordered according to formula 5. $RefSet_1$ is then ordered according to formula 8. The b_2 solutions stored in $RefSet_2$ are constructed as described in algorithm 4.
4: $NewElements \leftarrow true$, $iter \leftarrow 0$
5: **while** NewElements bfand $iter < Iter_{max}$ **do**
6:     Let be maxsubset, the number of subsets that include at least one new element
7:     $NewElements \leftarrow false$
8:     **for** $c = 1$ to maxsubset **do**
9:         Generate the next subset s from $RefSet$ with the Subset Generation Method
10:         Apply the solutions Combination Method to obtain the improved solution X^*.
11:         **if** $X^* \notin RefSet_1$ **and** $Fitness(X^*) < \max_{x \in RefSet_1}\{Fitness(x)\}$ **then**
12:             remove the worst element from $RefSet_1$
13:             $RefSet_1 \leftarrow RefSet_1 \cup X^*$
14:             NewElements←true
15:         **else if** $X^* \notin RefSet_2$ **and** $dmin(X^*) > dmin(x)$ for a solution $x \in RefSet_2$ **then**
16:             remove the worst element from $RefSet_2$
17:             $RefSet_2 \leftarrow RefSet_2 \cup \{X^*\}$
18:             NewElements←true
19:         **end if**
20:     **end for**
21:     $iter \leftarrow iter + 1$
22: **end while**

---

4   Experimental Results

4.1   Testing Methodology

In order to evaluate and compare results obtained by Scatter Search, two kinds of databases are used: artificial datasets [9] and real life datasets [1]. These datasets are supervised: for each object, we know its label which is only used to evaluate the method but which remains unknown from the method itself. To evaluate the accuracy of our algorithm we have used the following clustering error measure[8]: let denoted by $c(o_i)$ the label (or class) of object o_i and $c'(o_i)$, the label are found by the method we consider, the clustering error E_c is computed as follows:

$$E_c = \frac{2}{n(n-1)} \sum_{(i,j)\in\{1,...,n\}^2, i<j} \varepsilon_{ij} \qquad (10)$$

where :

$$\varepsilon_{ij} = \begin{cases} 0 \text{ if } & (c(o_i) = c(o_j) \wedge c'(o_i) = c'(o_j)) \\ & \vee (c(o_i) \neq c(o_j) \wedge c'(o_i) \neq c'(o_j)) \\ 1 \text{ else} \end{cases} \qquad (11)$$

This error considers all the couple of objects and is increased when two objects are not in the same situation than they were according their labels. This error has the advantage of taking into account the number of clusters that have been obtained by the studied method.

4.2   Results

The results produced by SSC are shown in table 4. Two major indicators of performance can be found in this table: E_c is the averaged classification error and k' is the average number of classes, σ_{E_c} and $\sigma_{k'}$ are the corresponding standard deviations. M represents the number of attributes, n represents the number of objects and K is the original number of clusters all attributes are normalized within $[0; 1]$.

We can see from the results that presented in this table , on artificial and real world datasets, all misclassification error rates are low. Furthermore, SSC sometimes obtains the real number of classes.

4.3   Original Size(OS_{size}) and Refset Size

In order to demonstrate the impact of OS_{size} parameter on the number of clusters k', different values of OS_{size} have been experimented. Figure 1 underlines

Table 4. Experimental results obtained by SSC averaged over 50 runs

Data	M	n	K	$OS_{size} = 50$	
				$E_c[\sigma_{E_c}]$	$k'[\sigma_{k'}]$
Art1	2	400	4	0.16 [0.03]	4.98 [1.73]
Art2	2	1000	2	0.27 [0.06]	5.04 [2.03]
Art3	2	1100	4	0.25 [0.05]	5.62 [2.99]
Art4	2	200	2	0.27 [0.04]	4.90 [1.06]
Art5	2	900	9	0.15 [0.04]	6.00 [1.67]
Art6	8	400	4	0.06 [0.05]	6.42 [3.07]
Iris	4	150	3	0.14 [0.03]	3.46 [0.82]
Wine	12	178	3	0.15 [0.05]	5.86 [2.23]
Glass	9	214	6	0.31 [0.03]	6.36 [2.04]
Pima	8	768	2	0.48 [0.02]	5.66 [2.47]
Soybean	21	47	4	0.10 [0.05]	6.00 [1.75]
Thyroid	5	215	3	0.36 [0.06]	2.40 [0.66]

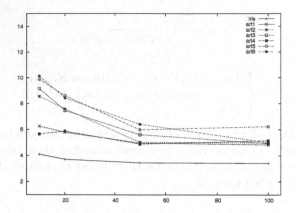

Fig. 1. The Effect of OS_{size} on k'

Table 5. The Effect of reference set size on k'

Dataset	b	k' $[\sigma_{k'}]$	b	k' $[\sigma_{k'}]$
Iris	10	3.4 [0.49]	15	3.40 [0.00]
Art1	10	4.86 [1.48]	15	4.84 [1.16]
Art2	10	5.04 [2.03]	15	4.98 [1.07]
Art3	10	5.52 [1.98]	15	4.94 [1.61]
Art4	10	5.03 [1.06]	15	5.16 [0.73]
Art5	10	6.00 [1.67]	15	6.24 [1.22]
Art6	10	6.24 [3.07]	15	5.00 [1.24]

SSC results with some datasets (Iris,Art1,Art2,Art3,Art4,Art5,Art6). The curves show that k' is sensitive to the value of OS_{size}: we have obtained better results for k' when the value of OS_{size} was large.

Unlike the population size in other evolutionary algorithm, the reference set size in scatter search is relatively small [3]. Therefore, we study(using some dataset) the impact of reference set size on k' parameter taken into consideration small values of b. The conclusion of this work according to table 5 is that a big reference set size has a best result.

4.4   Comparative Study

We have compared SSC with other clustering algorithms: Antclass [8], an artificial ant based clustering algorithm, and K-means algorithm initialized with 10 randomly generated initial clusters. This comparison was done based upon the effectiveness of the final clustering returned by the algorithm which is represented by computing E_c, and the quality of finding the correct number of clusters. The parameter setting for SSC shown in table 6 is: $OS_{size} = 100$, $b_1 = 10$, $b_2 = 5$, $Iter_{\max} = 20$, and $Maxcluster = 15$. From a general point of view, SSC gives an averaged error and number of clusters which are lower than Antclass and 10-means methods.

Table 6. Experimental results obtained by AntClass, 10-means, and SSC averaged over 50 run

Data	10-means		AntClass		SSC	
	$E_c[\sigma_{E_c}]$	$k'[\sigma_{k'}]$	$E_c[\sigma_{E_c}]$	$k'[\sigma_{k'}]$	$E_c[\sigma_{E_c}]$	$k'[\sigma_{k'}]$
Art1	0.18 [0.01]	8.58 [0.98]	0.15 [0.05]	4.22 [1.15]	0.13 [0.023]	4.84 [1.155]
Art2	0.38 [0.01]	8.52 [0.96]	0.41 [0.01]	12.32 [2.01]	0.29 [0.041]	4.98 [1.086]
Art3	0.31 [0.01]	8.28 [0.96]	0.35 [0.01]	14.66 [2.68]	0.26 [0.037]	4.94 [1.605]
Art4	0.32 [0.02]	6.38 [0.75]	0.29 [0.23]	1.68 [0.84]	0.29 [0.025]	5.16 [0.731]
Art5	0.08 [0.01]	8.82 [0.91]	0.08 [0.01]	11.36 [1.94]	0.13 [0.032]	6.24 [1.449]
Art6	0.10 [0.02]	8.46 [1.08]	0.11 [0.13]	3.74 [1.38]	0.02 [0.029]	5.00 [1.249]
Iris	0.18 [0.03]	7.12 [1.11]	0.19 [0.08]	3.52 [1.39]	0.13 [0.029]	3.42 [0.602]
Wine	0.27 [0.01]	9.64 [0.52]	0.51 [0.11]	6.46 [2.10]	0.15 [0.054]	6.06 [2.053]
Glass	0.29 [0.02]	9.44 [0.70]	0.40 [0.06]	5.60 [2.01]	0.10 [0.051]	7.08 [1.521]
Pima	0.50 [0.01]	9.90 [0.36]	0.47 [0.02]	6.10 [1.84]	0.48 [0.017]	6.24 [1.955]
Soybean	0.13 [0.02]	8.82 [0.97]	0.54 [0.17]	1.60 [0.49]	0.28 [0.032]	7.52 [2.109]
Thyroid	0.42 [0.02]	9.56 [0.57]	0.22 [0.09]	5.84 [1.33]	0.36 [0.050]	2.42 [0.493]

SSC performs better than Antclass for Art1, Art2, Art3, Art4, Art6, Iris, where the number of clusters is closer to the results obtained for Wine and Pima data, but SSC has a better classification error value than Antclass. The computational times for SSC are high compared to the two other methods, because the first two components of SSC spend most of the time to create the initial solutions.

5 Conclusion

In this paper we have described a new algorithm which is based on the Scatter Search algorithm that have ability to discover automatically the number of clusters and cluster centers without any prior knowledge of a possible number of class. This algorithm has been compared with the K-means and the Antclass algorithms, both in terms of clustering errors and the number of classes. Results show that SSC is quite efficient to identify the global optimal solution. Also SSC algorithm has the capability from skipping from the local optima.This was achieved from the inherent features of the Scatter Search algorithm which are represented by exploiting the useful information of the optimal solution contained in a diverse collection of elite solutions.

References

1. C.L. Blake and C.J. Merz. UCI Repository of Machine Learning Databases, University of California, Irvine, Dept. of Information and Computer Sciences, 1998. http://www.ics.uci.edu/~mlearn/MLRepository.html.
2. D. Corne, M. Dorigo, and F. Glover, editors. *New Ideas in Optimisation*. McGraw-Hill, London, UK, 1999.

3. F. Glover, M. Laguna and R. Martí. "Scatter search". Advances in Evolutionary Computation: Theory and Applications, A. Ghosh and S. Tsutsui (Eds.), Springer-Verlag, New York,pp. 519-537,2003.
4. J. Han, M. Kamber. Data Mining: Concepts and Techniques, Academic press,2001.
5. M. Laguna, and R. Martí."Experimental Testing of Advanced Scatter Search Designs for Global Optimization of Multimodal Functions", in Global Optimization,1997.
6. J.A. Lozano and P. Larrañaga. "Using Genetic Algorithms to Get the Classes and their Number in a Partitional Cluster Analysis of Large Data Sets",http://citeseer.ist.psu.edu/457425.html.
7. R. Martí, M. Laguna, V. Campos. Scatter Search vs. Genetic Algorithms: An Experimental Evaluation with Permutation Problems, In: Rego, C., Alidaee, B.(Eds.), Adaptive Memory and Evolution: Tabu Search and Scatter Search, Kluwer Academic Publishers,1997.
8. N. Monmarché. Algorithmes de fourmis artificielles : applications à la classification et à l'optimisation. Thèse de doctorat, Laboratoire d'Informatique, Université de Tours, décembre 2000.
9. N. Monmarché. Artificial datasets. Handicap et Nouvelles Technologies(HaNT), Laboratoire d'Informatique, htt://www.hant.li.univ-tours.fr/ webhant/index.php?pageid=55.
10. J. Pacheco, O. Valencia."Design of Hybrids for Minimum Sum-of-Squares Clustering Problem", in Computational Statistic and Data Analysis. 43(2),Pages 235-248,2003.
11. M. Sarkar, B. Yegnanafayana, D. Khemani."A Clustering Algorithm using an Evolutionary Programming-based Approach", Pattern Recognition letters, vol 18, page 975-986,1997.
12. B. Zhang, G. Kleyner, M. Hsu."A Local Search Approach to K-Clustering". HP-Lab Tech.Rep,1997.

Multi-objective Parameters Selection for SVM Classification Using NSGA-II

Li Xu and Chunping Li

School of Software, Tsinghua University, China
li-xu04@mails.tsinghua.edu.cn,
cli@tsinghua.edu.cn

Abstract. Selecting proper parameters is an important issue to extend the classification ability of Support Vector Machine (SVM), which makes SVM practically useful. Genetic Algorithm (GA) has been widely applied to solve the problem of parameters selection for SVM classification due to its ability to discover good solutions quickly for complex searching and optimization problems. However, traditional GA in this field relys on single generalization error bound as fitness function to select parameters. Since there have several generalization error bounds been developed, picking and using single criterion as fitness function seems intractable and insufficient. Motivated by the multi-objective optimization problems, this paper introduces an efficient method of parameters selection for SVM classification based on multi-objective evolutionary algorithm NSGA-II. We also introduce an adaptive mutation rate for NSGA-II. Experiment results show that our method is better than single-objective approaches, especially in the case of tiny training sets with large testing sets.

1 Introduction

Support Vector Machine was proposed by Vapnik [3] as a statistic learning method with promising generalization ability. It maps the training vectors into a high dimensional feature space, and constructs a hyperplane that maximizes the margin (maximizes the distance between the hyperplane and the closest training vector in feature space) [7]. SVM is widely used in the field of classification and pattern recognition.

As one of the learning methods, SVM's generalization ability depends on kernel parameters and tradeoff parameter. In order to find these parameters that minimize the generalization error of SVM, several techniques have been proposed [1][2][4]. On the one hand, the leave-one-out procedure as a standard experimental method gives an almost unbiased estimate of the expected generalization error [1][17]. On the other hand, the bounds for estimating generalization error can be deduced in theoretical ways. In practice, theoretical upper bounds of generalization error are used because of the high computational complexity of leave-one-out procedure.

On the assumption that removing a non-support vector from the training set does not change the solution computed by SVM, Vapnik [1][3] proposed a

P. Perner (Ed.): ICDM 2006, LNAI 4065, pp. 365–376, 2006.

bound on the number of errors made by leave-one-out procedure concerning support vector count. Jaakkola and Haussler [1][18] studied the non-threshold SVM optimization performance when computing the leave-one-out error and put forward Jaakkola-Haussler bound. Motivated by linear response theory, Opper and Winther [1][19] presented Opper-Winther bound for hard margin SVM without threshold. Chapelle [1][2] introduced the concept of span of support vectors which gave the exact number of errors made by the leave-one-out procedure on the previous assumption. Vapnik [1][5] demonstrated that the span bound could be linked with Jaakkola-Haussler bound, Radius-margin bound and Opper-Winther bound respectively.

Genetic Algorithms (GA) was proposed by Holland as a general-purpose heuristic search algorithm that mimicked the evolutionary process in order to find the fittest solutions [16]. The potential of GA in multi-objective optimization was initially hinted by Rosenberg in 1960s [21]. Recent literature has paid much attention on it because they deal simultaneously with a set of possible solutions which allow an entire set of Pareto-optimal solutions to be evolved in a single run. Nondominated Sorting Genetic Algorithm (NSGA) was suggested by Goldberg and implemented by Srinivas and Deb [16]. Although NSGA has been proved to be effective for multi-objective optimization problems, NSGA has its drawbacks such as high computational complexity of nondominated sorting, lack of elitism, and need for specifying the sharing parameter σ_{share} [8]. Aim at such problems, Deb [8] introduced NSGA-II as an improved method which overcame the original NSGA defects by alleviating computational complexity, by introducing elitist-preserving mechanism and employing crowded comparison operator.

The exhaustive search for parameters selection of SVM becomes intractable as the parameters exceeds two. Due to the ability to discover good solutions quickly for complex searching and optimization problems, GA has been proved to be effective for automatic selecting parameters of SVM [11]. However, traditional methods using GA to select the parameters of SVM are single-objective optimization problems. The fitness function of GA adopted is one of the various generalization error bounds. It is well known that support vector count bound (NS) depends on the number of support vectors, while span bound (SPAN) depends on the span of support vectors which indicates the maximal distance among the support vectors. Since above two criteria concern support vectors, it is obvious that they have influence with each other. Using either criterion as fitness function seems insufficient for parameters selection. The purpose of this paper is to extend single-objective optimization problems to multi-objective optimization problems under the framework of NSGA-II. We evaluate and discuss the performance of proposed method against the single-objective GA with single fitness function.

The paper is organized as follows. We briefly introduce the basics of SVM classification in Section 2. In Section 3, we describe the estimation performance of SVM. In Section 4 we give NSGA-II algorithm. The experiment conditions are described in Section 5. The main experiments on SVM classification and experiments analysis are shown in Section 6. In Section 7 we have concluding remarks.

2 Support Vector Machine Classification

The classification problem can be considered as two-class problem. Given the training data vectors $D = \{(x_1, y_1), \ldots, (x_l, y_l)\}$, $x_i \in R^n$ which belongs to a class labeled by $y_i \in \{-1, 1\}$, and the goal is to separate the two classes by the hyperplane (1) which is induced from available examples.

$$\langle w, x \rangle + b = 0. \tag{1}$$

where w is weight vector, b is threshold.

For non-linear problems, the optimization is to minimize the classification error as well as minimizing the bound on the VC dimension to the classifier. The optimal separating hyperplane with the constraints of

$$y_i[\langle w, x_i \rangle + b] \geq 1 - \zeta_i, \quad i = 1, \ldots, l. \tag{2}$$

minimizes the function

$$\phi(w, \zeta) = \frac{1}{2}\|w\|^2 + C(\sum_{i}^{l} \zeta_i). \tag{3}$$

where $\zeta = (\zeta_1, \ldots, \zeta_l)$, ζ_i is a measure of the misclassification errors, C is a constant which controls the tradeoff between the complexity of the decision function and the number of training examples misclassified.

The optimization problem (3) under the constraints of Equation (2) can be transformed to its dual problem [11]

$$Max : W(\alpha) = \sum_{i=1}^{n} \alpha_i - \frac{1}{2}\sum_{i=1}^{l}\sum_{j=1}^{l} y_i y_j \alpha_i \alpha_j K(x_i, x_j). \tag{4}$$

with constraints (5)(6)

$$ST : \sum_{i=1}^{n} y_i \alpha_i = 0. \tag{5}$$

$$0 \leq \alpha_i \leq C. \quad i = 1, \ldots, l. \tag{6}$$

where α_i is Lagrange multiplier.

SVM is a linear maximal margin classifier in a high-dimensional feature space where data are mapped through a non-linear function $\phi(x_1) \cdot \phi(x_2) = K(x_1, x_2)$ [1]. In order to get the optimal hyperplane in feature space, kernel function should be used. Usually, Radial Basis Function(RBF) is used as the kernel function

$$K(x_1, x_2) = exp\left(-\frac{\|x_1 - x_2\|_2}{2 \times \sigma^2}\right). \tag{7}$$

where σ is scaling factor.

The decision function given by a SVM is

$$f(x) = sgn\left(\sum_{i=1}^{l} \alpha_i^0 y_i K(x_i, x) + b\right). \tag{8}$$

where the coefficients α_i^0 are obtained when Equation (4) is maximized.

3 Expected Generalization Error on SVM

If one has enough data available, it is possible to estimate the true error on a validation set. This estimation is unbiased and its variance gets smaller as the size of the validation set increases [1]. Since the data to be trained for SVM are limited, we can not get the exact number of errors made by SVM. To describe the estimating performance of SVM, both experimental and theoretical methods are proposed to assess the generalization ability of SVM.

3.1 The Leave-One-Out Procedure

The leave-one-out procedure is executed as follows: pick one sample from the data set and then test it on the decision function formed by the remaining samples of the data set. The procedure is iterated until each sample is picked and tested [1]. Luntz [17] pointed that the leave-one-out procedure gave almost unbiased estimate of the expected generalization error.

3.2 The Expected Generalization Error Bounds

Although leave-one-out procedure has such advantages, its computational complexity is very high. Theoretical generalization error upper bounds are used to estimate the expected error rate of an SVM in practice.

Support vector count. According to Kuhn-Tucker conditions, we have

$$\alpha_i \Big(y_i \big[\langle w, x_i \rangle + b \big] - 1 \Big) = 0, \quad i = 1, \ldots, l. \tag{9}$$

The vectors corresponding with non-zero lagrange multipliers α_i are called Support Vectors (SV). For SVM can summarize the information contained in the data set produced by the SV, removing non-support vectors from the training set does not change the solution computed by SVM. The bound on the number of estimate error performed by leave-one-out procedure is

$$T = \frac{N_{SV}}{l}. \tag{10}$$

where T is the upper bound quantity and N_{SV} the number of support vectors.

Span bound. Given a set of support vectors $(x_1, y_1), \ldots, (x_l, y_l)$ and $\alpha^0 = (\alpha_1^0, \ldots, \alpha_l^0)$ is the lagrange multipliers of support vectors, we construct the set Λ_p as follows [5].

$$\Lambda_p = \{ \sum_{i=1, i \neq p}^{l} \lambda_i x_i : \sum_{i=1, i \neq p}^{l} \lambda_i = 1, \ and \ \forall i \neq p, \ \alpha_i^0 + y_i y_p \alpha_p^0 \lambda_i \geq 0 \}. \tag{11}$$

where set Λ_p is a linear combinations of the other support vectors and λ_i can be less than 0.

The span of the support vector x_p is defined as

$$S_p^2 = d^2(x_p, \Lambda_p) = \min_{x \in \Lambda_p} (x_p - x)^2.$$

Under the assumption that the set of support vectors remains the same during the leave-one-out procedure, the following equality holds.

$$y_p(f^0(x_p) - f^p(x_p)) = \alpha_p^0 S_p^2.$$ (12)

where S_p is the distance between the support vector x_p and set Λ_p, α_p^0 is the corresponding lagrange multiplier for the optimal hyperplane of support vector x_p.

Therefore the exact number of errors made by the leave-one-out procedure under the previous assumption can be deduced as follows.

$$T = \frac{1}{l} \sum_{p=1}^{l} \psi(\alpha_p^0 S_p^2 - 1).$$ (13)

where ψ is the step function : $\psi(x) = 1$ when $x > 0$ and $\psi(x) = 0$ otherwise.

4 Multi-objective Genetic Algorithms NSGA-II

4.1 Multi-objective Optimization Problem

The multi-objective optimization problem consists of a number of objective functions, which are to be optimized simultaneously. In the multi-objective optimization problem, no solution can achieve global optimum for all objectives. If the value of any objective function cannot be improved without degrading at least one of the other objective functions, the solutions is refered to Pareto-optimal or nondominated ones. Since Pareto-optimal solutions [8] can not be compared with each other, the optimality of Pareto-optimal solutions is described as: a solution u^1 dominates another solution u^2, if

$$J_i(u^1)! \prec J_i(u^2). \quad \forall i \in \{1, 2, \ldots, s\},$$

$$J_j(u^1) \succ J_j(u^2). \quad \exists j \in \{1, 2, \ldots, s\}.$$

where the operator $\prec$ denotes worse and $\succ$ denotes better. The solutions that are Preto-optimal within the entire search space constitute the Pareto-optimal set or Pareto-optimal front.

4.2 Description of NSGA-II

The NSGA was implemented by Srinivas and Deb as the method for solving the multi-objective problem. But the high computational complexity of nondominated sorting, lack of elitism and sharing parameter δ_{share} have been criticized for years. Deb [8] presented NSGA-II as an improvement of NSGA by introducing a fast nondominated sorting procedure with less computational complexity, an elitist-preserving mechanism and a parameterless niching operator for diversity preservation. NSGA-II also performs well for solving the constrained multi-objective optimization problems. The main steps of NSGA-II are described as follows.

Step 1 : Generate a parent population P_0 of size N at random.

Step 2 : Sort the population based on the nondomination.

Step 3 : Evaluate each individual of population P_0 and put a rank value based on its nondomination level.

Step 4 : Form child population Q_0 on the basis of population P_0 by performing binary tournament, crossover and mutation operations.

Step 5 : At the tth generation, produce population R_t of size N by integrating parent population P_t with child population Q_t.

Step 6 : Sort R_t on the basis of nondomination and assign corresponding rank.

Step 7 : Create new parent population P_{t+1} by filling the highest ranked front set until the size of the population size exceeds N.

Step 8 : Create child population Q_{t+1} according to population P_{t+1} by utilizing binary tournament, crossover and mutation operations.

Step 9 : Jump to *Step* 5 until the preset generation count is reached.

5   Implementation Conditions for Solving Parameters Selection of SVM Classification

There are several factors for controling the process of NSGA-II while searching the parameters of SVM. To apply NSGA-II to the SVM parameters tuning, we focus on the following issues.

5.1   Encoding Scheme

For genetic algorithms, one of the key issues is to encode a solution of the problem into a chromosome. Since the model selection of SVM is the optimization problem with constraints, and the real-coded scheme is able to perform better than binary-coded scheme in constrained optimization problems with contiguous search space. We here use real-coded scheme to represent to the kernel parameter σ and the tradeoff parameter C.

5.2   Produce the Initial Population

The size of initial population controls the search space of the algorithm, and the solution of the problem is initialized at random. The bigger of the population size, the more even dispersion of the solution. Small size of the population can cause the convergence of the search process at early runs and hence limit the search capability. In this paper, we define the population size 100 according to the standard population size setting proposed by De Jong [20].

5.3   Genetic Operator

Genetic operator consists of three basic operators, i.e., selection, crossover and mutation. In this paper, a new rate generator is presented to pick different mutation rate according to the generation counts during the run.

(1) Selection operator
Selection operator in NSGA-II is composed of picking child population from the parent population with the same size. The binary tournament selection runs a tournament between two individuals and selects the winner. It can obtain better result than the methods of proportional and genitor selection. Hence, binary tournament selection is adopted to select the next generation individual.

(2) Crossover operator
For real-encoding scheme is employed, the crossover operator is defined as follows.

$$P' = aP_1 + (1-a)P_2. \tag{14}$$

where P' is the offspring after crossover operation, P_1 and P_2 are the two parents to be implemented the crossover operation. a is a random number which belongs to (0,1).

(3) Mutation operator
According to the mechanism of GA, at the early stage of the process, search space needs to be enlarged in order to avoid the precocity. But at the end of the process, optimum solutions are found or the population is converged. Large mutation rate can separate the population and damage the Pareto-optimal solution, so mutation rate should be diminished according to the generation count. We here present the mutation rate as follows.

$$P_m = max\left\{ \frac{mod(Popsize, L)}{L}, Mr_{max} \right\} * \frac{Maxgen - gen}{Maxgen} + Mr_{min}. \tag{15}$$

where P_m is the mutation probability. Mr_{max} controls the maximum mutation rate, and Mr_{min} guarantees mutation rate above zero. $Popsize$ is the population size, L the dimension number of the dataset used to produce an alternative mutation rate, $Maxgen$ the maximum runtimes, and gen the current run count.

5.4   Fitness Function

Since the average performance of the SVM classifier depends on either support vector count or the span of support vectors. We choose Equation(10)(13) as fitness functions. The aim is to minimize the two measures of the expected error rate of SVM.

5.5   Stopping Criterion

It is important to define the stop condition for genetic algorithm because it would be time wasted after the population is converged. In this paper, we use metric Δ proposed by Deb [8] to measure the extent of spread achieved among the obtained solutions. Metric Δ is defined as follows.

$$\Delta = \frac{d_f + d_l + \sum_{i=1}^{N-1} |d_i - \bar{d}|}{d_f + d_l + (N-1)\bar{d}}. \tag{16}$$

where the parameters d_f and d_l are Euclidean distances between the extreme solutions and the boundary solutions of the obtained nondominated set. The parameter $\overline{d}$ is the average of all distances d_i, i=1,2,...,(N-1), assuming that there are N solutions on the best nondominated front. For the most widely and uniformly spread out set of non-dominated solutions, the value of Δ is zero. According to Deb [8], this diversity metric can be used on any set of solutions.

6   Experiments

This section shows the experimental details and evaluation on experiment results of NSGA-II on different test databases. To illustrate the performance of proposed method, we use heart database picked from the four test databases. Finally, we discuss the simulation results of the experiments.

6.1   Experiment Details

To evaluate the performance of our method, Experiments have been carried out using the databases in the benchmark database [1][11] which are available at: http://ida.first.gmd.de/~raetsch/data/benchmarks.htm.

For each test database in the benchmark we picked, the following test procedures are performed:

1. Tune the parameters of the SVM classifier with training sets in the database and test the classification performance with the testing sets in the database.

2. Tune the parameters of the SVM classifier with one training set randomly selected from the training sets in the database and test the classification performance with all testing sets in the database as follows.

In order to demonstrate the feasibility of our method, the experiments consist of following two parts corresponding to different test databases.

(a) The experiments are performed on the single-criterion GA with fitness function (10) and (13) respectively to select parameters for SVM classification and are stopped if the classification accuracy rate do not change in 30 generation runs.

(b) The experiments are performed on NSGA-II with fitness function (10) and (13) simultaneously for SVM classification.

We use the parameters in Table 1 to run experiments on different databases to validate the method.

6.2   Experiment Result and Evaluation

Table 2 shows the classification accuracy rates obtained using three algorithms, i.e., single-objective GA with fitness function(10)(NS-GA), single-objective GA with fitness function(13)(SPAN-GA), and NSGA-II on four different databases. NSGA-II performs the best in all testing problems with total training sets. SPAN-GA plays the second-best and gets close classification accuracy rate with

Table 1. Parameters of GAs used for classification

Features	Parameters
Population size	100
Encoding Scheme	real-coded Scheme
Selection strategy	binary tournament
Crossover type	Equation (14)
Crossover rate	0.5
Mutation type	Equation (15)
Minimum mutation rate	0.02
Maximum mutation rate	0.1
Termination criterion	Equation (16)
Maximum number of generation	500

Table 2. Experiments on four databases

	Size of the train data set	breast-cancer	diabetis	heart	titanic
NS-GA	Total traingroups	0.7421	0.7316	0.8243	0.7335
	one traingroup	0.7103	0.6634	0.7987	0.7013
SPAN-GA	Total traingroups	0.7884	0.7723	0.856	0.7939
	one traingroup	0.7662	0.7103	0.8312	0.7456
NSGA-II	Total traingroups	0.8111	0.7782	0.8682	0.8004
	one traingroup	0.7749	0.7048	0.8431	0.7886

NSGA-II in diabetis and titanic databases. The worst performance is observed with NS-GA. On most problems with one randomly training set, the NSGA-II is able to find better result than SPAN-GA and NS-GA, whereas in diabetis with one training set, the SPAN-GA performs little better than NSGA-II.

For illustration, we show the test result curves of heart database. The heart database was used in Zheng [11] to test the single-objective GA on the problem of parameters selection for SVM. Fig.1 shows the evolutionary process of three algorithms using total training sets. We can see from Fig.1 that NSGA-II gets best classification accuracy rate. NSGA-II classification accuracy rate moves up from start to approximately 350 generation, and maintains at this level until the program ends. SPAN-GA gets better classification result than NSGA-II at the beginning, but the classification accuracy rate fluctuates during the evolutionary process. The NS-GA performs worst among the three algorithms. The NS-GA gets its best classification performance around 350 generation. Fig.2 shows the classification accuracy rate of three algorithms on the same testing sets with one training set randomly picked from the training sets. NSGA-II classification accuracy rate goes upward steadily and maintains at a satisfactory level about 84%. Before first 60 generation, the classification accuracy rate of SPAN-GA is better than NSGA-II, and its classification accuracy rate finally maintains about 82%, wheras NS-GA gets its best classification results around 400 generation.

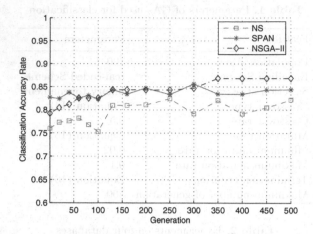

Fig. 1. Classification accuracy rate of SVM classifier with total training sets

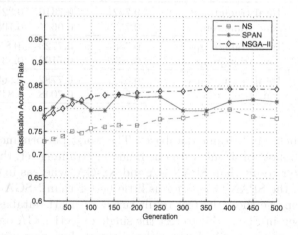

Fig. 2. Classification accuracy rate of SVM classifier with one training set

NSGA-II performs the best among these three methods because NSGA-II employs two fitness functions used in SPAN-GA and NS-GA. This fully utilizes both the number and the correlation of support vectors. SPAN-GA performs better than NS-GA in that span represents the maximum distance between the support vectors and it can give more accurate number of errors made by the leave-one-out procedure. NS-GA performs worst because it only focuses on the number of support vectors. We can also see that the NSGA-II classification accuracy rate moves up steadily. The reason is that NSGA-II uses the elitism-preserving mechanism to keep the elitist solution in the population. however, because lack of elitism mechanism, SPAN-GA and NS-GA fluctuate randomly. Even though SPAN-GA sometimes can get a solution that is better than NSGA-II, it can not preserve the elitist solution for later classification.

7 Conclusion and Future Work

By analyzing traditional methods using single-objective GA to select parameters for SVM classification, it can not take full advantage of various theoretical generalization error bounds in existence. In this paper, we show a computationally fast and elitist multi-objective Genetic Algorithm NSGA-II to tune parameters for SVM classification, two widely used generalization error bounds are applied as fitness functions of NSGA-II. We introduce a new mutation rate operator which enables the population more diversity in the process to avoid precocity. Experiments are taken to invest the feasibility of proposed method on four different databases. The results show that the NSGA-II is able to obtain a better classification results compared to two other single-objective GAs. The classification result is satisfactory especially when the number of train samples is tiny. The main contributions of the proposed method are: (1) Extend single-objective optimal problems to multi-objective problems by selecting parameters for SVM classification. (2) An adaptive mutation rate is integrated into the algorithm to get better results. (3) Validate this method is effective in the case of tiny training sets with large testing sets classification problems. From these points of view, the work presented in this paper is very useful in the field of SVM classification.

In the future work, we will focus on introducing parameterless method for SVM, which tries to get best classification results according to different datasets.

Acknowledgment

This work was supported by Chinese 973 Research Project under grant No. 2004CB719401.

References

1. Chapelle, O., Vapnik, V., Bousquet, O., Mukherjee, S.: Choosing multiple parameters for support vector machines.Machine Learning, Vol. 46. N.1 (2002) 131–159
2. Chapelle, O., Vapnik,V.: Model Selection for Support Vector Machines. Advances in Neural Information Processing Systems, Vol.12. MIT Press, Cambridge, MA, (2000)
3. Vapnik, V.: The nature of statistical learning theory. Berlin:Springer. (1995)
4. Vapnik, V.: Statistical learning theory. New York: John Wiley Sons. (1998)
5. Vapnik, V., Chapelle, O.: Bounds on Error Expectation for Support Vector Machines. Neural Computation, Vol. 12. N.9 (2000) 2013 – 2036
6. Lee, J.H., Lin, C.J.: Automatic Model Selection for Support Vector Machines. http://www.csie.ntu.edu.tw/cjlin/papers/modelselect.ps.gz, (2000)
7. Gunn, S.R.: Support Vector Machines for Classification and Regression. Technical Report, Image Speech and Intelligent Systems Research Group, University of Southampton (1997)
8. Deb, K., Ptatap, A.,Agarwal, S. Meyarivan, T. : A Fast and Elitist Multiobjective Genetic Algorithm NSGA-II. IEEE Transactions on Evolutionary Computation. Vol. 6. (2002) 182–197

9. Deb, K.: Multiobjective Optimization Using Evolutionary Algorithms. Chichester, U.K.:Wiley (2001)
10. Zhao, X.M., Huang, D.S., Cheung, Y.M., Wang, H.Q., Huang,X.: A Novel Hybrid GA/SVM System for Protein Sequences Classification. Intelligent Data Engineering and Automated Learning. Vol. 3177. (2004) 11–16
11. Zheng, C.H., Jiao, L.C: Automatic parameters selection for SVM based on GA. Intelligent Control and Automation, Vol. 2. Springer-Verlag, Berlin Heidelberg New York (2004) 1869 – 1872
12. Joachims, T.: Estimating the generalization performance of a SVM efficiently. In Proceedings of the International Conference on Machine Learning, San Francisco. Morgan Kaufman.
13. Joachims, T.: Making large-Scale SVM Learning Practical. In Advances in Kernel Methods-Support Vector Learning, chapter 11. MIT Press (1999)
14. Huaqing, L., Shaoyu, W., Feihu, Q.: SVM Model Selection with the VC Bound. Computational and Information Science: First International Symposium. Vol. 3314. (2004) 1067–1071
15. Ohn, S.Y., Nguyen, H.N., Kim, D.S., Park, J.S.: Determining Optimal Decision Model for Support Vector Machine by Genetic Algorithm. Computational and Information Science: First International Symposium (2004) 895–902
16. Khoa, D.T.: Elitist Non-Dominated Sorting GA-II(NSGA-II) as a Parameter-less Multi-Objective Genetic Algorithm. SoutheastCon Proceedings. IEEE (2005) 359–367
17. Luntz, A.& Brailovsky, V.: On estimation of characters obtained in statistical procedure of recognition. Technicheskaya Kibernetica. 3,(in Russian).(1969)
18. Jaakkola, T.S.&Haussler, D.: Probabilistic kernel regression models. In Proceedings of the 1999 Conference on AI and Statistics.(1999)
19. Opper, M.&Winther, O.: Gaussian processes and svm: Mean field and leave-one-out.Advances in large margin classifiers.Cambridge, MA: MIT Press.(2000)
20. K. A. De Jong.: An analysis of the behavior of a class of genetic adaptive systems. Ann Arbor: University of Michigan, 1975.
21. C.A.Coello.: A Short Tutorial on Evolutinary Multiobjective Optimization. In Proceedings of First International Conference on Evolutionary Multi-Criterion Optimization, 2001.

Effectiveness Evaluation of Data Mining Based IDS

Agustín Orfila, Javier Carbó, and Arturo Ribagorda

Carlos III University of Madrid,
Computer Science Department,
Leganés 28911, Spain
{adiaz, jcarbo, arturo}@inf.uc3m.es

Abstract. Data mining has been widely applied to the problem of Intrusion Detection in computer networks. However, the misconception of the underlying problem has led to out of context results. This paper shows that factors such as the probability of intrusion and the costs of responding to detected intrusions must be taken into account in order to compare the effectiveness of machine learning algorithms over the intrusion detection domain. Furthermore, we show the advantages of combining different detection techniques. Results regarding the well known 1999 KDD dataset are shown.

1 Introduction

According to ISO/IEC TR 15947 [1] intrusion detection is the process of identifying that an intrusion has been attempted, is occurring or has occurred. Thus, Intrusion Detection Systems (IDS) are technical systems that are used to identify and respond to intrusions in IT systems. Consequently, IDS attempt to identify actions that does not conform to security policy.

IDS analysis of the data sources can be done through different methods such as expert systems, statistical techniques, signature analysis, neural networks, artificial immune systems or data mining among others. Data mining is defined as the process of discovering patterns in data automatically. This technique deals well with big amounts of information what makes it appropriate for the intrusion detection task. In fact, the appliance of data mining to the intrusion detection field is an active research topic [2,3,4]. After the process of extracting the interesting characteristics from data sources, either supervised or unsupervised learning can be applied over the processed data. Supervised algorithms need a training set in order to build the model that will be used in operating conditions. At the training phase, the IDS can model either the normal behaviour of the system, the abnormal or both. The main advantages of IDS based on supervised learning are their ability to detect known attacks and minor variants of them. Weak points deal with the necessity of building proper training datasets and with the time consuming phase for building the models. On the other hand, unsupervised learning does not require a training dataset.

P. Perner (Ed.): ICDM 2006, LNAI 4065, pp. 377–388, 2006.

Evaluation of IDS effectiveness did not become an active topic until 1998. MIT Lincoln Laboratories (MIT/LL) led an ambitious evaluation of IDS [5,6]. A military network was simulated in order to test different proposals. These works and subsequent criticism [7,8] set down the main difficulties that research community had to face in order to evaluate IDS effectiveness [9]. A processed version of the data generated by MIT/LL was used to evaluate several machine learning algorithms in the 1999 KDD intrusion detection contest [10]. This dataset has been used extensively after the contest although its limitations (derives from a controversial dataset and the probability of intrusion that it shows is far away from what is expectable in a real scenario).

In order to measure IDS effectiveness the *Receiver Operating Characteristic* (ROC) has been widely used. ROC was introduced in signal theory to characterize the trade-off between hit rate and false alarm rate over a noisy channel. In data mining field, it has been used to measure machine learning algorithms performance when the class distribution is not balanced (i.e. accuracy is not a good measure). The main problem of ROC analysis is that it does not consider the costs of misclassification (wrong detections). Normally the cost of a false negative (failing to detect an intrusion) is much higher than the cost of a false positive (stating an event is hostile when it is not) so a different representation of effectiveness that takes this situation into account is necessary. In fact, if the ROC curves of two classifiers (detectors) cross, it could not be stated that one outperforms the other under any circumstances. Because of this, Drummond [11] proposed an alternative representation to the ROC in order to compare classifiers under different class distributions and error costs.

Ulvila works [12,13,14] showed that IDS effectiveness depends not only on the hit rate and false alarm rate but also on the hostility of the operating environment and on the cost of detection errors. Orfila [15] showed the need of including the response cost in order to evaluate IDS effectiveness properly.

The remainder of this paper is organized as follows. In section 2 we expose a methodology for comparing IDS effectiveness from a decision analysis perspective. Then in section 3 we propose a simple way to combine the detection capabilities of several machine learning techniques. Section 4 overviews 1999 KDD dataset that is used in section 5 for the experimental work. This experimental work compares different machine learning algorithms with the combined model proposed in section 3 by means of the methodology described in section 2. Finally, this paper ends up with the main conclusions.

2 Decision Model Analysis

Decision theory has been successfully applied in areas such as Psychology [16], Economy [17] or Meteorology [18]. In the computer security field, it has been used to face the intrusion detection task, in order to provide a way to compare different IDS and to determine the best operating point of an IDS under different operating conditions [12].

Table 1. Conditional probabilities that an IDS detects the system state

	System state	
Detector's report	No intrusion (NI)	Intrusion (I)
No alarm (NA)	FVN $(1-F)$	FFN $(1-H)$
Alarm (A)	FFP (F)	FVP (H)

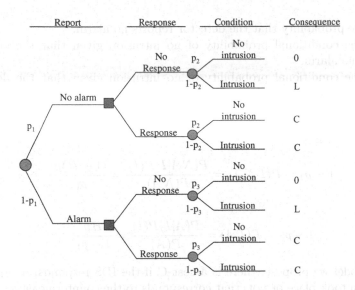

Fig. 1. Decision tree of the detector's expected cost that considers the response cost

In this section we propose a method to measure IDS effectiveness that considers both damage (produced by a successful intrusion) and response cost (the one incurred by taking actions in order to avoid an intrusion [15]). The comparison is made from an utility perspective, that means the best IDS is the one that better helps on minimizing expenses when defending a system.

The system we want to protect can be in two possible states: an intrusive state (I) or a non intrusive state (NI). Similarly an IDS, depending on the analysis of data sources, can report an alarm (A) or not (NA). The ROC of a detector is a plot of the conditional probabilities $P(A|I)$ (hit rate H) vs. $P(A|NI)$ (false alarm rate F) as shown in Table 1.

The expected cost of a detector on a certain operating point can be computed analyzing the decision tree of Figure 1.

Decision or action nodes, which are displayed as squares, are under control of the decision maker, who will choose which branch to follow. Conversely, the circles represent event nodes that are subject to uncertainty. A probability distribution represents the uncertainty about which branch will happen following an event node. Event nodes probabilities are defined as follows:

Table 2. Expected cost of responses vs. detector's report

Detector's report	Response	
	No	Yes
No alarm	$L(1-p_2) = \frac{L(1-H)p}{p_1}$	$Cp_2 + C(1-p_2) = C$
Alarm	$L(1-p_3) = \frac{LHp}{1-p_1}$	$Cp_3 + C(1-p_3) = C$

- p_1: is the probability that the detector reports no alarm.
- p_2: is the conditional probability of no intrusion given that the detector reports no alarm.
- p_3: is the conditional probability of no intrusion given that the detector reports an alarm.

Conditional probabilities $1 - p_2$ and $1 - p_3$ can be expressed in terms of hit and false alarm rates:

$$1 - p_2 = P(I|NA) = \frac{P(NA|I)P(I)}{P(NA)} = \frac{(1-H)p}{p_1} \tag{1}$$

$$1 - p_3 = P(I|A) = \frac{P(A|I)P(I)}{P(A)} = \frac{Hp}{1-p_1} \tag{2}$$

In the model we propose, there is a cost C if the IDS responds, irrespective the intrusion took place or not, that corresponds to the countermeasures taken. L represents the losses if there is a false negative. The decision maker (the own IDS if the response is automatic or the network administrator if it is not) will follow the strategy that minimizes the expected cost. In order to compute this expected cost it is necessary to calculate the expected cost conditional on the detector's report. The four possibilities are summarized in Table 2. The prior probability that an intrusion happens is represented by p (P(I)).

Thus, if the report of the detector is known, the minimal expected cost can be computed. If there is no alarm the expression for the expected cost under this condition is:

$$M_{NA} = \min\{L(1-p_2), C\} = \min\{\frac{L(1-H)p}{p_1}, C\} \tag{3}$$

Similarly, the expected cost given an alarm is:

$$M_A = \min\{L(1-p_3), C\} = \min\{\frac{LHp}{1-p_1}, C\} \tag{4}$$

Finally, the expected cost of operating at a given operating point (a point in the ROC curve), is the sum of the products of the probabilities of the detector's reports and the expected costs of operating conditional on the reports. Then the expression is:

$$p_1 \min\{\frac{L(1-H)p}{p_1}, C\} + (1 - p_1) \min\{\frac{LHp}{1-p_1}, C\} =$$
$$= \min\{L(1 - H)p, C((1 - F)(1 - p) + (1 - H)p)\} +$$
$$+ \min\{LHp, C(F(1 - p) + Hp)\} \tag{5}$$

Consequently, the expected cost by unit loss (M) is:

$$M = \min\{(1 - H)p, \frac{C}{L}((1 - F)(1 - p) + (1 - H)p)\} +$$
$$+ \min\{Hp, \frac{C}{L}(F(1 - p) + Hp)\} \tag{6}$$

It is important to note that this formulation includes the possibility of taking actions against the report of the detector if this action leads to a lower expected cost.

Next, a metric that measures the value of an IDS is introduced. First some concepts need to be defined.

The expected expense of a perfect IDS (the one that achieves H=1 and F=0) by unit loss is (from expression (6))

$$M_{per} = \min\{p, \frac{C}{L}p\} = p \min\{1, \frac{C}{L}\} \tag{7}$$

In addition, an expression is needed for the expected cost when only information about the probability of intrusion is available (no IDS working). In this situation, the decision maker can adopt two strategies: always protect taking some precautionary action (incurring in a cost C) or never protect (incurring in losses pL). Consequently, the decision maker will respond if $C < pL$ and will not if $C > pL$. Then, the expected cost by unit loss is:

$$M_{prob} = \min\{p, \frac{C}{L}\} \tag{8}$$

Accordingly, the value of an IDS is defined as the reduction it gives on the expected cost over the one corresponding to the only knowledge of the probability of intrusion, normalized by the maximum possible reduction.

$$V = \frac{M_{prob} - M}{M_{prob} - M_{per}} \tag{9}$$

As a result, if an IDS is perfect at detecting intrusions its value is 1. Conversely, an IDS that does not improve a predictive system solely based on the probability of intrusion has a value less or equal than 0.

The metric of value is very useful because it includes all the relevant parameters involved in the evaluation of IDS effectiveness. A similar metric was proposed in [19] but it did not manage the possibility that a decision is made contrary to the detector's report.

3   Parametric IDS

Several IDS can not be tuned to work at different operating points. This is a limiting feature. An operating point is defined by a pair (F,H). In order to adapt to different operating conditions, an IDS should be able to work at different operating points [20]. In consequence, we propose a very simple parametric IDS that consists on combining different non parametric detection techniques.

The question we want to answer is in what sense the mere combination of machine learning algorithms outperforms the individual approaches on intrusion detection domain. The way the parametric IDS works is the following. Let us consider an event happens on the monitored system. If the fraction of individual models that state the event is hostile is over a certain probability threshold p_t, then the parametric IDS will assume it as intrusive. p_t can be tuned from 0 to 1 in such a way that different predictions about the event are produced. In other words, the parametric detection depends on how many machine learning models predicted the event as hostile and on the threshold p_t.

Therefore, the hit rate and false alarm rate of the parametric IDS, computed over an event dataset, depend on this threshold p_t [19].

$$H = H(p_t) \quad F = F(p_t) \quad \forall p_t \in [0, 1] \tag{10}$$

Consequently, the value of the IDS, as defined in equation (9), also depends on p_t.

$$V = V(p_t) \quad \forall p_t \in [0, 1] \tag{11}$$

For a fixed $\frac{C}{L}$ relationship, the optimum value of the IDS is:

$$V_{opt} = \max_{pt} V(p_t) \quad \forall p_t \in [0, 1]. \tag{12}$$

4   Experimental Setup

The main problem to test IDS effectiveness is the absence of non controversial benchmarks. It is not an easy task to build such a benchmark because different requirements must be considered to test different IDS [9]. There are also problems in repeating experiments with real data (privacy problems) and simulated data is under suspicion because is hard to establish how close the artificial data is to the real one. The ad-hoc methodology that is prevalent in today's testing and evaluation of network intrusion detection systems makes it difficult to compare different algorithms and approaches [21]. Although the best way to evaluate any intrusion detection algorithm is to use live or recorded real traffic from the site where the algorithm is going to be deployed, there is a need of public datasets in order to evaluate proposals in a repeatable manner.

In order to model the sensor agents of our system , we needed a datFor the experiments we have used the well known 1999 KDD dataset[1] [10]. It derives from from MIT/LL 98 evaluation. Training and testing datasets were created at Columbia University. KDD dataset is the most frequently used dataset

---

[1] In fact the reduced version of the dataset (10% of the complete one).

Table 3. Attack and normal instances in original KDD training and test datasets

	Training	Test
Normal instances	97277	60593
Attack instances	396743	250436
Total	494020	311029
% of normal instances	19.69	19.48
% of attack instances	80.31	80.52

Table 4. Attack and normal instances in original training and test 1999 KDD datasets (after filtering)

	Training	Test
Normal instances	97277	60593
Attack instances	4887	2650
Total	102164	63243
% of normal instances	95.22	95.81
% of attack instances	4.78	4.19

to test machine learning algorithms on the intrusion detection domain (e.g. [22,23,24]). It was firstly employed for a machine learning competition in order to test different classifiers over the intrusion detection domain. A complete description of the data mining process can be found in [25]. They are currently available at California University website[2]. Next, we are going to review the dataset briefly (a general description can be found in [10]). Each connection record defines a TCP session and is described by 41 attributes (38 numeric and 3 nominal), and the corresponding class that indicates if the record represents normal or hostile activity. The number of normal and attack examples are summarized in Table 3. As it can be seen, the percentage of attacks is extraordinary high both on training and test datasets. This situation is not expectable in a real environment because, normally, the probability of intrusion is very low. However we have shown in previous sections the importance of the probability of intrusion when evaluating IDS effectiveness. Consequently the experiments we carried out have been done over original and filtered data. The filtering consisted on getting rid of the most common attack types both in training and test datasets. The resulting number of examples is summarized in Table 4. It is important to note that, after filtering, attack frequency remains under 5%.

We have experimented with 10 machine learning algorithms over the complete and the filtered datasets. Two of these algorithms are based on decision trees (*ADTree, J48*), five in rules (*ConjunctiveRule, DecisionStump, DecisionTable, OneR, PART*), one on bayesian learning (*NaïveBayes*) and two in simpler techniques (*HyperPipes, VFI*)[3]. Consequently, 10 models were built from training

---

[2] http://kdd.ics.uci.edu/databases/kddcup99/kddcup99.html
[3] The names correspond to the implementation name in WEKA software [26].

dataset and tested against the test dataset. The parametric IDS built from the individual models is tested against test dataset as well. The following section shows the results.

5 Experimental Results

Figure 2 shows the operating points of each machine learning model against the ROC points of the parametric IDS over the original dataset. The main conclusions from the analysis of this figure are:

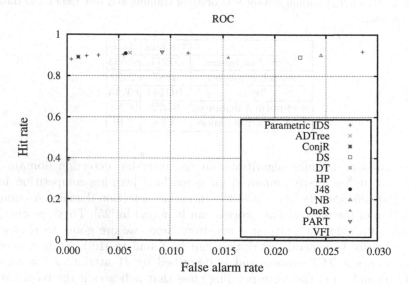

Fig. 2. ROC space of parametric IDS vs. individual models over original KDD test dataset

– Parametric IDS can work on different operating points.
– As p_t is increased, ROC points of the parametric IDS present lower H and F.
– It is difficult to state if the parametric model outperforms the non parametric components.

Then, in order to compare the different models, the metric of value we proposed in section 2 is used. Figure 3a) shows non parametric value curves while Figure 3b) shows those that correspond to the parametric IDS.

The main conclusions from these results are:

– *PART* is the machine learning model that achieves better results over a wider $\frac{C}{L}$ range. In addition, the greatest value of the non parametric IDS is also obtained by *PART*. The corresponding operating point is $(F, H) = (0.009, 0.916)$ with V=0.907 for $\frac{C}{L}$=0.805. This means that under these cost conditions and with the unrealistic probability of intrusion of the test dataset, *PART* is expected to have a value that is 90.7% of the perfect IDS.

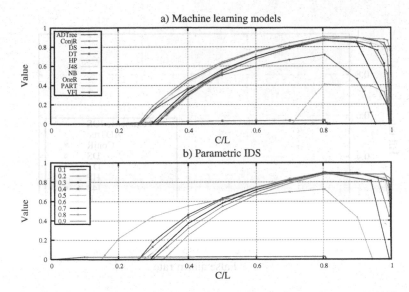

Fig. 3. Value curves over original KDD test dataset. a) Machine learning models and b) Parametric IDS.

- Parametric IDS obtains results that are similar to $PART$ for high $\frac{C}{L}$ relationships. But for lower $\frac{C}{L}$ the parametric system is much better. For instance, if $\frac{C}{L}=0.3$ the value of the parametric IDS is 0.441 ($p_t=0.2$). Under the same operating conditions, the best non parametric model ($PART$) has a value of 0.185. This means an increase of 25.6%. In addition, the $\frac{C}{L}$ range where the parametric is valuable is 25% wider than any of the individual models.

As we have stated, the probability of intrusion that KDD dataset shows is not realistic. Next results show the effectiveness of the systems tested after filtering the data as explained in section 4. Figure 4 shows the corresponding points on ROC space and Figure 5 exposes the value curves. From the ROC curves is difficult to say if $J48$ is more effective than $NaïveBayes$ or contrary. Figure 5a) shows that for $\frac{C}{L}>0.41$ $J48$ is preferred but for lower values $NaïveBayes$ is better. It is important to note that normally L is much bigger than C because the losses when an intrusion happens are usually bigger than the cost of taking some action of response. Therefore, it is important to study the behaviour for low $\frac{C}{L}$ relationships.

On the other hand, parametric IDS clearly outperforms any of the machine learning models. The envelope of the first includes the envelope of the composition of the second ones. To put it simply, there is no cost relationship where an individual algorithm outperforms the parametric IDS. In fact, the maximum of the parametric envelope is a 9.3% over the best non parametric curve. Furthermore, the range with value is also bigger for the parametric approach and, what is more important, for low $\frac{C}{L}$ relationships ($0.00012 < \frac{C}{L} < 0.018$) the combined model is valuable and none of its components separately has any value.

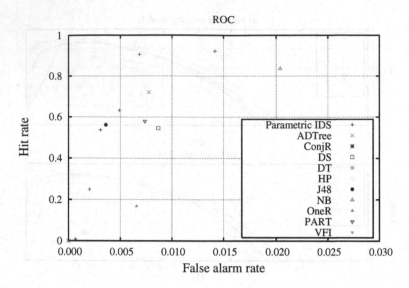

Fig. 4. ROC space of parametric IDS vs. individual models over filtered KDD test dataset

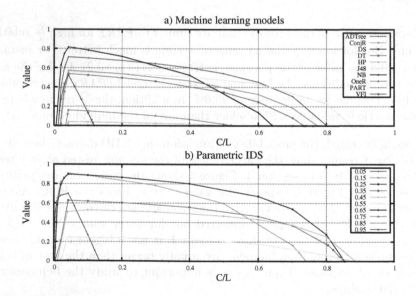

Fig. 5. Value curves computed over KDD filtered test dataset

6   Conclusions

This paper has proposed a method for comparing IDS effectiveness from a perspective of the utility of IDS detections. Experimental work has been done focusing on supervised machine learning algorithms. Results show that, generally, the best classifier highly depends on the operating conditions (summarized in the cost relationship and in the probability of intrusion). ROC curves are a good performance representation if an IDS has greater hit rate and lower false alarm rate than the one it is compared with. Else some alternative representation is needed. In fact, even when ROC curves are useful they do not give quantitative information about the dominance of one machine learning schema over another (this difference depends on the costs and on the probability of intrusion). The metric of value we propose gives a quantitative measure of how better a model is under different operating conditions. Furthermore, value curves state if a classifier is worthless (no better than a predictive system based on uncertainty) and allow to know how far a model is from a perfect one.

Results on the KDD dataset confirm that different classifiers stand out at different operating conditions. So, over the intrusion detection domain, it is very important to compare proposals considering the environment faced. In addition, the proper combination of different machine learning techniques produces a more effective IDS in the sense that it can operate under different scenarios (versatility) getting greater absolute values.

In conclusion, we encourage to adopt this evaluating methodology when evaluating and testing data mining approaches over the intrusion detection domain in order to avoid out of context conclusions.

References

1. ISO: Information technology - security techniques - it intrusion detection frameworks. Technical report (2002) ISO/IEC TR 15947.
2. Maloof, M.A.: Machine Learning and Data Mining for Computer Security: Methods and Applications (Advanced Information and Knowledge Processing). Springer Verlag, New York, Inc., Secaucus, NJ, USA (2005)
3. Sy, B.K.: Signature-based approach for intrusion detection. [27] 526–536
4. Giacinto, G., Perdisci, R., Roli, F.: Alarm clustering for intrusion detection systems in computer networks. [27] 184–193
5. Lippmann, R., Fried, D., Graf, I., Haines, J., Kendall, K., McClung, D., Weber, D., Webster, S., Wyschogrod, D., Cunningham, R., Zissman, M.: Evaluating intrusion detection systems: The 1998 DARPA off-line intrusion detection evaluation. In: Proceedings of the DARPA Information Survivability Conference and Exposition, Los Alamitos, California, USA, IEEE Computer Society Press (2000)
6. Lippmann, R., Haines, J.W., Fried, D.J., Korba, J., Das, K.: The 1999 darpa off-line intrusion detection evaluation. Computer Networks 34(4) (2000) 579–595
7. McHugh, J.: Testing intrusion detection systems: a critique of the 1998 and 1999 darpa intrusion detection system evaluations as performed by lincoln laboratory. ACM Transactions on Information and System Security 3(4) (2000) 262–294
8. Mahoney, M.V., Chan, P.K.: An analysis of the 1999 darpa/lincoln laboratory evaluation data for network anomaly detection. In Vigna, G., Jonsson, E., Krügel, C., eds.: RAID. Volume 2820 of Lecture Notes in Computer Science., Springer (2003) 220–237
9. Mell, P., Hu, V., Lippman, R., Haines, J., Zissman, M.: An overview of issues in testing intrusion detection (2003) National Institute of Standards and Technologies. Internal report 7007.

10. Elkan, C.: Results of the KDD'99 classifier learning contest. (1999)
11. Drummond, C., Holte, R.C.: Explicitly representing expected cost: an alternative to roc representation. In: Proceedings of the Sixth ACM SIGKDD International Conference on Knowledge Discovery and Data Mining, KDD '00, Nueva York, USA, ACM Press (2000) 198–207
12. Gaffney, J.E., Ulvila, J.W.: Evaluation of intrusion detectors: A decision theory approach. In: Proceedings of the IEEE Symposium on Security and Privacy, SP '01, Washington, DC, USA, IEEE Computer Society (2001) 50–
13. Ulvila, J.W., Gaffney, J.E.: Evaluation of intrusion detection systems. Journal of Research of the National Institute of Standards and Technology **108**(6) (2003) 453–473
14. Ulvila, J.W., Gaffney, J.E.: A decision analysis method for evaluating computer intrusion detection systems. Decision Analysis **1**(1) (2004) 35–50
15. Orfila, A., Carbó, J., Ribagorda, A.: Intrusion detection effectiveness improvement by a multi-agent system. International Journal of Computer Science & Applications **2**(1) (2005) 1–6
16. Swets, J.A., Dawes, R., Monahan, J.: Psychological science can improve diagnostic decisions. Psychological Science in the Public Interest **1**(1) (2000) 1–26
17. Sen, A.: Choice functions and revealed preferences. Review of Economic Studies **38** (1971) 307–317
18. Katz, R.W., Murphy, A.H.: Economic Value of Weather and Climate Forecasts. Cambridge University Press, UK (1997)
19. Orfila, A., Carbó, J., Ribagorda, A.: Fuzzy logic on decision model for ids. In: Proceedings of the Twelveth IEEE International Conference on Fuzzy Systems, FUZZ-IEEE '03. Volume 2., St. Louis, Missouri, USA (2003) 1237–1242
20. Axelsson, S.: The base-rate fallacy and the difficulty of intrusion detection. ACM Transactions on Information and System Security, TISSEC **3**(3) (2000) 186–205
21. Athanasiades, N., Abler, R., Levine, J.G., Owen, H.L., Riley, G.F.: Intrusion detection testing and benchmarking methodologies. In: Proceedings of the International Information Assurance Workshop, IWIA '03, Maryland, USA (2003) 63–72
22. Giacinto, G., Roli, F., Didaci, L.: Fusion of multiple classifiers for intrusion detection in computer networks. Pattern Recognition Letters **24**(12) (2003) 1795–1803
23. Sabhnani, M., Serpen, G.: Kdd feature set complaint heuristic rules for r2l attack detection. In: Security and Management. (2003) 310–316
24. Laskov, P., Düssel, P., Schäfer, C., Rieck, K.: Learning intrusion detection: Supervised or unsupervised?. In Roli, F., Vitulano, S., eds.: ICIAP. Volume 3617 of Lecture Notes in Computer Science., Springer (2005) 50–57
25. Lee, W., Stolfo, S.J.: A framework for constructing features and models for intrusion detection systems. ACM Transactions on Information and System Security **3**(4) (2000) 227–261
26. Witten, I.H., Frank, E.: Data mining: practical machine learning tools and techniques. Morgan Kaufmann Publishers Inc., San Francisco, California, USA (2005)
27. Perner, P., Imiya, A., eds.: Machine Learning and Data Mining in Pattern Recognition, 4th International Conference, MLDM 2005, Leipzig, Germany, July 9-11, 2005, Proceedings. In Perner, P., Imiya, A., eds.: MLDM. Volume 3587 of Lecture Notes in Computer Science., Springer (2005)

Spectral Discrimination of Southern Victorian Salt Tolerant Vegetation

Chris Matthews[2], Rob Clark[1], and Leigh Callinan[1]

[1] Dept of Primary Industries, PIRVic, Bendigo, Victoria, Australia
Rob.Clark@dpi.vic.gov.au,
Leigh.Callinan@dpi.vic.gov.au
[2] Faculty of Science, Technology & Engineering,
La Trobe University, P.O. Box 199 Bendigo 3552, Victoria, Australia
Tel.: +61 3 54447998, Fax: +61 3 54447557
c.matthews@latrobe.edu.au

Abstract. The use of remotely sensed data to map aspects of the landscape is both efficient and cost effective. In geographically large and sparsely populated countries such as Australia these approaches are attracting interest as an aid in the identification of areas affected by environmental problems such as dryland salinity. This paper investigates the feasibility of using visible and near infra-red spectra to distinguish between salt tolerant and salt sensitive vegetation species in order to identify saline areas in Southern Victoria, Australia. A series of classification models were built using a variety of data mining techniques and these together with a discriminant analysis suggested that excellent generalisation results could be achieved on a laboratory collected spectra data base. The results form a basis for continuing work on the development of methods to distinguish between vegetation species based on remotely sensed rather than laboratory based measurements.

1 Introduction

Dryland salinity is a major environmental problem in Australia. One important issue is the identification and mapping of the affected areas. One possible indicator of the severity of dryland salinity is the presence of salt tolerant and salt sensitive vegetation types in the landscape. However the mapping and monitoring of vegetation across broad landscapes by ground based field survey is labour intensive and therefore costly. Surveys are usually limited to observations at discrete points and rely on the ability to extrapolate data to provide a spatial context across the broader landscape. Remote sensing has the potential to provide a spatial context with its ability to capture data across broad swathes of landscape quickly and efficiently. Field surveys also rely heavily on local knowledge to identify sites and access to remote sites can be difficult. Remote sensing has the potential to ensure that all sites of interest are included in a survey. The main disincentive to using remotely sensed data is the ability to obtain a level of accuracy that is comparable with in field measurements. The research in this

P. Perner (Ed.): ICDM 2006, LNAI 4065, pp. 389–403, 2006.

project is a first step towards developing methodologies that could provide data of accuracy comparable to in situ measurements.

The project is intended to demonstrate that it is possible to discriminate vegetation genera/ species based on their innate characteristics. For the purpose of identifying species based on spectral responses the defining characteristics of vegetation can be identified as leaf pigmentation and internal structure and canopy architecture (i.e. the arrangement and alignment of leaves within the canopy). The data collected for this project looked at differences in leaf pigmentation and internal structure between species and genera. However the effect of canopy architecture was lost as a result of the way the measurements were made. The chosen vegetation included a number of salt tolerant and salt sensitive species common to much of Victoria, Australia. This data is to form the basis for further work that would allow the mapping of salt affected soil based on the presence of salt sensitive species and the absence of salt sensitive species. This mimics the field based method that is commonly used in Victoria to identify and map salt affected areas. A number of the salt sensitive species are common native grasses in Victoria and it is also intended to develop the ability to identify and map native grasses using this type of remotely sensed data.

2   Background

The visible and near infrared (VNIR) portion of the electromagnetic spectrum covers the range from around $400nm$ to just over $1000nm$ and the reflectance or radiation at particular wavelengths can give an indication of colour. Low reflectance in the visible range ($400 - 700nm$) is due to the absorption of radiation by leaf pigments, such as chlorophyll, and high reflectance near the IR range ($> 700nm$) indicates that the absorption by leaf pigments and cell walls is low. Wavelengths with maximum sensitivity to chlorophyll are $550 - 630nm$ and near $700nm$[4,12].

Remote and optical sensing using VNIR spectra has attracted interest across a range of problem domains. These include the determination of chlorophyll and other biochemical properties in plant leaves [4,7], the classification of the mineral composition of rocks [10], the identification of chemical and physical soil properties [13] and the monitoring of food quality during cooking in industrial ovens [11]. In each case a spectral database is built which can be used to establish some relationship between the properties of interest and the spectral signatures. This might simply be the ability to classify an example based on the spectral data or, in the case of a regression problem, the ability to estimate the value of some chemical or physical property. It may also involve the identification of particular wavelengths within the spectra that are important in the classification or estimation, or the removal of redundant and highly correlated components of the spectra in order to simplify the analysis.

The available analytical techniques fall into two broad categories: traditional statistical approaches and computational intelligence or data mining approaches. For example the on-line classifier used in monitoring food quality during cooking was built using a back propagation neural network [11] whereas step wise multiple regression analysis of the spectral data was used as a predictor for biochemical properties such as cellulose and protein in plant leaves [7]. A genetic algorithm was one of the techniques used to search for an optimum subset of wavelength ranges for mineral identification [10] while an established statistical technique such as principal components analysis was suggested as being suitable for reducing the dimensionality of plant spectra prior to database storage [3] or classification model development [11].

A related issue is the pre-processing options available prior to analysis. This is particularly relevant when we are building a classifier where we are attempting to distinguish between spectra of different classes. The use of higher order derivative data (e.g. 1st or 2nd order derivatives) estimated from the raw spectra in an effort to resolve overlapping spectral bands is well established in spectroscopy [1,9]. These derivatives give an indication of the slope and the rate of change of the slope in the original spectra and offer the possibility of greater discrimination between spectra. This approach has had some success as a pre-processing tool for building a neural network classifier model to identify the type and concentration of contaminants in waste water from UV-Vis spectra [2].

This project is concerned with the construction and analysis of a data base of VNIR spectra for a range of pasture and native vegetation species common to Southern Australia. In particular we are interested in the answers to the following:

1. Is it possible to build classification models which distinguish between species based on the spectral data collected under the same climatic conditions?
2. If so, which spectral characteristics(wavelengths) contribute most to the classification?

The paper is organised as follows. Section 3 outlines the collection and preparation of the specimens, and the measurement of the spectra leading to the construction of the spectral database. Section 4 describes the building and assessment of a series of classification models using the database in an effort to answer the first question. Section 5 describes the statistical analysis of the spectra carried out in order to seek an answer to the second question. Finally section 6 provides some concluding remarks and discusses the on-going work that arises from the results reported here.

3   Experimental Work

3.1   Collection and Preparation of Plant Samples

For the study, vegetation specimens were collected for 16 species. The plants fell into three categories: salt tolerant species, native grass species and pasture species common in the Hamilton district, Victoria, Australia. The species are listed in Table 1. Three separate field trips were made to collect vegetation samples, December 6 to December 9 2004 (known as week 1), December 20 to

December 22 2004 (week 2) and February 7 to February 11 2005 (week 3). It was intended that 20 samples of each species would be collected on each field trip, however there was some unintentional variation from this and the number of samples varied from 19 to 23 samples per specie. Some of the target species have an annual life cycle, and while all species were available on the first trip in early December, specie *balansa clover* was not available for collection by mid-December and species, *barley grass* and *sub clover* were not available by early February. In the course of the field vegetation collection it was noticed that three of the species, *cocksfoot*, *phalaris* and *tall wheat grass*, were sometimes grazed and at other sites were not grazed (rank). The grazed samples contained relatively little senesced vegetation material compared to the rank, ungrazed samples and thus it is possible that the spectral signatures might vary across the subgroups. It was for this reason it was decided to divide these species into grazed and rank sub-groups.

Each sample was cut, packed in a labelled plastic bag and stored in a refrigerator for transport back to the laboratory. All plants were kept refrigerated until their spectrum was measured. Spectra were measured for all plants within 3 hours of cutting to minimise deterioration of the plant material. When plants were collected in the field they were cut as low to the ground as possible and then cut into 15 to 20cm lengths if required. The basal section was placed in the bag first, with the next section placed on top of it. This continued until the uppermost section of the plant (generally containing the flower or seed heads) was placed on top of the plant material. Shorter species like *sub clover* did not require cutting in this manner, while species like *tall wheat grass* were frequently cut into five or six sections. When the plants were unpacked in the laboratory they were carefully arranged to cover the spectrometer field of view (FOV) so that the basal leaves were at the bottom of the pile and the flower/ seed heads sat on top of the pile. The aim was to arrange the plant material under the spectrometer in the laboratory in the same order as occurred in situ.

3.2   Measurement of Plant Spectra

Laboratory measurement of spectra was carried out in an environment where the amount and type of illumination could be controlled. To this end, a box was positioned over the spectrometer and the vegetation sample to exclude natural light. The inside of the box and all fittings inside the box were painted matt black to reduce reflectance from background materials on the spectrometer sensor. A pair of 50W Quartz-Tungsten Halogen lights powered by a 12 volt DC source to ensure a constant current, were installed inside the box 70 cm either side of the target area holding the vegetation samples and 90 cm above the sample. The spectrometer has a conical FOV of 25 degrees and was located so that the sensor aperture was 30 cm directly above the plate on which the vegetation samples were placed. At this height the diameter of the FOV was just over 13 cm. The plate was covered by a matt black material that contributed very little to the reflectance measurement. The instrument used to measure the vegetation spectra

Table 1. Plant species

species (common name)	category	week 1	week 2	week 3
Balansa clover	salt tolerant	y(20)	-	-
Barley grass	pasture	y(20)	y(20)	-
Broad leaf plantain	pasture	y(20)	y(20)	y(20)
Buck's horn plantain	salt tolerant	y(20)	y(20)	y(20)
Cocksfoot	pasture	y(20)	y(20)	y(20)
Danthonia	native grass	y(20)	y(20)	y(20)
Phalaris	pasture	y(20)	y(20)	y(20)
Perennial rye grass	pasture	y(20)	y(20)	y(20)
Sea barley grass	salt tolerant	y(20)	y(20)	y(20)
Spiny rush	salt tolerant	y(20)	y(20)	y(20)
Stipa sp.	native grass	y(21)	y(20)	y(20)
Sub clover	pasture	y(23)	y(20)	-
Sweet vernal grass	pasture	y(20)	y(20)	y(20)
Tall wheat grass	salt tolerant	y(19)	y(20)	y(20)
Kangaroo grass	native grass	y(20)	y(20)	y(20)
Yorkshire fog grass	pasture	y(20)	y(20)	y(20)
Total sample size		323	300	260

Table 2. ASD Fieldspec spectrometer: technical specifications

Number of bands	512
Spectral Range	325 - 1075 nm
Band Width at FWHM	1.6 nm
Spectral Resolution	3.5 nm @ 700 nm
Field of View	25 degrees

was an ASD FieldSpec HandHeld spectrometer. Table 2 lists the instrument specifications.

4   Classification Models

Although the spectral range of the spectrometer was $325nm$ to $1075nm$, measurements at each end of the range tended to be relatively noisy. The noisy data was excluded and data analysis was limited to a spectral range of $400nm$ to $1050nm$. The raw spectral data was preprocessed prior to model development. The reflectance values were sampled at $10nm$ intervals across the range and normalised, resulting in 66 inputs. For data set sizes of around 320 this is consistent with that delivered by the *subjects-to-variables* ratio, sometimes used in statistical analysis [5]. There are differences in the climatic conditions, such as temperature and humidity, between the collection points which may lead to differences in the spectral signatures within species. This is supported by reference to the spectra. For example figure 2 shows comparative spectra for samples of

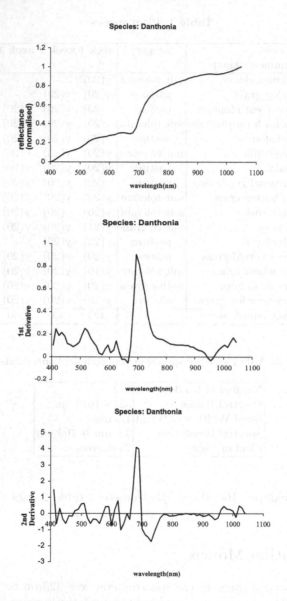

Fig. 1. Sample spectra for species *Danthonia*: normalised raw reflectance data and derivative data

species *Danthonia* collected during week 1 and week 3. Differences in the spectra, particularly in the visible range (400 to ≈ 700*nm*), can clearly be seen. It is for this reason that classification models described below focused on species identification within each collection point. Data sets were also prepared using 1st and 2nd derivative estimates from the normalised reflectance data. This resulted in the loss of one input for each higher order derivative estimate i.e 65 and 64

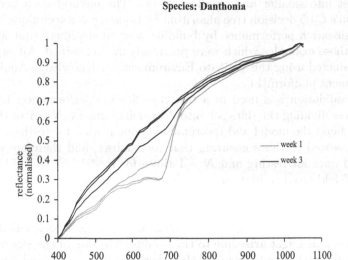

Fig. 2. Sample spectra for species *Danthonia*: week 1 and week 3

inputs for the 1st derivative and 2nd derivative data respectively. Figure 1 shows three derived spectra from one of the week 1 samples for species *Danthonia*. The possibility of increased discrimination between spectra obtained by using the derivative data can clearly be seen. As will be seen later this is supported by the experimental results.

4.1   Individual Species Classification

The first set of experiments involved the development of classifiers to distinguish between individual species. Initially the grazed and rank subgroups for species *cocksfoot, phalaris* and *tall wheat grass* were combined giving 16 target classes for the week 1 data set, 15 for week 2 and 13 for week 3. Four basic classification approaches were used. The first used a non-linear function approximator, in this case a single layer back propagation neural network. Networks of this type have the ability to learn from data, provided the target class is known. They are able to approximate the theoretical function between the inputs and the target and are robust in the presence of noisy and/or missing data. The second used linear logistic regression. This statistical approach estimates a relationship between a set of attributes (or predictors) and some categorical dependent variable based on the non-linear logistic function. The third approach used the instance based method, k-nearest neighbour classification. Here the classification is determined by the closeness of the unknown examples to k known examples as plotted in a n-dimensional space, where n represent the size of the attribute set. The final approach was rule induction, with and without boosting. Rule induction derives a set of production rules from a decision tree based on the continual partitioning of a data set into smaller and smaller subsets. The method used here is based on Quinlan's $C4.5$ decision tree algorithm[8]. Boosting is a technique used to improve classification performance by building a set of classifiers that focus increasingly on those examples which were previously miss-classified. All experiments were conducted using the Waikato Environment for Knowledge Analysis (*Weka*) development platform[14].

10-fold cross validation was used to assess classification performance. Cross validation involves dividing the data set into N disjoint subsets. $N - 1$ of these sets are used to build the model and the remaining one is used for testing. The experiment is repeated N times ensuring that each subset, and therefore each example, is used once for testing and $N - 1$ times for model building. This is referred to as N-fold cross validation. The literature suggests 10 as a suitable value for N, ensuring there is a balance between the computational requirements and the classification error [6]. Three 10-fold cross validation experiments were run for each approach on each data set and the results averaged. This was done to reduce any bias that might arise due to the random selection of the examples into each of the subsets. It should be noted that there was little variation between the results for a given experiment using the same classifier on the same data set. All results reported here are the (average) percentage of data set examples that were correctly classified when members of the *testing* set i.e an estimation of the generalisation performance of the classifier.

Some preliminary experimentation was carried out to determine an optimum set of operating parameters and architecture for the neural network models. It was found that single hidden layer networks with 27 units, trained using a learning rate of 0.3 and momentum of 0.2, trained for 500 epochs gave the best results. However network performance was not overly sensitive to increased hidden layer size or training time.

The detailed results for species classification are shown in table 3. The same trends were observed across the three data sets. The classification accuracy increases from the normalised to the first and second derivative data, with the second derivative data giving the best results in most cases. This confirms the view that the use of derivative data provides the possibility of greater distinction between spectra. The week 3 results, with only 13 target classes, were the best. In general, the best classification results were achieved using the neural network and the logistic regression approaches, although the nearest neighbour classifiers performed very well on the 2nd derivative data. Rule induction gave the worst results, even when boosting was used.

The experiments were repeated treating the subgroups for species *cocksfoot*, *phalaris* and *tall wheat grass* as separate classes. The results were marginally worse than those for the combined subgroups. For example, the average neural network classification results for the week 1 data (now having 19 rather than 16 target classes) were 90.2%, 96.7% and 98.2% for the normalised, 1st and 2nd derivative data sets respectively. The results for the other classification techniques followed a similar trend. This suggests that there is little difference in the

Table 3. Comparative results for individual species classification: 10 fold cross validation

Method (*Weka* implementation)	Normalised radiance data	1st Derivative data	2nd Derivative data
neural network (MultilayerPerceptron)			
week 1	92.6%	98.5%	99.7%
week 2	90.8%	98.1%	99.6%
week 3	94.5%	99.3%	100%
logistic regression (Logistic)			
week 1	95.9%	98.9%	99.7%
week 2	93.9%	99.6%	99.7%
week 3	96.9%	99.3%	99.0%
logistic regression (SimpleLogistic)			
week 1	91.4%	98.6%	99.6%
week 2	93.1%	97.1%	98.7%
week 3	96.0%	98.8%	99.1%
K-nearest neighbour (IBk, k = 3)			
week 1	78.6%	90.4%	98.6%
week 2	69.7%	87.7%	98.9%
week 3	82.8%	95.1%	100%
rule induction (PART)			
week 1	68.4%	69.7%	75.8%
week 2	59.2%	71.4%	75.2%
week 3	67.6%	81.8%	79.0%
rule induction (PART) with AdaBoostM1 (10 iterations)			
week 1	75.9%	84.9%	92.1%
week 2	73.3%	85.7%	92.6%
week 3	78.6%	90.7%	93.2%

spectra between grazed and non grazed examples within these three species, at least revealed by the techniques used here.

To see how much of this classification success may simply be due to random factors rather than to the properties inherent in the spectra signatures between species the experiments were repeated using random classes. The week 1 2nd derivative data set was taken and the examples were randomly assigned to one of 16 classes (identified as class A through to class P), in the same proportion as the original. Given that there are approximately 20 examples allocated to each random class, the probability of correctly selecting, at random, an example of a given class from the data set would be 20/323 or 0.062(6.2%). We would expect that classifiers built using this data set to perform almost as poorly. The results were as expected. For example, the average classification accuracy for the 10-fold cross validation experiments using a neural network model was only 9.0%, a result only slightly higher than if the classification was done totally randomly. The results for the other classifiers were similar.

4.2   Distinguishing Salt Tolerant from Salt Sensitive Species

The classification problem now becomes a two class problem. The proportion of salt tolerant to salt sensitive examples was 99 : 224 for the week 1 data set, 80 : 220 for week 2 and 80 : 180 for week 3. Only the 2nd derivative data sets were used in these experiments. The same classification approaches and evaluation methods were used and the results are shown in table 4. Overall the results are not as good as those for the individual species classification, although the differences seem marginal in some cases. The best technique across the three data sets is the 3-nearest neighbour classifier, with those using the week 3 double derivative data set giving a 100% average testing accuracy. It should also be noted that salt tolerance is the minority class and in many cases the classification error is higher for this than for the salt sensitive class.

Table 4. Comparative results for salt tolerant and salt sensitive classification: 10 fold cross validation using 2nd Derivative data

Method (Weka implementation)	week 1	week 2	week 3
neural network (MultilayerPerceptron)	97.8%	99.2%	96.2%
logistic regression (Logistic)	97.8%	95.9%	95.0%
logistic regression (SimpleLogistic)	97.0%	98.0%	92.3%
K-nearest neighbour (IBk, k = 3)	99.5%	99.9%	100%
rule induction (PART)	88.8%	88.9%	90.5%
rule induction (PART) with AdaBoostM1 (10 iterations)	94.8%	95.1%	95.1%

The experiments were repeated where the examples were randomly assigned to two classes in the same proportion as the original data set. In this case the minority class (class1) consisted of 99 examples and the majority class (class2) of 224 examples. Random selection should result in a 30.7% classification accuracy for class1 and 69.3% for class2. Again the results were as expected. For example a 10-fold cross validation neural network experiment carried out on the week 1 2nd derivative data gave a 34.3% classification accuracy for class1 and 72.3% for class2. This lends further support to the view that successful classification is due differences in the spectral signatures between species rather than random factors.

5   Analysis of Variance and Discriminant Analysis

Analysis of variance(ANOVA) is used to assess the statistical significance of the effect of one or more independent variables on one or more independent variables. In this case the effect of the reflectance at certain wavelengths on the species classification. Analysis of variance assumes that the data is normally distributed. Discriminant analysis can then be applied to obtain a classification accuracy using these wavelengths.

Each week's data was analysed separately, and within each week the reflectance data was split into a training set (around two thirds of the samples for each specie) and a test set (around one third of the samples for each specie). The full wavelength set was subject to this analysis. Exploration of the raw reflectance data showed that it was not normally distributed. A log transformation was applied to the reflectance data to ensure that it was normally distributed. Using only the training set of samples, log transformed reflectance values for each of the vegetation types (species) were analysed in one way ANOVAs (analysis of variance). The ANOVA calculated a variance ratio for each wavelength, which provides a measure of the separation between groups compared to the separation within each group. Graphing the variance ratio against the wavelength (see Figure 3 for an example, the week 1 training data set) shows a series of larger peaks and troughs and some relatively minor peaks and troughs. The peaks are of particular interest and indicate wavelengths where there is better discrimination between species compared to neighbouring wavelengths. Wavelengths selected after running an ANOVA for all species were known as primary wavelengths.

Using the training set, log transformed reflectance values for each of the primary critical wavelengths were subjected to a discriminant analysis. In discriminant analysis, canonical variates analysis (CVA) is used to get scores for the group means. CVA operates on a within-group sums of squares and products matrix, calculated from a set of variates (in this case, log transformed reflectances at selected wavelengths) and a factor that specifies the grouping of units (in this case, species). CVA finds linear combinations of the (sometimes standardised) variables that maximise the ratio of between group to within group variation, thereby giving functions to the original variables that can be used to discriminate between groups. CVA is used to obtain the scores for the group means and loadings for the variables, scores are then calculated for all the units. Maha-

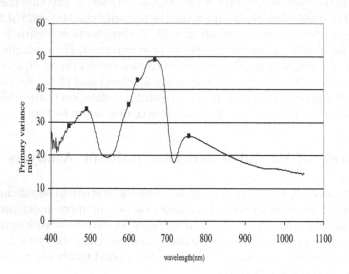

Fig. 3. Primary variance ratios for week 1 training data

lanobis squared distances between the units and the group means are calculated from the Canonical Variate scores. Finally, each unit is allocated to a group for which it has the smallest Mahalanobis distance to the group mean.

Examination of the results matrix output from the discriminant analysis may show confusion between certain groups of species. If the error count is considered to be unacceptable, species within these groups were subjected to another ANOVA (limited to the group of misclassified species) to identify a secondary batch of critical wavelengths. In this case, log transformed reflectance values for the secondary wavelengths were added to the primary group and used to improve the accuracy of the discriminant analysis. The aim was to obtain the best accuracy for the least number of wavelengths and various combinations of the primary and secondary wavelengths were tested. When a final set of wavelengths was identified using the training data set, log transformed reflectance values were calculated for the same wavelengths within the test data set. A discriminant analysis was run and the results, together with the reduced wavelength sets are shown in table 5. The testing results are consistent with those obtained using the neural network and logistic approaches and there is overlap between the wavelength sets across the three collection points.

The testing set results across the three weeks were then re-examined to determine a classification accuracy for the distinction between the salt tolerant and salt sensitive species. In this case only miss-classifications between salt tolerant and salt sensitive species were considered. The results are shown in table 6 and taken with those in table 4 suggest that a distinction between salt tolerance and salt sensitivity based on the spectral data is possible.

Table 5. Discriminant analysis for weeks 1,2 and 3, using the primary and secondary wavelength sets: individual species

	Training	Testing	wavelength set
week 1	93.8%	93.8%	$424nm$, $446nm$, $491nm$, $600nm$, $623nm$, $669nm$, $757nm$, $977nm$
week 2	89.7%	87.6%	$463nm$, $494nm$, $595nm$, $623nm$, $655nm$, $688nm$, $772nm$, $978nm$
week 3	93.5%	94.5%	$411nm$, $428nm$, $504nm$, $588nm$, $620nm$, $678nm$, $758nm$, $928nm$, $1031nm$

Table 6. Distinguishing between salt tolerant salt sensitive species using the discriminant analysis results

test set (size)	week 1 (112)	week 2 (105)	week 3 (91)
salt tolerant	97.1 %	96.4%	92.9%
salt non-tolerant	98.7 %	97.4 %	98.4%
overall	98.2%	97.1 %	96.7%

6   Conclusion and Future Work

The results demonstrate that at least in a laboratory, with pure samples of the plant species under conditions of controlled illumination and with no atmospheric effects, it is possible to discriminate between the target species with some confidence based on their spectral reflectance within the visible and near infrared portion of the spectrum. The classification models, particularly those built using the logistic regression and neural network approaches on 2nd derivative spectral data, provided excellent generalisation results for both the distinction between individual species and that between salt sensitive and salt tolerant species. The results in section 5 suggest that there are key areas in the spectral signatures which may be important in the classification. Further investigation is continuing in this area including the possible application of search techniques such as genetic algorithms to determine further subsets of wavelengths which can retain the classification accuracy of the original models. However the major focus of future work is the development of methods to enable the classification of species from spectral data derived from measurements made in the field.

The conditions under which the current data was collected vary considerably with those likely to be encountered when making in situ reflectance measurements. For in situ measurements canopy architecture will be intact and there will be some degree of mixing from various sources of reflectance within the field of view of the spectrometer. Illumination will be natural and the atmospheric effects may be significant. Measurement of spectra within the laboratory shows that reflectance signals influenced primarily by leaf pigmentation and internal structure allowed the target species to be distinguished with good accuracy. This work is the first step in the development of a methodology to map saline soils based on the presence of salt tolerant vegetation and the absence of salt sensitive vegetation. The next stage will be an attempt to correctly identify the indicator species in the field using hyperspectral imagery. For this exercise it is intended to use Hymap imagery which is captured using an aircraft based hyperspectral sensor. Hymap has 125 spectral bands with a spectral resolution of 10-20 nm, a swathe width of around 1.5 km and a spatial resolution of 3 metres. In order to identify individual plant genera or species atmospheric effects, natural illumination, canopy structure and more than one target type within each pixel will all need to be taken into account. There are a number of current techniques that may be applicable and it is of interest to determine if it is possible to use some of these to successfully identify plant genera/species that form less than whole pixels under these conditions. If successful we will be in a position to develop a model that assesses pixels as either saline or non-saline and possibly the level of salinity based on the amount and type of ground cover within each pixel. This work also has the potential to develop methodologies that could benefit from the ability to map and monitor vegetation by remote sensing such as mapping weeds, mapping and monitoring riparian vegetation or native grasslands or monitoring changes in land cover.

References

1. Luidmil Antonov and Stefan Stoyanov. Analysis of the overlapping bands in uv-vis absorption spectroscopy. *Allied Spectroscopy*, 47(7):1030–1035, 1993.
2. Boyle W.J.O. Benjathapanun N and Grattan K.T.V. Binary encoded 2nd-diffential spectrometry using UV-Vis spectral data and neural networks in the estimation of species type and concentration. *IEE Proceedings -Science, Measurement and Technology*, 144(2):73–80, 1997.
3. Ian E.Bell and Gladimir V.G. Baranoski. Reducing the dimensionality of plant spectral databases. *IEEE Transactions on Geoscience and Remote Sensing*, 42(3):570–576, 2004.
4. A.A. Gitelson, M.N. Merzlyak, and Y. Grits. Novel algorithms for remote sensing of chlorophyll content in higher plant leaves. In *Geoscience and Remote Sensing Symposium, 1996. IGARSS '96. 'Remote Sensing for a Sustainable Future.', International*, volume 4, pages 2355–2357. IEEE, 1996.
5. Laurence G. Grimm and Paul R. Tarnold, editors. *Reading and Understanding Multivariate Statistics*. American Psychological Association, Washington D.C., 1998.
6. Trevor Hastie, Robert Tibshirani, and Ferome Friedman. *The Elements of Statistical Learning: Data mining, Inference and Prediction*. Springer Series in Statistics. Springer, New York, 2003.
7. S. Jacquemoud, J. Verdebout, G. Schmuck, G. Andreoli, B. Hosgood, and S.E. Hornig. Investigation of leaf biochemistry by statistics. In *Geoscience and Remote Sensing Symposium, 1994. IGARSS '94. Surface and Atmospheric Remote Sensing: Technologies, Data Analysis and Interpretation*, volume 2, pages 1239–1241. IEEE, 1994.
8. Quinlan J.R. *C4.5: Programs for Machine Learning*. Morgan Kaufman, San Mateo CA, 1993.

9. Sommer L. *Analytical Absorption Spectophotometry in the Visible and UltraViolet: The Principles.* Studies in Analytical Chemistry 8. Elsevier, Amsterdam, 1989.
10. Jonathan Moody, Ricardo Silva, and Joseph Vanderwaart. Data filtering for automatic classification of rocks from reflectance spectra. In *Proceedings of the seventh ACM SIGKDD International Conference on Knowledge Discovery and Data Mining*, pages 347–352. ACM Press, 2001.
11. Marion O'Farrell, Elfred Lewis, Colin Flanagan, William B. Lyons, and N. Jackman. Design of a system that uses optical-fiber sensors and neural networks to control a large-scale industrial oven by monitoring the food quality online. *IEEE Sensors Journal*, 5(6):1407–1420, 2005.
12. Hans-Werner Olfs, Klaus Blankenau, Frank Brentrup, Jorg Jasper, Axel Link, and Joachim Lammel. Soil-and plant-based nitrogen-fertilizer recommendations in arable farming. *J. Plant Nutr. Soil Sci*, 168:414–431, 2005.
13. H. Preissler and G. Loercher. Extraction of soil properties from laboratory and imaging spectrometry data. In *Geoscience and Remote Sensing Symposium, 1995. IGARSS '95. 'Quantative Remote Sensing for Science and Applications', International*, volume 3, pages 1968–1970. IEEE, 1995.
14. Ian H. Witten and Eibe Frank. *Data Mining: Practical machine learning tools and techniques.* Morgan Kaufmann, San Francisco, 2nd edition, 2005.

A Generative Graphical Model for Collaborative Filtering of Visual Content

Sabri Boutemedjet and Djemel Ziou

DI, Faculté des Sciences
Université de Sherbrooke
Sherbrooke, QC, Canada J1K 2R1
{sabri.boutemedjet, djemel.ziou}@usherbrooke.ca

Abstract. In this paper, we propose a novel generative graphical model for collaborative filtering of visual content. The preferences of the "like-minded" users are modelled in order to predict the relevance of visual documents represented by their visual features. We formulate the problem using a probabilistic latent variable model where user's preferences and items' classes are combined into a unified framework in order to provide an accurate and a generative model that overcomes the new item problem, generally encountered in traditional collaborative filtering systems.

1 Introduction

There is a huge amount of multimedia content such as texts, images and video information available on the WWW. The improvements in mobile and display technologies make it possible to one to search visual documents from everywhere and every time using hand-held devices like Portable Digital Assistants (PDA). The usual scenario used in today's academic Content Based Image Retrieval (CBIR) systems [1] is to present a set of initial images from which a user selects one or more example images to form a search query. Then, the CBIR system returns the set of images that matches the query and the user may iterate through query refinement using a Relevance Feedback (RF) mechanism. By this way, a typical CBIR system responds to user's immediate needs expressed as queries in a reactive manner. User's long term needs related to visual documents were not the subject of many studies and need to be investigated. In fact, the information overload in current digital libraries creates new challenges in providing personalized and individualized services to users that help them in finding interesting visual documents (i.e. images) rapidly and improve her experience. When using small hand-held devices for image search, the interaction time with the CBIR system may be increased greatly. This is due essentially to the small number of example images that may be presented on the PDA's screen to start the retrieval. Since these devices are constrained by a limited battery life, we need thus a system able of predicting user's needs before starting the retrieval. After that, the user builds a search query from the set of suggested images that meet her needs. If the prediction process of these images is accurate then the user will

P. Perner (Ed.): ICDM 2006, LNAI 4065, pp. 404–415, 2006.

find the sought images quickly. To do that, we need to model user preferences related to the visual content. To explain that, let's take the following example. Assume two users Ali and Lucie with the following preference patterns. Ali is graphical designer and looks generally for images he uses in conceiving convivial user interfaces while Lucie student in medicine and interested generally by scientific pictures of human organs. It is natural to think that an effective CBIR system will start the retrieval by presenting images to each of the users according to their long term needs i.e. preferences instead of making random selections. This improves greatly user's experience since it provides a personalized search service. In literature, user modelling [2] is addressed mainly within the information filtering (IF) [3] community, a technology used in recommender systems. For example, Amazon makes personalized recommendations based on the books a user has bought and any explicit ratings of books expressed on a five star scale. Viscors [4] recommends cell-phone wall-paper images based on previously rated images. Both systems use memory-based collaborative filtering (CF) algorithms which build user neighborhoods using similarity measures such as Pearson Correlation Coefficients [5] or vector similarity [6]. Another class of CF consists of learning first a probabilistic model of users (e.g. user classes) and then use the learned model to predict ratings for items. Examples include the Aspect model [7] and the Flexible Mixture Model [8]. Collaborative filtering algorithms suffer from the *"new item problem"* where the incoming non rated items will never be suggested. In a content based filtering (CBF) approach such as [9], texts are recommended on the basis of the similarity between documents and user's profile. However, CBF techniques have the problem of *overspecialization* in the sense that recommended items are always similar to the user profile. Interesting documents different from the user's profile will never be recommended.

In our paper, we present a novel hybrid filtering approach which combines both model-based CF and CBF together in unified framework to overcome the *new item* and *overspecialization* problems. Indeed, user communities are identified on the basis of similar visual content (texture and color features) and not the basis of visual documents themselves. The filtering system we propose may be integrated to a CBIR system in order to "recommend" visual documents to the user according to her preferences. This model may be integrated into an email filter to bock for example user's undesirable objects such as pornographic images for not adults people. Information filtering systems that block uninteresting contents are referred to as passive filtering systems in literature [3].

This paper is organized as follows. In Sect. 2 we present our model of filtering visual contents using a probabilistic framework. After that, the estimation of model's parameters will be presented in Sect. 3 and experiments will be shown in Sect. 4.

2   The Proposed Model

The domains we consider are a set of users $\mathcal{U} = \{u_1, u_2, \ldots, u_{|\mathcal{U}|}\}$ and a set of visual documents $\mathcal{I} = \{i_1, i_2, \ldots, i_{|\mathcal{I}|}\}$, $|.|$ used to denote the cardinality of

Fig. 1. Collaborative filtering of visual content

a set. Let us consider a utility function s in $\mathcal{U} \times \mathcal{I}$ where $s(u,i)$ quantifies the relevance of a visual document i for the user u. This function may be for example, the number of times the user has accessed the visual document, or the time he spent in reading its content or an explicit rating captured using a relevance feedback mechanism. In this paper, we assume that users give explicit ratings to documents on certain scale. We denote by $\mathcal{R} = \{r_1, \ldots, r_{|\mathcal{R}|}\}$ this rating scale where r_1 (resp. $r_{|\mathcal{R}|}$) refers to the lowest (resp. highest) relevance. The problem of suggesting visual documents may be formulated as the the identification of visual documents with highest ratings for a given user. Mathematically, this may written as follows:

$$\arg \max_{i \in \mathcal{I}} s(u, i) \tag{1}$$

We propose to use a probabilistic framework in which we predict $s(u,i)$ on the basis of probabilities $p(u,i,r)$, the joint probability to observe a user u, attributes a rating r to a visual document i. More exactly, since we are interested by predicting document's relevance for a given user, we compute $s(u,i)$ on the basis of probabilities $p(i,r|u)$. One may think to use the mean prediction rule which computes a rating as $s(u,i) = \sum_r rp(r|i,u)$. According to Bayes' rule, it is easy to compute $p(r|u,i)$ on the basis of probabilities $p(i,r|u)$ as $p(r|u,i) = p(i,r|u)/\sum_r p(i,r|u)$. One can also use the maximum prediction rule which returns a rating with the highest probability. Mathematically, this may be formulated as $s(u,i) = \arg\max_r p(r|u,i)$. In this paper, we use the mean prediction rule for $s(u,i)$ and we focus hereafter on modelling $p(i,r|u)$.

We introduce a hidden (latent) variable z in order to model user communities (or preference patterns) and their related items. Indeed, we associate a state of the latent variable z for each observation $< u, i, r >$. This constitutes a flexible clustering method since the state of z is associated to a user, and an item and the rating together in order to explain such relation. In other words, we may find for example, $< u_1, i_1, r_{|\mathcal{R}|}, z_1 >$ and $< u, i_2, r_{|\mathcal{R}|}, z_2 >$. There is a great difference between the proposed model and Bayesian clustering (BC)[6]. In fact, in BC, users are assumed to belong to one class say z_1 and all user's ratings on items will be justified only by one state of z. We assume a conditional independence between a user and and item with his rating (i.e. $u \perp\!\!\!\perp (i,r)|z)^1$. This allows us to write $p(i,r|u)$ as:

$$p(i,r|u) = \sum_z p(i,r,z|u) = \sum_z p(z|u)p(i,r|z) \tag{2}$$

As presented in Eq.(2), the model is nothing else than the Aspect model [7] where i denotes the index of an item. One major problem of the Aspect model is the new *item problem* caused by the need to retrain the model for newer documents due to the unavailability of the probabilities $p(i,r|z)$. Moreover, if we are able to update online these probabilities, we need ratings for those newer documents which is not always possible. In other words, users must rate a document in order to be able to predict its relevance. With the exponentially growing digital image collections every day, the Aspect model as presented in Eq.(2) needs to be improved. We present a novel model able to predict ratings for newer documents even if they were not rated by users. The principle is to associate a state of the variable z to visual content classes instead of individual visual documents. In fact, visual documents have the advantage that of the ability of modelling their content such as the color and the texture co-occurrence vectors efficiently. The idea behind our principle is to build user communities around the class of visual contents. For example, a user may prefer snowy mountains or blue skies characterized by their dominating blue and white pixels. We propose to cluster the visual content by summarizing image collections using a finite mixture model [10]. Denoting by v^i the feature vector of the visual document i and by c its class, we summarize the collection into classes, using the finite mixture model as given in Eq.(3):

$$p(v^i) = \sum_c p(c)p(v^i|c) \tag{3}$$

We use the Dirichlet distribution (DD) in modelling $p(v^i|c)$ due to its advantages. First, the Dirichlet distribution is defined in a compact support which is an interesting property of densities. Colors are encoded in general within the interval $[0, 256]$ which makes color histograms compactly supported. Secondly, the Dirichlet distribution has many shapes and thus fits better the data. A visual feature is represented by a vector $v^i = (v^i_1, \ldots, v^i_n)$ of dimension n where n denotes for example the number of color bins in a color histogram. We say that v^i follows a DD with parameters $\alpha^c = (\alpha^c_1, \ldots, \alpha^c_n), \alpha^c_l > 0$ when $p(v^i)$ has the form of the density given in Eq.(4). This density is defined in the simplex $\{(v^i_1, \ldots, v^i_n), \sum_{l=1}^{n-1} v^i_l < A\}$ and we have $(v^i_n = A - \sum_{l=1}^{n-1} v^i_l)$. Notice that we have used a general form of the DD since we have put $\sum_{l=1}^{n} v^i_l = A$.

$$p(v^i|c) = \frac{\Gamma(|\alpha^c|)}{A^{|\alpha^c|-1} \prod_{l=1}^{n} \Gamma(\alpha^c_l)} \prod_{l=1}^{n} (v^i_l)^{\alpha^c_l - 1}, \quad \alpha^c_l > 0 \tag{4}$$

In order to build a generative model able of predicting ratings for incoming visual documents without re-estimation, we propose the following model under

---

^{1} Phil Dawid's notation of conditional independence.

the following assumptions. Firstly, we assume that a rating r and the visual document i are conditionally independent given the preference pattern z (i.e. $i \perp\!\!\!\perp r|z$). This is somewhat justified by the fact that when we associate a state of z to each observation (u, i, r), knowing z for a given user, allows the identification of i and r each independently. Secondly, in order to construct user communities on the basis of their preferences to similar contents instead of documents themselves, we associate a state of z to the class c of visual documents, the user u and the rating r. Another assumption is made about the conditional independence between visual features v^i and z given the class c (i.e. $v^i \perp\!\!\!\perp z|c$). Indeed, we assume that the visual content is generated from its class only. This is a reasonable assumption since we have summarized the collection based on the visual content. It is sufficient to know the classes of visual content a user would like, since documents may be identified from these classes. Under these assumptions and from Eqs. (3) and (2), we write our model which we call Visual Content Aspect (VC-Aspect) model, in the following:

$$
\begin{aligned}
p(v^i, r|u) &= \sum_z p(z|u)p(r|z) \sum_c p(c|z)p(v^i|c) \\
&= \sum_{z,c} p(z|u)p(r|z)p(c|z)p(v^i|c)
\end{aligned}
\tag{5}
$$

From Eq.(5), the generative process of a rating is to identify first the preference pattern through $p(z|u)$ for a given user, and then generates independently the class of visual documents c and his associated rating r. From the generated class c we finally identify which visual documents "suggest" (resp. to block) in the case of recommendation (resp. passive filtering) scenario. The graphical representation corresponding to the model in Eq.(5) is given in Fig.2

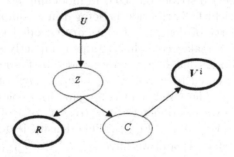

Fig. 2. Graphical representation of the VC-Aspect model

2.1   Recommendation

The goal of a visual content recommender is the suggestion of relevant unseen visual documents to an active user[2] u_a according to his profile. We define the

---

[2] The active user is the user that queries the CF system.

recommendation as the process of deciding which visual documents suggest for an active user. Most recommendation systems [7] [8] use the predicted rating as a criterion for suggestion. In other words, the content is suggested when his predicted rating is above a certain threshold. By this way, it is natural to see that two documents with the same predicted rating will have the same chance to be suggested even if they are too similar. We propose to construct a set of visual documents to suggest using a score computed on the basis of the predicted rating and also on the basis of the diversity constraint. We use information about visual document classes in order to suggest diversified content. A document class is identified using the Bayes' rule $p(c|v^i) \propto p(c)p(v^i|c)$. Indeed, documents that belong to different classes are associated their predicted ratings without changes. Penalties are applied to visual documents that belong to the same class when of them has been already selected for suggestion.

3   Maximum Likelihood Estimation

The problem of estimating parameters of models with hidden variables was the subject of multiple studies. During the last two decades, the Maximum Likelihood (ML) has become the most common approach to this problem. The natural choice for finding ML estimates for models with hidden variables is the use of the Expectation-Maximization (EM) algorithm [11]. The EM algorithm is an efficient optimization algorithm for solving the ML estimation problem with missing information (hidden preference patterns z and visual feature classes c variables in our case). This algorithm gives us an iterative procedure and the practical form is usually simple. To do that, we need independent and identically distributed (i.i.d.) observations $< u, i, r >$ which form our data set $\mathcal{D}$. This data set is nothing else than the history of users related to visual documents of the collection $\mathcal{D} = \{< u, i, r > | u \in \mathcal{U}, i \in \mathcal{I}, r \in \mathcal{R})\}$. In order to make derivatives clear, we consider Θ as the set of parameters to estimate $\Theta = (p(z|u), p(c|z), \alpha^c, p(r|z))$ and we give the likelihood $L(\Theta)$ of observations in $\mathcal{D}$ in the following:

$$L(\Theta) = \sum_{<u,i,r>} \ln[\sum_{z,c} p(z|u)p(c|z)p(v^i|c)p(r|z)] \tag{6}$$

Since the states of the hidden variables c and z are not known, we introduce a so called *variational probability function* $Q(z, c; u, i, r)$ over hidden variables z, c for every observation $< u, i, r >$ to get a lower bound $L^c(\Theta, Q)$ to be maximized. During the E-step, the model maximizes the this lower bound $L^c(\Theta, Q)$ with respect to Q and during the M-step, maximization is made with respect to Θ. We give the formula of EM steps in the following:

E-step:

$$Q^*(z, c; u, i, r; \hat{\Theta}) = \frac{p(z|u)p(c|z)p(v^i|c)p(r|z)}{\sum_{z,c} p(z|u)p(c|z)p(v^i|c)p(r|z)} \tag{7}$$

M-step:

$$p^{(t+1)}(z|u) = \frac{\sum_{<u',i,r>:u'=u} \sum_c Q^{*(t)}(z,c;u,i,r)}{\sum_{<u',i,r>:u'=u} \sum_{z,c} Q^{*(t)}(z,c;u,i,r)} \tag{8a}$$

$$p^{(t+1)}(c|z) = \frac{\sum_{<u,i,r>} Q^{*(t)}(z,c;u,i,r)}{\sum_{<u,i,r>} \sum_c Q^{*(t)}(z,c;u,i,r)} \tag{8b}$$

$$p^{(t+1)}(r|z) = \frac{\sum_{<u,i,r'>:r'=r} \sum_c Q^{*(t)}(z,c;u,i,r)}{\sum_{<u,i,r>} \sum_c Q^{*(t)}(z,c;u,i,r)} \tag{8c}$$

In order to estimate the α^c parameters, we use the Newton-Raphson method [12]. Its principle is to update the parameters at the time $t+1$ using their value at the time t and also on the basis of the gradient and hessian of the objective function, in our case this function is the lower bound of the log-likelihood $L^c(\Theta, Q)$ of the sample. To ensure that Dirichlet parameters α_l^c (l^{th} parameter of cth class) be always positive, we use transformation $\beta_l^c = e^{\alpha_i^c}$. The parameter's update formula is given by:

$$\begin{pmatrix} \hat{\beta}_1^c \\ \vdots \\ \hat{\beta}_n^c \end{pmatrix}^{(t+1)} = \begin{pmatrix} \hat{\beta}_1^c \\ \vdots \\ \hat{\beta}_n^c \end{pmatrix}^{(t)} + \begin{pmatrix} H_{11} & \cdots & H_{1n} \\ \vdots & \ddots & \vdots \\ H_{n1} & \cdots & H_{nn} \end{pmatrix}^{-1(t)} \begin{pmatrix} \frac{1}{\partial \beta_1^c} L^c \\ \vdots \\ \frac{\partial}{\partial \beta_n^c} L^c \end{pmatrix}^{(t)} \tag{9}$$

4   Experimental Results

In this section we present our method for evaluating the Visual Content Aspect model in filtering visual documents. We have made two kinds of evaluations. The first one focuses on measuring the rating's prediction accuracy while the second is concerned by evaluating the usefulness of visual content filtering in a concrete application. We have chosen to evaluate the filtering model within a CBIR system designed for mobile environments.

4.1   The Data Set

To be able to conduct experiments, we need a data set $\mathcal{D}$ of observations $< u, i, r >$. The novel nature of the proposed model in the sense that it models users preferences to visual documents makes its validation on concrete data a difficult task due to the absence of real-life data set. In our validations we have generated synthetically this data set.

The collection of visual documents we have used in experiments contains 3227 images collected in part from Washington University [13] and another part from collections of free photographs on the Internet. We have considered color histograms to represent the content of visual documents in the RGB $(red, green, blue)$ space. This feature space uses a binned version of the color histogram and thus each visual feature is represented by 27D vector. The constant

Table 1. An example of users community

user	image cluster	rating
1-10	1,2	2
11-21	3,4	2
21-30	5,6	2

A in Eq.(4) is considered as as the total number of pixel of a visual document. For convenience, we have preprocessed images of the collection so that all visual documents have the same resolution and thus the same number of pixels A. In our data set we have considered 30 users and a two star rating scale to represent the "dislikes" and "likes" patterns.

We have first summarized the image collection using the finite Dirichlet mixture model $p(v^i) = \sum_c p(c)p(v^i|c)$ where we have identified six image classes. Then, we generate observations $< u, i, r >$ as indicated in Tab. 1. For each user u, we select randomly an image i from the collection and we identify its class using the Bayes' rule $p(c|v^i) \propto p(c)p(v^i|c)$. If this image class matches the user preferences indicated in Tab. 1, then we generate the observation $< u, i, 2 >$ otherwise we generate $< u, i, 1 >$.

4.2   Evaluation of Rating'S Prediction Accuracy

This evaluation tries to answer the question *"does the proposed Visual Content Aspect model predicts accurate ratings?"*. A widely used scenario within the IF community [14] consists of using a small part $\mathcal{D}^L$ (10%) from a data set for learning the model and the remaining part $\mathcal{D}^E$ (90%) for evaluation. Then, we measure the error between the predicted and real ratings of observations in $\mathcal{D}^E$. The method consists of computing the Mean Absolute Error (MAE) between the predicted ratings and user's true ratings. In fact, MAE [14] a widely used accuracy metric in the evaluation of IF systems, measures the absolute average deviation between the predicted rating $s(u, i)$ and the user's true rating (from the data set) say $r(u, i)$ in the evaluation data set. This absolute deviation for a particular user is computed as:

$$|MAE_u| = \frac{\sum_{i=1}^{N_{test}} |s(u, i) - r(u, i)|}{N_{test}} \quad (10)$$

We have conducted two kinds of experiments. During the first one, we compare results with the the Aspect Model as presented in Eq.(2). We use the same visual documents during both learning and prediction due to the fact that the Aspect model does not handles new visual documents. The goal of this experiment is to compare the accuracy between our hybrid (collaborative content based) model with and a pure collaborative filtering model. Results are shown in Fig.3. The second experiment in other hand, evaluates the accuracy of the rating's prediction for newer documents. We use the previously generated data set with the following consideration. We divide each class c into two subsets of visual documents namely I_c^1 and I_c^2. During the learning phase, we use only observations

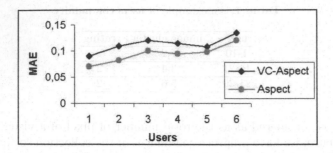

Fig. 3. Maximum absolute error curves for VC-Aspect and Aspect Models

from $< u, i, r >\in \mathcal{D}^L$ such as $i \in I_c^1$ for all the classes. Then, we compute the MAE for documents for users u such as $< u, i, r >\in \mathcal{D}^E$ and $i \in I_c^2$. Results are shown in Fig.5.

Discussion. Figure 3 illustrates how the proposed VC-Aspect model is close to the Aspect model. This may be interpreted mainly by the fact that when the content is the criterion of preferring images, representing images by their indices (or identifiers) is the same as their representation by visual features. This informs us also about the robustness of Dirichlet distribution in modelling the visual features. We can clearly see from Fig.5, the generative characteristic of the VC-Aspect model. Indeed, a slightly greater MAE for newer images is acceptable and allows the model to scale to these images though their visual features efficiently.

4.3   Evaluation in a CBIR System

We want also to validate the VC-Aspect model in a concrete CBIR system. For ground truth acquisition, we have used the log file of a Web-based version of a previously developed CBIR system (AtlasMobile) [15] designed for hand-held (HP iPAQ) devices. AtlasMobile provides a relevance feedback mechanism and the possibility to construct search queries with positive and negative examples. Two human subjects participate in experiments and their history is extracted from the log file of AtlasMobile and added to the previously generated data set. The visual content filtering system is integrated as a separate module with AtlasMobile in order to initialize the CBIR's page zero from which a user selects example images to build a search query. Figure 4 presents an example of the page zero for the two human subjects.

In order to evaluate the effectiveness of using the filtering system as an image selector for each user, we used the number of refinement iterations before the sought image is found (see Tab. 2) in conjunction with the precision. The precision is a defined as the percentage of representative images that allow the user to find the requested images when he uses them as search queries. Precision results for different page zero sizes are shown in Fig.6. Notice that we have made a comparison with another version of AtlasMobile in which the selection of initial pages is made randomly.

Fig. 4. CBIR initial pages for two users

Table 2. Number of iterations needed to locate a good image by two subjects

	S1	S2	Average
Trial 1			
Random	12	10	11
VC-Aspect	3	2	2.5
Trial 2			
Random	18	Fail	Fail
VC-Aspect	3	3	3

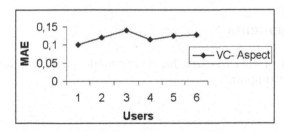

Fig. 5. MAE for newer visual documents

Discussion. We can see from Tab.2 and Fig.6 that incorporating the user model within a CBIR system, improves greatly the user's experience expressed in terms of a lower number of iterations and a higher precision. Particularly, Tab.2 shows that in some cases, the traditional CBIR systems may not be suitable for use within a mobile computing environment and fails to find good images. In fact, when using a visual content filtering module, the CBIR system, presents a small

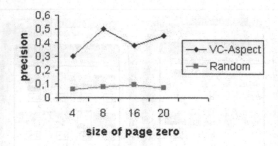

Fig. 6. Precision curves for two CBIR systems

window of relevant images to the user according to her preferences and thus allows her to find what she is looking for efficiently. The precision in other hand, is computed on the basis of representative images and not the sought images themselves. A good representative is the one which helps in finding sought images in few iterations. We can see that a precision of 30% for a window size of 4 is a great improvement since at least one image may be used to construct a search query.

5   Conclusion

We have presented a novel model for filtering visual documents such as images. The presented results indicate that our model is as accurate as the most model-based techniques and it preserves this accuracy for newer visual documents since user communities are built on the basis of the preferred visual content instead of documents. The VC-Aspect model allows to improve greatly the efficiency of CBIR systems designed for mobile computing environments.

Acknowledgements

The completion of this research has been made possible thanks to NSERC Canada for their support.

References

1. Kherfi, M.L., Ziou, D., Bernardi, A.: Image retrieval from the world wide web: Issues, techniques, and systems. ACM Computing Surveys **36**(1) (2004) 35–67
2. Kobsa, A.: Generic user modeling systems. User Modeling and User-Adapted Interaction **11**(1-2) (2001) 49–63
3. Hanani, U., Shapira, B., Shoval, P.: Information filtering: Overview of issues, research and systems. User Modeling and User-Adapted Interaction **11**(3) (2001) 203–259
4. Kim, C.Y., Lee, J.K., Cho, Y.H., Kim, D.H.: Viscors: A visual-content recommender for the mobile web. IEEE Intelligent Systems **19**(6) (2004) 32–39

5. Resnick, P., Iacovou, N., Suchak, M., Bergstrom, P., Riedl, J.: Grouplens: An Open Architecture for Collaborative Filtering of Netnews. In: In Proceeding of the ACM 1994 Conference on Computer Supported Cooperative Work. (1994)
6. Breese, J.S., Heckerman, D., Kadie, C.M.: Empirical analysis of predictive algorithms for collaborative filtering. In: In Proceedings of the Fourteenth Conference on Uncertainty in Artificial Intelligence, July 24-26, 1998, University of Wisconsin Business School, Madison, Wisconsin, USA. (1998) 43–52
7. Hofmann, T.: Probabilistic latent semantic indexing. In: Proceedings of Twenty-second Annual International SIGIR Conference. (1999)
8. Si, L., Jin, R.: Flexible mixture model for collaborative filtering. In: Machine Learning,Proceedings of Twentieth International Conference (ICML 2003), AAAI Press (2003) 704–711
9. Mooney, R., Roy, L.: Content-based book recommending using learning for text categorization. In: Proc. Fifth ACM Conf. Digital Libaries. (2000) 195–204
10. Bouguila, N., Ziou, D., Vaillancourt, J.: Unsupervised learning of a finite mixture model based on the dirichlet distribution and its applications. IEEE Transactions on Image Processing 13(11) (2004) 1533–1543
11. Dempster, A., Laird, N., Rubin, D.: Maximum likelihood from incomplete data via the em algorithm. Journal of the Royal Statistical Society, Series B 39 (1977) 1–38
12. Rao, C.R.: Advanced Statistical Methods in Biomedical Research. John Wiley and Sons, New York (1952)
13. (http://www.cs.washington.edu/research/imagedatabase/)
14. Herlocker, J.L.: Evaluating collaborative filtering recommender systems. ACM Transactions on Information Systems 22(1) (2004) 5–53
15. Kherfi, M., Ziou, D., Bernardi, A.: Combining positive and negative examples in relevance feedback for content-based image retrieval. Journal of Visual Communication and Image Representation 14(4) (2003) 428–457

A Variable Initialization Approach to the EM Algorithm for Better Estimation of the Parameters of Hidden Markov Model Based Acoustic Modeling of Speech Signals

Md. Shamsul Huda, Ranadhir Ghosh, and John Yearwood

School of Information Technology and Mathematical Science, University of Ballarat,
P.O. Box -663, Ballarat-3353, Victoria, Australia
mhuda@students.ballarat.edu..au,
{r.ghosh, j.yearwood}@ballarat.edu.au

Abstract. The traditional method for estimation of the parameters of Hidden Markov Model (HMM) based acoustic modeling of speech uses the Expectation-Maximization (EM) algorithm. The EM algorithm is sensitive to initial values of HMM parameters and is likely to terminate at a local maximum of likelihood function resulting in non-optimized estimation for HMM and lower recognition accuracy. In this paper, to obtain better estimation for HMM and higher recognition accuracy, several candidate HMMs are created by applying EM on multiple initial models. The best HMM is chosen from the candidate HMMs which has highest value for likelihood function. Initial models are created by varying maximum frame number in the segmentation step of HMM initialization process. A binary search is applied while creating the initial models. The proposed method has been tested on TIMIT database. Experimental results show that our approach obtains improved values for likelihood function and improved recognition accuracy.

1 Introduction

Estimation of the parameters of Hidden Markov Model (HMM) [1], [2] in acoustic modeling of speech signals is the most vital step while developing an Automatic Speech Recognition (ASR) system. Success of the recognizer depends heavily on how precisely the developed acoustic model can describe underlying phonemes in speech data which indirectly incorporates the appropriate estimation of the parameters of HMM based acoustic modeling. In other words, the recognition accuracy of an ASR system will be higher if the estimated acoustic model can describe the underlying phonemes more precisely. But the parameter estimation problem of HMM based acoustic modeling becomes difficult due to the complex feature characteristics of the phonemes found in the speech database. In a real recognition task, feature vectors from different instances of the same phoneme vary largely due to variations in speakers (e.g. sex, age, length of vocal tract), changes in context (e.g. right, write) of the words where pronunciations are same, changes in device (e.g. microphone, telephone), variation in the emotion of the speaker when the speech is produced (e.g.

P. Perner (Ed.): ICDM 2006, LNAI 4065, pp. 416–430, 2006.

read, prompted, conversational, excitement, stress) and noises in the environment. Therefore, it is very difficult to find an appropriate estimation for the parameters of HMM based acoustic model that can precisely represent all the phonemes having complex data structure in the underlying training data. Most of the modern ASR systems use the Baum-Welch (EM algorithm) [3], [4] approach for estimation of the parameters of HMM based acoustic modeling. The Baum-Welch (EM algorithm) [3], [4] re-estimation approach is attractive because of its iterative nature which guarantees an increment in the likelihood function with each iteration [5], [6]. Unfortunately, the estimation for HMM parameters computed by Baum-Welch (EM) approach is not always good enough and thereby use of the model estimated by EM may lower the recognition accuracy of ASR systems. The reason is that EM algorithm is strongly dependent on initial values of model parameters and is guaranteed to produce a local maximum of likelihood function [5], [6]. This gives a non-optimized estimation of the parameters of HMM and consequently lowers the recognition accuracy. Therefore, one of the important research question in parameter estimation of HMM based acoustic modeling is how do we choose initial values of the HMM parameters so that better estimation for HMM parameters and thereby higher recognition accuracy can be obtained.

Recently several approaches have been adopted to overcome the problem of EM and thereby for better estimation of HMM parameters. Chau, et al. [7] introduce a genetic based optimization method for HMM parameter estimation. However, it uses discrete HMM structure and can not be applied in HMM with a Gaussian mixture model. It also adopts a random initialization for the parameters of HMM. Martinez and Vitria [8], [9] proposes a combination of genetic algorithm [10], [11, [12] and EM algorithm for optimal estimation of the parameters of Gaussian mixture model. But it is not generalized for HMM and considers a randomly generated initial population for GA. It also assumes mixtures of same model are equi-probable. Thereby, it has no mixture weight in the model parameters. This is dissimilar with the Gaussian mixture based HMM used in acoustic modeling of speech signal in speech recognition where each mixture of Gaussian has a weight which is initially calculated by an incremental cluster splitting algorithm. Moreover, Random initialization can not give a good starting point for EM used in the estimation of HMM based acoustic modeling. Pernkofp and Bouchaffra [13] suggests genetic-based EM algorithm which uses Minimum Description Length (MDL) criterion for selecting the number of mixture in each Gaussian model. This method facilitates optimal estimation of model as well as selection of number of mixtures in the model. But it is also not generalized for HMM and genetic algorithm without constraint-based approach [10], [11, [12] is used. Both Martinez et al. [8], [9] and Pernkofp et al. [13] suggest GA based global optimization approach. But in these approaches, one model is trained at a time which comprises certain number of Gaussian mixtures. One individual of GA has parameters from the single Gaussian model. Total number of parameter per GA individual is small. Whereas Gaussian mixture based HMM has three states. Each state is represented with one Gaussian model. For better recognition accuracy more than ten Gaussian mixtures are taken in each HMM state [2], [14]. Thus one GA individual encounters the parameters from all mixtures of all states of HMM which give a high dimensional GA individual. If GA is applied on such high dimensional population with the satisfaction of the HMM constraints at each iteration of GA, excessive computation may be required for convergence of the GA.

This paper aims at developing a learning algorithm to obtain a better estimation for the parameters of Continuous Density HMM (CDHMM) as well as to improve the recognition accuracy of ASR systems using a "Variable Initialization Approach to EM" (VIA-EM) algorithm. Since the EM Algorithm is very much sensitive to initial point, we have created several starting points for EM and EM is applied on those starting points to generate a number of candidate HMM models. The final HMM model is chosen as the one with the highest value for likelihood function. Instead of generating the initial points randomly [15], we varied the maximum frame number per HMM state in constrained clustering segmentation (CSS) [16] step and then used an incremental cluster splitting algorithm (described in section-3) in the initialization process of HMM. A binary search [17] is applied while varying the maximum frame number in the HMM initialization process to find better initial points instead of applying a brute force approach. The rest of the paper is organized as follows. In the next section, a brief description of Hidden Markov Model (HMM) and the objective function for re-estimation of the parameters of HMM are discussed. Section 3 explains the "Variable Initialization Approach to EM" (VIA-EM) algorithm for HMM parameter estimation as well as binary search approach to find the better initial point in detail. The experimental procedure and the obtained results are delineated in Section 4. Section 5 describes analysis of the results. Conclusion of this study is given in the last section.

2 Hidden Markov Model and Objective Function for Re-Estimation of Its Parameter

Most of the modern ASR systems use HMM for acoustic modeling of speech signals. While developing the acoustic model, observation vectors for each instance of phoneme are extracted by feature extraction algorithm form speech data. These observation vectors are used in the HMM based acoustic modeling of speech signals. HMM is a doubly stochastic process where the states are invisible and evolution of states follows the property of first order Markov chain. The observations belonging to each state are the probabilistic function. HMM can be expressed as a set of five elements such as follows: $\lambda = \{S, O, A, B, \Pi\}$ where "S" is the set of states $S = \{S_1, S_2, S_3, ...S_N\}$. "O" is the set of observation vectors $O = \{O_1, O_2, O_3, ...O_M\}$. "A" is the state transition probability distribution matrix $A = \{a_{ij}\}$, "B" is the observation probability distribution matrix, $B = \{b_j(k)\}$ $b_j(k) = P(O_k | q_t = S_j)$ $1 \leq k \leq M$. "$\prod$" is the initial state distribution, $\Pi = \{\Pi_i\}$. The Fig. 1 gives a complete presentation of a HMM model and its parameters. Since the observations are continuous signal, observation probability distribution is considered as a mixture of Gaussian as follows: $b_j(O) = \sum_{n=1}^{M} c_j^n b_j^n(O)$, $\sum_{n=1}^{M} c_j^n = 1$, $c_j^n \leq 1$ instead of discrete probability distribution.

"M" is the total no mixture per state. c_j^n, μ_j^n, U_j^n =Mixture weight, Mean vector, variance for jth state and nth mixture.

$$b_j^n(O) = \frac{1}{\sqrt{(2\Pi)^p |U_j^n|}} exp\{-\frac{1}{2}(O-\mu_j^n)^T U_j^n (O-\mu_j^n)\}$$

(2.1)

"$b_j^n(O)$" is the probability of one observation vector in state "j" for nth mixture. The objective function used to re-estimate the model parameter is $P(O|\lambda)$ for one instance of one phoneme. Due to long sequence of multiplications (of value less than one) for $P(O|\lambda)$ under flow may occur. Hence instead of using the $P(O|\lambda)$, a logarithm of $P(O|\lambda)$ is used as objective function. Actual objective function is used as $P_{avg} = \frac{1}{L}\sum_{l=1}^{L} Log_e[P_l(O|\lambda)]$. "L" is the total number of instances per phoneme in training data. The detail of the computation for $P_l(O|\lambda)$ and P_{avg} are given in the next sections.

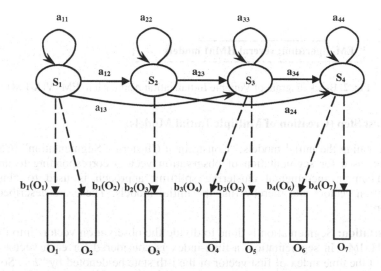

Fig. 1. Typical HMM model and its parameters

3 Detail Methodology of Variable Initialization Approaches to EM Algorithm (VIA-EM)

Variable initialization Approach to EM (VIA-EM) uses multiple starting points for EM to overcome its optimization problem in parameter re-estimation of HMM. For this purpose, multiple initial models are created. Then EM algorithm is applied on those initial models to find several candidate HMMs. The best model is chosen based on the highest value for objective function. The complete procedure can be easily clarified using the block diagram of Fig. 2. The complete algorithm is given in the Fig. 5. The detail methodology consists of two main components. These are described in the following:

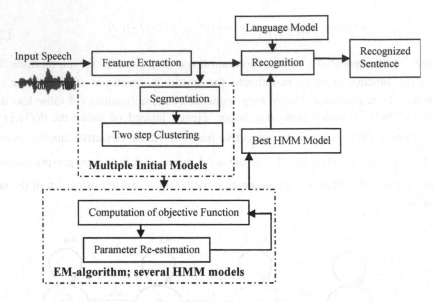

Fig. 2. Block diagram of Variable Initialization Approach to EM (VIA-EM)

3.1 First Step (Creation of Multiple Initial Models)

While creating the initial models, "Constrained Clustering Segmentation" (CSS) [16] has been used for segmentation of observation vectors corresponding to an HMM state. Then an incremental clustering splitting approach is used to cluster the observation vectors and thereby find the initial models. These are described in the following.

Segmentation: Segmentation is done to divide the observation vectors into the states of the HMM. In segmentation, a time-index is considered for each vector of each state. Let the time index of first vector of the i-th state be denoted by "b_i". So the i-th state begins with a feature vector at time "b_i" and ends with a feature vector "$b_{i+1} - 1$". The aim is to find some criterion the "P-1" boundaries of the "P" states $\{b_2, b_3, ..., b_{P-1}\}$ where "$b_1 = 1$" and "b_{P+1}" is total observation. Now the boundaries are found by Constrained Clustering Segmentation [16]. "b_i" has an upper and a lower limit. Minimum value of "b_i" is the minimum number of frames per HMM state and maximum value of "b_i" is the maximum number of frame per HMM state. At this stage, segmentation is done by finding the boundaries that minimizes the total distortion. Total distortion is as follows:

$$D_{tot} = \sum_{i=1}^{P} \sum_{n=b_i}^{b_{i+1}} \| O_n - m \|^2 \quad O_n = \text{where Observation vector} \tag{3.1}$$

The speech signals can be divided into a sequence of states corresponding to time variant patterns of the speech. Therefore, every state is represented by the mean vector "m" of observations belonging to the states. The mean of the HMM state is calculated by incremental cluster splitting algorithm. The clustering process is described in the following section.

Clustering: After the segmentation of observation vectors into HMM states, a Gaussian model of the observation vectors is obtained estimating the expected vector and the co-variance matrix for each HMM state. The expected vector represents the data centroid in the observation space. The Gaussian model is described in Fig. 3 by its level curve. The centroid is denoted by μ_Y. Now the eigenvector Σ_{max} of co-variance matrix is determined. The higher distortion direction is determined by the eigenvector Σ_{max} associated with the maximum eigen-value σ^2_{max}. Two new centroids μ_1 and μ_2 are optimally calculated as the couple of points at a distance " Δ " from the centroid μ_Y in the direction of maximal distortion. The " Δ " is computed as follows: $\Delta = \sqrt{\frac{2}{\Pi}}\sigma^2_{max}$.

The two new centroids μ_1 and μ_2 outline two clusters given by the observation vectors closer to each centroid according to a Euclidean distance measure. A Gaussian model is found for each of the two clusters by estimating the mean and covariance matrix.

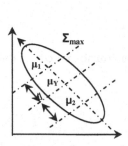

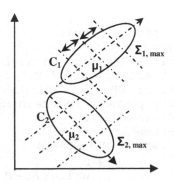

Fig. 3. Gaussian mixture models   **Fig. 4.** Creating (n+1) Gaussian mixture

Fig. 4 shows the two new clusters. The weight associated with each mixture component is given by the fraction of vectors belonging to each cluster. Now the distortion of each cluster is determined. The cluster with highest distortion is divided again. In the Fig. 4 cluster "C_1" has the highest distortion and is divided again. On the other hand, cluster "C_2" is taken as a Gaussian mixture of a particular HMM state of one initial model. Thus given a set of "n" cluster for a particular step, a set of "n+1" cluster is found, *i.e.* we are getting "n+1" mixtures of Gaussian for a particular HMM states of one initial model. The process is repeated until a pre-determined number of Gaussian mixtures are obtained. Thus, by repeating the above clustering process, we obtain the initial models for all states of HMM. The multiple initial models are created by varying the maximum number of frames per HMM state in the segmentation module. Maximum number of frames per HMM state depends on window length, sampling rate and the time length of a phoneme utterance. The number of frames varies in different instances of the same phoneme. Usually, while applying the EM algorithm for re-estimation of HMM parameters, approximately an average value is chosen for maximum frame number. The average value is the approximate average of the maximum number of frames per phoneme in the training data which is divided by the total number of HMM states used per phoneme. We varied the maximum number of frame per HMM state in Constrained Clustering Segmentation (CSS) [16]. For each value of maximum number of frames, we computed a separate segmentation and then applied the clustering approach to build the Gaussian mixtures for HMM state. This gives one initial model for that phoneme. The process is repeated for other values of maximum frame number per HMM state and other initial models are obtained for a particular phoneme.

```
Program Variable Initialization Approach to EM (VIA-EM)
Var:  LBLProb, ALProb, UBLProb, BLProb, BestLProb: Real;
      MFramePerState, AF, LB, UB: Integer;
      {ALProb =Log probability at Average Point, UBLProb
      =Log probability at Upper bound, LBLProb =Log
      probability at Lower bound, MFramePerState=Maximum
      Frame number per HMM state, LB=Lower Limit of
      Maximum Frame Number per HMM state, UB=Upper Limit
      Maximum Frame Number per HMM state, AF=Average
      Frame number per HMM state, BestLProb=Best Log
      probability};
  Begin
   InitialTraining_Data:=D
   Extract_Features( D)
   LB:=1; UB:=Two Third of the maximum number of frames
   in a phoneme in training data.
   AF:=(LB+UB)/2
   MFramePerState:=LB
      while (UB-LB>=2)
         begin
            1. while( P_new - P_old >= 1.0 )
               begin
                  a. Apply CSS for segmentation with
                     MFramePerState
                  b. Apply incremental Clustering
                  b. Initialize HMM parameters, λ
```

$$c. \ Find \ P_{old} := \frac{1}{L} \sum_{l=1}^{L=|D|} Log_e[\,P_l(O\,|\lambda\,)]$$

```
                  d. Re-estimate HMM parameters, λ'
```

$$e. \ Find \ P_{new} := \frac{1}{L} \sum_{l=1}^{L=|D|} Log_e[\,P_l(O\,|\lambda'\,)]$$

```
            2. end
            LBLProb:= P_new
            MFramePerState:=UB
            Repeat step-1 to step-2
            UBLProb:= P_new
            MFramePerState:=AF
            Repeat step-1 to step-2
            ALProb:= P_new
            3.if(LBLProb>= UBLProb)
               begin
               if(LBLProb>=ALProb)
```

```
        begin
        UB:=AF
        AF:=(LB+UB)/2
        end
    else
        begin
            If(ALProb>=UBLProb)
            begin
            LB:=AF-(AF-LB)/2
            UB:=AF+(UB-AF)/2
            end
        end
    end
else
    begin
    if(UBLProb>= ALProb)
        begin
        LB:= AF
        AF:=(LB+UB)/2
        end
    else
        begin
        If(ALProb >= ULProb)
            begin
            LB:=AF-(AF-LB)/2
            UB:=AF+(UB-AF)/2
            end
        end
    end
end
BestLProb:=Maximum(LBLProb,ALProb, UBLProb)
4.Final HMM model:=Model corresponding to the
maximum frame number at BestLProb.
end
```

Fig. 5. Algorithm for Variable Initialization Approach to EM (VIA-EM)

3.2 Second Step (Creation of Several HMM Models and Model Selection Using Binary Search)

While creating the multiple initial models by varying the maximum number of frames per HMM state, a brute force approach could have been applied by incrementing the maximum frame number and then creating one initial model at each point. This would involve excessive time to get a better initial model. We have applied a binary search [17] approach. One upper bound and one lower bound have been considered for maximum frame number per HMM state and their average is taken. For these three numbers, we created three initial models according to the segmentation and clustering technique described in the section 3.1. Three re-estimated models are computed by applying Baum-Welch (EM algorithm) [3], [4] re-estimation approach on three initial models. After computing three re-estimated models, the value for objective function is calculated for each of the models. The parameter re-estimation and corresponding computation for objective function is given at the end of this section. Now we select any of the branches (left or right) for next search space depending on the objective function values of three models. A detail of branch selection criterion is given in step 3 to step 4 of the algorithm in the Fig. 5. The search continues until lower limit and upper limit makes a difference of greater than or equal to two. The best model is selected from the last three models corresponding to lower, upper and average values of maximum frame number. The best model has the highest value for its objective function.

Computation for Objective Functions and Re-estimation of Parameters: For each initial model corresponding to each maximum frame number per HMM state, $Log_e[P(O|\lambda)]$ is calculated. Then parameters are re-estimated. We get one HMM from each initial model corresponding to each maximum frame number. Parameter re-estimation follows the steps 1 to 2 of the algorithm in Fig. 5. The computation for maximum likelihood function $Log_e[P(O|\lambda)]$ is done using veterbi [18] algorithm. These steps are described as follows: Consider $\phi_t(i) = P(O_1, O_2, \ldots \ldots O_t, q_t = S_i | \lambda)$. We can solve for the $\phi_t(i)$ inductively.

Initialization: $\phi_1(i) = \Pi_i b_i(O_1), \quad 1 \le i \le N, \ 1 \le j \le N, 2 \le t \le T$ (3.2)

Induction: $\phi_t(j) = \max_{1 \le i \le N} [\phi_{t-1}(i)a_{ij}]b_j(O_t)$ Termination: $P(O|\lambda) = \max_{1 \le i \le N} [\phi_T(i)]$ (3.3)

$$Log_e[P(O|\lambda)] = \max_{1 \le i \le N}[Log_e[\phi_T(i)]], \quad 1 \le j \le N, 2 \le t \le T \tag{3.4}$$

$$Log_e[\phi_T(j)] = \max_{1 \le i \le N}[Log_e[\phi_{T-1}(i)] + Log_e[a_{ij}]] + Log_e[b_j(O_T)] \tag{3.5}$$

Putting these into equation (3.4) we get $Log_e[P(O|\lambda)]$. Average value over all phoneme instances $P_{avg} = \frac{1}{L}\sum_{l=1}^{L} Log_e[P(O|\lambda)]$ can be easily calculated from equation (3.4). The re-estimation module starts from the initial models and calculates the value for objective function "P_{avg}". Then the parameter of the HMM model is re-estimated according to Baum-Welch re-estimation formula [2], [3], [4] as follows: $\overline{\Pi}_i = \gamma_i(i)$ =New Initial probability of ith state, $\gamma_i(i) = \sum_{j=1}^{N} \xi_i(i,j)$,

$$\xi_t(i,j) = \frac{\alpha_t(i)a_{ij}b_j(O_{t+1})\beta_{t+1}(j)}{\sum_{i=1}^{N}\sum_{j=1}^{N}\alpha_t(i)a_{ij}b_j(O_{t+1})\beta_{t+1}(j)} \quad \gamma_t(j,k) = \left[\frac{\alpha_t(j)\beta_t(j)}{\sum_{j=1}^{N}\alpha_t(j)\beta_t(j)}\right]\left[\frac{c_{jk}\Pi[O,\mu_{jk},U_{jk}]}{\sum_{j=1}^{M}c_{jm}\Pi[O,\mu_{jm},U_{jm}]}\right] \tag{3.6}$$

New transition Probability of ith state to jth state $\overline{a}_{ij} = \dfrac{\sum_{t=1}^{T-1}\xi_t(i,j)}{\sum_{t=1}^{T}\gamma_t(j)}$ (3.7)

New observation probability of "O" $\overline{b}_j(O) = \sum_{k=1}^{M}\overline{c}_{jk}\Pi[O,\overline{\mu}_{jk},\overline{U}_{jk}]$ (3.8)

$$\text{New Mixture Weight of jth state and kth mixture } \overline{c}_{jk} = \frac{\sum_{t=1}^{T} \gamma_t(j,k)}{\sum_{t=1}^{T} \sum_{k=1}^{M} \gamma_t(j,k)} \tag{3.9}$$

$$\text{New mean vector of jth state and kth mixture } \overline{\mu}_{jk} = \frac{\sum_{t=1}^{T} \gamma_t(j,k).O_t}{\sum_{t=1}^{T} \gamma_t(j,k)} \tag{3.10}$$

$$\text{New co-variance matrix } \overline{U}_{jk} = \frac{\sum_{t=1}^{T} \gamma_t(j,k).(O_t - \mu_{jk})(O_t - \mu_{jk})'}{\sum_{t=1}^{T} \gamma_t(j,k)} \tag{3.11}$$

After the re-estimation of parameters, again the objective values P_{avg} (new) are calculated and it is compared with P_{avg} (old). If their difference is greater than a convergence threshold, then the procedure is iterated otherwise it is stopped and one HMM model is found from one initial model. Other HMM models can be found by repeating this step. The best HMM model is chosen which has the highest value for objective function.

4 Experiments

The TIMIT [19] Acoustic Phonetic Speech Corpus has been used for both training and testing of "VIA-EM". The following settings have been used during the time of training and testing. Two different test sets have been used. One set include all sentences form TIMIT [19] test set (Test set-A) which has 1680 sentences. Another TIMIT [19] test set (Test set-B) has total 1344 sentences which excludes the SA sentences from the test set in TIMIT [19] corpus.

4.1 Settings

A Left-to-Right simple model with no node skip has been used for HMM topology. Context independent phoneme model has been considered. A single model training approach has been adopted for re-estimation. Maximum number of EM iteration has been taken as 10. During testing, a phonetic bi-gram grammar has been used. A beam search algorithm with Initial Beam Coefficient =10E-18 and Internal Beam Coefficient = 10E-16 has been set.

Table 1. Test set-A: Total insertion, Omission, Substitution of phonemes in the recognition result. Total number of phonemes in the solution: 64145

Mix.	Insertion		Omission		Substitution	
	VIA-EM	EM	VIA-EM	EM	VIA-EM	EM
3	1691	1695	8701	8744	15390	15429
5	1669	1736	8348	8400	14402	14620
8	1659	1680	8231	8164	13743	13857
10	1579	1550	8133	8044	13402	13569

Table 2. Test set-A: Recognition accuracy

Mix.	Percent Correct		Accuracy	
	VIA-EM (%)	EM (%)	VIA-EM (%)	EM (%)
3	62.44	62.32	59.81	59.67
5	64.53	64.11	61.93	61.41
8	65.74	65.67	63.16	63.05
10	66.43	66.31	63.97	63.89

Table 3. Test set-B: Total insertion, Omission, Substitution of phonemes in the recognition result. Total number of phonemes in the solution: 51681

Mix.	Insertion		Omission		Substitution	
	VIA-EM	EM	VIA-EM	EM	VIA-EM	EM
3	1466	1458	7119	7108	13419	13560
5	1365	1419	6892	6864	12695	12867
8	1416	1434	6797	6761	12396	12509
10	1347	1330	6709	6658	12068	12257

Table 4. Test set-B: Recognition accuracy

Mix.	Percent Correct		Accuracy	
	VIA-EM (%)	EM (%)	VIA-EM (%)	EM (%)
3	60.26	60.01	57.42	57.19
5	62.1	61.82	59.46	59.08
8	62.86	62.71	60.12	59.94
10	63.67	63.4	61.06	60.83

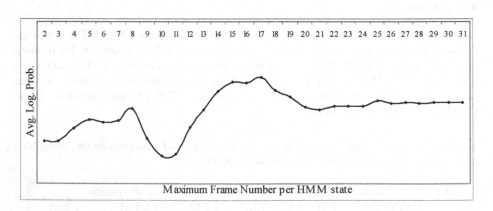

Fig. 6. Avg. Log. Probabilities of candidate HMM models at different Maximum Frame number of phoneme-"ay" for mixture 3 in a brute force approach where we varied maximum frame number per HMM state incrementally. At each Maximum Frame number we found one candidate HMM model.

Table 5. Maximum frame number and corresponding log probabilities of HMM models at different steps of binary search in VIA-EM for phoneme-"ay" for mixture-3 is given in the table. Three frame limits in any pass of the search are minimum (Min), maximum (Max) and average (Avg.). Corresponding maximum frame number per HMM state is also given.

Frame Limit	Maximum number of frames per HMM state	Avg. Log. Prob
	After First Pass	
Min.	2	-2278.28405184855
Avg.	16	-2278.19424149077
Max.	31	-2278.22440535373
	After Second Pass	
Min.	9	-2278.28002151153
Avg.	16	-2278.19424149077
Max.	23	-2278.23054662834
	After Third Pass	
Min.	13	-2278.23552199152
Avg.	16	-2278.19424149077
Max.	19	-2278.21598175755
	After Fourth Pass	
Min.	15	-2278.19301478461
Avg.	16	-2278.19424149077
Max.	17	-2278.18513757513
	After Fifth Pass (Convergence)	
Min.	16	-2278.19424149077
Avg.	16	-2278.19424149077
Max.	17	-2278.18513757513

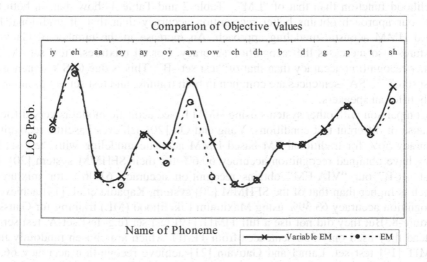

Fig. 7. Comparison of avg. Log. Probabilities obtained from the HMMs for different phonemes in "VIA-EM" and that EM for Gaussian mixture-5

4.2 Results

Recognition accuracy for different mixtures and corresponding insertion, omission and substitution of phonemes for both test sets are given in the Table 1, Table 2, Table 3 and Table 4. Results of brute force approach where the maximum number of frames per HMM state is varied incrementally for Gaussian mixture-3 have been given in Fig. 6. The results of binary search for Gaussian mixture-3 are given in the Table 5. A comparison of the values for objective function between "VIA-EM" and that of "EM" is given in Fig. 7.

5 Discussion

"VIA-EM" considers several initial points for EM which are created by varying the maximum number of frames per HMM state in segmentation step CSS [16] of HMM initialization module. Fig. 6 gives the average log probabilities for HMM models at different maximum frame number of phoneme-"ay" for mixture-3 obtained by a brute force approach where we incremented the maximum frame number. It shows that change in the avg. log probabilities of different HMM models obtained by increasing the maximum frame number is non-linear. Table 5 gives the average log probabilities of HMM models at different maximum frame number while applying the binary search of "VIA-EM" for phoneme-"ay" (Gaussian mixture-3). Fig. 6 and Table 5 show that "VIA-EM" with binary search converges in much less number of EM executions than that of taken by their brute force variant. Fig. 7 gives a comparison of average log probabilities of HMM models of different phonemes for Gaussian mixture-5 of "VIA-EM" and that of EM. A better value for likelihood function approaches more to zero. Fig. 7 shows that VIA-EM has obtained better values for likelihood function than that of "EM". Table 2 and Table 4 show that, in both test sets, our approach obtains better recognition accuracy than that of traditional EM based HMM acoustic modeling approach. An increase in the number of Gaussian mixtures also increases the recognition accuracy. For all mixtures, "test set -A" has higher recognition accuracy than that of "test set -B". This is due to SA sentences in "test set-A". "SA" sentences are common in both training and test set but pronounced with different speakers.

Comparison with other systems using HMM based acoustic model is very difficult, because of different test conditions. Yung and Oh [20] achieves baseline recognition accuracy 56% for traditional EM based HMM acoustic modeling with "test set-B". They have obtained recognition accuracy 60.6% for their SFHMM system [20]. For "test set-B" our "VIA-EM" obtains recognition accuracy 61.06% for mixture-10 which is higher than that of the SFHMM [20] system. Kapadia et al. [14] achieves a recognition accuracy 63.39% using Maximum Likelihood (ML) training for Gaussian mixture-8. But they did not use a full TIMIT [19] test set (e.g. test set-A, test set-B), instead they used only 336 sentences from TIMIT which are chosen randomly from TIMIT [19] test set. Lamel and Gauvain [21] achieve recognition accuracy 66.4% using a context dependent phoneme model with 61 phoneme set on TIMIT [19] "test set-B". We have used context independent model. Overall recognition accuracy could also be further increased by considering a context dependent phoneme model and increasing the number of Gaussian mixtures with the present approach. "VIA-EM" applies multiple initialization approach to EM to overcome the problems of EM and also improves recognition accuracy. However, only multiple initialization approach may not be able to solve the local optimization problem in EM completely. Some other hybrid method using global approach (e.g. Genetic Algorithm, GA) and local approach (e.g. EM) could also be investigated along with the multiple initialization approach of "VIA-EM" for further improvement of recognition accuracy.

6 Conclusion

This paper proposes a "Variable Initialization Approach to EM" algorithm (VIA-EM) for better estimation of the parameters of HMM based acoustic modeling of speech signal. Since EM is highly sensitive to initial models and better initial models help to estimate more appropriate values for the parameters of HMM, "VIA-EM" uses multiple start for EM. Then a number of candidate HMM models are build by applying EM on the initial models. The best HMM model is chosen as the one which has the highest value for the likelihood function. Multiple initial models are created by varying the maximum frame number per HMM state in the segmentation step of HMM initialization module. Instead of applying a brute force approach while varying the maximum frame number per HMM state, a binary search is applied. This helps to reduce the search space for initial models while building the candidate HMM models. Experimental results show that, in each phoneme, the average log probabilities of HMM models trained by "VIA-EM" are higher than that of the HMM models trained by traditional EM algorithm. While applying the best HMM model obtained by using "VIA-EM" to test the recognition accuracy, it gives recognition accuracy which is comparable to other systems [14], [20] and [21] and higher than that of the HMM model obtained by using standard EM. In the future, we will consider a hybrid algorithm using Genetic Algorithm [10], [11] and EM with multiple initial models for re-estimation of the parameters of HMM based acoustic modeling of speech signals.

References

1. Levinson S. E., Rabiner L.R., Sondhi M.M, An introduction to the application of the theory of probabilistic functions of a Markov process to automatic speech recognition, The Bell System Technical Journal, 62, No 4 (1983).
2. Rabiner, L.R., A tutorial on Hidden Markov Models and selected applications in speech recognition, in Proc. of IEEE, 77 (1989) 257-286.
3. Dempster, A.P., Laird, N.M., and Rubin, D.B., Maximum likelihood from incomplete data via EM algorithm, Journal of royal statistical society. Series B. (Methodological), 39 (1977) 1-38.
4. Ghahramami, Z. and Jordan, M.I., Learning from incomplete data, Technical Report AI Lab Memo No. 1509, CBCL Paper No. 108, MIT AI Lab,(1995).
5. Wu, C.F.J., On the convergence properties of the EM algorithm, The Annals of Statistics, 11 (1983) 95–103.
6. Xu, L. and Jordan, M.I., "On convergence properties of the EM algorithm for Gaussian mixtures". Neural Computation, 8 9 (1996)129–151.

7. Chau C.W, Kwong S., Diu C.K., Fahrner W. R., Optimization of HMM by a Genetic Algorithm, In Proc. of the 1997 IEEE International Conference on Acoustics, Speech, and Signal Processing (ICASSP '97).
8. Martinez, A.M. and Vitria, J., Learning mixture models using a genetic version of the EM algorithm". Pattern Recognition Letters, 21 (2000) 759–769.
9. Martinez, A. M. and Vitria, J., Clustering in image space for place recognition and visual annotations for human-robot interaction. IEEE Transactions on Systems, Man, and Cybernetics - Part B, 31(2001) 669–682.
10. Michalewicz, Z. and Schoenauer, M., Evolutionary Algorithms for Constrained Parameter Optimization Problems, Evolutionary Computation, Vol.4, No.1,(1996) 1-32.
11. Back T., Evolutionary Algorithm in Theory and Practice, Oxford University press (1996).
12. Back, T. and Schwefel, H., Evolutionary computation: An overview. In IEEE Conference on Evolutionary Computation,(1996) 20–29.
13. Pernkopf , F. and Bouchaffra, D., Genetic-Based EM Algorithm for Learning Gaussian Mixture Models, IEEE Trans. on Pattern Analysis and Machine Intelligence, vol-27, No 28, (2005).
14. Kapadia, S., Valtchev, V. and Young, S.J., MMI training for continuous phoneme recognition on the TIMIT database, Proc. of the IEEE Conference on Acoustic Speech and Signal Processing , Vol. 2 (1993) 491-494.
15. Rabiner, L.R., Juang, B.H., Levisnon, S.E. and Sondhi, M.M., Some properties of continuous Hidden Markov Model representation, AT & T Tech. Journal, Vol. 64, 6 (1985) 1251-1270.
16. Soong F.K., Svendsen T., On the Automatic Segmentation of Speech, Proc. ICASSP, (1987).
17. Ghosh, R., Connection topologies for combining genetic and least square methods for neural learning, Journal of Intelligent System, Vol. 13, 3 (2004) 199-232.
18. Veterbi, A.J., Error bounds for convolutional codes and an asymptotically optimal decoding algorithm, IEEE transaction on Information Theory, vol. IT-13, (1967) 260-269.
19. Garofolo, S.J., Lamel, L., and Fisher, M.W., TIMIT Acoustic-Phonetic Continuous Speech Corpus, ISBN: 1-58563-019-5, Linguistic Data Consortium, University of Pennsylvania.
20. Yung, Y.S., and Oh, Y.H., A segmental-feature HMM for continuous speech recognition based on a parametric trajectory model, Journal of Speech Communication, Vol 38, 1(2002) 115 – 130.
21. Lamel, L. and Gauvain J. L., High performance speaker-independent phone recognition using CDHMM, Proc. EUROSPEECH, (1993)121- 124.
22. Figueiredo, M.A.T. and Jain, A.K., Unsupervised learning of finite mixture models, IEEE Transactions on Pattern Analysis and Machine Intelligence, 24 (2002) 1–16.

Mining Dichromatic Colours from Video

Vassili A. Kovalev

Centre for Vision, Speech and Signal Processing
School of Electronics and Physical Sciences
University of Surrey, Guildford, Surrey GU2 7XH, United Kingdom
v.kovalev@surrey.ac.uk, vassili.kovalev@googlemail.com

Abstract. It is commonly accepted that the most powerful approaches for increasing the efficiency of visual content delivery are personalisation and adaptation of visual content according to user's preferences and his/her individual characteristics. In this work, we present results of a comparative study of colour contrast and characteristics of colour change between successive video frames for normal vision and two most common types of colour blindness: the protanopia and deuteranopia. The results were obtained by colour mining from three videos of different kind including their original and simulated colour blind versions. Detailed data regarding the reduction of colour contrast, decreasing of the number of distinguishable colours, and reduction of inter-frame colour change rate in dichromats are provided.

1   Introduction

With the advent of digital video revolution the volume of video data is growing enormously. The visual content is produced by different sources including the broadcasting and film industry, recent video communication systems and camera phones, the systems providing access to the content of vast film and video archives at broadcasters, museums, industries and production houses, by automated video surveillance systems, by the video-based business communications and, finally, by the remote education and e-learning systems [1]. The television broadcasting industry, home video systems, and mobile services slowly but surely transferring to an end-to-end digital video production, transmission and delivery. Lately, it was commonly recognised that the most powerful approaches for increasing the efficiency of visual content delivery are personalisation [1], [2], [3], [4], [5] and adaptation of visual content according to user preferences and his individual characteristics [6], [7], [8]. As a result, there has been enormous growth of research work and development of new technologies and industrial standards in this area (see [6] for an overview). For example, while MPEG-7 already can be used to describe user's preferences for visual content filtering, searching and browsing, the new MPEG-21 standard (part 7 "Digital Item Adaptation" [9]) expands these possibilities further to implement a user-centered adaptation of multimedia content to the usage environment. In particular [7] [2], it addresses the customization of the presentation of multimedia content based on user's

P. Perner (Ed.): ICDM 2006, LNAI 4065, pp. 431–443, 2006.

preferences for content display/rendering, quality of service as well as configuration and conversion with regard to multimedia modalities. It also facilitates adaptation of visual content to user's colour vision deficiency such as colour blindness and low-vision impairments as well as audition and audio accessibility characteristics.

In the last decade, the data mining research and developments provided various techniques for automatically searching large stores of data for discovery of patterns and new knowledge (eg, [10], [11]). These techniques has been successfully used for video data mining in a number of applications. For instance, it was demonstrated that for a specific kind of video data such as sport video it is possible to automatically identify high-level features for semantic video indexing [12] and to detect gradual transitions in various video sequences for temporal video segmentation [13]. As a result of an extensive study of colour and texture properties of video sequences [14], there have been suggested new descriptors that provide an efficient extraction, representation, storage, and similarity retrieval in video. These descriptors include a histogram descriptor that is coded using the Haar transform, a color structure histogram, a dominant color descriptor, and a color layout descriptor. The three texture descriptors include one that characterizes homogeneous texture regions and another that represents the local edge distribution [14]. All the descriptors are included in the MPEG-7 standard. Another kind of colour descriptors included in the standard are the descriptors discussed in [15] that were developed to reliably capture the color properties of multiple images or groups of frames. One family of such descriptors, called alpha-trimmed average histograms, combine individual frame or image histograms using a specific filtering operation to generate robust color histograms that can eliminate the adverse effects of brightness/color variations, occlusion, and edit effects on the color representation [15]. Based on so-called colour correlograms [16] or colour co-occurrence matrices [17] that capture the spatial structure of colour in still images, authors of work [18] have lately suggested colour descriptors involving a color adjacency histogram and color vector angle histogram. The color adjacency histogram represents the spatial distribution of color pairs at color edges in an image, thereby incorporating spatial information into the proposed color descriptor. The color vector angle histogram represents the global color distribution of smooth pixels in an image.

Thus, colour appears to play a key role in delivery of visual content and, in certain circumstances, may even be vital for correct perception and interpretation of visual data in professional applications. And yet, 8% of the population is suffering from a specific colour vision deficiency known as dichromasia [19], [20], [21]. These are the people who have some sort of colour blindness, and they usually can distinguish only two hues. They are the protanopic and deuteranopic viewers who have difficulties in seeing red and green respectively. Such people are collectively known as dichromats. A small fraction of people can only see a single hue, and these are the truly colour-blind people [19]. An important issue then arises, concerning the video as seen by these viewers, the way it appears to them, and whether the use of colour conveys to them the same information it conveys to normal viewers [22], [20]. Several studies have been done to answer this question, and indeed we know with pretty high confidence the way the world looks like through the eyes of such viewers (eg, [21]). Recently, quite a few studies have been made in the way colour coded information should be processed and displayed so that it is equally useful to all viewers (eg, [22], [23], [7], [24]). "An image is a thousand words", and an image conveys information by the relative colours and contrasts it contains. If a person does not see these contrasts caused by the use of different colours, the person may miss a significant part of the information conveyed by the image. Thus, methods and algorithms of converting colours for dichromats generally depend on the joint colour appearance in real video data as seen by dichromats compared to people with normal vision. However, the issue of statistical properties of colour contrast and temporal colour change has not received much attention yet.

In our previous works (eg, [24], [25]) we investigated influence of colour blindness to image retrieval results and have suggested an adaptive colour conversion technology for still images and other static media. The problem of converting colours was posed as an optimisation task with different cost function terms (achieved colour contrast, similarity to normal vision, etc). As yet, there are several points that need to be investigated for converting videos. They are concerned with specific aspects of temporal colour change. Industrial re-production of high quality videos adapted for dichromatic users supposes pre-calculation of some kind of dynamic look-up table based on a colour analysis performed prior to the conversion. Computation expenses for calculating an optimal conversion look-up table are generally function of the number of different colours presented in the media as well as their temporal change. Once computed, the specific look-up table can be used for colour conversion virtually for free.

In this work, we present results of a comparative study of colour contrast and characteristics of colour change between successive video frames for normal vision and two most common types of colour blindness: the protanopia and deuteranopia. The blue blindness known as tritanopia is not considered here because it is extremely rare [19]. The results were obtained by colour mining from three videos of different kind including their original and simulated colour blind versions. In our best knowledge this is the first work on mining dichromatic colours from video.

2   Materials

2.1   The Videos

In this study we used the following three videos that represent relatively different ways of spatial colour appearance:

- a lyrical-humorous love story film "The Love and Doves" by Mosfilm containing similar proportion of in-door and out-door scenes, which is conditionally referred here to as *V1-Ordinary*,
- a commonly known animation movie "The Lion King" by Walt Disney Pictures (*V2-Animation*),

Table 1. General technical characteristics of videos used for the analysis

Video	frame size (pixels)		number of frames	number of
	horisontal	vertical	included into the analysis	key frames
V1-Ordinary	640	368	150,600	842
V2-Animation	512	368	120,000	2324
V3-Nature	700	516	78,600	936

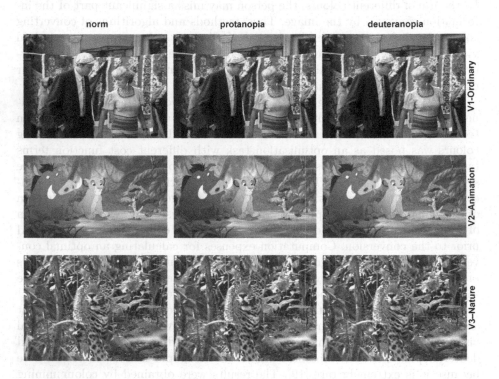

Fig. 1. Example frames taken from three videos (by rows) used in this study as seen by people with normal vision (left column) and individuals suffering from protanopia (central column) and deuteranopia (right column)

– a popular documentary movie "Cats", part 2 about the wild life of cat family animals from National Geographic (*V3-Nature*).

In all three occasions video frames with captioning textual data as well as frames containing no information (eg, black background only) were excluded from the analysis. General technical characteristics of mined videos are given in Table 1.

2.2   Simulating the Colour Blindness

To enable mutual comparisons, the original three videos were also converted to their protanopic and deuteranopic versions. Construction of dichromatic versions of colours was based on the LMS specification (the longwave, middlewave and the shortwave sensitive cones) of the primaries of a standard video monitor [23], [26]. The conversion from trichromatic to dichromatic colors itself was done using the *dichromat* package implemented by Thomas Lumley within the R, a language and software environment for statistical computing and graphics [27], [28]. Examples of video frames of three colour versions of all three videos are provided in Fig. 1.

3 Methods

3.1 Colour Space Conversion

Everywhere in this work the perceived difference between colours was measured using the Euclidean metric in Lab colour space [29]. The Lab and Luv colour spaces are standardised by the Commission Internationale d'Eclairage (CIE) and known to be approximately perceptually uniform [29], [30]. The Lab describe colors of objects, and so require specification of a reference "white light" color. The most commonly used are illuminant D65, which represents a standard indirect daylight, illuminant D50, which is close to direct sunlight, and illuminant A that corresponds to the light from a standard incandescent bulb. In this work we employed illuminant D65.

The original video frame colours were converted from sRGB colour space (ie, the RGB space of standard PC monitors) to the Lab in two steps. First, r, g, b components were converted into standard CIE XYZ space capable of representing all visible colors but not in a perceptually uniform way. At the second step we converted XYZ to the uniform Lab colours. Specifically, for a given RGB colour whose components are in the nominal range [0.0, 1.0], the following equations were used:

$$[XYZ] = [rgb][M],\qquad(1)$$

where

$$r = \begin{cases} R/12.92 & R \le t \\ ((R+0.055)/1.055)^{2.4} & R > t \end{cases}$$

$$g = \begin{cases} G/12.92 & G \le t \\ ((G+0.055)/1.055)^{2.4} & G > t \end{cases}$$

$$b = \begin{cases} B/12.92 & B \le t \\ ((B+0.055)/1.055)^{2.4} & B > t \end{cases}$$

and threshold $t = 0.04045$. For the reference white D65, the 3×3 conversion matrix M known also as "Adobe RGB (1998)" is

$$M = \begin{pmatrix} 0.576700 & 0.297361 & 0.0270328 \\ 0.185556 & 0.627355 & 0.0706879 \\ 0.188212 & 0.075285 & 0.9912480 \end{pmatrix}.$$

For given reference white $(X_r, Y_r, Z_r) = (0.3127, 0.3290, 0.3583)$, the Lab colour components are calculated as

$$L = 116f_y - 16, \quad a = 500(f_x - f_y), \quad b = 200(f_y - f_z), \quad (2)$$

where

$$f_x = \begin{cases} \sqrt[3]{x_r} & x_r > \varepsilon \\ \frac{kx_r+16}{116} & x_r \le \varepsilon \end{cases}, \quad f_y = \begin{cases} \sqrt[3]{y_r} & y_r > \varepsilon \\ \frac{ky_r+16}{116} & y_r \le \varepsilon \end{cases}, \quad f_z = \begin{cases} \sqrt[3]{z_r} & z_r > \varepsilon \\ \frac{kz_r+16}{116} & z_r \le \varepsilon \end{cases},$$

$$x_r = \frac{X}{X_r}, \quad y_r = \frac{Y}{Y_r}, \quad z_r = \frac{Z}{Z_r}, \quad \varepsilon = 0.008856, \quad k = 903.3$$

Finally, the perceived difference between any given pair of colours c_i and c_j was measured as the Euclidean distance in the Lab space:

$$d(c_i, c_j) = \sqrt{(L_i - L_j)^2 + (a_i - a_j)^2 + (b_i - b_j)^2} \quad (3)$$

3.2   Measuring Colour Contrast

Colour contrast C_{cntr} was measured within each frame of every video including its original, protanopic, and deuteranopic versions (ie, 3 videos × 3 versions = 9 videos in total). The contrast values C_{cntr} were computed by calculating the perceived colour difference (3) between the pairs of neighboring pixels p_i and p_j situated at the distances $d = \{1, 2, 3\}$ pixels apart. The scale for original r, g, b pixel intensity values was 0–255. All possible pixel pairs with no repetition were considered for given distance range according to computational procedure similar to the one used for calculating colour co-occurrence matrices discussed in [17], [24]. This particularly means that for each non-border pixel the number of pairs it participating in was 4 pairs for $d = 1$, 6 pairs for $d = 2$, and 7 pairs for $d = 3$. The mean contrast values computed over the whole frame with these three inter-pixel distances were then used as final contrast characteristics of the frame. The primary goal was to find out and to describe quantitatively the difference in contrast between the normal and colour blind versions of each video.

3.3   Measuring Colour Change Between Video Frames

The absolute value of colour change $C_{chang-A}$ between the two successive video frames was calculated as a sum of two numbers $C_{chang-A} = N_{gone} + N_{come}$. First number is the number of different colours that presented in the first frame but disappear in the second frame $N_{gone} = N_{F1} - N_{F1} \bigcap N_{F2}$. Oppositely, the second number is the number of new colours that appear in the second frame being not presented in the first one $N_{come} = N_{F2} - N_{F1} \bigcap N_{F2}$. The frequencies of colours (ie, the number of pixels with given colour) were not considered here. The exception was only that we used them for a thresholding: any colour was considered to be presented in a video frame if its frequency exceeds 4 what is equivalent to a minimal frame patch of 2 × 2 pixels in size.

It is clear that the range of $C_{chang-A}$ value depends on the number of distinguishable colours, ie, the colour quantisation scheme. In this work we used an uniform resolution of 6 bits per pixel for each of R, G, and B colour planes. Thus, the maximal number of different colours was $N_{col}^{max} = 262144$. As an additional feature we also employed a relative colour change $C_{chang-R}$ between the two frames, which was calculated as the absolute number of changed colours $C_{chang-A}$ normalised to the sum of different colours appeared in both frames (per cent):

$$C_{chang} = 100 \times C_{chang}/(N_{F1} \bigcup N_{F2})$$

Note that in the above expressions the intersection and union set operations are used in a simplified manner for brevity.

4   Results

4.1   Colour Contrast

Colour contrast C_{cntr} was measured for every frame of each of 9 videos. General characteristics of color contrast for inter-pixel distance $d = 1$ are summarised in Table 2 in form of descriptive statistics calculated over all the frames of each video. Note that the local contrast (ie, colour contrast computed for $d = 1$) normally plays the most important role in distinguishing colour borders. Contrast reduction score given in the last column of Table 2 is the ratio of the mean contrast of norm and mean contrast of corresponding dichromatic version of the video. As it can be immediately inferred from the results reported in Table 2, the reduction of colour contrast for deuteranopia is notably higher than in case of protanopia for all three types of videos. Most likely, the magnitude of contrast reduction score for every particular video depends on the amount of scenes containing various hues of red and green colours, which are seen as shadows of yellow by protanopes and deuteranopes. Similarly, an obvious asymmetry of temporal colour contrast distribution detected in videos $V2$ and $V3$ with characteristic high skewness values is rather individual feature of these videos. It can be explained by relatively large proportion of scenes with predominantly high and low colour contrast. Mean colour contrast values for inter-pixel distances $d = 2$ and $d = 3$ were always higher than those reported in Table 2 for $d = 1$ with approximately linear increase with d. For instance, mean contrast values of $V1$ video measured at distances $d = 2$ and $d = 3$ were equal to 472.6 and 577.1 for norm, 389.3 and 473.4 for protanopia, and 329.3 and 400.1 for deuteranopia respectively. Such a behavior was found to be well predictable considering the spatial colour correlation phenomena.

Descriptive statistics of colour contrast given in Table 2 provide general, meanwise information regarding the contrast in videos of different kind as well as contrast reduction ratio for colour blind viewers. More detailed, frame-wise information is presented in Table 3 in form of linear regression of video frame contrast of protanope C_{cntr}^{pro} and deuteranope C_{cntr}^{deu} versions of videos to the contrast of norm C_{cntr}^{nrm} for $d = 1$. As usual, the statistical significance of the

Table 2. Descriptive statistics of colour contrast calculated over all video frames

Video	version	colour contrast C_{cntr} for inter-pixel distance $d = 1$			
		mean	STD	skewness	contrast reduction score
	normal vision	323.4	101.6	-0.021	—
V1–Ordinary	protanopia	266.1	93.5	0.058	1.22
	deuteranopia	225.7	85.5	0.085	1.43
	normal vision	180.1	63.6	0.949	—
V2–Animation	protanopia	137.9	52.3	1.077	1.31
	deuteranopia	116.9	46.1	1.305	1.54
	normal vision	259.0	86.8	0.781	—
V3–Nature	protanopia	208.7	75.5	0.834	1.24
	deuteranopia	176.9	64.6	0.836	1.46

Fig. 2. Examples of video frames with extreme values of colour contrast taken from two videos: *V1–Ordinary* (top row) and *V2–Animation* (bottom row). (a), (c) Colour texture frames with high colour contrast. (b), (d) Low contrast frames with domination of homogeneous colour regions.

regression is measured with the help of squared correlation coefficient R^2, which provides linearity of significance scores. Note that in this particular case the regression significance is equivalent to the significance score of a *paired* Student's t–test.

Table 3. Linear regression of dichromatic colour contrast to the norm

Video	version	regression equation for $d = 1$	significance, R^2
V1–Ordinary	protanopia	$C_{cntr}^{pro} = 0.914 \cdot C_{cntr}^{nrm} - 29.6$	0.987
	deuteranopia	$C_{cntr}^{deu} = 0.822 \cdot C_{cntr}^{nrm} - 40.0$	0.953
V2–Animation	protanopia	$C_{cntr}^{pro} = 0.806 \cdot C_{cntr}^{nrm} - 7.3$	0.963
	deuteranopia	$C_{cntr}^{deu} = 0.682 \cdot C_{cntr}^{nrm} - 5.8$	0.887
V3–Nature	protanopia	$C_{cntr}^{pro} = 0.867 \cdot C_{cntr}^{nrm} - 15.8$	0.990
	deuteranopia	$C_{cntr}^{deu} = 0.731 \cdot C_{cntr}^{nrm} - 12.5$	0.961

Table 4. Descriptive statistics of the number of different frame colours

Video	version	number of distinguishable colours in frame, N_F				
		mean	STD	skewness	colour reduction score	mean, relative to 2^{18}, pro mil
V1–Ordinary	normal vision	2445.4	908.7	-0.162	—	9.33
	protanopia	499.8	152.9	0.094	4.89	1.91
	deuteranopia	473.7	142.4	0.095	5.16	1.81
V2–Animation	normal vision	2077.0	1179.1	1.102	—	7.92
	protanopia	449.6	242.8	0.937	4.62	1.72
	deuteranopia	389.7	232.3	0.989	5.33	1.49
V3–Nature	normal vision	3862.3	1602.4	0.034	—	14.73
	protanopia	814.9	424.1	1.358	4.74	3.11
	deuteranopia	689.2	344.5	1.300	5.60	2.63

Finally, specific examples of video frames with extreme values of colour contrast are shown in Fig. 2. Fig. 2(a) represents colour texture appeared highly contrasted for normal vision ($C_{cntr}^{nrm} = 480.8$), which loses 102.7 contrast units (21.4%) being observed by protanopes ($C_{cntr}^{pro} = 378.1$) and 178.6 units (37.1%) when observed by deuteranopes ($C_{cntr}^{deu} = 302.2$). The animation movie video frame presented in Fig. 2(c) demonstrates similar properties with the starting colour contrast value for norm as high as $C_{cntr}^{nrm} = 702.4$. On the contrary, the frame depicted in Fig. 2(b) has very low colour contrast value in norm $C_{cntr}^{nrm} = 87.1$, which is almost preserved on the same level for protanopia and deuteranopia observers ($C_{cntr}^{pro} = 83.4$ and $C_{cntr}^{deu} = 81.2$). This is because it is mostly occupied by shadows of blue colour, which are not distorted much in protanopic and deuteranopic vision. Despite the animation movie frame provided in Fig. 2(d) appears as pretty colourful, its contrast is also low because of domination of large homogeneous colour regions.

4.2   Colour Change Between Video Frames

At firs, we calculated the number of different colours (18 bit resolution) in each video frame N_F for all three versions of three videos involved in this study. Resultant descriptive statistics are summarised in Table 4. Colour reduction

Table 5. Regression of the number of different dichromatic and normal colours

Video	version	regression equation	significance, R^2
V1–Ordinary	protanopia	$C_{cntr}^{pro} = 0.132 \cdot C_{cntr}^{nrm} + 177.2$	0.615
	deuteranopia	$C_{cntr}^{deu} = 0.120 \cdot C_{cntr}^{nrm} + 179.3$	0.590
V2–Animation	protanopia	$C_{cntr}^{pro} = 0.158 \cdot C_{cntr}^{nrm} + 121.2$	0.589
	deuteranopia	$C_{cntr}^{deu} = 0.145 \cdot C_{cntr}^{nrm} + 89.4$	0.539
V3–Nature	protanopia	$C_{cntr}^{pro} = 0.201 \cdot C_{cntr}^{nrm} + 40.2$	0.574
	deuteranopia	$C_{cntr}^{deu} = 0.163 \cdot C_{cntr}^{nrm} + 60.3$	0.574

Table 6. Characteristics of inter-frame colour change

Video	version	number of changed colours			colour change reduction	mean, relative to colours in two frames, %
		mean	STD	skewness		
V1–Ordinary	normal vision	571.8	293.8	2.35	—	23.7
	protanopia	37.7	24.2	7.15	15.2	8.0
	deuteranopia	35.0	22.9	7.47	16.3	7.9
V2–Animation	normal vision	463.5	470.7	4.35	—	21.7
	protanopia	39.1	50.7	6.72	11.9	8.5
	deuteranopia	35.8	48.1	6.68	12.9	8.9
V3–Nature	normal vision	1125.9	866.0	2.50	—	14.73
	protanopia	81.3	88.4	4.30	13.8	3.11
	deuteranopia	66.5	71.2	4.34	16.9	2.63

score is the ratio of the mean number of colours in norm and dichromatic versions of videos. As it can be easily noticed from Table 4, the number of distinguishable colours is reduced dramatically in case of dichromatic vision. The reduction score achieves values in the range of 4.6–5.6 being sufficiently higher in deuteranopes comparing to protanopes: 5.16 vs. 4.89 for an ordinary video combining both in-door and out-door scenes, 5.33 vs. 4.62 for the animation video, and 5.60 vs. 4.74 for video about the nature. No obvious differences in the colour reduction score were observed depending on the type of video. The linear regression equations describing relationships between the number of different frame colours for normal vision, protanopia, and deuteranopia are included in Table 5 together with the squared correlation coefficient. Note the low values of regression coefficients and reasonably low significance scores R^2 suggesting relatively weak dependence.

At the second step we calculated the number of colours that changed between the pairs of successive video frames. Results are reported in Table 6 in the same way as for distinguishable colours in previous table. The rate of colour change reduction caused by dichromasia was found to be as high as 11.9–16.9 depending on the particular video and type of dichromasia. Again, relatively to the nor-mal vision, the reduction rate was worse in case of deuteranopia comparing to protanopia for every particular video (16.3 vs. 15.2, 12.9 vs. 11.9, and 16.9 vs. 13.8 respectively).

5   Conclusions

Results of mining dichromatic colours from video reported with this study allows us to draw the following conclusions.

1. Colour contrast of video frames perceived by subjects suffering from dichromasia is lower compared to people with normal vision. For the three videos of different type used in this study the mean contrast reduction score varied in the range of 1.22–1.54. Reduction of colour contrast for deuteranopia was always higher than in case of protanopia.

2. Most likely, the magnitude of colour contrast reduction score for every particular video depends on the amount of scenes containing various hues of red and green colours, which are seen as shadows of yellow by protanopes and deuteranopes.

3. Mean colour contrast values for inter-pixel distances $d = 2$ and $d = 3$ were always higher than those obtained for $d = 1$ with approximately linear increase with d.

4. The number of different colours in video frames reduces dramatically in observers with dichromatic vision. In this particular study, the reduction score achieved values in the range of 4.6–5.6 being sufficiently higher in deuteranopes comparing to protanopes: 5.16 vs. 4.89 for an ordinary video combining both in-door and out-door scenes, 5.33 vs. 4.62 for an animation video, and 5.60 vs. 4.74 for video about the nature. No obvious differences in the colour reduction score were found depending on the type of video.

5. For a colour quantisation scheme with the maximum of 262,144 distinguishable colours the mean value of colours changed in two successive frames varied in the range of 463–1126 colours for normal vision, 38–81 colours for protanopia, and 35–67 colours for deuteranopia. Again, relatively to the normal vision, the reduction of inter-frame colour change rate was worse in case of deuteranopia comparing to protanopia for every particular video (16.3 vs. 15.2, 12.9 vs. 11.9, and 16.9 vs. 13.8 respectively).

Acknowledgments

This work was supported by the grant number GR/R87642/01 from the UK Research Council and partly by the EU project INTAS 04-77-7036.

References

1. Hanjalić, A.: Content-based analysis of digital video. Kluwer Academic Publisher, Boston (2004) 194p.
2. Tseng, B.L., Lin, C.Y., Smith, J.R.: Using MPEG-7 and MPEG-21 for personalizing video. IEEE Trans. Multimedia 11 (2004) 42–52
3. Wu, M.Y., Ma, S., Shu, W.: Scheduled video delivery — a scalable on-demand video delivery scheme. IEEE Trans. Multimedia 8 (2006) 179–187

4. Feiten, B., Wolf, I., Oh, E., Seo, J., Kim, H.K.: Audio adaptation according to usage environment and perceptual quality metrics. IEEE Trans. Multimedia **7** (2005) 446–453
5. Smeulders, A.W.M., Worring, M., Santini, S., Gupta, A., Jain, R.: Content-based image retrieval at the end of the early years. IEEE Trans. Pattern Analysis Mach. Intel. **22** (2000) 1349–1380
6. Vetro, A., Timmerer, C.: Digital item adaptation: overview of standardization and research activities. IEEE Trans. Multimedia **7** (2005) 418–426
7. Nam, J., Ro, Y.M., Huh, Y., Kim, M.: Visual content adaptation according to user perception characteristics. IEEE Trans. Multimedia **7** (2005) 435–445
8. Ghinea, G., Thomas, J.P.: Quality of perception: user quality of service in multimedia presentations. IEEE Trans. Multimedia **7** (2005) 786–789
9. ISO: Information Technology. Multimedia Framework. Part 7: Digital item adaptation. (2004) ISO/IEC 21000–7.
10. Bozdogan, H., ed.: Statistical Data Mining and Knowledge Discovery. Chapman & Hall/CRC Press, Boca Raton, Florida (2004) 624p.
11. Abbass, H.A., Sarker, R.A., Newton, C.S., eds.: Data Mining: A Heuristic Approach. Idea Group Publishing, Hershey, London (2002) 310p.
12. Zhu, X., Wu, X., Elmagarmid, A.K., Feng, Z., Wu, L.: Video data mining: Semantic indexing and event detection from the association perspective. IEEE Trans. Knowl. Data Eng. **17** (2005) 665–677
13. Joyce, R.A., Liu, B.: Temporal segmentation of video using frame and histogram space. IEEE Trans. Multimedia **8** (2006) 130–140
14. Manjunath, B.S., Ohm, J.R., Vasudevan, V.V., Yamada, A.: Color and texture descriptors. IEEE Trans. Circ. Syst. Video Technol. **11** (2001) 703–715
15. Ferman, A.M., Tekalp, A.M., Mehrotra, R.: Robust color histogram descriptors for video segment retrieval and identification. IEEE Trans. Image Proc. **11** (2002) 497–508
16. Huang, J., Kumar, S., Mitra, M., Zhu, W.J., Zabih, R.: Image indexing using color correlograms. In: 16th IEEE Conf. on Computer Vision and Pattern Recognition, San Juan, Puerto Rico (1997) 762–768
17. Kovalev, V., Volmer, S.: Color co-occurrence descriptors for querying-by-example. In: Int. Conf. on Multimedia Modelling, Lausanne, Switzerland, IEEE Computer Society Press (1998) 32–38
18. Lee, H.Y., Lee, H.K., Ha, Y.H.: Spatial color descriptor for image retrieval and video segmentation. IEEE Trans. Multimedia **5** (2003) 358–367
19. Viénot, F., Brettel, H., Ott, L., M'Barek, A.B., Mollon, J.: What do color-blind people see? Nature **376** (1995) 127–128
20. Rigden, C.: The eye of the beholder - designing for colour-blind users. British Telecom Engineering **17** (1999) 2–6
21. Brettel, H., Viénot, F., Mollon, J.: Computerized simulation of color appearance for dichromats. Journal Optical Society of America **14** (1997) 2647–2655
22. Viénot, F., Brettel, H., Mollon, J.: Digital video colourmaps for checking the legibility of displays by dichromats. Color Research Appl. **24** (1999) 243–252
23. Meyer, G.W., Greenberg, D.P.: Color-defective vision and computer graphics displays. IEEE Computer Graphics and Applications **8** (1988) 28–40
24. Kovalev, V.A.: Towards image retrieval for eight percent of color-blind men. In: 17th Int. Conf. On Pattern Recognition(ICPR'04). Volume 2., Cambridge, UK, IEEE Computer Society Press (2004) 943–946

25. Kovalev, V., Petrou, M.: Optimising the choice of colours of an image database for dichromats. In Perner, P., Imiya, A., eds.: Machine Learning and Data Mining in Pattern Recognition. Volume LNAI 3587., Springer Verlag (2005) 456–465
26. Walraven, J., Alferdinck, J.W.: Color displays for the color blind. In: ISandT/SID Fifth Color Imaging Conference: Color Science, Systems and Appl, Scottsdale, Arizona (1997) 17–22
27. Becker, R.A., Chambers, J.M., Wilks, A.R.: The New S Language. Chapman and Hall, New York (1988)
28. Everitt, B.: A Handbook of Statistical Analyses Using S-Plus. 2nd edn. Chapman & Hall/CRC Press, Boca Raton, Florida (2002) 256p.
29. Hunt, R.W.G.: Measuring Color. 2nd edn. Science and Industrial Technology. Ellis Horwood, New York (1991)
30. Sharma, G.: Digital Color Imaging Handbook. Volume 11 of Electrical Engineering & Applied Signal Processing. CRC Press LLC, New York (2003) 800p.

Feature Analysis and Classification of Classical Musical Instruments: An Empirical Study

Christian Simmermacher, Da Deng, and Stephen Cranefield

Department of Information Science, University of Otago, New Zealand
{ddeng, scranefield}@infoscience.otago.ac.nz

Abstract. We present an empirical study on classical music instrument classification. A methodology with feature extraction and evaluation is proposed and assessed with a number of experiments, whose final stage is to detect instruments in solo passages. In feature selection it is found that similar but different rankings for individual tone classification and solo passage instrument recognition are reported. Based on the feature selection results, excerpts from concerto and sonata files are processed, so as to detect and distinguish four major instruments in solo passages: trumpet, flute, violin, and piano. Nineteen features selected from the Mel-frequency cepstral coefficients (MFCC) and the MPEG-7 audio descriptors achieve a recognition rate of around 94% by the best classifier assessed by cross validation.

1 Introduction

Research in music data retrieval for commercial or non-commercial applications has been very popular in the last few years. Even though speech processing applications are well established, the growing use and distribution of multimedia content via the Internet, especially music, imposes some considerable technical challenges and demands more powerful musical signal analysis tools. New methods are being investigated so as to achieve semantic interpretation of low-level features extracted using audio signal processing methods. For example, a framework of low-level and high-level features given by the MPEG-7 multimedia description standard [1] can be used to create application specific description schemes. These can then be utilised to annotate music with a minimum of human supervision for the purpose of music analysis and retrieval.

There are many potential applications to be found for instrument detection techniques. For instance, detecting and analysing solo passages can lead to more knowledge about different styles of musical artists and can be further processed to provide a basis for lectures in musicology. Also various applications for audio editing, audio and video retrieval or transcription can be supported. Other applications include music genre classification [2], play list generation [3], and using audio feature extraction to support video scene analysis and annotation [4]. An overview of audio information retrieval and relevant techniques can be found in [5].

P. Perner (Ed.): ICDM 2006, LNAI 4065, pp. 444–458, 2006.
© Springer-Verlag Berlin Heidelberg 2006

With this work we intend to eventually recognise classical instruments in solo musical passages with accompaniment, using features based on human perception, cepstral features, and the MPEG-7 audio descriptors. We try to find synergies and differences between these feature schemes so as to build a robust classification system. The performance of the feature schemes is assessed individually and in combination with each other.

This rest of the paper is organised as follows. Section 2 highlights a few recent relevant works on musical instrument recognition and audio feature analysis. Section 3 outlines the approach we adopted in tackling the problem of instrument classification, including feature extraction schemes, feature selection methods, classification algorithms used, as well as our experiment procedures and settings. Empirical results based on the proposed approach are then presented in Section 4, followed by a discussion. Finally, we conclude the paper in Section 5.

2   Related Work

Various feature schemes have been proposed and adopted in the literature, and different computational models or classification algorithms have been employed for the purpose of instrument detection and classification.

Mel-frequency cepstral coefficients (MFCC) features are commonly employed not only in speech processing, but also in music genre classification and instrument classification (e.g. [6,7,8]). Marques and Moreno [6] built a classifier that can distinguish between eight instruments with a 70% accuracy rate using Support Vector Machines (SVM). Eronen [7] assessed the performance of MFCC features and spectral and temporal features such as amplitude envelope and spectral centroid etc. for instrument classification. He conducted Karhunen-Loeve Transform to decorrelate the features and then used k-nearest neighbours (k-NN) classifiers whose performance was then assessed using cross validation. The results favoured MFCC features, and violin and guitar were among the most poorly recognised instruments.

The MPEG-7 audio framework targets on the standardisation of the extraction and description of audio features [1]. The sound description of MPEG-7 audio features was assessed in [9] based on their perceived timbral similarity. It was concluded that combinations of the MPEG-7 descriptors can be reliably applied in assessing the similarity of musical sounds. Xiong et al. [10] compared MFCC and MPEG-7 audio features for the purpose of sports audio classification, adopting hidden Markov models and a number of classifiers such as k-NN, Gaussian mixture models (GMM), AdaBoost, and SVM.

Brown and Houix [11] conducted a study on identifying four instruments of the woodwind family. Features used were cepstral coefficients, constant Q transform (CQT), spectral centroid, autocorrelation coefficients (AC), and time features. For classification a k-Means based GMM was used. Recognition success of the feature sets varied from 75%-85%.

Essid et al. [8] processed and analysed solo musical phrases from ten instruments. Each instrument was represented by fifteen minutes of audio material from various CD recordings. Spectral features, audio spectrum flatness, MFCC, and derivates of MFCC were used as features. SVM yielded an average result of 76% for 35 features. A subsequent work from the same authors [12] used the same experimental setup but employed different features including AC and CQT, as well as amplitude modulated features. A feature selection technique was presented and features were classified pairwise with an expectation-maximisation based GMM. Best average results showed an accuracy of around 80%.

In [13], spectral features were extracted while the classification performance was assessed using SVM, k-NN, canonical discriminant analysis, and quadratic discriminant analysis, with the first and last being the best.

Livshin and Rodet [14] evaluated the use of monophonic phrases for detection of instruments in continuous recordings of solo and duet performances. The study made use of a database with 108 different solos from seven instruments. A large set of 62 features (temporal, energy, spectral, harmonic, and perceptual) was proposed and subsequently reduced by feature selection. The best 20 features were used for realtime performance. A leave-one-out cross validation using a k-NN classifier gave an accuracy of 85% for 20 features and 88% for 62 features.

Eggink and Brown [15] presented a study on the recognition of five instruments (flute, oboe, violin and cello) in accompanied sonatas and concertos. GMM classifiers were employed on features reduced by a principal component analysis. The classification performance on a variety of data resources ranges from 75% to 94%, while mis-classification occurs mostly on flute and oboe (as violin).

In terms of feature analysis, some generic methods such as information gain (IG) and symmetric uncertainty (SU) were discussed in [16]. Grimaldi et al. [17] evaluated selection strategies such as IG and gain ratio (GR) for music genre classification. Some wavelet packet transform features, beat histogram features, and spectral features were extracted, selected, and classified by k-NN classifiers.

On the other hand, there are very limited resources available for benchmarking, so direct comparison of these various approaches would be hardly possible. Most studies have used recordings digitised from personal or institutional CD collections. McGill University Master Samples (MUMS) have been used in [13,15], while the Iowa music samples were used in [7,15].

3   Methodology

In this section, we present our computational approach for instrument classification. We will briefly introduce some common feature extraction schemes, the feature selection methods used, and the classification models. Our experiment model is then introduced, including data sources used, experiment procedures and resources made use of.

3.1   Feature Extraction

One of our main intentions is to investigate the performance of different feature schemes and find an optimal feature combination for robust instrument classification. Here, we use three different extraction methods, namely, perception-based features, MPEG-7 based features, and MFCC. The first two feature sets consist of temporal and spectral features, while the last is based on spectral analysis.

The perception-based approach represents the instrument sound samples in a physiological way by calculating a nerve image. Three main steps are involved: simulation of the filtering of the outer and middle ear, simulation of the basilar membrane resonance in the inner ear, and simulation of a hair cell model. A second-order low-pass filter is applied for the outer and inner ear filtering. It has a 4 kHz resonance frequency that approximately simulates the overall frequency response of the ear. The basilar membrane is implemented via arrays of band-pass filters. They are divided into 40 channels with frequencies from 141 to 8877 Hz. Finally, the hair cell model uses half-wave rectification and dynamic range compression to act like an amplifier.

Among the temporal features, *zero-crossing rate* (ZCR) is an indicator for the noisiness of the signal and is normally found in speech processing applications; the *root-mean-square* (RMS) feature summarises the energy distribution in each frame and channel over time; the *spectral centroid* measures the average frequency weighted by amplitude of a spectrum; *bandwidth* shows a signal's frequency range by calculating the weighted difference in a spectrum; *flux* represents the amount of local spectral change, calculated as the squared difference between the normalized magnitudes of consecutive spectral distributions.

In our approach we first use the Harmonic Instrument Timbre Description Scheme of the MPEG-7 audio framework, which consists of seven feature descriptors: Harmonic Centroid (HC), Harmonic Deviation (HD), Harmonic Spread (HS), Harmonic Variation (HV), Log-Attack-Time (LAT), Temporal Centroid (TC) and Spectral Centroid (SC). This is only a subset of the eighteen descriptors provided by the MPEG-7 audio framework.

To obtain MFCC features, a signal needs to be transformed from frequency (Hertz) scale to mel scale and a discrete cosine transform converts the filter outputs to MFCC. Here, the mean (denoted as MFCCnM) and standard deviation (as MFCCnD) of the first thirteen linear values are extracted for classification.

Table 1 lists the 44 extracted features. The first 11 features are perception-based, the next 7 are MPEG-7 feature descriptors, and the last 26 are MFCC features.

3.2   Feature Selection

Feature selection techniques are often applied to optimise the feature set used for classification. This way, redundant features are removed from the classification process and the dimensionality of the feature set is reduced to save computational time. However, care has to be taken that not too many features are removed. The effect of multiple features substituting each other could be desirable, since it is not exactly clear how musical timbre is described best.

To evaluate the quality of a feature for classification, a correlation-based approach is often adopted. In general, a feature is good if it is relevant to the class

Table 1. Feature Description

Feature No.	Description	Scheme
1	Zero Crossings	
2-3	Mean and standard deviation of ZCR	
4-5	Mean and standard deviation of RMS	Perception-
6-7	Mean and standard deviation of Centroid	based
8-9	Mean and standard deviation of Bandwidth	
10-11	Mean and standard deviation of Flux	
12	Harmonic Centroid Descriptor	
13	Harmonic Deviation Descriptor	
14	Harmonic Spread Descriptor	MPEG-7
15	Harmonic Variation Descriptor	Timbre Description
16	Spectral Centroid Descriptor	
17	Temporal Centroid Descriptor	
18	Log-Attack-Time Descriptor	
19-44	Mean and standard deviation of the first 13 linear MFCCs	MFCC

concept but is not redundant to other relevant features [18]. Eventually it boils down to the modeling of correlation between two variables or features. Based on information theory, a number of indicators can be developed.

Given a feature set, the 'noisiness' of the feature X can be measured as entropy, defined as

$$H(X) = -\sum_i P(x_i) log_2 P(x_i),$$ (1)

where $P(x_i)$ is the prior probabilities for all values of X. The entropy of X after observing another variable Y is then defined as

$$H(X|Y) = -\sum_j P(y_j) \sum_i (P(x_i|y_j) log_2 P(x_i|y_j)),$$ (2)

The Information Gain (IG) [19], indicating the amount of additional information about X provided by Y, is given as

$$IG(X|Y) = H(X) - H(X|Y)$$ (3)

IG itself is symmetrical, i.e., $IG(X|Y) = IG(Y|X)$, but it favours features with more values.

The gain ration method (GR) normalised IG with an entropy item:

$$GR(X|Y) = \frac{IG(X|C)}{H(Y)}$$ (4)

A better symmetrical measure is defined as the *symmetrical uncertainty* [20][18]:

$$SU = 2\frac{IG(X|Y)}{H(X) + H(Y)}$$ (5)

To calculate these feature selection indexes, the feature sets need to be discretized beforehand.

3.3   Classification

The following classification algorithms are used in this study: condensed k-NN, which is a lazy learning method with an edited set of prototypes [21]; multilayer perceptron (MLP), which is a feedforward neural network using error back-propagation for training; and support vector machine, which is a statistical learning algorithm and has been implemented in a number of machine learning toolboxes.

3.4   Experiment Settings

In this study we tackle the music instrument classification problem in two stages:

– Instrument tone classification using samples of individual instruments.
– Solo instrument detection and classification.

For these experiments all audio features are extracted using the IPEM Toolbox [22] and Auditory Toolbox [23], and an implementation of the MPEG-7 audio descriptors by Casey [24] is used. Weka [25] is used for feature selection, and for classification using SVM and MLP. The condensed k-NN algorithm is implemented separately in Java.

Single Instrument Classification. Samples used in the first experiment are taken from the Iowa Music Samples Collection. The collection consists of 761 single instrument files from 20 instruments which cover the dynamic range from pianissimo to fortissimo and are played bowed or plucked, with or without vibrato depending on the instrument. All samples recorded in the same acoustic environment (anechoic chamber) under the same conditions. We realise that this is a strong constraint and our result may not generalise to a complicated setting such as dealing with live recordings of an orchestra. The purpose of this experiment, however, is to test the behaviour of the feature schemes, evaluate the features using feature selection, and test the performance of different classifiers. It is also important for us to use some benchmark data also used in other research for this purpose.

Solo Instrument Classification. For the second experiment, instrument classification is to perform on solo samples. These sample phrases are often polyphonic, therefore more challenging than the first experiment. One representative instrument of each class is chosen. The instruments are: trumpet, flute, violin, and piano. To detect the right instrument in solo passages, a classifier is trained on short monophonic phrases. Ten-second long solo excerpts from CD recordings are tested on this classifier. The problem here is that the test samples are recorded with accompaniment, thus are often polyphonic in nature. Selecting fewer and clearly distinguishable instruments for the trained classifier helps to make the problem more addressable.

It is assumed that an instrument is playing dominantly in the solo passages. Thus, its spectral characteristics will be the most dominant and the features

Table 2. Data Sources used in solo instrument classification

Sources	Training set		Test set	
Trumpet (5)	9 min	270 samples	3.3 min	181 samples
Piano (6)	10.6 min	320 samples	4 min	219 samples
Violin (6)	10 min	300 samples	4 min	215 samples
Flute (5)	9 min	270 samples	3.3 min	185 samples
Total (22)	38.6 min	1160 samples	14.6 min	800 samples

derived from the harmonic spectrum are assumed to work. In order to get a smaller but more robust feature scheme, a feature selection algorithm is applied.

The samples for the four instruments are taken from CD recordings from private collections and the University of Otago Library. Each instrument has at least five sources and each source is taken either for training or testing to guarantee the independence of the data set. As seen in Table 2, three sources are used for the training set and at least nine minutes of two second monophonic phrases are extracted from them. The test set has two sources for trumpet and flute, and three sources for piano and violin. Passages of around ten-second length are segmented into two second phrases with 50% overlap. The difference in the number of test samples is due to this process.

The test set includes different recordings of the four instruments. Samples of the piano are pure solo passages. The trumpet passages sometimes have multiple brass instruments playing. The flutes are accompanied by multiple flutes, a harp or a double bass, and the violin passages are solos and sometimes with flute and string accompaniment.

4   Results

4.1   Instrument Tone Classification

Feature Selection. For this purpose, we first simply the instrument classification problem by grouping the instruments into four major classes: piano, brass, string and woodwind. For this 4-class task, the best 20 features of the three selection methods are shown in Table 3. All of them indicate that Log-Attack-Time (LAT) and Harmonic Deviation (HD) are the most relevant features. The following features have nearly equal relevance and represent the data collectively. It is necessary to mention that the standard deviation of the MFCC is predominantly present in all three selections. Also the measures of the centroid and bandwidth, as well as one representative of flux, zero crossings and energy can be found in each of them.

Choice of Classifier Scheme. Next, we work onto examining the choice of feature sets together with the classification algorithms, so as to determine a final classification scheme. Three data analysis methods (k-NN, SVM, MLP) are compared for this classification task. Each of them splits 66% of the data into training instances and takes the rest for testing. The percentage split takes the

Table 3. Feature selection for single tones

Rank	IG		GR		SU	
	Relevance	Feature	Relevance	Feature	Relevance	Feature
1	0.8154	LAT	0.531	LAT	0.4613	LAT
2	0.6153	HD	0.527	HD	0.3884	HD
3	0.419	FluxD	0.323	MFCC2M	0.2267	BandwidthM
4	0.3945	BandwidthM	0.297	MFCC12D	0.219	FluxD
5	0.3903	MFCC1D	0.27	MFCC4D	0.2153	RMSM
6	0.381	MFCC3D	0.266	BandwidthM	0.2084	MFCC1D
7	0.3637	RMSM	0.264	RMSM	0.1924	MFCC4M
8	0.3503	BandwidthD	0.258	MFCC13D	0.1893	MFCC11D
9	0.342	MFCC4M	0.245	MFCC2D	0.1864	MFCC3D
10	0.3125	MFCC11D	0.24	MFCC11D	0.1799	BandwidthD
11	0.3109	ZCRD	0.235	MFCC7D	0.1784	MFCC2M
12	0.2744	CentroidD	0.229	FluxD	0.1756	MFCC4D
13	0.2734	MFCC8D	0.224	MFCC1D	0.171	MFCC7D
14	0.2702	MFCC6D	0.22	MFCC4M	0.1699	MFCC12D
15	0.2688	MFCC7D	0.215	CentroidM	0.1697	ZCRD
16	0.2675	ZC	0.211	SC	0.1653	CentroidD
17	0.2604	MFCC4D	0.209	MFCC5M	0.161	CentroidM
18	0.2578	CentroidM	0.208	CentroidD	0.1567	MFCC13D
19	0.2568	MFCC10M	0.195	HC	0.1563	SC
20	0.2519	MFCC10D	0.191	MFCC1M	0.1532	MFCC8D

Table 4. Performance of three classifiers for the four classes

Feature Scheme	k-NN	SVM	MLP
All 44 features	65.15%	82.58%	92.65%
Best 30	63.64%	82.58%	91.91%
Best 20	58.33%	75%	91.91%
Best 10	56.06%	59.09%	88.97%

distribution of class values into account so that each class is reasonably well represented in both training and testing sets. In a first step a classifier is trained on all features. The first 30, 20 and ten features from the information gain filter are taken as the reduced feature set, since they show better results than gain ratio and symmetrical uncertainty. The results are given in Table 4.

The k-NN classifier achieved its best performance with three nearest neighbours. For all features and the best 30 features 200 prototypes are found, the best 20 have 217 prototypes and the best ten have 227. The SVMs use a polynomial kernel with an exponential of 9 and the C value is set to 10. Ninety-two support vectors are used for all features and the best 30, 133 for 20 features, and 235 for ten features. The MLP is trained over 500 epochs with a learning rate of 0.3 and a momentum of 0.2. The accuracy increases with the amount of features in all three classifications. The variance of the results in MLP is not as large as in the other two, and it also shows the highest recognition rate.

Table 5. Performance of the feature sets in classifying the 4 classes (10 CV)

Feature set	Piano	Brass	String	Woodwind	Average
MFCC (26)	99%	92%	87%	64%	85.5%
MPEG-7 (7)	99%	67%	57%	48%	67.75%
IPEM (11)	100%	76%	85%	36%	74.25%
MFCC-MPEG-7 (33)	100%	92%	95%	71%	89.5%
MFCC-IPEM (37)	98%	93%	92%	78%	90.25%
MPEG-7-IPEM (18)	99%	82%	93%	48%	80.5%
All (44)	100%	90%	97%	73%	90%

The performance of different feature set combinations are then assessed with the best classifier - MLP. A 10-fold cross validation process is employed to obtain the results as given in Table 5.

In terms of average performance, the MFCC-IPEM set shows the closest results compared to all 44 features. The 18 features from the MPEG-7-IPEM set have lowest combination result. Generally, the sum of features shows better results. However, between 33, 37 and 44 features there is not even one percent difference. MFCCs are included in all these, being probably the most significant features.

The piano could be classified by all feature sets near to perfect. The MPEG-7 and IPEM sets have problems identifying brass instruments, only the IPEM set could increase the performance of MFCC for this task. String instruments have a high recognition rate except for the MPEG-7 feature set. But combined with MFCC the rate improves to 95%, which is good considering the amount of features (33). All individual feature sets had problems classifying the woodwind class, which is probably because of the few samples in relation to the number of instruments. Only the combination of MFCC-IPEM upgraded the performance to a maximum of 78%. This capability of MFCC-IPEM makes it the best working combination on average for all four instrument classes.

Instrument Classification. Based on the result given above, MLP is chosen as the classifier for further experiments, in which all 20 instruments are directly differentiated against each other. The Iowa samples are used to train a classifier with all 44 features. The confusion matrix of the 20-instrument classification is given in Table 6, where the 10-fold cross validation results are shown. At the bottom it also shows the combined classification rate for the four instrument groups, with 'piano' being the best, and 'woodwind' the worst.

4.2   Solo Instrument Detection

Feature Selection. Again we apply the three feature selection measures for the training features. The result is shown in Table 7. All selection techniques indicate the same features (except MFCC6M and CentroidD) and also their ranking is nearly similar. It is to notice that nearly all IPEM features are represented (except CentroidD in information gain and symmetrical uncertainty), as well as

Table 6. Confusion matrix for all 20 instruments with 10-fold CV using all 44 features

Instrument	Classified As																			
	a	b	c	d	e	f	g	h	i	j	k	l	m	n	o	p	q	r	s	t
a=piano	100																			
b=tuba		20																		
c=trumpet			19			1														
d=horn	1			19																
e=tenoTrombone	1		1		18															
f=baseTrombone					6	14														
g=violin							25													
h=viola	1						1	24												
i=bass	1	1							23											
j=cello										25										
k=sax											8	1						1		
l=altoSax												6			1	1		2		
m=oboe	1									1			7					1		
n=bassoon														10						
o=flute															9		1			
p=altoFlute		1														8	1			
q=bassFlute																2	8			
r=bassClarinet	1								2	1	1				1			5		
s=bbClarinet										1		1			2			1	6	
t=ebClarinet												1	1		1				1	6
Combined	100%			90%				97%					73%							

the means of the first seven MFCC. For the MPEG-7 scheme SC, HC, HS, and HV work best.

Again, the three feature selection filters extract similar groups of features. It seems that among the 44 features, log-attack time, energy features and all standard deviations of the MFCCs are not or only minimal relevant. It is not surprising that LAT is not relevant, since the phrases are cut sequentially at two second intervals, thus there is no proper information of the instrument attack phase. Even if this information would be present, it could be horizontally masked by successive tones or other instruments. Apart from LAT, the standard deviation of the MFCCs as well as TD (MPEG-7) are discarded.

The dynamics of the phrase could also be the cause for the decline in relevance of energy features. Phrases are not static like the instrument tones in the first experiment. Composition and playing style may cause the instruments' dynamic ranges difficult to extract. Successive tones and other instruments can also mask the instrument vertically.

For this task the original feature set is reduced to only 28 features. It consists of the means of the MFCC, the MPEG-7 features without LAT, and the IPEM features without RMS. The new set of features was calculated from the 1160 training and 800 test samples. This accounts for a 59% split of the data set for training.

Table 7. Feature selection for solo passages

Rank	IG		GR		SU	
	Relevance	Feature	Relevance	Feature	Relevance	Feature
1	1.0028	SC	0.4653	MFCC2M	0.4819	MFCC2M
2	0.99748	MFCC2M	0.4413	SC	0.4699	SC
3	0.97115	HC	0.401	HC	0.4396	HC
4	0.82191	ZCRM	0.3477	ZC	0.3712	ZCRM
5	0.78518	ZC	0.338	ZCRM	0.3691	ZC
6	0.72037	MFCC3M	0.2808	HD	0.309	MFCC3M
7	0.62972	CentroidM	0.2702	MFCC3M	0.2954	HD
8	0.62191	HD	0.2631	CentroidM	0.2869	CentroidM
9	0.52701	ZCRD	0.2475	ZCRD	0.2555	ZCRD
10	0.51799	HS	0.247	HS	0.2531	HS
11	0.50303	MFCC4M	0.2337	MFCC1M	0.238	MFCC4M
12	0.43957	MFCC1M	0.231	MFCC10M	0.2268	MFCC1M
13	0.41417	MFCC10M	0.2255	MFCC4M	0.2186	MFCC10M
14	0.37883	FluxM	0.1793	FluxM	0.1844	FluxM
15	0.3643	MFCC5M	0.1752	MFCC7M	0.1752	MFCC7M
16	0.34954	MFCC7M	0.1573	MFCC5M	0.1689	MFCC5M
17	0.30444	BandwidthM	0.1517	BandwidthM	0.1521	BandwidthM
18	0.28482	FluxD	0.147	FluxD	0.1448	FluxD
19	0.22816	MFCC6M	0.1386	CentroidD	0.1175	BandwidthD
20	0.22358	BandwidthD	0.1235	BandwidthD	0.1147	MFCC6M

Table 8. Performance on feature sets in combination for four instruments

MLP	Trumpet	Piano	Violin	Flute	Average
MFCC (13)	93.4%	76.3%	97.7%	100%	91.38%
MPEG (6)	40.9%	69.9%	91.6%	82.2%	72%
IPEM (9)	48.6%	74.9%	93.5%	91.9%	77.9%
MFCC-MPEG-7 (19)	91.7%	88.6%	97.7%	99.5%	94.25%
MFCC-IPEM (22)	93.9%	74%	100%	99.5%	91.4%
MPEG-7-IPEM (15)	83.4%	68%	96.7%	94.1%	85.25%
All 28 features	95%	82.6%	98.1%	99.5%	93.5%

The evaluation of the feature set using a MLP to classify the four instruments is shown in Table 8. The MFCC set alone has a high recognition rate with only 13 features. They sometimes mistake trumpet for piano, but some more errors exist in the representation of piano; it is sometimes misinterpreted as violin or flute.

All 28 features achieved a 93.5% recognition rate. Furthermore, the sets of the selected best 20 and 10 features had a classification rate of 92.13% and 82.88% respectively. We can see that the higher the number of features the higher the increase in accuracy.

The highest average accuracy for detecting the four instruments is 94.25%, achieved by combining the MPEG-7 features with MFCCs. Interestingly, this

Table 9. Confusion matrix for four instruments classification with 28 features

Instruments	Predicted As			
	Trumpet	Piano	Violin	Flute
Trumpet	172	9	0	0
Piano	1	181	7	30
Violin	0	4	211	0
Flute	0	0	1	184

feature set of only 19 features performs better than the selected best 20 features, indicating that feature selection may not guarantee the exact best performance.

A change to shorter one second segments for training and testing shows similar results but with a tendency of reducing to lower recognition rates.

Piano is often misclassified as flute and trumpet is confused with violin using IPEM and MPEG-7 features alone. However, these two sets have less than ten features and probably do not capture all necessary information from the signal. Violin and flute are classified excellently by all feature sets. The IPEM and MPEG-7 feature sets have a low recognition rate for the trumpet samples. In combination the accuracy can be boosted to over 90%. The piano is the hardest instrument to classify, even though its training and test samples are mostly pure solo passages without accompaniment. The 88.6% accuracy of the MFCC-MPEG-7 set for piano makes it the best working combination on average.

The confusion matrix for the four instruments (Table 9) shows that even with all 28 features employed the classifier cannot fully distinguish between piano and violin, and piano and flute. Furthermore, sometimes trumpet and violin are misinterpreted as piano.

4.3 Discussion

The feature selection for the two classification problems given above produces similar results, agreeing to that MFCCs are the most important features for instrument classification. There are some interesting difference, however. In the solo passage experiments, e.g., the standard deviation features of MFCC are found to be irrelevant. Rather, the mean values of the MFCC are the most robust feature set.

In general, the solo instrument detection classification is a more challenging problem, dealing with mostly polyphonic samples. The highest recognition rate is achieved by a combination with the MPEG-7 set. Spectral Centroid and Harmonic Centroid from the MPEG-7 scheme have a high relevance in the feature selection and perhaps could capture more information in combination with the MFCC scheme. The combination MFCC-IPEM was found to be unable to improve the result achieved by MFCC alone.

Flute and violin are the instruments with the highest classification accuracy. This is different from the findings in [7] and [15]. The IPEM and MPEG-7 features sets have problems representing the trumpet. Better results are achieved with the MFCC set or generally with a combination of the feature sets. Throughout piano is detected with the lowest average accuracy of around 75%, contrary to the finding in the experiments on the samples of single instruments.

Generally, the high classification rates are possibly due to the distinctive acoustic properties of the instruments, since they originate from different families. It is not claimed that these results generalise. The accuracy is likely to decrease when more instruments and more sources of samples are introduced.

Using feature selection filters, the most informative features for solo passages are found to be the spectral and harmonic centroids, zero-crossing rate, and generally the first seven MFCCs. It is not surprising that, for instance, time-dependent features cannot represent the signal, since a strict sequential segmentation is applied, leaving incomplete spatial cues, and destroying the context of the temporal information.

Another possibility can be to employ segmentation at onset time, so that it make sense to apply time-dependent features again. However, the detection of onset is itself a challenging problem. Nevertheless, using spectral features alone can achieve a good performance as shown in our experiments, where a simple sequential segmentation of the solo passage was implemented.

5   Conclusion

In this paper, we studied feature extraction and evaluation for the problem of instrument classification. The main contribution is that we bring three major feature extraction schemes under investigation, have them analysed using feature selection measures based on information theory, and their performance assessed using classifiers undergoing cross validation. In the first experiment of instrument tone classification, a publicly available data set is used, allowing for the possibility of benchmark comparison. For instance, Iowa music samples were also used in [7], but our results on instrument family classification and instrument tone classification are much higher on almost all common instruments in both studies.

Three feature selection measures are adopted and produce similar feature selection outputs, which basically aligns with the performance obtained through classifiers, especially MLP. We note that the use of an MLP is rather uncommon for recognising musical tones and phrases as shown from the literature. It however produces favourable results both on tone and solo passage classification. This finding may not generalise, but we will assess its performance using more music samples, and compare the performance of more classification models. Also, by conducting linear and non-linear principal component analyses, their dimension reduction and de-noising effects may also enhance the final classification outcome.

We have covered only four instruments in the solo passage experiments. The intention is to distinguish major classical solo instruments in accompanied solo passages in concertos or sonatas. There are few works concentrating on polyphonic music without separating the signal into its sound or instrument sources. Detecting the range of orchestral instruments therein still needs a considerable effort of research. A comparison study on analysing musical passages is hard to achieve, as till now there is no free accessible common data set which could be used as a basis for further work.

In the future, we intend to investigate the feature extraction issue with more real-world music data, develop new feature schemes, as well as experiment on finding better mechanisms to combine the feature schemes and the classification models in order to achiever better performance on more solo instruments.

References

1. ISO/IEC Working Group: MPEG-7 overview. URL http:// www.chiariglione.org/mpeg/standards/mpeg-7/mpeg-7.htm (2004) Accessed 8.2.2006.
2. Tzanetakis, G., Cook, P.: Musical genre classification of audio signals. IEEE Transactions on speech and audio processing **10** (2002) 293–302
3. Aucouturier, J., Pachet, F.: Scaling up music playlist generation. In: Proc. ICME. Volume 1. (2002) 105 – 108
4. Divakaran, A., Regunathan, R., Xiong, Z., Casey, M.: Procedure for audio-assisted browsing of news video using generalized sound recognition. In: Proc. SPIE. Volume 5021. (2003) 160–166
5. Foote, J.: An overview of audio information retrieval. Multimedia Systems **7** (1999) 2–10
6. Marques, J., Moreno, P.: A study of musical instrument classification using gaussian mixture models and support vector machines. Technical Report CRL 99/4, Compaq Computer Corporation (1999)
7. Eronen, A.: Comparison of features for music instrument recognition. In: Proceedings of the IEEE Workshop on Applications of Signal Processing to Audio and Acoustics. (2001) 19–22
8. Essid, S., Richard, G., David, B.: Efficient musical instrument recognition on solo performance music using basic features. In: Proceedings of the Audio Engineering Society 25th International Conference. (2004) Accessed 22.11.2005.
9. Peeters, G., McAdams, S., Herrera, P.: Instrument sound description in the context of mpeg-7. In: Proc. of Inter. Computer Music Conf. (2000) 166–169
10. Xiong, Z., Radhakrishnan, R., Divakaran, A., Huang, T.: Comparing MFCC and MPEG-7 audio features for feature extraction, maximum likelihood HMM and entropic prior HMM for sports audio classification. In: Proc. of ICME. Volume 3. (2003) 397–400
11. Brown, J.C., Houix, O.: Feature dependence in the automatic identification of musical woodwind instruments. Journal of the Acoustical Society of America **109**(3) (2001) 1064–1072
12. Essid, S., Richard, G., David, B.: Musical instrument recognition by pairwise classification strategies. IEEE Trans. on Speech and Audio Processing (to appear) (2006) Accessed 2.12.2005.
13. Agostini, G., Longari, M., Poolastri, E.: Musical instrument timbres classification with spectral features. EURASIP Journal on Applied Signal Processing (1) (2003)
14. Livshin, A.A., Rodet, X.: Musical instrument identification in continuous recordings. In: Proceedings of the 7th International Conference on Digital Audio Effects. (2004)

15. Eggink, J., Brown, G.J.: Instrument recognition in accompanied sonatas and concertos. In: Proc. of ICASSP. Volume IV. (2004) 217–220
16. Yu, L., Liu, H.: Efficient feature selection via analysis of relevance and redundancy. J. Machine Learning Research **5** (2004) 1205–1224
17. Grimaldi, M., Cunningham, P., Kokaram, A.: An evaluation of alternative feature selection strategies and ensemble techniques of classifying music. In Mladenic, D., Paa, G., eds.: Workshop in Multimedia Discovery and Mining at ECML/PKDD-2003. (2003)
18. Yu, L., Liu, H.: Feature selection for high-dimensional data: A fast correlation-based filter solution. In: Proc. 20th Intl Conf. Machine Learning. (2003) 856–863
19. Qinlan, J.: *C4.5*: Programs for machine learning. Morgan Kaufmann (1993)
20. Press, W.H., Flannery, B.P., Teukolsky, S.A., Vetterling, W.T.: Numerical recipes in C. Cambridge University Press (1988)
21. Niemann, H.: Klassifikation von Mustern. Springer Verlag (1983)
22. IPEM: IPEM-toolbox. URL http://www.ipem.ugent.be/Toolbox (2005) Accessed 10.9.2005.
23. Slaney, M.: The Auditory Toolbox. Technical Report 1998-010, Interval Research Corporation (1998) URL http://rvl4.ecn.purdue.edu/~malcolm/interval/1998-010. Accessed 22.11.2005.
24. Casey, M.: MPEG-7 sound-recognition tools. IEEE Trans. on Circuits and Systems for Video Technology **11**(6) (2001) 737–747
25. Witten, I.H., Frank, E.: Data Mining: Practical machine learning tools and techniques. Second edn. Morgan Kaufmann, San Francisco (2005)

Automated Classification of Images from Crystallisation Experiments

Julie Wilson

York Structural Biology Laboratory, Department of Chemistry,
University of York, Heslington, York YO10 5YW, UK
julie@ysbl.york.ac.uk

Abstract. Protein crystallography can often provide the three-dimensional structures of macro-molecules necessary for functional studies and drug design. However, identifying the conditions that will provide diffraction quality crystals often requires numerous experiments. The use of robots has led to a dramatic increase in the number of crystallisation experiments performed in most laboratories and, in structural genomics centres, tens of thousands of experiments can be produced daily. The results of these experiments must be assessed repeatedly over time and inspection of the results by eye is becoming increasingly impractical. A number of systems are now available for automated imaging of crystallisation experiments and the primary aim of this research is the development of software to automate image analysis.

Keywords: classification, image analysis, protein crystallization, automation.

1 Introduction

The determination of protein structures by X-ray crystallography can provide insight into molecular function and facilitate manipulation of biological processes by effective drug design. The number of protein structures solved has increased significantly in recent years but represents only a small percentage of the sequenced genes now available. Structural genomics aims to implement high-throughput technologies to accelerate molecular structure determination and many steps in the process have been automated. Although the intense, highly focused X-rays available at synchrotron sources now allow the use of micron-sized crystals, the process of obtaining diffraction quality crystals remains a major bottleneck. Currently there is no *a priori* method to determine the optimum crystallisation strategy for a particular protein and the process remains highly empirical. Several important variables, which often interact, such as protein concentration, precipitant, pH and temperature must be tested in combination. Various buffers are available to maintain a specific pH and different salts, polymers or organic solvents may be used as precipitants. Detergents and other additives may also be needed to maintain protein solubility during crystallisation. Various sampling techniques have been proposed to reduce the number of possible combinations but the screening of conditions is largely a process of trial-and-error. The automation of nano-volume crystallisation has vastly increased the number of experiments performed in most laboratories and, in high-throughput

P. Perner (Ed.): ICDM 2006, LNAI 4065, pp. 459–473, 2006.

mode, robotic systems can successfully perform tens of thousands of experiments a day [1]. The results of these experiments must be assessed repeatedly over a period of time and incorporated into optimisation protocols. Visual inspection of the results is becoming increasingly impractical and the development of tools to automate analysis is essential.

Integrated storage and imaging systems allow the results of crystallisation trials to be recorded at regular intervals and can provide regulated temperatures and minimal movement of the crystallisation trays. Crystallographers can therefore view their experimental results via a computer in the comfort of their office rather than through a microscope in the cold room. However, analysing the many thousands of images produced is a monotonous task with the majority of experiments yielding negative results. Software to automatically analyse the images is now being developed by a number of research groups ([2], [3], [4], [5]) and should allow the images to be sorted so that only the highest scoring experiments need be checked by eye. In most cases the image analysis software is developed for a particular imaging system but the intention here is that ALICE (AnaLysis of Images from Crystallisation Experiments) should be generic software that can be adapted to the many different systems available. Whilst the identification of crystals is the primary objective, reliable classification of other experimental outcomes would provide information for subsequent trials. Therefore the aim of this research is to provide a score for each image reflecting how close the experimental conditions are to those required for crystal growth. This allows the images to be examined in order of merit and as soon as some high-scoring conditions are confirmed, no further images need be considered. Although human classification will always be superior, automated analysis promises to drastically reduce the number of images to be inspected. Equally important is the potential for the development of optimization procedures. Not only will promising initial conditions be identified but failed experiments will also be recorded allowing the possibility for automated screening protocols to be developed via data-mining and neural network techniques paper.

2   Imaging Systems

ALICE is being developed in collaboration with the Oxford Protein Production Facility (OPPF) at the University of Oxford where it is now used routinely to annotate images Many of the images shown were supplied by the OPPF where crystallisation experiments are performed in 96-well Greiner plates (micro-titre format) and the images are taken using an automated Oasis 1700 imaging system (Veeco, Cambridge, UK). Native images are 1024 × 1024 × 8 bit bitmap (BMP) images (~1 Megabyte in size, corresponding to a pixel width of about 3 μm.

Additionally, figure 1(a) shows an image of a 1μl drop in an Art Robbins Intelliplate (Hampton Research) acquired with the Tritek Crystal Pro imaging system at the Synchrotron Radiation Source in Daresbury. The original colour image (1280 × 1014 × 8 bit BMP) was converted to greyscale here. Figure 1(c) shows a 1024 × 768 × 8 bit BMP image of an experiment performed in a Greiner low-profile crystallisation tray and was supplied by the Nationaal Kanker Instituut, in Amsterdam. The image

(a)   (b)   (c)

(d)   (e)   (f)

Fig. 1. Experiments in three different crystallisation plates are shown. Image (a) shows a well from an Art Robbins Intelliplate, (b) shows a single well from a 96-well Greiner plate (micro-titre format) and (c) an experiment performed in a Greiner low-profile crystallisation plate.

was acquired using the BioTom storage and visualisation robot. Figure 3 shows a $2560 \times 1920 \times 8$ bit JPEG colour image, also in a 96-well Greiner plate, taken at EMBL in Grenoble with the RoboDesign imaging system.

3   Classes

A major issue in this particular classification problem is the fact that there are, in reality, no discrete classes. The experiments produce a continuum of results and the number of classes used is a somewhat arbitrary choice. In the extreme case we could have a two-class system, crystals and non-crystals. However this would give no information about the experiments that failed to produce crystals and therefore no information for subsequent trials. Research has shown that systematic addition of new components to initial conditions can yield better crystals [6]. In the absence of crystals, the occurrence of micro-crystals or spherulites, for example, indicate conditions that are very close to those required for crystallization. Phenomena such as phase separation can lead to crystal growth and should be recognized and even crystalline precipitate may be refined in optimization protocols. On the other hand, experiments resulting in heavy amorphous precipitate or denatured protein show that the conditions are inappropriate and this information is also valuable for further screening procedures.

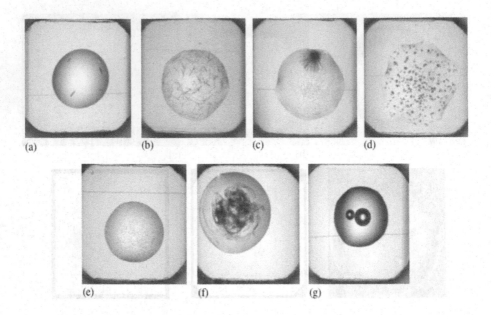

(a)   (b)   (c)   (d)

(e)   (f)   (g)

Fig. 2. Example images from the seven different classes used in this research are shown. The highest scoring class, consisting of single crystals of any size or shape and a score of 6, is represented by image (a). Class 5 images include piles of needle crystals, as in image (b), as well other types of crystal cluster. Image (c) shows the formation of a "sea-urchin" of micro-crystal needles but class 4 also includes tiny seed-like crystals. Class 3 is comprised of non-crystalline results considered better than precipitate such as phase-separation, oil-drops or the outcome of image (d) whereas all precipitates such as image (e) are assigned to class 2. Denatured protein as shown in image (f) and other unwanted objects such as skin on the drop or contaminants are given class 1 and empty drops class 0. Image (g) is classed as an empty drop even though it contains bubbles because it shows no experimental result. In most cases, bubbles can be identified and eliminated before object classification.

Attempts have been made to classify experimental results into as many as ten different categories including three separate grades of precipitate [7]. However, we found that agreement rates between any two crystallographers on the exact class of a series of images are rarely above 70% and that this decreases as the number of classes increases [8]. In particular, agreement rates drop dramatically when crystallographers are asked to distinguish between "good" and "bad" precipitates. No matter how many distinct classes are used there will always be border-line cases. When, for example should small crystals be considered as micro-crystals? We have found that, even when a traffic-light approach involving just three classes to describe the results as definitely worth pursuing, possibly worth pursuing or definitely not worth pursuing was used, the mean agreement rate for 34 volunteers was only 62%. After various trials with volunteers, a seven-class system, with scores ranging from 0 for an empty drop to 6 for good single crystals, was chosen for this research. Example images showing typical experimental results associated with each class are shown in Figure 2.

Table 1. Agreement rates between individual crystallographer's scores and the mean scores for each image. The figures given are percentages of the 1207×16 images classified, where 16 crystallographers each classified a set of 1207 images. The rows in the table correspond to the mean image-scores and the columns correspond to the class chosen by the 16 classifiers. Classifiers were given the option of leaving an image as unclassified and the column headed "–1" corresponds to such images (which were not used when calculating the mean score). The actual number of images in each class (according to the mean score) is given in the column headed "N".

	N	6	5	4	3	2	1	0	-1
Class 6	51	84.7	13.7	1.2	0.0	0.0	0.4	0.0	0.0
Class 5	87	11.2	68.5	17.7	1.5	0.1	0.3	0.4	0.3
Class 4	78	3.3	29.0	50.4	12.6	1.8	1.3	1.1	0.4
Class 3	113	0.6	2.0	18.9	46.7	23.5	6.5	1.4	0.4
Class 2	356	0.0	0.1	1.9	20.6	59.3	14.4	3.5	0.2
Class 1	87	0.1	0.0		8.5	18.1	39.5	32.5	0.6
Class 0	435	0.0	0.0	0.1	0.9	1.8	5.4	91.6	0.3

Studies to assess the reliability of human classification of images from crystallisation experiments not only show that agreement rates are surprisingly low, but that people are often not consistent with themselves when shown the same image on different occasions. Thus, no individual's data can be taken as the "correct" classification of an image and several people's results need to be combined when producing training data for classification algorithms. Table 1 shows a truth table for the scores provided by individual crystallographers in comparison to the mean score for each image. The rows in the table correspond to the mean image-scores and the columns correspond to the classes chosen by the 16 crystallographers. It can be seen that class 6 images (single crystals) have high agreement rates as might be expected, with 84.7% total agreement and another 13.7% being classified as class 5 (crystal cluster). Unsurprisingly class 0 (empty drops) also cause little difference of opinion with 91.6% exact agreement. Other classes however show more variation with images classified by the mean image-score as 3, 4 and 5 being assigned to every class possible. In many cases though, the scores that do not agree exactly with the mean score, differ by only one class. In this study, allowing agreement within one class gave an average agreement rate of 94.4% and allowing a two class difference gave close to total agreement at 99%. This diversity in human classification needs to be taken into account when assessing the classification success of software to analyse images from crystallisation experiments.

4   Image Pre-processing

Careful screening of crystallisation conditions involves conducting many experiments. This time-consuming and monotonous process made it an obvious candidate for automation and crystallisation robots are now used routinely in most laboratories. The experiments may be carried out using vapour diffusion [9] or microbatch [10] but each requires the combination of protein sample with a cocktail of crystallisation reagents. Liquid dispensing robots are able to dispense mirco-litre to nano-litre droplets into appropriate wells in crystallisation plates. These crystallisation drops are the subject of the analysis but may be relatively small in relation to the well in which they are deposited. Imaging systems must ensure that the crystallisation drop is entirely within the image and, even if centred originally, the drop may migrate across the well as the tray is moved. The image must therefore capture the entire well so that much of it is redundant as far as the experimental result is concerned. As tens of thousands of images can be produced on a daily basis, the speed of analysis is essential and, although parallel processing of the images is possible, each image must be evaluated within a few seconds. It is therefore important to identify the region of interest early in the analysis. In ALICE this is achieved in a two-stage process. First the edges of the well are identified and then the position of the crystallisation drop within the well. Many different crystallisation plates are available (see figure 1 for examples) and the identification of the well depends on the type of plate. Round wells are easily recognized using a Hough transform whereas wells with straight sides can be found using wavelets transforms. The use of wavelets in ALICE also allows the crystallisation drop to be identified on a coarse grid and therefore speeds up processing considerably.

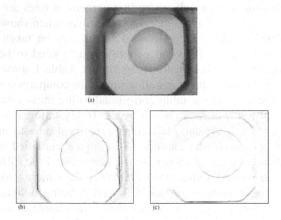

Fig. 3. Difference images obtained using wavelet transforms. The original image is shown in (a) with the horizontal differences in (b) and the vertical differences in (c).

Wavelets transforms have been used in many disciplines for a variety of purposes and the mathematics have been described in detail elsewhere (see [11] for example). Intuitively, for a one-dimensional signal, each level of the transform can be thought of as a pair of filters, a smoothing filter that provides a lower resolution approximation of the signal and a related filter that stores the differences between the approximation and the original signal. The wavelet transform uses basis functions or wavelets that are localised in both position and scale and therefore provides information about where in the signal the differences occur. In the multi-resolution analysis of Mallat, each approximation is decimated by a factor of two so that, for a signal of length, n, the first approximation can be represented in $n/2$ points. The differences, or details at this scale, can also be represented in $n/2$ points. For two-dimensional data, each level of the transform gives a smooth approximation reduced by a factor of four corresponding to a smoothing in both the horizontal and vertical directions. In this case detail information corresponding to differences in the horizontal, vertical and in both directions is output.

The ability of wavelets to detect vertical and horizontal differences can be exploited to identify the edges of the well. Many different wavelet bases are available and generally there is a trade-off between smoothness and how compactly supported the wavelet functions are. Here we are interested in the position of the largest

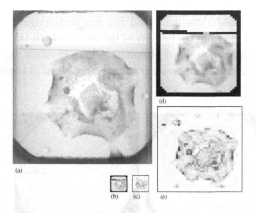

Fig. 4. The low-resolution approximation of the image in (a) is shown to scale in (b) to emphasize the data reduction achieved. Here an eight-level wavelet transform reduced the number of pixels to be considered by a factor of 256. A close-up of this same approximation is shown in (d). Black pixels indicate pre-masked areas of the image. The image, shown to scale in (c) and as a close-up in (e), was obtained by combining the three separate difference images from the eighth level of the transform.

differences rather than smooth approximations and therefore use the simplest wavelet functions originally due to Haar [12] and shown to belong to the Daubechies family of wavelet functions [13]. Figure 3 shows an image and the horizontal and vertical details obtained from it. The darkest pixels in the detail images correspond to the largest values and therefore give the positions of the greatest differences in intensity in the image. The edges of the well are obvious even though the shadow across the top of the well reduces the contrast to some extent. Summing the differences for each row allows the vertical sides to be identified and similarly the differences across columns give the positions of the horizontal sides. In addition to the well, the edge of the crystallisation drop is picked up in this image where the change in intensity is high due to the shadows caused by the curvature of the drop. This is not always the case however with certain additives in particular leading to less convex drops and lighting effects sometimes obscuring the drop boundary rather than emphasising it. In such cases the drop itself is not so clear in the difference images and therefore we do not attempt to identify it at this stage but simply crop the area of the image to be processed further to the size of the well.

Before attempting to define the drop boundary, it is worth removing unwanted artefacts that could cause problems in classification or affect the mask obtained for the drop [8]. Crystallisation plates can often have mould defects creating lines across the image (as can be seen in some of the images in figure 1) and could cause classification algorithms to produce many false positives. Although sometimes distorted by the lens effect of the drop, these lines are roughly horizontal (or vertical for some imaging systems) and, unlike crystals, extend beyond the crystallisation drop. This allows them to be recognized and eliminated before analysis in most cases. The appropriate difference image (horizontal or vertical) is used to identify such lines but with a lower threshold than that used for the well edges. The lines do not necessarily extend the full width (or height) of the well and allowance has to be made for this. In order to reduce the risk of eliminating long crystals that happen to lie in such a position, the differences are given greater weight close to the well edge.

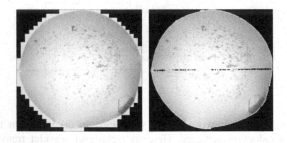

Fig. 5. The initial rough mask for the crystallisation drop obtained from a low-resolution wavelet image is shown in (a) and the refined mask in (b). Pixels identified as part of a horizontal line are also masked.

The power of wavelets for compression allows the crystallisation drop to be identified in a very low-resolution image and therefore speeds up processing significantly. Rather than the smooth approximation, an image at the same resolution combining the three possible difference images (horizontal, vertical and both directions) is used. Figure 4 shows that the crystallisation drop is easier to identify in this difference image. Here eight levels of the wavelet transform reduced the original 461,824 pixels by a factor of 256 to give an image with only 1,804 pixels in which the drop is clearly visible. The small droplets, which often occur with robotic dispensing, are also detectable but can be disregarded by considering connectivity. It can be seen that the line across the image due to the plastic plate has been masked and, in some cases, this could effectively cut the drop in half. The shape and expected size of the drop is therefore taken into account when determining the pixels to be used in the drop mask. This coarse mask can then refined as shown in figure 5.

5 Analysis of the Crystallisation Drop

With the analysis restricted to the crystallisation drop, characteristic features that can be quantified and used for classification must be determined. These may be features of the whole crystallisation drop or of individual objects or blocks within the drop. Straight lines are an obvious characteristic of crystals and can be detected using techniques such as the Hough transform [14], [2], [4] or the Radon transform [3] and used to compute classification variables. Other features include statistical descriptors such as the variation calculated over small blocks within the drop [2] and local smoothness [3]. Various measures related to texture can be defined in terms of the correlation between intensities at different scales and a few global parameters can be extracted from local texture measures [4].

Most methods for the analysis of crystallisation images take the drop-based approach but, in ALICE, individual objects are identified within the cryst-allisation drop. Objects are defined as connected sets of pixels above a threshold determined by the intensity statistics and each object is evaluated separately. Boundary-related variables include measures of curvature and the length of straight sections. Ordered patterns in the gradient direction anywhere within objects, in straight lines or blocks, indicate the presence of regular objects and various shape descriptors and statistical measures provide information about other types of object [15].

Table 2. Scoring system used for classification of objects within the crystallisation drop. The list is not exhaustive and, during training, any objects not listed would be assigned to the class with a score reflecting its significance in terms of the experimental outcome.

OBJECT	SCORE
single crystal	6
crystal cluster	5
pile of needle crystals	5
micro-crystals	4
sea-urchins	4
spherulites	4
phase-separation	3
oil drops	3
precipitate	2
skin	1
denatured protein	1
drop edge	0
Bubble	0

For any pattern recognition problem, the extracted features should have common values within a class and be discriminatory between classes. Unfortunately this is rarely the case with features extracted from crystallisation images. Although crystals may be expected to have straight edges and sharp angles, there is no fixed pattern that describes every crystal and in fact very irregular crystals have been found that diffract beautifully. Wrinkles in the skin on the drop can have similar angular features and denatured protein can create a variety of strange effects. Furthermore the features within a class may have totally unrelated values. For example, micro-crystals may appear as tiny seeds throughout the drop or cluster together at a single nucleation site forming spidery objects often referred to as sea-urchins (see figure 1(c)). For this reason, thirteen separate classes, listed in Table 2, are used for object classification. After the individual objects have been classified, the thirteen classes are reduced to the seven classes represented in Figure 1, using the scores shown in Table 2. Thus each object is assigned to a class with a score from 0 to 6 reflecting its significance in terms of the experimental outcome, where a score of zero is given to objects that are not related to experimental results, such as air bubbles and crystallization plate defects. The list is not comprehensive and other objects that were observed during training were assigned to the class with the most appropriate score in terms of the experiment.

6 Classification

Supervised learning algorithms are trained to associate a certain output with particular inputs so that the vector of values obtained from the classification variables, or feature vector, can be used to assign an object to a particular class. Training requires a set of input vectors that have been pre-classified by eye and an independent test set for validation to avoid problems with over-fitting. Unsupervised learning algorithms respond only to the input values and do not require output targets. Such networks are usually clustering algorithms and are useful for the identification of patterns and groupings within the input data. Self-organising maps are widely used unsupervised learning algorithms [16] and have been applied to the classification of crystallisation images [4], [5]. Each node or neuron in a two dimensional grid has a set of weights associated with it representing feature vectors from the training data. These weights are modified over a number of training cycles and the map organises itself so that physically close nodes have similar weight vectors. Although this clustering is unsupervised, self-organising maps can be used for classification by associating each node in the final map with the class of the closest training. New vectors can then be presented to the map for classification and the class of the node closest to the input vector assigned to it. Learning vector quantization is a related method and also provides a set of trained vectors against which new data can be compared.

Self-organising maps (SOMs) and learning vector quantization (LVQ) are both implemented in ALICE together with Bayesian probabilities. For each variable, the distribution of values in each class is calculated from the training data to give the probability of a particular value given the class, or $P(x_i/C_j)$ where x_i is the value of the *i*th variable and C_j is the *j*th class. Bayes theorem then gives the probability of a certain class given the value of the variable as

$$P(C_j/x_i) = \frac{P(C_j)P(x_i/C_j)}{\sum_k P(C_k)P(x_i/C_k)}.$$

The variables are unlikely to be independent but, for simplicity, this is assumed to be the case and the probabilities obtained for individual variables are multiplied together to give a probability for each class given a particular set of variables. In order to combine these probabilities with the results from SOMs and LVQs, probabilities are derived from both these methods. This is achieved by generating a series of ten self-organising maps (by randomising the training data) and adding a score of 0.1 to the class chosen by each map, giving a probability for each class rather than a single output class, Similarly, probabilities are obtained from ten sets of LVQs so that the three probabilities may simply be added and the result used to determine the final class of an object. An overall score is given to the image based on the scores for the individual objects within the crystallisation drop. As an image in which a crystal surrounded by precipitate should score as highly as an image containing only large crystals, the class of the highest scoring object determines the overall class of the image.

7 Results and Discussion

Table 3 shows the results from the same 1207 images that were classified by 16 crystallographers. None of these images were used in training and so form a completely independent test set. The test set here was not chosen carefully but consists of ten consecutive plates (960 images) that were produced at the OPPF with another 247 images added to increase the number of images with more favourable outcomes. The number of images in each class is therefore not balanced (see Table 1) but has many more empty drops and precipitate images as would be expected in a typical run.

In assessing the results the variation in human scoring should be taken into account and the results are also shown when a difference of one class is allowed for. It can be seen that the worst results are obtained for class 1 images, which are often scored too highly. As well as denatured protein and skin forming on the drop, this class includes any foreign bodies, such as lint and hairs that have contaminated the experiments. In terms of the classification variables, these objects look far more interesting than they actually are and attempts to reduce the number of these false positives would run the risk of increasing the number of false negatives. False positives mean that crystallographers may have to look at more images than necessary whereas false negatives could mean missing crystals and is therefore more serious. In fact some images containing crystals (5.9%) have been classified by ALICE as empty drops. This is due to crystals growing at the edge of the crystallisation drop as in Figure 5. The single object formed has many of the features of the edge of the drop and hence is given a score of zero. Extra checks are applied to any object classified as "drop edge" in order to avoid this but some small crystals can still be missed in this way. The other consequence of these safety checks is the number of empty drops classified too highly (12.2% in class 5 for example) due to shadows or other lighting effects at the edge of the drop and a balance must be found.

ALICE is being adapted to a number of different imaging systems and must be trained to recognise the variables expected for a particular set of images. Many factors influence the type of image to be analysed but lighting and resolution have the most dramatic effects for automated classification algorithms. Some of the differences can be dealt with by pre-processing the images, as can the problems associated with the variety of crystallisation plates used. Although pre-processing will reduce the variation between imaging systems, resolution in particular is an important factor that cannot be normalised. A training set of individual objects classified by eye is required and a graphical user interface allows the objects within an image to be identified by ALICE and selected by the user on the click of a mouse button. Selected objects can then be assigned to classes defined by the user and the

Table 3. Agreement of rates for the scores given by ALICE and the mean scores of 16 crystallographers. In (a) the figures given are percentages of the 1207 images classified. The rows in the table correspond to the mean image-scores and the columns correspond to the automated analysis. In (b) the results from neighbouring classes have been merged to show the agreement when a one-class difference is allowed for.

(a)

	6	5	4	3	2	1	0
Class 6	33.3	37.3	11.8	5.9	5.9	2.0	5.9
Class 5	11.5	66.7	16.1	3.4	1.1	0.0	1.1
Class 4	7.7	17.9	48.7	17.9	5.1	1.3	1.3
Class 3	0.9	8.0	34.5	38.1	17.7	0.9	0.0
Class 2	0.0	1.4	16.6	37.1	38.2	1.4	5.3
Class 1	0.0	2.3	17.2	36.8	25.3	18.4	0.0
Class 0	0.9	12.2	13.6	4.8	2.1	2.5	63.9

(b)

	6	5	4	3	2	1	0
Class 6	70.6		11.8	5.9	5.9	2.0	5.9
Class 5	94.3			3.4	1.1	0.0	1.1
Class 4	7.7	84.5			5.1	1.3	1.3
Class 3	0.9	8.0	91.2			0.9	0.0
Class 2	0.0	1.4	16.6	76.7			5.3
Class 1	0.0	2.3	17.2	36.8	43.7		
Class 0	0.9	12.2	13.6	4.8	2.1	66.4	

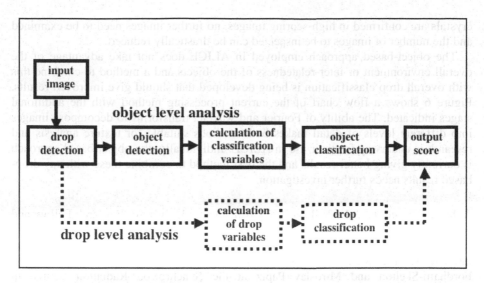

Fig. 6. Flowchart showing the various stages used for processing crystallisation images. The current object-based implementation is shown with solid lines and the planned drop-based stages indicated by broken lines.

associated variables stored for training. The collection of training data is still extremely tedious although it should not need to be performed more than once for each new system.

8 Conclusions

Crystallisation experiments give a continuum of results and classification by eye into any fixed number of discrete classes will lead to differences of opinion, particularly between neighbouring classes. With the seven-class system used in this study the difference is only one class in many cases but it has been found that agreement rates between crystallographers get worse if the number of classes is increased. However, allowing overlap between neighbouring classes when considering agreement rates is not the same as reducing the number of classes. Using a traffic-light system of just three classes to describe the results does not improve the agreement rates and, in this case, allowing overlap between classes would make the classification meaningless. The diversity in human classification needs to be taken into account when collecting training data and in assessing the classification success of software to analyse images from crystallisation experiments.

ALICE is still being developed and is not reliable enough to be depended upon completely. The aim however is to aid rather than replace human classification and the software is already used to annotate images at the Oxford Protein Production Facility. ALICE is sufficiently accurate in identifying empty drops that the many such images can already be ignored. A graphical user interface has been developed in Oxford [17] that allows users to order the images according to the scores. Thus, if crystals are confirmed in high-scoring images, no further images need to be examined and the number of images to be inspected can be drastically reduced.

The object-based approach employed in ALICE does not take advantage of the overall environment or inter-relatedness of the objects and a method to combine this with overall drop classification is being developed that should give improved results. Figure 6 shows a flow chart of the current processing method with the additional stages indicated. The ability of Fourier and wavelet transforms to decompose images into different levels of detail makes both methods suitable for texture analysis and research is underway for their use in ALICE. Individually, the object-based approach is currently giving better results and the best method to combine these with any drop-based results needs further investigation.

Acknowledgments. Julie Wilson is a Royal Society University Research Fellow and would like to thank the Royal Society for their support. Most images shown were supplied by the Oxford Protein Production facility in Oxford. The OPPF is funded by the UK Medical Research Council. The author would also like to thank Tony Fordham-Skelton and Miroslav Papiz at the Synchrotron Radiation Source in Daresbury, Anastassis Perrakis at the Nationaal Kanker Instituut, in Amsterdam and José Antonio Marquez at EMBL in Grenoble for supplying additional images.

References

1. Mayo, C.J, Diprose, J.M., Walter, T.S., Berry, I.M., Wilson, J., Owens, R.J., Jones, E.Y., Harlos, K., Stuart, D.I. and Esnouf, R.M. Benefits of automated crystallization plate tracking, imaging and analysis. Structure 13 (2005) 175-182.
2. Bern, M., Goldberg, D., Kuhn, P. and Stevens R. Automatic classification of protein crystallization images using a line tracking algorithm. J.Appl. Cryst. 37 (2004) 279-287.
3. Cumbaa, C.A., Lauricella, A., Fehrman, N., Veatch, C., Collins, R., Luft, J., DeTitta, G. and Juristica, I. Automatic classification of sub-microlitre protein-crystallization trials in 1536-well plates. Acta Cryst. D59 (2003) 1619-1627.
4. Spraggon, G., Lesley, S., Kreusch, A. and Priestle, J. Computational analysis of crystallization trials. Acta Cryst., D58 (2002) 1915-1923.
5. Wilson, J. Automated evaluation of crystallisation experiments. Cryst.Rev., 10, No.1 (2004) 73-84.
6. Qian, C., Lagace, L., Massariol, M.-J., Chabot, C., Yoakim, C., Déziel, R. and Tong, L. A rational approach towards successful crystallization and crystal treatment of human cytomegalovirus protease and its inhibitor complex. Acta Cryst. D56 (2000) 175-180.
7. Saitoh, K., Kawabata, K., Asama, H., Mishima, T., Sugahara, M., and Miyano, M. Evaluation of protein crysatllization states based on texture information derived from greyscale images. Acta Cryst., D61 (2005) 873-880.
8. Wilson J. and Berry, I. The use of gradient direction in pre-processing images from crystallisation experiments. J. Appl. Cryst. 38 (2005) 493-500.
9. Mueller, U., Nyarsik, L., Horn, M., Rauth, H., Przewieslik, T., Saenger, W., Lehrach, H. and Eickhoff, H. Development of a technology for automation and miniturization of protein crystallization. J. Biotech. 85 (2001) 7-14.
10. Chayen, N.E., Shaw Stwewart, P.D., Maeder, D.L., and Blow, D.M. An automated system for Micro-batch Protein Crystallization and Screening. J. Appl. Cryst. 23 (1990) 297-302.

11. Mallat, S. A theory for multi-resolution signal decomposition; the wavelet representation. IEEE Trans. Patt. Anal. And Mach. Intell., 11 (1989) 674-693.
12. Haar, A. Math. Annal., 69 (1910) 331-371.
13. Daubechies, I. Ten lectures on wavelets, Society for Industrial and Applied Mathematics, Philadelphia, PA.
14. Zuk, W. and Ward.K. Methods of analysis of protein crystal images. J. Cryst. Growth, 110 (1991) 148-155.
15. Wilson, J. Towards the automated evaluation of crystallisation trials. Acta Cryst., D58 (2002) 1907-1914.
16. Kohonen, T. Self-organization and associative memory. 2nd. Edn. Berlin: Springer (1987).
17. Mayo, C.J, Diprose,J.M., Walter, T.S.,Berry, I.M., Wilson, J., Owens, R.J., Jones, E.Y., Harlos, K., Stuart, D.I. and Esnouf, R.M. Benefits of automated crystallization plate tracking, imaging and analysis. Structure 13 (2005) 175-182.

An Efficient Algorithm for Frequent Itemset Mining on Data Streams

Xie Zhi-jun, Chen Hong, and Cuiping Li

School of Information, RenMin University, BeiJing, P.R. China 100872

Abstract. In order to mining frequent itemsets on data stream efficiently, a new approach was proposed in this paper. The memory efficient and accurate one-pass algorithm divides all the frequent itemsets into frequent equivalence classes and prune all the redundant itemsets except for those represent the GLB(Greatest Lower Bound) and LUB(Least Upper Bound) of the frequent equivalence class and the number of GLB and LUB is much less than that of frequent itemsets. In order to maintain these equivalence classes, A compact data structure, the frequent itemset enumerate tree (FIET) was proposed in the paper. The detailed experimental evaluation on synthetic and real datasets shows that the algorithm is very accurate in practice and requires significantly lower memory than Jin and Agrawal's one pass algorithm.

1 Introduction

Many real applications need to handle data streams, such as stock tickers, click streams, sensor net works and telecom call records. Mining frequent itemset forms the basis of algorithms for a number of other mining problems, including association mining, correlations mining[13].A main limitation of the existing work on frequent itemset mining is the high memory requirements when the support level is quite low or the distinct items is large .

In this paper, we present a new approach for frequent itemset mining on data stream. Our work addresses three major challenges in frequent itemset mining in a streaming environment. Firstly, we have proposed a method for finding frequent itemset while keeping limited memory,the most important of our algorithm is it can handle large number of distinct items and small support levels using a reasonable amount of memory. Secondly, we have developed an algorithm which is accurate in practice and in theory, At any time,the accuracy is 100% ,while other algorithms such as In-Core[11] developed by Jin and Agrawal which is the most accurate algorithm until now only in several cases can reach 100% and when ε increase ,the accuracy is decrement . Thirdly, we have designed a new data structure FIET(Frequent Itemset Enumeration Tree) and a novel approach to maintain it. A number of other implementation optimizations were proposed to support efficient execution. In the end, we have carried out a detailed evaluation using both synthetic and real dataset. Experiment results show that it has significant performance advantage over other approaches for mining frequent itemset in data streams.

P. Perner (Ed.): ICDM 2006, LNAI 4065, pp. 474–491, 2006.
© Springer-Verlag Berlin Heidelberg 2006

The rest of the paper is organized as follows: In Section 2,we will discuss the related work, In section 3, we will give the problem statement and give the maintenance algorithm in section 4.In section 5,the experiment result will be discussed.

2 Related Work

Processing of streaming data has received a lot of attention within the last couple of years [3, 5, 7, 9] .More recently, attention has been paid to the area of frequent itemset mining [8, 15].

The work closest to our work on handling streaming data is by Jin and Agrawal[11]. They have presented a one pass algorithm that does not allow false negatives and has a deterministic bound on false positives. They achieve this through an approach called in-core frequent itemset mining: At any given time, they maintain a set K of frequently occurring items and their counts. When read an element from the sequence, either increment its count in the set K or insert in the set with a count of 1.When |K|>1/θ,decrement the count of each element in the set K, and delete elements whose count has become zero. The difference between our approach and theirs are two aspects: first our algorithm is very accurate in theory and in practice, at any time, the accuracy is 100% while their algorithm only in several cases can reach 100% and when ε increase ,the accurate is decrement. Second our algorithm is very efficient in space requirements. We divided the frequent itemset into equivalent classes, and only maintain the frequent itemsets which represent the GLB(Greatest Lower Bound) and LUB(Least Upper Bound) of the classes, other frequent itemsets can be pruned .While in their algorithm, they must maintain all the 2-itemset and the count. Mankuand and Motwani[15] also presented a one pass algorithm that did not allow false negatives and has a provable bound on false positives. They achieved this through an approach called lossy counting. Their algorithm need an out-of-core structure, and lower than In-core [11 mentioned by Jin and Agrawal in accuracy and memory efficient. Giannella et al. had developed a technique for dynamically updating frequent patterns on streaming data[8].They create a variation of FP-tree,called FP-stream,for time-sensitive mining of frequent patterns.As our experimental results have shown, the memory requirements of our approach are significantly lower than those FP-tree. Comparing with the Apriori algorithm [2, 1], which require two or more passes. Several algorithms have required only two passes. This includes the FP-tree based approach by Han and Coworkers[13].The two pass algorithm does not extend to a one pass algorithm with any guarantees on accuracy, as our experimental results have shown, the memory requirements for maintaining the frequent patterns summary increase rapidly when the support levels are low. Our approach has the advantages when the number of distinct itemset is large and/or the support level is low.

3 Problem Statement

Given a set of items $\sum$(where the $\sum$ is not fixed) ,a data stream DS wherein each transaction is a subset of $\sum$,and a threshold s which is called the minimum support(minsup),0<s≤1, the frequent itemset mining problem is to find all itemsets that occur in at least s|DS| transactions. We assume that there is a lexicographical order among the items in $\sum$ and we use $X \prec Y$ to denote that item X is lexicographically smaller than item Y. Furthermore, an itemset can be represented by a sequence, wherein items are lexicographically ordered. For instance,{A,C,D} is represented by ACD,given $A \prec C \prec D$. We also use $\prec$ to denote the lexicographical order between two itemsets. For instance, $AC \prec ACD \prec CDE$.

Our problem is to mine frequent itmeset in the N transactions in a data stream. Suppose N is the length of data stream DS at present, i.e |N|=|DS|. Each transaction has a time stamp, which is used as the tid (transaction id) of the transaction. Figure 1 is an example with $\sum$={A,C,D,E,T,W},We use this example throughout the paper with minimum support s=1/2.

To find frequent itemset on a data stream we first construct a frequent itemset enumeration tree (FIET) in the memory, and then divide all itemsets into equivalence classes by their tid, then found the GLB and the LUB of every class and prune the other items except the frequent itemset represents the GLB and LUB of the class. Second we update the equivalence classes in FIET.

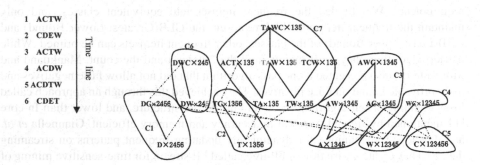

Fig. 1. A Running Example   **Fig. 2.** Lattice of frequent itemsets with equivalence classes

4 Mining and Maintenance Algorithm

In this section, we will give the mining and maintenance algorithm, we first give the concept and some properties of equivalence class in section 4.1, and then briefly explain the principles of maintenance and some implementation optimization in section 4.4.

4.1 Equivalence Class

According to the apriori property, any subset of a frequent itemset is also frequent, the number of frequent itemsets grows very quickly as the minimum support threshold is decrease. One of the solutions to these problems is closed itmest.

Let T and I ,T $\subseteq$ DS and I $\subseteq$ $\sum$,be subsets of all transactions until now and the set of all items respectively. The concept of closed itemset is based on the two following functions f and g:

$$f(T)=\{i \in I \mid \forall t \in T, i \in t\} \quad g(I)=\{t \in DS \mid \forall i \in I, i \in t\}$$

Function f returns the set of itemsets included in all the transactions belong to T, while function g returns the set of transactions supporting a given itemset I.

Definition 1(closure operator C). An itemset I is said to be closed if and only if

$$C(I)=f(g(I))=f \circ g(I)=I$$

Where the composite function c=f $\circ$ g is called Galois operator or closure operator C.

Lemma 1. Given an itemset X and any i $\in$ I ,if g(X)=g(i), $\Rightarrow$ i$\in$ C(x).

Proof. Since g(X$\cup$i)=g(x) $\cap$g(i),and g(x)=g(i), $\Rightarrow$ g(X$\cup$i)=g(x) ,

$$\Rightarrow \quad f(g(X\cup i))=f(g(X)),\text{Then } C(X\cup i)=C(x), \Rightarrow i \in C(x)$$

From the lemma 1 we know that the closure operator defines a set of equivalence classes over the lattice of frequent itemsets,i.e.,two itemsets belong to the same equivalence class iff they have the same closure,i.e.they are supported by the same set of transactions. So we can get the definition of equivalence class.

Definition 2(Equivalence class). A set of itemsets in a lattice of frequent itemsets is said to belong to the same equivalence class,C , if

1. Given any two items I and I' in C which satisfy I $\prec$ I', any intermediate items I'' satisfying I $\prec$ I'' $\prec$ I' will also be in C.

2. All the items with the same closure belong to the same equivalence class.

Figure 2 shows the lattice of frequent itemsets derived from the sample data stream reported in Figure 1 mined with min_sup=1/2.We can see that the itemset with the same closure are grouped in the same equivalence class. Each equivalence class contains elements sharing the same tidset .

All the possible frequent itemsets can be organized into the equivalence classes C and each frequent item is represented with an element of the equivalence class. An equivalence class is a partially order set (C, $\prec$), in which every pair of elements in C has a Least Upper Bound(LUB) and one or more Greatest Lower Bound(GLB) within C.

Definition 3(LUB and GLB). Given a set of elements E in an equivalence class C, the least upper bound(LUB) of E is an element u$\in$C such that e $\prec$ u for all e$\in$E and there exists no u' such that e $\prec$ u' for all e$\in$E and u' $\prec$ u . Likewise, the greatest lower bound(GLB) of E is an element $l \in C$ such that $l \prec e$ for all $e \in E$ and there exists no l'such that l' $\prec e$ for all $e \in E$ and $l \prec l'$. LUB are unique.

Lemma 2. Given two itemset X and Y,if $X \subset Y$,and g(X)=g(Y),then C(X)=C(Y).

Proof. If g(X)=g(Y),then f(g(X))=f(g(Y))   then C(X)=C(Y)

From the lemma 2, given a generator X, if we find an already mined Closed Itemsets Y that set_includes X,where X and Y has the same support and tidset, we can conclude that C(x)=C(Y). In a equivalence class,the closed itmeset Y is actually the LUB of the class[14], and all the other items in the equivalence class is the generator of LUB and the GLB is the most general among all generators[14]. Hence we can prune the generator except the GLB and LUB without losing any information. Since the frequent itemsets which has been pruned can be inferred from them. For instance, the equivalence class C7 in figure 2,its LUB is "TAWC"(which is unique in an equivalence class) and its GLB is "TA" and "TW".We call "TAC", "TAW" ,"TCW" ,"TA", "TW" the generator of"TAWC",but "TA","TW" is the minimal generator. So in a frequent class we can only store the GLB and the LUB. In this example, the generators TAC ,TWC and TAW can be inferred from the TAWC and TA, TC, since TA $\cup$ TW=TAW and TAWC-TAW=C ,so TAC =TA$\cup$C , TWC= TW$\cup$C .Hence we can prune all the other itemsets except for the itemsets which represent the GLB and the LUB in a equivalence class. Obviously, the number of LUB and GLB is much less than the number of items. Based of this concept, we first construct a FIET in the memory, plot out the equivalence classes in FIET, and prune redundant frequent items except for the itemsets which represent the GLB and LUB of equivalence classes.

A frequent equivalence class can be represented by a structure, C=(lup,tidset), in which lup is the least upper bound of the class and all the itemsets in the class has the same tidsets.We use C.lup and C.tidset to represent each component of C respectively. For example,the class C7 in Figure 1 is represented as C7=(TAWC,135).

4.2 The Frequent Itemset Enumeration Tree

We propose an in-memory data structure, the Frequent itemset enumeration tree(FIET),to monitor a dynamically selected set of itemsets that enable us to answer the query "what are the current frequent itemsets" at any time. Similar to prefix tree,each node n_I in a Frequent Itemset Enumeration Tree (FIET) represent a frequent itemset I. However, unlike a prefix tree, which maintains all itemsets, a FIET only maintains the frequent itemsets which represent the GLB and LUB in each equivalence classes. As long as the conceptual in the stream is not too dramatic, most itemsets do not change their status(from frequent to infrequent or from infrequent to frequent), and do not cause change of status of many involved nodes. If an itemset do not change its status, nothing needs to be done except for increasing or decreasing the counts of the involved itemsets. If it does change its status from infrequent to frequent, as we will show, the change must come through the boundary nodes (we call them sensitive nodes in FIET), which means the change to the entire tree structure is still limited. We further divide itemsets on the boundary into two categories,which correspond to the boundary between frequent and non-frequent; we divide all the infrequent boundary itemset into the same equivalence class and mark it as non-frequent classes, according to property 1,all the itemset in non-frequent class do not need to enumerate; actually, all the member of non-frequent class are single items(sensitive nodes) and the size of the non-frequent class is very small. As for the frequent itemsets, all the itmeset divided into the same equivalence class if they have the same tid, we pruned the redundant itemsets except for the itemsets represent the GLB and LUB. For instance, In figure 3 ,In frequent equivalence class C5, TAWC is the LUB of C5, and TA,TW is the GLB, other redundant itemset can be omitted, we mark them use double strikethrough. Equivalence class C1 is a non-frequent equivalence class, item "E" has only appeared in transaction 2 and transaction 6, which is infrequent, we simply put it into non-frequent equivalence class, according property 1, all the itemset in non-frequent equivalence class do not need to enumerate; When the new item appear the first time, we also put it into the non-frequent equivalence class. when the items in non-frequent equivalence class become frequent in the future, we will enumerate it with other active sensitive nodes to get the frequent itemsets. For frequent equivalence class ,we define specific actions to maintain them when there are concept drift in data streams (section 4.4.1).

Property 1 enable us to prune a large amount of itemsets from the FIET, which enable us to mine frequent itemsets using an efficient and compact data structure.

Property 1. If n_I is an infrequent node, then any node n_J where $J \supset I$ represent an infrequent itemset.

Proof. Property 1 is derived from the apriori property.

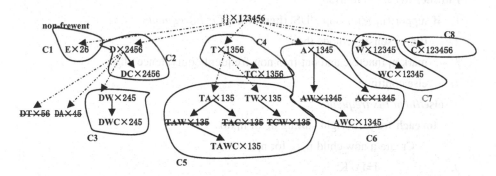

Fig. 3. The Frequent Itemset Tree Corresponding to the sample dataset

A FIET achieves its compactness and time efficiency by prune a large amount of the itemsets. It prunes the descendants of n_I and the descendants of n_I 's siblings' nodes that subsume itemset I. In Figure 3, If item E is infrequent, we do not enumerate the subtree under E , Further more, we do not union E with its siblings such as D, T ,A, W ,C to generate E's child nodes. AS for the frequent itemset , if the itemset is become infrequent during the enumerating, we can stop to enumerate it to generate its descendants. For instance, For the item D, when DT and DA is no longer frequent, we can stop to enumerate it. As a result, a large amount of the itemsets are pruned to reduce the enumerate time. Thus the space and time efficient is improved.

4.3 Building the Frequent Itemset Enumeration Tree

In a FIET,we store the following information for each node n_I : i)the itmeset I itself, ii)the tidset iii)the class type,which was marked by the node in a frequent equivalence classes or infrequent equivalence class. (Similar to the IT_Tree in the Charm[12],Each node in the FIET, represented by an itemset-tidset pair,$X \times t(X)$,show in Figure 3,such as TAWC$\times$135).In order to efficiently maintain the FIET, we use different set of buckets to store the equivalence classes. We only store the GLB and LUB for each of the classes in the buckets.

To build a FIET, we firstly create a root node n_0. Secondly, we create $|\Sigma|$ child nodes for n0, i.e., each $i \in \Sigma$ corresponds to a child node n_i, we call these nodes **sensitive nodes**. The sensitive node has two status,inactive and active. In general, they are inactive. They will be active when the new transaction has change their support (the detail will be discussed in section 4.4.1).After having built all the sensitive node, Enumerate procedure on each node n_i will be called. Pseudo code for the Enumerate algorithm is given in Figure 4. During the enumeration, we can divide all the frequent itemset into equivalence classes and prune the redundant itemsets except for those represent GLB and LUB. The result of Enumeration of the sample data in Figure 1 is shown on Figure 3.Note that before we create $|\Sigma|$ child nodes for n_0 ,we must sort these

Enumerate(n_I,DS,minsup)

1. **if** support(n_I)<minsup . |DS| **then** //Item I is infrequent
2.   if n_I is sensitive node then
3.   mark n_I inactive and put into non-frequent equivalence class
4.   else continue
5. **else**//Item I is frequent
6.   **foreach** frequent right sibling n_K of n_I **do**
7   Create a new child $n_{I \cup K}$ for n_I :
9.   I=I $\cup$ K
10.   T=t(I)$\cap$t(K)
11   Put I$\times$T into equivalence frequent class
12.   foreach child n_K of n_I do
13.   **Enumerate**(n_K,DS,minsup)

Fig. 4. The Enumerate algorithm

child nodes base on the weight of the items. The definition of the weight of an item is mentioned in Charm[12].For instance in Figure 3, the sequence of child nodes for n_0 sorted based on the weight is {E,D,T,A,W,C}.

Enumerate is a depth_first procedure that visits itemsets in lexicographical order. In lines 1-4 of Figure 4, if a node is found to be infrequent and is the sensitive node, it is marked as inactive ,and is put into non-frequent equivalence class. We do not enumerate it until the node become frequent in the future .However, when the node in non-frequent equivalence class become frequent, we will explore it at once. In lines 5-11, when items I is frequent, we do an enumerate operation with siblings nodes of I in lexicographical order,i.e.,we do a union operation of the itemset (in line 9) and perform intersection of tidsets(in line 10) and divide it into equivalence frequent class (line11).

4.4 Maintenance of FIET

In this section, we will first propose the underlying principles for maintaining the equivalence classes in the FIET, and then give some implementation optimization. At last we will give the maintain algorithm. We denote the set of frequent equivalence classes in the FIET as Ψ , and the new set of frequent equivalence classes as Ψ '.We consider the case that the incremental update when a new transaction is coming .

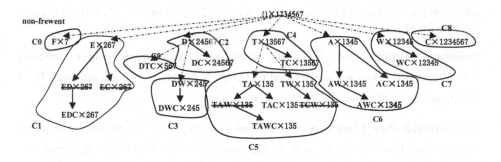

Fig. 5. The FIET after insertion of transaction(DEFTC)

4.4.1 The Principle of Maintenance

As we discussed before, we divide the equivalence class into two categories, frequent equivalence class and non-frequent class. New transaction t can affect both the frequent equivalence classes and non-frequent classes. For the frequent equivalence class, a new transaction t can affect an equivalence class in Ψ in several ways. First, it can cause the support of the equivalence class to change without affecting the partition of the lattices. Second, it might cause the equivalence class to split, creating some new equivalence classes.The final possibility is that the equivalence class might not be affected at all. We define the operation Match as follows:

Definition 3(matching). A transaction is said to match a itemset-tidset pair in FIET if the transaction match the itemset-tidset pair in all the itemset except for those tidset .Given a set of itemset-tidset pair,C,a transaction t is said to match C if it matches all the itemset-tidset pair in C.

For example,in Figure 4,the transaction t=(DEFTC) matches both the pair DC×2456 and the set of pairs in Class C4.

When a new transaction matches the least upper bound of an equivalence class, the new transaction t will cause the support of the equivalence to be changed. More importantly, we know that the transaction will match every pairs in the equivalence class since the class's least upper bound is the most specific pair in the whole equivalence class. In this case the equivalence class can't split.

Proposition 1 (Value Modified Class). Given an frequent equivalence class C in Ψ ,if a new transaction matches C.lup, C need not to be split and C.tidset muste be modified.

For example,in Figure 5,because C2.lup match new transaction t=(DEFTC),we update the tidset of C2 from "2456"to "24567".

When t matches only a certain portion of C.lup,i.e. t can only match a portion of the pairs in C, C must be split into two portions, one in which all pairs match t and one in which all pairs do not. A new transaction t partly affects a class C only if there is some intersection between t and C.lup.

Definition 4 (intersection). We say that transaction t has an intersection(or intersects) with a class C if t does not match C but t $\cap$C.lup$\neq\Phi$.Given Ψ ,we use intersect(Ψ ,t) to denote the set of classes in Ψ that intersect t.

Proposition 2 (New Class Generator). Given a new transaction t, an existing frequent equivalence class C must be split if (1)C intersects with t and C is the class that contributes to the GLB$\{Y|Y=C'$.lup$\cap t\}$,C'$\in \Psi$;and (2) there does not exist any class C''$\in \Psi$ such that C''.lup=C.lup$\cap t$; If these two conditions are satisfied, we call C a new class generator since the splitting will result in a new equivalence class.

The first condition of proposition 2 ensures that given all classes which generate the same upper bound for the new class C_n,the one that is the most general will be the new class generator, and the first condition according to the property 2 as follows.

Property 2. Given all classes which generate the same upper bound for the new class C_n,the one that is the most general (i.e the GLB) will be the new class generator.

Proof. Given any equivalence class C1 and C2 in FIET, suppose C1 is more general than C2,i.e,C1.lup $\subseteq$ C2.lup. For a new transaction t,t $\cap$ C1=t $\cap$ C2.If any itemset X in

C1 match transaction t,from lemma 2,we know that $X \subseteq C1.lup$,therefore $X \subseteq C2.lup$ since $C1.lup \subset C2.lup$.

For example, in Figure 4,given the new transaction t=(DEFTC),we have $C2 \cap t=C3 \cap t=\{DC\}$,Since C3 is the upper bound of $C2(DC \subseteq DWC)$,C2 will become a new class generator for t if it satisfies the second condition of proposition 2.Explaining the second condition in proposition 2 is more simple. Since $t\cap C$ represents the upper bound of the potential new class,there is no need to generate a new class if such an frequent equivalence class already exists as indicated by the existence of a class $C'' \in \Psi$ such that $C''.lup=t\cap C.lup$.The split operation of a class is defined as follows:

Definition 5 (Split Operation). Given a generator class $Cg(Cg \subseteq \Psi)$ and a new transaction t, the split operation on it, and Cg generates a new class Cn and a modified generator C'g ,the split operation as follows:

Cn.lup=Cg.lup$\cap$t ; Cn.tidset= Cg.tidset$\cup$t.tidset ; C'g.lup=Cg.lup ; C'g.tidset =Cg.tidset

The last proposition involves a simple category of equivalence classes that neither match nor intersect the new transaction t.

Proposition 3 (Dumb Class). If an equivalence class C in Ψ is neither a modified class nor a generator, there is no need to change C,We call C as a dumb class.

When the itemset in the frequent equivalence class become infrequent, we need to delete it at once. In fact, all the itemset in the same equivalence have the same support, If the items in a class become infrequent, all the items in the equivalence will become infrequent. Therefore we need to delete the whole equivalence class. However, if the classes contain a sensitive node, we must mark it infrequent and put it into non-frequent class. For example in Figure 5, if the item in C3 becomes infrequent, we only need to delete the class C3 simply. But if the items in class C6 become infrequent, we need put the sensitive node "A " into non-frequent class, because we can get the potentially frequent itemset in the future by enumerate the sensitive node "A " when it become frequent.

When a transaction contains the item which is appeared first time, we put it into the non-frequent class and mark it sensitive node. For example, in Figure 5,transaction (DEFTC) contain item "F", which is appeared first time, we only put it into non-frequent class and mark it sensitive node.

When the new transaction t affects the non-frequent class, it only cause the support of the items to change. Because all the members of non-frequent class are sensitive node and their status are inactive when the support of the items exceed the threshold of minsup,we need to chang their status to active and the procedure Enumerate will be called to create new frequent equivalence classes in the end.For example,in Figure 5,when the new transaction t(DEFTC) comes in, it increases the support of item "E" in non-frequent class, and causes the item "E" to change its status from infrequent to frequent. Then the procedure Enumerate is called and a new frequent equivalence class C1 is created.

Now,we discuss the sensitive node. The status of the sensitive nodes is inactive in general, it will be change to active in the follows conditions:(1)It is be changed to frequent from infrequent and it is in the non-frequent class; Such as the node "E" in class C1 in Figure 5. (2)Its support has been increased and it is in the frequent equivalence classes, such as the node "D" in class C2 and "T" in C5. We can recover some frequent itemsets which had been omitted previously ,and we can get them by re-enumerating the active sensitive nodes.For example,in Figure 5,when the new transaction t(DEFTC) comes in,the nodes "E" ,"ED","EC","EDC"in C1 and "DT" in C9 change to frequent,we can recover them only by re-enumerate the active sensitive nodes "E" "D" and "T".

Above all lay the foundation for maintaining the FIET .As we know, the maintenance time complexity is linear to the number of frequent equivalence classes,since the number of classes is much less than the number of the items, Our algorithm is much more time efficient than those algorithms linear to the number of items.

4.4.2 Implemention Optimization

As we have discussed in section 4.1, all the itemset and tidset pairs have the same tidset in the same frequent equivalence class.In order to improve the space efficiencies and and reduce redundant space , we use a structure C=(lup,tidset) represent the frequent equivalence class, and all the items in the same class can share the same tidset. If the number of the class is huge,the space cost is very large. We found that different equivalence class in FIET may share some base itemset and tidset,there are still some redundancies among them.In Figure 6 (a),the lup of class C2 is {DC} and the lup of Class C3 is {DWC}. It can be observed that {DC} is actually redundant between C2 and C3. As for the tidset, we can see that the tidset of

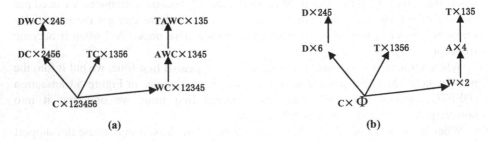

Fig. 6. Family relationship in FIET

C2 is {2456} while the tidset of C3 is {245}, and {245} is also redundant between C2 and C3.If we can remove this kind of redundancy, lots of storage space can be spared.According to the basic properties of itemset-tidset pairs mentioned by CHARM[12],We have found some interesting relationship between the frequent equivalence classes in the frequent lattice: suppose class C1 is more general than class C2,C1.tidset is the superset of C2.tidset,and C2.lup is the superset of C1.lup.As for the scenario of updating FIET,we can found the relationship also exists in the newly generated equivalence class and its generators according to the definition 7, i.e,generator.lup $\supset$ newClass.lup, newClass.tidset $\supset$ generator.tidset. Based on this property, we know that maintain the itemset-tidset pairs in the new frequent equivalence class can be done by simply storing the difference between the new class and the generator .The generator store the difference of the lup while the newly generated class store the difference of the tidset. We call this difference the increment set of the new equivalence class. For example, in Figure 6(b),suppose C3 ={DWC×245}is the generator of C2={DC×2456} ,so class C3 only store {W},and C2 only store {6}.There is a linkage between the new class and its generator since each new class has a unique generator,and all the linkages between the new class and its generator in the FIET is acuter a tree relationship,we call it a family tree relationship, show in Figure 6 (b).We can get the actual lup and tidset pair of a class by combining the node along its family linkage path from the node representing the class to the root. For example, in Figure 6(b),to found the lup of C5{ TAWC×135},we can combine{C} ∪ {W}∪ {A}∪ {T},if we want to found the tidset of C7{ WC×12345},we need to combine {135} ∪ {4}∪ {2}.When denote the family relationship in the FIET,we only need to add a domain in the node to represent this linkage.

4.4.3 The Realization of Maintenance Algorithm

In what follows,we will introduce the algorithm maintain, which updates the FIET and the set of equivalence classes for new transaction .

Algorithm maintain (Ψ ,t,DS,minsup)

{ Ψ *is the set of class in FIET,t is a new transaction,DS is the Data Stream,minsup is the threshold of support*}

1. Divide all frequent equivalence classes C with C's cardinality into buckets B[0]…B[n],non-frequent class in B[n+1].*//B[i] is the ith Bucket*

2.let B'[i]= $\emptyset$ (i=0,...n){*the set of bucket B' is for the new and modified classes*}

3.for i=0 to n do //*deal with frequent equivalence classes*

4.   for each class C in B[i] do

5.   if |C.tidset|<minsup.|DS| then// *if Class C is infrequent then delete it*

6.   if C contain the sensitive node and does not in B[n+1] then put the item into B[n+1],delete C

   else delete C

7.   else // *Class C is frequent*

8.   if t matches C.lup then

9.   C.tidset=C.tidset $\cup$ t

10.   else

11.   MaxMatch=C.lup $\cap$ t

12.   if |MaxMatch|=0 then break;// *C is dumb class*

13   if $\neg \exists X \in$ B'[j] (j=0..i-1,i+1..n) and X.lup=MaxMatch then //*C is a generator*

14.   Split C into Cn and Cg'

15.   Cn.parent=Cg',Cg'.child=Cn

16.   add Cn to B'[j] and Cg' to B'[i]

17   end if

18.   end if

19.   end for

20.   end for

21.   for each itemset-tidset pairs P in B[n+1] do

22.   if t match P.item then

23.   P.tidset=P.tidset $\cup$ t

24.   if |P.tidset|> minsup|DS| then

25.   mark p 's status to active

26.   end for

27.   for all the active itemset-tidset pairs P do

28.   Enuerate(P,DS,minsup)

In algorithm **maintain**, we apply the three propositions for updating the FIET, we first put all the classes into a set of buckets and sort the classes based on ascending cardinality according to property 2.We refer to |C.lup| as the cardinality of C. A different set of bucket B'[0]...B'[n] are initialized to store the updated and new equivalence classes. The main loop (line 3-20) iterates through the classes in each buckets. For each class C in bucket B[i], we first check whether the class become infrequent when the transaction comes in, If it becomes infrequent then it is deleted at once(line 6).In line 8-9,check for a value modified class and corresponding update is performed; in line 12 ,in the case of Class C is a dumb class,it is filtered off. In line 13-16,hasing confirmed C is a generator of new class, a split operation was carried on C based on definition 5. Line 21-26 is the case that an itemset in non-frequent class is changed to frequent when the transaction t comes in.

In addition, so far our algorithm only handles one transaction in one update. In reality, there are situations in which data are burst and multiple transactions need to be deleted during one update. However, it is not difficult to adapt our algorithm to handle multiple transactions in one update. Originally, if an update contains a batch of transactions, we can recursively partition on both the existing classes and the set of transactions, Each partition do the update similar to the algorithm maintain.

5   Experimental Results

In this section, we evaluate our new algorithm using a number of synthetic and real datasets.We focus on a number of different aspects of our algorithm:(1) Comparing the memory requirements of our algorithm with those of apriori and fp-tree based algorithms;(2) Evaluating the execution time and memory requirements of our new algorithms with increasing dataset size and decreasing support levels;(3) Evaluating the accuracy of our algorithm. For comparing our algorithm against the Apriori algorithm,we used a well-known public distribution from Borgelt[4].Earlier versions of this code have been incorporated in a commercial data mining tool called Clementine.For Comparisions with FP-tree based algorithm,the implementation we used is from Goethals[10].All of our experiments are conducted on a PC with Inel Pentium IV processor and 1 GB memory, which runs Windows XP professional operation system.

5.1   Synthetic Datasets

The synthetic datasets we used were generated using a tool from IBM[2].Datasets generated from this tool have been widely used for evaluating frequent itemset and association mining implementations.

First we will focus on two datasets where conventional offline algorithm has performed well and we will show our algorithms ablility to handle very low support levels and a large number of distinct itmset. The first dataset we used is T10I4.N10K.The number of distinct itemsets is 10000, the average number of items per transaction is 10, and the average size of large itemsets is 4.

Figure 7 shows the memory requirements of apriori, fp-tree and our algorithms as the support threshold is varied from 0.1% to 1.0%. The number of transaction is 12 million. Because of high memory requirements,fp-tree could not be executed with support levels lower than 0.4%.This limitiation of the fp-tree approach has been identified by other experimental studies also[7].Up to the support level of 0.6%,the memory requirements of all versions is quite similar, except for fp-tree's memory requirements increase rapidly when the support level is less than 0.6%.The important property of our algorithm is that the memory requirements do not increase significantly as the support level is decreased.

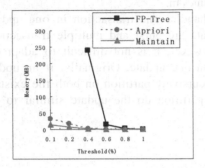
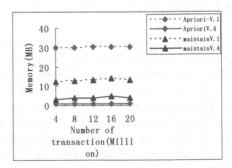

Fig. 7. Memory Requirements with changing Support level(T10.I4.N10K Dataset)

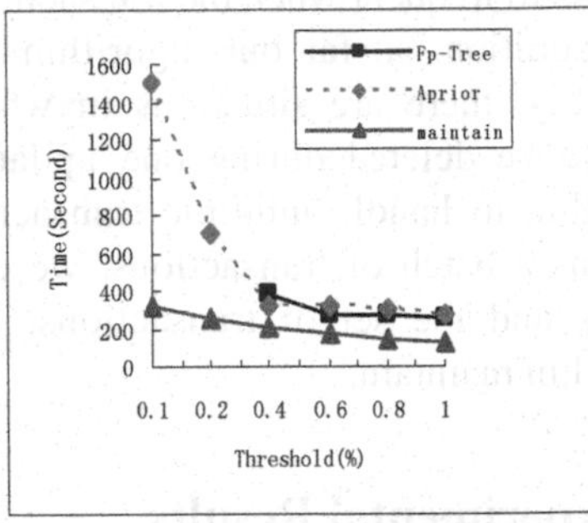

Fig. 8. Execution Time with changing Support Level (T10.I4.N10K Dataset)

Figure 8 compares the execution time. From the chart, we know that up to the support level of 0.4%,the execution time of all version is quite similar. However, appriori's execution time increase rapidly when the support level is less than 0.4%.As expected our algorithm has the lowest execution time among all of the algorithms.

Accuracy of an algorithm is defined as the fraction of reported frequent itemsets that are actually frequent.Obviously,the accuracy of apriori,fp-tree and maintain is always 100%,since any item in an equivalence classes will be deleted together with the whole class if it become infrequent in our algorithm.

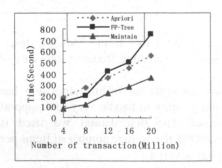

Fig. 9. Execution Time with Increasing Dataset Size(threshold=0.4%,T10.I4N10K)

Fig. 10. Memory requirements with increasing Datasize(T10.I4.N10k)

Figure 9 examine the execution times as the dataset is increased ,our algorithm is faster than apriori and fp-tree when the data size is varied.More importantly,our algorithms always give an accuracy of 100% when the threadhold is .4%.Figure 10 focuses on memory requirements with support level of .4% and .1%.Because of high memory requirements of fp-tree,our algorithm is only compared against apriori.At the support level of 0.4%,apriori is lower than our's,However,with threshold at.1%,our algorithm requires less than half the memory. Moreover, it is important to note that with 10,000 distinct items and a support level of .1%, the total memory requirements are only around 13 MB,which is less than the algorithm In-core[11] in the same environment, which requires 17 MB memory mentioned in [11].

The second dataset is T15.I6.N10k.We repeated the same set of experiments using this dataset.The results are shown in Figure 11,12,13 respectively.The key difference between this dataset and the previous dataset is the length of each transaction and each frequent itemset is higher.Our algorithm does not always outperform apriori with this dataset,especially in the case of up to the support level of 4% shown in Figure10. However,our algorithm does maintain very high accuracy of results on the datasets.With 12 million,16 million,20 million transactions,and with the support of .4%,our algorithm is faster than apriori.

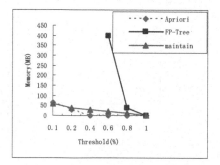

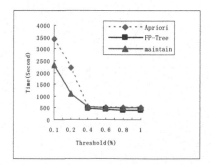

Fig. 11. Memory Requirements with changing Support level(T15.I6.N10K)

Fig. 12. Execution Time with changing Support Level (threshold=.4%,T15.I6.N10K)

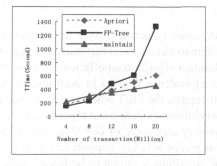

Fig. 13. Execution Time with Increasing Dataset Size(threshold=0.4%, T15.I6.N10K)

5.2 Real Dataset

The real dataset we use is the BMS-WEBView-1 dataset which contains several months of clickstream data from an e-commerce website,and is also used by Jin[11].The characteristics of the BMS-WebView-1 dataset are quite different from IBM synthetic datasets.The original dataset has almost 60,000 transactions and contains almost 500 distinct items.The maximum transation size is 267,while the average transaction size is just 2.5 .In our experiments,we duplicated and randomized the original dataset to obtain 1 million transactions,This has also been done in the In-core [11]. Because of the small size of data size and small number of distinct items,our algorithm is not always outperform apriori and fp-tree.However,our algorithm is still competitive in accurate and when the support level is very low ,just as show in Figrue 14,when the support level is lower than 0.4%,our algorithm is fast than apriori and fp-tree.In Figure 15,the memory cost of apriori is very low,because of the number of frequent itemset is relatively small.Although the cost of our algorithm is higher than that of apriori,we can see the absolute memory cost is not more than 10 MB. It is comes most from the initial data structure.

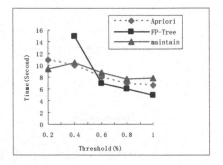
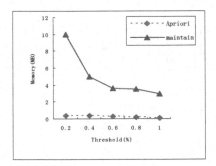

Fig. 14. Execution time with changing Support level(BMS-WebView-1)

Fig. 15. Memory requirements with Changing support level (BMS-WebView-1)

6 Conclusion

In this paper,we have developed a new approach for frequent itmeset mining.We have proposed a novel algorithm to discover and maintain all frequent itemsets for streaming environment. In the Maintain algorithm,an efficient in-memory data structure FIET is used to record all the equivalence Classes.In addition,we have developed efficient algorithm to incrementally update the FIET when newly-arrived transaction coming. Our detailed experimental evolution has shown our algorithm is very accurate in theory and practice, While the memory efficiency of our algorithm allow us to deal with large number of distinct items and/or very low support levels.At last,the memory usage and time complexity of our algorithm is shown to be linear in the number of equivalence classes in FIET.

References

1. R.Agrawal,H.Mannila,R.Srikant,H.Toivonent,and A.Inkeri Verkamo.Fast discovery of associantion rules.In U.Fayyad and et al,editors,Advances in knowledge Discovery and Data Mining,pages 307-328.AAAI press,Menlo Park,CA,1996.
2. R.Agrawal and R.Srikant. Fast algorithms for mining association rules.In Proc.1994 Int.conf.Very Large DataBases(VLDB'94),pages 487-499,Santiago,Chile,September 1994.
3. B.Babcock ,S.BAbu,M.Datar,R.Motwani,and J.Widom. Models and Issues in Data Stream systems.In Proceedings of the 2002 ACM Symposium on principles of Database Systems (PODS 2002)(Invited Paper).ACM Press,June 2002
4. Christan Borgelt.Apriori implementation.http://fuzzy.cs.UniMagdeburg.de/borgelt/ Software.
5. A.Dobra,J.Gehrke,M.Garofalakis,and R.Rastogi.Processing complex aggregate queries over data streams.In proc.of the 2002 ACM SIGMOD intl.Conf. on Management of Data,June 2002.
6. P.Domingos and G.Hulten.Mining high-speed data streams.In Proceedings of the ACM Conference on Knowledge and Data Discovery (SIGKDD),2000.
7. J.Gehrke,F.Korn,and D.Srivastava.On computing correlated aggregates over continual data streams.In Proc.of the 2001 ACM SIGMOD Intl.Conf.on Manaagement of Data,pages 13-24.acmpress,June 2001.
8. C.Giannella,Jiawei Han,Jian Pei,Xifeng yan,and P.S.Yu. Mining Frequent Patterns in Data Streams at Multiple Time Granularities.In Processding s of the NSF Workshop on Next Generation Data Mining,November 2002.
9. Phillip B.Gibbons and S.Tirthapura. Estimating simple functions on the union of data streams.In proc.of the 2001 ACM Symp.on parallel Algorithms and Architechtures,pages 281-291.ACM Press,August 2001.
10. Bart Goethals.Fp-tree implementation.http://www.cs.helsinki.fi/u/goethals/software/index. html.
11. R. Jin and G. Agrawal. An algorithm for in-core frequent itemset mining on streaming data. Submitted for Publication, 2004.
12. M.J.Zaki and C.Hsiao.Charm:An efficient algorithm for closed itemset mining.In 2nd SIAM Int'l confon Data Mining,2002
13. J.Han,J.Pei,and Y.Yin. Mining Frequent patterns without candidate generation.In Proceedings of the ACM SIGMOD Conference on Management of Data,2000.
14. Cuiping Li, Gao Cong, Anthony K. H. Tung, Shan Wang,"Incremental Maintainence of Quotient Cube for sum and Median" Proceedings of SIGKDD, p.226-235, August 2004 , Seattle,WA,USA
15. G.S.Manku and R.Motwain. Approximate Frequency Counts Over Data Streams. In proceedings of Conference on Very Large DataBase(VLDB),pages 346-357,2002.

Discovering Key Sequences in Time Series Data for Pattern Classification

Peter Funk and Ning Xiong

Department of Computer Science and Electronics
Mälardalen University
SE-72123 Västerås, Sweden
{peter.funk, ning.xiong@mdh.se}

Abstract. This paper addresses the issue of discovering key sequences from time series data for pattern classification. The aim is to find from a symbolic database all sequences that are both indicative and non-redundant. A sequence as such is called a key sequence in the paper. In order to solve this problem we first we establish criteria to evaluate sequences in terms of the measures of evaluation base and discriminating power. The main idea is to accept those sequences appearing frequently and possessing high co-occurrences with consequents as indicative ones. Then a sequence search algorithm is proposed to locate indicative sequences in the search space. Nodes encountered during the search procedure are handled appropriately to enable completeness of the search results while removing redundancy. We also show that the key sequences identified can later be utilized as strong evidences in probabilistic reasoning to determine to which class a new time series most probably belongs.

1 Introduction

Data mining attains growing importance to ease the knowledge acquisition bottleneck. It can be defined as efficiently discovering useful knowledge and information which are hidden somewhere in large databases. Extracting valuable knowledge from stored records/examples has been recognized as a non-trivial process of identifying novel, valid and potentially useful data patterns, and ideally also, to understand these data patterns for specific purpose [3].

Time series data bases present a relatively new research area for data mining. Unlike static databases where objects are described by attributes which are time independent, a time series database contains profiles of time-varying variables wherein pieces of data are associated with a timestamp and are meaningful only for a specific segment in a period. Analyses of time relevant data patterns are crucial for acquiring necessary knowledge to understand and predict the behavior of complex, dynamic processes.

Our paper studies the problem of key sequence discovery from symbolic time series data. The input is a collection of pairs of time series profiles and the associated classes. Each time series is a list of symbols corresponding to events that occurred in consecutive time segments. The task is to find all non-redundant sequences that are evaluated as frequent and indicative in discerning certain object classes. The non-

P. Perner (Ed.): ICDM 2006, LNAI 4065, pp. 492–505, 2006.
© Springer-Verlag Berlin Heidelberg 2006

redundancy of a sequence requires that it not contain any other sequence that has been identified to be indicative of the same class as it. A sequence that is both non-redundant and indicative is termed as a key sequence. The key sequences identified can later be utilized as strong evidences in probabilistic reasoning to determine to which class a new time series most probably belongs.

This study was primarily motivated by our AI project in stress medicine which aims at diagnosis of stresses based on sensor readings collected during patient respirations. Experimentally a patient is investigated through a series of 40-80 breathing cycles (including inhalation and exhalation). The classification of dysfunctional patterns for each breathing cycle has been implemented in the previous work using case based reasoning [12]. The next step is further to estimate the category of stress according to the series of breathing dysfunctions detected for successive respiration cycles. Related medical research has revealed that certain transitions of breathing patterns over time may possess high co-occurrence with stress categories of interest [16]. Finding such sequences from time series data is thus beneficial in offering valuable information to support clinical diagnoses.

Beside, there are many other application scenarios to which the work of this paper would be relevant. For instance, in health monitoring of engineering equipments, original sensor readings can be converted into discrete symbols [15], and some critical changes in time series of measurements like swell, sag, impulsive transients, might be signs indicating a present or potential anomaly. In telecommunications, useful information can be obtained from sequences of alarms produced by switches for analysis and prediction of network faults. In defense, sequences of deployments/actions of enemies would possibly betray their tactical intentions. Finally, in a medical scenario again, a data sequence of symptoms exhibited on a patient may help to forecast a disease that follows the emerging symptoms.

Some researches into time series data mining have been conducted recently. Three embedding methods were proposed by [5] to transform time series data into a vector space for classification purpose. Keogh and his colleagues addressed the issue of dimensionality reduction for indexing large time series databases [9] and also for fast search in these databases [10]. In [20] a family of three unsupervised methods was suggested to identify optimal and valid features given multivariate time series data. Similarity mining in time series was tackled by [8] and various methods for efficient retrieval of similar time sequences were discussed in [2, 6, 13, 19]. Algorithms for mining association rules were handled in [11, 14, 18] to model and predict time series behaviors in dynamic systems, and the application of association mining to disclose stock prices relations in time series was presented in [7].

This paper focuses on symbolic sequential data and proposes a novel approach to discovery of key sequences for time series classification. The remainder of the paper is organized as follows. In section 2 we briefly formulate our problem and show what kind of data sequences are targeted at. Sequences are evaluated in section 3 for distinguishing indicative ones. Section 4 details a sequence search algorithm with simulation results. Then, in section 5, we explain the utility of the discovered sequences in probabilistic diagnosis and classification. Finally the paper is concluded with summary remarks in section 6.

2 Problem Statements

To clearly present the proposed work, we now give descriptions of the various terms and concepts that are related. We begin with the definitions about time series, sequences, and time series databases, and then we precisely formulate the problem this paper aims to tackle.

Definition 1. A time series (profile) is a series of elements occurred sequentially over time, $X = \langle x(1), x(2), \cdots x(i), \cdots, x(n) \rangle$, where i indexes the time segment corresponding to a recorded element and n can be very large.

The elements x in time series can be numerical or symbolic values. Numeric values in time series may depict the evolution of a continuous variable as time elapsed, while symbolic values correspond to discrete events that happened or agent actions that were taken in successive time segments. In the following discussions we restrict our attention to symbolic time series consisting of discrete symbols.

Moreover, every time series profile has an inherent class. The previous time series data are assumed to have been classified and they are stored in a database together with their associated classes to facilitate data mining. A formal definition of time series database in the context of classification is given as follows:

Definition 2. A time series database is a set of pairs $\{(X_i, Z_i)\}_{i=1}^{K}$, where X_i denotes a time series profile and Z_i the class assigned to X_i and K is the number of time series cases in the database.

With a time series database at hand, the data mining process involves analyzing sequences that are included in the database. A sequence of a time series profile is formally described in definition 3.

Definition 3. A sequence S of a time series profile $X = \langle x(1), x(2), \cdots, x(n) \rangle$ is a list consisting of elements taken from contiguous positions of X, i.e., $S = \langle x(k), x(k+1), \cdots, x(k+m-1) \rangle$ with $m \leq n$ and $1 \leq k \leq n - m + 1$.

Usually there is a very large amount of sequences included in the time series database. But only a part of them that carry useful information for estimating consequences are in line with our interest. Such sequences are referred to as indicative sequences and defined in the following:

Definition 4. A sequence is regarded as indicative given a time series database provided that

1) it appears in sufficient amount of time series profiles of the database;
2) the discriminating power of it, assessed upon the database, is above a specified threshold.

A measure for discriminating power together with the arguments that lie behind this definition will be elaborated in the next section. The intuitive explanation is that an indicative sequence is such a one that, on one hand, appears frequently in the database, and on the other hand, exhibits high co-occurrence with a certain class.

Obviously, should a sequence be indicative, another sequence that contains it as subsequence may also be indicative for predicting the outcome. However, if these both are indicative of the same consequent, the second sequence is considered as redundant with respect to the first one because it conveys no more information. Redundant sequences can be easily recognized by checking possible inclusion between sequences encountered. The goal here is to find sequences that are not only indicative but also non-redundant and independent of each other.

Having given necessary notions and clarifications we can now formally define our problem to be addressed as follows:

Given a time series database consisting of time series profiles and associated classes, find a set of indicative sequences $\{S_1, S_2, ..., S_p\}$ that satisfy the following two criteria:

1) For any i, $j \in \{1, 2, ...p\}$ neither $S_i \subseteq S_j$ nor $S_j \subseteq S_i$ if S_i and S_j are indicative of a same consequent;

2) For any sequence S that is indicative, $S \in \{S_1, S_2, ..., S_p\}$ if S is not redundant with respect to S_j for any $j \in \{1, 2, ...p\}$.

The first criterion above requests compactness of the set of sequences $\{S_1, S_2, ..., S_p\}$ in the sense that no sequence in it is redundant by having a subsequence indicative of the same consequent as it. A sequence that is both indicative and non-redundant is called a key sequence. The second criterion further requires that no single key sequence shall be lost, which signifies a demand for completeness of the set of key sequences to be discovered.

3 Evaluation of Single Sequences

This section aims to evaluate individual sequences to decide whether one sequence can be regarded as indicative. The main thread is to assess the discriminating power of sequences in terms of their co-occurrence relationship with possible time series classes. In addition we also illustrate the importance of sequence appearing frequencies in the database for ensuring reliable assessments of the discriminating power.

Given a sequence S there may be a set of probable consequent classes $\{C_1, C_2, ..., C_k\}$. The strength of the co-occurrence between sequence S and class C_i $(i=1...k)$ can be measured by the probability, $p(C_i \mid S)$, of C_i conditioned upon S. Sequence S is considered as discriminative in predicting outcomes as long as it has a strong co-occurrence with either of the possible outcomes. The discriminating power of S is defined as the maximum of the strengths of its relations with probable consequents. Formally this definition of discriminating power PD is expressed as:

$$PD(S) = \max_{i=1\cdots k} P(C_i \mid S) \tag{1}$$

In addition we say that the class yielding the maximum strength of the co-occurrences, i.e., $C = \arg \max_{i=1\cdots k} P(C_i \mid S)$, is the consequent that sequence S is indicative of.

The conditional probabilities in (1) can be derived according to the Bayes theorem as:

$$P(C_i | S) = \frac{P(S | C_i) P(C_i)}{P(S)} \tag{2}$$

As the probability $P(S)$ is generally obtainable by

$$P(S) = P(S | C_i) P(C_i) + P(S | \overline{C}_i) P(\overline{C}_i) \tag{3}$$

equation (2) for conditional probability assessment can be rewritten as

$$P(C_i | S) = \frac{P(S | C_i) P(C_i)}{P(S | C_i) P(C_i) + P(S | \overline{C}_i) P(\overline{C}_i)} \tag{4}$$

Our aim here is to yield the conditional probability $P(C_i | S)$ in terms of equation (4). As $P(C_i)$ is a priori probability of occurrence of C_i which can be acquired from domain knowledge or approximated by experiences with randomly selected samples, the only things that remain to be resolved are the probabilities of S in (time series) cases having class C_i and in cases not belonging to class C_i respectively. Fortunately such probability values can be easily estimated by resorting to the given database. For instance we use the appearance frequency of sequence S in class C_i cases as an approximation of $P(S | C_i)$, thus we have:

$$P(S | C_i) \approx \frac{N(C_i, S)}{N(C_i)} \tag{5}$$

where $N(C_i)$ denotes the number of cases having class C_i in the database and $N(C_i, S)$ is the number of cases having both class C_i and sequence S. Likewise the probability $P(S | \overline{C}_i)$ is approximated by

$$P(S | \overline{C}_i) \approx \frac{N(\overline{C}_i, S)}{N(\overline{C}_i)} \tag{6}$$

with $N(\overline{C}_i)$ denoting the number of cases not having class C_i and $N(\overline{C}_i, S)$ being the number of cases containing sequence S but not belonging to class C_i.

The denominator in (4) has to stay enough above zero to enable reliable probability assessment using the estimates in (5) and (6). Hence it is crucial to acquire an adequate amount of time series cases containing S in the database. The more such cases available the more reliably the probability assessment could be derived. For this reason we refer the quantity $N(S) = N(C_i, S) + N(\overline{C}_i, S)$ as evaluation base of sequence S in this paper.

At this point we realize that two requirements have to be satisfied for believing a sequence to be indicative of a certain class. Firstly the sequence has to possess an adequate evaluation base by appearing in a sufficient amount of time series cases. Obviously a sequence that occurred randomly in few occasions is not convincing and can hardly be deemed significant. Secondly, the conditional probability of that class under the sequence must be dominatingly high, signifying a strong discriminating power. These explain why indicative sequence is defined by the demands on its appearance frequency and discriminating power in definition 4.

In real applications two minimum thresholds need to be specified for the evaluation base and discriminating power respectively, to judge sequences as indicative or not. The values of these thresholds are domain dependent and are to be decided by human experts in the related area. The threshold for discriminating power may reflect the minimum probability value that suffices to predict a potential outcome in a specific scenario. The threshold for the evaluation base indicates the minimum amount of samples required to fairly approximate the conditional probabilities of interest. Finally only those sequences that pass both thresholds are evaluated as indicative ones.

4 Discovering a Complete Set of Key Sequences

With the evaluation of sequences being established, we now turn to exploration of qualified sequences in the problem space. The goal is to locate all key sequences that are non-redundant and indicate. We first detail a sequence search algorithm for this purpose in subsection 4.1 and then we demonstrate simulation results on a synthetic database with the proposed algorithm in subsection 4.2.

4.1 A Sequence Search Algorithm

Discovery of key sequences can be considered as a search problem in a state space in which each state represents a sequence of symbols. Connection between two states signifies an operator between them for transition, i.e. addition or removal of a single symbol in time sequences. The state space for a scenario with three symbols a, b, c is illustrated in Fig. 1, where an arc connects two states if one can be created by extending the sequence of the other with a following symbol.

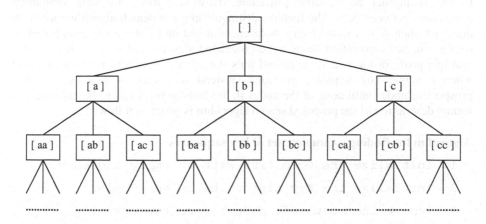

Fig. 1. The state space for sequences with three symbols

A systematic exploration in the state space is entailed for finding a complete set of key sequences. We start from a null sequence and generate new sequences by adding a single symbol to parent nodes for expansion. The child sequences are evaluated according to evaluation bases and discriminating powers. The results of evaluation determine the way to treat each child node in one of the following three situations:

i) If the evaluation base of the sequence is under a threshold required for conveying reliable probability assessment, terminate expansion at this node. The reason is that the child nodes will have even smaller evaluation bases by appearing in fewer cases than their parent node;

ii) If the evaluation base and discriminating power are both above their respective thresholds, do the redundancy checking for the sequence against the list of key sequences already identified. The sequence is redundant if at least one known key sequence constitutes its subsequence while both remaining indicative of the same consequent. Otherwise the sequence is considered as non-redundant and hence is stored into the list of key sequences together with the consequent it indicates. After that this node is further expanded with the hope of finding, among its children, qualified sequences that might be indicative of other consequents;

iii) If the evaluation base is above its threshold whereas the discriminating power still not reaching the threshold, continue to expand this node with the hope of finding qualified sequences among its children.

The expansion of non-terminate nodes are proceeded in a level-by-level fashion. A level in the search space consists of nodes for sequences of the same length and only when all nodes at a current level have been visited does the algorithm move on to the next level of sequences having one more symbol. This order of treating nodes is very beneficial for redundancy checking because a redundant sequence will always be encountered later than its subsequences including the key one(s) during the search procedure.

From a general structure, the proposed sequence search algorithm is a little similar to the traditional breadth-first procedure. However, there are still substantial differences between both. The features distinguishing our search algorithm are: 1) it does not attempt to expand every node encountered and criteria are established to decide whether exploration needs to be proceeded at any given state; 2) it presumes multiple goals in the search space and thus the search procedure is not terminated when a single key sequence is found. Instead the search continues on other prospective nodes until none of the nodes in the latest level needs to be expanded. A formal description of the proposed search algorithm is given as follows:

Algorithm for finding a complete set of key sequences

```
1. Initialize the Open list with an empty sequence.

2. Initialize the Key_List to be an empty list.

3. Remove the most left node t from the Open list.

4. Generate all child nodes of t
```

5.   For each child node, $C(t)$, of the parent node t

a) Evaluate $C(t)$ according to its discriminating power and evaluation base;

b) If the evaluation base and discriminating power are both above their respective thresholds, do the redundancy checking for $C(t)$ against the sequences in the *Key_list*. Store $C(t)$ into the *Key_list* if it is judged as not redundant. Finally put $C(t)$ on the right of the *Open* list.

c) If the evaluation base of $C(t)$ is above its threshold but the discriminating power is not satisfying, put $C(t)$ on the right of the *Open* list.

6. If the *Open* list is not empty go to step 3, otherwise return the *Key_list* and terminate the search.

Finally it bears mentioning that finding key sequences in our context differs from those [1, 4, 17] in the literature of sequence mining. Usually the goal in sequence mining is merely to find all legal sequential patterns with their frequencies of appearances above a user-specified threshold. Here we have to consider the cause-outcome effect for classification purpose. Only those non-redundant sequences which are not only frequent but also possess strong discriminating power will be selected as the results of search.

4.2 Simulation Results

To verify the feasibility of the mechanism addressed above we now present the simulation results on a synthetic database. A case in this database is depicted by a time series of 20 symbols and one diagnosis class as the outcome. A symbol in a time series belongs to {a, b, c, d, e} and a diagnosis class is either 1, 2, or 3. The four key sequences assumed are [a d c], [b c a], [d e b], and [e a e]. The first two sequences were supposed to have strong co-occurrences with class 1 and the third and fourth exhibit strong co-occurrences with classes 2 and 3 respectively. Each time series in the database was created in such a way that both sequences [a d c] and [b c a] had a chance of 80% of being reproduced once in the time series of class 1 while sequences [d e b] and [e a e] were added into class 2 and class 3 cases respectively with a probability of 90%. After stochastic reproduction of these key sequences, the remaining symbols in the time series of all cases were generated randomly. The whole database consists of 100 instances for each class. Presuming such time series cases to be randomly selected samples from a certain domain, a priori probability of each class is believed to be one third.

The sequence search algorithm was applied to this database to find key sequences and potential co-occurrences hidden in the data. The threshold for the discriminating power was set at 70% to ensure an adequate strength of the relationships discovered. We also specified 50 as the threshold of the evaluation base for reliable assessment of probabilities. The sequences found in our test are shown in table 1 below.

Table 1. Sequences discovered on a synthetic database

Sequence Discovered	Discriminating power	Evaluation base	Dominating Consequent
[a d c]	76.70%	103	Class 1
[b c a]	78.22%	101	Class 1
[d e b]	73.39%	124	Class 2
[e a e]	83.18%	107	Class 3

As seen from table 1 we detected all the four key sequences previously assumed. They were recognized to potentially cause the respective consequents with probabilities ranging from 73.39% to 83.18%. These relationships with a degree of uncertainty are due to the many randomly generated symbols in the database such that any sequence of symbols is more or less probable to appear in time series of any class. But such nondeterministic property is prevalent in many real world domains.

5 Applying Key Sequences in Probabilistic Reasoning

The discovered key sequences are treated as significant features in capturing dynamic system behaviors. Rather than enumerating what happened in every consecutive time segment, we can now characterize a dynamic time series in terms of what key sequences it includes as well as how many times each included key sequence has occurred. Further, as the key sequences have strong co-occurrences with a certain class, they can be used as discriminative evidences to update our beliefs concerning probabilities of classes an unknown time series may belong to.

Given a new time series X to be classified, the first task is characterization of the series according to the set of key sequences, say $\{S_1, S_2, ..., S_p\}$. Hence X has to be scanned thoroughly to detect all occurrences of key sequences in it. Every appearance of a key sequence S_j ($j=1...P$) in X is treated as an evidence for brief updating in classification. In view of this, the time series X can be characterized by a collection of evidences, i. e. $EV(X) = \{e_1, e_2, \cdots, e_T\}$ with $e_i \in \{S_1, \cdots, S_P)$ for any i from 1 to T. Important to note is that it is possible to have $e_i = e_j$ for $i \neq j$, implying that a key sequence appearing in X more than once is considered to cause multiple evidences.

The next task is to update the probabilities of different classes using detected evidences to reduce the uncertainty. Assuming conditional independence of key sequences occurrences under any class, the evidences available can be utilized separately for probability updating in individual steps. At every step we use a single evidence to revise prior probabilities according to the Bayes theorem and these updated probability estimates are then propagated as prior beliefs to the next step. Considering a two class problem without loss of generality, the procedure of probability updating using a set of evidences $\{e_1, e_2, \cdots, e_T\}$ is depicted by a series of equations as follows:

$$P(C \mid e_1) = \frac{P(e_1 \mid C)P(C)}{P(e_1 \mid C)P(C) + P(e_1 \mid \overline{C})P(\overline{C})} \quad (7)$$

$$P(C \mid e_1, e_2) = \frac{P(e_2 \mid C)P(C \mid e_1)}{P(e_2 \mid C)P(C \mid e_1) + P(e_2 \mid \overline{C})P(\overline{C} \mid e_1)} \quad (8)$$

$$P(C \mid e_1, \cdots, e_i) = \frac{P(e_i \mid C)P(C \mid e_1, \cdots, e_{i-1})}{P(e_i \mid C)P(C \mid e_1, \cdots, e_{i-1}) + P(e_i \mid \overline{C})P(\overline{C} \mid e_1, \cdots e_i)} \quad (9)$$

$$P(C \mid e_1, \cdots, e_T) = \frac{P(e_T \mid C)P(C \mid e_1, \cdots, e_{T-1})}{P(e_T \mid C)P(C \mid e_1, \cdots, e_{T-1}) + P(e_T \mid \overline{C})P(\overline{C} \mid e_1, \cdots e_{T-1})} \quad (10)$$

where the probabilities $P(e_i \mid C)$ and $P(e_i \mid \overline{C})$ for $i \in \{1,...,T\}$ can be estimated according to equations (5) and (6) respectively, as e_i is a sequence. The probability updated in equation (7) represents the probability for class C given evidence c_1, which is further updated in equation (8) by evidence e_2 producing a more refined belief considering both e_1 and e_2. Generally the probability $P(C \mid e_1, \cdots, e_i)$ is yielded by updating the prior probability $P(C \mid e_1, \cdots, e_{i-1})$ with a new evidence e_i in equation (9). Finally we obtain the ultimate probability assessment incorporating all available evidences by equation (10).

We now give a concrete example to illustrate how the above sequential procedure works in probability refinements using key sequence appearances as evidences. Consider a problem of classifying a time series X into one of the two classes. Suppose that two key sequences S_1 and S_2 are detected in X and both are indicative of a certain class C. The a priori probability of class C is 50% and the probabilities of sequences S_1, S_2 in situations of class C and its complementary are shown below:

$$P(S_1 \mid C) = 0.56 \qquad P(S_1 \mid \overline{C}) = 0.24$$

$$P(S_2 \mid C) = 0.80 \qquad P(S_2 \mid \overline{C}) = 0.40$$

Further we assume that sequence S_1 appears twice in X and S_2 appears once, hence the collection of evidences for X is notated as $EV(X) = \{S_1, S_1, S_2\}$. With these three evidences detected, the probability of class C for time series X is refined gradually in the following three steps:

Step 1: Update the a priori probability $P(C)$ with the first appearance of S_1 by

$$P(C \mid S_1) = \frac{P(S_1 \mid C)P(C)}{P(S_1 \mid C)P(C) + P(S_1 \mid \overline{C})P(\overline{C})} = \frac{0.56 \cdot 0.5}{0.56 \cdot 0.5 + 0.24 \cdot 0.5} = 0.70$$

Step 2: Refine the probability updated in step 1 with the second appearance of S_1, thus we have

$$P(C \mid S_1, S_1) = \frac{P(S_1 \mid C)P(C \mid S_1)}{P(S_1 \mid C)P(C \mid S_1) + P(S_1 \mid \overline{C})P(\overline{C} \mid S_1)} = \frac{0.56 \cdot 0.70}{0.56 \cdot 0.70 + 0.24 \cdot 0.30} = 0.8448$$

It is clearly seen that the belief in class C is increased from 0.70 to 0.8448 due to the key sequence occurring for the second time.

Step 3: Refine the probability updated in step 2 with the occurrence of S_2, and we acquire the final probability assessment taking into account all evidences by

$$P(C|S_1,S_1,S_2) = \frac{P(S_2|C)P(C|S_1,S_1)}{P(S_2|C)P(C|S_1,S_1)+P(S_2|\overline{C})P(\overline{C}|S_1,S_1)} = \frac{0.80 \cdot 0.8448}{0.80 \cdot 0.8448 + 0.40 \cdot 0.1552} = 0.9159$$

Here, the appearance of S_2 makes the probability be enhanced to an even higher value of 0.9159. As both sequences S_1 and S_2 are consistent in being indicative of the same consequence, each appearance of them contributes to increase the probability of C with a certain extent.

At last let us consider the order in which single evidences are used to refine probability assessments. This seems a fundamental issue and involves allocation of evidences to different steps of a sequential procedure. Fortunately our study has clarified that the order of evidences used in probability updating is completely indifferent. The final probability value remains constant as long as each piece of evidence is assigned to a distinct step. The claims as such are formally based on the following theorems.

Lemma. Let $\{e_1,\cdots e_T\}$ be a set of evidences representing appearances of the key sequences in a time series X. The final probability for X in class C is not affected if two adjacent evidences exchange their positions in the order of evidences used for probability refinements. This means that the relation $P(C|e_1,\cdots e_i,e_{i+1},\cdots,e_T) = P(C|e_1,\cdots e_{i+1},e_i,\cdots,e_T)$ holds for $i \in \{1,...T-1\}$.

A proof of the lemma is given in the appendix. Contemplating the implication of this lemma led us to a corollary presented below.

Corollary. Let $\{e_1,\cdots e_T\}$ be a set of evidences representing appearances of the key sequences in a time series X. The final probability for X in class C is independent of the order according to which single evidences $e_1, e_2, ..., e_T$, are used in probability refinements.

The proof of the above corollary is obvious. According to the lemma, an element in a given order of evidences can be moved to an arbitrary position by repeatedly exchanging its position with an adjacent one while not affecting the final probability assessments. As this can be done to every piece of evidence, we enable transitions to any orders of evidences without altering the classification result.

This corollary is important in providing theoretic arguments allowing for an arbitrary order of sequences to be used in probability refinement based on the Bayes theorem. The connotation is that when a key sequence occurred in the time series does not matter for the final result of classification. Instead only the numbers of appearances of key sequences effect our beliefs concerning the likelihoods of probable outcomes.

6 Conclusion

This paper tackles discovery of key sequences for time series data classification. The input is a symbolic database which consists of pairs of time series profiles and their associated classes. The problem is to find from the database a complete set of sequences that are both indicative and non-redundant. A sequence as such is called a key sequence in the paper.

Novel solutions are suggested here to deal with this problem. First we establish criteria to evaluate sequences in terms of the measures of evaluation base and discriminating power. The main idea is to accept those sequences appearing frequently and possessing high co-occurrences with consequents as indicative ones. Secondly a sequence search algorithm is proposed for exploration of indicative sequences in the problem space. One property of the search algorithm is that it always visits nodes of longer sequences after nodes of shorter ones such that redundant sequences can be detected easily for exclusion. The other property is that it terminates expansion only at the nodes where there is no prospect to find qualified sequences from their off-springs, guaranteeing the completeness of the search results.

The discovered key sequences are considered as important features in characterizing time series cases. We show that appearances of key sequences in time series can be used as evidences in probabilistic reasoning. A sequential procedure is presented to update beliefs for classification using found evidences. We also demonstrate that the order in which single evidences are used for brief refinements is indifferent to the final results.

References

1. Agrawal, R., Srikant, R.: Mining sequential patterns. In: Proceedings of the 11th International Conference on Data Engineering. (1995) 3-14
2. Chan, K. P., Fu, A. W.: Efficient time series matching by wavelets. In: Proceedings of the International Conference on Data Engineering. (1999) 126-133
3. Fayyad, U., Piatetsky-Shapiro, G., Smyth, P.: From data mining to knowledge discovery. In: Advances in Knowledge Discovery and Data Mining. MIT Press (1996) 1-36
4. Garofalakis, M. N., Rajeev, R., Shim, K.: SPIRIT: Sequential sequential pattern mining with regular expression constraints. In: Proceedings of the 25th International Conference on Very Large Databases. (1999) 223-234
5. Hayashi, A., Mizuhara, Y., Suematsu, N.: Embedding time series data for classification. In: Perner, P., Imiya, A. (eds.): Proceedings of the IAPR International Conference on Machine Learning and Data Mining in Pattern Recognition. Leipzig (2005) 356-365
6. Hetland, M. L.: A survey of recent methods for efficient retrieval of similar time sequences. In: Last, M., Kandel, A., Bunke, H. (eds.): Data Mining in Time Series Databases. World Scientific (2004)
7. Huang, C. F., Chen, Y. C., Chen, A. P.: An association mining method for time series and its application in the stock prices of TFT-LCD industry. In: Perner, P. (ed.): Proceedings of the 4th Industrial Conference on Data Mining. Leipzig (2004)
8. Huhtala, Y., Kärkkäinen, J., Toivonen, H.: Mining for similarities in aligned time series using wavelets. In: Data Mining and Knowledge Discovery: Theory, Tools, and Technology. SPIE Proceedings Series, Vol. 3695. Orlando, FL (1999) 150-160

9. Keogh, E., Chakrabarti, K., Pazzani, M., Mehrotra, S.: Locally adaptive dimensionality reduction for indexing large time series databases. In: Proceedings of ACM SIGMOD Conference on Management of Data. Santa Barbara, CA (2001) 151-162

10. Keogh, E., Chakrabarti, K., Pazzani, M., Mehrotra, S.: Dimensionality reduction for fast similarity search in large time series databases. Journal of Knowledge and Information Systems (2001)

11. Last, M., Klein, Y., Kandel, A.: Knowledge discovery in time series databases. IEEE Trans. Systems, Man, and Cybernetics --- Part B: Cybernetics 31 (2001) 160-169

12. Nilsson, M., Funk, P.: A Case-Based Classification of Respiratory Sinus Arrhythmia. In: Proceedings of the 7th European Conference on Case-Based Reasoning. Madrid (2004) 673-685

13. Park, S., Chu, W. W., Yoon, J., Hsu, C.: Efficient search for similar subsequences of different lengths in sequence databases. In: Proceedings of the International Conference on Data Engineering. (2000) 23-32

14. Pray, K. A., Ruiz, C.: Mining expressive temporal associations from complex data. In: Perner, P., Imiya, A. (eds.): Proceedings of the IAPR International Conference on Machine Learning and Data Mining in Pattern Recognition. Leipzig (2005) 384-394

15. Ray, A.: Symbolic dynamic analysis of complex systems for anomaly detection. Signal Processing 84 (2004) 1115-1130

16. von Schéele, B.: Classification Systems for RSA, ETCO2 and other physiological parameters. PBM Stressmedicine, Technical report, www.pbmstressmedicine.se, (1999)

17. Srikant, R., Agrawal, R.: Mining sequential patterns: Generalizations and performance improvements. In: Proceedings of the 5th International Conference on Extending Database Technology. (1996) 3-17

18. Tung, A. K. H., Lu, H., Han, J., Feng, L.: Breaking the barrier of transactions: Mining inter-transaction association rules. In: Proceedings of ACM Conference on Knowledge Discovery and Data Mining. (1999) 297-301

19. Wu, Y., Agrawal, D., Abbadi, A. EI: A comparison of DFT and DWT based similarity search in time series databases. In: Proceedings of the 9th ACM CIKM Conference on Information and Knowledge Management. McLean, VA (2000) 488-495

20. Yoon, H., Yang, K., Shahabi, C.: Feature subset selection and feature ranking for multivariate time series. IEEE Trans. Knowledge and Data Engineering 17 (2005) 1186-1198

Appendix: Proof of the Lemma

For proof of the lemma with the statement that $P(C|e_1,\cdots,e_{i-1},e_i,e_{i+1},\cdots,e_T) = P(C|e_1,\cdots,e_{i-1},e_{i+1},e_i,\cdots,e_T)$, we only need to establish the relation for $P(C|e_1,\cdots,e_{i-1},e_i,e_{i+1}) = P(C|e_1,\cdots,e_{i-1},e_{i+1},e_i)$, which is equivalent to the lemma.

We start to consider the probability $P(C|e_1,\cdots e_i,e_{i+1})$ which is acquired by updating the prior brief $P(C|e_1,\cdots e_i)$ with a new evidence e_{i+1}, hence it can be written as

$$P(C|e_1,\cdots,e_i,e_{i+1}) = \frac{P(e_{i+1}|C)P(C|e_1,\cdots,e_i)}{P(e_{i+1}|C)P(C|e_1,\cdots,e_i) + P(e_{i+1}|\overline{C})P(\overline{C}|e_1,\cdots,e_i)} \tag{11}$$

Further the probability $P(C|e_1,\cdots,e_i)$ is formulated by taking $P(C|e_1,\cdots,e_{i-1})$ as its prior estimate such that

$$P(C|e_1,\cdots,e_i) = \frac{P(e_i|C)P(C|e_1,\cdots,e_{i-1})}{P(e_i|e_1,\cdots,e_{i-1})} \tag{12}$$

Likewise we obtain

$$P(\overline{C}|e_1,\cdots,e_i) = \frac{P(e_i|\overline{C})P(\overline{C}|e_1,\cdots,e_{i-1})}{P(e_i|e_1,\cdots,e_{i-1})} \tag{13}$$

Combining (12) and (13) into equation (11) gives rise to a transformed formulation as

$$P(C|e_1,\cdots,e_i,e_{i+1}) = \frac{P(e_{i+1}|C)P(e_i|C)P(C|e_1,\cdots,e_{i-1})}{P(e_{i+1}|C)P(e_i|C)P(C|e_1,\cdots,e_{i-1}) + P(e_{i+1}|\overline{C})P(e_i|\overline{C})P(\overline{C}|e_1,\cdots,e_{i-1})} \tag{14}$$

Next we express the conditional probabilities $P(e_{i+1}|C)$, $P(e_{i+1}|\overline{C})$, $P(e_i|C)$, $P(e_i|\overline{C})$ with their Bayes forms by

$$P(e_{i+1}|C) = \frac{P(C|e_{i+1})P(e_{i+1})}{P(C)} \tag{15}$$

$$P(e_{i+1}|\overline{C}) = \frac{P(\overline{C}|e_{i+1})P(e_{i+1})}{P(\overline{C})} \tag{16}$$

$$P(e_i|C) = \frac{P(C|e_i)P(e_i)}{P(C)} \tag{17}$$

$$P(e_i|\overline{C}) = \frac{P(\overline{C}|e_i)P(e_i)}{P(\overline{C})} \tag{18}$$

where $P(C)$ and $P(\overline{C})$ denote the initial probability estimates for class C and its complementary without any evidences. Using the Bayes forms from (15) to (18), equation (14) is finally rewritten as

$$P(C|e_1,\cdots,e_i,e_{i+1}) = \frac{P^2(\overline{C})P(C|e_{i+1})P(C|e_i)P(C|e_1,\cdots,e_{i-1})}{P^2(\overline{C})P(C|e_{i+1})P(C|e_i)P(C|e_1,\cdots,e_{i-1}) + P^2(C)P(\overline{C}|e_{i+1})P(\overline{C}|e_i)P(\overline{C}|e_1,\cdots)} \tag{19}$$

Clearly we see from equation (19) that the order between e_i and e_{i+1} has no effect at all on the probability $P(C|e_1,\cdots,e_i,e_{i+1})$ assessed. It follows that

$$P(C|e_1,\cdots,e_{i-1},e_i,e_{i+1}) = P(C|e_1,\cdots,e_{i-1},e_{i+1},e_i) \tag{20}$$

and here from the lemma is proved.

Data Alignment Via Dynamic Time Warping as a Prerequisite for Batch-End Quality Prediction

Geert Gins[1], Jairo Espinosa[2], Ilse Y. Smets[1], Wim Van Brempt[3],
and Jan F.M. Van Impe[1]

[1] BioTeC, Dept. of Chemical Engineering,
Katholieke Universiteit Leuven,
W. de Croylaan 46, B-3001 Leuven, Belgium
{geert.gins, ilse.smets, jan.vanimpe}@cit.kuleuven.be
[2] Facultad de Minas, Universidad Nacional de Colombia,
Carrera 80 No. 65-223 Medellín, Colombia
jespinov@unal.edu.co, jairo.espinosa@ipcos.com
[3] IPCOS – ISMC office,
Technologielaan 11/0101, B-3001 Leuven, Belgium
wim.vanbrempt@ipcos.com

Abstract. In this work, a 4-phase *dynamic time warping* is implemented to align measurement profiles from an existing chemical batch reactor process, making all batch measurement profiles equal in length, while also matching the major events occurring during each batch run.

This data alignment is the first step towards constructing an inferential batch-end quality sensor, capable of predicting 3 quality variables before batch run completion using a multivariate statistical *partial least squares* model. This inferential sensor provides on-line quality predictions, allowing corrective actions to be performed when the quality of the polymerization product does not meet the specifications, saving valuable production time and reducing operation cost.

1 Introduction

In chemical industry, batch processes are widely used for flexible manufacturing. To obtain high quality consistency and safety, on-line monitoring of these batch processes is a necessity. Multivariate statistical methods, originally used for monitoring continuous processes, have recently been extended to batch processes [3,4,5,6]. In this work, *dynamic time warping* (DTW) is used to align measurement profiles from an existing chemical batch reactor, making all profiles equal in length.

This data alignment is the first step in constructing an inferential batch-end quality sensor to predict the quality of a polymerization product before a batch run is completed. This early prediction allows corrective actions to be performed during the batch run if the quality of the product is not satisfactory. Hence, less *off-spec* batches are produced, saving valuable production time and lowering operation costs.

In Section 2 of this paper, a description of the data set used in this work is given. Section 3 details the *dynamic time warping* data alignment algorithm. Section 4 discusses the alignment results. Finally, conclusions are drawn in Section 5.

P. Perner (Ed.): ICDM 2006, LNAI 4065, pp. 506–510, 2006.

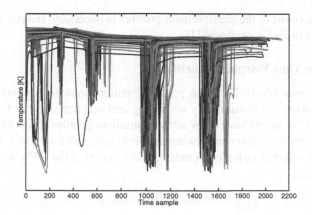

Fig. 1. Original alignment variable profiles. It is clear that all batches are not equal in length. Also, temperature drops are spread out over a large range.

2 Industrial Data

The data set used in this work is obtained by monitoring an industrial polymerization process. First, the polymerization process is described. Next, the available data are briefly discussed.

2.1 Production Process

After loading half of the monomer into the reactor, the batch is heated until polymerization is observed. After waiting approximately 10 minutes, the second half of the monomer is slowly added to the reactor. Extra initiator is added to the reactor about 2, 4 and 6 hours after detection of the polymerization. After 8 hours, the batch is cooled down and emptied.

2.2 Data Set

During each of the 246 available polymerization batches, 30 variables are monitored on-line, with a time delay of 15 seconds between each measurement. After batch completion, 3 quality parameters are measured off-line by means of lab analysis.

3 Data Alignment

When modelling batch processes, a first problem is encountered during the data gathering step: all batches –or batch phases– have a different duration. As a result, the major events observed during batch operation do not occur at the same sample point in every batch. This is illustrated in Figure 1 for one temperature measurement, where the temperature drops corresponding to the addition of new initiator to the reactor are spread out over a large time period.

Model identification, however, requires measurement profiles of identical length [3,4,5,6], with specific events always occurring at the same instants (or sample point).

Therefore, *alignment* of the measurement profiles is necessary. Hereto, the concept of *dynamic time warping* is exploited [1].

3.1   Dynamic Time Warping Algorithm

Dynamic time warping (DTW) is a powerful pattern matching algorithm rooted in speech recognition. By dynamically stretching and compressing the time axis of all batches, the DTW algorithm brings all measurement profiles to an identical length, while minimizing the difference between the observed profile and the reference profile of one or more selected variables. A detailed description of the DTW algorithm can be found in, e.g., [2].

3.2   Alignment Procedure

The first step of the DTW alignment consists in selecting an aligning variable, in this case, a temperature measurement.

Next, the batch run is divided into 5 phases using the operational procedure described in Section 2.1: the 10 minute delay after reaction detection, the addition of the second half of the monomer load, and each of the three following initiator introductions. However, because no exact information on the start of each of the batch phases is available, the start of each phase must be determined from the available measurement profiles. Furthermore, because the initiator introduction occurring 2 hours after the detection of the reaction is not observed in all batches, the second and third phase of the batch run are combined into a single phase, resulting in 4 batch phases.

Then, a reference temperature profile is selected for each of the 4 identified batch run phases. This reference profile has a close-to-average duration, and exhibits all special events. The resulting reference profile is depicted in Figure 2. A number of sudden temperature changes can be observed in this reference profile. The first two peaks correspond to the start and end of the slow monomer feed, while the remaining three temperature peaks are related to the introduction of additional initiator into the batch reactor.

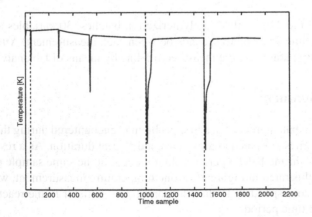

Fig. 2. Reference profile for alignment. This reference profile is composed of 4 separate phases (indicated by the vertical dashed lines).

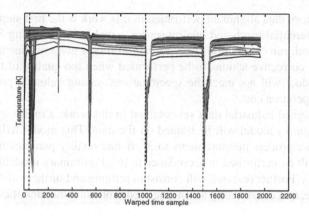

Fig. 3. Aligned temperature profiles obtained after performing the *dynamic time warping* for all 4 batch phases (indicated by the vertical dashed lines)

After selecting the reference profile, the different phases of the available batches are aligned with the selected reference profile. Afterwards, the individual phase warping paths resulting from the DTW algorithm are combined into a single warping path.

4 Alignment Results

In this section, the quality of the alignment obtained in Section 3.2 is investigated, and the aligned (warped) data set is discussed.

4.1 Alignment Results

As can be seen in Figure 3, the aligned temperature profiles all have identical lengths, and all temperature peaks are properly aligned, all starting at the same sample point, and having the same duration. Even the batches where not all temperature peaks are observed, are aligned properly, illustrating the power of the DTW algorithm.

4.2 Resulting Data Set

Using the aligned variables obtained from the DTW algorithm, a new, aligned, data set is constructed. This data set is composed of 246 batches of equal length, namely 1962 sample points. Each batch consists of 31 variables: the warped versions of the original 30 variables, augmented with the warped time vector of each batch, which indicates how strong the original time axis is compressed or expanded by the DTW algorithm.

5 Conclusions and Future Work

In this work, a 4-phase *dynamic time warping* is used to align measurement profiles from an existing chemical batch reactor process, making all batch measurement profiles equal in length, while also matching the major events of each batch run.

The satisfactory data alignment performed in this work is the first step towards constructing an inferential batch-end quality sensor, capable of predicting 3 quality variables before batch run completion. This inferential sensor gives on-line quality predictions, allowing corrective actions to be performed when the quality of the final polymerization product will not meet the specifications, saving valuable production time and reducing operation cost.

Using the aligned industrial data set obtained in this work, a multivariate statistical *partial least squares* model will be trained on the data. This model will relate the 30 available on-line process measurements to 3 off-line quality parameters. This model training step will be performed in accordance to [6]. Preliminary modelling results are very satisfactory. Further research will consist in refining and further validating the PLS model structure, and constructing an on-line predictor using the identified PLS model.

Acknowledgements

Work supported in part by IWT Project 040363 and Project OT/03/30 of the Research Council of the Katholieke Universiteit Leuven and the Belgian Program on Interuniversity Poles of Attraction, initiated by the Belgian Federal Science Policy Office. Ilse Smets is a postdoctoral fellow with the Fund for Scientific Research Flanders-Belgium (FWO-Vlaanderen). The scientific responsibility is assumed by its authors.

The authors would like to thank Jan De Wilde of CYTEC (Drogenbos, Belgium) for the data sets provided for this study.

References

1. A. Kassidas, J.F. MacGregor, and P.A. Taylor. Synchronization of batch trajectories using dynamic time warping. *AIChE J.*, 44(4):864-875, 1998.
2. A. Kassidas, P.A. Taylor, and J.F. MacGregor. Off-line diagnosis of deterministic faults in continuous dynamic multivariate processes using speech recognition methods. *J. Proc. Cont.*, 8(5-6):381-393, 1998.
3. J.H. Lee, and A.W. Dorsey. Monitoring of batch processes through state-space models. *AIChE J.*, 50(6):1198-1210, 2004.
4. N. Lu, Y. Yao, and F. Gao. Two-dimensional dynamic PCA for batch process monitoring. *AIChE J.*, 51(12):3300-3304, 2005.
5. P. Nomikos, and J.F. MacGregor. Monitoring batch processes using multiway principal component analysis. *AIChE J.*, 40(8):1361-1375, 1994.
6. P. Nomikos, and J.F. MacGregor. Multi-way partial least squares in monitoring batch processes. *Chemometr Intell Lab*, 30:97-108, 1995.

A Distance Measure for Determining Similarity Between Criminal Investigations

Tim K. Cocx and Walter A. Kosters

Leiden Institute of Advanced Computer Science (LIACS)
Leiden University, The Netherlands
tcocx@liacs.nl

Abstract. The information explosion has led to problems and possibilities in many areas of society, including that of law enforcement. In comparing individual criminal investigations on similarity, we seize one of the opportunities of the information surplus to determine what crimes may or may not have been committed by the same group of individuals.

For this purpose we introduce a new distance measure that is specifically suited to the comparison between investigations that differ largely in terms of available intelligence. It employs an adaptation of the probability density function of the normal distribution to constitute this distance between all possible couples of investigations.

We embed this distance measure in a four-step paradigm that extracts entities from a collection of documents and use it to transform a high dimensional vector table into input for a police operable tool. The eventual report is a two-dimensional representation of the distances between the various investigations and will assist the police force on the job to get a clearer picture of the current situation.

1 Introduction

The amount of data being produced in modern society is growing at an accelerating pace. New problems and possibilities constantly arise from this so-called data explosion. One of the areas where information plays an important role is that of law enforcement. Obviously, the amount of criminal data gives rise to many problems in areas like data storage, data warehousing, data analysis and privacy. Already, numerous technological efforts are underway to gain insights into this information and to extract knowledge from it. On top of this, useful information not only exists in structured tables but is often contained in unstructured data sources like written reports or intercepted emails.

This paper discusses new tools that deal with the extraction of logical concepts from police narrative reports and documents found on crime scenes in order to automatically establish an educated guess on what crimes may be committed by the same (group of) criminals. To this end we employ *text mining*, a *distance measure* and an *associative array clustering technique*. We discuss the difficulties in case-comparison and the specific distance measure we designed to cope with this kind of information.

P. Perner (Ed.): ICDM 2006, LNAI 4065, pp. 511–525, 2006.

The main contribution of this paper is the discussion in Section 7, where the distance measure is introduced.

2   Background

After a slow start, the number of data mining projects in the law enforcement area is now slowly increasing, both in- and outside of the academic world. Commercial players vary from very small to very large multi-nationals, like statistical software producer SPSS. One of the first large-scale academic projects is the COPLINK project in Arizona where some excellent work has been done in the field of entity extraction from narrative reports [3], the exploitation of data mining for cooperation purposes [2] and social network analysis [13,4]. In the often mentioned FLINTS project, soft (behavioral) and hard (fingerprints, DNA) forensic evidence was combined to give analysts the ability to build a graphical image of (previously unthought-of) relations between crimes and criminals. Another link-analysis program, FinCEN [6], aimed to reveal money laundering networks by comparing financial transactions. Also, Oatly et al. did some link analysis work on burglary cases in the OVER project [10]. Clustering techniques have also been employed in the law enforcement area. Skillicorn [11] did some work on the detection of clusters within clusters to filter the surplus of information on possible terrorist networks and present law enforcement personnel with a viable subset of suspects to work with. Adderly and Musgrove [1] applied clustering techniques and Self Organizing Maps to model the behavior of sex-offenders.

Our research aims to apply multi-dimensional clustering to investigations rather than persons in order to constitute similarity between them.

3   Project Layout

As discussed earlier, useful information exists in unstructured data like police narrative reports, intercepted emails and documents found on crime scenes. It would be desirable to employ this information for case comparison in order to supplement the forensic work done on-site and provide police officers with information about crimes that may be committed by the same perpetrators. However, this information is usually deeply hidden in the unstructured setup of such, often free-text, documents. Even after the employment of a suitable text miner, the enormous amount of extracted entities still poses many problems. As is common with police work, some cases suffer from a lack of data, while others bury the police in paper work. Comparing cases that differ extremely in size in terms of entities extracted from this unstructured data, is one of the challenges. Another is that of preparing the resulting data of this comparison, visualizing it and presenting it to the officers on the case. Our research aims to address both these challenges and to set up a police framework for comparing cases on the basis of collected or created documents.

4   System Architecture

Our case comparison system is a multiphase process that relies on a commercial text miner, a table transformation unit, a distance calculator and a visualization tool. We therefore describe our process as a *four-step paradigm* (see Figure 1) and will elaborate on the individual components and their in- and output in the following sections. Black boxed, the paradigm reads in a collection of unstructured documents and provides a comparison report to the end user.

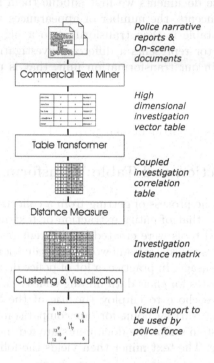

Fig. 1. Four-step paradigm

The documents we use as input for our case comparison system consist of two different types, both of which are provided by the individual regional police departments for analysis:

- Police narrative reports: one of the types contained in our document collection is that of the police written narrative reports. These reports are created to describe a crime, the people involved and the Modus Operandi (MO). Protocols exist how these reports should be written, but these rules are not always strictly followed. Also, these reports suffer from an abundance in police terminology (for example, almost all reports contain the words 'rep.' (report) and 'serial number') and they are likely to have typing mistakes in for example the way names are written. Some of these spelling mistakes are intentionally introduced by suspects to avoid cross referencing. Due to these effects, the police narrative reports are often reasonably polluted.

– Crime scene documents: digital documents found on crime scenes are often very rich in information. They contain valuable information like email contact lists that can give an idea of other people involved or lists of goods acquired to commit crimes. Since they are mostly created by the perpetrators themselves they are less likely to have errors or typing mistakes. Therefore, the crime scene documents are less noisy than the narrative reports, but are unfortunately also more rare.

When processing these documents we first subdue them to a text miner that yields a table with concepts, the number of appearances and the investigation they belong to. This table is then transformed to a high dimensional vector space, where each vector represents a different investigation. We then extract comparison numbers in our transformation unit, that is presented to our distance calculator. The distance matrix that results from this is now fed to the visualization and presentation tool, that can be operated by the analyst himself. The results will be presented visually and are ready to be interpreted and used by the individual police department that provided the documents.

5   Entity Extraction and Table Transformation

An important step in the process of getting from a collection of documents to a comparison overview is that of entity extraction or text mining. As mentioned earlier some specialized tools were created by different research programs. The INFO-NS program [9] suggests a framework for evaluation of commercial text mining tools for police usage. In practice, a lot of police departments employ one of these commercial suites for their data mining endeavours. In order to comply with this situation, we chose to employ the use of the SPSS Lexiquest text mining tool [12] as the starting point for our comparison framework. Through a simple operating system script the documents are fed into the text miner one investigation at a time. The text miner then yields the following table:

Entity	Investigation	Type	Amount

In this table Type refers to one of the types defined in Table 1 that also shows the percentage of these types in the dataset used for our experiments. The resulting table is primary keyed by both entity and investigation but since the final objective is the comparison of investigations it is necessary to transform this table to an investigation based one that contains all characteristics per investigation. The table should therefore contain information about what entities are present in each investigation. The table we are creating therefore has an integer field for every entity. If the key investigation-entity is present in the original table, the corresponding field in the new table will be equal to the contents of the Amount field and 0 otherwise. The number of distinct investigations we can retrieve from the table will be denoted by m. This yields the following high-dimensional vector table:

Investigation	Entity 1	Entity 2	...

where the number of dimensions, apart from the key attribute Investigation, is equal to the number of distinct entities in the previous table, which we will denote by n.

Table 1. Different types recognized by entity extractor

Type	Description	Percentage
K	License plate	0.90%
P	Person	5.34%
u	URL	0.02%
O	Organization	0.48%
L	Location	0.69%
e	Email address	0.04%
D	Product	0.03%
i	IP address	0.02%
U	Unknown	92.45%

This table contains highly accurate entity usage information per investigation, for it contains all available information. We can now employ this information to get insights into the way different cases are alike in terms of used concepts.

6   Multi-dimensional Transformation

The high dimensional table that resulted from the previous step can now be used to describe distances between the various investigations in n-dimensional space. Naturally, we need to transform this table into a two-dimensional representation of the given data in order to come to a useful visualization in our tool. In order to achieve this dimensional downscaling we assume similarity can be constituted by the sizes of the investigations in terms of entities extracted and the entities they have in common.

According to this assumption, we compare the investigations couple-wise on each individual entity (see Figure 2) and score the couples on the amount of common entities according to the following method: every time both investigations have a value larger than or equal to 1 in a column, the score for overlapping is raised by 1.

The algorithm treats every investigation as a subset of the total set of entities. The calculation of the amount of common entities in two investigations is therefore synchronous to the calculation of the amount of items in the intersection of both sets (see Figure 3), and goes as follows:

$$\text{Overlap} = |\text{Inv}_1 \cap \text{Inv}_2| \ ,$$

where Inv_i is the set of entities for investigation i ($i = 1, 2$). We also let Size_i denote $|\text{Inv}_i|$.

	John Doe	Jane Doe	J.doe@me.nl	The Duke	555-123456	Violent	Consigliere	1 Mystreet	Money	Narcotic	
Case A	0	0	0	0	0	0	2	0	0	0	...
Case B	0	1	0	0	0	0	2	0	0	0	...
Case F	1	1	3	1	2	0	0	0	0	0	...
Case G	0	0	0	2	0	0	0	1	0	0	...
Case I	2	0	0	0	1	0	0	0	0	0	...
Case K	0	0	2	0	0	1	0	0	0	0	...
Case M	0	0	1	0	0	0	3	0	0	0	...
Case N	0	0	0	0	0	0	0	2	0	2	...
Case Q	1	0	0	2	0	4	0	1	0	0	...

Fig. 2. Comparing the investigations on common entities

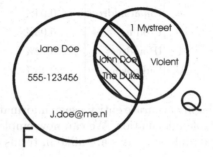

Fig. 3. Viewing the transformation process as calculating intersections

It is possible to utilize a filtering technique at this point to exclude all entities with type 'U' (unknown) from the comparing method. This will probably yield highly accurate results, due to the high expressive power of the recognized entities. For example two cases sharing the person 'John Doe' are more likely to be similar than two cases sharing the word 'money'. However, due to the high percentage of entities that are being classified as unknown, leaving them out can cause undesired shortcomings to the algorithm. For example: the word 'violent' may well be a key word in comparing two individual investigations, but is still categorized under type 'U'.

The mentioned algorithm provides a table with $\frac{1}{2}m(m-1)$ rows, where each row represents one couple of investigations. Each row consists of three columns: the size of the first investigation, the size of the second and the amount of common entities:

Size$_1$	Size$_2$	Overlap

This table is comparable to the ones used in data mining on shopping baskets where the goal is to determine which customers exhibit similar shopping behavior.

7   New Distance Measure

To constitute similarity between different investigations we introduce a distance measure, that calculates the distance between two such criminal cases. The distance measure we propose is a function over the parameters we stored in the table resulting from the previous step. The higher the function outcome and thus the distance, the less alike two investigations are. Our function yields a distance value between 0 and 1.

It is not just the amount of common entities that constitutes the distance between two investigations; the different sizes of the investigations should be taken into account as well. It is common practice in for example the analysis of the earlier mentioned shopping baskets, to let a difference in size have a negative effect on similarity. If we take a look at two shopping baskets, and we observe that one basket contains a newspaper and a bottle of wine and another basket contains the same paper and wine but also a hundred other items, no analyst would claim similar shopping behavior of the two customers, although 100% of one of the customer's acquisitions is also in the other one's basket. Therefore, distance measures like the symmetrical distance measure [7]:

$$\frac{(\text{Size}_1 - \text{Overlap}) + (\text{Size}_2 - \text{Overlap})}{\text{Size}_1 + \text{Size}_2 + 1}$$

that also incorporates size differences, are often employed in this area. However, this does not hold for the comparison of investigations. Although the size in terms of entities extracted may well be an indication of difference between two cases (many or few computers found on scene) it is, as mentioned earlier, not uncommon for law enforcement cases to differ largely in size while they still involve the same people (the police was at the scene very quickly vs. the criminals had time to destroy evidence).

As a consequence, the symmetrical distance measure mentioned above is not applicable in the area of case comparison. Naturally, the sole use of common entities is not applicable either. We therefore introduce a new distance measure specifically suited for the comparison of criminal investigations based upon entities extracted.

We propose a distance measure based upon the random amount of common entities two investigations would have if they were drawn randomly from the entire set of entities. The deviation between the size of the randomly selected intersection and the actual amount of common entities then constitutes distance. The size of the entire collection of entities, the universe of entities, will be denoted by A. In calculating this value we only count each distinct entity once instead of using each occurrence of a single entity in the table. This will more accurately represent the probability space for each individual investigation subset. We will denote the average size of the intersection of two randomly drawn subsets having sizes X and Y as E, which can be calculated as follows:

$$\frac{X}{A} \cdot \frac{Y}{A} = \frac{E}{A} \quad \Longleftrightarrow \quad E = \frac{X \cdot Y}{A^2} \cdot A = \frac{X \cdot Y}{A} \quad .$$

We can now easily calculate the difference (Differ) between the actual value Z and the expected value E as follows:

$$\text{Differ}(Z) = Z - E \ .$$

As is clear from the calculation of E, the expected value depends on the three variables X, Y and A. As a consequence, a very large universe A can lead to very low values of E and thus to very large differences between E and Z. This variation can be considered to be disruptive to the process in the following two cases:

- Some very large investigations without any relation to the other investigations, for example, two large Finnish investigations among a series of English investigations, are included in the list to be analyzed. The large number of unique entities these Finnish investigations would contribute to the universe A would implicate that all other investigations would have very low expected values and therefore very high differences. This can put all those investigations at a distance from each other that is far less than it should intrinsically be.
- When a lot of different investigations are to be compared, they all contribute a number of unique entities to the universe A. This means that, while the actual chance of two investigations having a certain overlap does not change, the calculated E would decrease approximately linearly to the amount of investigations included in the analysis. This can, as was mentioned above, lead to too small distances between the investigations.

As a measure for countering these effects we propose to calculate A from the actual overlapping values instead of just using the total amount of entities. We have implemented this method and compared it to the standard method described above.

We will base the alternative calculation of A upon the actual overlapping entities in all the possible couples, meaning that we calculate A out of X, Y and Z, instead of calculating E out of X, Y and A. Our method will then average all the individually calculated A's and use this number for A instead of the total amount of entities. Calculating A will go as follows:

$$A = \frac{\displaystyle\sum_{i=1}^{m} \sum_{j=i+1}^{m} \frac{X_i \cdot Y_j}{Z_{ij}}}{\frac{1}{2}m(m-1)} \tag{1}$$

In this summation we omit the pairs (i, j) with $Z_{ij} = 0$. Having obtained the differences we can calculate the distance between two investigations.

The normal distribution is the most widely used distribution in statistics and many statistical tests are based on the assumption of normality. One of the most used representations of this distribution is the probability density function (see Figure 4), which shows how likely each value of the random variable x is:

$$f(x) = \frac{1}{\sigma\sqrt{2\pi}} \exp\left(-\frac{(x-\mu)^2}{2\sigma^2}\right),$$

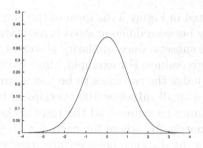

Fig. 4. Normal probability density function; $\sigma = 1, \mu = 0$

where σ denotes the standard variation and μ denotes the mean. Since we want to give a quantization of how notable the Differ function outcome is, we can take this function as basis for our distance function. We will thus employ an adaptation of that function to calculate the distance of two investigations by using the above mentioned function Differ. First, because we want to normalize our outcome between 0 and 1 we need to top of our function at $\frac{1}{2}$ by changing the factor before the exponential part of the function into $\frac{1}{2}$. Then we take the minimal value of X and Y as our standard deviation, since it is logical for the intersection of two large subsets to deviate more from the expected value than the intersection of two smaller subsets. We can flip the function part left of the mean to represent a positive deviation as a smaller distance between the two investigations. If we denote $\min(X, Y)$ as the minimum value of X and Y, our final distance function will look like this:

$$\text{Dist}(Z) = \begin{cases} \frac{1}{2} \exp\left(\frac{-\text{Differ}(Z)^2}{\frac{1}{2}\min(X,Y)}\right) & \text{if } \text{Differ}(Z) \geq 0 \\ 1 - \frac{1}{2} \exp\left(\frac{-\text{Differ}(Z)^2}{\frac{1}{2}\min(X,Y)}\right) & \text{otherwise} \end{cases}$$

This function calculates distance with respect to any size difference that may occur between two investigations while not incorporating any negatives effect for that difference. The proposed measure is symmetrical (X and Y can be exchanged). If two investigations are very much alike, their distance will approximately be 0; if they are very different their distance approaches 1.

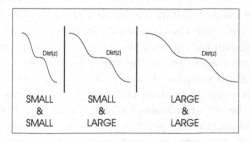

Fig. 5. Distance function of different sized couples of investigations

As is clearly illustrated in Figure 5 the form of the graph of the distance function differs significantly between different sized investigations. This enables us to compare different sized subsets, since similarity is constituted by the probability space rather than integer values. For example, three overlapping entities in two small subsets can now judge the two cases to be just as similar as 10 overlapping entities in a large and a small subset or 100 overlaps in two very large cases.

If we apply this distance measure to all the rows in the last table we are able to create a distance matrix M, where for each $1 \leq i \leq M$ and $1 \leq j \leq M$ element M_{ij} represents the distance between investigation i and j. Due to the fact that the distance between i and j is the same as between j and i our distance matrix is symmetrical. Having calculated all the distances we can display the investigations in our visualization tool.

8   Visualization

It is desirable for police personnel to be able to view the total picture in one glance. In most cases it is not possible to display a high dimensional situation, such as our initial vector table, perfectly in a two-dimensional plane, especially after the amount of transformations our data went through. We therefore employed the associative array clustering technique [8] to display (an approximation) of all the distances between the different investigations in one two-dimensional image. This technique can be viewed as Multi-Dimensional Scaling (MDS, see [5]), and is especially suited for larger arrays. The image we now have can be fed back to the officers on the case to enhance their understanding of the situation.

The associative array clustering technique strives for the creation of a flat image of all considered elements where the physical distance between them is linearly related to the distance in the matrix, while minimizing the error in that distance, sometimes referred to as "stress". It is an iterative process that starts off at a random situation and through a specified number of iterations tries to improve that situation until it reaches a more or less stable state. This is a state where the error made in the placement of the elements is at a (local) minimum.

The algorithm works as follows: starting at the earlier mentioned random position, where all the elements are in an arbitrary position, the algorithm investigates a random couple of elements and when the distance in the image is relatively larger than the requested distance, the pull operation is executed. If, on the contrary the current distance is smaller than the distance in the matrix the push operation will push the elements away from each other. As can be seen in Figure 6 the push and pull operations move the elements in the target image away from or towards each other on the line defined by the two elements.

In every iteration all couples of investigations will be evaluated and their respective distances corrected. Since the image usually can not be displayed entirely correct in the two-dimensional plane, the image might differ a bit depending on the random starting point, but is consistent enough to give a good overview of the similarity between investigations. Also note that rotations and reflections may be applied without affecting the outcome.

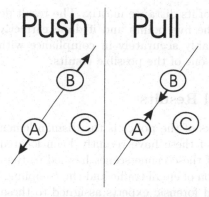

Fig. 6. Push and pull operations

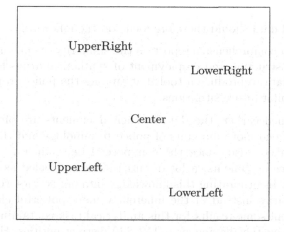

Fig. 7. Clustering of a centerpointed square based upon its distance matrix; visualized using labels

It is imperative for the tool that performs this task to be operable by the police officers that request the similarity analysis. The tool to be designed therefore needs to be extended by a graphical user interface (GUI). Developing a GUI not only serves the purpose of making the application usable by police personnel, but also gives insights in the formation of the image and enables us to detect problematic situations and improve the algorithm.

The tool we developed allows a number of settings and has a main screen where the user can see the image unfold in different speeds. The user can then output the images in PDF format for usage in a document. The user can customize the screen to display investigation labels of numbers if the titles overlap too much.

As a simple demonstration of the algorithm's possibilities, we tried to regain the image of four points forming the corners of a square and a fifth point in the center, by means of its distance matrix. The result depends on the random starting position of the five points and if done correctly would represent the original image reasonably accurately in compliance with rotation and mirror symmetry. Figure 7 is one of the possible results.

9   Experimental Results

One of the major tasks of the police is the dismantlement of synthetical drugs laboratories. Several of these have recently been located and rendered out of order. Investigation of these crime scenes has led to the acquirement of digital documents, interception of email traffic and the compiling of numerous narrative reports by officers and forensic experts assigned to these investigations. Given the nature of the different laboratory sites, case detectives suspect common criminals to be involved in exploiting some of these locations for the creation of synthetical drugs. Employment of a clustering technique should provide answers to the questions about common perpetrators in these and future cases. Research on the collected data should therefore focus on the following:

- Producing a comprehensive report on the similarity of current investigations into the construction and employment of synthetical drugs laboratories.
- Using the data to produce a tool that enables the police to perform similar tasks in similar future situations.

As was mentioned earlier, the data in such documents are often polluted by the inclusion of enormous amounts of police terminology and the large number of typing mistakes. Also, since the commercial text miner is not specifically trained on police documents, a lot of entities where labeled as unknown or as the wrong type. Incorporating this knowledge into our scripts we decided to use all types of entities instead of the inherently more powerful classified entities alone. We present some results for this analytical task containing $n = 28$ police investigations, together having $m = 152,820$ distinct entities. Here, A is either m, using just the amount of entities or is computed according to Formula (1).

Usage of our new distance measure on this data yielded distance matrices that indeed showed results that could indicate similarity between some of the individual investigations. The distance matrices showed some significant difference in distance values between the individual investigations. Application of our clustering approach to this newly generated matrix for both different calculation methods for A showed a clustering image (Figure 8 left and right) that indeed demonstrated that certain investigations are closer and therefore more similar to each other than others. We infer from these images that there is some relevant similarity between certain investigations and submitted the reports, outputted by our application to the investigation teams. We are currently in discussion with the domain experts about the validity of the outcome of both methods employed by our system.

In the comparison of both possible methods of calculating A, it is noteworthy that the distances represented in both images do not vary a lot between the different methods but show minor differences.

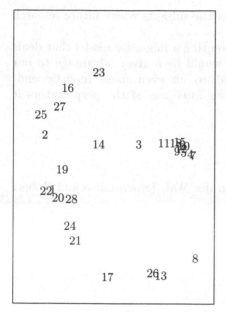
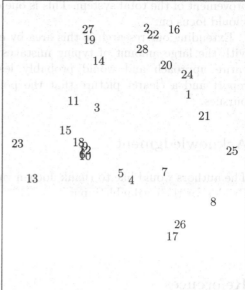

Fig. 8. Clustering of the database investigations using $A = n$, numbered 1 to 28 (Left) and clustering of the database investigations using Formula (1) for estimating A, numbered 1 to 28 (Right)

10   Conclusion and Future Directions

Data mining is a suitable solution for many problems and opportunities arising from the information explosion. In this paper we demonstrated the applicability of data mining in the comparison of individual criminal investigations to establish a quantity for similarity between them. We used a four-step paradigm to transform a set of documents into a clustering image that gives a full overview of the similarity between all investigations and is ready to be used by police experts. The new distance measure we introduced was specifically designed for this purpose. It incorporates the differences in information size between investigations while still maintaining a realistic comparison standard.

Future research will aim at getting a clearer picture about the computation method for A. Assigning n to A describes the situation with a true to reality universe of entities while using Formula (1) probably delivers better end-results for largely different or a large number of investigations. Both methods of assigning a value to A therefore have their own merits and more testing on different data sets is a prerequisite in deciding between them.

The commercial text miner used in this project was a source of problematic entries in our initial table. Incorporation of domain specific text miners such as used in the COPLINK project [3] would probably lead to a significant improvement of the total system. This is one of the subjects where future research should focus on.

Extending our research in this area by creating a linguistic model that deals with the large amount of typing mistakes would be a great advantage to our entire approach and would probably lead to an even more realistic end-report and a clearer picture that the police force has of the perpetrators it pursues.

Acknowledgment

The authors would like to thank Jochen van der Wal, Jeroen Laros and Robert Brijder for their valuable input.

This research is part of the DALE[1] project as financed in the ToKeN program from the Netherlands Organization for Scientific Research (NWO) under grant number 634.000.430.

References

1. R. Adderley and P. B. Musgrove. Data mining case study: Modeling the behavior of offenders who commit serious sexual assaults. In *KDD '01: Proceedings of the Seventh ACM SIGKDD International Conference on Knowledge Discovery and Data Mining*, pages 215–220, New York, 2001.
2. M. Chau, H. Atabakhsh, D. Zeng, and H. Chen. Building an infrastructure for law enforcement information sharing and collaboration: Design issues and challenges. In *Proceedings of The National Conference on Digital Government Research*, 2001.
3. M. Chau, J. Xu, and H. Chen. Extracting meaningful entities from police narrative reports. In *Proceedings of The National Conference on Digital Government Research*, 2002.
4. H. Chen, H. Atabakhsh, T. Petersen, J. Schroeder, T. Buetow, L. Chaboya, C. O'Toole, M. Chau, T. Cushna, D. Casey, and Z. Huang. COPLINK: Visualization for crime analysis. In *Proceedings of the The National Conference on Digital Government Research*, 2003.
5. M.L. Davison. *Multidimensional Scaling*. John Wiley and Sons, New York, 1983.
6. H.G. Goldberg and R.W.H. Wong. Restructuring transactional data for link analysis in the FinCEN AI system. In *Papers from the AAAI Fall Symposium*, 1998.
7. W.A. Kosters, E. Marchiori, and A. Oerlemans. Mining clusters with association rules. In *Proceedings of the Third Symposium on Intelligent Data Analysis (IDA99)*, LNCS 1642, pages 39–50. Springer, 1999.
8. W.A. Kosters and M.C. van Wezel. Competitive neural networks for customer choice models. In *E-Commerce and Intelligent Methods, Studies in Fuzziness and Soft Computing*, pages 41–60. Physica-Verlag, Springer, 2002.
9. N. Kumar, J. de Beer, J. Vanthienen, and M.-F. Moens. Evaluation of intelligent exploitation tools for non-structured police information. In *Proceedings of the ICAIL 2005 Workshop on Data Mining, Information Extraction and Evidentiary Reasoning for Law Enforcement and Counter-terrorism*, 2005.

---

[1] Data Assistance for Law Enforcement.

10. G.C. Oatley, J. Zeleznikow, and B.W. Ewart. Matching and predicting crimes. In *Proceedings of AI2004, the Twenty-fourth SGAI International Conference on Knowledge Based Systems and Applications of Artificial Intelligence*, 2004.
11. D.B. Skillicorn. Clusters within clusters: SVD and counterterrorism. In *Proceedings of the Workshop on Data Mining for Counter Terrorism and Security*, 2003.
12. SPSS LexiQuest website. http://www.spss.com/spssbi/lexiquest/.
13. Y. Xiang, M. Chau, H. Atabakhsh, and H. Chen. Visualizing criminal relationships: Comparison of a hyperbolic tree and a hierarchical list. *Decision Support Systems*, 41(1):69–83, 2005.

Establishing Fraud Detection Patterns
Based on Signatures

Pedro Ferreira[1], Ronnie Alves[1], Orlando Belo[1], and Luís Cortesão[2]

[1] University of Minho, Department of Informatics, Campus of Gualtar,
4710-057 Braga, Portugal
{pedrogabriel, ronnie, obelo}@di.uminho.pt
[2] Portugal Telecom Inovação, SA, Rua Eng. José Ferreira Pinto Basto
3810 - 106 Aveiro - Portugal
LCorte@ptinovacao.pt

Abstract. All over the world we have been assisting to a significant
increase of the telecommunication systems usage. People are faced day
after day with strong marketing campaigns seeking their attention to
new telecommunication products and services. Telecommunication companies struggle in a high competitive business arena. It seems that their
efforts were well done, because customers are strongly adopting the new
trends and use (and abuse) systematically communication services in
their quotidian. Although fraud situations are rare, they are increasing
and they correspond to a large amount of money that telecommunication
companies lose every year. In this work, we studied the problem of fraud
detection in telecommunication systems, especially the cases of superimposed fraud, providing an anomaly detection technique, supported by a
signature schema. Our main goal is to detect deviate behaviors in useful
time, giving better basis to fraud analysts to be more accurate in their
decisions in the establishment of potential fraud situations.

1 Introduction

Today communication is a common act of living. Recent telecommunications
market analysis show that companies have been working very well, especially in
the area of new products and services. Telecommunications companies have been
continuously and significantly improving their business incomes and extending
their influence in the market. However, some studies show that telecommunication companies lose large amounts of money every year due to a large diversity of
fraudulent cases. Due to the fact that fraud is continuously evolving and telecommunications networks generate huge amounts of data (sometimes of the order
of several gigabytes per day) the detection and identification of fraud cases is
extremely hard and costly, demanding for huge amount of resources (human and
material) to fight it. Essentially, two main types of fraud can be distinguished
[19]: *subscription* and *superimposition* fraud. In the former, the fraudsters (fak-
ing identifications) especially create a new account without having the intention
to pay for the used services. Typically, these cases reveal an intensive high-usage

P. Perner (Ed.): ICDM 2006, LNAI 4065, pp. 526–538, 2006.

right from the beginning. In the latter, the fraudsters make an illegitimate use of a legitimate account by different means. In this case, some abnormal usage is blurred into the characteristic usage of the account. This type of fraud is usually more difficult to detect and poses a bigger challenge to the telecommunications companies. Some of the telecommunications companies use since the 90's decade several kinds of approaches based on statistical analysis and heuristics methods to assist them in the detection and categorization of fraud situations. Additionally, some of them adopted the use and exploitation of data mining and knowledge discovery techniques.

Telecommunications scenarios pose big challenges to traditional data mining techniques. Here can we emphasize three of these challenges. 1) The abstraction level of the analysis. Fraud analysts are typically interested in the customer behavior and not in the call details. For each call, telecommunication systems generate a record - call detail record (CDR) - that has enough information to completely describe a call. However, a CDR is not by itself enough to detect a fraud situation. We are interested in studying the customer behavior and not individual phone calls. Thus, based on CDRs, we must use some kind of profiling techniques in order to reveal, with certain accuracy, the customer behavior along the time. Signature records that include a large diversity of features, such as number of calls, average call duration, average number of calls received, etc., can be used to establish customer profiles. Additionally, customer data (age, job, location, price plan and so on) which is of critical importance in this analysis can also be used in this profile construction. Therefore, we can resume three levels of data [18]: *call*, *behavior* and *client*. 2) Inappropriateness of data for supervised techniques. Data Mining techniques are more suitable to work only in the last two levels of data, and, typically, they can be divided in two categories: *Supervised* and *Unsurpervised Learning*. In supervised techniques there is a feedback to the system since the inputs and respective outputs are known. In this case all the instances in data have assigned a predefined class. In unsupervised techniques the system has no hints in how to find the correct answer since no apriori discrimination of the data exists. From the fraud detection point of view, where the goal is to discriminate between normal and fraudulent users, the supervised techniques seem to be more appropriate to the problem. Nevertheless, due to several reasons, like the inexistence of previously known fraud cases, or the imbalance (fraud occurs in a relative small number) of the data cases [18], the direct application of supervised techniques is not always possible. 3) The need for real time or almost real time update of the detection system information due to the high costs associated with fraud.

In order to capture the characteristics of an user behaviour the concept of *signature* can be applied. This concept has already been used successfully for anomalous detection in many areas like credit card usage [11], network intrusion [13,11] and in particular in telecommunications fraud [3,21,1,5]. A signature corresponds to a set of information that captures the typical behavior of a user. For example, the average number of calls, time of the calls, area where the calls are made and so on. Thus, if in a given moment, an user deviates from which is its typical behavior expressed by its signature, that can be a motive to trigger an alarm for further analysis of that user. In the fraud and intrusion detection systems, signatures can be used in two distinct ways:

- *Detection based in User Profiles* - The signature of the user is compared against a database of cases of known non legitimate use. This kind of method fits under the class of supervised learning technique.
- *Detection based in Signatures* - The user signature is used as a comparison basis. A possible differentiation between the actual behaviour of the user and its signature may reveal an anomaly situation.

In this paper we tackle the problem of superimposed fraud detection in telecommunication systems. We propose an anomaly detection technique based on the concept of signature. Our goal is to detect deviate behaviors in useful time, giving better basis to analysts to be more accurate in their decisions in the establishment of potential fraud situations. In the following sections, we describe the signature based detection models and algorithms developed as well as the current functional architecture of the proposed system.

2   Detecting Fraud Situations Based on Signatures

Our technique has as a core concept the notion of signature. We emphasize the work of Cortes and Pregibon [5], since it was the main inspiration for the use of signatures. In this section, we start by presenting our own definition of signature. Next, we present all its relevant elements and the theoretical background that allows computing the statistical-based distances of the signatures. Finally, we explain how the management (start and update) of the signatures is done.

2.1   Definition of Signature

A signature of a user corresponds to a *vector of feature variables* whose values are determined during a certain period of time. The variables can be *simple*, if they consist into a unique atomic value (ex: integer or real) or *complex*, if they consist in two co-dependent statistical values, typically the average and the standard deviation of a given feature.

A signature S is then obtained from a function φ for a given temporal window w, where $S = \varphi(w)$. We consider a *time unit* the amount of time in which the CDRs are accumulated and that in the end of this period are processed. The value of w is proportional to the time unit, $w = \alpha \times \Delta t$. For example, if we consider the Δt of one day we will have $\alpha = 7$ for a temporal window of one week.

In figure 1 we illustrate the scheme of the evolution of a signature through time. S corresponds to the initial value of the user signature. After a shift of one unit of time, the signature S is then updated to S', according to the new usage information (CDRs that happen between the end of S and S'). For a given set of CDRs (shadow area) verified in a unit of time Δt, a comparison against the most

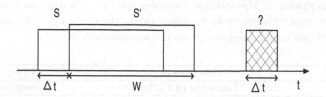

Fig. 1. Evolution of a signature through time

actual value of signature can be made in order to detect deviating behaviors. Since this information is processed to resume the user behavior in a certain time period we denote it as a *summary*. The reason for this denomination will be made more clear in the next sections.

The described type of processing is *time oriented*, since the set of user actions are accumulated, kept and processed during the time unit for posterior analysis. On the other hand, we can have an *action oriented* processing that makes the direct comparison of each new action (CDR) against the signature.

A signature can be updated according to one of these two modes. In [5] it is pointed that the most adequate model for the updating is the action oriented. This is mainly due to the elevated costs associated with fraud, which require a constant (for every call) update of the signature. In this work we choose the time oriented mode for signature updating. The reason for this is the high processing cost of this operation. As we will see in the following sections, signature processing requires the analysis of massive volumes of data. Since the used time unit can be made not too large (typically one day or less) a reasonable trade-off between processing cost and up to date information is achieved.

2.2   Elements of a Signature

Each of the signature feature variables is obtained directly from coded fields from one or more CDRs. These feature variables correspond to a statistical value which describe a certain aspect of the user behavior. Both a signature and a summary correspond to the set of all the variables. The main difference resides in the time window that they resume. In order to capture the user behavior in different situations a signature reflects a longer time window, like for example a week, a month or even half year period. On the other hand, by reasons already pointed out, a summary reflects a much smaller time period, like for example an hour, a half day or complete day.

Our proposed model contemplates simple and complex variables, a simple variable corresponds to an average value and a complex variable to the average and standard deviation of a certain feature. In table 1 we list the feature variables and the respective type.

The choice of the type of the variables depends on several factors, like the complexity of the feature described or the data available to perform such calculation. A feature like the duration of the calls shows a significant variability which is much better expressed through an average/standard-deviation parameter. A

Table 1. Description of the features variables used in signature and summary and the respective type. *Currently in Portugal exists three wireless telecommunications companies and one major company in fixed telecommunications.*

Description	Type
Duration of Calls	Complex
Number of Calls - Working days	Complex
Number of Calls - Weekends and Holidays	Complex
Number of Calls - Working Time (8h-20h)	Complex
Number of Calls - Night Time (20h-8h)	Complex
Number of Calls to the Different national networks*	Simple
Number of Calls as Caller (Origin)	Simple
Number of Calls as Called (Destination)	Simple
Number of International Calls	Simple
Number of Calls as Caller in Roaming	Simple
Number of Calls as Called in Roaming	Simple

feature like the number of international calls is typically much less frequent and thus an average value is sufficient to describe it.

2.3 Anomaly Detection

Given a set of CDRs, C, we would like to know if during the corresponding period of time the user deviates from its typical behavior. First of all, there is the need to process such information. The processing of C, P_C, basically consists in extracting from C the set of feature variables described in table 1. Once this step is performed, we have two vectors of feature variables, S(signature) and P_C, available for comparison. For the determination of the distance between these two vectors, the usual distance functions like the Euclidean distance can not be applied, since the vectors contain complex variables. Besides, we would like to look for the problem from a probabilistic point of view, i.e. the distance measure corresponds to some probabilistic value of P_C being different form S.

Since the features in the signature have different types, each variable has to be evaluated by a distinct sub-function. Thus, the *dist* function is composed by the several sub-functions: $dist = \phi(f_1, f_2, \ldots, f_n)$.

Next, we present through a semi-formal example the details of our distance function. Consider a simplification of a signature $S = \{(\mu_a, \sigma_a); \mu_b; \mu_c; (\mu_d, \sigma_d)\}$, where the first and the last feature variables are complex and the second and the third are simple variables. Let $P_C = \{(\mu'_a, \sigma'_a); \mu'_b; \mu'_c; (\mu'_d, \sigma'_d)\}$ a vector of variables from a period Δt already processed. The proposed distance function can be presented as:

$$dist(S, C) = \alpha_1 \cdot f_1(S.a, C.a) + \alpha_2 \cdot f_2(S.b, C.b) + \alpha_3 \cdot f_3(S.c, C.c) + \alpha_4 \cdot f_4(S.d, C.d) \quad (1)$$

The formula 1 is a linear combination of the distances observed in each of the feature variables. The constants α_i are a weighting factor for each of the variables and they can express the importance given to each feature when determining anomaly deviation. These values are provided by the fraud analyst. Since he/she may wants to observe different fraud's situations. Different distance functions can be provided, by setting the weighting factors α_i to different values. This way, the distance function is now defined as in 2.

$$Dist(S, C) = max\{dist_1(S, C), \; dist_2(S, C), \; \ldots, \; dist_m(S, C)\} \tag{2}$$

The main point of using a distance function is that if the distance between S and C exceeds a certain threshold, ξ defined by the analyst, i.e. $Dist(S, C) > \xi$ then an alarm should be raised to future inspection. Otherwise, the user is considered to be within its expected behavior.

2.4   Distance Between Feature Variables

From a statistical point of view, it is frequently acceptable that many random variables have likelihood distributions that can be appropriately described by a normal distribution, if the μ and σ are specified [16]. The normal distribution give us a reasonable approximation to many scientific variables that occur in real world situations. According to this , we suggest an adaptation of the normal distribution function to measure the distance between complex feature variables. For a given variable X, where $X \sim N(\mu, \sigma)$, the Z-score function provides the likelihood of X taking the value of x, $P(X = x) = P(Z = \frac{x-\mu}{\sigma})$. In our particular case, we want to measure for a feature variable X taking a value of x the distance from the typical behavior, i.e. the average value. The Z-score function provides a larger likelihood as the value of X tends to μ, being maximal if $X = \mu$. Since we are measuring a distance, we want that our distance function returns a value that is inversely proportional to the likelihood of X taking the value of μ. For that, we only need to subtract our likelihood value P to the accumulated likelihood, that is one, $f_{Normal} = 1 - P$. With this formula, distant values of X from μ have a smaller value of f_{Normal}. Considering the example of the last section, f_1 and f_4 correspond to f_{Normal} where μ_a and σ_a are the parameters that describe the normal distribution of the feature a and μ'_a the value being evaluated.[1] To measure the distance between simple feature variables we can use a simple distance or a any other distribution function measure. We propose the use of the Poisson non cumulative distribution [16,17,22]. This function has its most important application in the counting of the number of events that occur in a certain time interval or spatial region, when the events are independent from each other. The probability density function of a Poisson variable is given by formula 3. The constant e corresponds to the napier number, λ is the expected value that in our case correspond to the average value described by the signature and k corresponds to the observed value.

$$P(N = k) = \frac{e^{-\lambda}\lambda^k}{k!} \tag{3}$$

In order to measure the probabilistic distance of the observed value k and the expected value λ of a variable X is given by: $f_{Poisson} = dist(\lambda, k) = \frac{|P(X=\lambda) - P(X=k)|}{N}$.

---

[1] The value of σ_a will only be considered for updating of the signature.

N is the normalizing factor. Since the Poisson function is non-symmetric and only defined for values greater than zero, if $X \geqslant \lambda$ then $N = P(X = \lambda) - P(X = \infty) \simeq P(X = \lambda)$ and $N = P(X = \lambda) - P(X = 0)$ if $0 \leqslant X < \lambda$.

2.5 Signature Updating

Before describing how the update of a signature is performed, we should say that the initialization of a signature is a straightforward process. The initial signature S_0 corresponds to a summary for the period of the initial time window w_0. As we already mentioned in a previous section, the update can be performed in a time oriented or action oriented mode. The chosen mode for this work was the former. In either cases, it is necessary to weight the impact of the new action or set of actions in the new signature values. Following the ideas of [5,2], the update of a signature S_t in the instant $t + 1$, S_{t+1}, through a set of processed CDRs P_C is given by the formula 4.

$$S_{t+1} = \beta \cdot S_t + (1 - \beta) \cdot P_C \qquad (4)$$

The constant β indicates the weight of the new actions C in the values of the new signature. Depending on the size of the time window w this constant can be adjusted. In [5] it is pointed that a daily update with a value of $\beta = 0.85$ allows to account for the information of the last 30 days. With a value of $\beta = 0.5$ only the last 7 days are considered in the signature values. This constant can always be tuned by the fraud analyst.

In our system, in contrast to the system in [5], the value of the signature is always updated. If the $Dist(S_t, C) \leqslant \xi$ then the user is considered to have a normal behavior. If $Dist(S_t, C) > \xi$ then an alarm is triggered, but the signature continues to be constantly updated. The reason for this is that the alarm still needs to pass through the analysis of the company fraud expert. It can happen the case that the analyst considers it as a false alarm and the user behavior is within some expected behavior. The continuous update of that user signature avoids the loss of information that was gathered between the moment when the alarm was triggered and the moment the analyst gives the verdict.

3 Model Behavior

In the next two sections we describe how the signature and summary information is managed through the entire system.

3.1 Pseudo-algorithm

The functioning logic of the system is in "batch" mode, i.e. always that new summaries are available, like for instance at the end of the day, the list of summaries is traversed and a comparison against the respective signature is made. In algorithm 1, the foreach cycle between line 1 and 15 processes all the incoming summaries. Line 2 and 3 gets the respective user and signature identification.

Algorithm 1. Pseudo algorithm that performs the anomaly detection by comparing the new incoming summaries with the respective signatures

    input : SummList(List of New Summaries)

```
   /* Compare each Summary against the respective Signature and detect
      anomalous behaviors                                             */
1  foreach Summ in SummList do
2      userId = getUserId(Summ);
3      signId = getSignId(userId);
4      if signatureIsActive(signId) == TRUE then
5          w = createWindowTimeFrame();
6          Sign = loadSignature(signId);
7          if Dist(Sign, Summ) ⩽ ξ then
8              updateSignature(Sign, Summ, w);
9          else
10             updateSignature(Sign, Summ, w);
11             triggerAlarm(userId);
12             clientToQuarantine(userId);
13         end
14     end
15 end
```

Next, it is verified if the signature is in an active state, which corresponds to an up to date signature. Line 5 creates a referential for the window frame that is being analyzed and in line 6 all the information relative to user signature is fetched from the database. Lines 7 to 13 tests the distance between the user signature and summary. If an alarm is raised the user becomes part of a "Black List", which we call quarantine. In either cases the signature is always updated (lines 8 or 10).

3.2   Detecting Anomalies

The anomaly detection procedure consists in a process of several steps that is represented in figure 2. The process starts by the *loading* step, which is used to import the information to the database of the system. This information refers to the signature and summary information of each user. The signatures are imported once, when the system is started. All the signatures of a user are kept through time. Such information will be used for posterior analysis. A signature may have two status "Active" or "Expired". For each client only one signature can have the Active state, and it is the most up to date one. The *processing* step corresponds to the algorithm described in section 3.1, where the Active signatures are used for the anomaly detection. In this step, the active signature is updated (see section 2.5) and marked as active. If an alarm is raised, the client is put on the quarantine list. This corresponds to the *triggering alarm* step that can be described in the section 2.3 and in section 2.4. Finally, all the raised alarms have to pass through the analyst's verification in order to determine if this alarm corresponds or not to a fraud scenario.

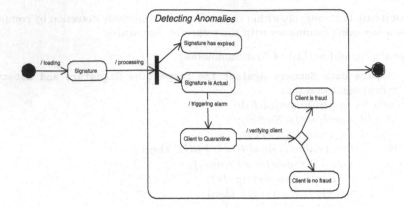

Fig. 2. State Chart of the Signature flow

4   Evaluating Alarms

The system interface is inspired on the ideas of a dashboard system, which shows a complete set of information to facilitate the evaluation process. The analyst has several tools to investigate those alarms. Here, we give a brief overview of three of proposed tools.

An alarm corresponds to a situation where the distance between the signature and a summary has exceed the threshold. It is interesting to analyze what were the feature variables with the greatest impact, which after verification, has caused an alarm. This impact can be calculated simply by the ratio of each feature variable (fv) in the overall distance (formula 1). Figure 3 (a) shows a piechart for the distribution of the impact of seven feature variables.

In order to have a more general overview of the impact of each feature variable, the TOP-K alarms associated to a given user grouped, and the aggregation $([sum(fv_1), sum(fv_2), \ldots, sum(fv_n)])$ of these impacts is calculated. Figure 3 (b) shows the aggregation of the impacts for the TOP 5 alarms of user A.

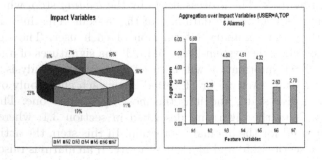

Fig. 3. (a) Impact of each feature variable; (b) Aggregation of the impact features of a given client

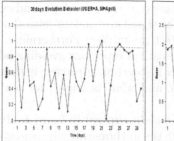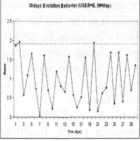

Fig. 4. Graph of the distance values(score) of two users in the time interval of one month

The type of information presented in figure 3 (a) and (b) is very important to the analyst because it supports the understanding of the user behavior and points toward the threshold values that should be used to capture the alarms.

In order to observe the behavior of a given client during a certain period of time the analyst can make use of a time series chart. In this graphic, all the calculated distances for the select time window can be used to study whether the client shows any particular trend in its behavior. Figures 4 (a) and (b) show two examples, for two different users during the period of one month. Note that in the points where the distance (also called score for output reasons) exceeded the threshold (dashed line) an alarm was raised. Two different threshold values were used for illustration purposes.

5   Related Work

Fraud detection can be done at two levels, call or behavior, and with two different approaches, user profile or signature based. Most of the techniques use the CDR data to create an user profile and to detect anomalies based on these profiles. The work from [9,8] is an example of this. They mined large amounts of CDRs in order to find patterns and scenarios of normal usage and typical fraud situations. These scenarios were then used to configure monitors that "observe" the user behavior with relation to that type of fraud. These monitors are then combined in a neural network, which raises an alarm when sufficient support of fraud exists. This type of system can be classified in a rule based approach, since it relies in the triggering of certain rules due to abnormal usage. The system presented in [18] is also an example of a rule based system that work in data behavior level. But as stated in [11], rule based systems have the drawback of requiring expensive management of rules. Rules need to be precise (avoid false positive alarms) and constantly evolving (detect new scenarios), which result in very time-consuming programming.

The most common and best succeeded methods [21] for fraud analysis are signature based. These methods detect the fraud based on deviation detection by comparing the recent activity with the user behavior data, which is expressed through the user signature. In this context, our work adapts and extends the work of [5] by reformulating the notion of signature and by introducing the notion of statistical-based distances to detect anomalies. Furthermore, we reduce the computation cost by using simple statistical functions avoiding processing costly histograms. A clear problem with a histogram approach is that discretization intervals or buckets must be chosen, and what is (right) for one customer may be (wrong) for another.

Other approaches have also been widely applied to fraud analysis, like for example neural networks [15,19]. In [20] the authors describe neural networks, mixture models, and Bayesian networks telecommunication fraud detection, derived from call records stored for billing. Another applied technique is link analysis. Here the clients links (called numbers) are updated over time, establishing a graph of called, "communities of interest" [4], that can easily reveal networks of fraudsters. These methods are based on the observation that fraudsters seldom change their calling habits, but are often closely linked to other fraudsters [14]. In [10] several methodologies are presented for outlier detection. Lately, there are some efforts to exploration of anomaly metadata [12], pre-defined stream selections with concept-drifting [6] and states approaches based on alarms [7].

6   Conclusions and Future Work

Fraud detection for mobile telecommunications is a relatively recent area of research. Due to its characteristics this type of fraud requires (nearly) real-time and individualized customer analysis. Literature in this area, points that customer signatures provide a mean to describe the current customer behavior and that can be used to efficiently detect fraud situations. In this work, we propose an anomaly detection system to support mobile telecommunications fraud detection. Signatures form the basis of the anomaly detection mechanism. We have adapted and extended the concept of signature in order to accurately capture the statistical information that describes the user behavior and to increase the precision on the anomaly detection. Thus, we provide a new definition of signature along with the respective statistical tools for its analysis. We also provide the computational details for the management of the signatures. It is expected that the proposed system will have a critical impact in the fraud prevention and detection procedures of the mobile telecommunications providers. The system constantly adapts to the user behavior patterns. Deviations from these patterns results in an indication to the fraud analyst that an anomalous and eventually fraud situation has occurred.

At the moment of this writing, the system implementation has been finished. This work is now in its experimental stage. Currently, we are studying the parameters tuning, the scalability issues and the analyst interaction with the system. We have also been investigating the application of the signatures for user segmentation. We have applied clustering techniques in order to find groups of related users. We believe that the analysis of cluster migrations could also shed light on fraud situations.

Acknowledgments

This work was financed by Portugal Telecom Inovação, S.A. under a service acquisition and knowledge transference protocol celebrated with University of Minho. The authors gratefully acknowledge Francisco Paz, João Lopes, Filipe Martins, Eduardo Taborda, and João Pias for their fruitful support on this work.

References

1. Richard J. Bolton and David J. Hand Statistical. Statistical fraud detection: A review. *Statistical Science*, 17(3):235–255, January 2002.
2. P. Burge, J. Shawe-Taylor, Y. Moreau, H. Verrelst, C. Stoermann, and P. Gosset. Fraud detection and management in mobile telecommunications networks. In *Proceedings of the 2nd IEEE European Conference on Security and Detection,*, volume 437, pages 91–96, London, April 1997. IEEE.
3. M. Cahill, D. Lambert, J. Pinheiro, and D. Sun. *Handbook of massive data sets*, chapter Detecting fraud in the real world, pages 911–929. Kluwer Academic Publishers, Norwell, MA, USA, 2002.
4. C. Cortes, D. Pregibon, and C. Volinsky. Communities of interest. *Intelligence Data Analysis*, 6(3):211–219, 2002.
5. Corrina Cortes and Daryl Pregibon. Signature-based methods for data streams. *Data Mining and Knowledge Discovery*, (5):167–182, 2001.
6. Kaustav Das, Andrew Moore, and Jeff Schneider. Belief state approaches to signaling alarms in surveillance systems. In *Proceedings of the tenth ACM SIGKDD international conference on Knowledge discovery and data mining*, pages 539–544, New York, NY, USA, 2004. ACM Press.
7. Wei Fan. Systematic data selection to mine concept-drifting data streams. In *Proceedings of the tenth ACM SIGKDD international conference on Knowledge discovery and data mining*, pages 128–137, New York, NY, USA, 2004. ACM Press.
8. Tom Fawcett and Foster Provost. Combining data mining and machine learning for effective user profiling. In Simoudis, Han, and Fayyad, editors, *Proceedings on the Second International Conference on Knowledge Discovery and Data Mining*, pages 8–13, Menlo Park, CA, 1996. AAAI Press.
9. Tom Fawcett and Foster Provost. Adaptive fraud detection. *Data Mining and Knowledge Discovery*, pages 1–28, 1997.
10. Victoria Hodge and Jim Austin. A survey of outlier detection methodologies. *Artificial Intelligence Review*, 22(2):85–126, 2004.
11. Y. Kou, T. Lu S. Sirwongwattana, and Y. Huang. Survey of fraud detection techniques. In *Proceedings of 2004 IEEE International Conference on Networking, Sensing and Control*, Taipei, Taiwan, March 2004. IEEE, IEEE.
12. Tysen Leckie and Alec Yasinsac. Metadata for anomaly-based security protocol attack deduction. *IEEE Trans. Knowl. Data Eng.*, 16(9):1157–1168, 2004.
13. T.F. Lunt. A survey of intrusion detection techniques. *Computer and Security*, (53):405–418, 1999.
14. John McCarthy. Phenomenal data mining. *Commun. ACM*, 43(8):75–79, 2000.
15. Yves Moreau, Herman Verrelst, and Joos Vandewalle. Detection of mobile phone fraud using supervised neural networks: A first prototype. In *ICANN '97: Proceedings of the 7th International Conference on Artificial Neural Networks*, pages 1065–1070, London, UK, 1997. Springer-Verlag.

16. Myers and Myers. *Probability and Statistics for Engineers and Scientists*. Prentice Hall, 6th edition.
17. Antonio Pedrosa and Silvio Gama. *Introdução Computacional a Probabilidade e Estatistica*. Porto Editora, 2004.
18. Saharon Rosset, Uzi Murad, Einat Neumann, Yizhak Idan, and Gadi Pinkas. Discovery of fraud rules for telecommunications challenges and solutions. In *Proceedings of the fifth ACM SIGKDD international conference on Knowledge discovery and data mining*, pages 409–413, New York, NY, USA, 1999. ACM Press.
19. J. Shawe-Taylor, K. Howker, P. Gosset, M. Hyland, H. Verrelst, Y. Moreau, C. Stoermann, and P. Burge. *In Business Applications of Neural Networks*, chapter Novel techniques for profiling and fraud detection in mobile telecommunications, pages 113–139. Singapore: World Scientific, 2000.
20. Michiaki Taniguchi, Michael Haft, Jaakko Hollmen, and Volker Tresp. Fraud detection in communications networks using neural and probabilistic methods. In *Proceedings of the 1998 IEEE International Conference on Acoustics, Speech and Signal Processing (ICASSP'98)*, number 2, page 12411244, 1998.
21. Gary M. Weiss. *Data Mining in Telecommunications*. kluwer, 2004.
22. Eric W. Weisstein. Poisson distribution. From MathWorld–A Wolfram Web Resource. http://mathworld.wolfram.com/PoissonDistribution.html, 2006.

Intelligent Information Systems for Knowledge Work(ers)

Klaus-Dieter Althoff[1], Björn Decker[2], Alexandre Hanft[1], Jens Mänz[1],
Régis Newo[1], Markus Nick[2], Jörg Rech[2], and Martin Schaaf[1]

[1] University of Hildesheim,
Institute of Computer Sciences,
Laboratory of Intelligent Information Systems
{althoff, hanft, maenz, newo, schaaf}@iis.uni-hildesheim.de
[2] Fraunhofer Institute for Experimental Software Engineering,
Department for Experience Management, Kaiserslautern
{decker, nick, rech}@iese.fraunhofer.de

Abstract. Our society needs and expects more high-value services. Such
"knowledge-intensive" services can only be delivered if the necessary organizational and technical requirements are fulfilled. In addition, the
cost-benefit analysis from the service provider point of view needs to be
positive. Continuous improvement and goal-directed (partial) automation of such services is therefore of crucial importance. As a contribution
to this we describe our current research vision for (partially) automated
support of knowledge work(ers) based on intelligent information systems
focusing on the use of experience. For the implementation of such a vision
we base on the integration of approaches from artificial intelligence and
software engineering. A "deep" integration of case-based reasoning and
experience factory is a first successful step in this direction [33,28]. We
envision the further integration of software product-lines and multi-agent
systems as the next one.

1 Introduction and Motivation

The shift of relative importance from more traditional product factors to the new,
increasingly important product factor "knowledge" characterizes the developing
new economical structure [24]. The use of external knowledge is achieving strategic importance for companies in order to adapt to the current structural change
(decentralization, more flexibility). Specialized, up-to-date knowledge is required
not only for the intended innovations but also for organization-internal changes
as well as the production and sales of products. However, such knowledge often
cannot be provided organization-internally.

Knowledge-intensive services and especially knowledge work [14,25] represent
a quickly increasing part of the service sector. "Knowledge-intensive work" includes activities that require an intensive education and experience on a specific subject that has been accumulated over many years [36,23]. "Knowledge-
intensive services" need the resource knowledge as their most important input

P. Perner (Ed.): ICDM 2006, LNAI 4065, pp. 539–547, 2006.

factor for delivering the respective service [18]. "Knowledge work" denotes activities that not only base their problem solving process on knowledge acquired once, but also necessarily have to revise, improve and update their knowledge [36,23]. Experience represents the success-critical knowledge for knowledge-intensive services and knowledge work [19].

Within this paper we describe our research vision of how to develop intelligent information systems for supporting knowledge work and knowledge-intensive services with a specific focus on the use of experience [20,2]. Our vision especially includes computer-based, fully and/or partially automated knowledge work. Besides the known application possibilities within service economics (for a lot of success stories see [13]) our research also contributes to achieve ambitious goals as being formulated by the European Union (e.g., the so-called ambient intelligence scenarios [21] or the scenarios described in the report on "converging technologies" [15]; also [29]). Fully or partially automating knowledge work has the additional advantage that the provided knowledge is not only knowledge for the user, but - to an increasing degree - also knowledge for the computer on which it is used. This enables automated processing of knowledge and offers a unique added-value if compared with more traditional approaches.

Many requirements have to be fulfilled while developing intelligent information systems. In addition, the service expectation of our society is increasing and this is not going to change in the near future. Future information systems users expect to be easily supported, information systems to behave "intelligently" and learn from experience, and to improve their behavior by this. As a consequence, such intelligent information systems should be flexible, modular, and easily to adapt and maintain. These systems should contain a lot of valuable knowledge understandable for both the user and the computer. That is why such systems are also called "knowledge-based".

Implementing such intelligent information systems involves numerous problems, a lot of which have already been solved in principle or exemplary for selected tasks. However, the corresponding solutions are mostly developed by different research communities that only have a restricted exchange/communication with one another. Nevertheless, past experience has proven that achieving major progress for fields like the implementation of intelligent information systems requires integrating methods and techniques from different (sub-) disciplines. We present a research vision that has been developed while the authors were working in the computer science sub-disciplines software engineering (SE), artificial intelligence (AI), and business information systems. As a consequence, our vision is basing on an integration of approaches from these fields.

This includes the SE approaches experience factory and software product-lines as well as case-based reasoning, intelligent agents, and machine learning from AI. In addition, there are a lot of relationships to knowledge management and business processes, which may be viewed as part of business information systems.

2   Integration of Agent Technology, Case-Based-Reasoning, Experience-Factory, and Sofware Product-Lines

Experience factory (EF) is a logical and/or physical infrastructure for continuous learning from experience (Fig. 1). It includes an experience base for knowledge storage and knowledge reuse. The experience factory concept was introduced in the mid 1980s to support the central process of SE, the software development process [12,16]. Basili and Rombach consider software development running in projects separate from the learning organization experience factory because these two sub-organizations have different goals. Projects have to achieve their project goals, that is, developing software according to the given requirements. Experience factory, however, supports learning across projects. From a project's perspective this can be viewed as additional effort and might lead to a goal conflict. Such a separation of learning and project organization is a characteristic feature of an experience factory [9] and has been validated in practice.

Experience factory bases on the so-called quality improvement paradigm, a goal-oriented learning cycle for the experience based improvement of project planning, project execution, and project learning. Goal-oriented measurement and evaluation is used as a systematic procedure for evaluation [10]. Figure 1 shows the separation between learning and project organization, the main interfaces between projects and experience factory as well as various roles within the experience factory. While the experience factory manager has the overall responsibility, the experience manager has associated the task of deciding about content development and structuring. The experience engineer is responsible for packaging and analyzing the experience base.

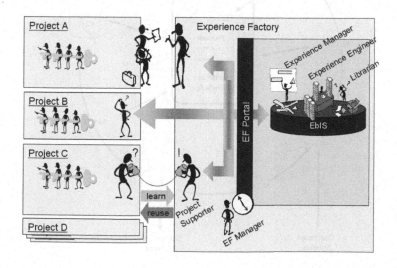

Fig. 1. Experience Factory

While the librarian cares about the technical and administrative tasks, the project supporter finally is the main contact for the respective projects.

Already before the invention of the experience factory approach, and until the mid 1990s also independently from it, case-based reasoning was introduced in the area of cognitive science and artificial intelligence in the late 1970s and the beginning 1980s. It was introduced as a model for human problem solving and learning [32,26]. Experiences are stored in the form of solved problems (case-specific knowledge, cases) in a so-called case base. A new problem is then solved by transferring the already known solution of a similar case from the case base to the new problem and adapting the solution if necessary (see Fig. 2).

Within AI, case-based reasoning effected a focusing of knowledge-based systems on experience [8,4,1,3] in the late 1980s and the 1990s. Incorporating the dynamic-memory-idea of Schank ensured a situation-based approach, which often led to a good user acceptance. Accordingly a number of commercial tools and many real-life applications were developed (e.g., [5] and [13,34]). Important problems in the mid 1990s were how to systematically develop a CBR system, how to operate it, how to integrate it into an industrial environment as well as how to evaluate it.

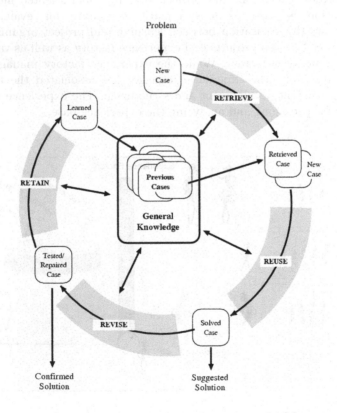

Fig. 2. Case-based reasoning process model [7]

From an experience factory perspective in the mid 1990s the basic approach was already introduced by Basili, Rombach et al. With NASA SEL a very successful and established application was available. In addition, there were also some other positive examples. Important problems in the mid 1990s were how to implement an experience base, how the necessary processes for developing an experience factory/base should look like in detail, as well as how experiments about implementation issues could be carried out.

The following integration of the experience factory and the case-based reasoning concepts [33] led to numerous advantages. Case-based reasoning provided an appropriate technology for implementing the experience base. In addition, a lot of detailed knowledge about the case-based reasoning processes was already available in the corresponding community and could be used as a very good starting point for describing experience factory processes. The experience factory approach provided knowledge about organizationally embedding case-based reasoning systems in commercial organizations. In addition, it contributed an approach that could be easily applied for evaluating case-based reasoning systems: goal-oriented measurement and evaluation [6].

Enhancing the integration of experience factory and case-based reasoning also led to the integration of systematic reuse into the software development process. As a consequence, the implementation of the experience/case base was based on the software product-line approach [28,30,27] and introduced as so-called "experience based information systems" (EbIS). Thus, an experience/case base was no more realized as single system but as a whole system family. The underlying system architecture is shown in Figure 3. As several of the presented components have different implementations, the architecture describes a family of systems, which definition is based on a number of responsibly designed, common features [31].

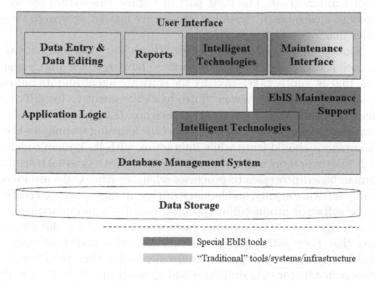

Fig. 3. Product-line architecture for EF/CBR systems [28]

3   Vision

The extraordinary significance of knowledge as a production factor of increasing importance was already pointed out in the beginning of this contribution. We emphasized as well our vision to develop intelligent information systems for supporting knowledge work and knowledge-intensive services, focusing on creating added-value through increasingly automated use of available knowledge. This resulted in the idea of a "knowledge product-line" (or short "knowledge-line"). A knowledge-line denotes the systematic application of the software product-line approach to the knowledge included in intelligent information systems.

Knowledge-lines enable the necessary "knowledge level modularization" for building potential variants in the sense of software product-lines. This is achieved through the use of multi-agent systems [17,35] as a basic approach for intelligent information systems. An intelligent agent is implemented as a case-based reasoning system, which besides experience can also include other kinds of knowledge. Each case-based reasoning system agent is embedded in an experience factory that is responsible for all necessary knowledge processes like knowledge inflow, knowledge outflow as well as knowledge analysis. Such an experience factory is potentially fully automated, because software agents are available for each role within the experience factory, and perform these roles in an increasingly automated way. For example, machine learning techniques are used for analyzing, evaluating, and maintaining the case base. As part of the vision both the case-based reasoning system agents as well as experience factory agents can learn from experience. As a consequence, the vision considers distributed learning systems as a model for future (intelligent) software systems.

Figure 4 presents a potential implementation of the vision. The left part of Figure 4 shows the case-based-reasoning-enabled operation of an experience factory for different subject areas. The right part of Figure 4 describes the systematic development of a case-based reasoning/experience factory system in the sense of a knowledge-line.

For each role within an experience factory there is at least one software agent. However, each software agent has an associated human coach who is responsible for the role that is jointly taken over by the software agent and its human coach (see Fig. 5). The human role owner "introduces the agent to his job" by taking over difficult decisions and providing his experience. Based on the case-based reasoning/experience factory approach and machine learning techniques the respective software agent should learn while interacting with its human coach and autonomously take over more and more tasks. This enables a gradual transition from purely human based processes to processes where routine tasks are increasingly taken over by software agents, and humans can spend more time on creative tasks.

Using the software product-line approach enables a modularization already on the knowledge level. The modules have associated the variabilities and requirements that they satisfy. As a consequence, such knowledge-line modules can be selected using a catalogue of requirements. By this, the development of further experience factories is simplified and speeded up. Nick [28] has identified an efficiency improvement by a factor > 4 for developing the design of an experi-

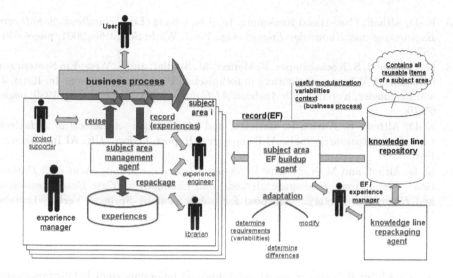

Fig. 4. Knowledge-line for developing intelligent information systems

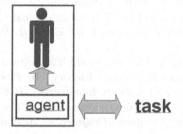

Fig. 5. Experience factory role owner as a coach for the respectively associated software agent

ence based information system. Further efficiency improvement for the build-up of experience factories is expected from increasing automation of an experience factory build-up agent.

References

1. D.W. Aha: The AAAI-99 KM/CBR Workshop: Summary of Contributions. *Proc. ICCBR 99 Workshops, II-37-II-44.* Technical Report, LSA-99-03E, TU Kaiserslautern, 1999.
2. K.-D. Althoff, J. Mänz, and M. Nick: Maintaining Experience to Learn: Case Studies on Case-Based Reasoning and Experience Factory. In *Proc. 6th Workshop Days of the German Computer Science Society (GI) on Learning, Knowledge, and Adaptivity (LWA 2005) Workshop on Machine Learning, Knowledge Discovery, and Data Mining,* Saarland University, Germany, Oct. 2005.

3. K.-D. Althoff: Case-Based Reasoning. In: S.K. Chang (Ed.), *Handbook on Software Engineering and Knowledge Engineering. Vol.1*, World Scientific, 2001; pages 549-587.

4. K.-D. Althoff, S. Kockskämper, F. Maurer, M. Stadler, and S. Wess: Ein System zur fallbasierten Wissensverarbeitung in technischen Diagnosesituationen. In: Retti, J. and Leidlmeier, K. (eds.), *5th Austrian AI-Conference*, Springer Verlag, 1989; pages 65-70.

5. K.-D. Althoff, E. Auriol, R. Barletta, and M. Manago: *A Review of Industrial Case-Based Reasoning Tools*. AI Perspectives Report, Oxford, UK: AI Intelligence, 1995.

6. K.-D. Althoff and M. Nick: *How to Support Experience Management with Evaluation - Foundations, Evaluation Methods, and Examples for Case-Based Reasoning and Experience Factory*. Accepted for publication by Springer Verlag, Lecture Notes of Computer Science/Artificial Intelligence (in progress)

7. A. Aamodt and E. Plaza: Case-based reasoning: Foundational issues, methodological variations, and system approaches. *AI Communications* 7(1), 1994, pages 39-59.

8. B. Bartsch-Spörl: Ansätze zur Behandlung von fallorientiertem Erfahrungswissen in Expertensystemen. *KI 4(1987)*, pages 32-36.

9. V. R. Basili, G. Caldiera, and H. D. Rombach: Experience Factory. In Mar-ciniak, J.J. (ed.), *Encyclopedia of SE, vol 1*, John Wiley & Sons; 1994; pages 469-476

10. V. R. Basili, G. Caldiera, and H. D. Rombach: Goal Question Metric Paradigm. In Marciniak, J.J. (ed.), *Encyclopedia of SE, vol 1*, Wiley & Sons, 1994; pages 528-532.

11. V. R. Basili, G. Caldiera, F. McGarry et al.: The Software Engineering Laboratory-An Operational Software Experience Factory. In *Proceedings of the Fourteenth International Conference on Software Engineering (ICSE 92)*, May 1992, 12 pages.

12. V. R. Basili: Quantitative evaluation of software methodology. In *Proceedings of the First Pan-Pacific Computer Conference*, Melbourne, Australia, September 1985.

13. R. Bergmann, K.-D. Althoff, S. Breen, M. Göker, M. Manago, R. Traphöner, and S. Wess: *Developing Industrial Case-Based Reasoning Applications*. Springer Verlag, LNAI 1612, 2003.

14. H.-J. Bullinger and R. Ilg: Leben und Arbeiten in einer vernetzten, mobilen Welt. In Uhr, W., Esswein, W. & Schoop, E. (Hrsg.), *Wirtschaftsinformatik 2003 Band I*, Physica Verlag, 2003, pages 1-8.

15. W. Bibel, D. Andler, O. Da Costa, G. Kppers, and I. D. Pearson: *Converging Technologies and the Natural, Social and Cultural World*. Report of the EU High Level Expert Group on "Forsighting the New Technology Wave" (FoNTWave), 30.6.2004.

16. V. R. Basili and H. D. Rombach: The TAME Project: Towards improvement-oriented software environments. *IEEE Transactions on SE, SE-14(6)*, 1988; pages 758-773.

17. H.-D. Burkhard: Software-Agenten. In Görz, G., Rollinger, C.-R. & Schneeberger, J., *Handbuch der Künstlichen Intelligenz*, 4. Auflage, pages 943-1020.

18. J. Cramer: Management wissensintensiver Dienstleistungen. In *[Her03a]*, pages 179-203.

19. C. Brasse and M. Uhlmann: Integration von Erfahrungswissen. In *[Her03a]*, pages 121-132.

20. B. Decker and K.-D. Althoff: Prozesslernen und Erfahrungsmanagement: Ergebnisse aus dem indiGo-Projekt. In *Proc. Lernen - Wissen - Adaptivität 2004 (LWA 2004)*, pages 138-145.

21. K. Ducatel, M. Bogdanowicz, F. Scapolo, J. Lejten, and J.-C. Burgelman: *Scenarios of Ambient Intelligence in 2010*. IST Advisory Group (ISTAG), European Commission Community Research, 2001.

22. S. Hermann, (Hrsg.): *Integrierter Schlussbericht - Verbundprojekt SIAM "Strategien, Instrumente und arbeitsorganisatorische Gestaltungsmodelle zur Förderung der Dienstleistungskompetenz in Unternehmen*, 2003. http://www.siam.iao.fraunhofer.de/intern/intern-berichte/siam-schlussbericht-final.doc (Accessed on Oct. 20, 2005).

23. S. Hermann: Produktive Wissensarbeit - Eine Herausforderung. In *[Her03a]*, pages 204-224.

24. M. Kiehl: *Arbeitsmarktentwicklung und wissensintensive Dienstleistungen im östlichen Ruhrgebiet*. Universitt Dortmund, LS VWL, insb. Raumwirtschaftspolitik, Arbeitskreis Strukturpolitik, 12.6.2003.

25. Bundesministerium für Forschung und Technologie, Bekanntmachung über die Förderung von Forschungsvorhaben auf dem Gebiet "Wissensintensive Dienstleistungen", 14.1.2000.

26. J. L. Kolodner: *Case-Based Reasoning*. Morgan Kaufmann Publishers, San Mateo, 1993.

27. D. Muthig: Systematischer Aufbau und Einsatz von Wissen zur effizienten Entwicklung von Software-Varianten. *KI (2)2005*, pages 5-11.

28. M. Nick: *Experience Maintenance through Closed-Loop Feedback*. PhD Thesis, Department of Computer Science, University of Kaiserslautern, 2005.

29. J. Rech and K.-D. Althoff: Artificial Intelligence and Software Engineering - Status and Future Trends. *Special Issue on Artificial Intelligence & Software Engineering, KI (3)2004*, pages 5-11.

30. K. Schmid: Systematische Wiederverwendung im Produktlinienumfeld - Ein Enscheidungsproblem. *Special Issue on Artificial Intelligence & Software Engineering, KI (3)2004*, pages 33-35.

31. K. Schmid: *Planning Software Reuse - A Disciplined Scoping Approach for Software Product Lines*. PhD thesis, University of Kaiserslautern, IRB Verlag, 2002.

32. R. C. Schank: *Dynamic Memory: A Theory of Learning in Computers and People*. Cambridge University Press, 1982.

33. C. Tautz: *Customizing Software Engineering Experience Management Systems to Organizational Needs*. PhD Thesis, Department of Computer Science, University of Kaiserslautern; Fraunhofer IRB Verlag, 2000.

34. I. Watson (ed.): *Applying Knowledge Management: techniques for building corporate memories*. Morgan Kaufmann Publishers Inc. San Francisco CA, 2003.

35. G. Wei (Ed.): *Multiagent systems. A modern approach to distributed artificial intelligence*. The MIT Press, 1999.

36. H. Willke: Organisierte Wissensarbeit. In *Zeitschrift für Soziologie* (1998) 3, pages 161-177.

Nonparametric Approaches for e-Learning Data

Paolo Baldini[1], Silvia Figini[2], and Paolo Giudici[3]

[1] University of Pavia,
27100 Pavia, Italy
paolo.baldini@unipv.it
[2] University of Pavia,
27100 Pavia, Italy
silvia.figini@eco.unipv.it
[3] University of Pavia,
27100 Pavia, Italy
giudici@unipv.it
http://www.datamininglab.it

Abstract. In the paper we propose nonparametric approaches for e-learning data. In particular we want to supply a measure of the relative exercises importance, to estimate the acquired Knowledge for each student and finally to personalize the e-learning platform. The methodology employed is based on a comparison between nonparametric statistics for kernel density classification and parametric models such as generalized linear models and generalized additive models.

1 Introduction

The concept of a probability density function is a central idea in statistics. Its role in statistical modelling is to encapsulate the pattern of random variation in the data which is not explained by the other structural terms of a model. In many settings this role, while important, is a secondary one, with the main focus resting on the nature of covariate or other effects. However, there are also situations where the detailed shape of the underlying density function is itself of primary interest. Smoothing techniques such as density estimation and non parametric regression have become established tools in applied statistics. There is now a wide variety of texts which describe these methods and a huge literature of research papers. Recent texts include Green and Silverman (1994), Wand and Jones (1995), Fan and Gijbels (1996), Simonoff (1996), Bowman and Azzalini (1997). A broader framework for the case of regression, known as generalized additive models, is also described by Hastie and Tibshirani (1990).

Modern statistical computing environments are generally geared towards vector and matrix representations of data. It is therefore a principal aim of this paper to provide simple matrix formulation of smoothing techniques which allow efficient implementation in this type of environment. A second aim of the paper is to adress the computational issues which arise when nonparametric methods are applied to large data set. This talk is structured as follow: in Section 2 we present methods on density estimation for exploring data; in Section 3

P. Perner (Ed.): ICDM 2006, LNAI 4065, pp. 548–560, 2006.

and Section 4 the properties of density estimates; in Section 5 we propose a method for feature selection in nonparametric spaces. Finally in Section 6 and Section 7 we show some inferential models and in Section 8 the results about our application.

2   Density Estimation for Exploring Data

The aim of this section is to explore techniques for describing data. The first method is based on construction of a histogram. This begins by dividing the sample space into a number of intervals. Each observation contributes a 'box' which is then placed over the appropriate interval.

If y denotes the point at which the density f must be estimated, the histogram may be written as:

$$\tilde{f}(y) = \sum_{i=1}^{n} I(y - \tilde{y}_i; h), \tag{1}$$

where $\{y_1, ..., y_n\}$ denote the observed data, $\tilde{y}_i$ denotes the centre of the interval in which y_i falls and $I(z; h)$ is the indicator function of the interval $[-h, h]$. Notice that further scaling would be required to ensure that $\tilde{f}$ integrates to 1.

Viewed as a density estimate, the histogram may be criticised in three ways.

- Information has been thrown away in replacing y_i by the central point of the interval in which it falls;
- In most circumstances, the underlying density function is assumed to be smooth, but the estimator is not smooth, due to the sharp edges of the boxes from which it is built;
- The behaviour of the estimator is dependent on the choice of width of the intervals used, and also to some extent on the starting position of the grid of intervals.

Rosenblatt (1956), Whittle (1958) and Parzen (1962) developed an approach to the problem which removes the first two of these difficulties. First, a smooth kernel function rather than a box is used as the basic building block. Second, these smooth functions are centred directly over each observation.

The kernel estimator is then of the form:

$$\hat{f}(y) = \frac{1}{n} \sum_{i=1}^{n} w(y - y_i; h), \tag{2}$$

where w is itself a probability density, called in this context a kernel function, whose variance is controlled by the parameter h. It is natural to adopt a function w which is symmetric with mean 0, but beyond that it is generally agreed that the exact shape is not too important. It is often convenient to use for w a normal density function, so that:

$$w(y - y_i; h) = \phi(y - y_i; h), \tag{3}$$

where $\phi(z; h)$ denotes the normal density function in z with mean 0 and standard deviation h. Because of its role in determining the manner in which the probability associated with each observation is spread over the surrounding sample space, h is called the *smoothing parameter* or *bandwidth*. Since properties of w are inherited by $\hat{f}$, choosing w to be smooth will produce a density estimate which is also smooth.

The third criticism of the histogram still applies to the smooth density estimate, namely that its behaviour is affected by the choice of the width of the kernel function, h.

The kernel method extends to the estimation of a density function in more than one dimension. As a descriptive exercise, a two-dimesional density estimate can be constructed by applying the first equation with a two-dimensional kernel function in the form:

$$\hat{f}(y_1, y_2) = \frac{1}{n} \sum_{i=1}^{n} w(y_1 - y_{1i}; h_1) w(y_1 - y_{2i}; h_2), \tag{4}$$

where $\{y_{1i} y_{2i}; i = 1, ..., n\}$ denote the data and (h_1, h_2) denote the joint smoothing parameters. It is possible also to study multivariate version of kernel function: Scott (1992) describes a variety of more sophisticated techniques for constructing and displaying density estimation that can be carried out in three, four and more dimensions.

3 Properties of Density Estimates

In order to go beyond the exploratory and graphical stage it is necessary first to understand more about the behaviour of these estimators and to derive some basic properties. Although many theoretical results exist, simple expressions for means and variances of the estimators are enough to allow ideas of interval estimation and hypothesis testing to be discussed, and to motivate techniques for choosing an appropriate bandwidth to employ with a particular dataset.

The mean of a density estimator can be written as:

$$E\left\{\hat{f}(y)\right\} = \int w(y - z; h) f(z) dz, \tag{5}$$

This is a convolution of the true density function f with the kernel function w. Smoothing has therefore produced a biased estimator, whose mean is a smoothed version of the true density. A Taylor series expansion then produces the approximation:

$$E\left\{\hat{f}(y)\right\} \approx f(y) + \frac{h^2}{2} \sigma_w^2 f''(y), \tag{6}$$

where σ_w^2 denotes the variance of the kernel function, namely $\int z^2 w(z) dz$.

Since $f''(y)$ measures the rate of curvature of the density function, this expresses the fact that $\hat{f}$ underestimates f at peaks in the true density and overestimates at troughs. The size of the bias is affected by the smoothing parameter

h. The component σ_w^2 will reduce to 1 if the kernel function w is chosen to have unit variance. Through another Taylor series argument, the variance of the density estimate can be approximated by:

$$var\left\{\hat{f}(y)\right\} \approx \frac{1}{nh}f(y)\alpha(w), \tag{7}$$

where $\alpha(w) = \int w^2(z)dz$. As ever, the variance is inversely proportional to sample size. In fact the term nh can be viewed as governing the local sample size, since h controls the number of observations whose kernel weight contributes to the estimate at y. It is also useful to note that the variance is approximately proportional to the height of the true density function.

The combined effect of these properties is that, in order to produce an estimator which converges to the true density function f, it is necessary that both h and $1/nh$ decrease as the sample size increases. A suitable version of the central limit theorem can also be used to show that the distribution of the estimator is asymptotically normal.

A similar analysis enables approximate expressions to be derived for the mean and variance of a density estimate in the multivariate case. In p dimension, with a kernel function defined as the product of univariate components w, and with smoothing parameters $(h_1, ..., h_p)$. Wand and Jones (1995) derive results for more general kernel functions.

It is helpful to define an overall measure of how effective $\hat{f}$ is in estimating f. A simple choice for this is the *mean integrated squared error* (MISE) which, in the one-dimensional case, is:

$$MISE(\hat{f}) = E\left\{\int \left[\hat{f}(y) - f(y)\right]^2 dy\right\} \tag{8}$$

$$= \int \left[E\left\{\hat{f}(y)\right\} - f(y)\right]^2 dy + \int var\left\{\hat{f}(y)\right\} dy, \tag{9}$$

This combination of bias and variance, integrated over the sample space, has been the convenient focus of most of theoretical work carried out on these estimates. In particular, the Taylor series approximations described allow the mean integrated squared error to be approximated as:

$$MISE(\hat{f}) \approx \frac{1}{4}h^4\sigma_w^4 \int f''(y)^2 dy + \frac{1}{nh}\alpha(w), \tag{10}$$

establishing the properties of the estimators which employ variable bandwidths, is more complex. Bowman and Foster (1993) avoided asymptotic calculations by employing numerical integration in the calculations of mean and variance. In order to construct a density estimate from the observed data it is necessary to choose a value for the smoothing parameter h. In this paper we describe only some methods employed to choose h for our application. An overall measure of the effectiveness of $\hat{f}$ in estimating f is provided by the mean integrated squared error. From the approximate expression given there it is straightforward to show that the value of h which minimizes MISE in an asymptotic sense is:

$$h_{opt} = \left\{ \frac{\gamma(w)}{\beta(f)n} \right\}^{1/5}, \tag{11}$$

where $\gamma(w) = \alpha(w)/\sigma_w^4$ and $\beta(f) = \int f''(y)^2 dy$. This optimal value for h cannot immediately be used in practice since it involves the unknown density function f. However, in our case, it is very informative in showing how smoothing parameters should decrease with sample size, namely proportionately to $n^{1/5}$, and quantifying the effect of the curvature of f through the factor $\beta(f)$.

These ideas involved in cross-validation are given a general description by Stone (1974). In the context of density estimation, Rudemo (1982) and Bowman (1984) applied these ideas to the problem of bandwidth choice, through estimation of the integrated squared error (ISE).

$$\int \left\{ \hat{f}(y) - f(y) \right\}^2 dy = \int \hat{f}(y)^2 dy - 2 \int f(y)\hat{f}(y)dy + \int f(y)^2 dy, \tag{12}$$

The last term on the right hand side does not involve h. The other terms can be estimated by:

$$\frac{1}{n} \sum_{i=1}^{n} \int \hat{f}_{-i}^2(y)dy - \frac{2}{n} \sum_{i=1}^{n} \hat{f}_{-i}(y_i), \tag{13}$$

where $\hat{f}_{-i}(y)$ denotes the estimator constructed from the data without the observation y_i. It is straightforward to show that the expectation of this expression is the MISE of $\hat{f}$ based on $(n-1)$ observations, omitting the $\int f^2$ term. The value of h that minimises this expression therefore provides an estimate of the optimal smoothing parameter. Stone (1984) derived an asymptotic optimality result for bandwidths which are chosen in this cross-validatory fashion.

Techniques known as *biased cross-validation* (Scott and Terrell 1987) and *smoothed cross-validation* (Hall et al. 1992) also aim to minimise ISE but use different estimates of this quantity. These approaches are also strongly related to the 'plug-in' approach. In our application we employed different methods with multivariate density estimates: Optimal smoothing, normal optimal smoothing, cross-validation and Sheather-Jones (Sheather and Jones, 1991) smoothing parameter. Jones et al. (1996) give a helpful and balanced discussion of methods of choosing the smoothing parameter in density estimation.

4   Feature Selection: A Nonparametric Smoothing Approach

The existence of density estimates gives the opportunity to explore dependence in a more flexible way. A general definition of independence is that the joint density of two variables decomposes into the product of the marginal densities:

$$f_{12}(y_1, y_2) = f_1(y_1) \times f_2(y_2), \tag{14}$$

An assessment of independence in a very general sense can then be performed by contrasting these joint and marginal density estimates. There are many ways in which this could be done. However, a natural approach is to construct a likelihood ratio expression:

$$\frac{1}{n} \sum \log \left\{ \frac{\hat{f}_{12}(y_{1i}, y_{2i})}{\hat{f}_1(y_{1i})\hat{f}_2(y_{2i})} \right\}, \tag{15}$$

A computational approach to the derivation of the distribution of this test statistic under the null hypothesis of independence is to apply a permutation argument, where values of y_{1i} are associated with randomly permuted y_{2i}. An empirical $p - value$ can be calculated as the proportion of statistics computed from the permuted data whose values exceed that of the observed statistic from the original data. Our ideas to reduce the dimensionality is based on Bjerve and Doksum(1993), Doksum et al.(1994) and Jones (1996) that suggest how dependence between *variables* can be quantified in a local way through the definition of correlation curves and local dependence function. In our application, see section for results, to show the similarity between two density function we use the previous methodology and we improve the results using a technique known as the smoothed boostrap, which involves simulating from $\hat{f}$ rather than resampling the original data. Taylor (1989) and Scott(1992) discusses and illustrates the role of the smoothed bootstrap in constructing confidence intervals.

After that it is possible to improve feature selection with a comparison between curves and surfaces. In a formal way, the hypotheses are:

$$H_0 : f(y) = g(y), \tag{16}$$

$$H_1 : f(y) \neq g(y), \tag{17}$$

In our case we use an approach for comparing two density estimates $\hat{f}$ and $\hat{g}$ is based on the following statistic:

$$Difference = \int \left\{ \hat{f}(y) - \hat{g}(y) \right\}^2 dy, \tag{18}$$

In the case of a test of normality, when normal kernel functions are used, it is possible to show how the integration can be carried out analytically, since the statistic can be represented as the sum of convolutions of normal curves. The same strategy can be applied to the previous expression. However, when the sample sizes are large it is more efficient, and sufficiently accurate, to approximate the value of the integral through numerical integration, using density estiamtes which are evaluated over a finily spaced grid along the horizontal axis.

When estimates of the densities are constructed individually this will lead to the use of two different smoothing parameter. There is however some potential advantage to be gained in using the same smoothing parameter for each estimate. This arises from the properties of denisty estimates, which were briefly described in Section 3. In particular, the means of the estimates are:

$$E\left\{ \hat{f}(y) \right\} = \int \phi(y - z; h) f(z) dz, \tag{19}$$

$$E\left\{\hat{g}(y)\right\} = \int \phi(y - z; h)g(z)dz, \tag{20}$$

Under the null hypothesis that the two density functions f and g are identical, these two means will therefore also be identical if the same smoothing parameter h is used in the construction of each. The distributional properties of the test statistic are difficult to establish when the null hypotesis is of such a broad form, with no particular shape specified for the common underlying density.

We compare more than two groups with the following statistic:

$$\sum_{i=1}^{p} n_i \int \left\{\hat{f}_i(y) - \hat{f}(y)\right\}^2 dy, \tag{21}$$

where $\hat{f}_1, ..., \hat{f}_p$ denote the density estimates for the groups, $\hat{f}$ denotes the density estimate constructed from the entire set of data, ignoring the group labels, and n_i denotes the sample size for group i. In order to preserve zero bias in the comparisons, a common smoothing parameter should again be employed, including in the combined estimate $\hat{f}$. We point out that in densities comparison is therefore crucial at any point y the quantity $var\left\{\hat{f} - \hat{g}\right\}$.

5   Kernel Density Estimation and Unsupervised Classification

Kernel density estimation is an unsupervised learning procedure, which historically precedes kernel regression. It also leads naturally to a simple family of procedures for nonparametric classification. One can use nonparametric density estimates for classification in a straightforward fashion using Bayes theorem. Suppose for a J class problem we fit nonparametric density estimates $\hat{f}_j(X)$, $j = 1, ..., J$ separately in each of the classes, and we also have estimates of the class priors $\hat{\pi}_j$ (usually the sample proportions). Then:

$$\hat{Pr}(G = j | X = x_0) = \frac{\hat{\pi}_j \hat{f}_j(x_0)}{\sum_{k=1}^{J} \hat{\pi}_k \hat{f}_k(x_0)}, \tag{22}$$

In our application we use Bayes theorem in a multavariate case and in particular we use a set of densities that come from the past feature selection (about 10 densities). In particular we assume that the densities are independent.

An other way to make classification is based on supervised methods. Regression models play an important role in many data analyses, providing prediction and classification rules, and data analytic tools for understanding the importance of different inputs. Although attractively simple, the traditional linear model often fails in these situations: in real life, effects are often not linear. This section describes more automatic flexible statistical methods that may be used to identify and characterize nonlinear regression effects. These methods are called generalized additive models. In the regression setting, a generalized additive model (Hastie and Tibshirani 1990) has the form:

$$E(Y|X_1...X_p) = \alpha + f_1(X_1) + ... + f_p(X_p), \tag{23}$$

As usual $X_1, X_2, ..., X_p$ represent predictors and Y is the outcome; the f_j's are unspecified smooth functions. Our approach : we fit each function using a scatterplot smoother (e.g., a cubic smoothing spline or kernel smoother), and provide an algorithm for simultaneously estimating all p functions. For two-class classification, as in our case, recall the *logistic regression model* for binary data. We relate the mean of the binary response $\mu(X) = Pr(Y = 1|X)$ to the predictors via a linear regression model and the logit link function:

$$log \frac{mu(X)}{1 - mu(X)} = \alpha + \beta_0 X_1 + ... + \beta_p X_p, \tag{24}$$

The *additive logistic regression model* replaces each linear term by a more general functional form:

$$log \frac{mu(X)}{1 - mu(X)} = \alpha + f_1 X_1 + ... + f_p X_p, \tag{25}$$

where again each f_j is an unspecified smooth function. While the nonparametric form for the functions f_j make the model more flexible, the additivity is retained and allows us to interpret the model in much the same way as before. The additive logistic regression model is an example of a generalized additive model. In general, the conditional mean $\mu(X)$ of a response Y is related to an additive function of the predictors via a link function g:

$$g\left[\mu(X)\right] = \alpha + f_1 X_1 + ... + f_p X_p, \tag{26}$$

Examples of classical link functions are the identity link, the probit link function for modeling binomial probabilities (the probit function is the inverse Gaussian cumulative distribution function), the logit link function for log-linear or log-additive models and for Poisson count data. All three of these arise from exponential family sampling models, which in addition include the gamma and negative-binomial distributions. These families generate the well-known class of generalized linear models, which are all extended in the same way to generalized additive models. In our application the target variable is binary, then we fit an additive logistic regression model. In this model the outcome Y can be coded as 0 or 1. We wish to model $Pr(Y = 1|X)$, the probability of an event given values of the covariates $X = (X_1, ..., X_p)$. The generalized additive logistic model has the form:

$$log(\frac{Pr(Y = 1|X)}{Pr(Y = 0|X)}) = \alpha + \beta_0 X_1 + ... + \beta_p X_p, \tag{27}$$

The functions $f_1, ..., f_p$ are estimated by a backfitting algorithm within a Newton Raphson procedure.

6   The Data

We want to supply a measure of the relative exercises importance, to estimate the acquired Knowledge for each student and finally to personalize the e-learning platform. The data are structured in 5 tables:

- IDUSER: the data related to the students that are enrolled to the course
- IDSESSION: the date and the initial and final time for every session in which a students is connected
- TREE: structure of the e-learning web site
- TRK1: transactional dataset of the lessons, as well as the final examination of each level and its evaluation
- TRK2: transactional dataset of the exercises and their evaluation.

To better understand the following analysis, is necessary to describe how the site is structured. It is formed by 15 levels and every level presents 11 unities (10 lessons and final examination): Assessment, Dialogue, Glossary, Introduction, Listening 1, Listening 2, Pronunciation, Reading, Use of English, Video and Vocabulary.

The descriptive analysis is mainly assembled on the data of the TRK2 table. Initially we have examined the variable Status that identifies which result has made the student in the different exercises. The acceptable values of this variable are C (completed), I (incomplete), F (Failure), P (passed). The results identify that the values of status C are relative to exercises that have been completed, but that they have not met the minimium threshold of evaluation. We have eliminated from the initial table only the anomalous observations and the values of status I. We have deleted 37203 observations from the 147432 of departure.

The second step has been to examine whether there are some errors in the assignment of the values P and F: there have not been found. In a next step, by assigning to each exercise its specific level it has become possible to understand how students are distributed among the levels. We have found that only 38 students are present in all levels. At this point we have considered only the data related to the level 1 that contained 463 students. To build the dataset we have united the observation of the table TRK1 related to the same level The final table contains 376 students and 17 variables.

7   Application

In order to explore the data available with particular focus on the exercices we compare histogram and kernel density estimation. This application concerns an e-learning platform used for english courses at the University of Pavia. The same course is proposed also for private companies. In our talk we analyze only private students. The course is divided in different type of exercises; some with evaluation (pronunciation, listening and assessment), the others without evaluation (grammar). The score of the first ranges between 0 and 100. The threshold to pass an exercise is 50. In Figure 1 we show the histogram and the relative

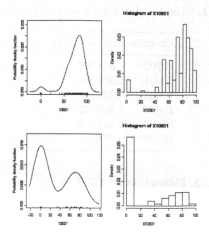

Fig. 1. Histogram and density for comprehension exercise

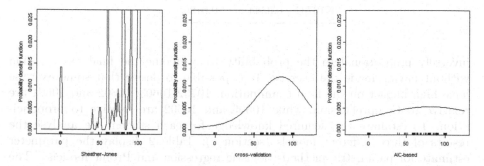

Fig. 2. Optimal smoothing parameter

density estimate for a comprehension exercise. The histogram is a widely used tool for displaying the distributional shape of a set of data. The left panel of Figure 1 displays an alternative estimate of the density function as a smooth curve. In the above part of Figure 1 it is possible to see the distribution of the students who have passed the final examination and in the lower part there who not. For kernel density estimation the choice of a bandwidth is a compromise between smoothing enough to remove insignificant bumps and not smoothing too much to smear out real peaks. In our application we have compared three differents methods (see Figure 2) to estimate optimal smoothing parameter (Sheather-Jones, Cross-Validation and AIC based methods). In particular, Sheather and Jones (1991) in our application produce an output very closed on the data. For our application, in order to find the best smoothing parameter, is better to use and compare Cross-Validation and AIC based methods.

To classify our exercises, we use the approach described in section 6. We present the results in Table 1 for the most critical exercises. We have supposed that it is possible to measure the relative importance for each exercise as

Table 1. Classification with posterior probabilities

Exercice	Pr(G=1|X=0)
10702	0.308166
10601	0.331919
10603	0.363216
10602	0.403032
10503	0.434726
10502	0,454616

Table 2. Estimation for Logit and probit model

Variable	GLM Logit	GLM Probit
Intercept	-2.3121	-1.3390
X10308	-0.0396	-0.0219
X10309	0.0291	0.0154
X10702	0.0344	0.0196

inversely proportional to the probability to overcome the final examination without having made the exercise. It is possible to derive that some exercise have high impact on the final examination. 10702 10603, 10602 and 10601 are relative to Comprehension, while 10503 and 10502 are relative to pronunciation. To estimate the acquired knowledge for each student we analyse the results of three different models (section 7). Table 2 display the parameter estimate for parametric methods: logistic regression and Probit models. The parametric models presents the same significative exercises. Table 3 show the outcome from generalized additive model. In our application we use the splines. For smoothing splines it would be possible to set up a penalized least-squares problem and minimize that, but there would be computational difficulties in choosing the smoothing parameters simultaneously. In our case an iterative approach is used with bakfitting algorithm. In order to choose the best predictive model we apply ANOVA analysis (Table 4). The best model under this measure evaluation is based on nonparametric approach. The confusion matrix (see e.g. Giudici 2003) is used as an indication of the properties of a classification

Table 3. Estimatation for GAM model

Spline	Chi-square	DF
s(X10308)	30.1602	3
s(X10309)	7.8260	3
s(X10601)	8.4466	3
s(X10602)	10.3671	3

Table 4. ANOVA for Model choice

Model	Residual deviance
GLM Logit	194.24
GLM Probit	194.52
GAM	128.20

(discriminant) rule. It contains the number of elements that have been correctly or incorrectly classified for each class. On its main diagonal we can see the number of observations that have been correctly classified for each class while the off-diagonal elements indicate the number of observations that have been incorrectly classified. If it is (explicitly or implicitly) assumed that each incorrect classification has the same cost. Finally in table 5 and table 6 we have the confusion matrix for the models. The confusion matrix for Logistic regression is equal to probit link.

Table 5. Confusion matrix for GLM models

	P(Y=0)	P(Y=1)
O(Y=0)	59	22
O(Y=1)	11	290

Table 6. Confusion matrix for GAM model

	P(Y=0)	P(Y=1)
O(Y=0)	67	14
O(Y=1)	6	285

In Table 5 and Table 6 the diagonal represents the correct predictions and we can see that the non parametric model is the best to predict student performance.

8 Conclusion

In this paper we have presented a new approach to personalize e-learning platforms through the analysis of the exercises performance. Our idea, based on generalized additive models gives for each exercise interesting measures of student performance and a probabilistic classification of exercises. Through this results we can personalize the e-learning platform near time and for each student suggest a personalized sequence of the lessons. Our proposal can be exetended also to others application area such as to predict credit risk and in general for forecasting.

Acknowledgment

This work has been supported by MIUR PRIN FUNDS "Data Mining for e-business approaches", 2004-2006.
The paper is the results of a close collaboration between the three authors. However section 1 has been written by Paolo Giudici, section 2,3,4,5 has been written by Silvia Figini and section 6,7 has been written by Paolo Baldini.

References

1. Azzalini, A. and Bowman, A. W.: Applied Smoothing Techniques for Data Analysis. Oxford Statistical Science Series, Oxford (1997)
2. Fan, J. and Gijbels, I.: Local Polynomial Modelling and Ist Applications. Chapman Hall, London (1996)
3. Giudici,P.: Applied data mining. Wiley (2003)
4. Green, P.J. and Silverman, B. W.: Nonparametric Regression and Generalized Linear Models: A Roughness Penality Approach. Chapman Hall, London (1994)
5. Hastie, T.J. and Tibshirani, R. J.: Generalized Additive Models. Chapman Hall, London (1990)
6. Scott, D.W.: Multivariate Density Estimation:Theory,Practice and Visualisation. Wiley, New York (1992)
7. Simonoff, J.S.: Smoothing Methods in Statistics. Springer Verlag, New York (1996)
8. Wand, M. P. and Jones, M. C.: Kernel Smoothing. Chapman Hall, London (1995)
9. Bjerve, S. , Doksum, K.: Correlation curves measures of association as functions of covariate values. Ann. Statist., 21, 890–902 (1993)
10. Bowman, A. W.: An alternative method of cross validation for the smoothing of density estimates. Biometrika., 711, 353–360 (1984)
11. Bowman, A. W. , Foster, P. J.: Adaptive smoothing and density based tests of multivariate normality. J. Amer. Statist. Assoc., 88, 529–573 (1993)
12. Doksum, K. , Blyth, S. , Bradlow, E. , Meng, X. L. , Zhao, H. : Correlation curves as local measures of variance explained by regression. J. Amer. Statist. Assoc., 89, 571–582 (1994)
13. Jones, M. C. , Marron, J. S. , Sheather, S. J. : A brief survey of bandwidth selection for density estimation. J. Amer. Statist. Assoc., 91, 401–407 (1996)
14. Parzen, E.: On the estimation of a probability density and mode. Ann. Math. Statist., 33, 1065–1076 (1962)
15. Rosenblatt, M.: Remarks on some noparametric estimates of a density function. Ann. Meth. Statist., 27, 832–837 (1956)
16. Rudemo, M.: Empirical choice of histograms and kernel density estimators. Scand. J. Statist., 9, 65–78 (1982)
17. Scott, D.W. , Terrell, G.: Biased and unbiased cross validation in density estimation. J. Amer. Statist. Assoc., 82, 1131–1146 (1987)
18. Sheather, S.J. , Jones, M.C.: A reliable data based bandwidth selection method for kernel density estimation. J. Roy. Statist. Soc. Ser. B, 53, 683–690 (1991)
19. Stone, M. A.: Cross validatory choice and assessment of statistical predictions. J. Roy. Statist. Soc. Ser. B, 36, 111–147 (1974)
20. Taylor, C. C.: Boostrap choice of the smoothing parameter in kernel density estimation. Biometrika, 36, 111–147 (1989)
21. Whittle, P.: On the smoothing of probability density functions. J. Roy. Statist. Soc. Ser. B, 55, 549–557 (1958)

An Intelligent Manufacturing Process Diagnosis System Using Hybrid Data Mining

Joon Hur[1], Hongchul Lee[1,*], and Jun-Geol Baek[2]

[1] Department of Industrial Systems and Information Engineering, Korea University,
Anam-dong, Sungbuk-gu, Seoul, 136-701, Republic of Korea
hclee@korea.ac.kr
[2] Department of Industrial Systems Engineering, Induk Institute of Technology,
Wolgye-dong, Nowon-gu, Seoul, 139-749, Republic of Korea

Abstract. The high cost of maintaining a complex manufacturing process necessitates the enhancement of an efficient maintenance system. For the efficient maintenance of manufacturing process, precise diagnosis of the manufacturing process should be performed and the appropriate maintenance action should be executed when the current condition of the manufacturing system is diagnosed as being in abnormal condition. This paper suggests an intelligent manufacturing process diagnosis system using hybrid data mining. In this system, the cause-and-effect rules for the manufacturing process condition are inferred by hybrid decision tree/evolution strategies learning and the most effective maintenance action is recommended by a decision network and AHP (analytical hierarchy process). To verify the hybrid learning proposed in this paper, we compared the accuracy of the hybrid learning with that of the general decision tree learning algorithm (C4.5) and hybrid decision tree/genetic algorithm learning by using datasets from the well-known dataset repository at UCI (University of California at Irvine).

1 Introduction

Despite the quality of a product being mostly dependent on intelligent facilities, any negligible error or disorder in the process can still cause a catastrophic system failure. Moreover, any unexpected process disorder can decrease production capability and the product quality. To avoid such an unexpected process disorder, effective maintenance is necessary to increase the reliability of the process. For the effective maintenance, the fault diagnosis is preceded before causing a catastrophic system failure.

In industry, failure-driven and time-based maintenance are two major approaches [15]. Failure-drive maintenance (FDM) is a reactive management approach, where corrective maintenance is often dominated by unplanned events, and is carried out only after the occurrence of an obvious functional failure, malfunction, or breakdown of equipment. However, this corrective maintenance often results in the unpredictable performance in a plant, i.e. high equipment downtime, high cost of restoring equipment, extensive repair time, high penalties associated with the loss of production, and a high spare parts inventory level [25]. Time-based maintenance (TBM) is preventive mainte-

---

* Corresponding author. (tel) +82-2-3290-3389.

P. Perner (Ed.): ICDM 2006, LNAI 4065, pp. 561–575, 2006.
© Springer-Verlag Berlin Heidelberg 2006

nance based on pre-defined time intervals. TBM assumes that the estimated failure behavior of the equipment, i.e. the mean time between functional failures (MTBF) is statistically or experientially known for equipment and machinery degrading in normal usage [8]. Although TBM can reduce the probability of system failure or the frequency of unplanned emergency repairs, it cannot eliminate the occurrence of random catastrophic failure. Condition-based maintenance (CBM) is a method used to reduce the uncertainty of maintenance activities and is carried out when the system deemed to be in abnormal condition. Compared to FDM and TBM, CBM is a more proactive maintenance which minimizes the maintenance cost and maximizes process availability [25].

For the effective CBM, the manufacturing process condition should be monitored and diagnosed precisely for the fault conditions. Condition monitoring is defined as the collection and interpretation of the relevant equipment parameters for the purpose of the identification of the state equipment changes from normal conditions and trends of the health of the equipment. Condition-based fault diagnosis is triggered by the detection of an equipment condition that is recognized as a deviation from the expected level. Then, fault diagnosis finds the causes about the current condition and figures out the possible maintenance actions for the abnormal condition. For the condition monitoring and fault diagnosis, a cause-and-effect knowledge (learning) must be preceded [25].

In recent years, various strategies have been reported for the diagnosis of manufacturing systems. Baek et al. [2] proposed cause-and-effect knowledge for online quality control of semiconductor manufacturing process using Statistical Batch based Decision Tree Learning (SBDL). Kim and May[11] employed evidential reasoning to identify malfunctions of semiconductor manufacturing equipment by combining evidence originating from equipment maintenance history, on-line sensor data, and in-line post-process measurements. Bohez and Thieravarut [4] used a hybrid reasoning approach between a deep model and a shallow model for the diagnosis of computer numerically controlled machines. Chevalier et al. [6] integrated casual reasoning and fuzzy logic reasoning for manufacturing line supervision and diagnosis. To some extent, these diagnostic strategies have successfully been used and have solved some practical problems. However, there is little evidence to suggest that all the fault data, as well as available diagnostic knowledge, has been integrated in manufacturing systems.

The intelligent systems used in condition-based fault diagnosis can be divided into three categories such as rule-based diagnostic systems, case-based diagnostic systems, and model-based diagnostic systems [7, 13, 22]. Rule-based diagnostic systems detect and identify incipient faults in accordance with the rules representing the relation of each possible fault with the actual monitored equipment condition. Case-based diagnostic systems use historical records of maintenance cases to provide an interpretation for the actual monitored conditions of the equipment. A model-based diagnostic systems use different mathematical, neural network, and logical methods to improve diagnostic reasoning based on the structure and properties of the equipment system. Among above three diagnostic systems, the rule-based systems usually consist of a bunch of IF-THEN rules, a bunch of facts, and some interpreter controlling the application of the rules, given the facts. Due to this structure that the humans can understand them easily, the analysis such as forward or backwards reasoning is easier than the other diagnostic systems. The current process condition can be inferred by forward reasoning with the current values of the attributes, and the possible maintenance actions can be figured out by backward reasoning.

Decision tree (DT) is simple to understand and interpret. The DT represents the rules which can be expressed as paths (IF-THEN rules) so that humans can understand them easily. Also, DT is robust; perform well with large data in a short time. Large amounts of data can be analyzed using personal computers in a time short enough to enable analysts to take decisions based on its analysis. However, the set of class boundaries is relatively inelegant (rough). Also, a decision tree model is nonparametric and has many more free parameters than a parametric model of similar power. Therefore this will require more storage and to obtain good estimates a large amount of training data is required [3, 14]. The hybrid learning has been adopted to solve this problem. First, Carvalho et al. [5] proposed a concept for the use of alternative learning bias, generally using hybrid approaches, for coping with the problem of small disjuncts. They used the decision tree and genetic algorithm to solve this problem. Wang et al. [24] presented a hybrid knowledge discovery model using decision tree and network for selecting dispatching rules of a semiconductor final testing factory. Dattilo et al. [7] presented hybrid data mining approach using decision trees and Bayesian clustering for the classification of balance-sheets.

In this paper, we present an intelligent manufacturing process diagnosis system as shown in Fig. 1.

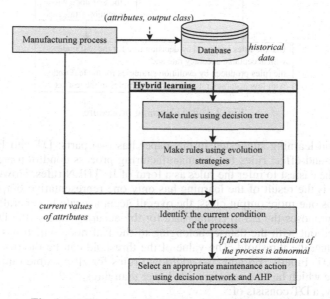

Fig. 1. Intelligent manufacturing process diagnosis system

As shown in Fig. 1, the hybrid learning module infers the cause-and-effect rules of the manufacturing process condition by hybrid decision tree /evolution strategies (ES) learning described in section 2. If the current condition of the process is diagnosed as abnormal condition by the cause-and-effect rules inferred by hybrid learning, an appropriate maintenance action is recommended by decision network and AHP (analytic hierarchy process). Section 3 describes how an appropriate maintenance action is recommended using a decision network and AHP. Finally, Section 4 presents the conclusions.

2   Hybrid Learning

In this paper, as shown in Fig. 2, the hybrid learning is used to infer the cause-and-effect rules for the manufacturing process diagnosis.

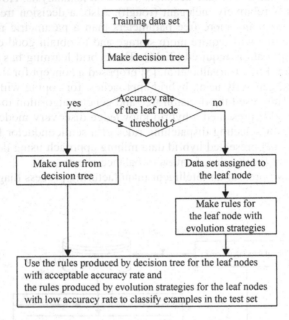

Fig. 2. Hybrid learning procedure

The hybrid learning suggested in this paper has two parts: DT and ES. First, the initial cause-and-effect rules for the manufacturing process condition are inferred by DT. DT is the easiest to infer the rules as a form of IF-THEN rules. However, the leaf node which is the result of the learning has only one representative output class. If a leaf node has one more output class, the overall accuracy rate is generally decreased. This paper proposes the ES to compensate for the accuracy rate of the DT. ES learning is carried out with the dataset belonging to the leaf node which has an accuracy rate lower than the threshold. The value of the threshold can be the overall accuracy rate of the DT. Finally, ES adds the additional rules for all possible output classes in the leaf node which has the accuracy rate lower than threshold.

Generally, a DT consists of:

- A leaf node that indicates a classification of output class.
- A non-leaf or decision node which contains an attribute name and branch to other decision nodes, one for each value of that attribute.

For constructing a DT, C4.5 [16, 17] is used generally. Information gain is used to select the test attribute at each node in the tree. Such a measure is referred to as a measure of the goodness of the split node. The attribute with the highest information gain (or greatest entropy reduction) is chosen as the test attribute for the current node. This attribute minimizes the information needed to classify the samples in the resulting partitions and reflects the least randomness or impurity in these partitions [9].

Evolution strategies (ES) were introduced by Ingo Rechenberg [18] and Hans Paul Schweffel [1] in the 1960s as a method for solving parameter-optimization problems. In its most general form, the phenotype of an individual is a vector $\vec{x}$ containing the candidate values of the parameters being optimized. The genotype of each individual is a pair of real-valued vectors $\vec{v} = \{\vec{x}, \vec{\sigma}\}$, where $\vec{x}$ is the above phenotypic vector (the genotype–phenotype distinction is thus somewhat degenerate with evolution strategies), and $\vec{\sigma}$ is a vector of standard deviations (SD) used to apply the mutation operator. The inclusion of the $\vec{\sigma}$ vector in the genome allows the algorithm to self-adapt the mutation operator while searching for the solution.

In ES, selection is performed after the genetic operators have been applied. The standard notations in this domain, $(\mu, \lambda) - \text{ES}$ and $(\mu + \lambda) - \text{ES}$, denote algorithms in which a population of μ parents generates λ offspring. The next generation is created by selecting the best fitted μ individuals. In the case of $(\mu, \lambda) - \text{ES}$ only the λ offspring are considered for selection, thus limiting the 'life' of an individual to one generation, while in the $(\mu + \lambda) - \text{ES}$ the μ parents are also considered for selection. Mutation is the major genetic operator in evolution strategies. It also plays the role of a reproduction operator given that the mutated individual is viewed as an offspring for the selection operator to work on. In its most general form, mutation modifies a genotype $\vec{v} = \{\vec{x}, \vec{\sigma}\}$, by first randomly altering $\vec{\sigma}$, and then modifying $\vec{x}$ according to the new values provided by $\vec{\sigma}$. This operation produces a new individual $\vec{v}' = \{\vec{x}', \vec{\sigma}'\}$, where $\vec{x}' = \vec{x}' + N(0, \vec{\sigma}')$. $N(0, \vec{\sigma}')$ denotes a vector of independent random Gaussian values with mean 0 and SD $\vec{\sigma}$. The crossover (or recombination) operator generates an offspring from a number of parents (usually two). There are two types of crossover operators: discrete and intermediate. In discrete recombination each component of $\vec{v}$, i.e. each pair of scalars $(\vec{x}_i, \vec{\sigma}_i)$, is copied from one of the parents at random. In intermediate recombination, the offspring values are a linear combination of all the parent vectors participating in the recombination process.

2.1 Individual (Genome) Presentation

For the ES learning suggested in this paper, the genome is constructed as shown in Fig. 3. The genomes represent the cause-and-effect rules for a given output class. To represent a variable-length rule antecedent (phenotype) we use a fixed-length genome, for the sake of simplicity.

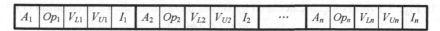

| A_1 | Op_1 | V_{L1} | V_{U1} | I_1 | A_2 | Op_2 | V_{L2} | V_{U2} | I_2 | $\cdots$ | A_n | Op_n | V_{Ln} | V_{Un} | I_n |

Fig. 3. Structure of the genome of an individual

For a given run of the ES, the genome of an individual consists of n genes, where $n = m - k$, m is the total number of predictor attributes in the dataset and k is the number of ancestor nodes of the DT leaf node for which the accuracy rate of the leaf node is below than the threshold.

Each gene represents a rule condition (phenotype) of the form $(A_i, Op_i, V_{Li}, V_{Ui})$, where the subscript i identifies the rule condition, $i = 1, ..., n$; A_i is the ith attribute; Op_i is a discrete/continuous presentation compatible with attribute A_i; V_{Li} is the lower bound of the target range in the domain of A_i; and V_{Ui} is the upper bound of the target range in the domain of A_i.

If a genome is encoded as seen on Fig. 4, each gene in a genome represent a rule condition for the each attributes. The first rule condition encoded in the genome could be a condition such as "$A_1 = Normal$", where attribute A_1 is a categorical(nominal) attribute, the value V_{L1} is "N" and the value V_{U1} is left as blank. The second and third rule condition encoded in the genome could be conditions such as "$100 \leq A_2 < 200$" and "$10 \leq A_3 < 20$", where attributes A_2 and A_3 are continuous (real-valued) attributes. The second condition, "$100 \leq A_2 < 200$" encoded for multi-interval range of the attribute using V_{L2} and V_{U2} where A_2 has overall range from 0 to 500. This multi-interval range gives more specific condition for the individual presentation (genome). The third condition, "$10 \leq A_3 < 20$" encoded for bi-interval range of the attribute using V_{L3} and V_{U3} where A_3 has overall range from 10 to 35. If the condition is bottom side, V_{Li} is the minimum value in attribute ranges; otherwise, V_{Ui} is the maximum value in attribute ranges.

A_1	D	N	Null	I_1	A_2	C	100	200	I_2	A_3	C	10	20	I_3

Fig. 4. An example of individual presentation for the multi-interval

I_i represents an active bit, which takes on the value 1 or 0 to indicate whether or not, respectively, the ith condition is present in the rule antecedent (phenotype). If 1 is allocated for I_i, this means the gene is active. If 0 is allocated for I_i, this means the gene is not active. Fig. 5 shows the active bit allocation algorithm.

Step 1. Compute $Prob(cond_i)$ for each ith gene of a genome.
Step 2. Repeat Step 2.1 ~ 2.2 until the number of iterations reaches the number of genes.
  Step 2.1 Generate random value (rv) with U (0, 1).
  Step 2.2 IF ($rv < Prob(cond_i)$) THEN Set I_i as 1.
    ELSE Set I_i as 0.

Fig. 5. Active bit allocation algorithm

In Fig. 5, $Prob(cond_i)$ is calculated by Bayes theorem as shown in equation (1).

$$P(C_i \mid X) = \frac{P(X \mid C_i)P(C_i)}{P(X)} \tag{1}$$

where, X is the number of target output classes in the datasets; C_i is the number of data which satisfied the given condition, $cond_i (A_i, Op_i, V_{Li}, V_{Ui})$ in the dataset; $P(X|C_i)$ is the posterior probability of X conditioned on C_i; and $P(C_i|X)$ is the posterior probability and is based on more information than the prior probability, $P(C_i)$ [23].

2.2 Evolution Strategies Learning Procedure

The ES proposed in this paper consists of the 9 procedures shown in Fig.6.

Step 1. Initialize (population)
Step 2. Evaluate (population)
Step 3. Select best fitted μ parents individuals
Step 4. Generate λ offspring individuals
  Step 4.1. Recombined offsprings
  Step 4.2. Mutated offsprings
Step 5. Adjust active bit in each gene for each genome of individuals
Step 6. Select best fitted μ individuals from the parent and offspring individuals.
Step 7. IF termination condition is satisfied THEN Stop.
      ELSE go to Step 3.

Fig. 6. ES learning procedure

In Step 1, the population is initialized with λ individuals which are the candidate rule. In Step 2, each individual of the population generated in Step 1 is evaluated according to the fitness given by equation (2).

$$fitness = \left(\frac{TP}{TP+FN} \right) \cdot \left(\frac{TN}{FP+TN} \right) \tag{2}$$

Let positive class be the class predicted by a given rule, and let negative class be any class other than the class predicted by the rule. *TP* (true positives) is the number of positive examples that were correctly classified as positive examples; *FP* (false positives) the number of negative examples that were wrongly classified as positive examples; *FN* (false negatives) the number of positive examples that were wrongly classified as negative examples; and *TN* (true negatives) the number of negative examples that were correctly classified as negative examples [10]. Then, in Step 3, μ individuals which have with highest fitness value are selected as a parent population. In Steps 4, the λ individuals are generated by recombination and mutation as an offspring population. Once the parent population is available, recombination allows for the creation of new individuals based on the previous generation. In the strategy presented here, we have chosen to use *generalized intermediate panmictic recombination* [21]. This technique consists in taking one individual from the parent population and holding it fixed while other parents are chosen to recombine with it. A new offspring population created by recombination operator has no new information has been inserted in the population but only old information has been recombined. In order to introduce new information into the population pool, the mutation operator is used. To optimized the convergence rate, the variance of the mutation operator is adjusted by *1/5 success rule* proposed by Recheberg [1,18]. In Step 5, the active bits are adjusted in given condition, $cond_i(A_i, Op_i, V_{Li}, V_{Ui})$ of the individual presentation as seen on Fig. 4. In Step 6, a new generation parent population is created by selecting the best fitted μ individuals from the parent and the offspring population. If the termination condition is satisfied, the ES learning is stopped, otherwise returned to Step 4. Termination condition is any one of the followings [12]:

- reaching a given number of generations,

- obtaining an individual with a fitness equal to or better than a given threshold,
- absolute or relative difference in fitness between the best and worst individuals is under a given threshold.

2.3 Case Study: Coil-Spring Manufacturing Process

This paper proposes the intelligent manufacturing process diagnosis system for a coil-spring manufacturing process as a case study. Real data and the characteristics of the attributes and output class were obtained from a coil-spring manufacturing company in Korea. As shown in Fig. 7, the coil-spring manufacturing process consists of six main operations.

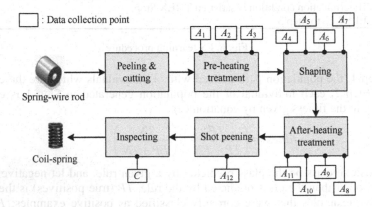

Fig. 7. Coil-spring manufacturing process

In the peeling and cutting station, spring-wire rod is peeled to the appropriate diameter and cut to the appropriate length. In the pre-heating treatment station, the rod from the peeling and cutting station undergoes a heat treatment to enable the spring-wire rod to be softened into a coil-spring shape more easily in the shaping station. The after-heating treatment station and shot peening station increase the product qualities such as intensity and tenacity. In the inspecting station, the produced coil-spring is inspected for height.

In Fig. 7, the data collection points are marked. A_i is the attribute ($i = 1, 2, ..., 12$) and C is the output class. The attributes and output class are explained in Table 1.

The attributes represent the status of the various stations in the process, and the output class represents the height of the coil-spring which is the process end-product. There are five output classes, EL (extra less target value), L (less target value), N (target value), H (over target value), and EH (extra over target value). Most of the attributes are located in the pre-heating treatment and shaping station because these stations affect the output class more strongly.

The initial cause-and-effect rules for the manufacturing process condition are generated from DT constructed by C4.5. We used the Enterprise-Miner® to generate a DT. Fig. 8 shows the DT for the coil-spring manufacturing process.

As shown in Fig. 8, four attributes, TB, ST, CT, and PH, are decision nodes for the coil-spring manufacturing process. The number in parenthesis is used to distinguish

Table 1. Attributes and output class for the coil-spring manufacturing process

	Name	Description	Type	Range of value
Attributes	$A_1(TB)$	Temp. of burner	Continuous	960±20 ℃
	$A_2(MS)$	Moving speed of working beam	Continuous	10.6±0.5 mm/min
	$A_3(ST)$	Staying time in pre-heating station	Continuous	49.8±5 min
	$A_4(CT)$	Coiling time	Continuous	106.6±1.5 sec
	$A_5(PH)$	Pressure of hydraulic power	Continuous	40~80 kg/m^2
	$A_6(SS)$	The status of the servo valve	Discrete	Normal/abnormal
	$A_7(TH)$	Temp. of hydraulic fluid	Continuous	30~55 ℃
	$A_8(TO)$	Temp. of the oil in the direct quenching tank	Continuous	40~60℃
	$A_9(PQ)$	Passing time in the direct quenching tank	Continuous	12.4±10 mm/min
	$A_{10}(TT)$	Temp. of the tempering	Continuous	420±10 ℃
	$A_{11}(PT)$	Passing time in tempering	Continuous	180±5 min
	$A_{12}(SP)$	The status of sand for shot peening	Discrete	Normal/abnormal
Output class	$C(TB)$	Height of coil-spring	Discrete	EL, L, N, H, EH

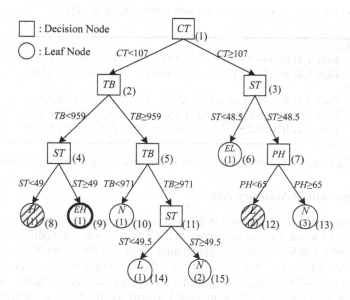

Fig. 8. A decision tree constructed by C4.5 for coil-spring manufacturing process

the leaf node with the same output class. The number in parenthesis sided by each node is the node number. From the DT in Fig. 8, eight rules are generated for the coil-spring manufacturing process condition as shown in Table 2.

The rules with an accuracy rate are below than the threshold are selected for the next learning: ES. The threshold is decided by the overall accuracy rate of the DT. In the case of coil-spring, the threshold is 78.92%. So, the datasets in the leaf nodes (the nodes are filled by oblique lines in Fig. 8) of Rule 1 and Rule 7 are selected for the ES learning because those accuracy rates are below than the threshold as shown in Table 2.

Table 2. The rules generated from the decision tree

Rule	Description	Accuracy
Rule 1	**IF** (*CT* < 107 AND *TB* < 959 AND *ST* < 49), **THEN** *HC* = *H*(1).	**75.3%**
Rule 2	**IF** (*CT* < 107 AND *TB* < 959 AND *ST* • 49), **THEN** *HC* = *EH*(1).	79.2%
Rule 3	**IF** (*CT* < 107 AND *TB* • 959 AND *TB* < 971), **THEN** *HC* = *N*(1).	91.8%
Rule 4	**IF** (*CT* < 107 AND *TB* • 971 AND *ST* < 49.5), **THEN** *HC* = *L*(1).	85.1%
Rule 5	**IF** (*CT* < 107 AND *TB* • 971 AND *ST* • 49.5), **THEN** *HC* = *N*(2).	80.4%
Rule 6	**IF** (*CT* • 107 AND *ST* < 48.5), **THEN** *HC* = *EL*(1).	81.5%
Rule 7	**IF** (*CT* • 107 AND *ST* • 48.5 AND *PH* < 65), **THEN** *HC* = *L*(2).	**69.9%**
Rule 8	**IF** (*CT* • 107 AND *ST* • 48.5 AND *PH* • 65), **THEN** *HC* = *N*(3).	87.7%

In our ES learning, we set the population size, μ, as 10, the number of off-springs, λ, as 3μ, and the replacement policy, R, as $(\mu + \lambda)$. $(\mu + \lambda)$ means μ individuals are select from the parent population (μ) and the offspring population (λ). The result of ES learning for rule 1 and 7 is as shown in Fig. 9. These additional rules are added to the initial cause-and-effect rules inferred by the DT.

· **Rule 1:**
　　· **Rule 1.1:** IF ((46.3 • *PH* < 50.6) AND (43.1 • *TH* < 49.3)) THEN *H*(4).
　　· **Rule 1.2:** IF ((48.1 • *TH* < 52.4) AND (12.7 • *PQ* < 14.1)) THEN *EH*(2).
· **Rule 7:**
　　· **Rule 7.1:** IF ((945 • *TB* < 952) AND (33.1 • *TH* < 34.9)) THEN *N*(4).
　　· **Rule 7.2:** IF ((38.8 • *TH* < 40.1) AND (11.0 • *PQ* < 15.2)) THEN *L*(2).
　　· **Rule 7.3:** IF ((50.2 • *TH* < 53.6) AND (25.7 • *PQ* < 31.4)) THEN *EL*(2).

Fig. 9. Additional rules generated by ES for coil-spring manufacturing process

2.4 Comparison of Accuracy Rate

We evaluated our hybrid learning rule-based system on eight public domain datasets from the well-known dataset repository at UCI (University of California at Irvine): Adult, Connect, CRX, Hepatitis, Segmentation, Splice, Voting and Wave. These data-sets are available on the internet at the: http://www.ics.uci.edu/~mlearn/MLRepository.html. In addition, we added a coil-spring data set to evaluate our system.

To verify the efficiency of the proposed hybrid learning, we compared the accuracy of the suggested hybrid decision tree + evolution strategies (DT+ES) with that of the general DT learning algorithm (C4.5) and hybrid decision tree/genetic algorithm (DT+GA) [5] by data from the UCI repository and coil-spring.

The results are shown in Table 3. The first column of this table indicates the datasets, the second the accuracy rate on the test set achieved by C4.5, the third the accuracy rate on the test set achieved by DT+GA hybrid learning and the last the accuracy rate on the test set achieved by hybrid DT+ES learning algorithm proposed in this paper.

As shown in Table 3, DT+GA and DT+ES showed somewhat better accuracy than C4.5 in 7 out of the 9 datasets, although not all results were statistically significant. Nevertheless, we concluded that these hybrid learning increase the accuracy of C4.5. Among the hybrid learning, DT+ES showed a better accuracy rate than DT+GA in 6 out of the 7 datasets for two reasons. Generally, ES perform very well in numerical domains, since they are dedicated to the real function optimization problems [10]. Compared to the individual of DT+GA, which divides the search space into bi-interval, the individual of DT+ES divides the search space into a multi-interval. This feature makes that DT+ES has better accuracy rate than DT+GA. Therefore, DT+ES can classify the condition more specifically than DT+GA3.

Table 3. Accuracy rate of DT(C4.5), hybrid DT+GA, and hybrid DT+ES system

Dataset	DT(C4.5)	DT+GA	DT+ES
Wave	75.46	79.60±2.0	**80.87±2.0**
Hepatitis	82.96	84.97±6.0	**85.25±5.0**
Adult	78.87	**79.83±0.1**	79.55±2.0
CRX	84.71	86.12±4.0	**86.37±2.0**
Voting	**94.73**	92.30±1.0	91.72±2.0
Connect	73.75	75.93±0.8	**77.19±0.2**
Splice	45.95	46.45±0.9	**47.70±2.0**
Segmentation	**97.61**	93.62±0.8	93.16±1.0
Coil-spring	78.92	81.22±2.1	**83.18±1.6**

3   Manufacturing Process Condition Diagnosis

As shown in Fig. 1, the current attributes are applied to the cause-and-effect rules inferred by hybrid learning. If the current condition of the process is diagnosed as an abnormal condition, maintenance action should be performed. To select an appropriate maintenance action, we construct a decision network which represents possible paths from the detected abnormal node (abnormal condition) to the normal node (normal condition) based on the cause-and-effect rules inferred by hybrid learning. Using a decision network, each possible maintenance action is identified as forming a path to correct the abnormal condition. The most appropriate maintenance action is selected by AHP (Analytical Hierarchy Process).

Methods for constructing a decision network and selecting an appropriate maintenance action will be presented in detail for the coil-spring manufacturing process. There are two methods of abnormal detection: loose and tight. The former is concerned with a severe condition such as EH and EL, while the latter is concerned with a possible abnormal condition such as H and L including severe condition. The possible abnormal condition is usually accepted to its customers, automobile manufactures, as a normal. In our paper, we are dealing with the loose detection.

3.1   Decision Network

The decision network identifies the possible maintenance actions from the cause-and-effect rules inferred by hybrid learning. It is easy to transform it to a readable maintenance action. The construction procedure of a decision network is simple. When the abnormal condition is detected by loose detection, the decision network is constructed according to the procedure in Fig. 10.

Step 1. Find the detected abnormal node.	
Step 2. Find the normal nodes.	
Step 3. Create paths from the detected abnormal node to each normal node.	

Step 1. Find the detected abnormal node.
Step 2. Find the normal nodes.
Step 3. Create paths from the detected abnormal node to each normal node.
Repeat sub-steps 3.1~3.3 by the number of normal nodes founded in step 2.
> **Step 3.1** Set the current location of the detected abnormal node and targeted normal node.
> **Step 3.2** Find the split node for the detected abnormal node and targeted normal node.
> **Step 3.3** Add the arc from the split node to the targeted normal node.

Step 4. Construct decision network.

Fig. 10. The procedure for constructing a decision network

When the current condition of the process is diagnosed as abnormal condition (i.e., bold lined node, *EH* (1) in Fig. 8), the decision network is constructed as shown in Fig. 11 according to the procedure for constructing a decision network.

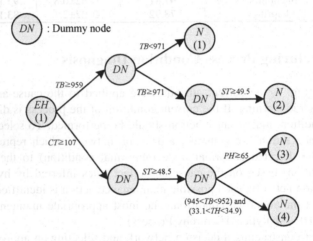

Fig. 11. Decision network for abnormal condition *EH*(1)

In the decision network, the source node is the abnormal node and the target nodes are the normal nodes. To consider the arcs in decision network the split node is found from the source node and the target node. The arcs are added from the split node to the target node. The end node of each path will be the normal node for each path. Dummy nodes are necessary between arcs as internal nodes. From the decision network, possible maintenance actions are illustrated in a readable form as presented in Table 4.

Table 4. Possible maintenance actions for the abnormal condition *EH*(1)

Maintenance Action	Description of Maintenance action
MA1 [*EH*(1)•*N*(1)]	Adjust(*TB*)
MA2 [*EH*(1)•*N*(2)]	Adjust(*TB*) & Adjust(*ST*)
MA3 [*EH*(1)•*N*(3)]	Adjust(*CT*) & Adjust(*ST*) & Adjust(*PH*)
MA4 [*EH*(1)•*N*(4)]	Adjust(*CT*) & Adjust(*ST*) & Adjust(*TB*) & Adjust(*TH*)

3.2 Select an Appropriate Maintenance Action Using AHP

The Analytic Hierarchy Process (AHP) is a decision analysis method that ranks alternatives based on a number of criteria. Its robust design enables the decision-maker to incorporate subjectivity, experience, and knowledge intuitively and naturally into the decision process. AHP considers both qualitative and quantitative information and combines them by decomposing unstructured problems into systematic hierarchies. AHP provides the final weighted average score for each alternative. In addition, the analyst finds the weight of each criterion and the scores for each alternative on each criterion. This information provides insight into elements of the process, thereby giving the analyst a better understanding of the final decision. With the decision aid for preference structuring the user can approach the problem with a technique called the AHP. In AHP the problem is described in the form of a hierarchy where overall objectives are represented by the topmost element in the hierarchy. The next level in the hierarchy consists of criteria or subgoals that are important for these objectives. The alternatives are at the lowest level. In AHP, pairwise comparisons are made on each level. Each goal and subgoal is given local weights which describe the importance of lower level elements with respect to the element in question [20].

To select an appropriate maintenance action for the coil-spring manufacturing process, the AHP has been applied to suggest an intelligent manufacturing process

Table 5. Pairwise comparison of factors

	Number of attributes	Maintenance time	Maintenance cost
Number of attributes	1	3	7
Maintenance time	1/3	1	5
Maintenance cost	1/7	1/5	1

Table 6. Pairwise comparison of the maintenance actions for each factor

Number of attributes				
	MA1	MA2	MA3	MA4
MA1	1	1/3	1/5	1/9
MA2	3	1	1/3	1/5
MA3	5	3	1	1/3
MA4	9	5	3	1
Maintenance time				
	MA1	MA2	MA3	MA4
MA1	1	1/5	1/3	1/7
MA2	5	1	3	1/3
MA3	3	1/3	1	1/5
MA4	7	3	5	1
Maintenance cost				
	MA1	MA2	MA3	MA4
MA1	1	1/3	3	1/5
MA2	3	1	5	1/3
MA3	1/3	1/5	1	1/7
MA4	5	3	7	1

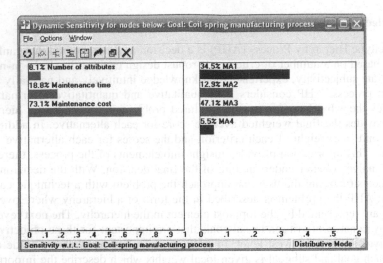

Fig. 12. Alternative maintenance action selected using AHP

diagnosis system. We conducted interviews and undertook a questionnaire survey to the number of experts in the company. The survey results indicated that the most important factors are the number of attributes, maintenance time, and cost. Table 5 is the pairwise comparison of these factors, and Table 6 is that of the maintenance actions for each factor.

We select an appropriate maintenance action using the Export Choice®, one of the AHP tools based on the pairwise comparison illustrated in Tables 5 and 6.

According to the results shown in Fig. 12, MA3 is the most appropriate maintenance action among the four possible maintenance actions. The suggested intelligent manufacturing process diagnosis system orders the workers to do MA3: Adjust (*CT*) & Adjust (*ST*) & Adjust (*PH*), that is ($CT \geq 107$, $ST \geq 48.5$, and $PH \geq 65$).

4   Conclusion

This paper presented an intelligent manufacturing process diagnosis system using hybrid data mining. This diagnostic model consists of two modules: one for learning and another for selecting the appropriate maintenance action. In the learning module, the hybrid DT+ES learning infers the cause-and-effect rules for the process. We compared the accuracy rates of hybrid DT+ES with the other learning methods such as DT and DT+GA. The result of accuracy test indicated that proposed hybrid DT+ES outperforms DT and DT+GA among tested datasets. With the cause-and-effect rules inferred by hybrid DT+ES learning, if the current condition of the process is diagnosed as an abnormal condition, the appropriate maintenance action should be followed. The decision network represents the possible paths from the detected alarm node to the normal nodes. Using a decision network, each possible maintenance action is identified as a path to correct the abnormal condition. Among the various possible maintenance actions, the most appropriate is selected by AHP.

References

1. Back, T., Hoffmeister, F., and Schwefel, H.P.: A survey of Evolution Strategies. In Proceedings of the Fourth International Conference on Genetic Algorithms, Morgan Kaufmann Publishers, San Mateo, CA. (1991) 2-9
2. Baek, J. G., Kim, C. O., and Kim, S. S.: Online learning of the cause-and-effect knowledge of a manufacturing process. International Journal of Production Research, Vol. 40, No. 14 (2002) 3275-3290
3. Berry, M. J. A. and Linoff, G.: Data Mining Techniques: For Marketing, Sales, and Customer Support. John Wiley & Sons (1997)
4. Bohez, E. L. J. and Thieravarut, M.: Expert system for diagnosing computer numerically controlled machines: a case-study. Computers in industry, Vol. 32, No. 3 (1997) 233-248
5. Carvalho, D. R. and Freitas, A.: A hybrid decision tree/genetic algorithm method for data mining. Information Science, Vol 163 (2004) 13-35
6. Chevalier, E., Martin, J.A., Colomb , Blanch i, and Laserna, J. M. L.: Hybrid manufacturing line supervision and diagnosis by means of fuzzy rules connected with a causal graph. In Proceedings of the Sixth IEEE International Conference on Fuzzy Systems, Vol. 3 (1997) 1259-1264
7. Dattilo, G., Greco, S., Masciari, E., and Pontieri, L.: A Hybrid Technique for Data Mining on Balance-Sheet Data. Lecture Notes in Computer Science, Vol 1874 (2000) 419-424
8. Gertsbakh , I. B.: Models of Preventive Maintenance. North-Holland (1977)
9. Han, J. and Kamber, M.: Data Mining: Concepts and Techniques. Morgan Kaufmann (2001)
10. Hand, D. J.: Construction and Assessment of Classification Rules. John Wiley&Sons (1997)
11. Kim, B. and May, G. S.: Real-time diagnosis of semiconductor manufacturing equipment using a hybrid neural network expert system. IEEE Transaction on Components, Packaging, and Manufacturing Technology-Part C, Vol. 20, No. 1 (1997) 39-47
12. Michalewicz, Z.: Genetic Algorithms + Data Structures = Evolution Programs. Third Edition. Springer-Verlag (1996)
13. Milne, R: Strategies for diagnosis. IEEE Transaction Systems, Man and Cybernetics, Vol. 17, No. 3 (1989) 333–339
14. Mitchell, T. M.: Machine Learning. McGraw-Hill (1997)
15. Moubray , J.: Reliability-Centered Maintenance, Second Edition. Industrial Press (1997)
16. Quinlan, J. R.: C4.5: Programs for machine learning. Morgan Kaufmann (1993)
17. Quinlan, J. R.: Induction of decision trees. Machine Learning, Vol 1(1986) 81-106
18. Rechenberg, I.: Evolution strategy-nature's way of optimization. in: Bergmann, (1989) 106-206
19. Russell, S. and Norvig, P.: Artificial Intelligence: A Modern Approach. Prentice Hall (1997)
20. Saaty, T. L.: The Analytic Hierarchy Process. McGraw-Hill (1980)
21. Schwefel, H. P.: Evolution and Optimum Seeking. John Wiley & Sons (1991)
22. Tse, P.: Neural networks based robust machine fault diagnostic and life span predicting system. PhD thesis, The University of Sussex, UK (1998)
23. Walpole, R. E., Myers, R. H., Myers, S. L., Ye, K., and Yee, K.: Probability & Statistics for Engineers and Scientists. Prentice Hall (2002)
24. Wang, K. J.,Chen, J. C., and Lin, Y. S.: A hybrid knowledge discovery model using decision tree and neural network for selecting dispatching rules of a semiconductor final testing factory. Production planning & control. Vol. 16, No. 7 (2005) 665–680
25. Williams, J. H., Davies, A., and Drake, P. R.: Condition-based Maintenance and Machine Diagnostics. Chapman and Hall (1994)

Computer Network Monitoring and Abnormal Event Detection Using Graph Matching and Multidimensional Scaling

H. Bunke[1], P. Dickinson[2], A. Humm[1,3], Ch. Irniger[1], and M. Kraetzl[2]

[1] Institut für Informatik und angewandte Mathematik, University of Bern
Neubrückstrasse 10, CH-3012 Bern, Switzerland
{bunke, irniger}@iam.unibe.ch
[2] Intelligence, Surveillance and Reconnaissance Division,
Defence Science and Technology Organisation, Edinburgh SA 5111, Australia
{peter.dickinson, miro.kraetzl}@dsto.defence.gov.au
[3] Department of Informatics, University of Fribourg
Bd de Pérolles 90, CH-1700 Fribourg, Switzerland
andreas.humm@unifr.ch

Abstract. Computer network monitoring and abnormal event detection have become important areas of research. In previous work, it has been proposed to represent a computer network as a time series of graphs and to compute the difference, or distance, of consecutive graphs in such a time series. Whenever the distance of two graphs exceeds a given threshold, an abnormal event is reported. In the present paper we go one step further and compute graph distances between all pairs of graphs in a time series. Given these distances, a multidimensional scaling procedure is applied that maps each graph onto a point in the two-dimensional real plane, such that the distances between the graphs are reflected, as closely as possible, in the distances between the points in the two-dimensional plane. In this way the behaviour of a network can be visualised and abnormal events as well as states or clusters of states of the network can be graphically represented. We demonstrate the feasibility of the proposed method by means of synthetically generated graph sequences and data from real computer networks.

Keywords: computer network monitoring, abnormal event detection, graph matching, multidimensional scaling.

1 Introduction

Intranets have been continuously growing in size and numbers because companies and organisations are becoming more and more information centred today. Consequently, intranet availability, reliability, and security are becoming important issues. Ensuring a high degree of availability, however, requires sophisticated tools for computer network monitoring and anomalous event detection. In the

P. Perner (Ed.): ICDM 2006, LNAI 4065, pp. 576–590, 2006.

beginning, the identification of network anomalies has relied upon ad-hoc methods developed by skilled network operators. Recently, however, anomalous event detection in computer networks has become an area of active research.

A number of principled methods for the detection of abnormal events in computer networks have been proposed in the literature. Some of these methods make use of signatures [1]. Signature based methods match current network patterns against abnormalities that have occurred in the past. Variants of signature based methods are rule-based methods [2], and case-based reasoning [3]. A further approach presents a data mining technique for discovering masquerader intrusion. User/system access data are used as a basis for deriving statistically significant event patterns. These patterns could be considered as a user/system access signature [4]. A shortcoming of signature based abnormal event detection is that anomalies that have not been observed in the past, and thus are not stored in the database of the system, remain undetected. Another approach to anomalous event detection is based on finite state machines [5]. However, a problem with this approach is that the number of states may grow very large when complex abnormalities need to be modelled. A number of other approaches make use of statistical methods [6,7], including auto-regressive processes [7,8,9], hidden Markov models [10], wavelets [11], and Bayesian networks [12]. In [13] it is shown that network alarms produced by Intrusion Detection Systems (IDSs) attains a high-level description of threats. As the number of alarms is increasingly growing, automatic tools for alarm clustering have been proposed to provide such a high level description of the attack scenario. It has been shown that effective threat analysis requires the fusion of different sources of information, such as different IDSs, firewall logs, etc.

In our previous work, we used graph theoretic methods for network anomaly detection [14,15,16]. The basic idea of this approach is to represent a computer network by a graph where the nodes represent servers and clients, and the edges represent physical or logical connections in the network. If the network is sampled at regular points in time, $t_1, t_2, ..., t_i, ...$, a time series of graphs, $g_1, g_2, ..., g_i, ...$ is obtained, which formally represents the network. Using graph distance measures originally developed in the domain of structural pattern recognition [17], one can compute the amount of change, or distance, between consecutive graphs in such a time series. If the distance $d(g_{i-1}, g_i)$ between two consecutive graphs, g_{i-1} and g_i, is above a given threshold, it is assumed that an abnormal event has occurred in the network between time t_{i-1} and time t_i. Because all clients and servers can be uniquely identified in the application, the underlying graphs have the property of unique node labels. This property ensures that all required graph operations can be very efficiently computed and the method can deal with large graphs [18].

The approach proposed in [14,15,16] has proven effective in identifying abnormal network behaviour. Nevertheless, it is limited in that it can only classify network change as normal or abnormal, but can not identify individual states, or clusters of states, of the network. In the context of this paper, the state of a network is defined by a certain subset of the nodes and edges within a graph. When dealing with a time series of graphs, this subset of graph elements will exist in adjacent graphs as long as the network remains in the same state. Assume that $d(g_{i-1}, g_i) > \theta$ and $d(g_i, g_{i+1}) > \theta$ where θ is a threshold that indicates an abnormal event. Clearly, in this case we conclude that two abnormal events have occurred in the network, one between time t_{i-1} and t_i, and the other between time t_i and t_{i+1}. However, we do not know if at time t_{i+1} the network is in the same, or a similar, state as it was at time t_{i-1}. That is, we do not know whether the changes that led from g_i to g_{i+1} are inverse to the changes that led from g_{i-1} to g_i, such that g_{i+1} is equal or similar to g_{i-1}. Information of this kind would be extremely valuable for a network operator. If it was known, for example, that the state at time t_{i-1} was a normal network state, then one could be sure that after two abnormal events, between time t_{i-1} and t_i as well as t_i and t_{i+1}, the network has returned to a normal state again.

In the current paper we introduce a new visualisation method for computer networks. This method not only makes abnormal events graphically visible, but also individual network states. Given a time series of graphs, $g_1, g_2, ..., g_i, ...$ representing a computer network, we first compute all pairwise distances $d(g_i, g_j)$ for $i \neq j$. Then we use multidimensional scaling (MDS) [19,20] to map each graph g_i to a point p_i on the two-dimensional real plane $\mathbb{R}^2$. One of the essential properties of MDS is that the pairwise distances between the points in the two-dimensional plane represent the original distances between the graphs as closely as possible. Under the method proposed in this paper, individual graphs from a sequence $g_1, g_2, ..., g_i, ...$ are not only represented by points $p_1, p_2, ..., p_i, ...$ in the two-dimensional plane, but a pair of points will also be connected by an edge if the corresponding graphs are adjacent in time, i.e. p_{i-1} and p_i will be connected. In this way not only the time series of graphs, but also the dynamic evolution of the network over time can be visualised. Returning to the example from the previous paragraph, if $d(g_{i-1}, g_i) > \theta$ and $d(g_i, g_{i+1}) > \theta$ then we expect the Euclidean distance between both pairs of points, p_{i-1} and p_i as well as p_i and p_{i+1} to be large. Moreover, if p_{i-1} and p_{i+1} have a large distance, it can be concluded that the network has changed state at time t_{i+1}. On the other hand, if the distance of p_{i-1} and p_{i+1} is small, then g_i was an outlier and the network returned to a state that is the same as, or similar to, the state it was in before the outlier occurred. We argue that the visualisation of network states, or clusters of similar states, is a valuable novel tool for computer network monitoring and abnormal event detection.

The remainder of this paper is organised as follows. In Section 2, we introduce some basic concepts of graph distance computation. Next, in Section 3, a brief introduction to MDS will be given. The combination of graph distance and MDS for the purpose of abnormal event detection will be described in Section 4. Experimental results are presented in Section 5. Finally, conclusions, a discussion and suggestions for future work will be given in Section 6.

2   Graph Matching Preliminaries

In this paper we consider graphs consisting of a finite number of nodes, V, and a finite number of edges, E. The edges are pairs of vertices, i.e. $E \subseteq V \times V$. Often, attributes are assigned to the nodes and/or edges of a graph. Let L_V and L_E denote two sets of node and edge labels, respectively. An attributed graph is a 4-tuple $g = (V, E, \alpha, \beta)$ where $\alpha : V \rightarrow L_V$ and $\beta : V \rightarrow L_E$ are the node and the edge labelling functions, respectively.

In many applications there is a need to compare graphs with each other. Graph comparison is also known as graph matching. It includes the computation of graph isomorphism, subgraph isomorphism and maximum common subgraph [21,22]. In the present paper we are concerned with a more general problem, namely, the computation of graph difference, or graph distance. One well-known distance measure for graphs, which has emerged in the domain of pattern recognition, is graph edit distance [17]. In graph edit distance computation, one applies a sequence of edit operations on the two given graphs so as to make the first graph identical, or isomorphic, to the second one. The length of the shortest edit sequence of this kind is defined as the edit distance of the two graphs under consideration. Often a cost is assigned to each edit operation. In this case, edit distance is defined as the cost of the cheapest sequence of edit operations that make the two graphs identical to each other.

The particular graph edit distance measure we use in this paper is quite simple. Given two graphs, $g_i = (V_i, E_i, \alpha_i, \beta_i)$ and $g_j = (V_j, E_j, \alpha_j, \beta_j)$, their distance is defined as:

$$D(g_i, g_j) = |V_i| + |V_j| - 2|V_i \cap V_j| + |E_i| + |E_j| - 2|E_i \cap E_j| \qquad (1)$$

In this equation $|V|$ denotes the number of nodes in set V, and $|E|$ the number of edges in E. Therefore this distance measure is equal to the number of nodes plus the number of edges that occur in only one of the two graphs, but not in both. In other words, if the set of edit operations consists of a node insertion, a node deletion, an edge insertion and an edge deletion, then Eq. 1 reflects the minimum number of edit operations needed in order to make g_i and g_j identical. More generally, the distance measure is equal to the minimum cost needed to make the two graphs identical to each other provided each edit operation has a cost equal to one. Note that $d(g_i, g_j)$ is small if g_i and g_j have many nodes and edges in common. In the extreme case, when g_i and g_j are identical, we get $d(g_i, g_j) = 0$. On the other hand, if both graphs have no node and no edge in common, then the distance assumes its maximum value, i.e. $d(g_i, g_j) = |V_i| + |V_j| + |E_i| + |E_j|$.

As an example, consider graphs g_i and g_j in Fig. 1. In order to make g_i and g_j identical, we have to remove node c and its two incident edges from g_i, and insert nodes d and e together with their incident edges in g_j. Assuming a cost equal to one for each edit operation, the total cost amounts to 8, i.e. $d(g_i, g_j) = 8$.

In general, graph edit distance computation has a high computational complexity. In the present paper, however, we make the assumption that the node labels

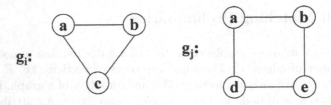

Fig. 1. Two graphs used to demonstrate a measure of graph distance

are unique. That is, no two nodes in a graph have the same label. This assumption is justified by the application considered in Section 4, where nodes represent the names of clients or servers in a computer network. Consequently, there is a unique one-to-one correspondence between the nodes of a pair of graphs, which reduces the computational complexity of graph edit distance computation and other graph matching tasks from exponential to linear (with respect to the number of nodes plus the number of edges in the given graphs) [18]. Basically all that is needed for the implementation of Eq. 1 in the context of this paper is the intersection of two sets and a function that returns the cardinality of a given set.

3   Multidimensional Scaling (MDS)

MDS refers to a class of methods often used in the visualisation of high-dimensional data [19,20]. Consider n objects $o_1, ..., o_n$ in some space and assume that the only information we are given about these objects is their pairwise distances, i.e. the objects may not be explicitly given. Let d_{ij} denote the distance between objects o_i and o_j, where $d_{ii} = 0$ and $d_{ij} = d_{ji}; i, j = 1, ..., n; i \neq j$. The starting point of MDS is an $n \times n$ distance matrix $\mathbf{D} = [d_{ij}]$. The goal of MDS is to reconstruct points $p_1, ..., p_n$ in the m-dimensional Euclidean space $\mathbb{R}^m$ such that the Euclidean distance between p_i and p_j approximates d_{ij} as closely as possible for all pairs i and j. In order to facilitate visualisation, the dimension m of the target space is usually chosen $m = 2$ or $m = 3$. In this paper we will exclusively consider the case $m = 2$.

There are several variations of MDS known from the literature. In this paper we will focus on metric scaling. Let d_{ij}^2 be the squared distance between object o_i and o_j, and let $\widehat{\mathbf{D}} = [d_{ij}^2]$ be the $n \times n$ matrix of pairwise squared distances. Define matrix $\mathbf{J} = \mathbf{I} - n^{-1}\mathbf{11}'$, where $\mathbf{I}$ is the identity matrix, and let $\mathbf{1}$ be an n-dimensional column vector of 1's. We use $\mathbf{x}'$ and $\mathbf{X}'$ to denote transpose of column vector $\mathbf{x}$ and matrix $\mathbf{X}$, respectively. From matrix $\widehat{\mathbf{D}}$ we want to recover matrix

$$\mathbf{X} = \begin{pmatrix} x_{11} & \cdots & x_{1m} \\ \vdots & \ddots & \vdots \\ x_{n1} & \cdots & x_{nm} \end{pmatrix} \tag{2}$$

where $\mathbf{x_j} = (x_{j1}, ..., x_{jm})$ is the location of object o_j in $\mathbb{R}^m$. Because $d_{ij}^2 = (\mathbf{x_i} - \mathbf{x_j})'(\mathbf{x_i} - \mathbf{x_j}) = \mathbf{x_i'x_i} - 2\mathbf{x_i'x_j} + \mathbf{x_j'x_j}$, matrices $\widehat{\mathbf{D}}$ and $\mathbf{X}$ are related via the equation $\widehat{\mathbf{D}} = \mathbf{c}\mathbf{1}' + \mathbf{1}\mathbf{c}' - 2\mathbf{X}\mathbf{X}'$ where $\mathbf{c} = (\mathbf{x}_1'\mathbf{x}_1, ..., \mathbf{x}_n'\mathbf{x}_n)'$. After multiplication of this equation with $\mathbf{J}$ from the left and from the right, and after some simplification, we obtain at $\mathbf{B} = -\frac{1}{2}\mathbf{J}\widehat{\mathbf{D}}\mathbf{J} = \mathbf{X}\mathbf{X}'$. Now the term in the middle is factored by eigendecomposition, yielding $\mathbf{B} = \mathbf{Q}\mathbf{\Lambda}\mathbf{Q}' = (\mathbf{Q}\mathbf{\Lambda}^{1/2})(\mathbf{Q}\mathbf{\Lambda}^{1/2})' = \mathbf{X}\mathbf{X}'$, and $\mathbf{X} = \mathbf{Q}\mathbf{\Lambda}^{1/2}$. Here, $\mathbf{\Lambda}$ is a matrix that contains the eigenvalues $\lambda_1, ..., \lambda_n$ of $\mathbf{B}$ in its diagonal and 0's elsewhere. By convention, we assume the eigenvalues being ordered such that $\lambda_1 \geq ... \geq \lambda_n \geq 0$. Matrix $\mathbf{Q}$ contains the eigenvectors of $\mathbf{B}$ as its columns. Now the coordinates $\mathbf{x}_i = (x_{i1}, x_{i2})$ of all objects o_i in the two-dimensional plane can be retrieved from the first two columns of matrix $\mathbf{X}$ (see Eq. 2).

4   Combining Graph Matching and MDS for Network Behaviour Visualisation

In the method proposed in this paper, the underlying network is first modelled as a graph, where the nodes represent either groups of users in common business domains or individual servers and clients. Graph edges represent logical links between nodes used for data transfer. It is straightforward to use edge labels to indicate the amount of data transferred over a certain link. In the current paper, however, we are only interested in network topology, i.e. in the presence or absence of nodes and edges in the network. Consequently we consider only graphs with unlabelled edges in the paper. The method described in the following is based on the assumption that anomalous network behaviour manifests itself in large graph distances. Given a graph sequence $g_1, ..., g_n$ it was proposed in [14,15,16] to compute all distances between pairs of consecutive graphs, $d(g_1, g_2), ..., d(g_{n-1}, g_n)$ and consider the change between g_{i-1} and g_i as abnormal if $d(g_{i-1}, g_i) > \theta$, where θ is a threshold that needs to be chosen by the network operator based on prior observations and experience.

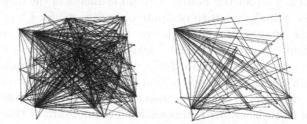

Fig. 2. Snapshots of computer network at two consecutive points in time

Snapshots of a computer network at two consecutive points in time are given in Fig. 2. A plot of distances between pairs of consecutive graphs of a whole time series of graphs is shown in Fig. 3. There is one prominent peak in the distance plot of Fig. 3 at time $t = 50$, and this peak corresponds in fact to an abnormal event in the network (similar to the change between the two graphs shown in Fig. 2). A closer look at Fig. 3 reveals, however, that a large graph distance occurs not only at time $t = 50$, but also at $t = 51$. This leads to the conjecture that the network topologies at time $t = 49$ and $t = 51$ may be similar to one another, i.e. the changes that led to the topology at time $t = 51$ may be inverse to the changes that led to the topology at time $t = 50$. However this conjecture cannot be verified given only the information provided in Fig. 3.

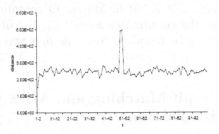

Fig. 3. Graph distance plot of the network over 102 consecutive points in time

Fig. 4. MDS plot of the network

In order to reveal similarities in network topology between pairs of graphs g_i and g_j that have a distance in time greater than one, i.e. $j > i + 1$, we propose to compute all pairwise distances $d(g_i, g_j)$ for $i, j = 1, ..., n; i \neq j$. This results in an $n \times n$ distance matrix $\mathbf{D} = [d_{ij}]$. As a matter of fact, from Eq. 1 it can be seen that $\mathbf{D}$ is a symmetric matrix with all elements in the diagonal equal to zero. Hence one actually needs to compute only $d(g_i, g_j)$ for $i > j$.

Mapping the graphs of the sequence underlying Fig. 3 into the two-dimensional plane by means of MDS yields the plot shown in Fig. 4. In addition to merely depicting the individual graphs, we show temporal relations by linking, through edges, pairs of points that belong to two consecutive graphs. In this figure one can identify one large cluster of points and one prominent outlier. As a matter of fact, the outlier corresponds to the network at time $t = 50$. This suggests that by means of the MDS plot shown in Fig. 4, the conjecture that the network returns to its original state after the abnormal event, can be verified, i.e. the network topologies at time $t = 49$ and $t = 51$ are similar to each other. To illustrate the behaviour of the network in greater detail, we show snapshots of the evolution of both the distance plot and the MDS plot in Fig. 5. Fig. 5a shows the network at time $t = 40$ before the abnormal event occurred. Next, Fig. 5b illustrates the network at time $t = 50$ immediately after the abnormal event has happened, and Fig. 5c corresponds to time $t = 60$. In the MDS plot it can be clearly seen that the abnormal events cause a large distance between consecutive

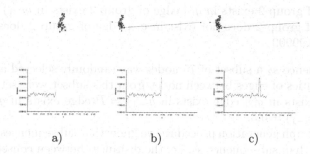

a)   b)   c)

Fig. 5. Dynamic evolution of MDS and graph distance plots over time

graphs (which can be seen in the graph distance plot as well). However, after the abnormal event has occurred, the network's topology becomes similar to the topology before the abnormal event as the corresponding points in the MDS plot belong to the same (i.e. the large) cluster. This phenomenon is only visible in the MDS plot, but not in the graph distance plot.

5   Experimental Results

In order to investigate the visualisation method proposed in this paper in a more systematic way, we generated a number of synthetic graph sequences with specific properties and applied the proposed method. In our first simulation, a sequence of 100 graphs was generated. All graphs had 150 nodes with randomly distributed edges. The sequence was divided into three subsequences, s_1, s_2, and s_3, including graphs g_1 to g_{39}, g_{40} to g_{70}, and g_{71} to g_{100}, respectively. Sequences s_1 and s_3 had the same statistical properties, but for s_2 different parameters were used in the graph generation process.

In many real networks, there exist a number of nodes that communicate with each other frequently while others communicate only occasionally. Throughout this paper we will refer to links arising from frequent communication as group 1 edges of the network. Conversely, links between pairs of nodes that communicate infrequently will be called group 2 edges. The two groups of edges are identified from the initial graph. The initial graph is generated in the following way. Firstly, $N = 150$ nodes are generated. Out of the N^2 possible edges, 5 percent are randomly chosen as edges for the initial graph. The edges chosen are designated to be edges of group 1. Conversely, the edges not chosen are designated as edges of group 2. No self-loops are admitted in the graph generation process.

The two groups of edges then have different change probabilities applied to them. Given graph g_{i-1}, the edges of the next graph g_i are chosen according to the following conditional probabilities:

- P(edge of group 1 exists in g_i | edge of group 1 exists in g_{i-1}) = 0.9
- P(edge of group 1 does not exist in g_i | edge of group 1 does not exist in g_{i-1}) = 0.3

- P(edge of group 2 exists in g_i | edge of group 2 exists in g_{i-1}) = 0.3
- P(edge of group 2 does not exist in g_i | edge of group 2 does not exist in g_{i-1}) = 0.99999

In subsequence s_2 a subset of 75 nodes was randomly selected and all transition probabilities of edges between nodes from this subset were set equal to 0.5, i.e. P(edge exists in g_i | edge exists in g_{i-1}) = P(edge exists in g_i | edge does not exist in g_{i-1}) = 0.5.

From the graph generation procedure we know that subsequences s_1 and s_3 are less dynamic than subsequence s_2, i.e. the distances between consecutive graphs in s_2 are expected to be higher than in s_1 and s_3. Fig. 6 shows both the MDS and the graph distance plot. Our expectation of s_2 exhibiting larger graph distances than s_1 and s_3 is confirmed in the graph distance plot. In the MDS plot we see, in addition to some outliers, a compact cluster of points in the right-hand side, and a somewhat diffuse cluster in the left-hand side. Fig. 7 shows three snapshots of the evolution of both plots over time. The three snapshots were taken at time 20, 50, and 80, i.e., during subsequence s_1, s_2, and s_3, respectively. From Fig. 7 we can conclude that the compact cluster corresponds to subsequences s_1 and s_3, while the diffuse cluster represents the network during subsequence s_2. Note that in the compact cluster many points are printed on top of each other. Hence this cluster appears smaller than the diffuse cluster, although in fact it includes more points. We conclude that both the distance and the MDS plot reflect our expectation and describe the behaviour of the network very well. The MDS plot, however, includes additional information that is not evident from the graph distance plot. First, it shows that there are two clusters of similar network states. Secondly, it indicates that the network states of subsequences s_1 and s_3 are very similar.

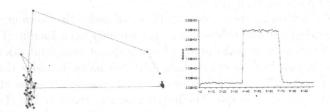

Fig. 6. MDS and graph distance plot of a simulated graph sequence

In the second simulation, we generated a sequence of 100 graphs based on the same parameters that were used for the generation of subsequences s_1 and s_3 in the first experiment. Once the whole sequence was generated, a subset of 75 nodes were randomly selected, and each node of this subset that occurred in any of the graphs g_{40}, ..., g_{70} was deleted together with all its incident edges. Due to this procedure one would expect distances between consecutive graphs to have similar values in subsequences $s_1 = g_1, ..., g_{39}$ and $s_3 = g_{71}, ..., g_{100}$, but be smaller in subsequence $s_2 = g_{40}, ..., g_{70}$, due to the reduced number of

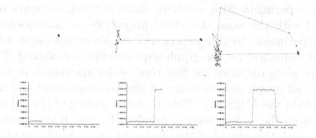

Fig. 7. Dynamic evolution of MDS and graph distance plots over time

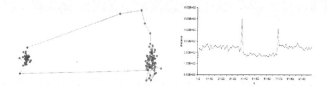

Fig. 8. MDS and graph distance plot of second simulated graph sequence

nodes and edges involved. This behaviour can be observed in the graph distance plot of Fig. 8. In addition, the two large peaks coincide with the points at which the subset of selected nodes, and their incident edges, were deleted and later re-inserted. In the MDS plot we identify two clusters and a few spurious points. The compact cluster in the left-hand side of the figure corresponds to sequence s_2 (smaller graph distances lead to smaller distances between points in the MDS plot), while the diffuse cluster in the right-hand side represents s_1 and s_3. The transition between the two clusters occurs at points in the sequence corresponding to the large peaks in the graph distance plot. Similarly to the first experiment, we can clearly see from the MDS plot that there are two major states. Furthermore, it can be observed that the network returns to the first state after having changed from the first to the second state. Information of this kind is not evident from the graph distance plot.

In the third experiment, again a graph sequence of length 100 was generated using the same statistical parameters as for subsequences s_1 and s_3 in the first experiment. At time $t = 50$ the graph was significantly distorted by randomly selecting a subset V' of 75 nodes, deleting all edges existing between the nodes of V' and inserting an edge between any pair of nodes from V' that were not connected before. Such a graph would be considered an outlier with respect to adjacent graphs in the sequence. In this experiment one would expect the graph distances $d(g_{49}, g_{50})$ and $d(g_{50}, g_{51})$ being significantly larger than all other graph distances. As a matter of fact, this experiment corresponds to Figs. 3 to 5. Our expectation is confirmed in the graph distance plot shown in Fig. 3. In the MDS plot we clearly identify the outlier that corresponds to the graph at time $t = 50$. One can also see that the topology of the network before and after time $t = 50$ is similar because the corresponding points are in the same cluster.

In our last experiment with synthetic data, a graph sequence of length 100 was generated with the same statistical properties as subsequences s_1 and s_3 in the first experiment. In this experiment no abnormal event was implanted into the graph sequence, i.e. the graph sequence was not altered. The MDS and graph distance plots obtained for this time series are shown in Fig. 9. As one would expect, all graph distances are of similar magnitude and no individual clusters emerge in the MDS plot. Note that the scaling of the MDS plot in Fig. 9 is different from the scaling used in previous figures. If the same scaling as in Fig. 8 was applied, the spread of the cluster in Fig. 9 would be about the same as the spread of the diffuse cluster in Fig. 8.

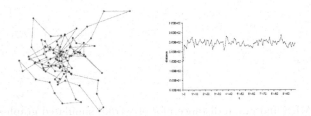

Fig. 9. MDS and graph distance plot of fourth simulated graph sequence

Finally, two experiments were conducted with time series of graphs obtained from real networks. The first network used in the study connects some $120,000$ users around Australia. Origin-Destination (OD) traffic statistics were collected using network monitoring tools, whereby five probes were placed on links in the core of an enterprise intranet. Probes were positioned on links in the network in such a way as to achieve wide coverage of traffic on the network. The number of nodes in the network was reduced to 150 by aggregating IP addresses to business domains. The OD traffic data for a single day was used to generate a graph representing the *logical* state of the network, in terms of topology and traffic, over a one day period. A time series of 102 graphs was derived using traffic data from 102 adjacent days of traffic. Average graph size was 70 nodes.

MDS and graph distance plots of this time series are shown in Fig. 10. Contrary to the synthetically generated sequences, minimal 'ground truth' data existed for this time series, i.e., we do not have a description for many of the abnormal events that have occurred within the recorded period of time. In the graph distance plot we clearly observe three prominent peaks. The second peak coincides with the introduction of a new electronic pay system. Before the first peak, the plot looks rather dynamic, but between the first and second, the second and third, and after the third peak, graph distances are somewhat smaller. From the MDS plot we can draw a number of conclusions that cannot be inferred from the graph distance plot. There are two rather dense clusters of points in the MDS plot, one in the upper right and one in the lower right part. The upper cluster corresponds to the period between the first and second peak, while the

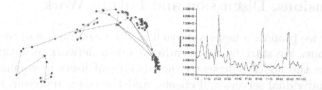

Fig. 10. MDS and graph distance plot of first sequence obtained from a real network

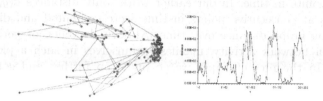

Fig. 11. MDS and graph distance plot of second sequence obtained from a real network

lower one represents both the period between the second and third, and after the third peak in the graph distance plot[1]. This means that the network has a different topology before and after the first peak. Likewise, the topology is different before and after the second peak. However, the network topology is similar before and after the third peak.

The second graph sequence based on real data was obtained from a wireless LAN used by delegates during the World Congress for Information Technology (WCIT) held in Adelaide, Australia, in 2002. The time series consists of 202 graphs with an average size of about 100 nodes each. Here each node represents an individual IP address. A graph was constructed from 30 minutes of traffic data. The sequence of graphs was therefore produced from traffic in adjacent time intervals. In the graph distance plot shown in Fig. 11, one can clearly observe a periodic behaviour of the network. There are five highly dynamic and four less dynamic periods, corresponding to day and night time, respectively.

In the MDS plot in Fig. 11 we observe one large and compact cluster in the right-hand side, and two rather diffuse clusters, one in the upper left and the other in the lower left part of the plot. The large compact cluster mainly corresponds to the network during the four less dynamic periods and to the first two dynamic periods. This cluster formed due to a reduced influence from traffic arising from user behaviour. The upper diffuse cluster represents the network during the third dynamic period and the lower diffuse cluster during the fourth and fifth dynamic periods[1]. Obviously this kind of information cannot be inferred from the graph distance plot.

---

[1] This information is conveyed much clearer if we display the evolution of the graph distance and the MDS plot as a function of time, see Fig. 5. An even better visualisation is achieved through displaying the evolution as a movie.

6   Conclusions, Discussion and Future Work

In this paper we propose a novel approach to the visualisation of computer network behaviour. We start by representing a given network as a time series of graphs, where the nodes represent either groups of users in common business domains or individual servers and clients, and the edges represent logical links between nodes. A graph distance measure originally developed in the domain of pattern recognition is used to compare graphs that represent the network at different points in time. In our earlier work, only distances $d(g_i, g_{i+1})$ between graphs at consecutive points in time were computed and displayed as a plot showing graph distance over time. Abnormal events, or periods of abnormally high network activity, manifest themselves in such a plot through high values. In the present paper we go one step further and compute distances between all pairs of graphs in a sequence. In this way not only local, but global network behaviour, with respect to time, is taken into consideration. The pairwise graph distances are submitted to a multidimensional scaling procedure that renders a two-dimensional visualisation of the graph sequence. In this visualisation, each graph in the sequence is represented by a point in such a way that the distances between points in the two-dimensional plane resemble the distances between the underlying graphs as closely as possible. By means of this procedure, not only anomalous network change can be represented, but also clusters of network states and the transition between states can be visualised.

A number of open issues remain to be addressed in future research. For example, in the current paper edge labels have been ignored. But it is a natural extension to include edge labels, or edge weights, in the underlying graphs so as to represent the amount of data transmitted over the links. As a matter of fact the considered graph edit distance measure can be easily extended such that edge labels are taken into account.

A limitation of the current method is imposed by the fact that a complete graph sequence must be given in order to apply the MDS procedure. This restricts the visualisation procedure to working exclusively in the 'off-line' mode. From the application oriented point of view, however, more flexibility would be achieved if an MDS plot could be built incrementally as new graphs of the time series are acquired. Such an approach could be applied in a streaming environment.

All steps required in the production of an MDS plot can be executed without user intervention. However, the interpretation of an MDS plot, i.e., the identification of clusters, abnormal events, etc. is left to a human operator. The automatic interpretation of MDS plots is therefore an interesting task to be addressed in future work. One essential step in such an automatic interpretation will be automatic clustering of the points in an MDS plot [23]. Alternatively, clustering could be performed on the high-dimensional data before reducing to 2-dimensions, using a clustering algorithm such as density based clustering [24]. The resulting cluster membership of each graph in the sequence could be overlayed onto the 2-dimensional visual display described in this paper.

References

1. Kruegel, C. and Toth, T: Using decision trees to improve signature-based intrusion detection. RAID, 2003.
2. Mahoney, M. and Chan, P.: Learning rules for anomaly detection of hostile network traffic. In ICDM 2003: Third IEEE International Conference on Data Mining, pages 601-604, Washington, DC, USA, 2003. IEEE Computer Society.
3. Lewis, L.: A case based reasoning approach to the managment of faults in communications networks. In IEEE INFOCOM, volume 3, pages 1422-1429, San Francisco, CA, March 1993.
4. Bon, K. S.: Signature-Based Approach for Intrusion Detection. In MLDM 2005: 4th International Conference, pages 526-536, Leipzig, Germany, 2005.
5. Lazar, A., Wang, W. and Deng, R.: Models and algorithms for network fault detection and identification: A review. In ICC, Singapore, November 1992.
6. Barford, P. and Plonka, D.: Characteristics of network traffic flow anomalies. In IMW '01: Proceedings of the 1st ACM SIGCOMM Workshop on Internet Measurement, pages 69-73, San Francisco, California, USA, 2001. ACM Press.
7. Thottan, M. and Ji, C.: Proactive anomaly detection using distributed intelligent agents. IEEE Network, 12(5):21-27, September 1998.
8. Cabrera, J.B.D., Lewis, L., Qin, X., Lee, W., Prasanth, R.K., Ravichandran B., and Mehra, R.K.: Proactive detection of distributed denial of service attacks using mib traffic variables - a feasibility study. In 2001 IEEE/IFIP International Symposium on Integrated Network Management Proceedings, pages 609-622, May 2001.
9. Hellerstein, J. and Watson, T.J.: An approach to selecting metrics for detecting performance problems in information systems. Proceedings of Second IEEE International Workshop on Systems Management, pages 30-39, 1996.
10. Hood, C.S. and Ji, C.: Intelligent network monitoring. In Proceedings of the 1995 IEEE Workshop on Neural Networks for Signal Processing, pages 521-530, 1995.
11. Magnaghi, A.,Hamada, T., and Katsuyama, T.: A wavelet-based framework for proactive detection of network misconfigurations. In SIGCOMM 2004, pages 253-258, August 2004.
12. Hood, C.S. and Proactive, C.Ji.: Network-fault detection. IEEE Trans. Reliability, 46(3):333-341, 1997.
13. Giacinto, G. and Perdisci, R. and Roli, F.: Alarm Clustering for Intrusion Detection Systems in Computer Networks. In MLDM 2005: 4th International Conference, pages 184-193, Leipzig, Germany, 2005.
14. Bunke, H., Kraetzl, M., Shoubridge, P., Wallis, W.D.: Detection of abnormal change in time series of graphs, Journal of Interconnection Networks, Vol.3, Nos 1&2, 2002, 85-101
15. Dickinson, P., Bunke, H., Dadej, A., Kraetzl, M.: Median graphs and anomalous change detection in communication networks, Proc. Int. Conference on Information, Decision and Control, Adelaide, 2002, 59 - 64
16. Bunke, H., Kraetzl, M.: Classification and detection of abnormal events in time series of graphs, in Last M., Kandel, A., Bunke, H. (Eds.): Data Mining in Time Series Databases, World Scientific, 2004, 127 - 148
17. Sanfeliu, A., Fu, K.S.: A distance measure between attributed relational graphs for pattern recognition, IEEE Trans. SMC, 13, 1983, 353-363
18. Dickinson, P., Bunke, H., Dadej, A., Kraetzl, M.: Matching graphs with unique node labels, Pattern Analysis and Applications 7(3), 2004, 243 - 254
19. Cox, T.F. and Cox, M.A.A.: Multidimensional Scaling. Chapman & Hall, 1995

20. Borg, I., Groenen, P.: Modern Multidimensional Scaling, Springer, 1997
21. Ullman, J.: An Algorithm for subgraph isomorphism, Journal of the Association for Computing Machinery, 23(1), 1976, 31-42
22. McGregor: Backtrack search algorithms and the maximal common subgraph problem, Software-Practice and Experience, 12, 1982, 23–13
23. Jain, A., Murty, M., Flynn, P.: Data clustering: a review. ACM Computing Surveys 31 (1999) 264-323
24. Ester, M., Kriegel, H., Sander, J., Xu, X.: A density-based algorithm for discovering clusters in large spatial databases with noise, Knowledge Discovery and Data Mining, (1996) 226-231

Author Index

Lecture Notes in Artificial Intelligence (LNAI)

Vol. 3849: I. Bloch, A. Petrosino, A.G.B. Tettamanzi (Eds.), Fuzzy Logic and Applications. XIV, 438 pages. 2006.

Vol. 3848: J.-F. Boulicaut, L. De Raedt, H. Mannila (Eds.), Constraint-Based Mining and Inductive Databases. X, 401 pages. 2006.

Vol. 3847: K.P. Jantke, A. Lunzer, N. Spyratos, Y. Tanaka (Eds.), Federation over the Web. X, 215 pages. 2006.

Vol. 3835: G. Sutcliffe, A. Voronkov (Eds.), Logic for Programming, Artificial Intelligence, and Reasoning. XIV, 744 pages. 2005.

Vol. 3830: D. Weyns, H. V.D. Parunak, F. Michel (Eds.), Environments for Multi-Agent Systems II. VIII, 291 pages. 2006.

Vol. 3817: M. Faundez-Zanuy, L. Janer, A. Esposito, A. Satue-Villar, J. Roure, V. Espinosa-Duro (Eds.), Nonlinear Analyses and Algorithms for Speech Processing. XII, 380 pages. 2006.

Vol. 3814: M. Maybury, O. Stock, W. Wahlster (Eds.), Intelligent Technologies for Interactive Entertainment. XV, 342 pages. 2005.

Vol. 3809: S. Zhang, R. Jarvis (Eds.), AI 2005: Advances in Artificial Intelligence. XXVII, 1344 pages. 2005.

Vol. 3808: C. Bento, A. Cardoso, G. Dias (Eds.), Progress in Artificial Intelligence. XVIII, 704 pages. 2005.

Vol. 3802: Y. Hao, J. Liu, Y.-P. Wang, Y.-m. Cheung, H. Yin, L. Jiao, J. Ma, Y.-C. Jiao (Eds.), Computational Intelligence and Security, Part II. XLII, 1166 pages. 2005.

Vol. 3801: Y. Hao, J. Liu, Y.-P. Wang, Y.-m. Cheung, H. Yin, L. Jiao, J. Ma, Y.-C. Jiao (Eds.), Computational Intelligence and Security, Part I. XLI, 1122 pages. 2005.

Vol. 3789: A. Gelbukh, Á. de Albornoz, H. Terashima-Marín (Eds.), MICAI 2005: Advances in Artificial Intelligence. XXVI, 1198 pages. 2005.

Vol. 3782: K.-D. Althoff, A. Dengel, R. Bergmann, M. Nick, T.R. Roth-Berghofer (Eds.), Professional Knowledge Management. XXIII, 739 pages. 2005.

Vol. 3763: H. Hong, D. Wang (Eds.), Automated Deduction in Geometry. X, 213 pages. 2006.

Vol. 3755: G.J. Williams, S.J. Simoff (Eds.), Data Mining. XI, 331 pages. 2006.

Vol. 3735: A. Hoffmann, H. Motoda, T. Scheffer (Eds.), Discovery Science. XVI, 400 pages. 2005.

Vol. 3734: S. Jain, H.U. Simon, E. Tomita (Eds.), Algorithmic Learning Theory. XII, 490 pages. 2005.

Vol. 3721: A.M. Jorge, L. Torgo, P.B. Brazdil, R. Camacho, J. Gama (Eds.), Knowledge Discovery in Databases: PKDD 2005. XXIII, 719 pages. 2005.

Vol. 3720: J. Gama, R. Camacho, P.B. Brazdil, A.M. Jorge, L. Torgo (Eds.), Machine Learning: ECML 2005. XXIII, 769 pages. 2005.

Vol. 3717: B. Gramlich (Ed.), Frontiers of Combining Systems. X, 321 pages. 2005.

Vol. 3702: B. Beckert (Ed.), Automated Reasoning with Analytic Tableaux and Related Methods. XIII, 343 pages. 2005.

Vol. 3698: U. Furbach (Ed.), KI 2005: Advances in Artificial Intelligence. XIII, 409 pages. 2005.

Vol. 3690: M. Pěchouček, P. Petta, L.Z. Varga (Eds.), Multi-Agent Systems and Applications IV. XVII, 667 pages. 2005.

Vol. 3684: R. Khosla, R.J. Howlett, L.C. Jain (Eds.), Knowledge-Based Intelligent Information and Engineering Systems, Part IV. LXXIX, 933 pages. 2005.

Vol. 3683: R. Khosla, R.J. Howlett, L.C. Jain (Eds.), Knowledge-Based Intelligent Information and Engineering Systems, Part III. LXXX, 1397 pages. 2005.

Vol. 3682: R. Khosla, R.J. Howlett, L.C. Jain (Eds.), Knowledge-Based Intelligent Information and Engineering Systems, Part II. LXXIX, 1371 pages. 2005.

Vol. 3681: R. Khosla, R.J. Howlett, L.C. Jain (Eds.), Knowledge-Based Intelligent Information and Engineering Systems, Part I. LXXX, 1319 pages. 2005.

Vol. 3673: S. Bandini, S. Manzoni (Eds.), AI*IA 2005: Advances in Artificial Intelligence. XIV, 614 pages. 2005.

Vol. 3662: C. Baral, G. Greco, N. Leone, G. Terracina (Eds.), Logic Programming and Nonmonotonic Reasoning. XIII, 454 pages. 2005.

Vol. 3661: T. Panayiotopoulos, J. Gratch, R. Aylett, D. Ballin, P. Olivier, T. Rist (Eds.), Intelligent Virtual Agents. XIII, 506 pages. 2005.

Vol. 3658: V. Matoušek, P. Mautner, T. Pavelka (Eds.), Text, Speech and Dialogue. XV, 460 pages. 2005.

Vol. 3651: R. Dale, K.-F. Wong, J. Su, O.Y. Kwong (Eds.), Natural Language Processing – IJCNLP 2005. XXI, 1031 pages. 2005.

Vol. 3642: D. Ślęzak, J. Yao, J.F. Peters, W. Ziarko, X. Hu (Eds.), Rough Sets, Fuzzy Sets, Data Mining, and Granular Computing, Part II. XXIII, 738 pages. 2005.

Vol. 3641: D. Ślęzak, G. Wang, M. Szczuka, I. Düntsch, Y. Yao (Eds.), Rough Sets, Fuzzy Sets, Data Mining, and Granular Computing, Part I. XXIV, 742 pages. 2005.

Vol. 3635: J.R. Winkler, M. Niranjan, N.D. Lawrence (Eds.), Deterministic and Statistical Methods in Machine Learning. VIII, 341 pages. 2005.

Vol. 3632: R. Nieuwenhuis (Ed.), Automated Deduction – CADE-20. XIII, 459 pages. 2005.

Vol. 3630: M.S. Capcarrère, A.A. Freitas, P.J. Bentley, C.G. Johnson, J. Timmis (Eds.), Advances in Artificial Life. XIX, 949 pages. 2005.

Vol. 3626: B. Ganter, G. Stumme, R. Wille (Eds.), Formal Concept Analysis. X, 349 pages. 2005.

Vol. 3625: S. Kramer, B. Pfahringer (Eds.), Inductive Logic Programming. XIII, 427 pages. 2005.

Vol. 3620: H. Muñoz-Ávila, F. Ricci (Eds.), Case-Based Reasoning Research and Development. XV, 654 pages. 2005.

Vol. 3614: L. Wang, Y. Jin (Eds.), Fuzzy Systems and Knowledge Discovery, Part II. XLI, 1314 pages. 2005.

Vol. 3613: L. Wang, Y. Jin (Eds.), Fuzzy Systems and Knowledge Discovery, Part I. XLI, 1334 pages. 2005.

Vol. 3607: J.-D. Zucker, L. Saitta (Eds.), Abstraction, Reformulation and Approximation. XII, 376 pages. 2005.